W9-CTT-347

Microsoft® Office 2000

Advanced Course™

Sandra Cable

Connie Morrison
Instructional Technology Consultant

Catherine Skintik
CEP, Inc.

VISIT US ON THE INTERNET
www.swep.com

South-Western Educational Publishing
an International Thomson Publishing company I(T)P®
www.thomson.com

Cincinnati • Albany, NY • Belmont, CA • Bonn • Boston • Detroit • Johannesburg • London • Madrid
Melbourne • Mexico City • New York • Paris • Singapore • Tokyo • Toronto • Washington

LARRY N. DAVIS
1130 Stonybrook Dr.
Napa, CA 94558-5243
707-

Library of Congress Cataloging-in-Publication Data

Cable, Sandra
    Microsoft Office 2000 advanced course / Sandra Cable, Connie
Morrison, Catherine Skintik.
    p. cm.
  Includes index.
  ISBN 0-538-68828-9 (spiral bound)
  ISBN 0-538-68847-5 (softcover)
  ISBN 0-538-68829-7 (perfect bound)
    1. Microsoft Office. 2. Business—Computer programs. I. Morrison,
Connie. II. Skintik, Catherine H.
  HF5548.4.M525 C33 1999
  005.369—dc21
                  99-23145
                  CIP

Team Leader: Karen Schmohe

Managing Editor: Carol Volz

Project Manager: Dave Lafferty

Production Coordinator: Angela McDonald

Art Coordinator: Mike Broussard

Consulting Editor: Custom Editorial Productions, Inc.

Marketing Manager: Larry Qualls

Production: Custom Editorial Productions, Inc.

Copyright © 2000

By SOUTH-WESTERN EDUCATIONAL PUBLISHING/ITP
Cincinnati, Ohio

ALL RIGHTS RESERVED

The text in this publication, or any part thereof, may not be reproduced or transmitted in any form or by any means, electronic or mechanical, including photocopying, recording, storage in an information retrieval system, or otherwise, without the prior written permission of the publisher.

ISBN: 0-538-68828-9, Spiral Cover Text
ISBN: 0-538-68847-5, Soft Cover Text
ISBN: 0-538-68829-7, Soft Cover Text/Data CD Package

2 3 4 5 6 BM 03 02 01 00 99

Printed in the United States of America

IP®

International Thomson Publishing

South-Western Educational Publishing is a division of International Thomson Publishing, Inc. The ITP® registered trademark is used under license.

Microsoft® is a registered trademark of Microsoft Corporation.

The names of these and all commercially available software mentioned herein are used for identification purposes only and may be trademarks or registered trademarks of their respective owners. South-Western Educational Publishing disclaims any affiliation, association, connection with, sponsorship, or endorsement by such owners.

WARNING: Reproducing the pages of this book by any means may be a violation of applicable copyright laws. Illegal copying robs authors and publishers of their proper revenues and makes educational materials expensive for everyone. South-Western Educational Publishing is interested in knowing about violations of copyright laws. If you know of materials being illegally copied and distributed, please contact us.

Microsoft and the Office logo are either registered trademarks or trademarks of the Microsoft Corporation in the United States and/or other countries. South-Western Educational Publishing is an independent entity from Microsoft Corporation and not affiliated with Microsoft Corporation in any manner. This text may be used in assisting students to prepare for a Microsoft Office User Specialist exam (MOUS). Neither Microsoft Corporation, its designated review company, nor South-Western Educational Publishing warrants that use of this publication will ensure passing the relevant MOUS exam.

Open a Window to the Future!

With these (exciting new products) from South-Western!

Our exciting new **Microsoft Office 2000** books will provide everything needed to master this software. Other books include:

 NEW! Microsoft® Office 2000 for Windows® Introductory Course by Pasewark & Pasewark
75+ hours of instruction for beginning through intermediate features

0-538-68824-6	Text, Hard Spiral Bound
0-538-68825-4	Text, Perfect Bound, packaged with Data CD-ROM
0-538-68826-2	Activities Workbook
0-538-68827-0	Electronic Instructor Package (Manual and CD-ROM)
0-538-68934-X	Testing CD-ROM Package

 NEW! Microsoft® Office 2000 for Windows® Advanced Course by Cable, Morrison, & Skintik
75+ hours of instruction for intermediate through advanced features

0-538-68828-9	Text, Hard Spiral Bound
0-538-68829-7	Text, Perfect Bound, packaged with Data CD-ROM
0-538-68830-0	Activities Workbook
0-538-68831-9	Electronic Instructor Package (Manual and CD-ROM)
0-538-68934-X	Testing CD-ROM Package

 NEW! Microsoft® Word 2000 for Windows® Complete Tutorial by Morrison & Pasewark
75+ hours of beginning through advanced features

0-538-68832-7	Text, Hard Spiral Bound
0-538-68833-5	Text, Perfect Bound, packaged with Data CD-ROM
0-538-68834-3	Activities Workbook
0-538-68835-1	Electronic Instructor Package (Manual and CD-ROM)
0-538-68934-X	Testing CD-ROM Package

 NEW! Microsoft® Excel 2000 for Windows® Complete Tutorial by Cable & Pasewark
35+ hours of beginning through advanced features

0-538-68836-X	Text, Soft, Spiral Bound
0-538-68837-8	Text, Perfect Bound, packaged with Data CD-ROM
0-538-68838-6	Activities Workbook
0-538-68839-4	Electronic Instructor Package (Manual and CD-ROM)
0-538-68934-X	Testing CD-ROM Package

 NEW! Microsoft® Access 2000 for Windows® Complete Tutorial by Cable & Pasewark
35+ hours of beginning through advanced features

0-538-68841-6	Text, Soft, Spiral Bound
0-538-68842-4	Text, Perfect Bound, packaged with Data CD-ROM
0-538-68843-2	Activities Workbook
0-538-68844-0	Electronic Instructor Package (Manual and CD-ROM)
0-538-68934-X	Testing CD-ROM Package

A new feature available for these products is the **Electronic Instructor**, which includes a printed Instructor's manual and a CD-ROM. The CD-ROM contains tests, lesson plans, all data and solutions files, SCANS correlations, portfolio analysis, scheduling, and more!

South-Western
Educational Publishing

Join Us On the Internet **http://www.swep.com**

PREFACE

You will find much helpful material in this introductory section. The *How to Use This Book* pages give you a visual summary of the kinds of information you will find in the text. The *What's New* section summarizes features new in this version of Microsoft Office. Be sure to review *Guide for Using This Book* to learn about the terminology and conventions used in preparing the pages and to find out what supporting materials are available for use with this book. If you are interested in pursuing certification as a Microsoft Office User Specialist (MOUS), read the information on *The Microsoft Office User Specialist Program*.

An Ideal Book for Anyone

Because computers are such an important subject for all learners, instructors need the support of a well-designed, educationally sound textbook that is supported by strong ancillary instructional materials. *Microsoft Office 2000: Advanced Course* is just such a book.

The textbook includes features that *make learning easy and enjoyable*—yet challenging—for learners. It is also designed with many features that *make teaching easy and enjoyable* for you. Comprehensive, yet flexible, *Microsoft Office 2000: Advanced Course* is adaptable for a wide variety of class-time schedules.

The lessons in this course contain the following features designed to promote learning:

- Objectives that specify goals students should achieve by the end of each lesson.
- Concept text that explores in detail each new feature.
- Screen captures that help to illustrate the concept text.
- Step-by-Step exercises that allow students to practice the features just introduced.
- Summaries that review the concepts in the lesson.
- Review Questions that test students on the concepts covered in the lesson.
- Projects that provide an opportunity for students to apply concepts they have learned in the lesson.
- Critical Thinking Activities that encourage students to use knowledge gained in the lesson or from PowerPoint's Help system to solve specific problems.

Each unit also contains a unit review with the following features:

- A Command Summary that reviews menu commands and toolbar shortcuts introduced in the unit.
- Review Questions covering material from all lessons in the unit.
- Applications that give students a chance to apply many of the skills learned in the unit.
- An On-the-Job Simulation that proposes real-world jobs a student can complete using the skills learned in the unit.

This book is ideal for computer courses with learners who have varying abilities and previous computer experiences. Each lesson offers an estimated completion time. Actual completion time depends on how well your students know computers in general and the current application in particular.

Acknowledgments

The authors of this book would like to make the following acknowledgments and dedications:

Sandy Cable: This book is the result of efforts of many people and I thank each and every one of you. To all the students I have taught and for all that they have taught me, I thank you. This book is dedicated to my brother, Keith Albright. Thank you for always being there for me.

Connie Morrison: Although the cover of this book identifies three authors, in reality *Microsoft Office 2000: Advanced Course* represents a true team effort involving several dedicated publishing experts at Custom Editorial Productions, Inc. My appreciation goes to that entire team who made this book possible. I especially want to thank my editor Cat Skintik for her support, patience, and understanding. Thanks also to my colleagues, and friends who offered constant encouragement. I am also very grateful to my family, Gene, Al, Amy, and Chris for their steadfast love and support.

Catherine Skintik: Thanks to the entire hard-working development and production team at Custom Editorial Productions, Inc., for providing support and jokes when desperately needed. Thanks to Betsy Newberry for support in times of crisis and for keeping the entire structure of the Office 2000 series straight at all times. Thanks especially to Ed and to Emma for putting it all into proportion.

About the Authors

Sandy Cable owns her own computer consulting company and works with companies such as Southwest Airlines, IAMS, and Memorex Telex just to name a few. She has many years of writing experience with South-Western Educational Publishing, which has resulted in eleven books. Sandy travels nationwide to speak at seminars and in classrooms promoting simple approaches to teaching computer applications.

Connie Morrison has over 25 years of combined experience in education and educational publishing. She has taught students at all levels from elementary through college levels, and she has provided training in industry.

Catherine Skintik has over 20 years of editorial experience, the last seven of which have involved developing and writing software tutorials for the education market.

How to Use This Book

W hat makes a good computer instructional text? Sound pedagogy and the most current, complete materials. That is what you will find in *Microsoft Office 2000: Advanced Course*. Not only will you find an inviting layout, but also many features to enhance learning.

Objectives—Objectives are listed at the beginning of each lesson, along with a suggested time for completion of the lesson. This allows you to look ahead to what you will be learning and to pace your work.

SCANS (Secretary's Commission on Achieving Necessary Skills)—The U.S. Department of Labor has identified the school-to-careers competencies. The eight workplace competencies and foundation skills are identified in exercises where they apply. More information on SCANS can be found on the *Electronic Instructor*.

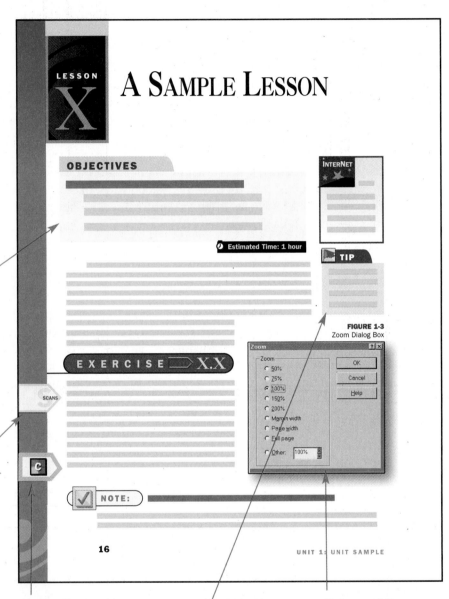

FIGURE 1-3
Zoom Dialog Box

16

Certification Icon— This icon is shown wherever a criteria for Microsoft Office User Specialist (MOUS) certification is covered in the lesson. A correlation table with page numbers is provided elsewhere in this book and on the *Electronic Instructor*.

Marginal Boxes— These boxes provide additional information for Hot Tips, fun facts (Did You Know?), Concept Builders, Internet Web Sites, Extra Challenges activities, and Teamwork ideas.

Enhanced Screen Shots—Screen shots now come to life on each page with color and depth.

How to Use This Book

Summary—At the end of each lesson, you will find a summary to prepare you to complete the end-of-lesson activities.

Review Questions—Review material at the end of each lesson and each unit enables you to prepare for assessment of the content presented.

Lesson Projects—End-of-lesson hands-on application of what has been learned in the lesson allows you to actually apply the techniques covered.

Critical Thinking Activities—Each lesson gives you an opportunity to apply creative analysis and use the Help system to solve problems.

Command Summary—At the end of each unit, a command summary is provided for quick reference.

End-of-Unit Applications—End-of-unit hands-on application of concepts learned in the unit provides opportunity for a comprehensive review.

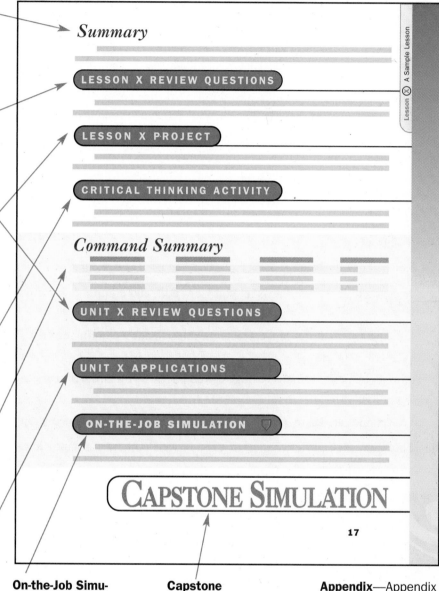

Summary

LESSON X REVIEW QUESTIONS

LESSON X PROJECT

CRITICAL THINKING ACTIVITY

Command Summary

UNIT X REVIEW QUESTIONS

UNIT X APPLICATIONS

ON-THE-JOB SIMULATION

CAPSTONE SIMULATION

Lesson X   A Sample Lesson

17

On-the-Job Simulation—A realistic simulation runs throughout the text at the end of each unit, reinforcing the material covered in the unit.

Capstone Simulation—Another simulation appears at the end of the text, to be completed after all the lessons have been covered, to give you an opportunity to apply all of the skills you have learned and see them come together in one application.

Appendix—Appendix includes Microsoft Office User Specialist Program.

WHAT'S NEW

Microsoft Office 2000 has many features that help you to be more productive and to enjoy using your computer. Some of the new Office 2000 features covered in this Advanced Course are listed below.

- All Office documents can be saved in HTML format so that anyone with a Web browser can view the documents just as they were created. You can "round trip" documents to HTML and back without losing Office file formats.

- Publishing to the Web is easier than ever. You can save a document to a Web server as easily as you would save to a hard drive.

- Web themes make it easier to create Web pages from Office 2000 applications.

- New tools make it possible to collaborate online with other members of a workgroup across intranets and the Web.

- New data analysis components allow you to use Excel features in Microsoft Internet Explorer.

- Access's Data Access Pages let you view, edit, and contribute information within a browser window.

- Office 2000 identifies and corrects installation and operating errors.

- The Office 2000 Clipboard lets you copy up to 12 different pieces of text or graphics from one or more documents, e-mail messages, Web pages, or other documents, and then paste them individually or all at once.

- Word tables are easily placed within a document and text can be wrapped around them.

- The Slide, Outline, and Notes views in PowerPoint are combined into a single screen.

- You can e-mail directly from each program.

START-UP CHECKLIST

HARDWARE

Minimum Configuration

- ✓ PC with Pentium processor
- ✓ 32 Mb RAM
- ✓ Hard disk with 200 Mb free for typical installation
- ✓ CD-ROM drive
- ✓ VGA monitor with video adapter
- ✓ Microsoft Mouse, IntelliMouse, or compatible pointing device
- ✓ 9600 or higher baud modem
- ✓ Printer

Recommended Configuration

- ✓ Pentium PC with greater than 32 Mb RAM
- ✓ Super VGA 256-color monitor
- ✓ 28,800 baud modem
- ✓ Multimedia capability
- ✓ For e-mail, Microsoft Mail, Internet SMTP/POP3, or other MAPI-compliant messaging software

SOFTWARE

- ✓ Windows 95, 98, or NT Workstation 4.0 with Service Pack 3.0 installed
- ✓ For Web collaboration and Help files, Internet Explorer 5 browser or Windows 98

JOIN US ON THE INTERNET

WWW: **http://www.thomson.com**
E-MAIL: **findit@kiosk.thomson.com**

South-Western Educational Publishing is a partner in *thomson.com,* an on-line portal for the products, services, and resources available from International Thomson Publishing (ITP). Through our site, users can search catalogs, examine subject-specific resource centers, and subscribe to electronic discussion lists.

South-Western Educational Publishing is also a reseller of commercial software products. See our printed catalog or view this page at:

http://www.swep.com/swep/comp_ed/com_sft.html

For information on our products visit our World Wide Web site at:

http://www.swep.com

To join the South-Western Computer Education discussion list, send an e-mail message to: **majordomo@list.thomson.com.** Leave the subject field blank, and in the body of your message key: SUBSCRIBE SOUTH-WESTERN-COMPUTER-EDUCATION <your e-mail address>.

A service of I(T)P®

GUIDE FOR USING THIS BOOK

Please read this *Guide* before starting work. The time you spend now will save you much more time later and will make your learning faster, easier, and more pleasant.

Terminology

This text uses the term *keying* to mean entering text into a computer using the keyboard. *Keying* is the same as "keyboarding" or "typing."

Text means words, numbers, and symbols that are printed.

Conventions

The different type styles used in this book have special meanings. They will save you time because you will soon automatically recognize from the type style the nature of the text you are reading and what you will do.

WHAT YOU WILL DO	TYPE STYLE	EXAMPLE
Text you will key	**Bold**	Key **Don't litter** rapidly.
Individual keys you will press	**Bold**	Press **Enter** to insert a blank line.

WHAT YOU WILL SEE	TYPE STYLE	EXAMPLE
Filenames in book	**Bold upper and lowercase**	Open **IW Step2-1** from the student data files.
Glossary terms in book	***Bold and italics***	The ***menu bar*** contains menu titles.
Words on screen	*Italics*	Highlight the word *pencil* on the screen.
Menus and commands	**Bold**	Choose **Open** from the **File** menu.
Options and areas in dialog boxes	*Italics*	Key a new name in the *File name* box.

Data CD-ROM

All data files necessary for the Step-by-Step exercises, end-of-lesson Projects, end-of-unit Applications and Jobs, and Capstone Simulation exercises for this book are located on the Data CD-ROM supplied with this text. Data files for the *Activities Workbook* are also stored on the Data CD-ROM.

Data files are named according to the first exercise in which they are used and the unit of this textbook in which they are used. A data file for a Step-by-Step exercise in the Advanced Microsoft Word unit would have a filename such as **AW Step1-1**. This particular filename identifies a data file used in the first Step-by-Step exercise in Lesson 1. Other data files have the following formats:

- End-of-lesson projects: **AW Project1-1**
- End-of-unit applications: **AW App2**
- On-the-Job Simulation jobs: **AW Job3**

Electronic Instructor® CD-ROM

The *Electronic Instructor* contains a wealth of instructional material you can use to prepare for teaching Office 2000. The CD-ROM stores the following information:

■ Both the data and solution files for this course.

■ Quizzes for each lesson and unit, and answers to the quizzes, lesson and unit review questions, and activities workbook.

■ Copies of the lesson plans that appear in the instructor's manual, as well as student lesson plans that can help to guide students through the lesson text and exercises.

■ Copies of the figures that appear in the student text, which can be used to prepare transparencies.

■ Grids that show skills required for Microsoft Office User Specialist (MOUS) certification and the SCANS workplace competencies and skills.

■ Suggested schedules for teaching the lessons in this course.

■ Additional instructional information about individual learning strategies, portfolios, and career planning, and a sample Internet contract.

■ PowerPoint presentations showing Office 2000 features for Word, Excel, Access, and PowerPoint.

Additional Activities and Questions

An *Activities Workbook* is available to supply additional paper-and-pencil exercises and hands-on computer applications for each unit of this book. In addition, testing software is available separately with a customizable test bank specific for this text.

SCANS

The Secretary's Commission on Achieving Necessary Skills (SCANS) from the U.S. Department of Labor was asked to examine the demands of the workplace and whether new learners are capable of meeting those demands. Specifically, the Commission was directed to advise the Secretary on the level of skills required to enter employment.

SCANS workplace competencies and foundation skills have been integrated into *Microsoft Office 2000: Advanced Course*. The workplace competencies are identified as 1) ability to use *resources*, 2) *interpersonal* skills, 3) ability to work with *information*, 4) understanding of *systems*, and 5) knowledge and understanding of *technology*. The foundation skills are identified as 1) basic communication skills, 2) thinking skills, and 3) personal qualities.

Exercises in which learners must use a number of these SCANS competencies and foundation skills are marked in the text with the SCANS icon.

THE MICROSOFT OFFICE USER SPECIALIST PROGRAM

APPROVED COURSEWARE

What Is Certification?

The logo on the cover of this book indicates that the book is officially certified by Microsoft Corporation at the **Expert** user skill level for Office 2000 in Word, Excel, Access, and PowerPoint. This certification is part of the **Microsoft Office User Specialist (MOUS)** program that validates your skills as knowledgeable of Microsoft Office.

Why Is Getting Certified Important?

Upon completing the lessons in this book, you will be prepared to take a test that could qualify you as an **Expert** user of Microsoft Office in Word, Excel, Access, and PowerPoint. This can benefit you in many ways. For example, you can show an employer that you have received certified training in Microsoft Office 2000, or you can advance further in education or in your organization. Earning this certification makes you more competitive with the knowledge and skills that you possess. It is also personally satisfying to know that you have reached a skill level that is validated by Microsoft Corporation.

You can also be certified as a **Core** user of Microsoft Office. The difference between Expert and Core users is the level of competency. Core users can perform a wide range of basic tasks. Expert users can do all those same tasks, plus more advanced tasks, such as special formatting.

Where Does Testing Take Place?

To be certified, you will need to take an exam from a third-party testing company called an **Authorization Certification Testing Center**. Call **800-933-4493** to find the location of the testing center nearest you. Learn more about the criteria for testing and what is involved. Tests are conducted on different dates throughout the calendar year.

South-Western Educational Publishing has developed an entire line of training materials suitable for Microsoft Office certification. To learn more, call **800-824-5179**. Also, visit our Web site at **www.swep.com**.

TABLE OF CONTENTS

UNIT   INTRODUCTION

UNIT   ADVANCED MICROSOFT WORD

UNIT · ADVANCED MICROSOFT EXCEL

UNIT   ADVANCED MICROSOFT ACCESS

UNIT

INTRODUCTION

lesson 1   2 hrs.

Office 2000 and the Internet

Estimated Time: 2 hours

OFFICE 2000 AND THE INTERNET

OBJECTIVES:

Upon completion of this lesson, you should be able to:

■ Apply basic Microsoft Word, Excel, Access, PowerPoint, and Outlook features.

■ Identify the advanced tools and options in each application.

■ Start Internet Explorer.

■ Search the Web.

■ Save Web sites to the Favorites folder.

■ View a history of the Web sites you have visited.

⏱ **Estimated Time: 2 hours**

Microsoft Office 2000 is a complete set of computer applications that equips you with the tools you need to produce a variety of documents and files, explore the vast resources on the World Wide Web, and streamline your everyday computing activities. In this course, you will build upon your understanding of the basic features and options in the Word, Excel, Access, PowerPoint, and Outlook applications. This course focuses on the more complex and advanced capabilities of these applications. In this lesson, you will review basic features. Then you will learn more about Internet Explorer and how to use it to access resources on the World Wide Web.

 Did You Know?

The Microsoft Office 2000 premium version also includes the Microsoft FrontPage Web site creation application, Publisher desktop publishing program, and PhotoDraw business graphics software.

Advanced Word Features

As you know, Microsoft Word is a powerful full-featured word processor. You've already learned many of the basic features that enable you to complete common word processing documents. The Word lessons in this course introduce you to features that will enable you to further enhance the appearance of your documents and save you time in preparing and editing your documents.

You will learn how to sort and calculate and how to customize tables. The lesson on mail merge will introduce you to the many features you can use to personalize documents and merge documents.

You will also learn about formatting special effects, including sizing and positioning graphics, balancing columns of text, formatting drop caps, and creating watermarks.

Word also provides some tools for copying and cutting text when you are working with multiple documents and long documents. You'll learn how to use these tools and work efficiently when creating and editing long documents.

On the job, you will likely be involved in many collaborative projects, and you and your co-workers will share documents. Word offers many tools for tracking changes and adding comments to documents. You'll learn how to combine several small documents into one master document, how to route documents to others, and how to protect documents from being permanently changed.

Before you begin to explore these and other advanced features in Word, however, complete the following Step-by-Step, which reviews many basic Word skills.

STEP-BY-STEP ▷ 1.1

1. Open the data file **IN Step1-1** from the student files and save the document as **Class Schedule Memo** followed by your initals.

2. Open the **File** menu and choose **Page Setup**. Click the **Margins** tab, if necessary, set the left and right margins at 1 inch, and then click **OK**.

3. Position the insertion point at the beginning of the first line of the document and press **Enter**. Then position the insertion point in the new blank line.

4. Key and format a memorandum heading:
   a. Key **MEMORANDUM**.
   b. With the insertion point in the line of text, click the **Center** button on the Formatting toolbar.
   c. Select the heading text (including the trailing paragraph mark), select **Arial** in the Font box, and then choose **26** in the *Font Size* box on the Formatting toolbar.
   d. With the text still selected, click the **Bold** button.
   e. Deselect the text and position the insertion point at the end of the heading.
   f. Press **Enter** twice and then change the font to **Times New Roman**, **12** pt.
   g. If necessary, click the **Bold** button to turn off the bold format and click the **Align Left** button to align the paragraph at the left margin.

5. Add the memo headings for **To**, **From**, **Date**, and **Subject**.
   a. Click the tab alignment button on the ruler until the Right Tab is displayed. Point and click at the 0.75 inch mark on the ruler to set a right-aligned tab.
   b. Click the tab alignment button on the ruler until the Left Tab is displayed. Point and click at the 1 inch mark on the ruler to set a left-aligned tab.
   c. Press **Tab** and key **To:**, press **Tab** and key **Fitness Trainers**, and then press **Enter**.
   d. Press **Tab** and key **From:**, press **Tab** and key **Pat Swearingen**, and then press **Enter**.
   e. Press **Tab** and key **Date:**, press **Tab** and key **September 1,** followed by the current year, and then press **Enter**.
   f. Press **Tab** and key **Subject:**, press **Tab** and key **Class Schedule**, and then press **Enter**.
   g. Select the heading **To:** and change the case to all caps. (Choose **Font** on the **Format** menu and then click the **All caps** font effect.) With the text still selected, press the **Bold** button.

6. Repeat the format on remaining headings:
   a. With the **To:** heading selected, double-click the **Format Painter** button on the Formatting toolbar.

(continued on next page)

b. Drag the pointer across the remaining headings **From:**, **Date:**, and **Subject:**. As you drag, be sure to include the colon that follows each heading name.

7. Edit the document as shown in Figure 1-1.

8. Use the Click-Shift-Click method to select text: Click the insertion point at the beginning of the first course title. Scroll down until you can see the last course description. Hold down **Shift** and click at the end of the last course description.

9. Click the **Bullet** button on the Formatting toolbar to create a bulleted list.

10. Use the Click-Shift-Click method to select the three questions, and then click the **Numbering** button on the Formatting toolbar to format an enumerated list.

11. Indent the enumerated list: With the enumerated list still selected, drag the left indent markers on the ruler to 1.5 inches. Then drag the right indent marker to 4.5 inches on the ruler.

FIGURE 1-1
Editing a Word document

For many months we have anticipated the opening of the new Family Fitness Facility in Columbus, and we are now counting down the days for our grand opening on October 1. Today we received confirmation that the fitness equipment for the facility will be delivered on September 11. All equipment will be assembled and installed as quickly as possible. We will then test and inspect each peice of equipment to make sure it is functioning properly and safely.

As we approach our grand opening day, I am ~~completing~~ *finishing* the class schedule for the family lifestyle center. You will recall that when we met last week I asked you to think about whether we should offer classes on health and nutrition. *↑each of*

Specifically, I am considering adding the following classes:

Weight Management will help individuals identify their recommended weight. The focus will be on sound advice for exercise and diet programs that will help individuals add or take off pounds to acheive ideal body weight.

Cooking for Good Health will provide tips on selecting and preparing food. Participants will learn about the nutritional benefits of a variety of foods from organic products to frozen dinners. The focus will be on making good choices, cooking foods properly, and creating wholesome menus.

Reading Food Labels will be a short class defining the information included in food labels and explaining its relevance to diet.

Value of Vitamins will explore the advantages and disadvantages of suplementing diets with vitamins. The benefits of each vitamin will be described.

Strengthening Your Imune System will explore how regular exercise, a healthy diet, and reduce ~~strength~~ *stress ing* emotional help strengthen the imune system.

I would like to hear your thoughts about these ~~lasses~~ *c proposed*. Please respond to the following questions:

Are these classes necessary, and will they complement our instruction on nutrition?

Do you think our family members will be interested in these classes?

Should we offer more than one class on cooking and ~~design~~ *target* the instructions ~~for~~ *to* specific age groups?

I would also like to hear your suggestions for any other classes that you think we should offer. Please write down your thoughts and send them to me, or stop by my office at any time *this week*.

12. Position the insertion point in front of the paragraph beginning *I would like to hear . . .* and press **Ctrl+Enter** to insert a hard page break.

13. Create a header for the second page of the document: Open the **View** menu and choose **Header and Footer**. In the Header and Footer dialog box, key **Class Schedule**, press **Tab,** key **September 1,** followed by the current year, press **Tab**, key **Page**, and then click the **Insert Page Number** button on the Header and Footer toolbar.

14. To adjust the header for the new margins you set in step 2, drag the center-aligned tab stop in the center of the ruler one-quarter inch to the right and drag the right-aligned tab stop at the right of the ruler one-half inch to the right (or flush with the right margin).

15. Click the **Page Setup** button on the Header and Footer toolbar, turn on **Different first page**, and click **OK**. Then close the Header and Footer dialog box.

16. Open the **Tools** menu and choose **Spelling and Grammar** and then complete the spelling and grammar check.

17. Save the changes, print the document, and then close the file and Word.

Advanced Excel Features

Excel is the spreadsheet application in the Microsoft Office suite. Spreadsheets are used primarily for calculating and analyzing data. You should be familiar with the basic features for creating, editing, and formatting worksheet information. Excel's advanced features, however, enable you to orchestrate complex calculations and in-depth analysis that you'd normally leave up to an economist or mathematician!

With Excel's data analysis tools, you can generate reports, charts, and tables that are every bit as professional-looking and accurate as those created by the experts. In this course, you'll become familiar with Excel's scenarios, Goal Seek, auditing, and PivotTable and PivotChart features.

Before you venture into the advanced features of Excel, complete the following Step-by-Step to review Excel basics.

STEP-BY-STEP ▷ 1.2

1. Open the **IN Step1-2** workbook from the student data files and save it as **Trendy Resort Sales Summary** followed by your initials.

2. Enter formulas that will sum both the columns and rows of information.

3. Change the title to a **bold**, **italic** format with a size of **14**.

4. Change the subtitle to an **italic** format with a size of **12**.

5. Add a heading of **Total** to the data in column N.

6. Bold the column and row headings. Center the column headings.

7. Apply a **currency** format to the numeric data.

8. Create a 3-D pie chart on its own page using the data in the Division and Total columns only. Add the title **Projected Total Sales by Division** to the chart. Format the chart parts as you feel is appropriate.

9. Print the worksheet and the chart sheet in landscape orientation.

10. Save the file and then close it and Excel.

Advanced Access Features

Access is the database application in the Office suite. Databases are used for storing and organizing information. They are made up of objects, including tables, queries, forms, reports, macros, and data access pages. You should be familiar with the basic techniques for creating these objects. Once you have created them, you can apply a number of advanced features that give you even more control over how database records are viewed and used.

You will learn how to design advanced forms that streamline data entry and editing. The report object can be used not only to present data in an attractive, reader-friendly manner, but also to provide an analysis of the data. Access's grouping and sorting options, as well as its Chart Wizard, are practical tools for illustrating record data and enhancing reports.

The query object lets you search scores of records to find those that meet even the most stringent or specific criteria. This course introduces you to advanced query design techniques and how to use them to extract only the information you need.

A new feature in Access 2000 is the data access page. This object enables you to build a Web page using an existing database table, form, or report. Then Internet users can access and even manipulate the object.

Before you start exploring Access's advanced features, do the following Step-by-Step to review basic skills and features.

STEP-BY-STEP ▷ 1.3

1. Open the **IN Step1-3** database from the student data files.

2. Open the **Employees** table in Design view.

3. Insert a field named **Department** between the **Employee ID** and **Last Name** fields. Define it as **Text** type. Change the Field Size property to **15**.

4. Insert the department in which each employee works, as listed below:

Crawford	Marketing
Dominquez	Marketing
Gonzalez	Administrative
Keplinger	Sales
Pullis	Accounting
Thomsen	Sales
Wong	Sales
Mancini	Accounting

5. Add a new record to the table using the information below.

Employee ID:	9
Department:	Sales
Last Name:	Barkin
First Name:	Dave
Salary:	$45,000
Home Phone:	608-555-5555
Social Security:	123-45-6789
Date Hired:	5/20/2000

6. Adjust the column widths as necessary. Then print the table in landscape orientation. Close the table.

7. Run an advanced filter on the **Products** table that displays only those products that have a price greater than $10. Adjust the column widths in the datasheet if necessary and then print the results of the filter. Close the table.

8. Use the Form Wizard to create a form from the **Transactions** table. Include all the fields in the form, select the **Columnar** layout, the **Industrial** style, and name the form **Transactions**.

9. In the form's Design view, change the properties of the *Shipping Charge* field to **Currency**

with two decimal places. Insert a title for the form in the *Page Header* section and format it as you feel is appropriate.

10. Move, resize, and format controls on the form as you feel is necessary.

11. Print the form for record **6** and then close the form.

12. Use the Report Wizard to create a report from the **Employees** table. Include all the fields except the *Salary*, *Social Security*, and *Date Hired* fields. Group the records by *Department*. Sort by *Last*

Name. Select the **Stepped** layout and **Portrait** orientation. Choose the **Corporate** style and name the report **Employees**.

13. Modify the design of the report as you feel is appropriate. Be sure to rearrange the fields so that they are in the following order: *Department, Employee ID, Last Name, First Name, Home Phone*.

14. When you are satisfied with the appearance of the report, print it and then close the report and the database.

Advanced PowerPoint Features

Microsoft PowerPoint is a presentation graphics program that allows you to create materials for presentations of many kinds, including slide shows using a projector and online presentations that everyone on a network can view. In the PowerPoint unit, you will explore some of PowerPoint's more advanced features.

You can present text on a slide in many different ways. Besides the headings and bulleted lists you already might have worked with, you can create numbered lists. You can add a text box anywhere on a slide to position text exactly where you want it. You can use tabs and indents to position text more exactly on a slide. You can add symbols to your text to make your meanings more precise. You can work with existing text on your slides by finding and replacing words or phrases and copying and moving words or phrases on or between slides. You can insert hyperlinks that you can access during a presentation to take you to another presentation, a document, or a site on the Internet.

To make your presentations more interesting and meaningful, you can add tables, charts, drawings, sounds, video clips, and pictures to your slides.

PowerPoint also offers many customizing features. You can create your own color schemes, backgrounds, and design templates. You can customize slide masters to present information just as you want it and add items to the masters that will display on every slide.

When preparing for your final presentation, you can set up options for displaying the slides and even record narration for your slides. You can use action settings to help you or the person viewing your slides navigate through the slides and access other documents or the Internet. You can set up your presentation to run on a company network or on the Internet and you can invite others to participate in a discussion about your slides. While presenting the slides, you can take notes on issues that come up and delegate tasks to be completed after the presentation. You can even pack up your slides to deliver your presentation on a computer that does not have PowerPoint installed.

Before you explore these advanced PowerPoint features, complete the following Step-by-Step to review your PowerPoint skills.

1. Start PowerPoint. In the PowerPoint dialog box, choose to open an existing presentation.

2. Open the **IN Step1-4** file from the student data files. Save the presentation as **Historic Preservation** followed by your initials.

3. Add a new slide by clicking the **New Slide** button on the Standard toolbar. In the New Slide dialog box, click **OK** to accept the Bulleted List slide type.

4. Click the title placeholder of the new slide and key **Definitions**. Click the bulleted list placeholder and key the following definition: **Stabilization is reestablishing structural stability to an unsafe property while maintaining its essential form.**

5. Press **Enter** to move to start a new bulleted item and key: **Preservation is sustaining the existing form, integrity, and material of a building.**

6. Press **Enter** and key: **Rehabilitation is returning a property to a state of utility through repair or alteration.** Italicize the words **Stabilization, Preservation, and Rehabilitation**.

7. Add another new bulleted list slide. Key the title **Solving Preservation Problems**. Insert the following bullet items on the slide. To create the subentries under *Conduct literary research*, press **Tab** to indent for the level 2 bullet items. Press **Shift**+**Tab** to return to the level 1 bullet items. Note that as you complete the last bulleted item, PowerPoint reduces the font size to fit all the bullet items in the placeholder.

```
Conduct literary research
   Primary source material
   Secondary source material
Conduct physical research
Establish list of elements to preserve
Decide on appropriate treatments
Develop priorities and work schedule
Carry out the plans
```

8. Click the **Apply Design Template** button on the **Common Tasks** drop-down menu and choose the **Fireball** design template. Click **Apply** to apply the new design to your slides.

9. With slide 1 on the screen, open the **Slide Show** menu and click **Slide Transition**. Apply the **Blinds Vertical** transition at a **Slow** speed to all slides in the presentation.

10. Run the slide show and observe your transitions.

11. Save your changes. Print the slides as handouts with 4 slides per page. Close the presentation and PowerPoint.

Advanced Outlook Features

Microsoft Outlook is a desktop information management program. Using Outlook, you can keep track of e-mail messages, appointments, meetings, contact information, and tasks you need to complete.

Outlook allows you to create items from existing items of a different type, so that you can, for example, use contact information to set up an appointment. You can attach documents or other Outlook items to existing items to keep track of many kinds of information.

Each of the Outlook folders offers some advanced features that can help you keep your work and personal life organized and efficient. In this book, you will explore some of Outlook's more advanced features:

■ Using Calendar, you can schedule multiday events such as conferences and seminars. You can plan meetings and send e-mail invitations to the persons you want to invite.

- Using Task Manager, you can set up recurring tasks that regenerate each time you complete them, so that you have a constant reminder to perform tasks you do on a regular basis. You can delegate tasks to other members of a workgroup or subordinates and track progress on those tasks.

- You can use shortcuts to add contacts to your Contacts folder and then you can communicate with them in a number of ways. You can phone contacts, send them e-mail, send them memos or letters, invite them to meetings, and even use the contact information to complete mail merge operations. You can create lists of contacts to make it easier to communicate with groups of contacts.

- You can customize e-mail messages with stationery and signatures and you can create templates for e-mail messages you use frequently.

If you use Outlook with the Microsoft Exchange Server, you have many other advanced options available. You can, for instance, use e-mail messages as a voting tool, and you can manage your e-mail messages from remote locations. In the Outlook unit in this book, you will use Outlook features available to any user.

Before you explore Outlook's advanced features, complete the following Step-by-Step to review basic Outlook skills.

STEP-BY-STEP ▷ 1.5

1. Start Outlook. Outlook opens the Inbox so you can check for e-mail messages. If you have any, read them and delete them.

2. Click **Outlook Today** in the Outlook Bar. Review any Outlook items active on the current date.

3. Click **Calendar** in the Outlook Bar. Display the calendar for a week from the current date. Create an appointment with your dentist for 10:00 AM and set a reminder. The appointment should last half an hour (if you're lucky). Click **Save and Close** to insert the appointment in the Calendar.

4. Click **Contacts** in the Outlook Bar. Double-click in the contact pane and add to your current contacts the name, address, and phone number of your dentist.

5. Click **Tasks** in the Outlook Bar. Double-click in the tasks pane and create a new task to look up your past dental bills to submit for insurance. Give the task high priority and specify that it be completed within a week.

6. Return to the Calendar and delete the appointment by moving to the date a week from the current date, clicking the appointment to select it, and clicking **Delete** on the **Edit** menu.

7. Delete the contact information for your dentist: move to the Contacts folder and click the dentist's name to select it. Press **Delete**.

8. Delete the insurance task. Close Outlook.

Accessing Internet Resources

Microsoft Office 2000 is designed to give you quick and easy access to the World Wide Web, regardless of which Office application you are currently using. *Internet Explorer*, the browser program included in the Office suite, gives you the capability to access, view, and download data from the Web.

You can start Internet Explorer in one of the following ways:

- Double-click its icon on the desktop.

- Click the Launch Internet Explorer Browser button on the Quick Launch toolbar.

- Display the Web toolbar in any of the Office applications, and click the Start Page button, the Search the Web button, or key a URL in the Address box. Figure 1-2 shows the Web toolbar.

FIGURE 1-2
Web toolbar

Examining the Explorer Window

The screen you see when you launch Internet Explorer depends on the Web page address you entered in the Address box, or the page, if any, that you've designated as your home page. An example of the opening Explorer screen is shown in Figure 1-3.

FIGURE 1-3
Example of opening Explorer screen

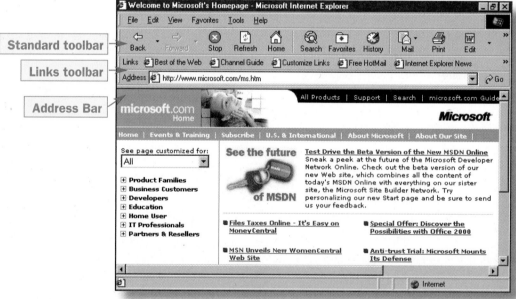

In addition to the Menu bar, the Explorer window features the Standard toolbar, the Links toolbar, and the Address Bar.

- The Standard toolbar contains buttons primarily for navigating, displaying, and printing Web pages. The Mail button lets you send and receive e-mail; the Print button lets you print the content of Web pages; and the Edit button lets you open the Web page in an application in which you can edit and modify it.

- The Links toolbar contains buttons, referred to as *quick links*, that let you quickly connect to specific Web sites. You can customize the toolbar by adding or removing buttons that link to your favorite Web sites. To add a quick link button to the toolbar, you must first display the Web page address in the Address Bar. Then drag the icon for the Web page from the Address Bar to the Links toolbar. To delete a quick link, simply right-click on it, and select Delete on the shortcut menu.

■ The Address Bar contains the Address box where you can key a URL for the Web page you want to visit.

STEP-BY-STEP ▷ 1.6

1. Start Internet Explorer using one of the three methods listed in the preceding text.

2. Click a quick link of your choice on the Links toolbar.

3. Click the **Back** button to return to your home page.

4. In the Address Bar, key **http://www.microsoft.com** and then press **Enter**.

5. Read through the page and click a hyperlink of your choice.

> **Hot Tip**
>
> A hyperlink is normally identified by underlining or a different color text. Also, if your mouse pointer turns into a hand with a pointing index finger, that means it is positioned on a hyperlink.

6. Click the **Back** button and remain in this screen for the next Step-by-Step.

Conducting a Search

When you click the Search button on the Standard toolbar, the Explorer window splits into two panes, as shown in Figure 1-4. The left pane, referred to as the Search Assistant pane, displays options for searching the Web, while the right pane displays the active Web page.

The Search Assistant lists a number of categories that allow you to narrow your search. Click a category, key the search information in the text box, and then click the Search button. The search is conducted using a predetermined search provider, or search engine. A *search engine* is a tool that processes requests for information and then searches for Web sites that satisfy the request. Some examples of search engines are InfoSeek, Dejanews, and Encarta. The search engine that Explorer uses depends on the category option you select in the Search Assistant pane.

> **Concept Builder**
>
> You can also conduct a search by keying **go**, **find**, or **?** followed by the word or phrase for which you are searching in the Address box.

FIGURE 1-4
Search window

S TEP-BY-STEP ▷ 1.7

1. Click the **Search** button on the Standard toolbar.

2. In the Search Assistant pane, click the **Find a Company/organization** option.

3. In the text box, key the name of your long-distance telephone service provider and then click the **Search** button.

4. Read through the Web page, click a link if one in particular interests you, and remain in this screen for the next Step-by-Step.

Saving Favorite Web Pages

As you rely more and more on the Web as a primary source of information on any topic, you'll find that there are sites you visit frequently or that you know you'll want to access again. You can place these sites in the Favorites folder, thereby giving you access to them at the click of the mouse. As you're probably aware, you can open the Favorites folder from the Start menu, from Windows Explorer or My Computer, from the Open dialog box in any Office application, or from the Internet Explorer window.

To save a Web page to the Favorites folder, first locate the page and display it in the browser window. Open the Favorites menu and select Add to Favorites. In the Add Favorite dialog box, key a new name for the page, if desired, and click OK.

To view files in the Favorites folder from Internet Explorer, you can click the Favorites button on the Standard toolbar. The window splits into two panes, with the contents of the folder displayed in the Favorites pane.

Tracking Web Sites Visited

You have probably noticed that when you click the arrow at the end of the Address Bar, a list of the Web sites you've visited is displayed. Internet Explorer keeps track of the Web sites you visit by adding them to this list. You can easily revisit any site on the list by selecting it.

In the Internet Explorer window, you can also view the history list by clicking the History button on the Standard toolbar. The window splits into two panes. In the History pane on the left, the sites you've visited are organized into folders for the previous week, the current day, and the day before. Click a folder to open it and click the Web site to revisit it.

S TEP-BY-STEP ▷ 1.8

1. A Web page for your long-distance phone company should still be displayed in the browser window. Click the **Favorites** button on the Standard toolbar.

2. Open the **Favorites** menu and select **Add to Favorites**. In the Add Favorite dialog box, key a new name for the Web page, if desired. If you want to save the page to a folder other than the Favorites folder, select it in the dialog box or click the **New Folder** button to create a new folder for the page. Click **OK** to close the dialog box.

3. Click the **History** button on the Standard toolbar. Notice that the Web page is listed under the folder for the current day's Web sites.

4. Close Internet Explorer.

5. Click the **Start** button, select **Favorites** on the **Start** menu, and check to see that the Web page for your long-distance company is saved to the Favorites folder. Close the **Start** menu.

Summary

In this lesson, you learned:

■ Microsoft Word is a powerful full-featured word processor. Its advanced features include sorting, calculating, and customizing tables; mail merge; formatting special effects, including sizing and positioning graphics, balancing columns of text, formatting drop caps, and creating watermarks; working with multiple documents and long documents; sharing documents; recording and running macros; and professionally formatting footnotes, endnotes, indexes, and tables of contents.

■ Excel is the spreadsheet application in the Microsoft Office suite. Spreadsheets are used primarily for calculating and analyzing data. Excel's advanced features include sorting and searching worksheet data; recording and running macros; and using data analysis tools to generate reports, charts, and tables that are every bit as professional-looking and accurate as those created by the experts.

■ Access is the database application in the Office suite. Databases are used for storing and organizing information. Access's advanced features include the ability to change field properties in order to control the values entered in a field; modify the design of forms and reports to enhance data entry efficiency and the presentation of data; design queries that let you search scores of records to find those that meet even the most stringent or specific criteria; and design data access pages that let you publish database objects to the World Wide Web.

■ Microsoft PowerPoint is a presentation graphics program that allows you to create materials for presentations of many kinds, including slide shows using a projector and online presentations that everyone on a network can view. Its advanced features include formatting text on a slide using numbered lists, tabs and indents, text boxes, and symbols that help precisely illustrate your points; inserting hyperlinks that you can access during a presentation; adding tables, charts, drawings, sounds, video clips, and pictures to your slides; customizing features that let you create your own color schemes, backgrounds, and design templates; a number of options for displaying the slides; and even recording narration for your slides.

■ Microsoft Outlook is a desktop information management program. Using Calendar, you can schedule multiday events such as conferences and seminars. You can plan meetings and send e-mail invitations to the persons you want to invite. Using Task Manager, you can set up recurring tasks that regenerate each time you complete them, so that you have a constant reminder to perform tasks you do on a regular basis. You can use shortcuts to add contacts to your Contacts folder and then you can communicate with them in a number of ways. You can customize e-mail messages with stationery and signatures and you can create templates for e-mail messages you use frequently.

■ Microsoft Office 2000 is designed to give you quick and easy access to the World Wide Web, regardless of which Office application you are currently using. Internet Explorer, the browser program included in the Office suite, gives you the capability to access, view, and download data from the Web.

LESSON 1 REVIEW QUESTIONS

TRUE/FALSE

Circle T if the statement is true or F if the statement is false.

T F 1. Mail merge is a feature you would use most often in Microsoft Excel.

T F 2. An Access database consists of objects, such as worksheets, forms, and charts.

T F 3. You can insert objects, such as Excel worksheet data, in a PowerPoint slide presentation.

T F 4. InfoSeek and Encarta are examples of Web browsers.

T F 5. The Links toolbar is a feature of Internet Explorer.

MATCHING

Match the most appropriate application in Column 2 to the activity in Column 1.

Column 1	Column 2
_____ 1. Create templates for e-mail messages you use frequently.	**A.** Microsoft Word
_____ 2. Create an employee handbook that contains a number of graphics, including tables that calculate data.	**B.** Microsoft Excel
_____ 3. Store names, addresses, and phone numbers of employees.	**C.** Microsoft Access
_____ 4. Create a list of data that can be calculated, sorted, searched, and charted.	**D.** Microsoft PowerPoint
_____ 5. Create an attractive report using data stored in a table.	**E.** Microsoft Outlook
	F. Internet Explorer

LESSON 1 PROJECTS

PROJECT 1-1

1. Open the file **IN Project1-1** from the student data files and save the document as **Follow-up** followed by your initials.

2. Make the changes indicated in Figure 1-5.

3. Justify the paragraphs in the body of the letter.

4. Indent 1.75 inches from the left each of the nine items in the list of features that guests will enjoy.

5. Spell and grammar check, proofread, and make any necessary corrections.

6. Save and then print the letter. Remain in this screen for the next Project.

PROJECT 1-2

1. In the Word window, display the Web toolbar, if necessary.

2. Click the **Search the Web** button.

3. Display the Search Assistant pane, if necessary.

FIGURE 1-5

BLACKFOOT CONFERENCE RESORT
Route 2
Butler, OH 44822-0712
1-800-555-5436

[handwritten: Arial 14 pt bold]

[handwritten: change left and right margins to 1.25"]

[handwritten: Current Date]

Mr. Gary Ferreira
Spectrum Media Corporation
1454 West 30th Street
Minneapolis, MN 55402-1884

Dear Mr. Ferreira:

[handwritten: Blackfoot Conference Resort has]

Thank you for considering Blackfoot Conference Resort as the site for your summer national conference scheduled for June 6-10. You need to concentrate on planning your meeting, and the last thing you need or have time for is to worry about whether the facility you choose is able to meet your needs. We have everything from meeting room size and configuration to dining and recreation, and we are in the business to help you make your meeting more productive.

[handwritten: year-round] [handwritten: more focused and]

We offer you a resort where your group members will enjoy luxurious accommodations, a warm and hospitable atmosphere, seasonal sports of every kind, and memorable meals. We are centrally located between Columbus and Cleveland.

[handwritten: fully equipped]

We designed everything about our resort around training. We have a convention center with over 20 separate meeting rooms to accommodate from 10 to 500 persons. In addition, we offer you...

- A personal conference coordinator to assist you in planning every detail of the meeting
- The latest audio-visual equipment and audio-visual technicians to assist you with your special needs
- Small rooms for break-out sessions
- A copy center including services for fax, copying, graphics, and photography

[handwritten: ← Insert a hard page break]

Guests enjoy our modern air-conditioned suites complete with TV, VCR, and phones. Each suite has a private balcony with a scenic view. In addition, guests will enjoy...

[handwritten: Mr. Gary Ferreira   Current Date   Page 2]

- an indoor and an outdoor pool
- whirlpool spa
- full-facility exercise room
- tennis courts
- basketball court
- a recreational lake for boating and fishing
- two area downhill and cross-country ski resorts
- horseback riding
- 18-hole golf course

[handwritten: Sincerely, Elizabeth A. Noack Sales Manager]

We are responsive to your needs. We pay attention to details and provide quality service.

Make your meeting a memorable success. Choose our facility with no reservations. We will treat your conference like it is the most important event we have ever had!

[handwritten: Format header on second page only ↑]

4. Search the Web for other Ohio-based conference resort sites.

5. When you find a site containing the information, save it to your Favorites folder.

6. Print the information, if desired. Then close the browser and close Word.

SCANS

ACTIVITY 1-1

Your company just purchased a copy of Microsoft Office 2000 and you are responsible for training employees on its use. Before you train employees on how to use the individual applications, you want to explain how the programs as a whole can be used in the office environment. Write a brief essay that explains each of the various applications included in Office 2000 and provide examples of how employees can apply each application in their daily computing activities.

UNIT

ADVANCED MICROSOFT® WORD

SORTING AND CALCULATING

OBJECTIVES

Upon completion of this lesson, you should be able to:

- Sort a one-column list.

- Sort a multiple-column list created with tabs.

- Sort paragraphs.

- Sort a table.

- Create calculations in tables.

- Update calculations in tables.

⏱ Estimated Time: 1.5 hours

Sorting Text

Word allows you to rearrange your text ***alphanumerically*** (numbers first, then letters), by numbers only, or by date. You can sort tables, paragraphs, or lists created with commas, tabs, spaces, or other separators. You can sort in either ascending or descending order. ***Ascending order*** is from A to Z, from 1 to 10, or from the earliest date to the latest date. ***Descending order*** is from Z to A, from 10 to 1, or from the latest date to the earliest date. You can turn on the ***Case sensitive*** option so words beginning with the same letter will be sorted with uppercase before lowercase letters. You can sort by as many as three criteria at a time.

Any blank paragraph marks you have inserted between paragraphs in your document will automatically be moved to the top or bottom of the selection during the sort.

Hot Tip

Each time you sort during a Word session, the previous sort settings are retained. Be sure to check all settings before you click OK to sort.

Sorting Single-Column Lists

When entering text, you do not need to enter list items in order. You can use Word's Sort feature to reorder list items in a number of ways.

To sort a list (or to perform any other kind of sort), open the Table menu and choose Sort. The Sort Text dialog box opens, similar to Figure 1-1. Perform a simple sort by selecting the item to sort by (usually Paragraphs) and the type of item to sort (Text, Number, or Date). Choose the Ascending or Descending option and then click OK. Notice that you can sort by more than one criterion using the additional *Then by* boxes.

FIGURE 1-1
Sort Text dialog box

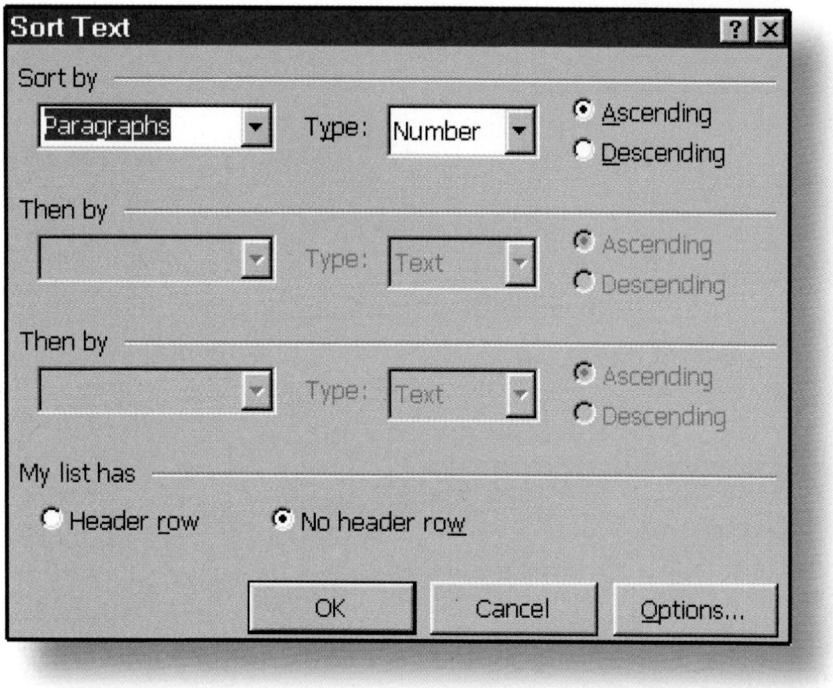

Clicking the Options button in the Sort Text dialog box opens the Sort Options dialog box, shown in Figure 1-2. In this dialog box, Word gives you additional options for controlling the sort. For paragraphs that contain more than single words, you can instruct Word to sort text by *fields*. Tabs, commas, or other characters may separate the fields. Click the *Case sensitive* option to have Word sort by both upper- and lowercase letters.

FIGURE 1-2
Sort Options dialog box

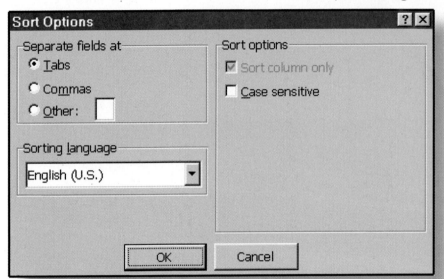

 S TEP-BY-STEP ⟹ 1.1

SCANS

1. Key the document shown in Figure 1-3. Use the **Numbering** button on the Formatting toolbar for each list of names.

2. Save the document as **Sorted Lists** followed by your initials.

3. Sort the list of numbers in ascending order:
   a. Select the list of numbers at the top of the document. (Do not select the paragraph mark below the list.)

💡 Did You Know?

Word will automatically number your enumerated lists after you key the first numbered line. To automatically number lists as you key, open the **Format** menu and choose **AutoFormat**, click **Options**, select the **AutoFormat As You Type** tab, and make sure *Automatic numbered lists* is checked.

FIGURE 1-3

```
8341906
6323611
4135608
5341789
7445213
9873398
3211657
2786534
1266768

1. Lewis, Julie Kay
2. Macnamara, Lorenzo
3. Jurgrau, William
4. Smith-Williams, Susan
5. Yamasaki, Roberta
6. Chien, Benjamin
7. Smith, Susan M.
8. Durkee, Ross
9. MacNamara, Lorenzo
10. Smith, S.
11. Kimura, Taro
12. Toepfer, John
13. Ortiz, Luis
14. Smith, Susan

1. Jeffrey D. Jones
2. Alice Rodriquez
3. Jeffrey Jones
4. Janet McDaniels
5. Jeffrey Rodriquez Jones
6. Kay M. Jones
7. Jeffrey David Jones
```

b. Open the **Table** menu and choose **Sort**. The Sort Text dialog box opens.

c. Make sure Word is using default settings: Click **Options** to open the Sort Options dialog box. In the *Separate fields at* box, the *Tabs* option should be selected. In the *Sort options* box, *Case sensitive* should not be checked. Click **OK**.

d. In the Sort Text dialog box, the *Sort by* entry should be **Paragraphs**, the *Type* entry should be **Number**, and the *Ascending* option should be chosen. Click **OK** to sort the list of numbers. The list should now be sorted from the lowest to the highest number.

4. With the list of numbers still selected, open the **Table** menu and choose **Sort** again. Change the sort order to **Descending** and then click **OK**. The list is now sorted from the highest to the lowest number.

5. Sort the first list of names by both last name and first name. Notice that the last name field and the first name field are separated by commas.

a. Select the first list of names. (Do not select the blank paragraph marks above and below the list. You will not be able to select the numbers.)

b. Open the **Table** menu and choose **Sort**.

c. Click **Options** to open the Sort Options dialog box. Click the *Commas* option to tell Word to sort by the first field (the last name) and then by the field following the comma (the first name). Click **OK**.

d. In the Sort Text dialog box, the *Sort by* entry should be **Paragraphs**, the *Type* entry should be **Text**, and the sort order should be **Descending**. Click **OK**. The list is sorted by last name from the end of the alphabet to the beginning. Notice that Word properly sorted by last name and then by first, and then renumbered the list.

> ### Hot Tip
>
> If you have only *Paragraphs* and *Word 1* available in the *Sort by* list box, click **Options** again and rekey the space in the *Other* box. Then try step 7f again. If **Word 3** is still not available in the *Sort by* list box, close the Sort Text dialog box and reopen it. **Word 3** should then be available.

(continued on next page)

6. Sort the list again in ascending order.

7. Now sort the second list of names. Notice that these names are not separated by a comma. In this list, the fields are separated by the spaces between the first, middle, and last names.

   a. Select the second set of names. (Do not include paragraph marks above or below the list.)

   b. Open the **Table** menu and choose **Sort**. Then click **Options**.

   c. If necessary, turn off *Case sensitive*. Then, if necessary, click *Other* under *Separate fields at*.

   d. Click in the text box next to *Other*, delete the entry in the box (if any), and press the **spacebar** once (indicating that you want the separator to be a space).

   e. Click **OK**.

   f. In the Sort Text dialog box, click the down arrow in the *Sort by* box and click **Word 3** (indicating that you want to sort first by the third word in each item).

   g. To sort by additional criteria, open the first *Then by* list box and click **Word 1**. This tells Word to sort by the first name when the last names are the same. Open the second *Then by* list box and click **Word 2** to indicate that the middle name is to be used when the first and second criteria are the same. Click **OK**.

8. Word sorts the list and automatically renumbers it. The list is not sorted properly, however, because some items in the list do not have a third word. You can fix this by inserting extra spaces for items that have only two fields. Deselect the list. Then, for Alice Rodriquez, Janet McDaniels, and Jeffrey Jones, add an additional space between the first and last names. (Word will consider the blank spaces a second word when you sort.)

9. Sort the list again using the same settings as before. The list is now sorted and numbered properly.

10. Delete the spaces you added.

11. Save your changes. Print the document and close it.

Sorting Multiple-Column Lists Created with Tabs

To sort a multiple-column list created with tabs, follow the same procedures as for a single-column list, but be sure to specify *Tabs* for the *Separate fields at* option and select the desired column (Field number) in the *Sort by* box. If you want to sort a single column without rearranging the rows for the entire list, select only the one column and turn on *Sort column only* in the Sort Options dialog box.

S TEP-BY-STEP ▷ 1.2

1. Open **AW Step1-2** from the student data files and save it as **Order** followed by your initials.

2. Sort based on the second column (the first column is a blank column of tab symbols):
   a. Select the list (do not include the blank paragraph mark below the list). Then open the **Table** menu and choose **Sort**.
   b. Click **Options**. If necessary, click **Tabs** and turn off *Case sensitive*. Click **OK**.
   c. In the *Sort by* box, click **Field 2**. If necessary, select **Text** (for *Type*) and the **Ascending** option.
   d. Click **OK**.

3. Item *CJ2541* is now first in the list. Delete the two paragraph marks at the top of the selection.

4. Sort in descending order based on the fifth column (remember that the first column is blank). Item *JX14W* is now first in the list.

5. Save your changes. Print and close the document.

Sorting Paragraphs

Word sorts paragraphs the same way it sorts lists. Word sorts by the first word in each paragraph. If you want to specify a different field number (for example, the second word in each paragraph), the text must be separated by spaces, commas, tabs, or some other character.

S TEP-BY-STEP ▷ 1.3

1. Open **AW Step1-3** from the student data files and save as **Product List** followed by your initials.

2. Select from *HS 50/50 R* down to the end of the *KB 120* description (do not include the paragraph mark below the last paragraph).

3. Open the **Table** menu and choose **Sort**. If necessary, select **Paragraphs** (for *Sort by*), **Text** (for *Type*), and **Ascending**. Click **OK**. The *HK 300* product is now the first item in the list.

4. Delete six of the nine paragraph marks above *HK 300*.

 Concept Builder

The Product List contains manual line break characters that are used here to control line breaks and to keep parts of a paragraph together—the part number and the description. These characters will not affect the sorting because paragraph marks are used to separate the actual items to be sorted—the product numbers only.

[Handwritten margin notes:] MANUAL LINE BREAK ← TO VIEW TOOLS→ OPTIONS→ VIEW → Pick Marks you want to see

5. Insert a blank line in front of each item number beginning with *HS 50/50 R*.

6. Save your changes. Print and close the document.

Sorting Tables

C When sorting table data, you can sort a single column or the entire table. When you want the entire table sorted based on the first column, you can use a button on the Tables and Borders toolbar to perform the sort automatically. If the result is not what you expect, you can open the Table menu, choose Sort, and check the settings.

STEP-BY-STEP ▷ 1.4

1. Open **AW Step1-4** from the student data files and save it as **Employees** followed by your initials.

2. If necessary, open the **View** menu, choose **Toolbars**, and then select **Tables and Borders** to display the Tables and Borders toolbar.

3. Click anywhere within the first column of the table and then click the **Sort Ascending** button on the Tables and Borders toolbar. The table is sorted based on the first column.

4. Sort *only* the fourth column of the table by date.
   a. Select the fourth column in the table. (Position the mouse pointer above the column and click when you see the column selection pointer.)
   b. Note before you sort that the *Date Hired* entry for *Richard Derrenberger* is *4-6-90.*
   c. Open the **Table** menu, choose **Sort**, and then click **Options**.
   d. If necessary, click *Sort column only* and then click **OK**.
   e. If necessary, change *Sort by* to **Column 4**, select **Date** as the *Type*, and select the **Ascending** option.

   f. Select *Header row* under *My list has.* When *Header row* is selected, Word does not include the table column headings in the sort.
   g. Click **OK**.

5. You sorted only the fourth column. The other columns remain unchanged. Notice that the *Date Hired* entry for *Richard Derrenberger* is now *12-17-89* rather than *4-6-90.* Undo the sort.

6. Sort the entire table by date based on the fourth column:
   a. Select the entire table. (Position the insertion point in the table, open the **Table** menu, click **Select**, and then click **Table** on the submenu.)
   b. Open the Sort Text dialog box.
   c. Select **Date Hired** (for *Sort by*), **Date** (for *Type*), and the **Ascending** option. Make sure *Header row* is selected.
   d. Click **OK**. Deselect the text. The table should now look like Figure 1-4.

7. Save your changes. Print and close the document.

FIGURE 1-4
Table sorted by date, based on fourth column

Name¤	Title¤	Department¤	Date·Hired¤	¤
¤	¤	¤	¤	¤
Lisa·Foster-Hale¤	Director¤	Legal¤	3-15-71¤	¤
Roger·Lee¤	Director¤	Public·Relations¤	4-5-80¤	¤
Terry·Curran¤	Manager¤	Personnel¤	7-14-82¤	¤
Shelley·Metzger¤	Administrative·Assistant¤	Finance¤	6-30-85¤	¤
Larry·Graszl¤	Sales·Representative¤	Marketing¤	12-17-89¤	¤
Richard·Derrenberger¤	Clerk·III¤	Accounting¤	4-6-90¤	¤
Mildred·Rush¤	Sales·Representative¤	Marketing¤	2-7-91¤	¤
Anne·Pfeifer¤	Receptionist¤	Personnel¤	9-14-92¤	¤

Performing Math Calculations

W ord provides a calculation feature that enables you to add numbers in text and in tables. When calculating sums in a paragraph of text, you simply select the paragraph and then choose the Table Formula command on the Table menu. When calculating sums in a table, Word provides an easy shortcut to total the columns and/or rows.

Calculating in Tables

To perform a calculation in a table, position the insertion point in the *cell* where the total (result) is to appear, open the Table menu, and choose Formula. Word opens the Formula dialog box, similar to Figure 1-5. Then, either key a *formula* in the *Formula* text box or accept the proposed formula. You can also specify number formats or choose a function from Word's list of frequently used functions.

You can also calculate a sum by clicking the AutoSum button on the Tables and Borders toolbar. Word automatically adds numbers in cells above the cell containing the insertion point or in cells to the left of the cell containing the insertion point. However, when it is possible to add from either direction, Auto-Sum may not choose the direction you want. Therefore, always check the accuracy of the result when using AutoSum.

FIGURE 1-5
Formula dialog box

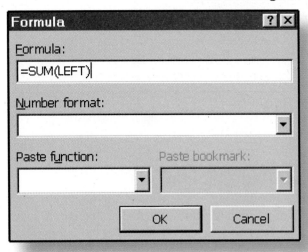

S TEP-BY-STEP ▷ 1.5

1. Open **AW Step1-5** from the student data files and save it as **Sales Figures** followed by your initials.

2. To calculate the total for the *Mary Colace* row:
   a. Position the insertion point in the last cell in the *Mary Colace* row.
   b. Open the **Table** menu and choose **Formula**. The Formula dialog box opens, with the proposed formula **=SUM(LEFT)**.
   c. Click **OK** to accept the proposed formula. The result (total) of **174,262** is automatically inserted in the current cell.

3. To quickly insert the same formula in the other cells of the *Total* column, click in each cell, open the **Edit** menu, and choose **Repeat Formula**. Do not insert a formula for the *TOTAL* row.

4. Calculate the total of the *April* column:
   a. Position the insertion point in the last cell in the *April* column.
   b. Open the **Table** menu and choose **Formula**. Word proposes **=SUM(ABOVE)**.
   c. Click **OK**. The total of **444,418** is automatically inserted.

5. Repeat the calculation process for the other three columns. The *TOTAL* row should now look like Figure 1-6.

6. Save your changes and leave the document open for the next Step-by-Step.

 Hot Tip

If you are calculating the sum of a column of a table in which some of the cells are empty, Word will stop calculating at the first blank cell. To make sure your results will be correct, you can enter zeroes in the empty cells before executing the Formula command.

FIGURE 1-6
TOTAL row completed with sums inserted

•TOTAL¤		444,418¤	495,700¤	512,510¤	1,452,628¤¤

Updating Calculations

After creating a table and calculating totals, you may discover that you need to change amounts. Word does not automatically update calculations as does a spreadsheet program such as Excel. Rather than recalculate each individual total in each column and row, Word provides a shortcut that enables you to recalculate an entire table quickly. When you use the Formula command on the Table menu, Word inserts hidden fields for each total. To recalculate, you simply select the cells containing those fields and update the fields by pressing the Update Field key, F9.

STEP-BY-STEP ▷ 1.6

SCANS

1. Change the *June* amounts to the following:

Colace	69,804	Josephs	47,996
Fracassa	73,168	Petitt	47,767
Guetle	92,544	Stewart	44,131
Homminga	79,007	Weston	70,305

2. Select the table. Note that the final total in the *Total* column is **1,452,628**.

3. Press the Update Field key, **F9**. All sums are automatically recalculated. Note that the final total in the *Total* column is now **1,464,840**.

4. Save your changes. Print and close the document.

Creating Formulas in a Table

You can also perform other complex math calculations in tables such as subtracting, multiplying, dividing, averaging, and calculating a percentage. For calculations, Word assigns letters to columns and numbers to rows, just as in a worksheet. Cells are named for their intersecting rows and columns. For example, A2 would be the intersection of the first column (A) and the second row (2). B3 would be the intersection of the second column and third row, and so on.

STEP-BY-STEP ▷ 1.7

SCANS

1. Open **AW Step1-7** from the student data files and save the document as **Payroll** followed by your initials.

2. If necessary, display the Tables and Borders toolbar.

3. Calculate the earnings for *Benitez*:
   a. Position the insertion point in the first blank cell in the *Earnings* column (*Benitez, L.*).
   b. Open the **Table** menu and choose **Formula**.
   c. Word proposes **=SUM(LEFT)**. If you accepted this formula, Word would add the hourly rate and the regular hours.
   d. Delete the proposed formula, and then key **=c2*b2**. This formula instructs Word to multiply the regular hours in row 3 times the hourly rate in row 3.
   e. Click the down arrow in the *Number format* list box and select **$#,##0.00; ($#,##0.00)**.
   f. Click **OK**. Word inserts the total *$ 574.40*.

4. Calculate the earnings for *Daniel* in the same way, changing the formula to **=c3*b3**.

5. Enter formulas in the *Earnings* cells for *Huang*, *O'Neil*, and *Parker*.

6. Position the insertion point in the last row of the *Regular Hours* column and click the **Auto-Sum** button on the Tables and Borders toolbar. Word automatically calculates the sum of all the numbers above.

7. Position the insertion point in the last row of the *Earnings* column and click the **AutoSum** button.

8. Insert a new row at the bottom of the table. Key **AVER. HOURS** in the first cell.

9. Press **Tab** twice to move the insertion point to the *Regular Hours* column. Open the **Table** menu and choose **Formula**.

10. Delete the proposed formula and then key **=AVERAGE(c2:c6)**. This formula instructs Word to calculate the average of the hourly rates in rows 2 through 6 in the *Regular Hours* column.

11. Save your changes. Print and close the document.

Summary

In this lesson, you learned:

- Text can be rearranged alphanumerically (numbers first, then letters).

- Lists, tabular columns, paragraphs, and text can be sorted in ascending or descending order.

- When turned on, the *Case sensitive* feature sorts text so words beginning with the same letter will be sorted with uppercase before lowercase letters.

- Paragraphs of text are sorted by the first word in each paragraph. The text must be separated by spaces, commas, tabs, or some other character.

- Sorts can be based on as many as three criteria at a time.

- When sorting a single column, the data in the other table columns is not rearranged.

- Before performing a calculation in a table, the insertion point should be positioned in the cell where the total (result) is to appear.

- The Update Field key, F9, updates calculations in a table.

- The Formula command on the Table menu enables you to perform complex math calculations in tables such as subtracting, multiplying, dividing, averaging, and calculating a percentage.

LESSON 1 REVIEW QUESTIONS

TRUE/FALSE

Circle T if the statement is true or F if the statement is false.

Punc, numbers, text

T **(F)** 1. An alphanumeric sort places letters before numbers.

(T) F 2. Word automatically renumbers paragraphs after a sort if the paragraphs are numbered using the Numbering button.

T **(F)** 3. After calculating a total, you must paste it into your document.

T **(F)** 4. Word always calculates the numbers in the table cells directly above the cell where the insertion point is positioned.

FILL IN THE BLANKS

Complete the following sentences by writing the correct word or words in the blanks provided.

1. If you have selected an entire table but do not want the table to be sorted based on the first column, you can specify a different column number in the ___Sort By___ list box of the Sort Text dialog box.

2. To sort a single column and leave the rest of the table or list unchanged, select the column and turn on ___Sort Column Only___ in the Sort Options dialog box.

3. To sort from the beginning of the alphabet, the lowest number, or the earliest date, select ___Ascending___ in the Sort Text dialog box.

4. To sort from the end of the alphabet or from the highest number to the lowest, select ___Descending___ in the Sort Text dialog box.

5. To perform a calculation, open the ___Table___ menu and choose ___Formula___.

6. If you change numbers in a table for which you have already calculated totals, select the table and press ___F9___ to update the calculations.

LESSON 1 PROJECTS

SCANS

PROJECT 1-1

1. Open a new document window. Key the document illustrated in Figure 1-7. Set appropriate tabs to create the two columns of information.

FIGURE 1-7

CAREER SEMINAR

Guest Speaker Expenses

Speaker	Expenses
Kindle, Barbara	1,239.48
Rhoden, Glen	548.00
Snyder, Charles	229.34
Vaccaro, Donna	882.67
Jolivet, Vance	1,328.78
Fletcher, Patsy	335.50
Marquez, Consuelo	756.12

2. Save the document as **Speaker Expenses** followed by your initials.

3. Underline the column headings.

4. Sort the table so that the speakers are listed in ascending alphabetical order by last name.

5. Save your changes. Print and close the document.

PROJECT 1-2

1. Open a new document window. Key the report illustrated in Figure 1-8.

FIGURE 1-8

FIRST QUARTER EXPENSE REPORT

Item	January	February	March
Advertising Expense	2,865.40	3,112.59	1,796.44
Delivery Expense	785.55	602.31	861.94
Insurance Expense	250.00	250.00	250.00
Interest Expense	4,031.13	4,029.55	4,300.67
Maintenance Expense	3,321.54	1,566.18	2,479.86
Miscellaneous Expense	678.59	505.37	891.40
Office Salaries Expense	85,678.84	85,886.45	84,959.32
Sales Salaries Expense	52,115.90	1,563.66	1,345.89
Utilities Expense	3,918.77	3,877.65	3,943.97
TOTAL			

2. Save the document as **Expense Report** followed by your initials.

3. Calculate the total for the *January* column. Then repeat the process for the other two columns.

4. Center and bold the column headings.

5. Right-align the amounts in each column.

6. Save your changes. Print and close the document.

PROJECT 1-3

1. Open a new document window. Create a table and key the information illustrated in Figure 1-9.

2. Save the table as **Account Info** followed by your initials.

FIGURE 1-9

Account	Balance	Date Due
G & B Industries	1,345.66	12-04
Fowler Manufacturing, Inc.	345.82	12-19
G & L Industries	3,452.19	12-22
Webbs Plastics, Inc.	5,446.78	12-03
Fox & Company	987.09	12-09
Richland Products	2,669.92	12-15
Weston Manufacturing	1,202.33	12-04
Kissinger Distributors	1,565.44	12-01
Warren Plastics and Film	445.42	12-08
A-1 Plastics	3,445.87	12-12
Allen Studios	2,229.54	12-09
ADCO Plastics Company	623.79	12-10
WW Supply	1,407.06	12-11
R & S Plastics and Film	2,985.39	12-05
Guenther Film Products	4,020.31	12-28
AVERAGE BALANCE		

3. Calculate the average balance for the second column. =AVERAGE(b:b)

4. Sort in ascending order based on the *Account* column. (Select only the rows to be included in the sort. Do not include the row with the column headings, the blank row, and the *AVERAGE BALANCE* row in the selection.)

5. Set a decimal tab for the amounts in the second column. Center the dates in the third column.

6. Change the words *AVERAGE BALANCE* to **TOTAL** and then delete the average calculation in the last row of the *Balance* column. Insert a new formula to calculate the total.

7. Sort the table based on the *Date Due* column in ascending order. Use Date as the *Type*.

8. Save your changes. Print and close the document.

ACTIVITY 1-1

Suppose you want to calculate the sum of two table cells, but the table cells are not adjacent to each other. How do you reference the cells? What formula would you key to calculate the sum of the data in the two cells? Use the Help feature to find the answer. *= SUM(a1, a3, a4)*

ACTIVITY 1-2

If you were to sort the following list in ascending order using Text as the *Type*, in what order would Word place the paragraphs and why? Use the Help feature to find the answer.

3 Smith, Robert

2 43

1 $45.20

punctuation
↓
numbers
↓
Text

CUSTOMIZING TABLES AND CREATING CHARTS

OBJECTIVES

Upon completion of this lesson, you should be able to:

- Center and AutoFit a table.

- Adjust column width and row height manually.

- Convert text to a table.

- Insert, delete, and move rows and columns.

- Merge and split table cells.

- Add custom table borders and shading.

- Change the direction and alignment of text in a table cell.

- Link and embed an Excel worksheet in a Word document.

- Create and modify a chart.

- Import Excel worksheet data into a chart.

Estimated Time: 2 hours

Customizing Tables

You will often want to customize the layout and design of your Word tables. Word offers some powerful features to help you format tables quickly and easily.

Using AutoFit and Alignment Options

When you create tables, Word inserts the number of columns specified but makes all the columns approximately the same width. You can adjust the width of each column automatically using the *AutoFit* feature. Word offers five AutoFit options. In this lesson, you will practice three of those options.

When you choose to AutoFit to Contents, Word automatically adjusts all column widths as needed to accommodate the contents within the cells. If you choose the AutoFit to Window option, Word will automatically resize a table for a Web page when you change the window size.

You can choose alignment options for a table in the Table Properties dialog box, shown in Figure 2-1. Open the Table menu, click Table Properties to open the dialog box, and then choose an alignment in the *Alignment* section of the Table tab. The alignment options in this dialog box determine the horizontal alignment of a table. By default, Word left aligns tables, but you can also center or right align the table.

FIGURE 2-1
Change alignment in the Table Properties dialog box

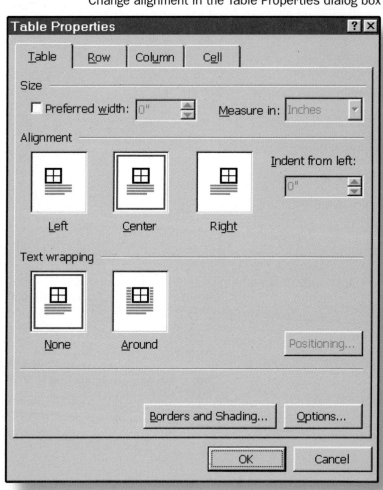

S TEP-BY-STEP ▷ 2.1

1. Open **AW Step2-1** from the student data files and save the document as **Staff Data** followed by your initials.

2. Position the insertion point anywhere inside the table.

3. Open the **Table** menu, choose **AutoFit**, and then choose **AutoFit to Contents** on the submenu. Word adjusts the width of each column to accommodate the contents within that column.

4. With the insertion point still positioned in the table, open the **Table** menu and choose **Table Properties**. If necessary, click the **Table** tab.

5. Click **Center** and then click **OK**. Word centers the table horizontally on the page.

6. Save your changes and leave the document open for the next Step-by-Step.

Hot Tip

The option to wrap text around a table is especially useful if you need to save space on a page such as in a newsletter.

Adjusting Column Width and Row Height Manually

Generally, when you need to adjust the width of a column, you can simply drag a column border. In the following steps, however, you will experiment with some techniques that give you more control over how the other columns adjust. If you want to see column measurements as you drag on the ruler, hold down Alt as well as the keys listed in steps 4–6 below. Be sure you release the mouse button before all other keys in the following steps, or your results may differ.

There may be times when you want rows or columns to be spaced evenly throughout the table. Word provides shortcuts for you to distribute the spacing of the rows and columns evenly: the Distribute Rows Evenly and Distribute Columns Evenly buttons on the Tables and Borders toolbar. To use these buttons, you must first select the rows or columns you want to adjust.

STEP-BY-STEP ▷ 2.2

1. Widen the first column using the column border:
   a. Position the mouse pointer at the border (the vertical gridline) between the first and second columns until you see the gridline pointer.

   `+|+Address¤`

   b. Drag the border about half an inch to the right.
   c. Notice that the first column width is increased and the second column width is decreased. The third and fourth columns remain the same width, and the overall table width remains the same.

2. Widen the second column using the ruler:
   a. Position the mouse pointer on the ruler at the column marker (the box) between the second and third columns.
   b. When you see the two-headed arrow (or the ScreenTip *Move Table Column*), drag the marker about half an inch to the right.

   c. Notice as you drag that the ruler shifts, rather than just the markers. After you release, notice that this time only the second column width changed. All other columns remained the same, and the overall table width increased.

3. Open the **Undo** list box and drag to undo both column width edits.

Hot Tip

You can double-click on the right border of a column to quickly resize a column to accommodate the longest entry in the column. In some tables, however, you may have to narrow one or more columns before you can double-click to widen another.

(continued on next page)

4. Adjust the height of the first row:

   a. Position the pointer on the bottom line of the first row.

   b. When the pointer changes to the gridline pointer, drag the line down about half an inch and release. The height of the first row increases.

5. If necessary, display the Tables and Borders toolbar.

6. Position the insertion point anywhere in the table and click the **Distribute**  Rows Evenly button on the Tables and Borders toolbar. The rows are now all the same height.

7. With the insertion point still positioned in the table, click the **Distribute Columns Evenly** button on the Tables and Borders toolbar. The columns are automatically adjusted to equal width.

8. Equal width columns do not work well in this table. Click the **Undo** button.

9. Save your changes. Print and close the document.

Converting Text to a Table

Generally you will use Word's Insert command on the Table menu or the Draw Table tool to create tables. However, there may be occasions when you want to convert existing text to a table. Word can quickly convert text separated by commas, tabs, spaces, or other separators into a table with cells.

To create a table from existing text, select the text and then open the Table menu and choose Convert. Then choose Text to Table from the submenu. The Convert Text to Table dialog box opens, similar to the one shown in Figure 2-2. Choose how many columns and rows to create from your selected text. You can also select AutoFit and AutoFormat options. In the *Separate text at* section, make sure the proper separator is chosen.

FIGURE 2-2
Convert Text to Table dialog box

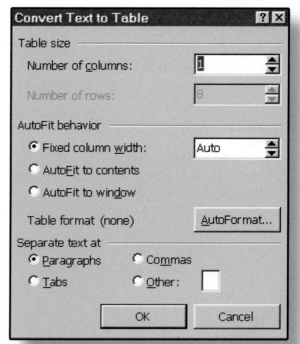

S TEP-BY-STEP ▷ 2.3

1. Open **AW Step2-3** from the student data files and save the document as **Test Results** followed by your initials.

2. Select the entire document except for the ending paragraph mark.

3. Open the **Table** menu and choose **Convert**. Then choose **Text to Table** on the submenu. The Convert Text to Table dialog box opens.

4. If necessary, select the **Tabs** option in the *Separate text at* section of the dialog box. Then click **OK**.

5. Deselect the table. Save your changes and leave the document open for the next Step-by-Step.

 Did You Know?

You can convert a table to text using the same Convert command. Word then allows you to specify how to separate the cell data to create text.

Inserting and Deleting Rows and Columns

You can quickly insert a new row in a table by pressing Tab in the last cell of the table. You can also quickly insert or delete multiple rows and columns in one edit by selecting the desired number of rows or columns you want to add or delete and then choosing the appropriate Table command.

S TEP-BY-STEP ▷ 2.4

1. Position the insertion point in the last cell in the table below the column heading *Pounds*.

2. Press **Tab**. A new row is inserted.

3. With the insertion point positioned in the new row you just created, open the **Table** menu and choose **Delete**. Then choose **Rows** on the submenu.

4. Select the last two rows in the table.

5. Open the **Table** menu and choose **Insert**. Then choose **Rows Above** on the submenu. Two new rows are inserted.

6. Key the following data in the two new rows. (To insert the inch marks and the multiplication signs, click **Symbol** on the **Insert** menu, or copy the symbols from other entries in the *Dimensions* column.)

```
119080 A1 14 microns 33" × 40" 70-75
119081 A2 17 microns 38" × 60" 80-85
```

7. Position the insertion point in the *Dimensions* column and then open the **Table** menu and choose **Insert**. Choose **Columns to the Right** on the submenu.

8. Key the following data in the new column:

```
Weight
80
30
40
50
35
110
```

9. Save your changes and leave the document open for the next Step-by-Step.

Moving Rows and Columns

You can move rows and columns using drag and drop in the same way you move text in a document. Select the entire row or column using the row selection pointer or the column selection pointer. Then click in the selected row or column and drag. You will see the drag-and-drop pointer just as when you drag and drop text. Move the pointer to the first cell in the row *below* where you want the moved row to appear or in the column to the *right* of where you want the moved column to appear.

You can also use the Cut and Paste commands to move rows and columns. Cut the row or column you want to move and then position the insertion point in the row below or the column to the right of where you want the moved row or column to appear. Then click Paste.

STEP-BY-STEP 2.5

1. Select the entire fourth row of the table (the first cell is *119082*).

2. Click in the selected row and drag the pointer to the first cell in the last row (*119083*). Release the mouse button.
   The moved row is now the second-to-last row.

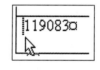

3. Select the entire seventh row (the first cell is *119079*).

4. Cut the row, position the insertion point in the *119080* cell, and paste. The row you cut is pasted in the new location. Note that the stock numbers are now in the correct order.

Hot Tip

If you dropped the row in the wrong location, click the **Undo** button and try the move again.

5. Now move the *Rating* column to become the sixth column. Select the *Rating* column. Drag the pointer *outside* the right table boundary and just to the left of the last set of column markers. Release the mouse button.

6. Save your changes and leave the document open for the next Step-by-Step.

Merging Table Cells

Word enables you to remove the boundary between any two cells. When you remove this boundary, it is called *merging cells*. You can merge cells horizontally or vertically. A quick way to merge cells is to use the Eraser tool on the Tables and Borders toolbar. As you erase cell borders in the table, the cells are merged.

STEP-BY-STEP ▷ 2.6

1. Click the **Eraser** button on the Tables and Borders toolbar. The pointer changes to an eraser.

2. Click on the right cell border of the first cell. The cell border is deleted and the first two cells are merged. Click on the remaining cells until the first row is a single cell.

3. Center and AutoFit the table to its contents.

4. Save your changes and leave the document open for the next Step-by-Step.

Adding Custom Table Borders and Shading

In most cases, the default $\frac{1}{2}$-pt single-line border will be appropriate for the tables you create. However, there may be occasions when you want to customize the border and add *shading* to some of the table cells.

You can make a number of border and shading changes using the Tables and Borders toolbar. Some toolbar buttons, such as Outside Border and Shading Options, have a down arrow you click to see a submenu of choices. If you know you want to make a number of choices from the submenu, you can "float" the menu away from the Tables and Borders toolbar. Click on the submenu's title bar and drag the menu to a new location. Figure 2-3 shows the Borders menu floating in this way. This menu stays open on the screen so that you don't have to click the down arrow again each time you want to make a new selection.

FIGURE 2-3
Borders menu floating under Tables and Borders toolbar

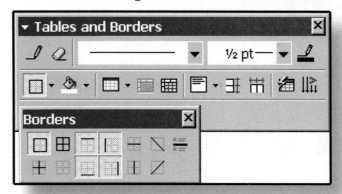

STEP-BY-STEP ▷ 2.7

1. Select the table.

2. Customize the table border:
   a. Click the down arrow next to the **Outside Border** button on the Tables and Borders toolbar. Several border options appear on a submenu. Click the submenu's title bar and drag down and to the right slightly to float the menu as shown in Figure 2-3.

   b. Select the **No Border** option on the **Borders** floating menu.
   c. Deselect the table and then select the row containing the column headings.
   d. Click the down arrow next to the **Line Weight** box on the Tables and Borders toolbar and select **1$\frac{1}{2}$ pt**.

(continued on next page)

e. Select the **Bottom Border** option on the **Borders** floating menu. Close the floating menu by clicking its close box.

3. Add shading to alternate rows in the table:

   a. With the row containing the column headings still selected, click the down arrow next to the **Shading Color** button on the Tables and Borders toolbar. A color palette opens.

   b. Select the third option in the first row (*Gray-10%*). The shading is applied to the row. Notice that the Shading Color button now shows this shading option.

   c. Select the row beginning *119079* and click the Shading Color button to apply the *Gray-10%* shading.

   d. Select the rows beginning *119081* and *119083* and apply the *Gray-10%* shading.

Hot Tip

Color shading adds interest to documents that will be viewed primarily on the screen or online. If you have a color printer, you can print color shading.

4. Click anywhere in the table to see the new shading. Save your changes. Print and close the document.

Extra Challenge

Save the document under a new name and experiment with different colors, border styles, and shading.

Drawing a Table and Splitting Table Cells

In addition to merging table cells, Word allows you to *split* table cells. Splitting is converting a single table cell into multiple cells. You can split a cell into two or more rows and/or into two or more columns.

The Draw Table tool allows you to use a pen pointer to draw a table boundary of just the size you want and then draw column and row lines within the boundary. To use the pen pointer to draw the boundary, click and drag down and to the right as if you were using the Rectangle drawing tool. To draw a column or row border, start from the boundary and drag down or across. Word completes your line for you and automatically makes it straight.

S TEP-BY-STEP ⟹ 2.8

1. Open a new document and, if necessary, display the Tables and Borders toolbar.

2. Use the Draw Table tool to create the table illustrated in Figure 2-4. You do not need to draw exact dimensions. Use the horizontal and vertical rulers on your screen to estimate the size of the table and the width and height of the columns and rows. Follow these general steps:

   a. Click the **Draw Table** tool on the Tables and Borders toolbar if it is not already active.

The pointer changes to a pencil and Word automatically changes to Print Layout view.

   b. Position the pointer at the left edge of the screen and drag down and to the right to create a table boundary. Release when the table (box) is approximately 6 inches wide by 2 inches high. Use the rulers on the top and left edges of the window to estimate the size.

c. Point toward the top border of the table and drag down to create the two vertical lines.

d. Point toward the first vertical line and drag to the right to create the two horizontal lines.

FIGURE 2-4
Use the Draw Table tool to create this table

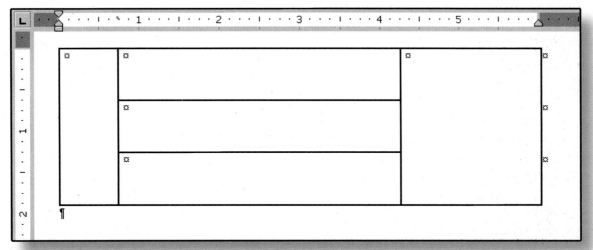

3. Save the document as **Recycling Rate** followed by your initials.

4. Split table cells:
   a. Select the middle column and click the **Split Cells** button on the Tables and Borders toolbar.
   b. In the Split Cells dialog box, change the number of columns to **1** and change the number of rows to **5**.
   c. Click **OK**. There are now five rows in the middle column.
   d. Click in the third column (it has only one cell). Click the **Split Cells** button. In the Split Cells dialog box, leave the number of columns set at **2**. Leave the number of rows set at **5**. Click **OK**.
   e. There are now a total of four columns. All columns except the first column have five rows.

5. Use the **Draw Table** tool to add cell boundaries in the first column as instructed in Figure 2-5.

Erase the cell border in the first row as shown in Figure 2-5.

FIGURE 2-5

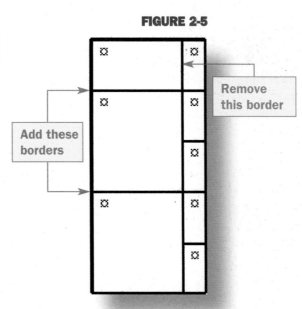

(continued on next page)

6. Complete the table as shown in Figure 2-6.

7. Save your changes and leave the document open for the next Step-by-Step.

FIGURE 2-6

Recycling·Rate¤		1998¤	1999¤
PET¤	Soft·drink·bottles¤	55%¤	57%¤
	Vegetable·oil·bottles¤	15%¤	21%¤
HDPE¤	Milk·jugs¤	34%¤	38%¤
	Bleach·and·laundry·detergent·bottles¤	19%¤	21%¤

Changing Text Alignment and Rotating Text

The Tables and Borders toolbar contains buttons you can use to align text in cells in a number of different ways. You can align text at the top, center, or bottom of a cell, as well as left, centered, or right using the alignment options shown in Figure 2-7.

You can quickly change the direction of text in a table cell by clicking the Change Text Direction button on the Tables and Borders toolbar. The Change Text Direction button toggles between three text positions. The third position is the horizontal placement of text with which you began.

FIGURE 2-7
Cell Alignment options

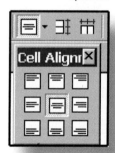

1. Align the text in the first table cell:
    a. Position the insertion point in the *Recycling Rate* cell.
    b. Click the down arrow to the right of the **Align Top Left** button on the Tables and Borders

toolbar. Several alignment options appear. Point to the title bar in the submenu options and drag down and to the right slightly to float the menu under the Tables and Borders toolbar.

c. Select the **Align Center** option. The text is centered between the left and right cell borders and between the top and bottom borders of the cell.

2. Select the four rows in the second column and then select the **Align Center Left** option.

3. Select all the rows in the *1998* and *1999* columns and then select the **Align Center Right** option.

4. Change text direction and align text in the first column:

a. Position the insertion point in the *PET* cell.

b. Click the **Change Text Direction** button on the Tables and Borders toolbar. The text is now rotated onto its side. (Don't worry if you still see the cell entry in its original position as well as in its rotated position.)

c. Click the **Change Text Direction** button again. The text is rotated again.

d. Click the **Align Center** option on the **Cell Alignment** floating menu. Notice the op-

tions are rotated to reflect the rotation of text in the cell.

e. Position the insertion point in the *HDPE* cell.

f. Click the **Change Text Direction** button twice. Click the **Align Center** option.

5. Bold all the text in the first row (*Recycling Rate, 1998*, and *1999*) and in the first column (*PET* and *HDPE*).

6. Close the Cell Alignment floating menu.

7. Center the table.

8. Save your changes. Print and close the document.

Hot Tip

When formatting table cells, you can position the insertion point in a table cell and right-click to access a shortcut menu. The shortcut menu includes options for formatting text direction, cell alignment, AutoFit, and table properties.

Integrating Word and Excel

W ord provides several ways to *import* Excel data into a Word document. You can copy and paste worksheet data, or you can insert the worksheet as a linked or embedded object. When transferring data from one application to another, the document in which you originally created the data is called the *source file*. The document to which you are transferring the data is called the *destination file*.

The simplest way to insert Excel data is to copy it in Excel and paste it in Word. When pasted in a Word document, the worksheet data becomes a table. You can edit the data just as you would any other Word table data.

You can also insert a worksheet as an embedded or linked object. An *embedded* object becomes part of the destination file. You can edit the object from the destination file by double-clicking it. Double-clicking opens the application that created the data and displays that application's toolbars and menus. When you have finished your modifications, click outside the embedded object again to return to Word.

To save file space, you can choose to insert the source file as a *linked* object. A linked object does not become a part of the destination file. When you link an object, you create a connection between the source file and the destination file. If you update the table in the source file, the object in the destination file is automatically updated because the files are linked.

Creating and Modifying a Worksheet in a Table

You have seen that Word tables can become pretty sophisticated. However, at times you might need a more complex table in which you can calculate and instantly recalculate numbers. The easiest way to create such a table in your word document is to embed an Excel Worksheet. The worksheet gives you access to all of Excel's data formatting and calculation options.

To insert an Excel worksheet, use the Insert Microsoft Excel Worksheet button on the Standard toolbar. After you select the number of rows and columns for the worksheet, the worksheet object appears in your document, as shown in Figure 2-8. Enter the data in the worksheet just as you would when working in Excel.

FIGURE 2-8
A worksheet object inserted in a document

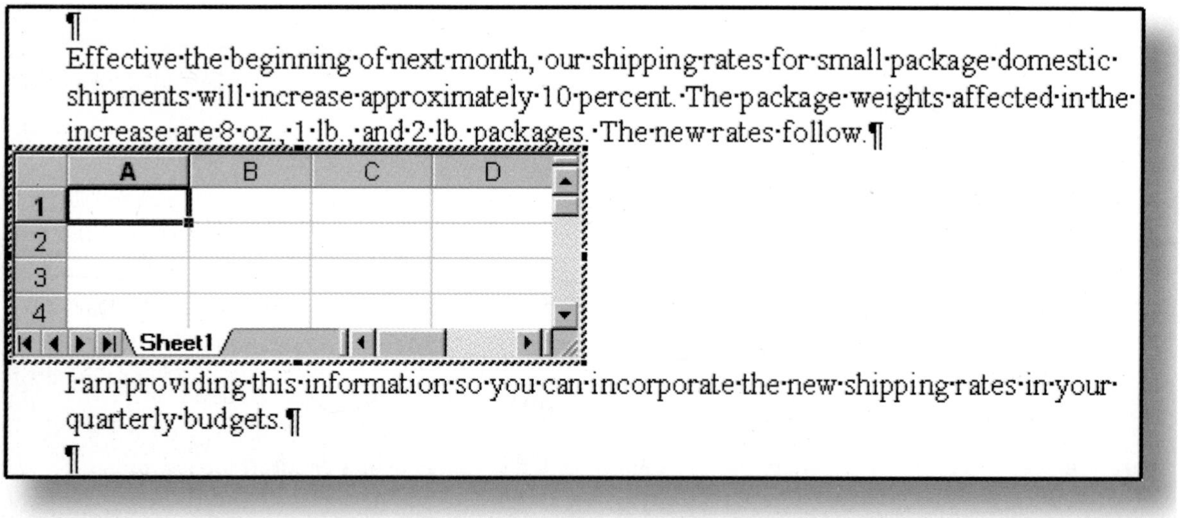

STEP-BY-STEP ▷ 2.10

1. Open **AW Step2-10** from the student data files and save the document as **Shipping Rates** followed by your initials.

2. Position the insertion point in the second blank paragraph between the two paragraphs in the body of the memo.

3. Embed an Excel worksheet:
   a. Click the **Insert Microsoft Excel Worksheet** button on the Standard toolbar.
   b. Drag down and across to create a 4 x 4 grid. The worksheet is inserted in the document.

4. Key the following data in the worksheet cells:

```
Weight   Next AM   Next PM   2nd Day
8 oz.    7.15      5.36      3.58
1 lb.    8.79      6.59      4.4
2 lb.    9.75      7.31      4.88
```

5. Click outside the worksheet. The worksheet displays like a table with no borders.

6. Click in the table once to select it and then click the **Center** button on the Formatting toolbar to center the table in the body of the memo.

7. Edit the worksheet as follows:
   a. Double-click the worksheet.
   b. Format the number entries for currency with two decimal places by first selecting cell range **B2:D4**. Open the **Format** menu and click **Cells**. On the **Number** tab, click the **Currency** option and specify two decimal places and the dollar sign. Click **OK**.
   c. Click in the cell for the 2nd Day rate for 1 lb. and key **4.83**. Click in the cell for the 2nd Day rate for 2 lb. and key **5.85**.

8. Click outside the worksheet to view the table in the document.

9. Key your initials at the end of the document.

10. Save your changes. Print and close the document.

Using the Object Command to Import a Worksheet in a Table

Another easy way to embed (or link) a worksheet in a document is to use the Object command on the Insert menu. This command enables you to create a new object or link or embed an object that already exists.

You can create a link between the source file and your current document. You can also choose to display the object as an icon in your current document.

1. Open **AW Step2-11a** from the student data files and save it as **Sales Memo** followed by your initials.

2. Open data file **AW Step2-11b** in Excel and save it as **Sales** followed by your initials. Select the cell range **A1:E5**.

3. Switch to the **Sales Memo** document in Word.

4. Position the insertion point at the end of the document, then open the **Insert** menu and choose **Object**.

5. Click the **Create from File** tab.

6. Click **Browse** and then locate the Excel file **Sales**. Select the file name when you locate the document and click **Insert**. The file name appears in the *File name* box on the **Create from File** tab.

7. To link this file to your current document, click the *Link to file* box and then click **OK**.

8. The worksheet appears in your document. Click the object once to select it.

9. Click the **Center** button on the Formatting toolbar to center the table horizontally.

10. Save your changes and then switch to the **Sales** document in Excel.

11. Use AutoSum to calculate the totals in the *Total* column and the *TOTAL* row. Save the changes and close the worksheet. Close Excel.

12. Return to the **Sales Memo** document in Word. Notice that the worksheet in the **Sales Memo** document is updated with the totals.

13. Key your initials at the bottom of the memo.

14. Save your changes. Print and close the document.

Creating a Chart

Charts provide a visual display of data and often make the material easier to understand. Word enables you to convert table data into colorful, three-dimensional charts. There are several options for chart types (column, bar, line, pie, and so forth). You can also format charts with titles, legends, and labels.

Creating and Modifying a Chart

You can create a chart from a table in Word, or you can create a chart from an Excel worksheet and paste or embed the chart in a Word document. In the next activity, you will create a chart from a Word table.

To create a chart, open the Insert menu, click Picture, and then click Chart on the submenu. Word creates the chart from your data and displays it along with the *datasheet*, a worksheet-like grid that contains the data used to prepare the chart. If you need to modify data for the chart, you do so in the datasheet.

After you create a chart, you can modify it in a number of ways. You can change the chart type in the Chart Type dialog box, shown in Figure 2-9. Each chart type has several subtypes you can choose from to present your data just as you want it. You can also resize the chart by dragging its selection handles and move it by dragging it to any location.

You can also change options used to format a chart using the many options in the tabs of the Chart Options dialog box, shown in Figure 2-10. For example, you can insert a title for the chart or the axes, you can add labels for the data, and you can change the font and location of the chart's legend.

Hot Tip

Microsoft Graph 2000 Chart must be installed in order for you to complete this exercise.

FIGURE 2-9
Standard Types folder in the Chart Type dialog box

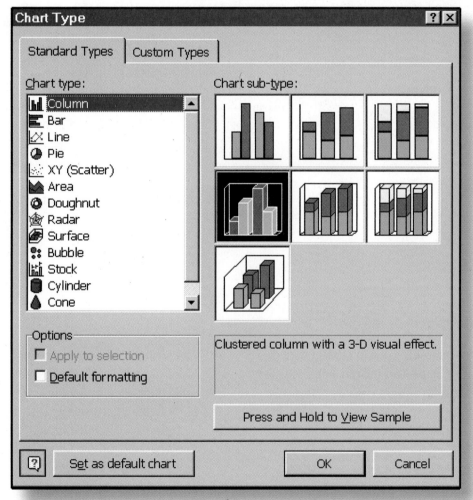

FIGURE 2-10
Chart Options dialog box

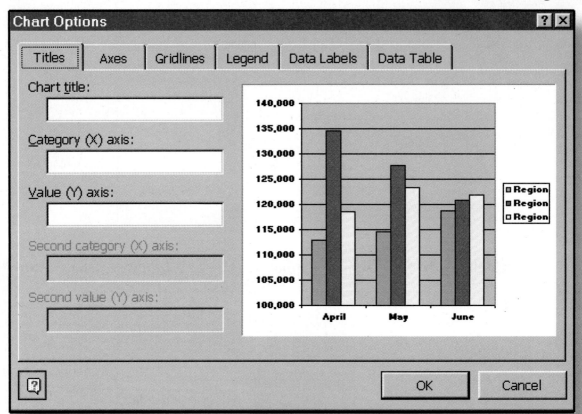

STEP-BY-STEP ▷ 2.12

1. Open **AW Step2-12** from the student data files and save it as **Second Quarter Sales** followed by your initials.

2. Select the table.

3. Open the **Insert** menu, choose **Picture**, and then choose **Chart** on the submenu.

4. Word displays a chart and the datasheet. Click the datasheet's close box.

5. Notice that Word automatically created a column chart to display the data contained within the table. Change the chart type:

a. With the chart selected (a cross-hatched border surrounds the chart), open the **Chart** menu and choose **Chart Type**. The Chart Type dialog box opens.

b. Under *Chart type*, **Column** should be chosen. Select the first option in the first row and then click **OK**.

6. Change the chart options:

   a. Open the **Chart** menu and choose **Chart Options**. The Chart Options dialog box opens.

   b. In the *Chart title* box on the **Titles** tab, key **Second Quarter Sales**.

   c. In the *Category (X) axis* box, key **Months**.

   d. In the *Value (Z) axis* box, key **Sales Volume**.

   e. Click the **Legend** tab. Change the placement of the legend to **Bottom** and click **OK**.

7. Click in the table above the chart. Open the **Table** menu, choose **Delete**, and then choose **Table** on the submenu to remove the table.

8. Click the chart to select it and then click the **Center** button on the Formatting toolbar to center the chart horizontally. Click the middle handle on the bottom border and drag downward about an inch to resize the chart.

9. Save your changes and leave the document open for the next Step-by-Step.

Importing Data into a Chart

Once you have created the chart, you can edit the data on the datasheet, import data from a text file, import an Excel worksheet, or copy data from another program. In this activity you will import data from an Excel worksheet.

To import data into a datasheet, display the datasheet and click the Import File button on the Standard toolbar. The Import Data Options dialog box opens, as shown in Figure 2-11. Here you can select a particular sheet to import data from and decide whether to import all data on a sheet or only a selected range. If the *Overwrite existing cells* box is checked, your existing data will be replaced by the imported data.

FIGURE 2-11
Import Data Options dialog box

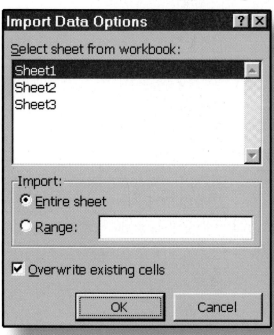

1. If necessary, double-click the chart to select it and display a cross-hatched border. The menus and toolbars now show the Microsoft Graph menus and buttons.

2. Import new data into the chart:

   a. In Excel, open **AW Step2-13** from the student data files to view its contents. Note that this worksheet contains information for the month of June in cells D1 through D4.

   b. Close the Excel worksheet.

   c. If the datasheet is not displayed in the Word document, click the **View Datasheet** button.

   ### Hot Tip

   When you want the imported data inserted in a cell other than the upper left cell on the datasheet, you must first select the cell.

   d. Click in the cell to the right of the *May* column heading in the datasheet.

   e. Click the **Import File** button on the Standard toolbar.

   f. In the *Look in* box, locate the Excel file **AW Step2-13**. Select the file name when you locate the document and click **Open**. The Import Data Options dialog box opens.

   g. Select **Range** under *Import* and then key **d1:d4** in the *Range* box. Turn off *Overwrite existing cells* and then click **OK**. The June figures are imported into the chart.

3. Close the datasheet. Click outside the chart to deselect it.

4. Save your changes. Print and close the document.

Summary

In this lesson, you learned:

- Word's AutoFit feature will automatically adjust column width and row height to fit a table to its contents or to the window.

- Text separated by commas, tabs, or spaces can be converted into a table format.

- Tables can be modified by inserting, deleting, and moving rows and columns.

- Merging cells combines two or more cells into a single cell; splitting cells divides a single cell into two or more cells.

- There are several options available on the Tables and Borders toolbar for changing borders, shading, and the direction and alignment of text in a table cell.

- An embedded object becomes part of the destination file.

- A linked object saves file space and creates a connection between the source file and the destination file. When the source file is updated, the destination file is also updated.

- Excel worksheets can be embedded and modified in Word documents.

- The chart feature enables you to create a variety of chart types of worksheet or table data.

LESSON 2 REVIEW QUESTIONS

TRUE/FALSE

Circle T if the statement is true or F if the statement is false.

T **F** 1. You can quickly insert or delete multiple rows and columns in one edit by selecting the desired number of rows or columns you want to add or delete and then choosing the appropriate Table command.

T **F** 2. You can use the Draw Table tool to add or delete cell boundaries. *Add with "Draw Table" Delete with "Eraser"*

T **F** 3. Converting a single table cell into multiple cells is called splitting the cell.

T **F** 4. A linked object becomes part of the destination file. *embedded*

T **F** 5. You can move rows and columns in a table the same way you move text in a document.

T **F** 6. You can align text within a table cell only as left, centered, or right. *9 alignments*

FILL IN THE BLANKS

Complete the following sentences by writing the correct word or words in the blanks provided.

1. To quickly insert a new row at the end of a table, press ___Tab Key___.

2. To automatically resize a table, select the table, open the ___Table___ menu, and choose ___Auto Fit___.

3. To convert text to a table, open the _____Table_____ menu and choose _____Convert_____.

4. When transferring data from one application to another, the document in which you originally created the data is called the _____Source_____ file. The document to which you are transferring the data is called the _____destination_____ file.

LESSON 2 PROJECTS

PROJECT 2-1

complete

1. Create a table and key the document illustrated in Figure 2-12.

2. Save the document as **Officers** followed by your initials.

3. Insert a third column at the end of the table.

4. Key the column heading **Corporation** and the following list of company names:
```
KOT, Inc.
Savannah Innovations
South-West Tech
National Plastics Corporation
Mears Manufacturing
The Kissinger Company
```

FIGURE 2-12

Name	Title
Fujio Shinoda	President
Curtis Sullivan	President-elect
Alberta Suarez	Past President
Isabel Guzman	Secretary/Treasurer
Tanya Sheehan	Board Member
Paul Rees	Board Member

5. Move the *Title* column to the left of the *Name* column.

6. Center the table and AutoFit the width of the columns for a more attractive layout.

7. Add two new rows above the column headings. In the first row, key the title **NATIONAL ALLIANCE OFFICERS**.

8. Merge the cells in the top row. Center the heading and change it to **Arial 16-pt bold**.

9. Center and bold the column headings.

10. Remove the table borders.

11. Save your changes. Print and close the document.

PROJECT 2-2

1. Use the Draw Table tool to create the table illustrated in Figure 2-13.

2. Save the document as **Products** followed by your initials.

3. Use the following features to format the table:

   Distribute rows evenly
   Cell alignment
   Shading color
   AutoFit
   Center table

4. Save your changes. Print and close the document.

FIGURE 2-13

PRODUCTS MADE FROM RECYCLED PLASTICS	
Automobile	Batteries and battery accessories
	Ice scrapers
	Motor oil
	Oil funnels
	Windshield washer solvent bottles
Toys and Sports	Backpacks
	Bait containers
	Bicycle racks
	Playground equipment
	Sandboxes
Clothing	Hats
	Jackets
	Jeans
	Sweatshirts
	T-shirts

PROJECT 2-3

1. Open **AW Project2-3a** from the student data files and save as **Countries** followed by your initials.

    Select table first   insert picture > chart

2. Create a bar chart from the table data. The title of the chart is **Requests by Country**. The Value Z axis is **# of Requests**.

3. Import the data for France from data file **AW Project2-3b** (an Excel worksheet) so that the information appears after Switzerland.

4. Delete the table so the document contains only the chart.

5. Center the chart horizontally and resize the chart if desired.

6. Save your changes. Print and close the document.

CRITICAL THINKING

SCANS

ACTIVITY 2-1

Carol is preparing an itinerary for her supervisor before she leaves on a 10-day business trip. The itinerary will provide her boss with pertinent information about her destinations and schedule for the next several days as well as telephone numbers where she can be reached. Carol created a table to organize the information and she created column headings in the first row of the table. The information is quite detailed and her table is long and wraps to a second page. How can Carol repeat the table headings on subsequent pages without keying them again? Use the Help feature to find the answer.

ACTIVITY 2-2

After Carol completed the itinerary, she noticed that one of the rows contained several lines of text. The row was positioned at the bottom of the first page and the content in that row wrapped to the second page. Carol does not want to split the information in that row. How can she prevent a table row from breaking across pages? Use the Help feature to find the answer.

MERGING FORM DOCUMENTS, MAILING LABELS, AND ENVELOPES

OBJECTIVES

Upon completion of this lesson, you should be able to:

- Create a main document.

- Create and edit a data source.

- Preview the merged documents.

- Merge the main document and data source.

- Sort and filter records to be merged.

- Prepare mailing labels with a merge.

- Prepare envelopes with a merge.

- Create catalogs and lists.

⏱ **Estimated Time: 1.5 hours**

Creating Mail Merge Documents

Mail merge documents are documents with ***boilerplate text*** (text that remains constant) and variable text (text that is individualized from document to document). The merge process combines the variable information (such as names and addresses) from a data source with a generic document. The result is a set of personalized documents, such as form letters, mailing labels, or envelopes. You can also use mail merge to create a single document, such as a catalog or membership directory.

Creating the Main Document

To begin the mail merge process, you must first create the generic document (called the main document). The ***main document*** contains the boilerplate text, with ***merge fields*** at the locations where variable text is to be inserted. To create a main document, you can begin with a new document or open an existing document. Then open the Tools menu and click Mail Merge to open the Mail Merge Helper dialog box, as shown in Figure 3-1.

FIGURE 3-1
Mail Merge Helper dialog box

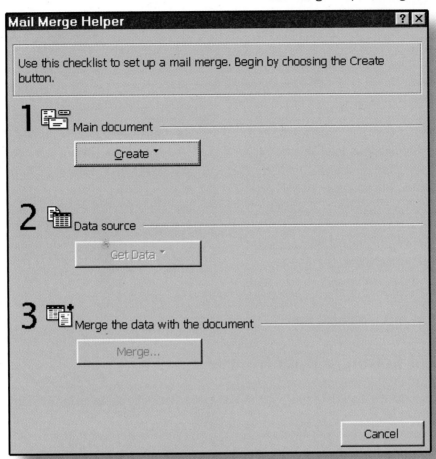

Click Create in the *Main document* area to see a drop-down list of possible main documents. After you choose one, Word displays the prompt shown in Figure 3-2. Click Active Window if you want to use your current document as the main document (even if you have not entered any text yet). Click New Main Document to open a new document for your main document.

FIGURE 3-2
Click a choice here to specify a main document

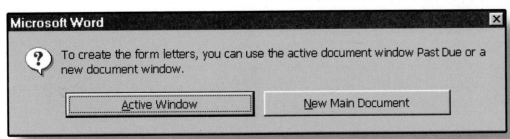

In Step-by-Step 3.1 through Step-by-Step 3.5, you will set up documents for mail merge and then perform the merge. These activities should be completed in a single class session. You will need approximately 40 minutes.

STEP-BY-STEP ▷ 3.1

1. Open **AW Step3-1** from the student data files and save the document as **Past Due** followed by your initials. Take a moment to glance through the letter. The letters *xx* indicate locations where you will insert merge fields later.

2. Indicate the current letter as the main document to be used for the form letters:

   a. Open the **Tools** menu and choose **Mail Merge**. The Mail Merge Helper dialog box opens.

   b. Under *Main document*, click **Create**. Then select **Form Letters** from the menu.

   c. Click **Active Window** in the prompt box.

3. Leave the Mail Merge Helper dialog box on the screen for the next Step-by-Step.

Creating and Editing a Data Source

The *data source* is the document containing the variable text to be merged into the main document. You can either open an existing data source or create a new data source. In Step-by-Step 3.2, you will create a new data source.

To create a new data source, you click Get Data in the *Data source* area of the Mail Merge Helper dialog box, and then click Create Data Source on the menu. Word opens the Create Data Source dialog box, shown in Figure 3-3. Like a database, the data source stores information in *fields*. Each field is identified by a *field name*.

Your first step in creating a data source is to identify the field names to be used in the main document. Word displays common field names in the *Field names in header row* list box. You can use these field names, delete those you do not need, or add different field names. Although it is not necessary for field names to be in a particular order in the data source, it is often more convenient to rearrange the list so that the field names are in the order in which they will appear in the main document.

After you have created the data source, you save it just as you would save any other Word document. Word displays another prompt (Figure 3-4) to remind you that your new data source contains no data. You will add records in Step-by-Step 3.3.

Hot Tip

Multiple merge documents can share the same data source. Some of the merge documents will use more fields than others. (For example, for this exercise, some letters will have departments and others will not.) You must be sure to include all fields in this dialog box that will be used for any of the form documents.

FIGURE 3-3
Create Data Source dialog box

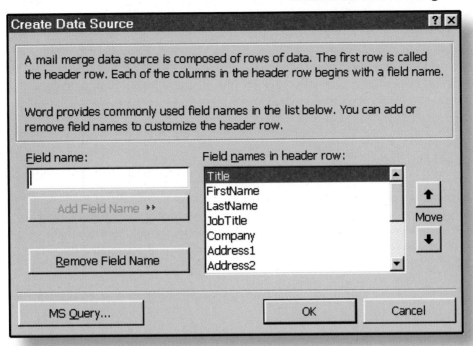

FIGURE 3-4
Prompt to edit data source or main document

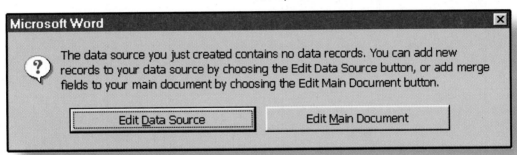

S TEP-BY-STEP ▷ 3.2

1. In the Mail Merge Helper dialog box, click **Get Data** under *Data source*.

2. Click **Create Data Source**. The Create Data Source dialog box opens.

3. You need the first three field names for your data source, but you do not need the fourth. Remove the *JobTitle* field as follows:
   a. Click the *JobTitle* field name in the *Field names in header row* list box.
   b. Click **Remove Field Name**.

(continued on next page)

4. Click the down arrow on the scroll bar (not the down arrow under *Move*). Click on and remove the field names *Country*, *HomePhone*, and *WorkPhone*.

5. Add a new field name:
   a. Key **Middle** in the *Field name* box.
   b. Click **Add Field Name**.

6. Add the following field names. Do not space between words.

```
Department
InvoiceAmount
InvoiceNumber
InvoiceDate
Officer
```

7. Move a field name up in the list:
   a. Click the *Middle* field name.
   b. Click the *Move* up arrow to the right of the list box. Continue to click the *Move* up arrow until *Middle* is immediately above

the *LastName* field name. (If you accidentally move the field name up too far, click the *Move* down arrow.)

8. Move the *Department* field name immediately above *Company*.

9. Click **OK**.

10. Your list of field names is complete. The Save As dialog box appears for you to name your data source file. Save the document as **Accounts Receivable** followed by your initials.

11. When the prompt to edit the data source or the main document appears, click **Edit Data Source** to indicate that you want to work with the data source.

12. Leave the Data Form dialog box on your screen for the next Step-by-Step.

The Data Form dialog box (Figure 3-5) now displayed on your screen is where you insert data into your data source. At the far left are the field names you saved. A blank box (field) follows each field name.

FIGURE 3-5
Data Form dialog box

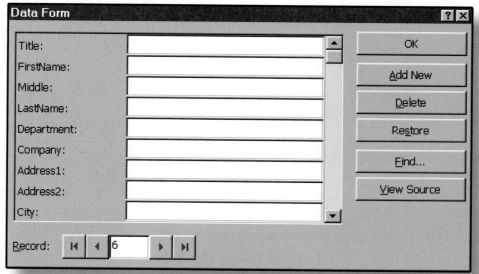

Each data form you complete becomes a *data record*. Each data record will be merged with the main document to create an individualized form letter. Notice the record number at the bottom of the dialog box. This number will change each time you add a new data record.

STEP-BY-STEP ▷ 3.3

Figure 3-6 lists the information you will key for each data record. The field names appear in the first column. Each of the other columns contains the information for a single record. Leave field boxes blank where shown in Figure 3-6.

FIGURE 3-6

Title	Mr.	Ms.	Mr.	Mr.	Ms.
FirstName	Gabriel	Cindy	Roy	Krikor	Tien
Middle	J.	A.	R.	H.	
LastName	Castillo	Shonrock	Henson	Selian	Pai
Department	Accounts Payable	Accounting Department			
Company	American Plastic Parts	Smith's Plastics, Inc.	The Plastic Factory		Eckert Specialty Plastics
Address1	7007 North Main Street	155 Churchill Drive	2245 West Roosevelt	165 Kempton Drive	424 Collins Avenue
Address2				Suite 3004	
City	Niles	Simi Valley	Jackson	Chicago	Karstad
State	IL	CA	MS	IL	MN
PostalCode	60648-3008	93065-1997	39215-0901	60650-1241	56732-2069
InvoiceAmount	4,047.20	11,673.11	1,345.78	9,766.38	2,677.01
InvoiceNumber	26928	28799	32567	31244	31005
InvoiceDate	March 23	May 4	February 16	May 1	April 14
Officer	Richard Trudeau	Sue Mitrovich	Nancy Valaas	Marie Frauenhei	Richard Trudeau

1. Key the information for the first data record:
   a. Key **Mr.** for *Title*.
   b. Press **Enter** or **Tab**, and key **Gabriel** for *FirstName*.
   c. Continue to key the information shown in the second column of Figure 3-6. (Note that after you key the street address for the *Address1* field, you will need to press **Enter** or **Tab** twice to leave the *Address2* field blank.)

2. After keying the officer's name (*Richard Trudeau*), click **Add New** or press **Enter** to display a new blank data form.

3. Key the information for the next four records.

4. After keying the information for the last record, click **View Source** to view the completed data source.

5. Save the data source and leave it open for the next Step-by-Step.

The data source appears on your screen in table form, as shown in Figure 3-7. The first row of your data source (known as the **header row**) contains the field names you will use to merge the main document with the data source. Each remaining row is a data record.

FIGURE 3-7
Portion of completed data source in table form

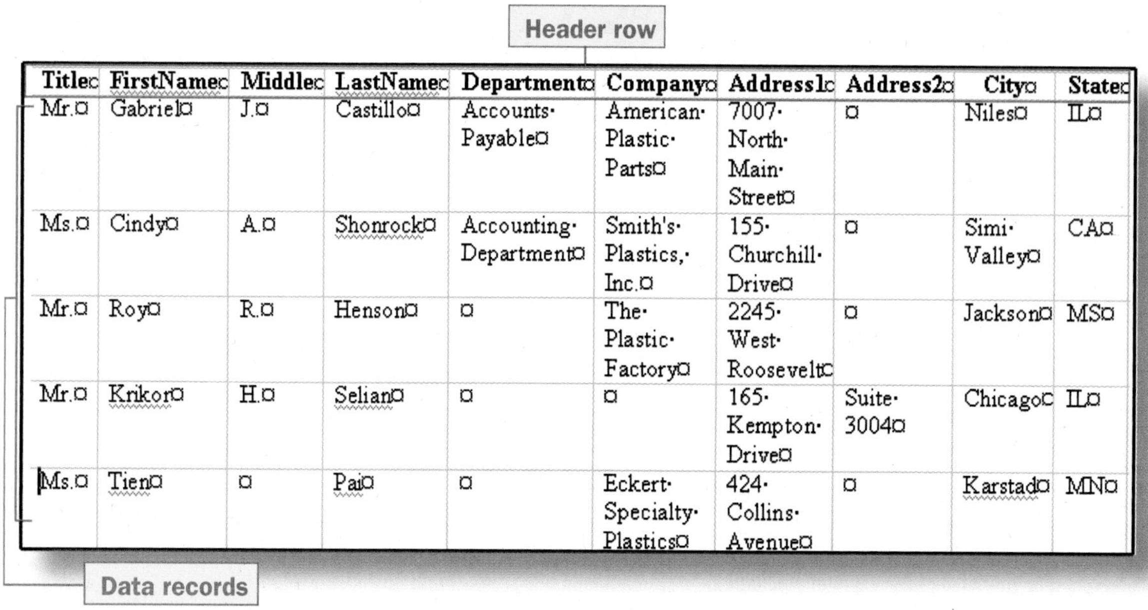

Header row

Title	FirstName	Middle	LastName	Department	Company	Address1	Address2	City	State
Mr.	Gabriel	J.	Castillo	Accounts Payable	American Plastic Parts	7007 North Main Street		Niles	IL
Ms.	Cindy	A.	Shonrock	Accounting Department	Smith's Plastics, Inc.	155 Churchill Drive		Simi Valley	CA
Mr.	Roy	R.	Henson		The Plastic Factory	2245 West Roosevelt		Jackson	MS
Mr.	Krikor	H.	Selian			165 Kempton Drive	Suite 3004	Chicago	IL
Ms.	Tien		Pai		Eckert Specialty Plastics	424 Collins Avenue		Karstad	MN

Data records

Do not be concerned about the appearance of the table. Although text wraps as necessary to fit the table boundaries, you do not need to adjust the table column widths. The information will print appropriately on the merge letters.

A new toolbar, the database toolbar (Figure 3-8), also appears. You can use the tools on this toolbar to manipulate data in your data source and assist you in the mail merge process.

FIGURE 3-8
Database toolbar

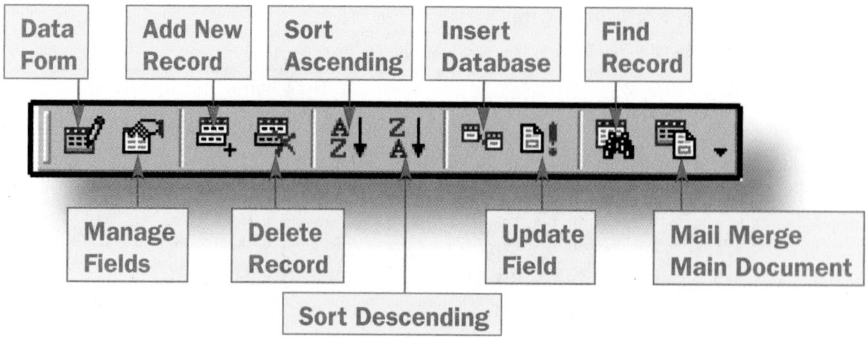

Data Form

Add New Record

Sort Ascending

Insert Database

Find Record

Manage Fields

Delete Record

Update Field

Mail Merge Main Document

Sort Descending

Inserting Merge Fields in the Main Document

To complete the main document, you need to substitute field names for the letters *xx* throughout the document. You do this using buttons on the Mail Merge toolbar in your main document window (Figure 3-9).

Hot Tip

The *xx*s appear in this document to help you see where merge fields should be inserted. You do not need to key *xx*s in your form documents.

FIGURE 3-9
Mail Merge toolbar

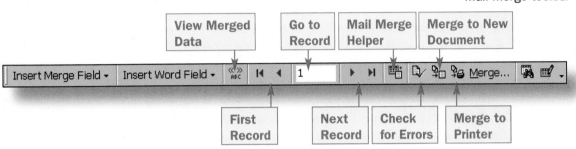

With the main document on the screen, position the insertion point where you want to insert a merge field. Then click the Insert Merge Field button on the Mail Merge toolbar. A drop-down list of the field names from the data source appears (Figure 3-10). Click the field name to insert it in your document.

FIGURE 3-10
Merge field drop-down list

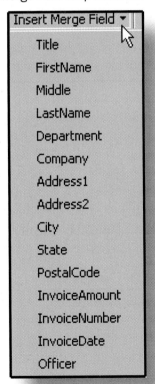

1. Click the **Mail Merge Main Document** button on the database toolbar to switch from the data source to the main document.

2. Insert a merge field:
   a. Scroll toward the top of the letter.
   b. Delete the first occurrence of the letters *xx,* but do not delete the paragraph mark.
   c. Click the **Insert Merge Field** button on the Mail Merge toolbar.
   d. On the drop-down menu, click the first field to be inserted (*Title*). *Title* is inserted as a merge field surrounded by chevrons (« »).

3. Press the **spacebar**, click the **Insert Merge Field** button, and click **FirstName**.

4. Press the **spacebar**, click the **Insert Merge Field** button, and click **Middle**.

5. Press the **spacebar**, click the **Insert Merge Field** button, and click **LastName**.

6. On the next four lines, delete the *xx* and insert the fields *Department, Company, Address1,* and *Address2*.

7. On the last line for the inside address, delete the *xx* and insert the field *City*. Then key a comma, press the **spacebar**, and insert the field *State*. Press the **spacebar** twice and insert the field *PostalCode*.

8. Delete the *xx* in the salutation (do not delete the colon) and insert the fields *Title* and *LastName*, with a space between the fields. Your inside address and salutation lines should now look like Figure 3-11.

FIGURE 3-11
Inside address and salutation with merge fields

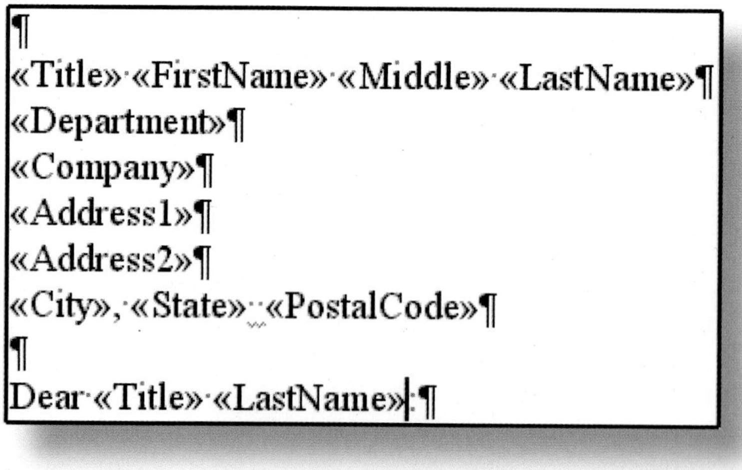

¶
«Title» «FirstName» «Middle» «LastName»¶
«Department»¶
«Company»¶
«Address1»¶
«Address2»¶
«City», «State» «PostalCode»¶
¶
Dear «Title» «LastName»:¶

9. Delete the first *xx* in the body of the letter (do not delete the dollar sign or the period). Then insert the field *InvoiceAmount*.

10. Replace the next two *xx*s with the fields *InvoiceNumber* and *InvoiceDate*.

11. Scroll down and replace the *xx* in the closing lines with the field *Officer*.

12. Save your changes to the main document and leave it open for the next Step-by-Step.

Previewing, Merging, and Printing the Form Documents

Although it is not necessary to preview before you merge and print your form documents, you may find it useful to preview one or two form documents before you print the entire set. If you are satisfied with the way your merged documents look, you can go ahead and perform the merge. To preview your merged documents, click the View Merged Data button on the Mail Merge toolbar. Data from your data source then appears in the main document instead of the merge fields. You can scroll through all records of your data source using the Next Record button on the Mail Merge toolbar. When you have finished previewing, click the View Merged Data button again to turn it off.

You have several options for the final merge. If you click Merge to New Document on the Mail Merge toolbar, Word creates a new document containing all of your merged items. You can then review them in the new document before printing and save the document with a new name. If you click Merge to Printer on the toolbar, Word sends the merged items directly to the printer.

You do not need to print all the documents from a merge. When merging to a new document, Word places each merged item in a section. You can tell Word to print a specific merged document by choosing the *Pages* option in the Print dialog box and then keying the section number of the document you want to print with the letter *s*. For example, to print only the fourth merged letter, key *s4*. You can see what section a particular merged item is by looking at the *Sec* number on the status bar.

STEP-BY-STEP 3.5

1. Move the insertion point to the top of the main document.

2. Preview the first two form documents:
   a. With the number *1* displayed in the *Go to Record* box, click the **View Merged Data** button on the Mail Merge toolbar. The button will stay highlighted.
   b. Scroll through the displayed letter and notice that the merge fields have been replaced with the variable information from Mr. Castillo's data record.
   c. Click the **Next Record** button on the Mail Merge toolbar.

   d. Scroll through the displayed letter and notice that the merge fields have been replaced with the variable information from Ms. Shonrock's data record.

 Hot Tip

If you get unexpected spaces or punctuation in your merged documents, you may have keyed spaces or punctuation in the data source records. Switch to the data source, view the data source (in table form), and make any necessary corrections. Save the changes to the data source, go back to the main document, and repeat the merge.

(continued on next page)

3. Click the **Previous Record** button on the Mail Merge toolbar.

4. Click the **View Merged Data** button to turn it off. The field names (rather than the variable information) are again displayed.

5. Click the **Merge to New Document** button on the Mail Merge toolbar.

6. Print only the first form letter:
   a. Open the **File** menu and choose **Print**.
   b. In the Print dialog box, click the *Pages* option and key **s1** in the *Pages* box.
   c. Click **OK**.

7. Close the document. Leave the **Past Due** document open for the next Step-by-Step.

Hot Tip

To save space on your drive, save merged documents only if you will use them frequently. If you save the main document and the data source, you can run the merge each time you need the merged documents.

Sorting and Filtering Data Sources

In Step-by-Step 3.5 you merged *all* the data records according to the order in which they appeared in the data source. To merge in a different order or to print only letters with data records meeting a certain criterion, Word allows you to sort and *filter* (select specific) data records.

To filter and sort records, you use options in the Query Options dialog box, shown in Figure 3-12. You display this dialog box by clicking the Mail Merge Helper button on the Mail Merge toolbar and then clicking Query Options in the Mail Merge Helper dialog box.

FIGURE 3-12
Filter Records tab in the Query Options dialog box

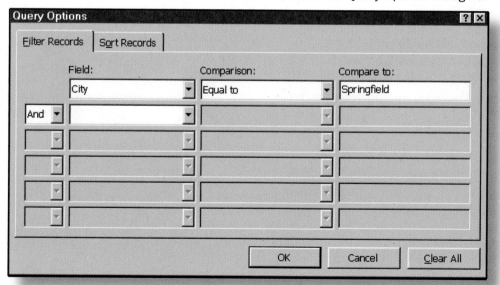

On the Filter Records tab, set up conditions that records must meet in order to be merged. Suppose, for example, you want to merge records only for persons who live in the city of Springfield. On the Filter Records tab, click the *Field* down arrow and select the City field. In the *Comparison* list box, the entry should be *Equal to*, because you want the city name to be the same as (or "equal to") Springfield. In the *Compare to* text box, key the text you want to use for the filter (in this example, you would key *Springfield*). This filter will find all records in which the city is Springfield and use them in the merge.

Notice that you can specify more than one criterion by using additional boxes on the tab. Use the *And* operator to add a criterion to your filter. For example, you might want to merge all records where the city is Springfield *and* the balance is greater than $2,000. Only records that meet both these conditions will be merged. You can also use the *Or* operator to filter for two different conditions. For example, you can specify a merge for records where the city is Springfield *or* the balance is greater than $2,000. This filter would merge all Springfield records as well as any record where the balance is greater than $2,000.

You can use the Sort Records tab in the Query Options dialog box to sort records before the merge (Figure 3-13). Notice that you can sort in ascending or descending order by up to three fields in the records.

FIGURE 3-13
Sort Records tab in the Query Options dialog box

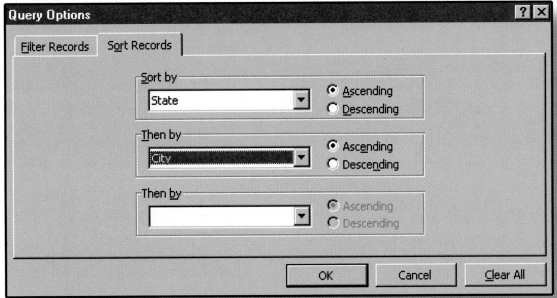

After you have selected query options such as a filter or sort, the Mail Merge Helper dialog box shows that query options have been set. These options remain in effect until you change them. You can remove query options by returning to the Query Options dialog box and clicking Clear All on any tab where you set a query option.

You can also return to the data source and use sorting buttons on the Database toolbar to sort entries in any field.

SCANS

1. If the **Accounts Receivable** document does not appear on your taskbar, click the **Edit Data Source** button on the Mail Merge toolbar. Then, in the Data Form dialog box, click **View Source**.

2. Sort by a single data field:
   a. Click anywhere in the *LastName* column.
   b. Click the **Sort Ascending** button on the Database toolbar.

3. Undo the sort.

4. You want to merge only records for clients in the state of Illinois. Apply a filter that will specify this criterion:
   a. Click the **Mail Merge Main Document** button on the Database toolbar to switch to the main document.
   b. Click the **Mail Merge Helper** button on the Mail Merge toolbar.
   c. Click **Query Options**. The Query Options dialog box opens with the Filter Records tab showing.
   d. In the *Field* box, click the down arrow and select **State**. The *Comparison* and *Compare to* boxes become active.
   e. *Equal to* is the comparison operator you want in the *Comparison* list box. Key **IL** in the *Compare to* text box.

5. Sort the data source by more than one field:
   a. Click the **Sort Records** tab in the Query Options dialog box.
   b. Click the down arrow for the *Sort by* list box to open the list box. Scroll down and click **State**. If necessary, click the **Ascending** option next to the list box.
   c. Open the first *Then by* list box. Scroll down and click **City**. If necessary, click the **Ascending** option. Do not select anything for the second *Then by* list box.
   d. Click **OK** to return to the Mail Merge Helper dialog box. Notice that *Options in Effect* now shows *Query Options have been set*.
   e. Click **Close** to return to the main document.

6. Click **Accounts Receivable** on the taskbar. The data source should now be sorted first by state and then by city. Notice there are two IL records (Mr. Selian's and Mr. Castillo's), so Word then sorted by city (first Chicago, then Niles).

7. Return to the **Past Due** document. Merge to a new document and scroll through the document to see that it contains only the two form letters for clients in the state of Illinois.

8. Print the document. Close it without saving.

9. Return to the Query Options dialog box and click **Clear All** on both the **Filter Records** and **Sort Records** tabs. Close the dialog box.

10. Close all other open documents and save changes to them if prompted.

Extra Challenge

Try printing selected records. Open the main document and then select Merge in the Mail Merge Toolbar. Under Records to be merged, key a record number (for example, 2) in the *From* box and a record number (for example, 3) in the *To* box.

Preparing Mailing Labels and Envelopes

To create merged mailing labels or envelopes, you can use addressee information from an existing data source or you can create a new data source. You can use any data source totally separate from any merge document connected to the data source.

Hot Tip

It is not necessary to use the actual mailing labels or envelopes for these exercises. You can print on regular paper.

Preparing Mailing Labels

To prepare mailing labels, you use many of the same steps you took to create form letters. After clicking Mail Merge on the Tools menu, click Create and then choose Mailing Labels from the drop-down menu. Specify the main document and then locate or create the data source for the labels. You will then see a prompt to set up your main document (Figure 3-14). To set up your main document, you first change or approve options in the Label Options dialog box (Figure 3-15).

FIGURE 3-14
Prompt to set up main document

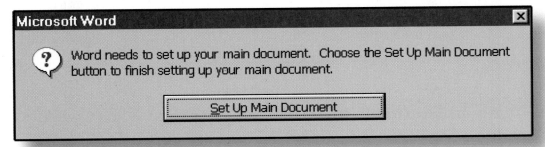

FIGURE 3-15
Label Options dialog box

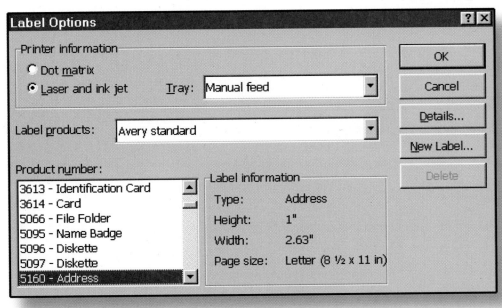

After you set label options, the Create Labels dialog box opens, as shown in Figure 3-16. Insert fields into the *Sample label* box in the same way you inserted merge fields in the form letter. Notice that you can also choose to insert postal bar codes for each label. If you choose to insert the postal bar code, you will need to tell Word which field contains the ZIP code and which field contains the street address (Figure 3-17). You are then ready to merge the labels.

FIGURE 3-16
Create Labels dialog box

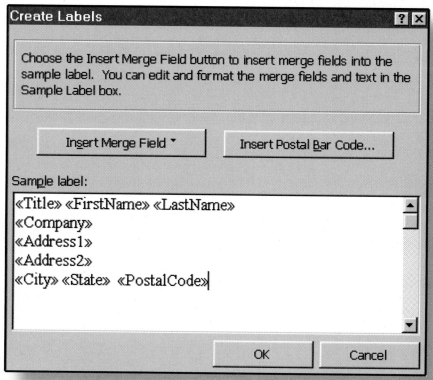

FIGURE 3-17
Insert Postal Bar Code dialog box

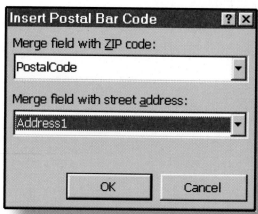

Whether or not you have mailing labels available, you should always print a sample on plain paper and compare the sample sheet of labels to see if you need to position the labels differently in the printer or if you need to adjust your main document settings (such as margins, page length, and column width).

STEP-BY-STEP ▷ 3.7

1. In a new document window, open the **Tools** menu and choose **Mail Merge**.

2. In the Mail Merge Helper dialog box, click **Create** and then click **Mailing Labels**. Click **Active Window** to indicate your current document will be the main document.

3. Attach (open) the existing data source for the mailing labels:
   a. Under *Data source*, click **Get Data**.
   b. Click **Open Data Source**.
   c. Locate the **Accounts Receivable** data source. Select it and click **Open**.

4. Choose label options:
   a. At the prompt, click **Set Up Main Document**.
   b. In the Label Options dialog box, select the type of printer, if necessary.
   c. If necessary, change the *Tray* (label feed) selection to match how you will actually print.
   d. Select *Avery standard* for the *Label products* list box, if necessary. Under *Product number*, click **5162** for a laser printer or **4146** for a dot-matrix printer.
   e. Click **OK**. The Create Labels dialog box opens.

5. Insert merge fields for the label:
   a. With the insertion point positioned in the *Sample label* box, click **Insert Merge Field** and insert the *Title, FirstName, LastName, Company, Address1, Address2, City, State,*

and *PostalCode* fields. Because you are formatting the delivery address, do not use any punctuation. Your sample label should look like the one shown in Figure 3-16.
   b. Click **Insert Postal Bar Code**. The Insert Postal Bar Code dialog box appears for you to identify the delivery address for the POSTNET bar code.

 Did You Know?

Using the POSTNET bar code speeds mail delivery. The FIM (Facing Identification Mark) is printed on the front side of a courtesy reply envelope that is preprinted with the sender's name and address.

   c. In the *Merge field with ZIP code* box, scroll down and click **PostalCode**.
   d. In the *Merge field with street address* box, click **Address1**.
   e. Click **OK** to return to the Create Labels dialog box and then click **OK** again to return to the Mail Merge Helper dialog box.

6. Merge the labels:
   a. In the Mail Merge Helper dialog box, click **Merge**.
   b. If necessary, select **New document** in the *Merge to* list box.

(continued on next page)

c. If necessary, click **All** under *Records to be merged*.

d. Click **Merge**.

7. Save the new document as **Merged AR Labels** followed by your initials. Print the labels on plain paper and then close the document.

8. Save the main document as **Labels** followed by your initials. Leave the document open for the next Step-by-Step.

Did You Know?

You can distribute merged documents to e-mail addresses or fax numbers. Click Merge in the Mail Merge Helper. Then instead of merging to a new document or to the printer, select **Electronic mail** in the *Merge to* list box.

Merging an Alternate Data Source

You can select a different data source for an existing main document. It is important, however, that the field names used in the header row of the new data source match the merge fields in the main document. You select the new data source in the Mail Merge Helper dialog box.

Concept Builder

You can use an Access database as a data source. In the Open Data Source dialog box, change the *Files of type* entry to MS Access Databases. Then locate the database. You can then select the table or query you want to use for the mail merge.

1. Click on the **Mail Merge Helper** button to display the Mail Merge Helper dialog box.

2. Note that under *Data source*, **Accounts Receivable** is displayed as the current data source. Click **Get Data**.

3. Click **Open Data Source** and locate **AW Step3-8** in the student data files. Select it and click **Open**.

4. Merge to a new document and save the merged document as **Merged Sales Labels** followed by your initials.

5. Print the labels. Close all open documents and save changes if prompted.

Preparing Envelopes by Merging a Data Source

You can prepare multiple envelopes by creating a main document and merging a data source. The process is very similar to creating mailing labels. Instead of specifying label options, you specify options for your envelopes in the Envelope Options dialog box, shown in Figure 3-18. After you specify envelope options, the Envelope address dialog box opens, similar to the Create Labels dialog box. Insert merge fields in the *Sample envelope address* box in the same way you inserted fields for the labels.

FIGURE 3-18
Envelope Options dialog box

Envelope Options ? X

| Envelope Options | Printing Options |

Envelope size:

Size 10   (4 1/8 x 9 1/2 in) ▼

If mailed in the USA
☐ Delivery point barcode
☐ FIM-A courtesy reply mail

Delivery address
Font...   From left: Auto ▲▼
             From top: Auto ▲▼

Return address
Font...   From left: Auto ▲▼
             From top: Auto ▲▼

Preview

OK   Cancel

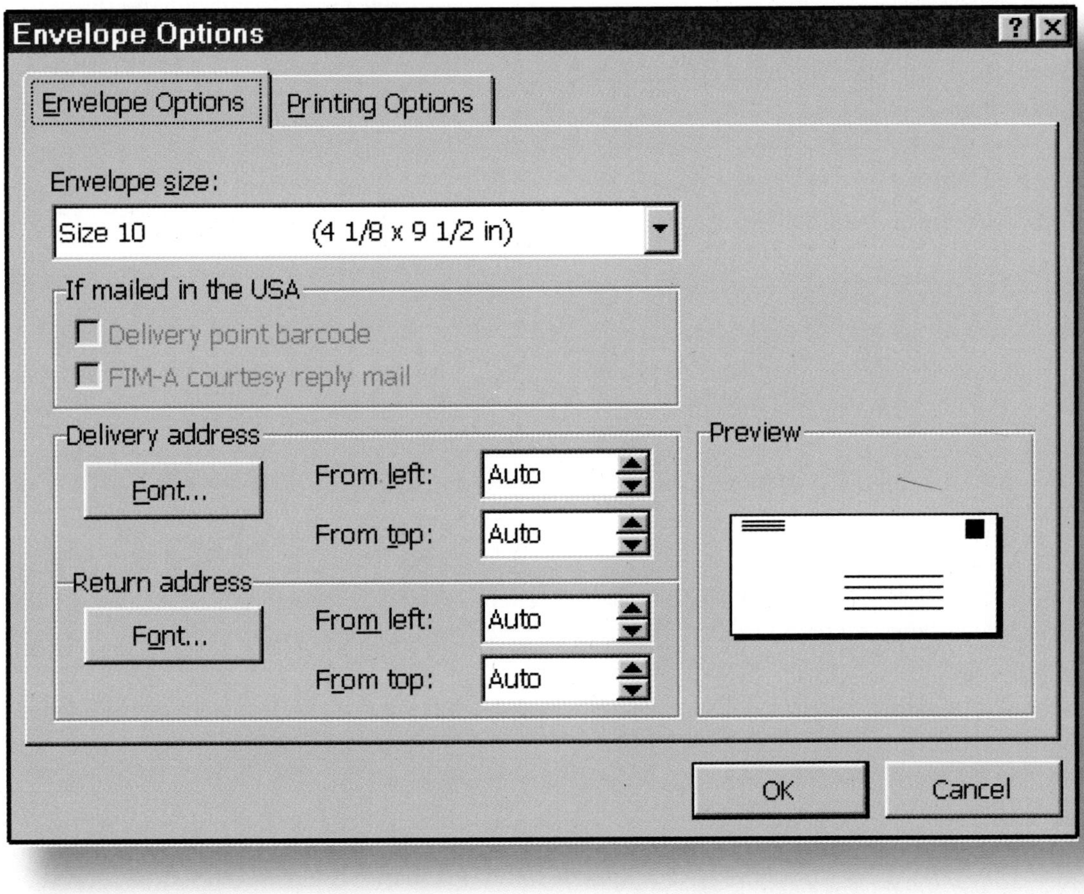

After you have set up the envelope address, you can choose to edit your main document by clicking Edit in the Mail Merge Helper dialog box. Word displays your envelope on the screen. You can add your return address in this view. Then select a merge option from the Mail Merge toolbar.

1. Open a new document window. Open the **Tools** menu and choose **Mail Merge**. The Mail Merge Helper dialog box is displayed.

2. Click **Create** and then click **Envelopes**. When prompted, choose **Active Window**.

3. Under *Data source*, click **Get Data**. Click **Open Data Source** and select **Accounts Receivable**.

4. When prompted, click **Set Up Main Document**. The Envelope Options dialog box opens.

5. On the **Envelope Options** tab, select *Size 10* for the *Envelope size*. If necessary, change the settings in the Printing Options folder for the way your printer will print the envelopes.

6. Click **OK**. The Envelope address dialog box opens.

7. With the insertion point positioned in the *Sample envelope address* box, click **Insert Merge Field** and insert the same fields you inserted for mailing labels, with the addition of the *MiddleName* field. Because you are formatting the delivery address, do not use any punctuation.

8. Click **Insert Postal Bar Code**. Select the ZIP code and street address fields as you did for labels.

9. Click **OK** to close the Insert Postal Bar Code dialog box and then click **OK** to close the Envelope address dialog box. The Mail Merge Helper dialog box is still displayed.

10. Under *Main document*, click **Edit** and then click the envelope document. The envelope document is displayed. Do not be concerned if you see *ZIP Code not valid* where the Postal Bar Code should be.

11. Edit the return address to read:

    Nu-Tech Plastics, Inc.
    1680 Oxford Road
    Mansfield, MA 02048-4314

12. Click the **Merge to New Document** button on the Mail Merge toolbar. You should see five addressed envelopes. Use the vertical scroll bar to view all of the envelopes.

13. Save the new document as **Merged Envelopes** followed by your initials. Print only the first envelope on plain paper.

14. Save the main document as **Envelopes** followed by your initials.

15. Close all open documents and save changes if prompted.

Creating Catalogs and Lists

The merge feature is also convenient for creating a catalog or price list. For example, a company may release a product price list at the beginning of each month. If the product information is stored in a data source, you can easily update the product information and merge it into a catalog form document.

Catalogs offer the same flexibility as other merge documents. Before merging and printing the catalog, you can update the data source records, add or delete records, and sort and filter the records. When you apply a format to the merge fields in the main document, the formats will be applied to the variable data when it is merged. You can also edit the main document and data source in the same way you edit other documents. In the next Step-by-Step, you will use the Find command to locate a record and then change the data for that record.

STEP-BY-STEP ▷ 3.10

1. Open a new document.

2. Create a catalog form document:
   a. Open the **Tools** menu and choose **Mail Merge**. Click **Create** and then select **Catalog**. When prompted, select **Active Window**.
   b. Click **Get Data** and then click **Open Data Source**.
   c. Select and open the data source **AW Step3-10**.
   d. When prompted, click **Edit Main Document**.

3. Format and key the catalog:
   a. At the top of the document and at the left margin, insert the merge field **ProductName**.
   b. Press **Enter** and insert the merge field **ProductNumber**.
   c. Press **Enter** and insert the merge field **Description**.
   d. Press **Enter** and insert the merge field **Price**.
   e. Press **Enter**.
   f. Select the entire first paragraph **Product-Name** and add the bold format.
   g. Indent the second paragraph *ProductNumber* 0.5 inch from the left and indent the third paragraph (*Description*) 1 inch from the left.

   h. Click in the third paragraph **Description** and format it for justified alignment.
   i. Click in the fourth paragraph **Price** and format it to align at the right margin. Select the entire paragraph and add the italic format.

4. Save the document as **Price List** followed by your initials.

5. Before merging the data records, you need to find a record in the data source and make some changes. Edit the data source:
   a. Click the **Edit Data Source** button on the Mail Merge toolbar.
   b. Click **Find** in the Data Form dialog box. The Find in Field dialog box opens.
   c. In the *Find what* box, key **PEAC 200** and then select **ProductNumber** in the *In field* box.
   d. Click **Find First** and then click **Close** in the Find in Field dialog box.
   e. Change the price for this record from $550 to **$575**. Click **OK**.

6. Merge all data records to a new document.

(continued on next page)

7. Save the new document as **Merged Price List** followed by your initials.

8. Move the insertion point to the top of the document, press **Enter** twice, and then move the insertion point to the first blank paragraph. Center

and key the heading **PRICE LIST**. Add the bold format and change the font size to **18** pt.

9. Save the changes to **Merged Price List**. Print the document and close it. Close **Price List** and save changes if prompted to do so.

Summary

In this lesson, you learned:

- You can use the mail merge feature to create personalized form letters, mailing labels, and envelopes. You can also use mail merge to create single documents such as catalogs and lists.

- A data source contains variable information. The first row in a data source (the header row) contains field names. Each remaining row in a data source contains a data record.

- You insert field names from the data source in the main document.

- You can preview documents before you complete a merge.

- You can sort data records before you merge them with a main document.

- You can merge all or selected records to a new document, the printer, or electronic mail.

LESSON 3 REVIEW QUESTIONS

FILL IN THE BLANKS

Complete the following sentences by writing the correct word or words in the blanks provided.

1. Each row of the completed data source except the first is called a(n) _data record_.

2. The _main document_ contains the boilerplate text, with field names where variable text will be inserted.

3. The _data source_ contains the variable text that will be merged into the main document.

4. The top row of the data source containing all the field names is called the _header row_.

5. Up to _three_ fields can be sorted for the data source.

MATCHING

Match the correct term in Column 2 to its description in Column 1.

Column 1

E 1. Selects specific data records

G 2. Speeds mail delivery

D 3. Identifies a field

A 4. Indicates where variable text is to be inserted

C 5. A completed data form

Column 2

A. Merge field

B. FIM (Facing Identification Mark)

C. Data record

D. Field name

E. Filter

F. Sort

G. POSTNET bar code

LESSON 3 PROJECTS

SCANS

PROJECT 3-1

1. In a new document window, change all margins to 1 inch.

2. Key the letter shown in Figure 3-19 with the indicated changes. If space allows, add a few blank lines below the date, but do not allow the letter to wrap to a second page.

3. Use the spelling checker, proofread the letter, and then save it as **Join Letter** followed by your initials.

4. Begin the merge process for a form letter, indicating the active window as the main document.

5. Create the data source with the following field names: Title, FirstName, LastName, Address1, City, State, and PostalCode.

6. Save the data source as **Prospects** followed by your initials.

7. Complete the data records using the following information:

```
Mr. Erik Stein
P. O. Box 11567
Lahaina, HI  96761-1567

Ms. Patti Ruiz
684 Fifth Avenue
New York, NY  10022-2245
```

FIGURE 3-19

OUR WORLD
1900 Fifth Avenue, Suite 500
New York, NY 10021-0491 } *Bold and Center*

Current Date

xx
xx
xx

Dear xx:

special
Right now you can become part of a unique relationship committed to preserving our
world. It is a relationship shared by more than 100,000 members throughout the nation. *nationwide*
Our World is a thriving and vital organization working to preserve the environment.
Members of Our World support environmental education programs, pollution controls,
recycling programs, environmental research, and water, land, and wildlife conservation.
You're invited to join Our World now and become part of this significant relationship.

Our World members benefit directly through:

italic
Preserving the Environment, a contemporary environmental resource
Local charters that promote community programs
Professional interaction with others concerned about the preservation of the environment
And much, much more!

today *will*
Become a member of Our World now. You'll be able to contribute your ideas, energy,
and talents to a worthwhile cause. Joining is easy! Indicate your membership choice on *bold*
the enclosed card and return it in the envelope provided. Or call our Membership Hotline
at 1-800-555-JOIN or 708-555-2284, Monday through Friday, 8 a.m. to 5 p.m., Eastern
time. ^EDT

Sincerely
Cordially,

David
D. J. Bronson
CEO *Chief Executive Officer*

xx

Enclosures

Dr. Barry Gross
41121 Laiolo Road
Fremont, CA 94538-7786

Mrs. Becky Laws
3947 Broadway
Grove City, OH 43123-2332

Dr. Joanna Dillon
P. O. Box C-320
Richmond, VA 23261-0320

8. View the data source and sort the records in ascending order by *LastName*. Then save the changes.

9. Switch to the main document and insert the appropriate fields for the inside address and the salutation.

10. Merge to a new document and save as **Merged Join Letter** followed by your initials.

11. Print only the first form letter. Close all documents, saving if prompted.

PROJECT 3-2

SCANS

1. Create a main document for merging envelopes.

2. Attach the data source **Prospects** that you created in Project 3-1.

3. Format the envelope for Size 10. Insert the delivery address merge fields and add the postal bar code.

4. Edit the main document to include the following return address:

```
OUR WORLD
1900 Fifth Avenue, Suite 500
New York, NY  10021-0491
```

5. Merge to a new document and save as **Merged Prospects Envelopes** followed by your initials. Print only the first envelope on plain paper.

6. Save the main document as **Prospects Envelopes** followed by your initials. Close all open documents, saving if prompted.

PROJECT 3-3

SCANS

1. Create a main document for merging mailing labels.

2. Attach the data source **AW Project3-3a**. This data source contains the names and addresses of customers.

3. Set up the main document. Use Avery labels product number 5162 for a laser printer or 4146 for a dot-matrix printer. Insert the following fields appropriately in the sample. Format a postal bar code if your printer can print one.

```
Title FirstName LastName
Address1
City State  PostalCode
```

4. Edit the records in the data source. Change the name *Mrs. Dawn Bixler* to **Ms. Dawn Schuette**. Miss Haru Fujiwara has a new business address:

```
Cyber Solutions
1350 Ocean Avenue
Emeryville, CA  94608-1128
```

5. View the data source and sort the records in ascending numerical order by *PostalCode*. Then, save the the edited data source as **Customer List** followed by your initials.

A W - 6 3

6. Switch to the main document and save the main document as **Mailing Labels** followed by your initials.

7. Merge to a new document, save the new document as **Merged Customer Labels**, and print.

8. Close the new merged document but keep the main document open.

9. The **Employees** table in the Access database **AW Project3-3b** contains information about company employees. You can use this database to create mailing labels using the same main document:
    A. Click the **Mail Merge Helper** button on the Mail Merge toolbar. Click **Get Data** in the Mail Merge Helper dialog box.
    B. Click **Open Data Source**. In the Open Data Source dialog box, change the *Files of type* entry to **MS Access Databases**. Click the **AW Project3-3b** database in your student data files and then click **Open**.
    C. When prompted, select the **Employees** table in the database.

10. In the Mail Merge Helper dialog box, click **Query Options**. Create a filter to merge only the records for employees who live in Grand Blanc.

11. Merge to a new document, save as **Merged Employee Labels** followed by your initials, and print.

12. Close all open documents and save changes if prompted.

CRITICAL THINKING

SCANS

ACTIVITY 3-1

Henry works for a large distribution company. The company periodically sends catalogs and promotional items to its established customers. Each customer is assigned a code and this code appears on all mailing labels. When the data source containing customer information was created, this customer code was entered in a field named *Code*. Recently the company started assigning a second number to all customers, and this second number is referred to as *Source Code*. Therefore, it is necessary to change the data source so that it will contain two different fields for the customer codes. How can Henry rename the existing *Code* field *Customer Code* and add a new field for *Source Code*? Use the Help feature to find the answer.

ACTIVITY 3-2

Henry's company recently printed custom-sized address labels with preprinted information including the company's address and logo. When Henry sets up the main document to print the mailing labels, he cannot find a label in the Product Number box that matches dimensions and layout of the new address labels. How can Henry create custom labels for the merge process? Use the Help feature to find the answer.

FORMATTING COLUMNS AND SECTIONS

OBJECTIVES

Upon completion of this lesson, you should be able to:

- Create a banner.
- Create a combination of multicolumn formats.
- Balance column length.
- Delete section breaks.
- Change section formats.
- Copy section formats.
- Keep text in columns together.
- Format nonbreaking spaces and nonbreaking hyphens.
- Find and replace special characters, formats, and nonprinting characters.

Ø Estimated Time: 2 hours

Formatting Columns

A *section* in a document controls the column formats. When you create a new document in Word, the document has just one section and the section formats apply to the entire document. If you want to create a combination of column formats in the same document, you must create a different section for each column format. This is especially useful for formatting newsletters and brochures. For example, you can have a three-column article and a two-column article on the same page.

When you divide a document into sections, the section breaks are displayed as double dotted lines. When there is enough space, the words "Section Break" are also displayed with the lines. The section break controls the section formatting for the text that precedes it. If the document has only one section, no section break is displayed and the section formats are stored in the last paragraph mark in the document.

Creating a Banner over Multiple Columns

One way to create a new section is to select text within a document and apply a different column format. When you select text and apply a new column format, Word formats the selected text as a new section. Figure 4-1 shows a document in which a heading is formatted in one column and the text in two columns. A heading formatted this way is called a *banner*.

Concept Builder

When working with columns in a document, you will want to display the document in Print Layout view to display the text in the column layout. Word sometimes automatically switches you to Print Layout view when you apply a column format. If the document does not display the column layout, click the Print Layout View button at the bottom left of the Word window.

FIGURE 4-1
Text formatted as a banner

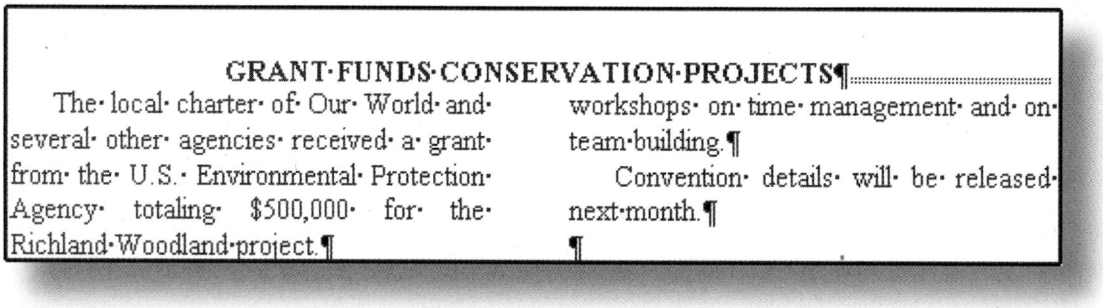

GRANT·FUNDS·CONSERVATION·PROJECTS¶
The· local· charter· of· Our· World· and· several· other· agencies· received· a· grant· from· the· U.S.· Environmental· Protection· Agency· totaling· $500,000· for· the· Richland·Woodland·project.¶

workshops· on· time· management· and· on· team·building.¶
Convention· details· will· be· released· next·month.¶
¶

STEP-BY-STEP ▷ 4.1

1. Open **AW Step 4-1** from the student data files and save the document as **Articles** followed by your initials.

2. If necessary, switch to Print Layout view. Notice that the entire document is formatted in two columns of equal width.

3. Select the heading for the first article (*GRANT FUNDS CONSERVATION PROJECTS*). Be sure to include the paragraph mark at the end of the heading in the selection.

4. Click the **Columns** button on the Formatting toolbar and select a single column format. The title becomes a part of a new section and spreads across the two columns of text in the section below.

5. Notice that the section break lines display at the end of the paragraph mark following the heading. Your document should look similar to Figure 4-1.

6. Save your changes and leave the document open for the next Step-by-Step.

Creating a Combination of Multiple-Column Formats

You can also create a new section by opening the Insert menu and choosing the Break command to display the Break dialog box, shown in Figure 4-2. You can choose from four different types of section breaks. A Next page section break begins at the top of the next page. A Continuous section break starts immediately below the preceding section on the same page. If the section is formatted with a Continuous section break, Word will automatically balance the text in the columns. Sections also can be formatted to start on the next odd or even page.

When you use the Break command to create a new section, the section break is inserted at the location of the insertion point and the section formats apply to the section above the section break.

FIGURE 4-2
Break dialog box

STEP-BY-STEP ▷ 4.2

1. Position the insertion point in front of the heading for the second article (*VICE-PRESIDENT PONTI ANNOUNCES RESIGNATION*).

2. Open the **Insert** menu and choose **Break**. The Break dialog box opens.

3. Under *Section break types*, select **Next page** and then click **OK**. The second heading and the text below it are moved to the top of the next page.

4. Scroll through the document. Notice that the text on both pages is formatted in two columns but neither page has enough text to wrap to the second column.

5. Position the insertion point at the beginning of the third heading (*MARK YOUR CALENDAR*) on the second page.

6. Open the **Insert** menu, choose **Break**, select **Continuous** under *Section break types*, and click **OK**. Notice the heading and the two paragraphs above the new section break are still formatted in two columns and now those columns are balanced because you inserted a Continuous section break.

7. Position the insertion point at the beginning of the first paragraph in the second article that begins *Anna Ponti, . . .* and insert a Continuous section break.

8. Click in the new section containing the heading *VICE-PRESIDENT PONTI ANNOUNCES RESIGNATION*. The two lines of text are formatted in two columns and the columns are balanced. Notice that the status bar displays *Sec 3*.

(continued on next page)

9. Format the heading for a single column. When the text changes to a one-column format, you have created a second banner.

10. Click in the section containing the paragraphs below the second banner. Open the **Format** menu, choose **Columns**, and format a **Left** preset with a line between the columns. Click **OK**.

11. Position the insertion point in front of the first paragraph in the third article that begins *You*

won't want . . . and insert a Continuous section break.

12. Click in the new section containing the heading *MARK YOUR CALENDAR* and format the article as a banner.

13. Save your changes and leave the document open for the next Step-by-Step.

Balancing Column Lengths

As you just learned, when you insert Continuous section breaks Word automatically balances the columns of text above the section break. On the last page of a section or document, the last column may be empty or partially filled. Balancing the columns will make the page more attractive. You can balance the columns manually by inserting a Continuous section break at the end of the last column.

Hot Tip

If the columns are not exactly balanced after you apply a Continuous section break, you can even up the columns by adjusting the spacing above headings or other text items.

STEP-BY-STEP ▷ 4.3

1. Position the insertion point in front of the blank paragraph at the end of the document.

2. Insert a Continuous section break. Word balances the columns.

3. Click in the section containing the paragraphs for the third article. Format the section for three

columns of equal width. Word adjusts the column lengths so they are approximately equal.

4. Save your changes and leave the document open for the next Step-by-Step.

Formatting Sections

Columns are only one example of section formats. Other section formats are margins, paper size or orientation, paper source for a printer, page borders, vertical alignment, headers and footers, page numbering, line numbering, and footnotes and endnotes. All of these section formats are stored in the section break.

Deleting Section Breaks

If you delete a section break, you also delete the formatting for the text above the section break. When a section break is deleted, the text becomes part of the section that follows. For example, assume that you have two sections in a document. Text in the first section is formatted in three columns. Text in the second section is formatted in two columns. If you delete the section break at the end of the first section, the text in the first section will take on the format of the next section below it. In this case, the text from the first section will be formatted in two columns.

S TEP-BY-STEP ▷ 4.4

1. Click on the first section break at the top of the document following the heading *GRANT FUNDS CONSERVATION PROJECTS*.

2. Press **Delete**. The heading becomes part of the two-column section immediately below.

3. Delete the section breaks following the second and third headings.

4. Save your changes and leave the document open for the next Step-by-Step.

Changing Section Formats

There may be occasions when you want to change section formatting. For example, you may choose to change the margin settings in one section of the document. When you change a section format in a document that contains more than one section, you can choose to apply the format to selected sections of the document or to the whole document.

To change section formatting, you double-click on the section break to open the Page Setup dialog box, shown in Figure 4-3. In this dialog box you can change section formats including margins, headers and footers, page borders, and page layout. You can also change the type of section break.

FIGURE 4-3
Page Setup dialog box

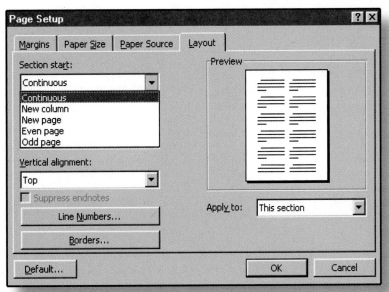

1. Double-click the section break at the end of the first article that ends with *1-800-555-6691*. The Page Setup dialog box opens.

2. Click the **Margins** tab and change the left and right margins to **1.5**.

3. Click the **Apply to** down arrow and select **This point forward**. Then click **OK**.

4. Click the **Print Preview** button to view the document. Notice that the margins for the second and third articles are wider than the first article.

5. Close Print Preview.

6. Double-click the section break after the first article again and change the left and right margins to **1.0**. Under *Apply to*, select **Whole document** and then click **OK**.

7. Look at the document in Print Preview to make sure all the sections have the same margins.

8. Save your changes and leave the document open for the next Step-by-Step.

Copying Section Formats

After you've formatted a section, you can save time by copying the section formatting to other parts of the document. To copy a section format, the document must be displayed in Normal view. You select the section break containing the formats you want to copy, click the Copy button on the Standard toolbar, and then paste the section break where you want to apply the section formats.

1. Insert a Continuous section break in front of the first paragraph in the first article that begins *The local charter . . . .*

2. Format the new section containing that heading as a banner.

3. Click the **Normal View** button at the bottom left of the Word window to switch to Normal view.

4. Select the section break below the heading *GRANT FUNDS CONSERVATION PROJECTS.*

> **Hot Tip**
>
> To select the section break, you can use the selection bar or click on the dotted lines and then drag across them.

5. Click the **Copy** button.

6. Position the insertion point in front of the first paragraph in the second article that begins *Anna Ponti, . . .* and click the **Paste** button. A new section is created and the heading for the second article is formatted in a single column.

7. Position the insertion point in front of the first paragraph in the third article that begins *You won't want . . .* and click the **Paste** button.

8. Click the **Print Layout View** button to switch back to Print Layout view.

9. Insert three blank paragraphs before and one blank paragraph after each of the banner headings.

10. Save your changes and leave the document open for the next Step-by-Step.

Controlling Column Breaks

When you work with columns in a document, you may want to control how the text flows from one column to the next. You can keep text together within a column and you can format a break in the middle of a paragraph so the text continues in the next column. When you manually split a paragraph between columns, there should be at least two lines of text and at the bottom of the first column and at least two lines of text should be carried over to the top of the next column.

Keeping Text in Columns Together

To keep portions of text together in a column, insert a hard column break where you want to end a column. To insert a hard column break, open the Insert menu, choose Break, and then select the Column break option.

Did You Know?

When the last line of a paragraph appears at the top of a page or column, it is called a *widow*. An *orphan* is the first line of a paragraph left at the bottom of a page or column.

S TEP-BY-STEP ▷ 4.7

1. The second article contains a widow at the top of the second column. Position the insertion point at the beginning of the second paragraph in the second article that begins *Ms. Ponti's . . .*

2. Open the **Insert** menu and choose **Break**.

3. Under *Break types* select **Column break**, and then click **OK**. Your document should look similar to Figure 4-4.

4. Save your changes and leave the document open for the next Step-by-Step.

FIGURE 4-4
Columns balanced with a column break

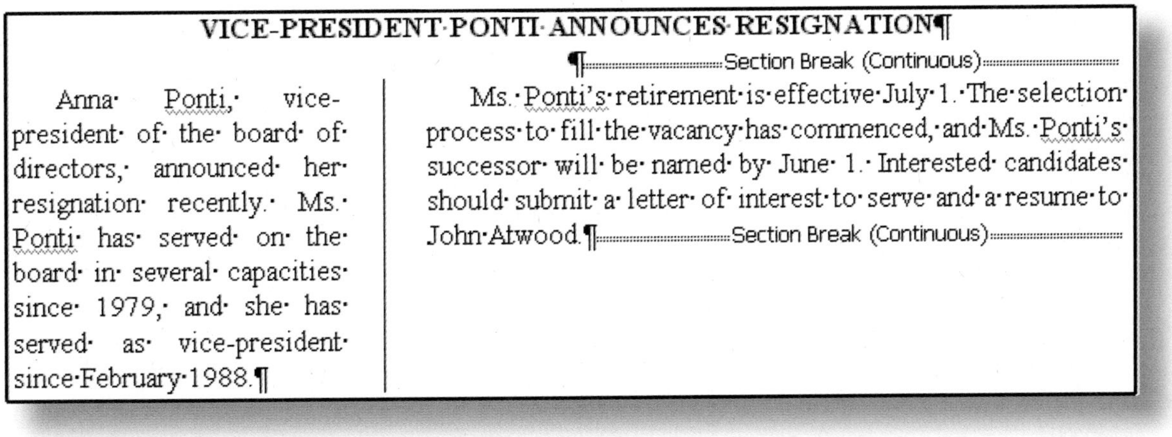

VICE-PRESIDENT·PONTI·ANNOUNCES·RESIGNATION¶

¶════════════Section Break (Continuous)════════════

Anna· Ponti,· vice-president· of· the· board· of· directors,· announced· her· resignation· recently.· Ms.· Ponti· has· served· on· the· board· in· several· capacities· since· 1979,· and· she· has· served· as· vice-president· since·February·1988.¶

Ms.·Ponti's·retirement·is·effective·July·1.·The·selection· process·to·fill·the·vacancy·has·commenced,·and·Ms.·Ponti's· successor· will· be· named· by· June· 1.· Interested· candidates· should· submit· a· letter· of· interest· to· serve· and· a· resume· to· John·Atwood.¶════════════Section Break (Continuous)════════════

Formatting Nonbreaking Spaces and Nonbreaking Hyphens

When text is formatted in multiple columns, undesirable line breaks often occur because of the short line lengths. *Nonbreaking spaces* are used to indicate words that should not be split between lines, such as dates and measurements. *Nonbreaking hyphens* are used to indicate hyphenated words that should not be split if the hyphen falls at the end of a line. Although you may not notice any undesirable line breaks in your document, it is wise to format nonbreaking spaces and hyphens in advance. Then if you edit the document, you do not need to be concerned about possible undesirable line breaks.

To create a nonbreaking space, hold down Ctrl and Shift and then press the spacebar. When Show/Hide ¶ is turned on, Word will display a symbol to indicate the nonbreaking space, but this symbol does not print when the document is printed.

To create a nonbreaking hyphen, hold down Ctrl and Shift and then key a hyphen. Although a nonbreaking hyphen displays larger than a normal hyphen, the hyphen prints the same as a normal hyphen.

S TEP-BY-STEP ▷ 4.8

1. If necessary, turn on Show/Hide ¶ to display nonprinting characters. Locate the toll-free phone number at the end of the third paragraph in the first article.

2. Delete each of the hyphens and then insert nonbreaking hyphens by holding down **Ctrl** and **Shift** as you press the hyphen key.

3. Find the date *July 1* in the second paragraph in the second article.

4. Delete the space between *July* and *1* and replace the space with a nonbreaking space by holding down **Ctrl** and **Shift** as you press the **spacebar**.

5. Find the date *June 1* also in the second paragraph of the second article. Change the space between *June* and *1* to a nonbreaking space.

6. Find the dates *April 11-13* in the first paragraph of the third article and change the hyphen to a nonbreaking hyphen.

7. Automatically hyphenate the document.

8. Save your changes. Print and close the document.

Find and Replace Formats, Special Characters, and Nonprinting Elements

The Find and Replace options on the Edit menu allow you to search for and replace character and paragraph formats, special characters, and nonprinting elements. You can search for combined formats such as bold and italic. When you need to replace multiple occurrences of the same text or format, you can use Replace to replace each occurrence automatically.

Any combination of search and replace can be used. For example:

■ You can key text in the *Find what* box and key no text in the *Replace with* box. You can then select a format so that the text you search for will be formatted automatically.

■ You can leave both the *Find what* box and the *Replace with* box blank and search for and replace formats only.

■ You can even leave the *Replace with* box blank (and select no format), in which case the text you specify in the *Find what* box will be deleted automatically.

To see options for finding and replacing text and formats, click the More button in the Find and Replace dialog box. The dialog box expands, as shown in Figure 4-5.

FIGURE 4-5
Replace tab in the Find and Replace dialog box

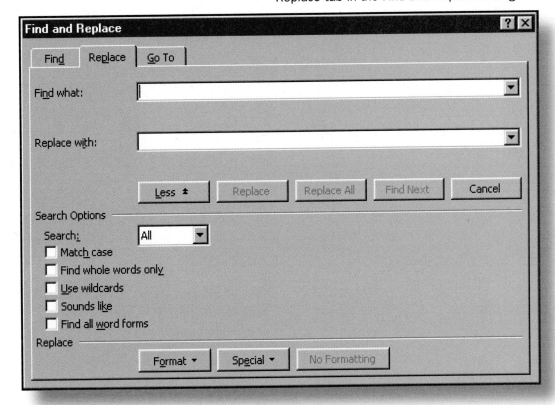

1. Open **AW Step4-9** from the student data files and save the document as **News Release** followed by your initials.

2. Open the **Edit** menu and choose **Replace**. If necessary, click **More** to display the dialog box shown in Figure 4-5.

3. If necessary, delete any text in the *Find what* box and click **No Formatting** so Word will not search for formats specified in an earlier search.

4. In the *Find what* box, key a hyphen.

5. Position the insertion point in the *Replace with* box and then click **Special**. In the pop-up menu, select nonbreaking hyphen. The special characters for a nonbreaking hyphen (^~) are inserted in the *Replace with* box.

6. Click **Replace All**. Word replaces all nine occurrences of normal hyphens with nonbreaking hyphens.

7. In the *Find what* box, key **March** and press the **spacebar** once.

8. Position the insertion point in the *Replace with* box and key **March**. Then, without keying a blank space, click **Special** and select nonbreaking space. The special characters for a nonbreaking space (^s) are inserted in the *Replace with* box.

9. Click **Replace All**. Both occurrences are replaced.

10. Delete the text in the *Find what* box. Click **Format**, and then select **Font** in the pop-up menu. In the Font dialog box, select the single underline format and then click **OK**.

11. Position the insertion point in the *Replace with* box. Delete any text and click **Format**. Select **Font** in the pop-up menu and click the **Bold Italic** font style. In the *Underline style* box, select **(none)**. Click **OK**.

12. Click **Replace All** in the Find and Replace dialog box. Word reformats all underlined text with bold and italic effects.

13. Save your changes. Print and close the document.

Summary

In this lesson, you learned:

- You can quickly create a banner above multicolumn formats by selecting the heading text and changing it to a single-column format.

- You can format sections to continue on the same page, to begin on a new page, or to begin on an even or odd page.

- By inserting a Continuous section break at the end of the last column in a document, you can balance the columns in that section.

- Once you have applied section formats, you can copy those formats to other parts of the document.

- You can control where columns break by inserting column breaks.

- You can control line breaks by formatting nonbreaking spaces and nonbreaking hyphens.

- The Find and Replace feature enables you to automatically replace formats, special characters, and nonprinting elements.

LESSON 4 REVIEW QUESTIONS

TRUE/FALSE

Circle T if the statement is true or F if the statement is false.

T ~~F~~ 1. If you want to change multicolumn text to a single column, you must first insert a section break.

T **F** 2. Columns are an example of a paragraph format. *section*

T F 3. The section break controls the format of the preceding section.

T **F** 4. To change a Continuous section break to a Next page section break, you must choose Break on the Insert menu. *Double Click on the break*

T F 5. The character for nonbreaking spaces does not print.

FILL IN THE BLANKS

Complete the following sentences by writing the correct word or words in the blanks provided.

1. To end a column, open the Insert menu, choose Break, and then select _Column Break_.

2. To balance columns, position the insertion point at the end of the last column, open the Insert menu, choose Break, and then select _Continous Break_.

3. A(n) _nobreaking hyphen_ is used to tell Word not to break a hyphenated word at the end of a line.

4. A(n) _no breaking space_ is used to indicate two words that should be kept together.

5. To copy a section format, the document must be displayed in _Normal_ view.

PROJECT 4-1

1. Open **AW Project4-1** from the student data files and save the document as **Soil** followed by your initials.

2. Format the document in two equal columns with a line between the columns.

3. Format the title (and the two blank paragraphs below it) as a banner over the two columns of text.

4. Insert manual column breaks so the *Pollution-Eating Bacteria* heading appears at the top of the second column and the *Thermal Desorption* heading appears at the top of page 2.

5. Balance the columns on the second page.

6. Format page numbers to print at the top right of all pages except the first.

7. Save your changes. Print and close the document.

PROJECT 4-2

1. Open a new document and key and format the document as illustrated in Figure 4-6.

2. Be sure to balance the list of courses in the two-column format.

3. Center the document vertically.

4. Save the document as **Courses** followed by your initials.

5. Print and close the document.

PROJECT 4-3

1. Open **AW Project4-3** from the student data files and save the document as **Study** followed by your initials.

2. Go to the section break following the paragraphs under the heading *THE STUDY* and change the section format from Next page to Continuous.

3. Copy the section format for the banner heading at the top of the document and then paste the formatting to change the remaining headings to banners.

4. Format the paragraphs below the headings *INTRODUCTION*, *THE STUDY*, and *CONCLUSION* in two columns. Balance the columns in the last section.

FIGURE 4-6

Lesson ④ Formatting Columns and Sections

Since the environmental education field is relatively new and ever-changing, you might wonder what courses an environmental education curriculum would include. Course titles and programs vary, of course, but the following list suggests the variety and range of courses that you might find offered in a program of study.

Field Ecology	Biology
Natural History	Geology
Native American Concepts of Nature	Mathematics
Wildlife Biology	Physical and Applied Sciences
Earth Science	Marketing
Human Development	Environmental Law
Humanities	Ethics for Business
Outdoor Leadership	Economics of the Environment
Chemistry	Handling Hazardous Substances

Obviously, the best way to prepare for an environmental career is to gain as much knowledge and training as possible. Until recently, there were limited resources for learning about the environment. Today, however, there are numerous opportunities available to study the environment ranging from university training to on-the-job-training.

5. Find all occurrences of the word *percent* and replace the space before the word with a nonbreaking space.

6. Find all occurrences of a hyphen and replace the normal hyphen with a nonbreaking hyphen.

7. Find all occurrences of bold text and replace the character formats with bold italic text in 14 pt.

8. Automatically hyphenate the document.

9. Save your changes. Print and close the document.

ACTIVITY 4-1

Julie created a multipage report that included bulleted lists and a table. After she prepared the entire report formatted in a single column, she decided to format the body of the report in two columns. When she applied the column format, she could still see the bulleted lists, but the table had disappeared. What happened to the table? Describe how Julie can display a table within a columnar format. Use the Help feature to find the answer.

ACTIVITY 4-2

Julie is working with a document that contains several nonbreaking spaces. Is there a quick way for Julie to remove all the nonbreaking spaces and replace them with normal spaces?

FORMATTING GRAPHICS AND TEXT BOXES

OBJECTIVES

Upon completion of this lesson, you should be able to:

- Add and crop a graphic.

- Wrap text around a graphic.

- Position a graphic precisely.

- Delete a graphic.

- Create a watermark.

- Create and modify page borders.

- Create a sidebar.

- Format paragraph and section shading.

- Create a pull quote.

- Change the orientation of text in a text box.

- Repeat text box contents on multiple pages.

- Create drop caps.

- Use AutoShapes to create objects.

- "Round trip" documents from Word to to HTML format.

⏱ **Estimated Time: 2 hours**

Formatting Graphics

Word supplies many pictures and graphics, and you can insert them by opening the Insert menu, clicking the Picture command, and then choosing Clip Art. You can also import pictures and other graphics from other sources. To insert a picture from a file, choose the Picture command on the Insert menu, choose From File, locate and select the desired file, and then click Insert.

After you import the graphic, you can use many Word features to format the graphic. You can crop graphics, position them exactly, and wrap text around them. You can also insert graphics as *watermarks* so they print as backgrounds behind the main body of text.

Adding and Cropping a Graphic

When you *crop* a graphic, you cut off portions of the graphic that you do not want to show. You can use the Crop button on the Picture toolbar to quickly crop a picture. This feature makes cropping easy because you can see the effects of the crop on the screen. To crop a graphic to exact dimensions, open the Format menu, click the Picture command, and select the Picture tab in the Format Picture dialog box (Figure 5-1). Then key the dimensions in the text boxes provided in the dialog box.

FIGURE 5-1
Picture tab in the Format Picture dialog box

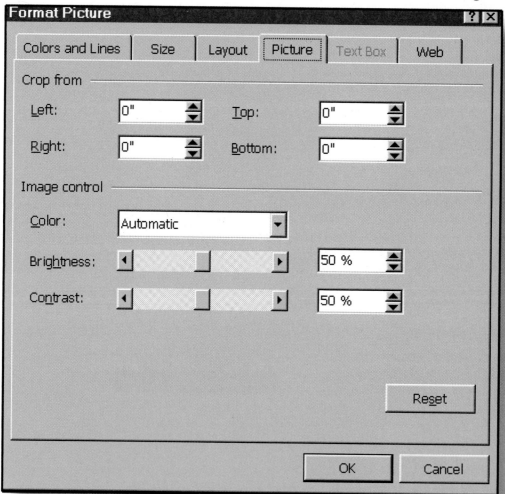

STEP-BY-STEP ▷ 5.1

1. Open **AW Step5-1** from the student data files and save the document as **T-shirt** followed by your initials.

2. Open the **Insert** menu and choose **Picture**. Then click **From File** on the submenu.

3. In the Insert Picture dialog box, locate the data files for this lesson. Click the **T-shirt** file and then click **Insert**.

Hot Tip

If the **T-shirt** file is not displayed in the list, change the *Files of type* to **All Pictures**.

4. Click the graphic to select it. Notice that the Picture toolbar displays when the graphic is selected.

5. Click the **Crop** button on the Picture toolbar. The pointer changes to a cropping box.

6. Position the mouse pointer on the middle handle at the right side of the graphic. When the cropping box surrounds the handle, drag the handle to the left until the border is close to the shirt.

7. Click the **Crop** button again to turn off the Crop function.

8. Double-click the picture to display the Picture tab in the Format Picture dialog box.

9. In the *Bottom* box under *Crop from*, key **.75**. Click **OK**. Your graphic should no longer have excess white space around the t-shirt image.

10. Save your changes and leave the document open for the next Step-by-Step.

Extra Challenge

Experiment with Word's cropping feature to add white space around a graphic. Open a new document and insert a clip art image. Display the Picture toolbar, click the **Crop** button, and drag the borders of the image to add white space.

Wrapping Text Around a Graphic

When you insert a graphic in a document, it is inserted in line with the text where the insertion point is positioned. You can format the text in the document to wrap around the graphic. Click the Text Wrapping button on the Picture toolbar to see a list of several options for wrapping the text around the graphic or in front of or behind the graphic. You can also choose text wrapping options in the Format Picture dialog box.

STEP-BY-STEP ▷ 5.2

1. If necessary, select the T-shirt graphic.

2. Click the **Text Wrapping** button on the Picture toolbar to display a menu of text wrapping options.

3. Select **Behind Text**. The graphic is positioned behind the text and the text overlays the graphic. (You might have to select this option again to send the graphic behind the text.)

(continued on next page)

4. Click the **Text Wrapping** button again, and this time select **Square**. The text no longer overlays the graphic, and the text wraps to the right of and below the graphic.

5. Drag the picture to the center of the document. Notice that the text wraps around the picture on all four sides.

6. Save your changes and leave the document open for the next Step-by-Step.

Positioning a Graphic Precisely

You already know that you can reposition a graphic anywhere within the printable area of the page by dragging it. By using the Picture command on the Format menu, you can position a graphic exactly relative to a reference point such as a margin, a page, a paragraph, or the edge of a column.

Position a graphic by clicking the Advanced button on the Layout tab in the Format Picture dialog box. The Advanced Layout dialog box opens, as shown in Figure 5-2. Key measurements in the *Horizontal* and *Vertical Absolute position* boxes and specify points of reference for *to the left of* and *below*.

FIGURE 5-2
Advanced Layout dialog box

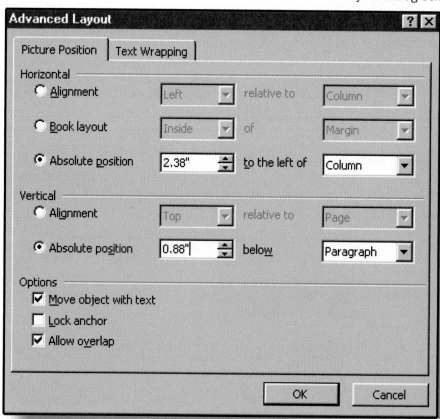

When you select a graphic, an anchor displays to the left of the paragraph where the graphic is anchored. Generally, when you move the graphic, the anchor moves to the paragraph nearest to the new position. You can attach the graphic to the paragraph to which it is anchored. Then, when you move the paragraph, the graphic will move with it.

Concept Builder

To attach a graphic to a paragraph, turn on the *Move object with text* check box in the Format Picture dialog box. If you want the graphic to remain anchored to the same paragraph, even if you move the graphic, turn on the *Lock anchor* check box in the Format Picture dialog box.

S TEP-BY-STEP ▷ 5.3

1. If necessary, select the graphic. Notice that there is an anchor displayed at the left of the first paragraph. The anchor is only displayed when the picture is selected.

2. Double-click the picture and then click the **Layout** tab. Click the **Advanced** button. The Advanced Layout dialog box opens.

3. Under *Horizontal*, click the down arrow in the *to the left of* list box. Choose **Margin**. In the *Absolute position* box, key **5.25**.

4. In the *Absolute position* box under *Vertical*, key **4.1** and, if necessary, select **Paragraph** for *below*.

5. Click **OK** twice to close the dialog boxes. The graphic is aligned horizontally 5.25 inches from the left margin and vertically 4.1 inches down from the first line in the paragraph to which it is anchored.

6. Save your changes and print the document. Leave the document open for the next Step-by-Step.

Deleting a Graphic

To delete a graphic, you select it and then press either Delete or Backspace. If you want to cut the graphic to the Clipboard, you can click the Cut button on the Standard toolbar. If you want to replace the graphic with another object, select the graphic and then choose the Picture command on the Insert menu to insert a new picture.

S TEP-BY-STEP ▷ 5.4

1. Select the graphic and press **Delete**. The graphic is removed and the text is again formatted with the normal line length.

2. Save your changes and leave the document open for the next Step-by-Step.

Creating a Watermark

A *watermark* is a ghost image that appears behind the printed text on each page of the document. Watermarks are often used to print logos or text such as *CONFIDENTIAL* on company stationery. A watermark can be created from text or a graphic. To create a watermark, you must insert the graphic or text in a header or footer. However, the watermark contents do not need to appear at the top or bottom of the page. A watermark can be positioned anywhere on the page.

After you insert the graphic in a header or footer, you format the graphic as a watermark on the Picture tab of the Format Picture dialog box. Just as you format other graphics, you can format the watermark image by choosing various options in the Color and Lines, Size, and Layout tabs. To view a watermark, display the document in Print Layout view.

Hot Tip

If your watermark prints too dark or too light, you can adjust the brightness and contrast controls under *Image control*. To lighten watermark text, change the font to a lighter color such as light gray. To lighten a watermark graphic, select the graphic and choose Picture on the Format menu. On the Colors and Lines tab, change the fill color to a lighter gray shading. If this doesn't work, edit the graphic in the program that was used to create it.

STEP-BY-STEP ▷ 5.5

1. Open the **View** menu and choose **Header and Footer**.

2. Click the **Show/Hide Document Text** button on the Header and Footer toolbar. The document will no longer be displayed on the screen, making it easier for you to work with the watermark image.

3. With the insertion point positioned in the Header pane, insert the clip art file **T-shirt** from the data files for this lesson.

4. Select the clip art in the Header pane and crop the white space around the picture.

5. Double-click the picture to display the Format Picture dialog box. In the *Color* box under *Image control*, select **Watermark**.

6. Click the **Layout** tab and select the **Behind text** wrapping option. Also on the Layout tab, select **Center** under *Horizontal alignment*.

7. Click the **Size** tab and scale the height and width to **500%**.

8. Click **OK**.

Concept Builder

If you are using a color printer, color graphics print in a lighter shade. However, if you are not using a color printer, color graphics may appear too dark when printed. If you do not have access to a color printer, you may find black and white graphics will work better as watermarks.

9. Click the arrow next to the **Zoom** box on the Standard toolbar and change the view to **25%**. You should now be able to see the entire page.

10. Select the watermark image and drag it down to center it vertically in the document.

11. Change the view back to **100%**.

12. Close the Header and Footer toolbar, and if it is still displayed, close the Picture toolbar.

13. Save your changes. Leave the document open for the next Step-by-Step.

 **Hot Tip**

If you want to go back and change the format of the clip art in the header, choose **Header and Footer** on the **View** menu and double-click the picture.

Adding a Page Border

You can also make documents more attractive by adding page borders. You can add page borders in many line styles and colors, as well as a variety of graphical borders. A page border is a section format. The border can be formatted for any or all sides of each page in a document, for pages in a section, for the first page only, or for all pages except the first.

The border will print on all the pages in the section formatted with a page border. To format a page border, you choose the Borders and Shading command on the Format menu and select options on the Page Border tab, shown in Figure 5-3.

FIGURE 5-3
Page Border tab in the Borders and Shading dialog box

Borders and Shading

| Borders | Page Border | Shading |

Setting:

None

Box

Shadow

3-D

Custom

Style:

Color:
Automatic

Width:
½ pt

Art:
(none)

Preview

Click on diagram below or use buttons to apply borders

Apply to:
Whole document

Options...

Show Toolbar   Horizontal Line...   OK   Cancel

1. Position the insertion point in the first paragraph.

2. Open the **Format** menu and choose **Borders and Shading**.

3. Click the **Page Border** tab.

4. Under *Style*, select the last option in the list box. Notice how the border looks in the *Preview* area of the dialog box.

5. Under *Width*, select **6 pt**.

6. Click the left and right borders in the *Preview* box to remove them.

7. Click **OK**.

8. Save your changes. Print and close the document.

Formatting Text Boxes

M any types of documents include special sections of text relating to the subject matter that are formatted differently from the rest of the document. For example, newsletters and magazine articles often include sections that summarize the contents of the article, highlight specific text, and draw the reader's attention to specific content.

You can use text boxes to position these special sections of text and to apply various formats such as font styles, line fills, and shadows. Within the text box, you can change the alignment of text. If the text box is not large enough to display all the text, you can either drag the sizing handles or you can format the text box precisely using the Text Box command on the Format menu.

Hot Tip

To position a text box more precisely, select the text box, click **Draw** on the Drawing toolbar, then click **Nudge** and select one of the four options to move the text box or object slightly.

Creating a Sidebar

A *sidebar* is supplemental text that is added to a document such as a magazine or newspaper article. A sidebar can be used to list the names of officers in a club newsletter or it can be used to summarize the contents of a magazine article. Sidebars are usually displayed in a boxed area and they are sometimes shaded.

Use a text box to create a sidebar. If the sidebar text already exists in the document, select the text and then click the Text Box button on the Drawing toolbar. The selected text appears in the text box. You can then position the text box as desired. If you need to key the contents for the sidebar, you can insert and position an empty text box and then enter the text in the text box.

STEP-BY-STEP ▷ 5.7

1. Open **AW Step5-7** from the student data files and save the document as **Lead** followed by your initials.

2. Select the first heading *History* and the paragraph mark that follows the heading. Do not select the section break. Press **Delete**.

3. Select the paragraph beginning *The Greeks were the first . . . .*

4. Click the **Text Box** button on the Drawing toolbar to insert a text box around the selected text.

5. Double-click the text box border. On the Size tab in the Format Text Box dialog box, change the height to **5.0** and the width to **4.5**.

6. Click the **Layout** tab and then click **Advanced**. Under *Horizontal*, change the *Absolute position* to **3** *to the left of* **Page**. Under *Vertical*, change the *Absolute position* to **4.25** *below* **Page**.

7. Click the **Text Wrapping** tab and select **Square** and then click **OK** twice. The text box is positioned in the lower right corner of the page. Reposition the sidebar text box if necessary so the text wraps around the text box only at the top and left.

8. Save your changes and leave the document open for the next Step-by-Step.

Applying Shading to Paragraphs and Sections of Text

You can set apart paragraphs or sections of text from the rest of a document by applying shading. Color highlights and shading are most effective when the recipient of the document reviews the document online or on a color printout. If the document is to be printed in black and white, light colors and shading patterns work best.

To add shading to an entire paragraph, you simply click anywhere within the paragraph and then apply the shading formats. To add shading to a word or group of words, you first select the text. Then, choose the Borders and Shading command on the Format menu and click the Shading tab to select the desired shading option.

To apply the shading formats to a text box, click the text box to select it. Then click the Fill Color button on the Drawing toolbar and select a shading.

STEP-BY-STEP ▷ 5.8

1. If necessary, click on the sidebar text box to select it.

2. Click the **Fill Color** button on the Drawing toolbar.

3. Select **Gray-25%**. The shading is applied to the entire text box. Your text box should look like the one in Figure 5-4.

(continued on next page)

FIGURE 5-4
Shaded text box

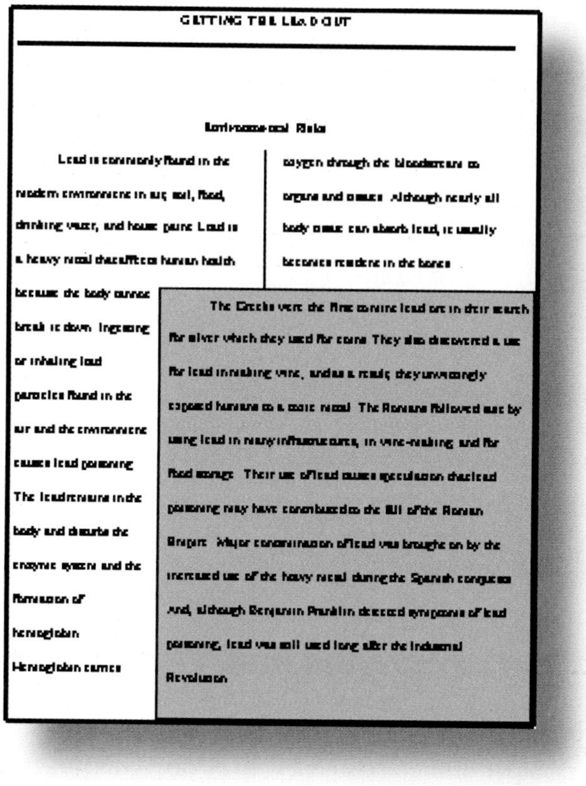

4. Select the bulleted list on page 2.

5. Open the **Format** menu, choose **Borders and Shading**, and then click the Shading tab.

6. Under *Fill*, select **Gray-25%** and click **OK**.

7. Save your changes and leave the document open for the next Step-by-Step.

Creating Pull Quotes

Pull quotes are often used in magazine and newsletter articles to highlight specific text included within the article. A pull quote is usually positioned on the same page and close to where it is referenced.

To create a pull quote, first insert an empty text box. Then copy the text you want to highlight into the textbox. The pull quote text is often formatted in a different font style, size, or color to add emphasis. A pull quote often has a border around it, but it can also be formatted without a border.

STEP-BY-STEP 5.9

1. Move the insertion point to the top of the document. Use **Find** to search for the sentence that begins *Lead poisoning is a health problem . . . .* When Word locates the sentence, close the Find and Replace dialog box and select the sentence (do not include the tab).

2. Copy the sentence to the Clipboard.

3. Scroll up and position the insertion point in the first paragraph in the left column on page 3.

4. Insert a text box approximately 1.5 inches square in the middle of the paragraph.

5. Click inside the text box, and then paste the sentence from the Clipboard.

6. Select the pull quote text and change it to **14 pt bold**.

7. If necessary, resize the text box to display the entire sentence. Apply the **Square** wrapping style.

8. Use **Print Preview** to reposition the text box in the middle of the page:
   a. Click the **Magnifier** button on the Print Preview toolbar.
   b. Point to a border of the text box and drag the text box to position it in the middle of the page.
   c. Close Print Preview.

9. With the text box selected, click the down arrow to the right of the **Line Color** button on the Drawing toolbar and then select **No Line**. Your pull quote should now look similar to that in Figure 5-5. (The text on both sides may vary.)

10. Move the insertion point to the top of the document and use **Find** to search for the sentence that begins *At this time . . . .* Copy the entire sentence and then deselect the text.

FIGURE 5-5
Pull quote positioned in center of page

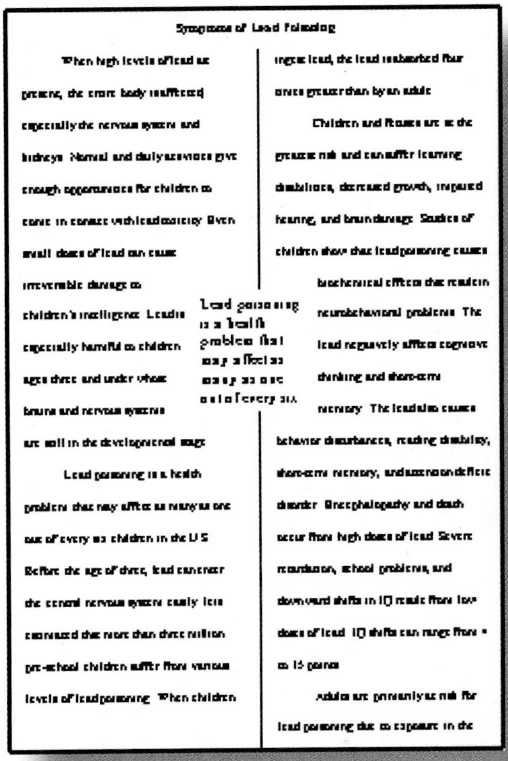

11. Position the insertion point in the paragraph that begins *Adults are primarily at risk . . .* and create a text box approximately 1.5 inches square.

12. Paste the sentence in the text box and change the text to **14 pt bold**. If necessary, resize the text box to reduce the amount of white space in the text box.

13. Position the text box in the center of the two columns on page 4 and remove the line around the text box.

14. Save your changes and leave the document open for the next Step-by-Step.

Changing the Orientation of Text in a Text Box

When you insert text in a text box, the default orientation for the text is horizontal. You can, however, change the orientation of text in a text box. The Text Direction command on the Format menu provides two different options for displaying the text vertically.

When you select this command, the Text Direction dialog box opens, as shown in Figure 5-6. Note that you can display text with a vertical orientation so that the text reads from bottom to top or from top to bottom.

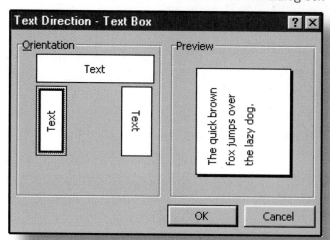

FIGURE 5-6
Text Direction dialog box

S TEP-BY-STEP ▷ 5.10

You must complete Step-by-Step 5.11 immediately after you complete this Step-by-Step.

1. Move the insertion point to the top of the document. Insert a text box approximately 0.5 inch wide by 3.5 inches high. Use the horizontal and vertical rulers to judge the size of the text box.

2. With the text box selected, open the **Format** menu and choose **Text Direction**. Select the *Bottom to top* option. (This option is shown selected in Figure 5-6.)

3. Change the font size to **20 pt bold** and then key **HEALTH WATCH**.

4. Center the text and remove the text box border.

5. With the text box selected, click the cross-hatched border to change it to small dots and then click the **Cut** button.

6. Save your changes. Leave the document open for the next Step-by-Step.

Repeating Text Box Contents on Multiple Pages

You can repeat text box contents on every page of a document or section of a document by inserting a text box item in a header or footer and positioning the text box where you want the contents to print. For example, you may want to print a title in the left margin on each page of a document.

STEP-BY-STEP ▷ 5.11

1. Open the **View** menu and choose **Header and Footer**.

2. With the insertion point positioned in the *Header -Section 1-* box, click the **Paste** button.

3. Drag the text box down and to the left so it is positioned in the margin to the left of the document text. Align the top border of the text box with the heading *Environmental Risks*. See Figure 5-7.

FIGURE 5-7
Text box inserted in header

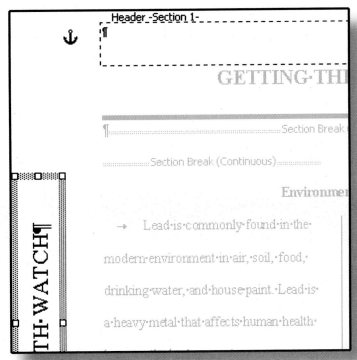

4. Click **Close** on the Header and Footer toolbar.

5. Click the **Print Preview** button to view the document in Print Preview. Click the **Multiple Pages** button on the Print Preview toolbar and drag across the grid until you see *2 x 3 Pages* and

then release the mouse button. Notice that the text box appears in the left margin on every page of the document. Close Print Preview.

6. Save your changes. Print and close the document.

Creating Drop Caps

Drop caps are often used to draw attention to the beginning of an article in a newsletter or magazine. The drop cap format can be added to the first letter in the first word of a paragraph or it can be added to the entire first word. To format the entire word, you must first select the word.

[handwritten: NOT WITH COLUMNS]

To apply a drop cap format, open the Format menu and choose Drop Cap. The Drop Cap dialog box opens, as shown in Figure 5-8. Use this box to determine the size, font, and position of the drop cap. You can position the drop cap(s) in the paragraph or in the margin. However, drop caps cannot be positioned in the margin when the text is formatted in columns.

FIGURE 5-8
Drop Cap dialog box

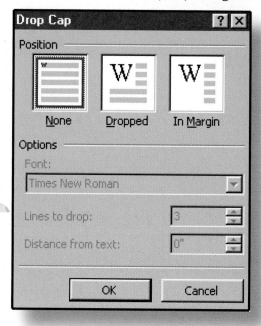

STEP-BY-STEP ▷ 5.12

1. Open **AW Step5-12** from the student data files and save the document as **Fitness** followed by your initials.

2. Position the insertion point in the word *Getting* in the first paragraph.

3. Open the **Format** menu and choose **Drop Cap**. Word displays the Drop Cap dialog box. Notice that the default setting is *None*.

4. Under *Position*, click **Dropped**.

5. Open the *Font* box in the dialog box. Scroll up and click **Arial**.

6. For the *Lines to drop* box, click the down increment arrow to change the number to **2**. This setting specifies the height of the drop cap in lines of text.

7. For *Distance from text*, click the up increment arrow to change the distance to **0.1**. This setting controls the amount of space between the drop cap and the text that follows it.

8. Click **OK**. The drop cap is formatted in a frame in the top left corner of the paragraph.

9. Position the insertion point in the first word in the second paragraph.

10. Choose **Drop Cap** from the **Format** menu. Select **Margin** and click **OK**.

11. Compare the two drop caps. You decide to use the format from the first drop cap. Click **Undo**.

12. Click on the drop cap in the first paragraph to select it.

13. Choose **Drop Cap** from the **Format** menu and then click **OK** without changing any of the options.

14. Click in the first word of the second paragraph. Open the **Edit** menu and click **Repeat** (or press **F4**).

15. Save your changes. Print and close the document.

Using AutoShapes to Create Objects

Word's AutoShape feature enables you to create a variety of drawing objects quickly and easily. To create an AutoShape, you choose an object such as a star, an arrow, or a callout from a pop-up menu on the Drawing toolbar. The pointer changes to a crosshair. If you want to insert a predefined size of the object, you simply click in the document window at the approximate location where you want to insert the AutoShape. Or you can drag the crosshair to create an object the size you want. If you hold down Shift as you drag a corner handle, the object will be sized proportionally for height and width. Once you have created the AutoShape object, you can resize it, position it, and rotate or flip it as you would other graphics.

To add text to an AutoShape object, right-click the object and then choose Add Text and key the desired text. The text becomes part of the object and moves with the object when you reposition it. If you rotate or flip the object, however, the orientation of the text will not change. To rotate the text, choose the Text Direction command on the Format menu.

The Callouts choice on the AutoShapes pop-up menu gives you a number of choices for creating callouts. *Callouts* let you insert text to label or point out an item. Notice that each callout has a leader you can use to point out the item you are labeling.

When you create a callout with an AutoShape object, the callout is automatically formatted as a text box. If you reposition the text box, the position of the leader does not change. To reposition the leader, drag the yellow diamond symbol at the end of the leader.

S TEP-BY-STEP ▷ 5.13

1. Open a new document window and display the Drawing toolbar if necessary.

2. Click **AutoShapes** on the Drawing toolbar and then select **Stars and Banners** in the pop-up menu.

3. In the **Stars and Banners** menu, select the first banner in the third row. The pointer changes to a crosshair and Word changes to Print Layout view.

4. Click at the top left corner of the document to insert the object. A predefined size of the banner is inserted at the location where you clicked. Drag the middle handle on the right side of the object to stretch the banner across the top of the page.

 **Hot Tip**

To resize the object proportionally, you must hold down **Shift** as you drag a corner handle.

(continued on next page)

5. Right-click the AutoShape and then choose **Add Text** in the shortcut menu.

6. In the text box, key **All Stars**. Center the text and change the font size to **26 pt**.

7. Double-click the AutoShape object. On the Size tab, scale the height and width to **150%** and then click **OK**. Notice that the AutoShape increases in size, but the text inside the Auto-Shape remains the same size.

 Hot Tip

To change the margin around text in an AutoShape or text box, click the **Text Box** tab in the Format AutoShape dialog box and adjust the measurements under *Internal margin*.

8. Drag one of the AutoShape borders to position the object in a new location. Notice that the text moves with the object.

9. Click **AutoShapes** on the Drawing toolbar, select **Callouts**, and then select any one of the objects in the first row.

10. Point to the center of the document window and drag down and to the right to create the callout object.

11. Key **Hello!**

12. Click on the object to select it and then click on the cross-hatched border to change it to small dots.

13. Drag the yellow diamond symbol at the tip of the leader to the opposite side of the object to change the direction of the leader and then release.

14. Insert a clip art image and experiment adding callouts and positioning the callouts next to the graphic.

15. Close the document without saving.

Round-Trip Documents from HTML

You save a Word document in HTML format so users can view the document with a Web browser. If you edit the HTML document, Word enables you to "round-trip" the document back into the Word program without losing the document formats.

Word allows you to build a Web page directly in Word. Saving the document as a Web page lets you see how your Web page will look in a browser. Most formatting options you apply to your text in Word will be retained in the Web page. If a formatting option is not available in the browser, Word substitutes another similar formatting option. For example, text formatted with the shadow font effect will be formatted as bold instead.

You can edit the HTML code while in your browser to make changes to your Web page. Then, you can save your HTML document back to Word format and see that the change you made in the browser is still in effect.

In the following Step-by-Step, you will format a document as a Web page, make a simple change to the HTML code, and then save the Web document as a regular Word document again.

S TEP-BY-STEP ▷ 5.14

SCANS

You can complete this Step-by-Step if you have access to a Web browser. Specific instructions are supplied for Internet Explorer. If you are using a different browser, ask your instructor for specific directions.

1. Open **AW Step5-14** from the student data files and save it as **Museum** followed by your initials.

2. Open the **File** menu and click **Save as Web Page**. Save the document using the same file name.

3. Open the **Format** menu and click **Background**. Choose a background color for the Web page. Change the color of the Web page title if desired using the *Font color* option in the Font dialog box.

4. Insert one or two clip art graphics to illustrate the Web page text. Resize the graphics appropriately and wrap text around them. You might need to add extra blank lines below each paragraph to get text to wrap properly around the graphics.

5. Start your Web browser and open the **Museum** HTML document. Your Web page should open with your formatting options displayed. (*Note:* Some browsers will not display the drop caps correctly, but you should be able to read all the text and see the graphics.)

6. Make a simple change to the HTML code for the Web page:
   a. Open the **View** menu and click **Source**. A notepad document opens containing the HTML code for the page.
   b. Scroll halfway down the HTML code until you find the page title *MUSEUM NEWS* enclosed in HTML coding brackets similar to

   ```
   <p class=MsoTitle><b><span
   style='color:maroon'>MUSEUM
   NEWS<
   ```

   c. Change the title from all caps to initial caps: **Museum News**. Open the **File** menu and click **Save**. Close the Notepad window. To see your change, click the **Refresh** button on the toolbar. Close your browser.

7. Open the HTML document in Word and save the document as a Word file titled **Web Museum**.

8. Print and close the document.

Summary

In this lesson, you learned:

- You can crop a graphic by dragging one of its borders or by indicating a precise measurement in the Format Picture dialog box.

- Word offers many options for wrapping text around graphics.

- To create a watermark, you format text or a graphic in a header or footer.

- Page borders can be formatted for any or all sides of each page in a document, for pages in a section, for the first page only, or for all pages except the first.

- Text boxes enable you to format sidebars, pull quotes, and drop caps.

- AutoShapes provide an easy way to create objects including stars, arrows, and callouts.

- "Round tripping" allows you to save a Word document for use on the Web, edit the HTML code, and resave the HTML file as a Word document.

LESSON 5 REVIEW QUESTIONS

TRUE/FALSE

Circle T if the statement is true or F if the statement is false.

T F 1. Text boxes can be positioned in headers and footers.

T F 2. When you insert text in a text box, Word automatically adjusts the size of the text box to fit the text you inserted. *Only if you don't drag the box to size it.*

T F 3. When you create a callout with an AutoShape, you must insert a text box inside the object.

T F 4. The drop cap format can only be added to the first letter of a word. *Select whole word to drop word.*

T F 5. If a document is to be printed in black and white, light colors and shading patterns work best.

FILL IN THE BLANKS

Complete the following sentences by writing the correct word or words in the blanks provided.

1. Supplemental text that is added to a magazine or newspaper article is called a(n) *Side bar*.

2. A(n) *watermark* is a ghost image that appears behind the printed text.

3. A(n) *pulled quote* emphasizes a passage from a document such as a magazine article.

4. *crop* means to cut off portions of a graphic.

5. A(n) *anchor* indicates the reference point for positioning a graphic.

LESSON 5 PROJECTS

PROJECT 5-1

1. Key the document illustrated in Figure 5-9 and save as **Trees** followed by your initials.

FIGURE 5-9

CAN YOU IMAGINE YOUR CITY WITHOUT TREES?

Whether we realize it or not, trees are significant to our survival and welfare. Most important, trees purify the air we breathe. They absorb the gases we exhale and in return provide large quantities of oxygen.

Trees cool the atmosphere in hot weather and provide welcome shade on a hot summer day. They render shelter for wildlife. Numerous recreational parks are situated in forests.

Planting trees can help solve environmental problems. New trees can help reduce erosion, restore damaged ecosystems, and provide habitat for wildlife.

For information on national and local tree planting programs, call 1-800-555-TREE.

2. Format the heading as a banner and format the paragraphs below the heading in two columns. Justify the paragraphs and insert a hard column break to move the last two paragraphs to the second column.

3. Create a watermark using the **Oak** file from the data files for this lesson. Crop the white space around the clip art. Increase the image size and position the image in the middle of the paragraphs in the document.

4. Format the first letter in the first paragraph as a drop cap. Use Times New Roman as the font, drop the cap two lines, and change the distance from text to 0.1 inch.

5. Save your changes. Print and close the document.

PROJECT 5-2

1. Open **AW Project5-2** from the student data files and save it as **Top Ten** followed by your initials.

2. Find and select the text *put nutritious fruits and vegetables on your plate five times a day.*

3. Format the selected text in a pull quote at the left edge of the second paragraph (and above the enumerated list). Format the pull quote text in a larger font and centered within the text box. If you have a color printer, format the text in red. Apply the square wrapping style and align the text box horizontally at the left. Remove the text box border.

4. Create a text box with the words *HEALTHY LIVING* oriented vertically from top to bottom. Format the text box in the document header to repeat on all pages. Position the text box horizontally 6 inches *to the left of* the margin and 5.5 inches *below* the paragraph.

5. Save the changes to the document and clear the screen.

PROJECT 5-3

1. Research the Web for information about a national competition that interests you. For example, you can choose a topic involving a sport, academics, music, or science.

2. Choose an appropriate title and write two or three paragraphs to summarize the events and the winner(s) of the competition.

3. Create the graphic illustrated in Figure 5-10 so it is approximately 3 inches high and 3 inches wide.
   A. Use AutoShapes and text boxes to create the object.
   B. Order the objects as illustrated in the figure.
   C. If you have access to a color printer, fill the objects with colors and/or format the AutoShape lines in color.

FIGURE 5-10

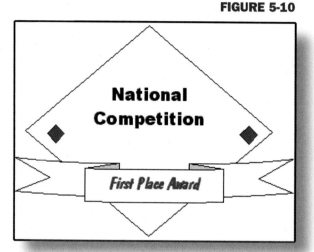

4. Position the object for an attractive layout and wrap the text around the document.

5. Save the document as **Award** followed by your initials. Print and close the document.

CRITICAL THINKING

ACTIVITY 5-1

Becky's supervisor asked her if she would prepare a company newsletter. Becky compiled all the articles into one document and began formatting the columns and adding text boxes. Before long, she was having difficulty determining the column and text box boundaries in the newsletter document. How could Becky view these boundaries as she works with the document? Use the Help feature to find the answer.

Text Layout View >> Tools > Options > Print + Web Layout Options
Text boundaries

ACTIVITY 5-2

As Becky continued working on the newsletter, she scanned photos and imported numerous clip art images. Soon she realized that the graphics were sometimes quite large and the size of the newsletter document had increased substantially. Scrolling through the document was very slow. What can Becky do to reduce the size of the document when she inserts so many graphics? How can Becky increase the scrolling speed when a document contains so many graphics? Use the Help feature to find the answers.

linking graphics, use black + white, lower resolution

AW-98

ADVANCED MICROSOFT WORD

WORKING WITH LONG DOCUMENTS

OBJECTIVES

Upon completion of this lesson, you should be able to:

- Move or copy text between documents.
- Format text flow options.
- Create and edit styles and use the document Organizer.
- Use the Document Map.
- Create a hyperlink.
- Create footnotes and endnotes.
- Revise footnotes and endnotes.

⏱ **Estimated Time: 1.5 hours**

Working with Multiple Documents

When long documents such as reports, studies, and proposals are prepared, the information in those documents is often compiled from several different documents. Word allows you to open multiple documents and keep them open so you can easily switch between documents. When you have two or more documents open, you can use the *Clipboard* to cut, copy, and paste from one document to another without having to open and close documents separately. Alternatively, you can use the *Spike* to combine pieces of documents. A third alternative, if you want to combine all of one file with another, is to use the File command on the Insert menu.

Opening Multiple Documents

The number of windows you can open depends on available system memory. You can open several documents at the same time by selecting all of the document file names in the Open dialog box. To select multiple file names, click on the first file name, hold down Ctrl, and click on each additional file name that you want to include in the selection. If the desired file names are listed together in the dialog box, you can click on the first file name in the range, hold down Shift, and click at the end of the range.

When you have multiple documents open, only one document is displayed. However, titles of all the open documents are displayed as buttons on the Windows taskbar. To switch between documents, you simply click on the document title in the taskbar. When you have several open documents, there is not enough space to display the full file name in the taskbar. To view the file names, point to one of the document buttons and wait for the ScreenTip to display the file name.

STEP-BY-STEP ▷ 6.1

As you work through Step-by-Steps 6.1 through 6.4, do not be concerned with paragraph spacing and unnecessary blank paragraphs in documents. You will adjust the spacing later.

1. Open **AW Step6-1a** from the student data files and save the document as **Pharmacy** followed by your initials.

2. Click the **Open** button on the Standard toolbar and locate the data files for this lesson.

3. Click **AW Step6-1b** to select it but do not click Open yet.

4. Hold down **Shift** and click **AW Step6-1e** (scroll as needed, but do not use the direction keys). Now **AW Step6-1b** through **AW Step6-1e** are all highlighted.

5. Hold down **Ctrl** and click on **AW Step6-1f**. Five file names are now included in the selection.

6. Click **Open**. All five files should open, one at a time. Do not save them with new names.

7. Click the **Pharmacy** button in the taskbar to switch to that window. Leave all documents open for the next Step-by-Step.

Using the Clipboard to Copy and Paste Multiple Items

When you display the Clipboard toolbar (Figure 6-1), you can view up to 12 of the last items that were copied or cut. If you dock the Clipboard toolbar, you need to click the *Items* down arrow to display the contents of the Clipboard. You can select any one of the items and paste it or you can choose the Paste all button to paste all the Clipboard items at once. If you choose the Clear All button, all the contents are removed from the Clipboard.

FIGURE 6-1
Clipboard toolbar

S TEP-BY-STEP ▷ 6.2

1. Open the **View** menu and choose **Toolbars**. Then select **Clipboard** to display the Clipboard toolbar.

2. If any documents are displayed on the toolbar, click the **Clear Clipboard** button. If the toolbar is docked, you will need to click the down arrow next to *Items* to view the contents.

3. Click on the **AW Step6-1b** button on the taskbar to switch to that document.

4. Select the heading *Education* and the first paragraph below the heading. Be sure to include the ending paragraph mark.

5. Click the **Copy** button to copy the text to the Clipboard. The Clipboard toolbar displays one item of copied text.

6. Click the **AW Step6-1c** button. Triple-click in the selection bar (the blank space to the left of the document) to select all the text in the document, including the ending paragraph

mark. Copy the text to the Clipboard.

7. Click the **AW Step6-1f** button and select the entire document. Copy the text to the Clipboard.

8. Click the **Pharmacy** button and position the insertion point at the end of the document.

9. Click the **Paste All** button on the Clipboard toolbar. The three items are pasted into the **Pharmacy** document.

10. Notice that the items are still stored on the Clipboard toolbar. Click the **Clear Clipboard** button to clear the contents of the Clipboard.

11. Close the Clipboard toolbar or drag it to the edge of the window to dock it.

12. Save your changes and leave all documents open for the next Step-by-Step.

Using the Spike to Cut and Paste Multiple Items

The Spike works very similar to the Clipboard. With the Spike, you remove two or more items from one or more documents so you can insert the items as a group in a new location or document. To cut each item to the Spike, you select the item and then press Ctrl + F3. The items are stored in the Clipboard in the order you cut them. To insert the items as a group, position the insertion point and press Ctrl + Shift + F3. When you insert the items this way, the contents are removed from the Spike.

The contents of the Spike are stored as an AutoText entry. If you want to insert the contents of the Spike and also keep the contents in the Spike, you must insert the Spike contents as an AutoText entry. Choose AutoText on the Insert menu, select Spike, and click Insert.

Sometimes it can be difficult selecting large sections of text or text that wraps from one page to the next page. The click-Shift-click method is easy to use. Click where you want the selection to begin, scroll to the end of the selection, hold down Shift, and click.

Hot Tip

You can close multiple windows at once by holding down **Shift** and opening the **File** menu. Instead of the usual command Close, the menu will display Close All.

Spike – to add Ctrl + F3
to insert Ctrl + Shift + F3

1. Click the **AW Step6-1d** button and select the entire document.

2. Press the Spike keys **Ctrl** + **F3** to send the text to the Spike.

3. Click the **AW Step6-1b** button. Click in front of the heading *Licenses*, scroll to the end of the document, hold down **Shift**, and then click at the end of the document. Press **Ctrl** + **F3** to send the text to the Spike.

4. Click the **AW Step6-1e** button. Select the entire document and send the text to the Spike.

5. Switch to the **Pharmacy** document and make sure the insertion point is positioned at the end of the document.

6. Press **Ctrl** + **Shift** + **F3** to insert the contents of the Spike and at the same time remove the contents from the Spike.

7. Save the changes to the **Pharmacy** document only.

8. Hold down **Shift**, open the **File** menu, and choose **Close All**. When prompted, do not save changes to any documents except **Pharmacy**.

Inserting a File

You can insert the entire contents of a file without even having to open that file. Position the insertion point where the file contents should be inserted. Then open the Insert menu and choose File. In the Insert File dialog box (Figure 6-2), select the file you want to insert. Then click Insert.

FIGURE 6-2
Insert File dialog box

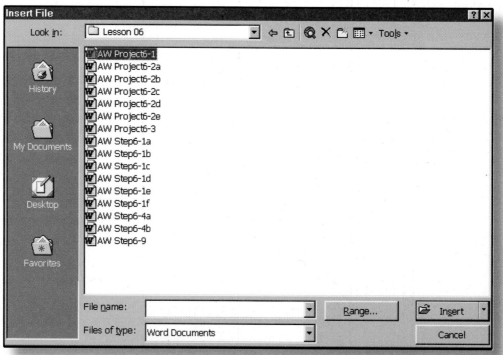

S TEP-BY-STEP ⊳ 6.4

1. Open the document **Pharmacy**.

2. Position the insertion point in the blank paragraph above the heading *Education* on the first page.

3. Open the **Insert** menu and choose **File**. The Insert file dialog box opens. Locate the data files for this lesson.

4. Select **AW Step6-4a** and click **Insert**. The entire contents of the file are inserted at the insertion point.

5. Position the insertion point at the end of the document and insert the file **AW Step6-4b**.

6. Scroll through the document and delete all blank lines (except for one blank line at the end of the document).

7. Select the entire document and change the spacing to single.

8. Save your changes and leave the document open for the next Step-by-Step.

Using Text Flow Options

When you work with documents that contain headings and other special paragraphs, you can adjust the spacing above and below the paragraphs in the Indents and Spacing tab in the Paragraph dialog box. In Figure 6-3, for example, the entry in the *After* box in the *Spacing* section will add 6 points of space after the current paragraph (or paragraphs, if several are selected).

FIGURE 6-3

Indents and Spacing tab in Paragraph dialog box

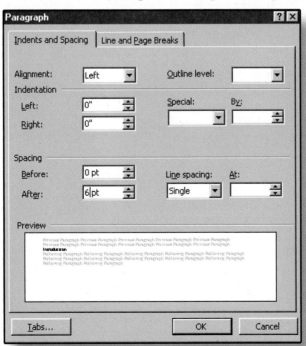

You can also control the flow of paragraphs from one page to the next. The text flow options are on the Line and Page Breaks tab in the Paragraph dialog box, shown in Figure 6-4. When you select text and click the option *Keep lines together*, Word makes sure the selected lines are not divided between two pages. When you select the option *Keep with next*, the paragraph is not split from the following paragraph. The *Page break before* option moves the paragraph to the top of the next page. A small box is displayed to the left of the paragraph when pagination formats are applied.

Concept Builder

When you want to keep two or more paragraphs together using a text flow option, do not select the last paragraph of the group, because you do not want to keep it with the next paragraph.

FIGURE 6-4
Line and Page Breaks tab in Paragraph dialog box

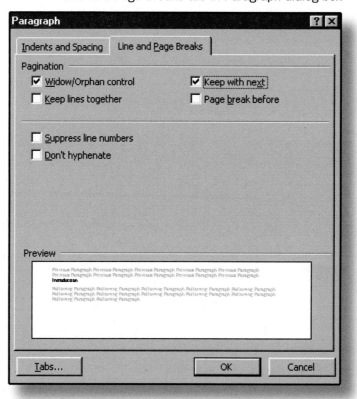

These text flow options are especially useful when you have headings and bulleted lists in a document. It's a good idea to apply these formats as you create the document. Then if you move text around in the document, the headings are not separated from related paragraphs and bulleted lists are not split between two pages.

Hot Tip

When you want to select text from the location of the insertion point to the beginning or the end of the document, hold down **Shift** and then press either **Ctrl + Home** or **Ctrl + End**.

ADVANCED MICROSOFT WORD

S TEP-BY-STEP ▷ 6.5

1. Position the insertion point in front of the heading *Introduction*. Hold down **Shift** and then press **Ctrl + End**. The text is selected from the location of the insertion point to the end of the document.

2. Open the **Format** menu and choose **Paragraph**. If necessary, click the **Indents and Spacing** tab.

3. Under *Spacing*, change 0 pt to **6 pt** in the *After* box.

4. Click **OK**. Scroll through the document. You can now clearly see where each paragraph begins and ends.

5. Position the insertion point in the heading *Introduction* near the top of the document.

6. Open the **Format** menu and choose **Paragraph**. Select the **Line and Page Breaks** tab.

7. Click in the **Keep with next** check box and, if necessary, click in the **Widow/Orphan control** check box. Click **OK**.

8. Click in the heading *History*. Open the **Format** menu and choose **Paragraph**. This time turn on **Keep with next** and **Page break before** and click **OK**.

9. Click in the heading *Education*. Open the **Edit** menu and click **Repeat Paragraph Formatting** (or press **F4**).

10. Format the following headings with the **Keep with next** option: *Course of Study, Internships and Externships, Skills,* and *Licenses*.

11. Format the following headings with the **Keep with next** and **Page break before** options: *Opportunities, Benefits,* and *Conclusion*.

12. Go to the bottom of page 3 (or the top of page 4). Select the bulleted list. Format the paragraphs with the **Keep lines together** and **Keep with next** options.

13. Save your changes. Leave the document open for the next Step-by-Step.

Working with Styles

A *style* is a set of formatting instructions that tells Word how to format text in a document. By applying styles to text, you can make sure that parts of your document such as headings look the same throughout the document. By default, Word applies several styles to any new document and lists them in the Style dialog box, shown in Figure 6-5. When you begin keying in a new document, you are using the Normal style. The *Description* area of the Style dialog box shows you the formatting instructions for the style selected in the *Styles* list.

FIGURE 6-5
Style dialog box

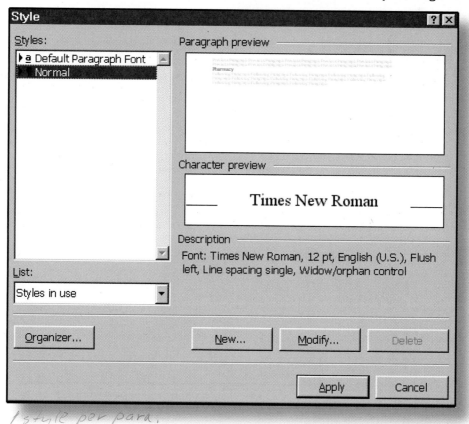

*1 style per para,
many character styles*

You can create your own styles to format items in your document just the way you want them. You can create styles for either characters or paragraphs. Only one paragraph style can be applied to each paragraph, but you can apply multiple character styles within a paragraph. When a paragraph is moved or copied within a document, styles are moved or copied with the text and do not need to be reapplied.

A *style sheet* is the list of all styles that are part of a document or document template. Style sheets are automatically saved with each Word document so you can print the document at any computer without having to remember to load a style sheet.

 **Hot Tip**

To display the styles used in a document, switch to Normal view, choose **Options** on the **Tools** menu, and click the **View** tab. Key a measurement (for example, .75) in the **Style area width** box and then click **OK**. The style names appear in an area at the left side of the document window.

Creating a Style

There are three main ways to create a style: You can create a style based on formatted text, you can use formatting commands, or you can base a style on an existing style.

■ To create a style based on formatted text, select the text you want to style and apply formats to it. Then open the Format menu and click the Style command. In the Style dialog box, click New. Word opens the New Style dialog box, shown in Figure 6-6. Key a name for the style in the *Name* box and specify in the *Style type* drop-down list whether the style is a character or paragraph style. Click OK and then click Apply to apply the style to your selected text.

FIGURE 6-6
New Style dialog box

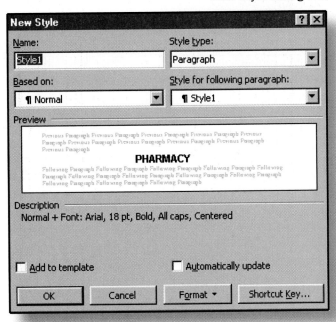

You can also create a style in the New Style dialog box itself. Click in the paragraph you want to style (or select characters), open the Style dialog box, and then click New. After you name the style and specify its type, click the Format button at the bottom of the dialog box. On the pop-up Format menu are commands for Font, Paragraph, Tabs, Border, and Numbering, among others. Click commands as desired to select formatting options. When you have finished building your style, click OK and then Apply.

After you have already created a style, you can create a new style based on that style by selecting it in the Style dialog box and then clicking New. In the New Style dialog box, key a name for the new style. Make any necessary formatting changes and then click OK and Apply. The new style will have all the formatting of the original style, plus your new changes.

As you define styles, the Style dialog box displays a description of the style and the Preview box shows how the text will look with the new style.

Concept Builder

The *Style for following paragraph* list box lets you specify a style for the paragraph that follows your current paragraph. For example, if you are defining a style for a heading, you can tell Word to apply the Normal style (or any other style you choose) to the paragraph after the heading. Styles are applied in this way only when you are keying a document.

1. Select the title *Pharmacy*. Open the **Format** menu and click **Font**. In the Font dialog box, select **Arial**, **Bold**, and **18** for the font size. Click the **All caps** option and then click **OK**.

Concept Builder

You must set capitalization options in the Font dialog box if you want them to be part of the style.

2. With the title still selected, open the **Format** menu and choose **Style** and then click **New** to display the New Style dialog box.

3. In the *Name* box, key **Title font**. Under *Style type*, click the down arrow and select **Character**.

4. Click **OK** to return to the Style dialog box and then click **Apply**.

5. Click in the first bulleted item on page 4. Open the **Format** menu and choose **Style** and then click **New**. In the *Name* box, key **Bulleted item**. Leave **Paragraph** selected under *Style type*. Click **OK** and then click **Apply**.

6. Click in the second bulleted item. Click the down arrow in the **Style** box on the Formatting toolbar and select the new **Bulleted item** style. Apply the style to the last bulleted item.

7. Position the insertion point in the heading *Introduction*. Open the **Format** menu and choose **Style**, and then click **New**. In the *Name* box, key **Side heading 1**. Leave **Paragraph** selected under *Style type*.

8. Open the *Based on* box, scroll to the top of the list, and select **(no style)**, because you want to create the style with formatting commands rather than basing it on the Normal style.

9. Define the character formats for the new style: Click **Format** and then click **Font**. If necessary, click the **Font** tab. Select the following formats: **Times New Roman**, **Bold**, **14 pt**. Click **OK**.

10. Define the paragraph formats for the new style: Click **Format** and then click **Paragraph**. If necessary, click the **Indents and Spacing** tab and select **Centered** alignment. Set the spacing before at **6 pt** and the spacing after at **6 pt**. Click **OK** twice and then click **Apply**.

11. Position the insertion point in the heading *History*. Click the down arrow in the **Style** box on the Formatting toolbar and select the new **Side heading 1** style.

12. Apply the Side heading 1 style to the following headings: *Education, Opportunities, Benefits,* and *Conclusion*. Notice that the formatting of the new style overwrites the text flow options you put in place earlier, so these headings no longer begin on new pages.

13. Position the insertion point in the heading *Course of Study*. Open the **Format** menu, choose **Style**, and click the **Side heading 1** style to select it. Click **New**. Under *Name*, key **Side heading 2**. Leave Paragraph selected under *Style type*. Under *Based on*, select the new **Side heading 1** style.

14. Click **Format** and then click **Font**. Change the font to **Times New Roman**, **12 pt**. Select the **Bold Italic** format. Click **OK** twice, and then click **Apply**.

15. Apply the **Side heading 2** style you created to the following headings: *Internships and Externships, Skills,* and *Licenses*.

16. Save your changes. Leave the document open for the next Step-by-Step.

Editing a Style and Printing a Style Sheet

After you create a style, you can easily modify it. In the Style dialog box, select the style you want to edit and click the Modify button. Word opens the Modify Style dialog box, which looks very similar to the New Style dialog box. Here you can change the style name or click the Format button to change formatting options for the style. After you click OK and Apply, the changes in the style are applied to all occurrences of that style in the document.

There may be occasions when you want to see a list of all the styles used in a document. You can print the style sheet for a document by opening the Print dialog box and selecting Styles in the *Print what* box.

S TEP-BY-STEP ▷ 6.7

1. Position the insertion point in the heading *Introduction*. Open the **Format** menu and choose **Style**. Notice that the **Side heading 1** style is already selected in the *Styles* list. Click **Modify** to open the Modify Style dialog box.

2. Click the **Format** button and click **Paragraph**. Change the alignment to **Left**. Click **OK** twice and then click **Apply**. Notice that all the headings styled with the Side heading 1 style are now left aligned. The Side heading 2 headings are also left aligned, because that style was based on Side heading 1.

3. Position the insertion point in the heading *Course of Study* and then open the **Format** menu and choose **Style**. In the Style dialog box, click **Modify**. Click **Format**, select **Paragraph,** and then change the spacing before to **3 pt**. Click **OK** twice and then click **Apply**.

4. Click in the first bulleted item on page 2. Open the **Format** menu, click **Style**, and click **Modify**.

In the Modify Style dialog box, click **Format** and then **Numbering**. Click **Customize**. Under *Bullet position*, change *Indent at* to **.25**. Under *Text position*, change *Indent at* to **.5**. Click **OK** twice and then click **Apply**. Notice that all the bullet items are now indented.

5. Open the **Insert** menu and choose **Page Numbers**. Under *Position*, select **Bottom of page (Footer)**. Under *Alignment*, select **Center**. If necessary, turn off *Show number on first page* and then click **OK**.

6. Save your changes. Print the document.

7. Print the style sheet attached to the document: Open the **File** menu, choose **Print**, select **Styles** under *Print what*, and then click **OK**.

8. Leave the document open for the next Step-by-Step.

Using the Document Organizer

When you create a style, the new style is stored in the document style sheet. If you want to remove a single style, you can do so in the Style dialog box by selecting the style name and clicking Delete. If you want to remove multiple styles, however, the document organizer makes the task easier. In the Style dialog box, click Organizer to open the Organizer dialog box, shown in Figure 6-7. Styles available for your current document are listed at the left side of the Styles tab in the *In* list box. To quickly remove a style from the document's style sheet, select the style and click Delete. To delete more than one style, click the first, hold down Ctrl, and click additional styles. When you delete a style, the text format reverts to the Normal style.

FIGURE 6-7

Styles tab in the Organizer dialog box

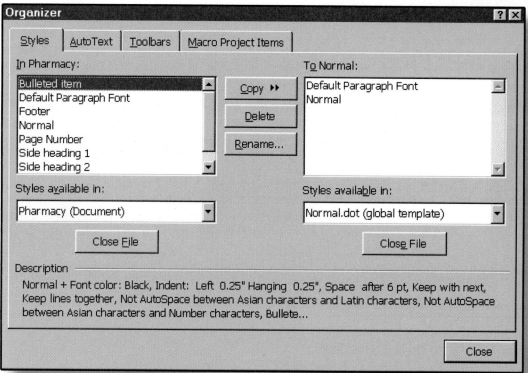

Although you will not be instructed to do so in this course, you can also use the document organizer to copy styles to the Normal template so you can apply those styles in other documents. You can also use the document organizer to rename styles you have created.

SCANS

S TEP-BY-STEP ▷ 6.8

1. Open the **Format** menu and choose **Style**. In the Style dialog box, click **Organizer**.

2. Notice the styles listed for *Pharmacy* in the *In Pharmacy* list box. Click the first style you created (*Bulleted item*), hold down **Ctrl**, and click each of the other styles you created: *Side heading 1, Side heading 2*, and *Title font*. (You will have to scroll down to select the *Title font* style.)

3. Click **Delete**. When prompted to confirm the deletion, click **Yes to All**.

4. Click **Close**. Notice that all the styles have been removed from the document.

5. Close the document without saving the changes.

Extra Challenge

The AutoFormat command on the Format menu automatically analyzes a document and applies appropriate styles to it. Open your *Pharmacy* document again, delete the styles as you did in Step-by-Step 6.8, and use AutoFormat to apply new styles to the document.

Navigating Through a Document

Moving around in a long document can become tedious, and finding information can be very time consuming. The Document Map feature provides an outline of the contents within the document as you work with it. Hyperlinks also provide convenient shortcuts to navigate within the same document and also to link to other documents and applications.

Using the Document Map

The Document Map is a view that enables you to quickly navigate through a document and keep track of your location in the document. Display the Document Map by clicking the Document Map button on the Standard toolbar or by clicking Document Map on the View menu.

When you display the Document Map, a *pane* displays a list of headings in the document, as shown in Figure 6-8. (For best results, the headings should be formatted with a standard heading style.) When you click a heading in the Document Map, Word moves the insertion point to the corresponding heading in the document, displays it at the top of the window, and highlights the heading in the Document Map.

FIGURE 6-8
Document with Document Map displayed

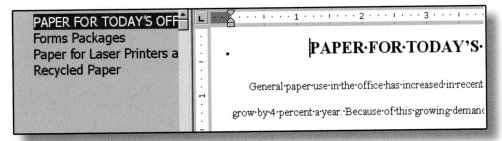

As you edit the document, the Document Map pane updates to include new headings or show deletions. Also, when you move the insertion point in the document, the Document Map highlights the appropriate heading to show your location in the document.

STEP-BY-STEP ▷ 6.9

1. Open **AW Step6-9** from the student data files and save the document as **Paper** followed by your initials.

2. Click the **Document Map** button on the Standard toolbar. The Document Map pane is displayed on the left side of your document.

3. In the Document Map pane, click the heading *Recycled Paper*. The insertion point moves to the heading on the second page of the document.

4. Scroll up in the document and position the insertion point in the heading *Paper for Laser*

Printers and Copiers. Notice that the highlight moves in the Document Map to reflect the new position of the insertion point.

5. Position the insertion point at the end of the title on the first page and press **Enter**.

6. Key **Economical and Environmental Concerns**. Notice that the Document Map is updated to show the new subheading. Drag the vertical border of the Document Map pane to the left to show more of your document.

7. Save your changes. Leave the document open for the next Step-by-Step.

Integration: Creating a Hyperlink

You already know that when you click on a hyperlink it takes you to a new location. You can use a hyperlink to move quickly to a location in your current document or to another existing document. Hyperlinks can also be used to jump from one application to another. You can use a hyperlink in Word, for example, to jump to an Excel worksheet or a PowerPoint presentation.

By default, Word creates a hyperlink if you key a Web or Internet address in a document. Or you can select any text or object in a document and create a hyperlink by clicking the Insert Hyperlink button on the Standard toolbar. In the Insert Hyperlink dialog box, you can then specify the document or address to link to. You can also create a hyperlink between applications by dragging selected text or graphics. When the text or graphic is copied, Word recognizes the location of the information and creates the link.

The Insert Hyperlink dialog box offers you several options for linking. You can link to any existing document or file, to a location in the current document (as shown in Figure 6-9), to a new document, or to an e-mail address. If desired, you can click ScreenTip in the Insert Hyperlink dialog box to key a ScreenTip that will appear when you move the mouse pointer onto the hyperlink.

FIGURE 6-9
Hyperlink options for the current document

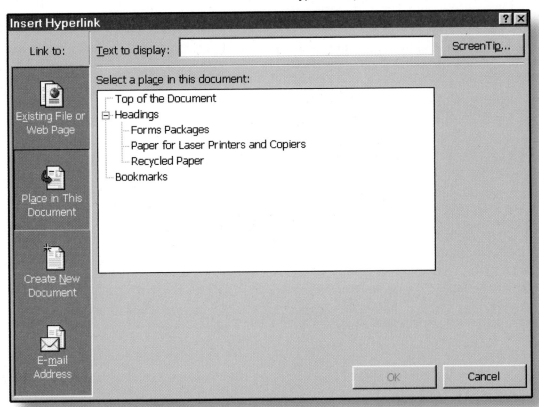

STEP-BY-STEP ▷ 6.10

SCANS

1. Position the insertion point in front of the tab character at the beginning of the first paragraph that begins *General paper . . .* and then press **Enter**. Move the insertion point to the new blank paragraph and key the following three lines:

   ```
   Forms Packages
   Paper for Laser Printers and Copiers
   Recycled Paper
   ```

2. Change the line spacing of these three lines to **1.5** and remove the first-line indent.

3. Select the words *Forms Packages*. Do not select the trailing paragraph mark. Then click the **Insert Hyperlink** button on the Standard toolbar.

4. If necessary, click *Place in This Document* to display the dialog box shown in Figure 6-9. Under *Select a place in this document*, click on the heading *Forms Packages*. Notice that the *Text to display box* shows the same text as the hyperlink.

5. Click **ScreenTip**. In the Set Hyperlink ScreenTip dialog box, key **Go to Forms Packages**. Click **OK** twice.

(continued on next page)

6. Select the words *Paper for Laser Printers and Copiers* and create a hyperlink with the following customized ScreenTip: **Go to Paper for Laser Printers and Copiers**. Select the words *Recycled Paper* and create a hyperlink with the following customized ScreenTip: **Go to Recycled Paper**.

7. To see how Word automatically formats a Web address you key, position the insertion point at the end of the document and key **For more information on this topic, go to http://www.ourworld.net.** (This hyperlink will not take you to an existing Web page.) Notice that the Web address is automatically formatted as a hyperlink. (If the address does not appear as a hyperlink, press the **spacebar** once.)

8. Scroll up and select the heading *Recycled Paper*. Click **Insert Hyperlink** and select the *Existing File or Web Page* option. Click the **File** button and locate the **Amazing Facts** data file (this is a PowerPoint presentation). Click **OK**.

9. Scroll to the top of the document and try your hyperlinks. Clicking the hyperlinks at the top of the document should take you to the headings within the document. The *Recycled Paper* hyperlink should open a PowerPoint presentation. Scroll through the slides, and then close the presentation and PowerPoint.

10. Save your changes and leave the document open for the next Step-by-Step.

Creating and Revising Footnotes and Endnotes

Footnotes and endnotes allow you to add information to a document or give the source of a quotation or other text. Footnotes appear at the bottom of the page where they are referenced. Endnotes are grouped at the end of a document.

Creating Footnotes/Endnotes

To insert a footnote or endnote, you position the insertion point at the location where you want the reference mark to appear in the document. Then open the Insert menu and choose the Footnote command to display the Footnote and Endnote dialog box, shown in Figure 6-10. Select the *Footnote* or *Endnote* option. You can choose to use Auto-Numbered references or a custom mark such as an asterisk or other symbol that you select. After selecting all options, click OK. If you are working in Normal view, Word opens a pane at the bottom of the window so you can key the note. If you are working in Print Layout view, Word moves you to the proper location in the document for your note.

When you add a footnote or endnote to a document that already contains notes, Word automatically numbers the new note and renumbers existing notes if the order has been affected.

FIGURE 6-10
Footnote and Endnote dialog box

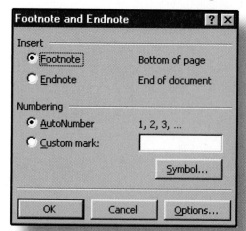

STEP-BY-STEP ⬭ 6.11

1. If necessary, switch to Print Layout view. Scroll through the document and notice that there are already three footnotes in the document. The first footnote is referenced on page 1, and the other two footnotes are referenced on page 2.

2. Select the heading *Forms Packages* in the Document Map and then position the insertion point following the period at the end of the first sentence (*. . . computer forms packages.*).

3. Open the **Insert** menu and choose **Footnote**. The Footnote and Endnote dialog box opens.

4. If necessary, select **Footnote** and **AutoNumber** and then click **OK**. A footnote reference mark (number 2) is inserted at the insertion point and at the bottom of the page. The insertion point moves to the bottom of the page after the new AutoNumbered footnote number.

5. Without moving the insertion point, key the following footnote text: **Joseph Kolinski,**

"Paperless Office," *Computer Tech,* **February 1998, pp. 17–20.**

Concept Builder

When referring to ranges of pages or other measurements in footnote text, it is proper to use an en dash (–). You can quickly key an en dash by pressing Ctrl + - on the numeric keypad.

6. Notice that the other footnotes are automatically renumbered.

7. Save your changes. Leave the document open for the next Step-by-Step.

Hot Tip

Pressing Alt + Ctrl + F is a shortcut to insert an AutoNumbered footnote, bypassing the Footnote and Endnote dialog box.

Viewing and Editing Footnotes

When you double-click a note reference mark in a document, Word scrolls to the bottom of the page or end of the document to show the note text. If you click a note number at the bottom of a page, or at the end of the document, Word repositions the insertion point at the location of the note reference mark in the document.

To quickly locate a specific footnote, you can use the Go To command. Double-click the page number in the status bar to display the Go To dialog box. Under *Go to what*, select Footnote or Endnote (Figure 6-11), key the note number, and then click Go To. If you don't know the number of the note, but you know how many notes you want to move relative to your current location, key a plus or minus and the number. For example, if you want to skip ahead to the third note, key +3.

Footnote: Note citing a particular source or a brief explaination placed at bottom of page
Endnote: same as above only at end of paper.

FIGURE 6-11
Go To tab in the Find and Replace dialog box

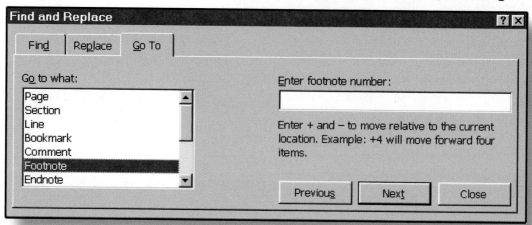

S TEP-BY-STEP ▷ 6.12

1. Double-click the footnote number to the left of the footnote text that you just keyed. The insertion point returns to the footnote reference mark in the document.

2. Double-click the page number on the status bar. In the *Go to what* list box, click **Footnote**.

3. Key **3** and then click **Go To**. Click **Close** in the Find and Replace dialog box.

4. The insertion point is now at the third footnote reference mark in the document.

Point to the reference mark. A ScreenTip displays the footnote text.

5. Double-click the footnote reference mark. The insertion point moves to the footnote entry at the bottom of the page.

6. Change the page numbers in the footnote text to **145–147**.

7. Save your changes. Leave the document open for the next Step-by-Step.

Revising Footnotes and Endnotes

If you rearrange your text or move, copy, or delete a note, Word will automatically renumber the note references in the document and rearrange the order of the notes.

To quickly copy a note, select the note reference mark, press the Copy button, and then paste the contents in a new location. Word will automatically format the pasted contents as a note and assign a new number or use the custom reference mark you used in the original note.

If you delete the note text, the note reference mark still remains. To delete both the note reference and the note text, you must select the note reference and press Delete or Backspace.

Deleting Note + Ref, pick note ref

STEP-BY-STEP ▷ 6.13

1. Note that there are four footnotes in the document in the following order: *Gubbels*, *Kolinski*, *Gonzales*, and *Ito*.

2. In the Document Map, click *Forms Packages*. Select the paragraph above the heading *Forms Packages*, cut the text, and paste the paragraph at the end of the document (before the paragraph containing the hyperlink).

3. Notice that the footnote moves with the paragraph and the footnote is renumbered *4*.

4. Drag to select the reference mark number and then click the **Copy** button.

5. Position the insertion point at the end of the first sentence in the same paragraph (it ends *. . . in the future.*) and click the **Paste** button.

6. Notice that there are now two footnotes for *Gubbels*, but they have different numbers (4 and 5).

7. Select the number 4 reference mark in the document pane at the end of the first sentence (the one you just pasted) and press **Delete**. The copied footnote is deleted and the footnotes are again renumbered.

8. Open the **Insert** menu and choose **Page Numbers**. Under *Position*, select *Bottom of page (Footer)* and under *Alignment* select *Center*. Turn off *Show Number on First Page* so the page number does not print on the first page. Click **OK**.

9. Check your document in Print Preview.

10. Close Print Preview and save your changes. Leave the document open for the next Step-by-Step.

Converting Footnotes to Endnotes

After you insert footnotes in a document, you can change them to endnotes, and vice versa. You can convert an individual note or change all notes by choosing the Footnote command on the Insert menu and clicking Options in the Footnote and Endnote dialog box. The Note Options dialog box opens. To convert footnotes to endnotes, click the All Endnotes tab (Figure 6-12), select options for the endnotes, and click the Convert button. The Convert Notes dialog box opens to show you the conversion option you have selected. Click OK twice to complete the conversion.

To print endnotes on a separate page, insert a page break or Next page section break just before the endnotes in the document.

FIGURE 6-12
All Endnotes tab in the Note Options dialog box

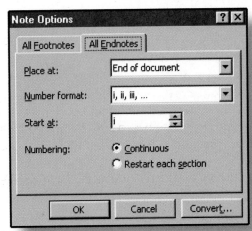

1. Open the **Insert** menu and choose **Footnote**.

2. Click **Options**. The Notes Options dialog box opens.

3. Click the **All Endnotes** tab.

4. In the *Number format* box, select the **1,2,3** number format.

5. Click **Convert**. The Convert Notes dialog box opens. Make sure that *Convert all footnotes to endnotes* is selected in this dialog box.

6. Click **OK** twice.

7. Click **Close** to close the Footnote and Endnote dialog box.

8. Change to Print Layout view if necessary to see the endnotes.

9. Save your changes. Print and close the document.

Summary

In this lesson, you learned that:

■ You can copy up to 12 multiple items to the Office Clipboard and then paste them all into a document.

■ The Spike enables you to remove two or more items from one or more documents and then insert the items as a group in a new location or document.   *Ctrl+F3*   *Shift+Ctrl+F3*

■ To combine all of one file with another, you use the File command on the Insert menu.

■ You can control page breaks by choosing text flow options.

■ You can create your own character and paragraph styles to make formatting documents easier and quicker.

■ The Document Map enables you to quickly navigate through a document and keep track of your location in the document.

■ Hyperlinks take you to new locations in the same document, to other documents or files, and to Web and Internet addresses.

■ Word automatically numbers footnotes and endnotes, and if you rearrange the order of text in the document, Word automatically renumbers the notes when they are moved to a new location.

■ You can easily convert footnotes to endnotes and vice versa.

LESSON 6 REVIEW QUESTIONS

TRUE/FALSE

Circle T if the statement is true or F if the statement is false.

T **(F)** 1. To collect multiple items to move from one open document to another open document, you must use the Spike.

T **(F)** 2. To create a style, you must base the style on formatted text.

(T) F 3. You can create hyperlinks to files created in other applications.

T **(F)** 4. To delete a footnote, delete the footnote text in the footnote pane. *this would leave the reference delete the ref. to remove all*

T **(F)** 5. You can view only three documents at a time.

FILL IN THE BLANKS

Complete the following sentences by writing the correct word or words in the blanks provided.

1. *footnotes* are references that are printed at the end of the section or document.

2. You can use the Office Clipboard to collect and paste up to *twelve* multiple items.

3. To format extra spacing above a paragraph, open the *format* menu and choose *paragraph* .

4. A(n) *Style* is a list of rules for automatically formatting characters or paragraphs.

5. To combine all text from one file with another, open the *insert* menu and choose *file* .

LESSON 6 PROJECTS

PROJECT 6-1

1. Open the data file **AW Project6-1** and save the document as **Accomplishments** followed by your initials.

2. Use the Spike to rearrange the order of the bulleted paragraphs: *Cntrl + Shft + F3*
   A. Cut each of the bulleted paragraphs in the sequence indicated in Figure 6-13. Note that although the bulleted paragraphs are numbered, you are not to key the numbers.

FIGURE 6-13

SELECTED PROFESSIONAL ACCOMPLISHMENTS

2 ▪ Restructured computer system for accounting office including evaluating current needs, analyzing products, designing new database, dismantling of outdated system, and installation and setup of new system.

7 ▪ Developed education material for operation and troubleshooting of basic computer systems. Materials used for professional training and individual consultations.

4 ▪ Designed and implemented an efficient method of access data for tax use. This project translated into $100,000 savings in first year and increased customer satisfaction, measured by customer survey.

9 ▪ Directed team in creating department-specific information system. Developed computer screens for interdepartmental functions; involved working closely with team leaders and project coordinators.

8 ▪ Presented model of quality improvement program. Development of presentation included developing a storyboard and creation of multimedia slide presentation.

5 ▪ Conceived, designed, and oversaw the development and implementation of an accounting system for two hospitals.

1 ▪ Researched, developed, and instituted a billing system that saved a medical center $500,000 in the first two years.

3 ▪ Planned and coordinated the installation of a 550-station telecommunications system, serving a 500,000-square-foot healthcare facility.

6 ▪ Received a personal letter from the CEO of Systems Advantage for outstanding achievement.

    B. With the insertion point positioned in the last (blank) paragraph in the document, empty the contents of the Spike.

    C. Delete the blank paragraphs after each of the bulleted paragraphs.

3. Save your changes. Print and close the document.

PROJECT 6-2

1. Open the data file **AW Project6-2a** and save the document as **Waste** followed by your initials.

2. Open the following data files: **AW Project6-2b**, **AW Project6-2c**, **AW Project6-2d**.

3. Copy the heading and the first paragraph from each open document to the Office Clipboard in the following sequence: **AW Project6-2b**, **AW Project6-2c**, and **AW Project6-2d**.

4. Paste all the contents in the Clipboard at the end of the **Waste** document.

5. Insert the file **AW Project6-2e** at the end of the document.

6. Change the entire document to double spacing and remove all blank lines except the one after the title and the one at the end of the document (add a blank line at the end if necessary).

7. Create a style **Side heading** using the following formats:
   A. Change the font to Arial 13 pt, Bold Italic, All caps.
   B. Format the headings with 12 pt spacing before and 3 pt spacing after. Turn on *Keep with next.*

8. Apply the style to all the side headings.

9. Format page numbers at the top right of all pages except the first.

10. At the end of the document, create a hyperlink to go to the top of the document. Customize the ScreenTip to read **Go back to the beginning**. (*Hint:* In the Insert Hyperlink dialog box, click *Place in This Document* and then **Top of the Document** under *Select a place in this document.*)

11. Save your changes. Print and close the document. Close all other open documents. 3/15/04

PROJECT 6-3

1. Open **AW Project6-3** and save the document as **Landfills** followed by your initials.

2. Add a footnote after the last sentence in the paragraph that begins *Currently, there is . . .* : **Douglas Brown, "The Future of Today's Landfills,"** *Today's Environment,* **March 1998, p. 4.**

3. Select the first footnote reference and move it up to the end of the first sentence in the same paragraph, which begins *Solid waste is . . . .* Adjust the spacing before and after the footnote reference number if necessary. (There should be no space between the period at the end of the sentence and the footnote reference mark.)

4. Delete the second Garcia footnote.

5. Convert the footnotes to endnotes using the 1,2,3 format.

6. Format the title with 12 pt spacing after the paragraph. Modify the **Text** style so that the text is **11 pt** rather than 12 pt.

7. At the end of the paragraph beginning *Approximately 40 to 50 percent . . .*, create a hyperlink to the Excel worksheet **Trash**. Use the last word in the paragraph (*waste*) for the hyperlink and create a ScreenTip that reads **For more information, click here.**

8. Test your hyperlink. Read the chart in Excel and close the worksheet and Excel.

9. Save your changes. Print and close the document.

CRITICAL THINKING

ACTIVITY 6-1

Justin was editing a document that was routed to him through the company intranet. He noticed that several of the paragraphs had small boxes to the left of them, indicating that they had special paragraph formats. It became a tedious task for Justin to click on each paragraph and open the Paragraph dialog box to view the format settings for each paragraph. Is there a shortcut Justin can use to view paragraph format settings for a particular paragraph? Use the Help feature to find the answer.

ACTIVITY 6-2

Juanita just completed a research paper for a class assignment. She formatted several endnotes for the report. She inserted a hard page break to print the endnotes on a separate page at the end of the document. There are so many endnotes, however, that they fill all of one page and part of another. How can Juanita format an endnote continuation notice to indicate that the endnotes are continued on the next page? Use the Help feature to find the answer.

EDITING IN WORKGROUPS

OBJECTIVES

Upon completion of this lesson, you should be able to:

- Set the file location for workgroup templates.
- Add comments to the file properties of a document.
- Route documents.
- Create multiple versions of a document.
- Track changes in a document.
- Combine revisions.
- Review and accept/reject changes.
- Compare documents.
- Add and edit comments to a document.
- Protect a document.
- Create and edit a master document.

⏱ Estimated Time: 1.5 hours

Sharing Documents

In many organizations, workgroups are formed for special projects, and documents may be created and reviewed by several individuals. Members of the workgroup may choose to edit a document or add comments to the document and then they can send the document to other members in the workgroup.

In this section, you will explore Word features that make it easy for members of a workgroup to work together on a document.

Setting the Default File Location for Workgroup Templates

For efficiency and consistency, members of workgroups often use *templates* to create their documents. A template stores frequently used text, graphics, and formats, and it is used as a pattern to create other similar documents. To make these document templates easily accessible for workgroups, they are usually stored in a default location. This location is specified in the File Locations tab of the Options dialog box (Figure 7-1).

Tools > Options > File Locations

FIGURE 7-1
File Locations tab in the Options dialog box

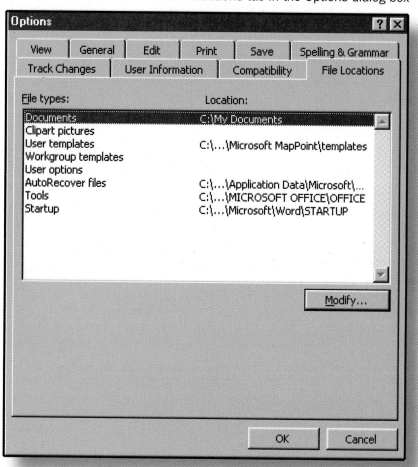

To protect these templates from being altered, they can be saved as **read-only recommended** or the access to the document can be restricted with a password. When a user opens a read-only recommended document, the user sees a dialog box asking to open the document as read only. If the user chooses to open the document as read only, the document can be edited. However, to save the changes, the user must save the document using a new file name. When access to a document is restricted with a password, the user must enter a password to open the document and/or enter a password to modify the document.

To save a document as read-only recommended or to restrict access to the document with passwords, click the Tools button in the Save As dialog box and then select General Options from the submenu.

In the next Step-by-Step you will open the File Locations tab to see where you would set the default file location but you will not make any changes. Then you will open a document template that is read-only recommended and that requires a password for access.

STEP-BY-STEP ▷ 7.1

SCANS

1. Open **AW Step7-1** from the student data files. When the prompt for the password is displayed, key **a1rs2** and click **OK**.

2. When the prompt to enter the password to modify or to open as read only is displayed, click **Read Only**.

3. Key your name for *Team Member.* Position the insertion point below *Update Remarks* and key the following:

   I have received and reviewed bids from several telemarketing companies. I am prepared to share this information and make a recommendation at our team meeting next Tuesday.

4. Save the document under a new file name and remove the passwords and the read-only recommendation:
   a. Open the **File** menu and choose **Save as**. Click the **Tools** button in the Save As dialog box and select **General Options** in the submenu.
   b. Select and delete the entries in the *Password to open* and *Password to modify*

boxes and turn off *Read-only recommended* if necessary. Click **OK**.
   c. Key **Status Report** in the *File name* box and then click **OK**.

5. Open the **Tools** menu and choose **Options** and then click the **File Locations** tab.

6. Under *File types*, click on **Workgroup templates**. The location for Workgroup templates will vary depending on your system setup.

7. Click **Modify**. If you were changing the location, you would identify the folder in the *Look in* box or key the path in the *Folder name* box. You are not making any changes at this time, so click **Cancel** and then click **Close**.

8. Print and close the document.

Concept Builder

Passwords are case sensitive and can contain up to 15 characters. The characters can be any combination of letters, numerals, spaces, and symbols.

Adding Comments to the File Properties of a Document

File properties such as the document title, the author name, and keywords provide descriptive information about a document. To view or change properties for a file, open the File menu and click Properties. The Properties dialog box opens, similar to the one shown in Figure 7-2. (The document name also appears in the dialog box's title bar.) By default, the dialog box opens with the Summary tab selected.

On the Summary tab, you can specify title, subject, author, manager, and company information. You can assign the document to a category and select keywords that will make it easier for you to search for the document. The *Comments* text box toward the bottom of the Summary tab lets you insert additional information that is saved with the file.

FIGURE 7-2
Properties dialog box

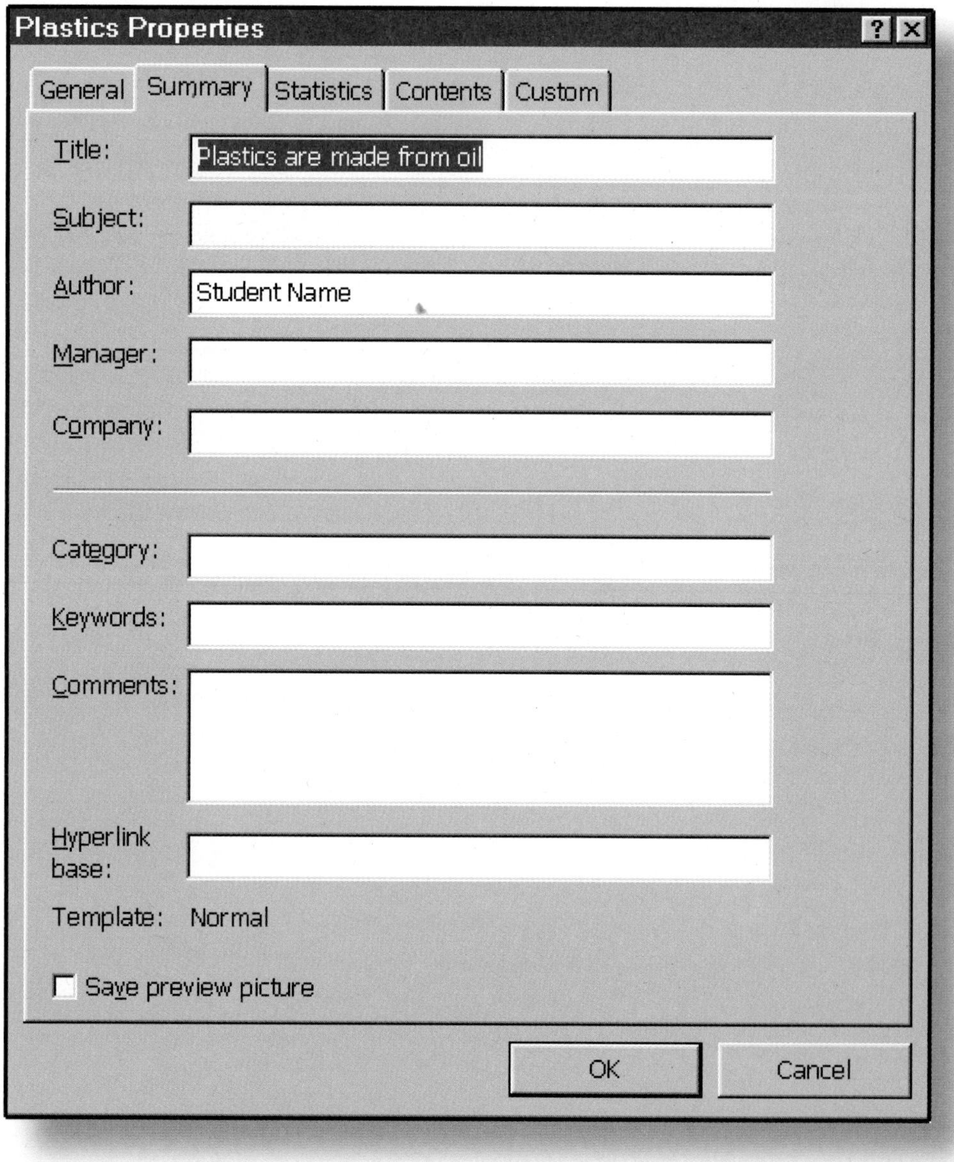

STEP-BY-STEP ▷ 7.2

SCANS

1. Open **AW Step7-2** from the student data files and save it as **Plastics** followed by your initials.

2. Open the **File** menu and choose **Properties**. The Plastics Properties dialog box opens.

3. In the *Title* box, key **Recycling Plastics**.

4. In the *Comments* box, key **Created by Workgroup 1 for the public relations brochure.**

5. Click **OK**. Leave the document open for the next Step-by-Step.

FILE > SEND TO >

Routing Documents

It is common for individuals to send documents online via electronic mail systems. Word's routing feature allows you to control the process of sending a document to a number of people who need to review it.

To route a document, open the File menu, choose Send To, and then select Routing Recipient. Word displays a Routing Slip dialog box similar to the one shown in Figure 7-3.

To quickly add a recipient whose e-mail address you already have stored, click the Address button and then select the recipient from your Address Book. Use the Move buttons to change the order of recipients in the *To* box. You can choose to have recipients receive the document one after the other in the order you have indicated in the *To* box or you can send the document to all of your designated recipients at once. You have additional options to return the document after the last recipient has viewed it and to track the progress of the document as it is routed from person to person. The *Protect for* drop-down list lets you control changes to it. Recipients of the documents can add to the document or simply comment on the document.

After you insert a recipient's name in the *To* box, the OK command button changes to Add Slip and the Route button becomes active. To carry out the routing process, click Route. To attach the routing slip to the document so it can be sent later, click Add Slip.

FIGURE 7-3
Routing Slip dialog box

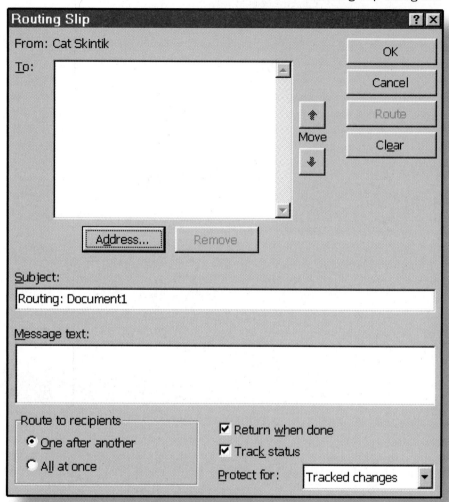

STEP-BY-STEP 7.3

You can view the Routing Slip dialog box in this Step-by-Step even if you don't have access to e-mail. If you do have access to e-mail, complete steps 3 and 4.

1. Open the **File** menu, choose **Send To**, and then select **Routing Recipient**. The Routing Slip dialog box opens.

2. Click the **Address** button to see addresses in your Address Book, if you have access to e-mail.

3. Click the name of a person in your Address Book and then click **To** to add that name to the recipients list. Click additional names in the Address Book to add them to the list.

4. Select **One after another** so that the recipients will receive the document in the order shown.

5. To route the document immediately, click **Route**.

6. Leave the document open for the next Step-by-Step.

Creating Multiple Versions of a Document

Word's versioning feature allows you to save multiple versions of the same document and record information about each version. For example, you may need to edit a document while also keeping the original document intact. You can save a version of the document each time you open, edit, and close it. You can tell Word to automatically save a new version each time the document is closed or you can save a version any time you want.

Versions are recorded in the Versions dialog box. Open the File menu and click Versions. If you have not saved a version of your document previously, this dialog box will be blank. If you want to save a version each time you close the document, click in the *Automatically save a version on close* box. Click Save Now to save a version. Word displays the Save Version dialog box shown in Figure 7-4. Here you can insert any comments you want to appear in the Versions dialog box. After you click OK, both the Save Version and the Versions dialog boxes close.

The next time you click the Versions command on the File menu, you will see the version you previously saved, as shown in Figure 7-5. Notice that Word records the date and time the version was saved, plus the name of the person who saved the version, and any comments keyed in the Save Version dialog box.

After saving multiple versions, you can review, open, print, and delete earlier versions. However, you cannot edit an earlier version of a document. To revise an earlier version, you must first open that version and save the document under a new name.

Concept Builder

The *Saved by* name is the name listed on the User Information tab in the Options dialog box. You will learn how to change this name later in this lesson.

FIGURE 7-4
Save Version dialog box

Save Version [?] [X]

Date and time: 2/11/99 11:08 AM
Saved by: Student Name

Comments on version:

| OK | Cancel |

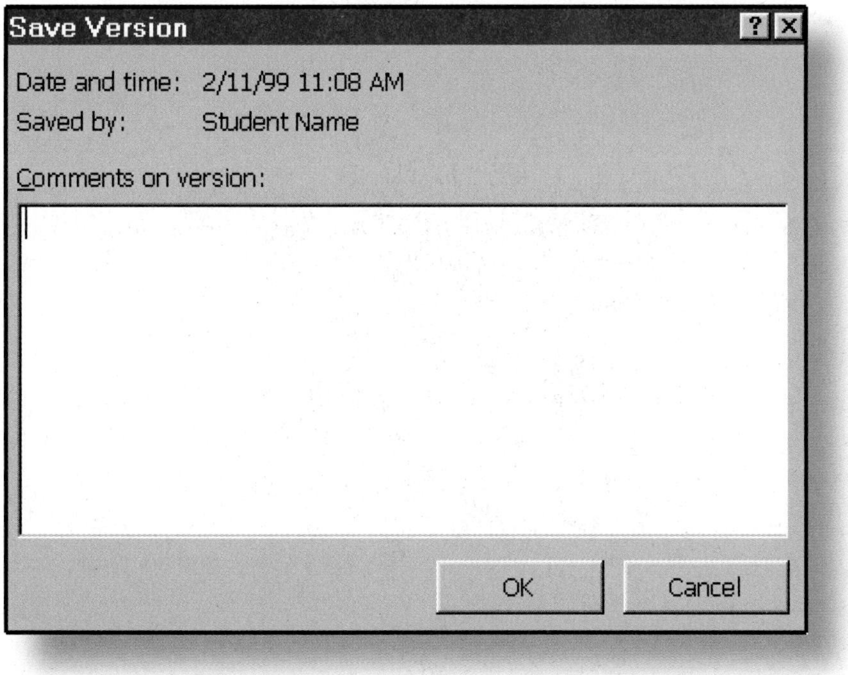

FIGURE 7-5
Versions in Plastics dialog box

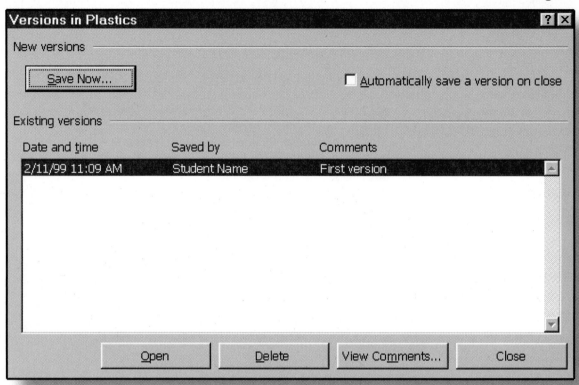

 TEP-BY-STEP ▷ 7.4

1. Save the current state of the document:
   a. Open the **File** menu and choose **Versions**. The Versions in Plastics dialog box is displayed. Because this is the first time you have indicated to save versions of the document, there are no existing versions listed.
   b. Click **Save Now**. The Save Version dialog box opens. (Do not be concerned about the name displayed for *Saved by*.)
   c. In the *Comments on version* box, key **first draft**.
   d. Click **OK**.

2. To see the current version information, open the **File** menu again and click **Versions**. The Versions dialog box now shows the date and time that you saved the first draft version of the document.

Concept Builder

You will work more with versions in the next Step-by-Step.

3. Click **Close**. Remain in this screen for the next Step-by-Step.

Tools> Track (Changes> Highlight

Tracking Changes to a Document

The Track Changes feature enables you to track suggested changes from reviewers and then merge all the revisions into the original document. Word uses **revision marks** to indicate tracked changes. The revision marks appear in a different color. Word assigns a different color for up to eight different reviewers. When there are more than eight reviewers, Word reuses the colors.

Turn revision tracking on by opening the Tools menu and clicking Track Changes. Then click Highlight Changes on the submenu. Word opens the Highlight Changes dialog box (Figure 7-6). To show revision marks while you are editing, click in the *Track changes while editing* box. After you click OK in this dialog box, your revisions will be displayed in the text. Text you delete displays in color (usually blue) with a strikethrough effect. Text you add displays in a different color (usually red) with an underline. A vertical line called a revision bar appears in the margin wherever revisions have been made.

FIGURE 7-6
Highlight Changes dialog box

To see who has made a revision in a document and when the revision was made, rest the I-beam over the revision. Word displays a ScreenTip giving information about the revision. The name given in the ScreenTip is the name listed on the User Information tab in the Options dialog box.

The Reviewing toolbar (Figure 7-7) offers a number of tools that can speed the reviewing process. You can turn tracking on and off easily using the Track Changes button. Click the Save Version button to quickly save a version of your document. To emphasize a portion of text, you can use the Highlight button.

FIGURE 7-7
Reviewing toolbar

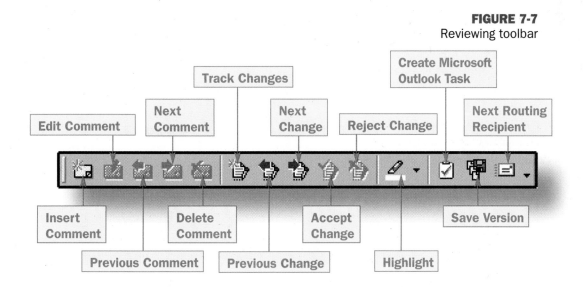

current
settings: NVAS
Initials: N

1. Set tracking options in the Options dialog box:

  a. Open the **Tools** menu and choose **Options**. The Options dialog box opens.

  b. Click the **User Information** tab. Write down the information in the *Name* and *Initials* boxes so you can restore the information later.

  c. Key your name and initials in the text boxes. You do not need to change the Mailing Address.

  d. Click the **Track Changes** tab. In the *Inserted text* and *Deleted text* areas, click the down arrow on the *Color* boxes and select the **By author** option. (This will allow you to see insertions and deletions from different authors in different colors.)

  e. Click **OK**.

2. Turn on Track Changes before you begin editing:

  a. Open the **Tools** menu, choose **Track Changes**, and then select **Highlight Changes**. The Highlight Changes dialog box opens.

  b. Click the **Track changes while editing** check box.

  c. If necessary, click **Highlight changes on screen** and **Highlight changes in printed document**.

  d. Click **OK**.

  e. If the Reviewing toolbar does not appear, click **Toolbars** on the **View** menu and then clicking **Reviewing**.

3. Notice that *TRK* is now highlighted on the status bar to indicate tracking is on. On the Reviewing toolbar, the **Track Changes** button is highlighted.

4. Edit the document:

  a. In the first sentence, position the insertion point at the beginning of the word *oil* and key **petroleum**.

 Hot Tip

As you revise your document with Track Changes turned on, you will not be able to use OVERTYPE. You will only be able to insert or delete text.

  b. Without spacing, delete the word *oil* (do not delete the period or the following space). Notice that the word *petroleum* is underlined and the word *oil* is shown with the strikethrough format. Also, a revision bar appears at the left edge of the screen.

  c. Point at the revision marks. Word displays the name of the reviewer and the date and time the revision was inserted.

  d. Make the same correction in the second sentence (key **petroleum** and delete *oil*).

  e. In the third sentence of the first paragraph, add the word **the** and a space between the words *and pollution*.

  f. In the same sentence, add the phrase **generated through the manufacturing**

process plus a space between *pollution* and *can be reduced*.

g. Move the second paragraph to make it the next-to-last paragraph. Notice that the original paragraph takes on the strike-through effect because it has actually been deleted. The paragraph in the new location has the underline style because it has been inserted.

5. Click the **Save Version** button on the Reviewing toolbar. Key **second draft** under *Comments on version*. Click **OK**.

6. Continue editing the document:

a. In the paragraph that begins *Collecting plastics . . .* , change *a difficult* to **not an easy**.

b. In the second sentence of the same paragraph, change *Plastic containers* to **Although plastic containers** and delete the word *but* and the space that follows.

c. In the following paragraph (the new location for the paragraph you moved), change *of the used plastics* to **of recycled plastics**.

d. In the second sentence of the same paragraph, change *important* to **necessary**.

e. In the last paragraph, position the insertion point on *minimize* and use the Thesaurus to replace *minimize* with a synonym of your choice.

f. In the same paragraph, change *kinds* to **types**.

7. Click the **Save Version** button, key **third draft** under *Comments on version*, and click **OK**.

8. Open a previous version of the document:

a. Open the **File** menu and choose **Versions**. You should see three versions of the document. The most recent version (*third draft* under *Comments*) is selected because that version is the active document.

b. Click on the first draft.

c. Click **Open**.

9. Word displays two windows for the document. One window contains the third draft and the other window contains the first draft. The first draft window is the active window. Notice that the first draft window does not show revision marks. The third draft window does.

10. Hold down **Shift** and open the **File** menu. Choose **Close All** to close all open documents. Remain in this screen for the next Step-by-Step.

Combining Revisions

If several reviewers have tracked their changes for the same document, you can combine all the changes into one document. If you have saved multiple versions of the document and you want to compare these versions to the original document, you must first save the earlier version as a separate file under a different name.

Then open the document you want to merge changes into. Open the Tools menu and choose Merge Documents. Word opens the Select File to Merge Into Current Document dialog box. Use this dialog box to locate the file you want to merge into your current document. After you click the Open button, Word merges any revisions in that document into your current document. If changes were made by different authors, they will show up in different colors in the current document.

All versions are saved in same file so...

To Compare Original to newer versions:

1. Save Original with different name

SCANS

S TEP-BY-STEP ▷ 7.6

1. Open **AW Step7-2** from the student data files and save the document as **Revised Plastics** followed by your initials.

2. Open the **Tools** menu and choose **Merge Documents**.

3. Locate and select **Plastics** and click **Open**. Word adds changes for the revisions marked in **Plastics**. (Don't worry if some words run together in your document. You will fix this later.)

 Hot Tip

If you see a dialog box indicating there are unmarked changes, the documents have differences in addition to those changes marked with revision marks. If this happens while you are completing the exercises in this lesson, you can click OK and continue with the exercise.

4. Merge changes from a second document edited by a different reviewer: Open the **Tools** menu and choose **Merge Documents**. Locate and select the **AW Step7-6** data file and click **Open**. Notice that the insertions from this reviewer are in a different color.

5. Point at a revision mark in the document to display the reviewer's name and the date and time the revision was inserted.

 Concept Builder

If the reviewer information does not appear above the revision, choose Options on the Tools menu, click the View tab, and turn on *ScreenTips*.

6. Save your changes and leave the document open for the next Step-by-Step.

Reviewing Revisions

After a document has been revised using Track Changes, you must decide whether to accept or reject the changes. You can review revisions easily using the Reviewing toolbar. To move to the next revision, click Next Change. The revision becomes highlighted. You can then click the Accept Change button to accept the revision or the Reject Change button to restore original wording. To return to a previous revision, click the Previous Change button.

Hot Tip

A quick way to accept or reject a revision is to right-click on the revision and then select a choice from the shortcut menu.

You can also review revisions using the Accept or Reject Changes dialog box. Open the Tools menu and click Track Changes. Then click Accept or Reject Changes on the submenu. The Accept or Reject Changes dialog box opens, as shown in Figure 7-8. Use the Find buttons to locate the next or previous revision and then use the command buttons to accept or reject the changes. You can also choose to accept all changes or reject all changes.

TOOLS > TRACK CHANGES > ACCEPT OR REJECT CHANGES

FIGURE 7-8
Accept or Reject Changes dialog box

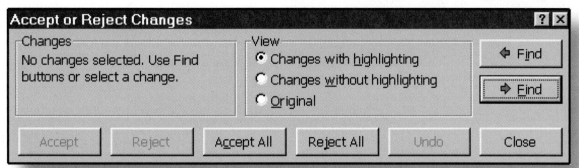

STEP-BY-STEP ▷ 7.7

1. If necessary, position the insertion point at the beginning of the document and display the Reviewing toolbar.

2. Click the **Next Change** button on the Reviewing toolbar. The first revision is highlighted.

3. Click the **Accept Change** button on the Reviewing toolbar. The new word *petroleum* is inserted and the underline format is removed.

4. Click the **Next Change** button on the Reviewing toolbar. The next revision (strikethrough *oil*) is highlighted.

5. Click the **Accept Change** button. The word *oil* is deleted.

6. Click the **Next Change** button. The next revision (strikethrough *oil* or underline *petroleum*, depending on how you made this change) is highlighted.

7. Click the **Reject Change** button on the Reviewing toolbar. The inserted text is deleted or the strikethrough is removed.

8. Click the **Undo** button on the Standard toolbar.

9. Move the insertion point to the top of the document.

10. Open the **Tools** menu and choose **Track Changes** and then select **Accept or Reject Changes**. The Accept or Reject Changes dialog box opens.

(continued on next page)

11. Click **Accept All**. Click **Yes** when you see the prompt about accepting changes without reviewing them. Word makes all the changes and removes the revision marks.

12. Close the Accept or Reject Changes dialog box.

13. If necessary, turn off Track Changes by clicking the **Track Changes** button on the Reviewing toolbar.

14. Make any necessary adjustments for spacing between words where changes were made and remove the highlight.

15. Save your changes. Print the document and leave it open for the next Step-by-Step.

Comparing Documents

If you did not track changes but you want to compare an edited document with its original version, you can compare the two documents to see where changes were made. With the edited document on the screen, open the Tools menu, choose Track Changes, and then click Compare Documents on the submenu. Word immediately displays revision marks in the edited document to show changes made from the original document.

You'll recall that **Revised Plastics** originated from the data file **AW Step7-2**. Changes were merged from two other documents and the document changes were accepted and saved. There are no longer any revision marks displayed in the document. In the following Step-by-Step, you will compare the edited document with the original version.

Edited Doc. on Screen > TOOLS > TRACK CHANGES > COMPARE DOCS SELECT THE ORIGINAL FOR COMPARISON

STEP-BY-STEP 7.8

1. Open the **Tools** menu and choose **Track Changes** and then select **Compare Documents**.

2. Locate and open **AW Step7-2** from the student data files. Word shows the changes with revision marks.

3. Close the document without saving the changes.

Inserting Comments in a Document

Comments are notes that are added within a document by the author and reviewers. They are similar to footnotes except that they are formatted as **hidden text**. The comment feature provides an easy way for reviewers to share their ideas and suggestions without changing the document.

Insert a comment by clicking the Insert Comment button on the Reviewing toolbar (or by opening the Insert menu and clicking Comment). A comment pane opens at the bottom of the screen. Your initials and the number 1 appear in both the comment pane and the document pane. The selected word and your initials are highlighted in the document pane, as shown in Figure 7-9. Key your comment in the comment pane. You can leave the pane open if you intend to add more comments or close it when you have finished keying the comment.

FIGURE 7-9
Key a comment in the comment pane

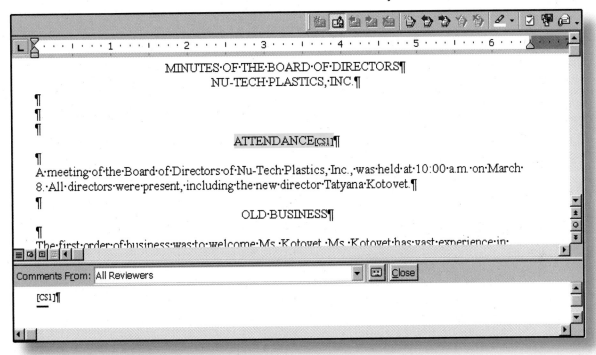

You can print comments along with the text of a document if desired. To print comments, click Options on the Tools menu, click the Print tab in the Options dialog box, and make sure a check mark appears in the *Comments* check box in the *Include with document* section of the tab. Comments are printed starting on a new page after the document has finished printing.

 Extra Challenge

If you have a sound board and a microphone, explore inserting voice comments. Click the Insert Sound Object button in the comment pane and then record the comment.

1. Open **AW Step7-9** from the student data files and save the file as **Board Minutes** followed by your initials.

2. If necessary, display the Reviewing toolbar.

3. Add a comment:
   a. Select the word **ATTENDANCE**.
   b. Click the **Insert Comment** button on the Reviewing toolbar.
   c. With the insertion point positioned after the comment mark in the comment pane, key **These centered headings may look better left aligned and bold with a larger font size.**
   d. Click **Close** in the comment pane.

4. Open the **Tools** menu and choose **Options**. Click the **User Information** tab and change the name to **Joan C. Kestella**, change the initials to **jck**, and then click **OK**.

5. Scroll down and select the name **Donald Goldstein** in the *Sales* paragraph.

6. Click the **Insert Comment** button. Notice that the comment reference mark now has the initials *jck* rather than your initials and it has been assigned the next available comment number (2).

7. Key **Donald Goldstein decided not to accept our offer for employment. Please change this name to Matthew Wang.**

8. Close the comment pane.

9. Open the **Tools** menu and choose **Options**. Change the name and initials in User Information back to your name and initials. Click the **Print** tab and make sure there is a check in the *Comments* box in the *Include with document* section. Click **OK**.

10. Scroll up two paragraphs and select the paragraph heading **Finance**. (Drag to select so that you include the period in your selection.)

11. Click the **Insert Comment** button. Notice that this becomes the second comment and the *jck* comment is automatically renumbered as the third comment.

Concept Builder

Comments, like footnotes, are automatically rearranged when you insert, delete, move, or copy them.

12. Key **These paragraph headings should either be underlined or set off as separate paragraphs.**

13. Close the comment pane. Save your changes and leave the document open for the next Step-by-Step. *cont. here from 3/16/04*

Viewing and Editing Comments

You can easily edit both comments and text by leaving the comment pane open. You can then move from the comment pane to the document pane by simply clicking in the desired pane.

You do not have to have the comment pane open to read comments inserted in a document, however. When you point to the highlighted text or the comment mark, the pointer changes to show the Insert Comment icon. If you keep the pointer positioned over the highlighted text, the user name and the comment text display in a box above the highlighted text.

You can use buttons on the Reviewing toolbar to help you view and edit comments. Use the Next Comment button to move to the next comment in your text. To return to a previous comment, click the Previous Comment button. Use the Edit Comment button to jump to the next comment and automatically open the comment pane for editing.

To delete a comment, click next to the comment mark in the document pane and click the Delete Comment button on the Reviewing toolbar. Note that deleting all the text in the comment pane does *not* remove the comment mark in the document pane. You must delete the comment mark in the document pane to remove a comment.

Hot Tip

You can also locate a comment mark by double-clicking the page number on the status bar, clicking *Comment* in the *Go to what* list box, and then clicking *Next* or *Previous*. Note that you can also go to a specific reviewer's comment by selecting the user's name in the *Enter reviewer's name* box.

STEP-BY-STEP 7.10

1. Move the insertion point to the top of the document.

2. Point to the highlighted text *ATTENDANCE.* After a moment, the comment text displays in a ScreenTip.

3. Locate a comment mark and open the comment pane:
   a. Click the **Next Comment** button on the Reviewing toolbar. Word scrolls to the highlighted text for the second comment. (If the insertion point moves to the beginning of the highlighted text for the first comment, click **Next Comment** again to move to the second comment.)

   b. Click the **Next Comment** button. Word scrolls to the highlight for the third comment.
   c. Click the **Previous Comment** button. Word scrolls to the highlight for the previous comment.
   d. Double-click the comment mark next to *ATTENDANCE* to open the comment pane to the first comment.

4. Click an insertion point in each comment mark in the comment pane, ending with the third comment. Notice that each time you click on a comment mark in the comment pane, Word scrolls to display the related comment mark in the document pane.

(continued on next page)

5. Close the comment pane.

6. Click the **Edit Comment** button on the Reviewing toolbar to go directly to the comment pane. Word locates the first comment in the document and opens the comment pane.

7. Edit the comment text for the second comment to read **These paragraph headings should be bold and underlined.**

8. Delete a comment:
   a. Move the insertion point to the third comment in the comment pane.
   b. Click next to the comment mark in the document pane.

c. Click the **Delete Comment** button on the Reviewing toolbar. The comment mark in the document pane is removed and the comment mark and text in the comment pane are also removed.

9. Undo this change and then close the comment pane.

10. Format page numbers at the bottom right but do not print a page number on the first page.

11. Save your changes and leave the document open for the next Step-by-Step.

3/16/04
1325

Protecting Documents

Before allowing others to review a document, you may choose to restrict access to the document. When you *protect* a document, you can control the kinds of changes a reviewer can make to the document. Protect a document by opening the Tools menu and clicking Protect Document. The Protect Document dialog box opens as shown in Figure 7-10.

FIGURE 7-10
Protect Document dialog box

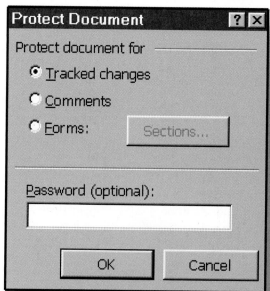

The *Tracked changes* option allows others to make changes, but all changes are shown with revision marks. With this option selected, the reviewer can also insert comments. If you want to let others insert only comments and not change the contents of the document, select the *Comments* option. To permit only authorized reviewers to make changes and add comments to the document, key a password.

Turn off protection for a document in the same way you applied it: Open the Tools menu and click Unprotect Document.

Hot Tip

A password can contain any combination of letters, numerals, spaces, and symbols. It can be up to 15 characters in length. Passwords are case sensitive. As you key the password, Word will display an asterisk (*) for each character you strike.

S TEP-BY-STEP ▷ 7.11

1. Protect the document from changes:
   a. Open the **Tools** menu and choose **Protect Document**. The Protect Document dialog box opens.
   b. Click **OK**.
   c. Key your first name at the top of the document. Notice that your name appears underlined as a tracked change.
   d. Select and delete your name.

2. Open the **Tools** menu and choose **Unprotect Document** to turn off the document protection.

3. Save your changes. Print the document. Note that your comments appear on a separate sheet of paper following the document. Close the document.

Working with Master Documents

A *master document* enables you to organize and maintain a long document by dividing it into smaller *subdocuments*. Each subdocument is a separate document file. There are a number of benefits to setting up a long document this way. Members of a workgroup can work on the individual subdocuments at the same time. As part of the master document, these individual subdocuments can then be given consecutive page numbers and consistent formatting. They can be printed with one click of the Print command, rather than have to be opened up separately and printed. You can use the Document Map to reorganize the master document by moving subdocuments. And, as in an outline, you can easily collapse and expand subdocuments to save time in reorganizing the master document.

Creating Master Documents

You have two options for creating a master document:

- If you have not yet created any subdocuments for the master document, you can begin creating a master document with an outline in Outline view. You then designate headings in the outline as subdocuments. When you save the master document, Word creates the subdocuments for you and assigns them names based on your outline headings.

- If you have already created subdocuments you want to combine into a master document, create the master document in Outline view and then use the Insert Subdocument button on the Outlining toolbar to add the existing subdocument to the master document.

The Outlining toolbar contains the tools you need to work with master documents and subdocuments. Figure 7-11 shows the portion of the toolbar that contains the master document tools. (You might need to click more buttons to see these tools.) In the next Step-by-Step, you will use these tools to create a master document and subdocuments.

Outlining Toolbar for Master/Sub Docs

FIGURE 7-11

Master document tools on the Outlining toolbar

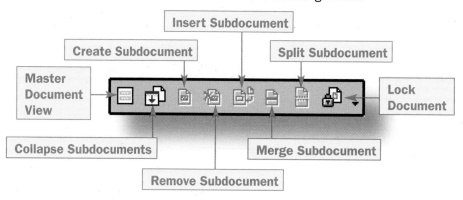

STEP-BY-STEP ▷ 7.12

1. Open a new document window.

2. Switch to Outline view. The Outlining toolbar displays.

3. If necessary, click the **Master Document View** button on the Outlining toolbar to change to Master Document view.

4. Key **HEALTH PROFESSION CAREERS** and then press **Enter**.

5. Click the **Demote** button to demote the new paragraph to a Level 2 heading.

6. Key the following headings, pressing **Enter** after each heading. Make sure you press **Enter** after the last heading.

   ```
   Sports Medicine
   Therapeutic Recreation
   Physical Therapy
   Fitness Training
   Geriatrics
   Immunology
   ```

7. Create subdocuments from the Level 2 headings:
   a. Click the heading **Sports Medicine**.
   b. Click the **Create Subdocument** button on the Outlining toolbar.

c. Word displays a Subdocument icon at the left of the heading. Word also displays a box around the heading. Also note the section breaks inserted before and after the subdocument. Each subdocument is a separate section in your master document.

d. Select each of the remaining Level 2 headings and format each as a subdocument.

8. Save the master document as **Careers** followed by your initials and leave it open for the next Step-by-Step.

Editing a Master Document

Your subdocuments currently consist only of headings. To enter text in a subdocument, change to Normal or Print Layout view and key the text. You can work with subdocuments in the same way you work with any other Word document. To work with a subdocument in a separate window, double-click the subdocument icon to the left of the subdocument title. You can edit and save the changes while this subdocument is open in another window and you can print just this subdocument while it is open in another window.

To make it easy to work with the subdocuments in a master document, you can collapse them. When subdocuments are collapsed, you can move them around in the master document, merge one or more into a single subdocument, or split portions of a subdocument into separate subdocuments. All subdocuments are locked when they are collapsed and display the lock icon under the subdocument icon at the left of the subdocument title. If a subdocument is locked, you can view the document but you cannot make changes.

Collapsed subdocuments appear in the master document as hyperlinks, as shown in Figure 7-12. You can click the hyperlink to display the subdocument in a separate window. To return to the master document, click the Back button on the Web toolbar.

To print a master document, expand or collapse the headings to display the document as you want it to print and then click Print.

Did You Know?

One of the most efficient ways to work on a master document is to store it on a network with file sharing privileges on. This allows members of a workgroup to access the master document's subdocuments. When a member of the workgroup is working on a particular subdocument, the document is locked so that no one else can access it. You can view the subdocument, but you can't modify it until your colleague closes it.

FIGURE 7-12
Master document with collapsed subdocuments

⊕ **HEALTH·PROFESSION·CAREERS¶**

Section Break (Continuous)

C:\My·Documents\Sports·Medicine.doc¶

Section Break (Continuous)

C:\My·Documents\Therapeutic·Recreation.doc¶

Section Break (Continuous)

C:\My·Documents\Physical·Therapy.doc¶

Section Break (Continuous)

C:\My·Documents\Fitness·Training.doc¶

Section Break (Continuous)

C:\My·Documents\Geriatrics.doc¶

Section Break (Continuous)

C:\My·Documents\Immunology.doc¶

¶

S TEP-BY-STEP ▷ 7.13

1. Click the **Collapse Subdocuments** button on the Outlining toolbar to collapse the subdocuments. Notice that the file names Word assigned are displayed as hyperlinks and each subdocument shows the lock icon to indicate it is locked.

Concept Builder

By default, Word collapses all subdocuments when you open a master document.

2. Click the **Expand Subdocuments** button to expand the subdocuments.

3. Add an existing document to the master document:

    a. Position the insertion point in the blank paragraph at the end of the document.

Hot Tip

Make sure you position the insertion point on a blank line between existing documents. If you position the insertion point within a subdocument, the document will be inserted within the subdocument.

    b. Click the **Insert Subdocument** button on the Outlining toolbar. The Insert Subdocument dialog box opens.

    c. Locate and open **AW Step7-13a** from the student data files.

4. If necessary, click the **All** button to expand the text below the heading *Nursing*.

5. Position the insertion point in the blank paragraph at the end of the document, click the **Insert Subdocument** button again, and open the **AW Step7-13b** data file.

6. Click the **All** button twice to collapse the text below headings in the subdocuments. (If the text does not collapse, move the insertion point into another subdocument and try clicking the All button again.)

7. Double-click the subdocument icon next to the heading *Nursing* to open the document in another window. Save the document as **Nursing** in the folder containing the master document. Close the subdocument.

8. Double-click the subdocument icon next to the heading *Pharmacy* to open the document in another window. Save the document as **Pharmacy** in the folder containing the master document. Close the subdocument.

9. Change the order of the subdocuments:
   a. Scroll to the top of the document.
   b. Drag the subdocument button for the heading *Fitness Training* to position the heading just above the blank paragraph mark at the end of the document. As you drag, an arrow and a horizontal line will display to indicate the new position (Figure 7-13).

Hot Tip

If the subdocument does not display at the end of the document, you may have dragged it within a section for another subdocument. Click **Undo** and try again.

FIGURE 7-13
Dragging a subdocument to a new location

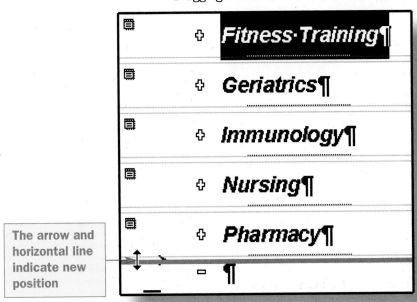

The arrow and horizontal line indicate new position

(continued on next page)

10. Combine two subdocuments:

    a. Select the subdocuments **Pharmacy** and **Fitness Training**. (Click **Pharmacy**, hold down **Shift**, and click **Fitness Training**.)

    b. Click the **Merge Subdocument** button on the Outlining toolbar. Notice that the two headings are now contained in one subdocument. Word saves the combined subdocuments with the name of the first subdocument (in this case, *Pharmacy*).

    c. Deselect the text.

11. Split a subdocument:

    a. Position the insertion point in front of the heading *Fitness Training*.

    b. Click the **Split Subdocument** button on the Outline toolbar. The subdocument is split at the location of the

insertion point and Word assigns a file name to the new subdocument.

12. Position the insertion point in the master document title (*HEALTH PROFESSION CAREERS*). Insert a header for the entire document with the document title at the left margin and the page number at the right margin. Use Print Preview to see how the subdocuments appear and how the pages are numbered consecutively throughout the master document.

13. Save your changes. Close the document.

Concept Builder

If subdocuments you want to merge or split are locked, you must first unlock them.

Summary

In this lesson, you learned:

- You can change the location where workgroup templates are stored. To protect templates that members of a workgroup use, you can save them as read-only recommended or restrict access with a password. *TOOLS > OPTIONS > FILE LOCATIONS*

- Comments can be added to the file properties of a document to provide additional information. *THIS CAN BE DONE FROM EXPLORER ALSO. OR FILE > PROPERTIES*

- Documents can be routed to others for review. If desired, you can specify the order in which the documents are received and you can track the status. *SEND TO > ROUTING RECIPIENT*

- Multiple versions of a document can be created so you can keep the original version intact. *FILE > VERSIONS*

- Word will track changes in a document and display them in up to eight different colors to help distinguish multiple reviewers. *TOOLS > TRACK CHANGES*

- Once workgroup members have reviewed and tracked changes, you can combine the revisions in one document. *TOOLS > MERGE DOCS*

- You can accept or reject changes in documents individually or you can accept or reject them all at one time. *VIEW > TOOLBARS > REVIEWING OR RIGHT CLICK ON REVISION OR TOOLS > TRACK CHANGES > ACCEPT OR REJECT CHANGES*

- If you don't track changes and you want to see what changes have been made in a document, you can compare the edited document with its original version. *NEED TO SAVE ORIG UNDER NEW NAME.*

- The protect feature enables you to restrict access to the document. *TOOLS > PROTECT DOC*

- A master document organizes subdocuments into a single document.

LESSON 7 REVIEW QUESTIONS

TRUE/FALSE

Circle T if the statement is true or F if the statement is false.

T **F** 1. Deleting the comment text in the comment pane also removes the comment mark from the document pane. *DELETE THE COMMENT MARK FROM THE DOC.*

T F 2. Comments are always formatted as hidden text.

T **F** 3. Once revisions are made in a document, all the changes must be either accepted or rejected at one time.

T F 4. When subdocuments are collapsed in the master document, each subdocument appears as a hyperlink.

MATCHING

Match the correct term in Column 2 to its description in Column 1.

Column 1	Column 2
D 1. Command you use to prevent reviewers from making changes to a document	**A.** Compare Documents
B 2. Changes in font color or style to show modifications	**B.** Revision marks
E 3. A document containing smaller sections	**C.** Comment
A 4. Command used to show how an edited document differs from the original document	**D.** Protect Document
G 5. Distributing a document to a list of recipients	**E.** Master document
C 6. Notes added within a document by an author or a reviewer	**F.** Merge Documents
	G. Routing

SCANS

PROJECT 7-1

1. Open **AW Project7-1** from the student data files and save the document as **Sales** followed by your initials.

2. Review the revisions. Accept each revision except where *$30,000* is changed to *$45,000*.

3. Highlight the second sentence in the third paragraph in the body of the memo that begins *In order to deliver . . . .* Use the highlight color yellow.

4. Save your changes. Print and close the document.

PROJECT 7-2

SCANS

1. Open **AW Project7-2** from the student data files and save the document as **Will-v1** followed by your initials.

2. Save the current state of the document as **version 1**.

3. Turn on Track Changes.   *Tools → track changes*

4. Edit the document as indicated by the proofreaders' marks in Figure 7-14.

5. Save the current state of the document as **version 2**.

6. Change the User Information as follows: the user name is **Reviewer Number 2** and the initials are **rn2**.

7. At the end of paragraph 5, key the following sentence: **Because my mother, Janice Henson Valarde, is financially stable and is well provided for, I am intentionally omitting her from this will.**

8. Save the current state of the document as **version 3** and close the document.

FIGURE 7-14

Lesson ⑦ Editing in Workgroups

LAST WILL AND TESTAMENT

1. I, William James Valarde, a resident of the State of Ohio, declare and publish this as my Will and revoke all previous Wills and Codicils.

2. I am married. My wife's name is LaDonna Becker Valarde. I have two daughters, Linda Valarde Lewis and Laura Suzanne Valarde, and one son, Russell Anthony Valarde *and Phillip Michael Valarde* ~~two~~ ~~s~~

3. I want a simple and inexpensive burial with a graveside service. *I want my body buried in Rosewood Cemetry in Centerville, Ohio, where I have already purchased a burial plot.*

4. I want any debts, taxes, and expenses of my estate to be paid out of my estate before any property is distributed to anyone under this Will ~~except that if the land still has a mortgage on it at the time of my death, my son, Russell Anthony Valarde, should be solely responsible for that mortgage.~~

5. I want my interest in my house located at ~~554 East Fifth Street,~~ *1074 Fairfield* Centerville, Ohio 45458-0931, excluding any of the personal property in the home, to go to my son, Russell Anthony Valarde. *and Phillip Michael Valarde* ~~two~~ ~~s~~ If he dies before me, it should go to ~~each~~ *one of them* of my daughters, Linda Valarde Lewis and Laura Suzanne Valarde, to be divided equally. In addition, I give all the personal property in the home to my children to be divided equally. I give ~~fifteen~~ *fifty* thousand dollars (\$~~15~~*50*,000) to each of my children. If one of my children dies before me and said child does not have any children surviving at the time of my death, my deceased child's share of my estate shall be divided equally among my surviving children at the time of my death. *the surviving son. In the event that both sons die before me, it should go to*

- 1 -

FIGURE 7-14
Continued.

6.   I appoint my wife, LaDonna Becker Valarde, as executrix of my estate. If she cannot serve as executrix, I appoint my brother, Daniel Roger Valarde, as executor. I give them the power to sell or not sell and to deal with my property in any way they feel is in the best interest of my estate. *I wish them to serve without bond.*

7.   If my wife, LaDonna Becker Valarde, dies before me, I appoint my sister, MaryJane Valarde Torres, and her husband, John Andrew Torres, as guardians of my minor children and their property. *I wish them to serve without bond.*

8.   Dated this 6th day of May, ----.

_____
Testator

The above Will was signed, declared, and published as his Will by William James Valarde in our presence, and at his request we have signed our names to this Will as witnesses, this 6th day of May, ----.

Witness_____

Residing_____

_____

Witness_____

Residing_____

_____

-2-

9. Open the **AW Project7-2** data file and save the document as **Will-v2** followed by your initials.

10. Turn on Track Changes.

11. Change the User Information back to the original settings before you added your own name and initials.

12. Add comments to the document as follows:
    A. Select the sentence in paragraph 3, and using your own initials, add this comment: **The family has already been informed about the burial arrangements.**
    B. In paragraph 6, select the second sentence (beginning *If she cannot serve . . .*), and add this comment: **Has Daniel Valarde been informed that he is the alternate executor of this will?**

13. Save the changes and close the document.

14. Open the **AW Project7-2** data file and save the document as **Will-v3** followed by your initials.

15. Combine the revisions from **Will-v1** and **Will-v2** with **Will-v3**.

16. Accept all the revisions, and if necessary, adjust the spacing between words where changes were made.

17. If necessary, insert a hard page break at the beginning of the last paragraph in the document (beginning *The above Will . . .*) to keep the paragraph and the signature lines together on the same page.

18. Save your changes. Print and close the document.

PROJECT 7-3

SCANS

1. Open **AW Project7-3a** from the student data files and save the document as **Lease** followed by your initials.

2. Compare the document to the **AW Project7-3b** data file (the original document).

3. Save your changes. Print the document with the revision marks and close it.

ACTIVITY 7-1

Mary is the manager of an insurance office and is responsible for updating the company's office procedures manual. Mary wants to route the current file for the manual to several workers in the office. How can Mary protect the document to enable reviewers to read it, make revisions, and add comments, but prohibit them from permanently changing the document?

ACTIVITY 7-2

Mary is not satisfied with the way revision marks display on the screen. To make it easier for her to view the changes, she would like to change the way revision marks look in a document. How can Mary make these changes? Use the Help feature to find the answer.

CREATING FORMS

OBJECTIVES

Upon completion of this lesson, you should be able to:

- Create and format a printed form document.

- Insert symbols.

- Create and modify an online form template using form controls.

- Insert online form fields for text boxes, check boxes, and drop-down lists.

- Format responses in text form fields.

- Add help text for an online form.

- Protect an online form.

- Fill in an online form.

⏱ **Estimated Time: 1.5 hours**

Forms can be used to collect a variety of information. To organize the information in a useful format, you can utilize text boxes, check boxes, and drop-down list boxes. Before creating a form in Word, you should design the layout of the form or use an existing form as a guide. To be useful, the information requested on the form should be well defined. The parts of the form should be arranged in an easy-to-follow order, and the questions should be easy to understand and answer.

The first decision you need to make is whether the user will complete the form on paper or online. If the form is to be printed, the tools you use to create the form will be different from those you use to create an online form.

Creating a Printed Form

When you create a printed form, the user completes the form on paper. You can format the form with text, graphics, and symbols. Use check boxes when one or more specific responses are available. Use blank lines for variable written responses. Be sure you allow sufficient space for the user to write on blank lines. If desired, you can further enhance the form with borders and shading.

Entering the Form Text

In Step-by-Step 8.1, you will create the form shown in Figure 8-1. To create a printed form, you key text just as you would for any other document. The best way to create the lines used for filling in information is to use right-aligned tabs with the underline leader. Using tabs with leaders lets you align your blank lines precisely at the right margin.

FIGURE 8-1

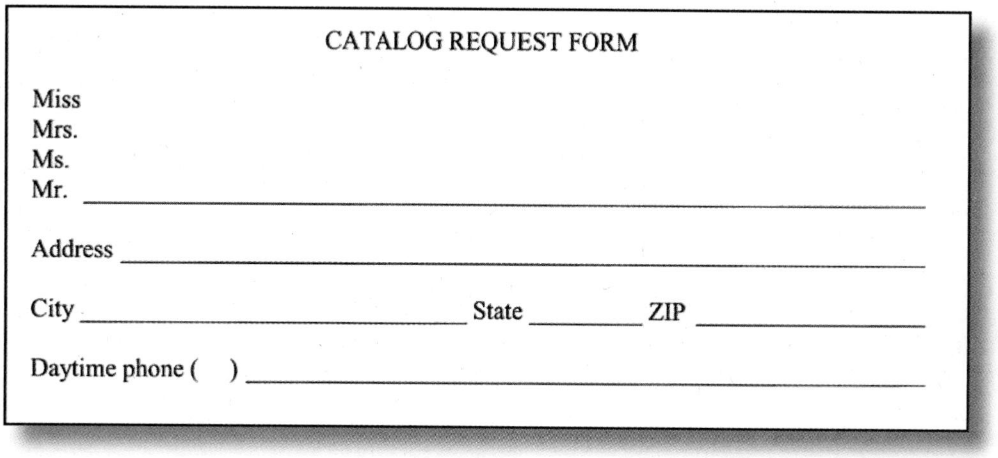

CATALOG REQUEST FORM

Miss
Mrs.
Ms.
Mr. _____

Address _____

City _____ State _____ ZIP _____

Daytime phone (   ) _____

S TEP-BY-STEP ▷ 8.1

1. Open a new document window and key the document illustrated in Figure 8-1. Be sure to leave a blank paragraph at the end of the document.

2. To create the blank lines, set a right-aligned tab at the 6-inch mark on the ruler and specify the underline leader.

3. Save the document as **Catalog Request Form** followed by your initials. Leave the document open for the next Step-by-Step.

Inserting Symbols and Special Characters

You can add symbols and special characters to create graphic items on the form. The symbols available are dependent on the printer you are using. To insert a symbol, open the Insert menu and click Symbol. The Symbol dialog box opens, as shown in Figure 8-2. To insert one of the symbols shown in the dialog box, click it and then click Insert. You can see symbols in other fonts by clicking the down arrow next to the Font list box and then choosing a font.

The Special Characters tab in this dialog box lets you easily insert characters such as em dashes, optional hyphens, and various kinds of spaces. Select a character and click Insert to insert it in your document.

 Did You Know?

If you want to insert more than one symbol, you can leave the Symbol dialog box open while you work. After you have finished inserting symbols, click the **Close** button.

ADVANCED MICROSOFT WORD

FIGURE 8-2
Symbols tab in the Symbol dialog box

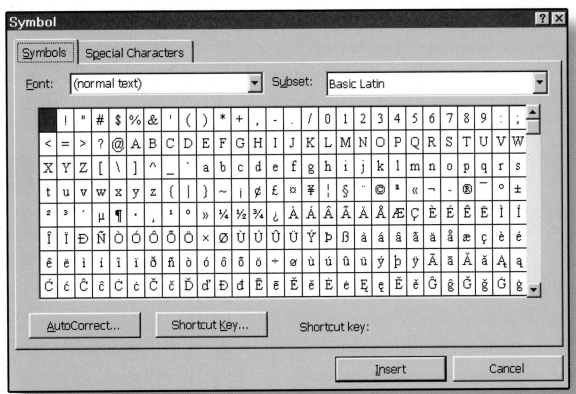

STEP-BY-STEP 8.2

1. Insert a symbol to indicate the user should clip the form from the printed page:

   a. Position the insertion point at the top of the document. Press **Enter** three times and then select the three blank paragraphs you just created.

   b. Change to left alignment.

   c. With the paragraph marks still selected, change the font to **Times New Roman 22 pt**.

   d. Deselect the paragraph marks and position the insertion point in the first blank paragraph.

   e. Open the **Insert** menu and choose **Symbol**. If necessary, click the **Symbols** tab. Do not be concerned if your dialog box looks different

   from the one shown in Figure 8-2. The symbols available will vary depending on your printer.

   f. If necessary, change the font in the *Font* box until you see a symbol that you can use to suggest cutting (for example, a pair of scissors). You can find such a symbol in the Monotype Sorts font and in the Wingdings font.

   g. If you cannot find an appropriate symbol, click **Close** and go on to step 4.

   h. Click the symbol in the dialog box.

   i. Click **Insert** and then click **Close.** The symbol is inserted in the document at the location of the insertion point.

(continued on next page)

2. To create a dashed "cut" line that extends from the symbol to the right margin, set a right-aligned tab at the 6-inch mark on the ruler and specify the dashed line leader.

3. Press **Tab**.

4. Insert a symbol to indicate a *Yes* response:

    a. Position the insertion point in the blank paragraph below the dashed line.

    b. Choose **Symbol** from the **Insert** menu. Locate and insert a checkmark symbol.

Hot Tip

Click on a symbol to see a larger view of it.

    c. Key **Yes!**

    d. Change the font size to **12 pt italic**, press the **spacebar**, and then key **Please send me a free catalog so I can learn more about your products.**

    e. Select the checkmark symbol, open the **Format** menu, and choose **Borders and Shading**. Add a $^1/_2$-pt shadow border to all four sides of the symbol.

5. Insert check boxes in front of the four titles (*Miss, Mrs., Ms.,* and *Mr.*):

    a. Position the insertion point to the left of *Miss* and insert a symbol that looks like a check box. (Any empty square or box will do. If available, you can choose a box with a shadow.)

    b. Repeat the symbol to the left of the other three titles by opening the **Edit** menu and choosing **Repeat Symbol**.

6. Save your changes and leave the document open for the next Step-by-Step.

Adding Borders and Shading to the Form

Shading in forms can help users quickly identify the areas to which they need to respond. To add shading to a printed form, select the text you want to emphasize and then add the shading format.

STEP-BY-STEP ⇨ 8.3

1. Select the paragraphs for title, address, city, and daytime phone. Be sure to select the blank paragraph at the end of the document.

2. Add Gray-10% shading and a $^1/_2$-pt box border.

3. Save your changes. Print the form and close the document.

Creating an Online Form Using Form Controls

An online form is distributed and collected via e-mail or another type of network. Because the user completes the form at the computer, you have many more tools you can utilize when designing and creating the form. Word provides form fields that enable you to quickly format areas of the form for a variety of responses including text, check boxes, and drop-down lists. You can even add Help messages to provide instructions for the user who is completing the form.

Creating a Template Form

The online form must be created as a *template*. The user creates a new document based on the template, so the template remains unchanged and can be used again and again.

In the following Step-by-Step, you will create the template for the form using the information shown in Figure 8-3.

FIGURE 8-3

INVOICE

NU-TECH PLASTICS, INC.
1680 Oxford Road
Mansfield, MA 02048-4314
Phone: 508-555-4021 Fax: 508-555-4029

Invoice #
Invoice Date

S TEP-BY-STEP ▷ 8.4

1. Create a new document template:
   a. Open the **File** menu and choose **New** to display the New dialog box.
   b. If necessary, click the **General** tab and then select **Blank Document**.
   c. Click **Template** in the bottom right corner of the dialog box and then click **OK**.

2. Key the document illustrated in Figure 8-3 as follows:
   a. Format the heading **Arial 16 pt bold centered**.

   b. Format all remaining text **Arial 12 pt bold**.
   c. Format the single line border **6 pt**.
   d. Set a right-aligned tab at the right margin to align *Invoice #* and *Invoice Date*.

3. Save the template as **Invoice Form** followed by your initials. Do not change the default location in the *Save in* box. Leave the document open for the next Step-by-Step.

Inserting Text Form Fields and Modifying Form Controls

A text form field enables users to enter text. You can specify a default entry so the user can change the response, eliminating the need for the user to key an entry.

You enter all form fields using options on the Forms toolbar, shown in Figure 8-4. Position your insertion point where you want the field to appear and then click the appropriate form field option on the Forms toolbar. Word inserts the field with visible shading to make it easy to distinguish fields from text. Although this shading displays on the screen, the shading will not show when the form document is printed.

Hot Tip

If you do not want the form fields shaded, click the Form Field Shading button on the Forms toolbar to turn off the option.

FIGURE 8-4
Forms toolbar

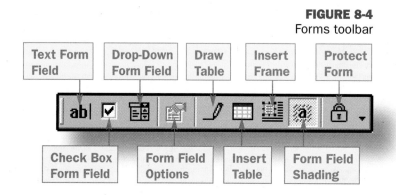

To modify a form field or specify formatting for it, click the Form Field Options button on the Forms toolbar to display an Options dialog box. Figure 8-5 shows the Text Form Field Options dialog box. In this dialog box, you can specify a format type for text, a maximum length for the text entry, and a default entry that will display in the field until the user inserts new text.

FIGURE 8-5
Text Form Field Options dialog box

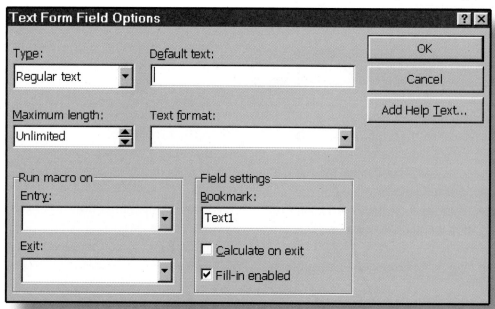

1. Display the Forms toolbar by right-clicking any toolbar and selecting **Forms** from the shortcut menu.

Hot Tip

If the Forms toolbar is floating in the middle of your screen, drag it to a side of the window to dock it so it won't be in your way while you are working.

2. Insert a text form field for the date:
   a. Position the insertion point immediately following *Invoice Date*.
   b. Press the **spacebar**.
   c. Click the **Text Form Field** button on the Forms toolbar. Word inserts a field at the location of the insertion point. (Don't worry if the field extends out into the margin.)

Hot Tip

If field codes are displayed instead of form fields, press Alt + F9.

   d. Notice that the **Form Field Shading** button on the Forms toolbar is now highlighted.
   e. Click the **Form Field Options** button on the Forms toolbar. The Text Form Field Options dialog box opens. (If the Form Field Options button is not available, click in the *Invoice Date* form field to activate the button.)
   f. In the *Type* box, select **Current date**. This field will display the current date automatically when the user selects the field.
   g. In the *Date format* box, click the down arrow and select **M/d/yy** from the drop-down list.
   h. Click **OK**.

3. If necessary, select the form field and click the **Bold** button on the Formatting toolbar to turn off the bold format.

4. Insert text form fields for the customer name and address:
   a. Position the insertion point left of the tab for the paragraph containing *Invoice #*. (Your insertion point should be at the left margin.) Click the **Bold** button on the Formatting toolbar to turn off the bold format.
   b. Click the **Text Form Field** button. Then click the **Form Field Options** button.
   c. In the *Default text* box, key **Enter customer name here.**
   d. Click the down arrow in the *Text format* box and select **Uppercase**. The user's response will be formatted in all caps, regardless of the way the user enters the information.
   e. Click **OK**.
   f. Position the insertion point left of the tab for the paragraph containing *Invoice Date*. Turn off bold formatting.
   g. Click the **Text Form Field** button and then click **Form Field Options**.
   h. In the *Default text* box, key **Enter customer address here.**
   i. Format the text uppercase and click **OK**.
   j. Position the insertion point in the blank paragraph at the end of the document. Turn off bold formatting.
   k. Click **Text Form Field** and then click **Form Field Options**.
   l. In the *Default text* box, key **Enter city, state, and ZIP here.**
   m. Format the text uppercase and click **OK**.

5. Save your changes and leave the document open for the next Step-by-Step.

Hot Tip

To change the options for a form field, double-click the form field to display the Form Field Options dialog box.

Inserting a Table on a Form

The Draw Table and Insert Table buttons are available on the Forms toolbar because tables are frequently used when creating a form. When inserting a table on a form, you first create the table structure and then insert text form fields in each cell of the table where you want the user to be able to insert information. You can speed the process of inserting text form fields in a table by copying fields from cell to cell.

You can also include calculations in the table. To insert a calculation in a table on a form, open the Form Field Options dialog box and select *Calculation* from the *Type* drop-down list. The dialog box then displays an *Expression* box you can use to key your calculation expression, as shown in Figure 8-6. You cannot copy calculated fields, because you need to key a new expression for each row of the table.

FIGURE 8-6
Create a calculation in a form field

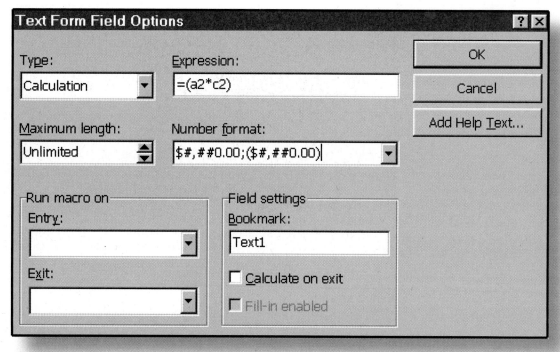

STEP-BY-STEP ▷ 8.6

1. Press **Enter** twice and insert a table grid with eight rows and four columns.

2. Key the following column headings: **Qty.**, **Description**, **Unit Price**, and **Total**. Format the headings bold. Center the *Qty.* and *Description* headings. Right-align the *Unit Price* and *Total* headings. Remove all borders for the entire table.

3. Format the table columns as follows: The *Qty.* column should be approximately 0.75 inch wide. The *Description* column should be approximately 3 inches wide. The *Unit Price* column should be approximately 1 inch wide. The *Total* column should be approximately 1.5 inches wide.

4. Position the insertion point in row 2 of the *Qty.* column, click **Text Form Field**, and then click **Form Field Options**. In the *Type* box, select **Number**. In the *Maximum length* box, key **6**. In the *Number format* box, select **0**. Click **OK**.

5. With the number form field you just created still selected, click the **Copy** button. Paste the number form field in the next four rows in the *Qty.* column.

6. Position the insertion point in row 2 of the *Description* column and create a regular text form field. Copy the field into the next four rows in the *Description* column.

7. Position the insertion point in row 2 of the *Unit Price* column and insert a number form field with a maximum length of **8**. Click **Text Form Field**, and then click **Form Field Options**. In the *Number format* box, select **0.00** and then click **OK**.

8. Copy the number form field to the next four rows in the *Unit Price* column. Right align the number form fields in the *Unit Price* column.

9. Position the insertion point in row 2 of the *Total* column and insert a calculation form field. Click **Text Form Field** and then click **Form Field Options**. In the *Type* box, select **Calculation**. In the *Expression* box, position the insertion point to the right of = and key **(a2*c2)**. In the *Number format* box select **$#,##0.00;($#,##0.00)**, and then click **OK**.

10. Insert a text form field to calculate each total in rows 3 through 6 of the *Total* column.

11. Position the insertion point in row 7 of the *Description* column and key **Sales Tax**. Format the text bold and right-align the text in the cell.

12. Position the insertion point in row 7 of the *Total* column and insert a form field to calculate sales tax. For *Type*, select **Calculation**. For *Expression*, key **sum(d2:d6)*.06**. This formula adds the amounts in the *Total* column and multiplies the sum by 6 percent. For *Number format*, select **$#,##0.00;($#,##0.00)** and then click **OK**.

13. Position the insertion point in row 8 of the *Description* column and key **TOTAL**. Format the text bold and right-align the text in the cell.

(continued on next page)

14. Position the insertion point in row 8 of the *Total* column and insert a text form field to calculate the total. For *Type*, select **Calculation**. For *Expression*, key **sum(d2:d7)**. For *Number format*, select **$#,##0.00;($#,##0.00)** and then click **OK**. Right align the form fields in the *Total* column.

15. Your screen should look like the one shown in Figure 8-7. Save your changes and leave the document open for the next Step-by-Step.

FIGURE 8-7
Your form should resemble the one shown here

INVOICE¶

¶
NU-TECH·PLASTICS,·INC.¶
1680·Oxford·Road¶
Mansfield,·MA··02048-4314¶
Phone:·508-555-4021··Fax:·508-555-4029¶

¶
ENTER·CUSTOMER·NAME·HERE.   →   Invoice·#¶
ENTER·CUSTOMER·ADDRESS·HERE.   →   Invoice·Date 2/1/99¶
ENTER·CITY,·STATE,·AND·ZIP·HERE.¶
¶

Qty.#	Description#	Unit·Price#	Total##
ooooo◌	ooooo◌	◌	$0.00◌◌
ooooo◌	ooooo◌	◌	$0.00◌◌
ooooo◌	ooooo◌	◌	$0.00◌◌
ooooo◌	ooooo◌	◌	$0.00◌◌
ooooo◌	ooooo◌	◌	$0.00◌◌
◌	Sales·Tax# ◌		$0.00◌◌
◌	TOTAL# ◌		$0.00◌◌

Creating a Drop-Down Form Field

A drop-down form field restricts available choices to those you create. If necessary, the user can scroll through the list to see the available choices and then click one to select it.

Click the Drop-Down Form Field option on the Forms toolbar to create a drop-down form field. To insert the items you want to appear on the drop-down list, click Form Field Options to display the Drop-Down Form Field Options dialog box, as shown in Figure 8-8. Key each item you want on your drop-down list in the *Drop-down item* box. Click Add to add it to the *Items in drop-down list* box. You can rearrange items in the list by selecting an item and clicking one of the Move buttons to move the item up or down. Remove an item by selecting it in the list and then clicking the Remove button.

FIGURE 8-8
Drop-Down Form Field Options dialog box

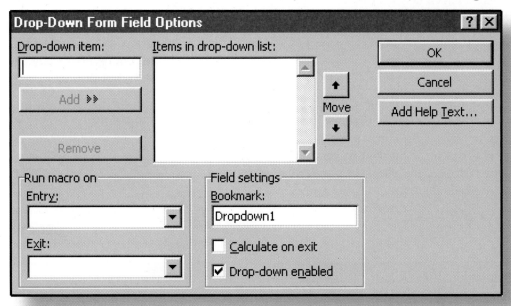

The drop-down form field by default displays the first item on the list in the form. The user can click the arrow to the right of the field to display the entire list.

STEP-BY-STEP ⟩ 8.7

1. Insert a drop-down form field:
   a. Position the insertion point at the end of the document. Turn on bold formatting and press **Enter** twice.
   b. Key **Payment:** and press the **spacebar** twice.
   c. Click the **Drop-Down Form Field** button on the Forms toolbar.

2. Format the drop-down form field:
   a. Click **Form Field Options**. The Drop-Down Form Field Options dialog box opens.

   b. In the *Drop-down item* box, key **On account**.
   c. Click **Add** (or press **Enter**).
   d. Key **Due upon receipt** and click **Add**.
   e. Key **Net 30 days** and click **Add**.
   f. Click the up arrow to the right of the *Items in drop-down list* box twice to move *Net 30 days* to the top of the list.
   g. Click **OK**.

3. Save your changes and leave the document open for the next Step-by-Step.

Creating a Check Box Form Field

You use a check box next to an independent option that is to be selected or cleared. To insert a check box next to a group of choices, select the items and then create the check box.

Click the Check Box Form Field button on the Forms toolbar to insert a check box. You can then format the check box form field in the Check Box Form Field Options dialog box, shown in Figure 8-9. In this dialog box, change the size of the check box and specify whether it will be checked or unchecked by default. Unless you specify an exact size, the check box is formatted to the size of the surrounding text.

Concept Builder

You cannot use drop-down form fields or check boxes while you are creating a form. They will work properly only after the form has been protected. You will learn how to protect the form document in Step-by-Step 8.10.

FIGURE 8-9
Check Box Form Field Options dialog box

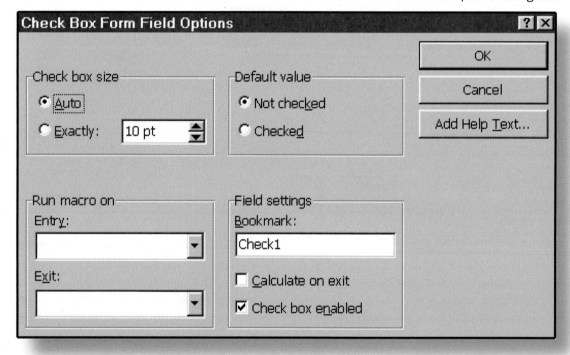

1. Insert a check box form field:
   a. Position the insertion point at the end of the drop-down form field.
   b. Press **Enter** twice.
   c. Click the **Check Box Form Field** button on the Forms toolbar.

2. Format the check box form field:
   a. Click **Form Field Options**. The Check Box Form Field Options dialog box opens.
   b. Select the **Exactly** option and change the text in the box to **14** pt.
   c. Click **OK**. A check box is inserted in the document.

   d. Position the insertion point to the right of the check box.
   e. Press the **spacebar** and key **Order was shipped via ground transportation.**
   f. Press **Enter**.
   g. Select and copy the check box form field to the new blank paragraph.
   h. Press the **spacebar** and key **Order was shipped via air transportation.** Press **Enter.**

3. Save your changes and leave the document open for the next Step-by-Step.

Adding Help Text to a Form Field

Help messages provide instructions for the user to complete the form. To add a help message to your form, click the Add Help Text button in any Form Field Options dialog box. Word displays the Form Field Help Text dialog box, shown in Figure 8-10. Notice the two tabs in the dialog box. To have a help message appear when the user presses F1, add your help text to the Help Key (F1) tab. To have the message appear in the status bar, add your help text to the Status Bar tab.

FIGURE 8-10
Help Key (F1) tab in the Form Field Help Text dialog box

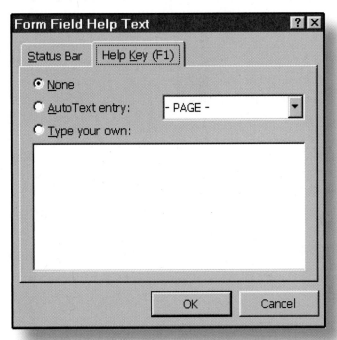

STEP-BY-STEP 8.9

1. Position the insertion point to the right of *Invoice #:* and press the **spacebar**. If necessary, turn off the bold format.

2. Insert a text form field with a help message:
   a. Click **Text Form Field**. Click **Form Field Options**.
   b. In the *Type* box, select **Number**.
   c. In the *Maximum length* box, key **8**.
   d. Click **Add Help Text**. The Form Field Help Text dialog box opens. Then click the **Help Key (F1)** tab.

   e. Select **Type your own**.
   f. In the text box, key **Enter the next sequential number. Invoice numbers are assigned when the invoice is created.**
   g. Click **OK** twice. If users do not know what text to enter for the Invoice #, they can press **F1** to see the Help screen.

3. Save your changes and leave the document open for the next Step-by-Step.

Protecting the Form Template

To prevent users from changing the content of the form template, you must protect the form. Protecting the form template allows users to move quickly from one form field to another. When a form is protected, many of the commands on the menus are not available.

To protect a form, click the Protect Form button on the Forms toolbar. You can then move from field to field in the form by pressing Tab or using the arrow keys.

STEP-BY-STEP 8.10

1. Position the insertion point at the beginning of the document.

2. Click the **Protect Form** button on the Forms toolbar. The first form field is selected.

3. Move from one form field to another:
   a. Press **Tab**. Word moves the insertion point to the next form field and selects the field. In this case, the next form field is for the Invoice #.
   b. Press the down or up arrow key to move between form fields.

   c. Press **Shift** + **Tab** to move to the previous form field.
   d. Move to each form field in the document. Notice that you cannot move to the calculation form fields. Word will automatically calculate the totals when you print the form. Also notice that when you move to the drop-down form field, a drop-down arrow appears.

4. Save your changes. Print the document and close it.

Filling in an Online Form

To fill in a protected form, users must create a new document based on the template. By default, Word saves templates in the Microsoft Office Templates folder. You can locate and open your template by clicking New on the File menu and then clicking the template on the General tab in the New dialog box.

STEP-BY-STEP ▷ 8.11

1. Open **File** and click **New**. Click the **Invoice Form** template on the **General** tab and click **OK**.

2. Save the new document as **Completed Invoice** followed by your initials.

3. Use **Tab** and the up and down arrows to move to each of the form fields and complete the form using the following information:

Customer Name	Direct Connections
Invoice #	11345
Customer Address	5883 Eden Park Place
City, State, ZIP	San Jose, CA 95138
Qty.	10
Description	#36 plastic bags
Unit Price	0.94
Payment	On account

Concept Builder

The *Total* fields will not show calculations until the form is printed.

4. Move to the first check box for ground transportation. Click in the check box to turn it on. When the check box is turned on, there is an X in the box.

5. Move the insertion point to the *Invoice #* form field. Press **F1** to see the Help message. Then click **OK** to close the Help dialog box.

6. Save your changes and leave the document open for the next Step-by-Step.

Saving and Printing Online Form Data

You can save the entire form document or you can save only the form data to a text file. If you save only the variable data entered by the user, the data can be imported to a database file. To save only the form data, choose Options on the Tools menu, click the Save tab, and turn on *Save data only for forms*.

STEP-BY-STEP ▷ 8.12

1. Save the entire form document.

2. Print the document. When the document is printed, the calculations are updated.

3. Close the document.

Concept Builder

If the calculations are not updated after printing, choose **Print** on the **File** menu, click **Options**, and make sure *Update fields* is turned on under *Printing options*.

Summary

In this lesson, you learned:

- You can use symbols and special characters to create check boxes and graphics in printed forms.

- Word provides form fields that enable you to quickly format areas of the form for a variety of responses.

- The online form must be created as a template.

- Text form fields enable users to enter text for their response.

- Drop-down list boxes restrict available choices to those you create.

- Check boxes are positioned next to independent options that are to be selected or cleared.

- You can format Help messages to provide instructions for the user to complete the form.

- You must protect the form template to prevent users from changing the content of the form. Form fields do not function correctly until the form template is protected.

LESSON 8 REVIEW QUESTIONS

TRUE/FALSE

Circle T if the statement is true or F if the statement is false.

T F 1. You cannot format a symbol after it is inserted in the document.

T **F** 2. To move from one form field to the next, press Shift + Tab.

T F 3. An online form is distributed and collected via e-mail or another type of network.

T F 4. If a form field is formatted for uppercase text, the text will automatically be formatted if a user enters lowercase letters.

T F 5. You cannot cut, copy, or paste form fields.

FILL IN THE BLANKS

Complete the following sentences by writing the correct word or words in the blanks provided.

1. To give users a choice of items in a field, use a(n) _drop down field_

2. You can insert special characters in a form or other document by opening the _insert_ menu and clicking the _symbol_ command.

3. An online form must be created as a(n) _template_ .

4. To modify a form field, click the _Form Field Options_ button on the Forms toolbar.

5. Users can see a Help message either by pressing the _F1_ key or by looking at the _Status Bar_.

LESSON 8 PROJECTS

PROJECT 8-1

1. Open a new document and key the form illustrated in Figure 8-11.
   A. Use right tabs and underscore leaders to create spaces for written responses.
   B. Insert symbols to create the check boxes.
   C. Apply a Gray-10% shading to the paragraphs containing blank lines for the user to fill in.
   D. Format two 6-pt single line borders as shown in the illustration.

2. Save the document as **Survey Form** followed by your initials. Print the form and then close it.

FIGURE 8-11

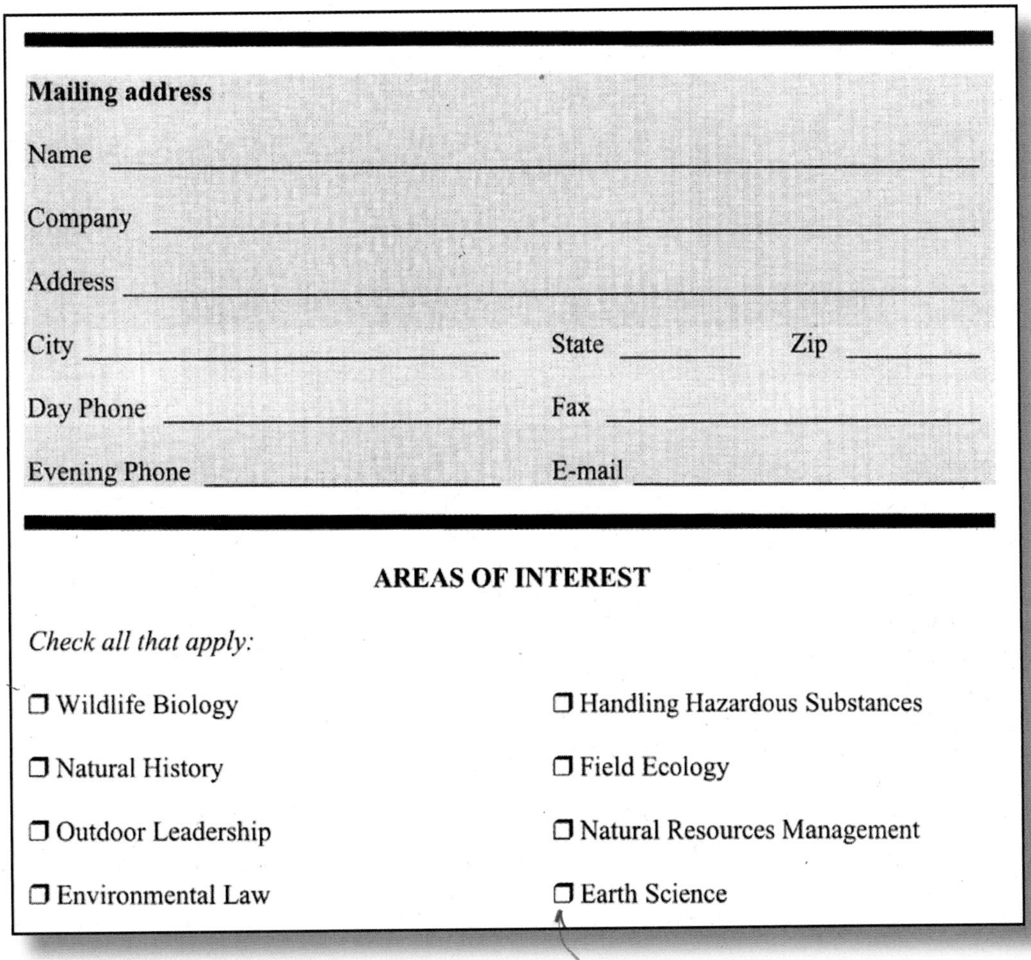

Mailing address

Name _____

Company _____

Address _____

City _____ State _____ Zip _____

Day Phone _____ Fax _____

Evening Phone _____ E-mail _____

AREAS OF INTEREST

Check all that apply:

❏ Wildlife Biology   ❏ Handling Hazardous Substances

❏ Natural History   ❏ Field Ecology

❏ Outdoor Leadership   ❏ Natural Resources Management

❏ Environmental Law   ❏ Earth Science

See pg. AW 156

PROJECT 8-2

1. Create a new document template.

2. Key the form illustrated in Figure 8-12. Double-space the entire form and format the title Arial 16 pt bold.

FIGURE 8-12

CHECK REQUEST FORM *Arial 16 pt Bold*

dbl spc.

Person requesting check:

Date of request:

Amount of check:

Make check payable to:

Explain what the check is for:

Date approved:

Amount approved:

Account number:

Date check written:

Check number:

3. Save the form template as **Check Request Form** followed by your initials.

4. Insert form fields as follows:
   A. Press **spacebar** before each form field.
   B. Insert a Regular text form field with unlimited Maximum length for *Person requesting check*.
   C. Insert a Current date form field formatted for M/d/yy for *Date of request, Date approved*, and *Date check written*.
   D. Insert a Number form field formatted for $#,##0.00;($#,##0.00) for *Amount of check* and *Amount approved*.
   E. Insert a Regular text form field formatted in 14 pt text for the *Make check payable to*.
   F. Insert a Regular text form field for *Explain what the check is for*.
   G. Insert a Number form field formatted for a maximum of three characters for *Account number*.
   H. Insert a Number form field formatted for a maximum of six characters for *Check number*. Add the following Help message to appear in the status bar: **Check number must match the number recorded in the check register.**

5. Protect the document.

6. Save your changes and close the document.

7. Open a new document based on the form template **Check Request Form**.

8. Save the document as **Completed Check Request** followed by your initials.

9. Use the following responses to complete the form:

Person requesting check:	Lowry Brown
Amount of check:	330.66
Make check payable to:	Lowry Brown
Explain what the check is for:	Equipment Repairs
Amount approved:	330.66
Account number:	566
Check number:	1298

10. Save your changes. Print and close the document.

PROJECT 8-3

1. Create a new document template.

2. Key the form illustrated in Figure 8-13.
   A. Use a 12 pt font.
   B. Double-space the entire form.
   C. Format the title Arial 16 pt bold.

FIGURE 8-13

REVENUE RECEIPT FORM — *ARIAL 16pt BOLD*

12 pt

Double Space

Received from:
Date:
Amount:
To be applied to the following revenue account:
    Fundraisers:
        Nut sales
        Bottle drive
        Vg's receipts
    Logo clothing
    Project donations
    Show donations
    Activities and banquet
    Miscellaneous:

3. Save the document as **Revenue Receipt Form** followed by your initials.

4. Insert form fields as follows:
   A. Press the **spacebar** before inserting each form field.
   B. Insert a Regular text form field for *Received from* and key the default text **Enter name here.** Format the form field for 13 pt italic text.

C. Insert a Current date form field for *Date*.

D. Insert a Number form field with the $#,##0.00;($#,##0.00) format for *Amount*.

E. Insert check box form fields before each of the revenue accounts. Leave a space between the check box and the account name.

F. Press the **spacebar** after *Fundraisers* and insert a drop-down form field for the three options shown in Figure 8-13.

G. Rearrange the items in the drop-down list box so they are in ascending alphabetical order.

H. Insert a Regular text form field for *Miscellaneous* and key the default text **Enter explanation here.** Format the form field for 13 pt italic text.

5. Protect the document.

6. Save your changes and close the document.

7. Open a new document based on the form template **Revenue Receipt Form**.

8. Save the document as **Completed Revenue Receipt** followed by your initials.

9. Use the following responses to complete the form:

Received from: Jenny Lambrecht
Amount: 3121.50

The money received was from Nut sales in the Fundraisers account.

10. Save your changes. Print and close the document.

11. Move any templates you created in this lesson to the location of your other solution files.

CRITICAL THINKING

SCANS

ACTIVITY 8-1

Tony's supervisor asked him to create an online form to gather information from people who visit the company's Web site. The information requested on the form includes title, name, address, phone, e-mail address, and so forth. Tony created check box fields for *Married* and *Single* status. Tony wondered if he could automate the check box field so that if the user selected the Married check box, a new text form field would display asking for *Name of spouse*. Can Tony automate the template? If so, how? Use the Help feature to find the answer.

ACTIVITY 8-2

Tony's supervisor was impressed with the online form he created for the Web site, so she asked Tony to create another form to be used on the company's intranet. This new form requires a calculation. Tony needs to calculate the difference between the value in the cell in the 6th row of column D and the value in the cell in the 27th row of column E. What function should Tony use to perform the calculation? Write the formula.

CUSTOMIZING FEATURES

OBJECTIVES

Upon completion of this lesson, you should be able to:

- Create a personal template.
- Attach your personal template to a document.
- Customize toolbars.
- Create a macro.
- Create a toolbar button to run a macro.
- Run a macro.
- Edit a macro.
- Copy, rename, and delete a macro.
- Use a macro to create a template.
- Set AutoCorrect exceptions.
- Create a custom dictionary.

⏱ Estimated Time: 1 hour

You have learned many ways to automate routine tasks in Office. You can use wizards, templates, and AutoText entries. However, you might perform some tasks repeatedly that are time consuming because they require a series of Word commands and instructions. A *macro* enables you to group these commands and instructions together as a single command to complete the task automatically. You can quickly access a macro by clicking a toolbar button or using a shortcut keyboard combination. Word provides macros ready for you to use or you can create your own.

Macros are stored in Word's templates. Before you begin creating macros, you need to understand more about Word's templates.

Working with Templates

Every Microsoft Word document is based on a template. The template affects the basic structure of a document and contains document settings such as AutoText entries, fonts, and page layout. The two basic types of templates are *global templates* and *document templates*. Global templates contain settings that are available to all documents. Word's default global template is the *Normal template*. Document templates contain settings that are available only to documents based on that template.

The macros Word provides are stored in the Normal template, so you can use the macro with every Word document. For example, each time you insert a footnote or AutoFormat a table, Word runs a macro to complete the task. When you create your own macros in this lesson, you will store the macro in a personal template that you will create in the next Step-by-Step.

Concept Builder

If prompted to save changes to the global Normal template upon exiting Word, click **No**.

Creating a Personal Template

By default, Word stores macros in the Normal template. Because you may share your computer with students in other classes, you will create an individual personal template in which to store the macros you create in this lesson.

You already know how to create a template using the Blank Document in the New dialog box. (You used this feature in Lesson 8 to create form templates.) You will use the same procedure here to create a personal template. To prompt Word to alert you to changes in the Normal template, you will turn on the option shown in Figure 9-1. Turning on this prompt will remind you to save changes to your personal template rather than to the Normal template.

FIGURE 9-1
Save tab in the Options dialog box

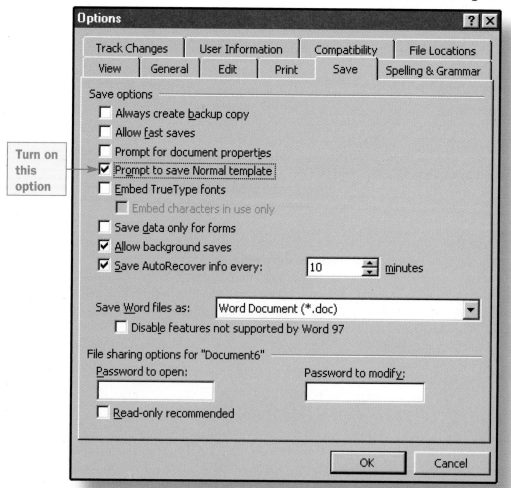

S TEP-BY-STEP ▷ 9.1

1. Open the **File** menu and choose **New**.

2. Click the **General** tab, if necessary, and select **Blank Document**.

3. In the *Create New* box, click the **Template** option.

4. Click **OK**. A new, blank template document opens on your screen.

5. Click the **Save** button.

6. You should save this template file in the root directory for the location of your data and solution files. In the *Save in* box, select the drive that contains your data and solution files.

7. In the *File name* box, key your first and last name.

8. Notice that the *Save as type* box displays *Document Template*. Word will automatically add the extension .dot because this is a template file.

9. Click **Save**.

10. Open the **Tools** menu and choose **Options**.

11. Click the **Save** tab, and if necessary, turn on *Prompt to save Normal template*. Then click **OK**.

12. Close the document.

Attaching Your Personal Template to a Document

Before you begin to create and save macros, you need to attach your personal template to the document in which you will create the macros. Also, when you plan to run a macro that is saved in your personal template, you must first attach your personal template to the document.

To attach your personal template, open the Tools menu and click Templates and Add-Ins. The Templates and Add-ins dialog box opens, as shown in Figure 9-2. Click Attach to open the Attach Template dialog box. Locate your personal template in this dialog box, select it, and then click Open. The name of your personal template should then display in the *Document template* box in the Templates and Add-ins dialog box. Click OK to close the dialog box.

FIGURE 9-2
Templates and Add-ins dialog box

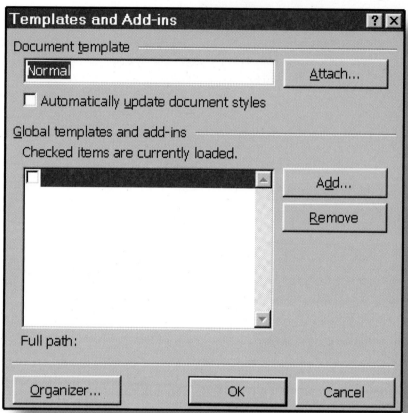

S TEP-BY-STEP ▷ 9.2

1. Click the **New** button to open a new document window.

2. Open the **Tools** menu and choose **Templates and Add-Ins**. The Templates and Add-ins dialog box opens.

3. Click **Attach** to display the Attach Template dialog box.

4. In the *Look in* box, select the drive that contains your data and solution files.

5. Select the desired template (your personal template, in this case).

6. Click **Open**. Your personal template should now display in the *Document template* box in the Templates and Add-ins dialog box, as shown in Figure 9-3.

7. Click **OK**. Leave the document open for the next Step-by-Step.

FIGURE 9-3
Dialog box with personal template selected

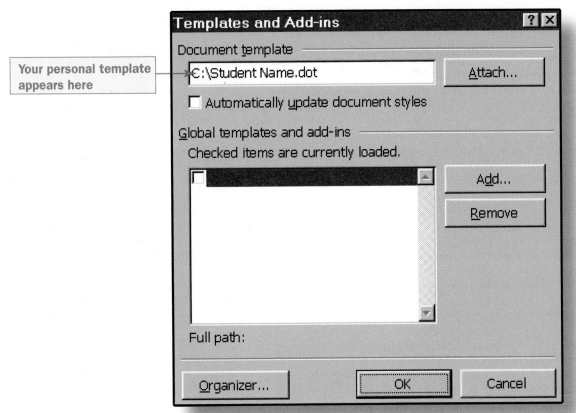

Your personal template appears here

Customizing Toolbars

As you become more proficient in Word, you may find that you frequently use commands that are not provided in the toolbars available. You have two options. You can customize the buttons that are displayed on the toolbars that Word provides, or you can create your own toolbar. Not only can you customize the toolbars with Word's built-in commands, you can also assign macros, fonts, styles, and AutoText entries to toolbars.

Create your own toolbar to customize by opening the Tools menu and clicking Customize. In the Customize dialog box, click the Toolbars tab, as shown in Figure 9-4, and then click the New button. The New Toolbar dialog box opens. Here you can key a name for the toolbar and choose a template to store it in. After you click OK, you can click the Commands tab to add buttons to the toolbar. In the *Categories* list, choose a category. The toolbar buttons available for that category appear in the Commands pane of the dialog box. To add one of these buttons to your toolbar, simply click on it and drag it to your toolbar.

FIGURE 9-4
Toolbars tab in the Customize dialog box

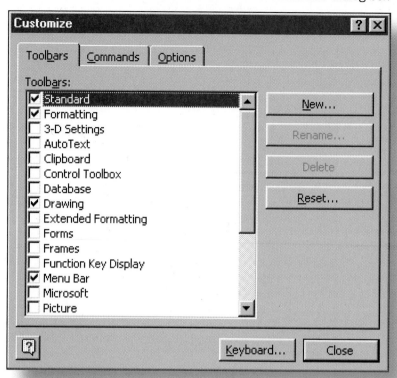

When you create a toolbar, you can make it available to the Normal template or to any other template that you specify. The toolbar is then available whenever the document is based on the template or when the template is attached to the document. At any time, you can modify the toolbar and/or delete it. In the following Step-by-Step, you will create your own custom toolbar to use in this lesson.

Hot Tip

To delete a custom toolbar that you created, select the toolbar name in the Toolbars tab of the Customize dialog box and then click **Delete**. When prompted, click **OK** to delete the toolbar and then click **Close** in the Customize dialog box.

S TEP-BY-STEP ▷ 9.3

1. Open the **Tools** menu, choose **Customize**, and then click the **Toolbars** tab.

2. Click **New** to open the New Toolbar dialog box. Key your initials in the *Toolbar name* box and select your personal template in the *Make toolbar available to* box.

3. Click **OK** to close the New Toolbar dialog box, but leave the Customize dialog box open. The new toolbar (a small box) will float on your screen.

4. Click the **Commands** tab. Under *Categories*, select **Edit**. Under *Commands*, select **Repeat**, and then drag the button to the new toolbar.

5. Under *Categories*, select **View**. Under *Commands*, select **Header and Footer**, and then drag the button to the new toolbar.

6. Under *Categories*, select **Insert**. Under *Commands*, select **Page Break**, and then drag the button to the new toolbar.

7. Click **Close** to close the dialog box. Leave the document open for the next Step-by-Step.

Working with Macros

To create a macro, you record the sequence of actions to complete a task. When recording a macro, you can use the mouse to choose commands and click icons. However, you cannot record mouse movements within the document window. For example, you cannot click the mouse to position an insertion point or drag to select text. Instead, you must use keystrokes to complete these actions.

Recording a Macro

Before you begin to create a macro, plan the steps you will record. Any mistakes and corrections you make as you record will be saved in the macro. Avoid messages Word might display that require a response from you. For example, if you record an action to close a document, Word may ask you to save the changes to the document. To avoid this message, record a step to save the document before closing it.

To record a macro, open the Tools menu, click Macro, and then choose Record New Macro from the submenu. The Record Macro dialog box opens, as shown in Figure 9-5. In this dialog box, you key a name for the macro, indicate where it should be stored, and if desired key a description of the macro's actions. You can also assign the macro to a toolbar button or to a keyboard shortcut to save time in running the macro.

Hot Tip

Macro names must begin with a letter and can contain up to 80 letters and numbers. The name cannot contain spaces or symbols.

If you choose to assign the macro to a keyboard shortcut, the Customize Keyboard dialog box opens, similar to the one in Figure 9-6. To assign a shortcut key combination for the macro, click in the *Press new shortcut key* box and then press the keys you want to use for the shortcut. If you choose shortcut keys that are already assigned to other commands or functions, Word will display a message indicating that those keys have already been assigned. Click Assign to assign the macro to your shortcut keys. You must then tell Word what template to save the shortcut in by clicking the down arrow in the *Save changes in* list box. To store the shortcut in your personal template, make sure you select your template in this drop-down list, as shown in Figure 9-7.

You do not have to assign your macro to a keyboard shortcut (or a toolbar button). If you do not assign either, you can run your macro by opening the Tools menu, choosing Macro, selecting Macros, selecting the macro name, and clicking Run.

FIGURE 9-5
Record Macro dialog box

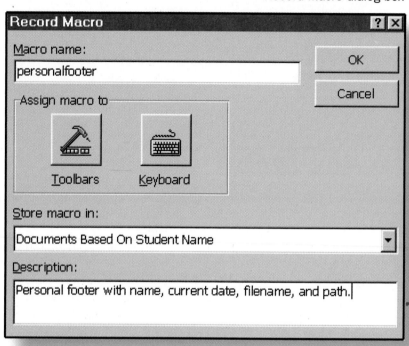

FIGURE 9-6
Customize Keyboard dialog box

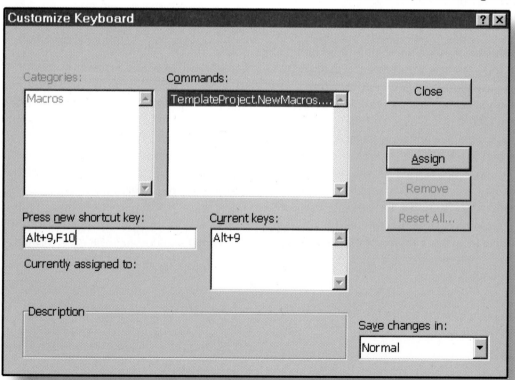

FIGURE 9-7
Select your personal template
under *Save changes in*

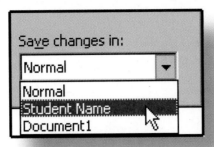

S TEP-BY-STEP ▷ 9.4

1. Open the **Tools** menu and choose **Macro**.

2. Select **Record New Macro**. The Record Macro dialog box appears.

3. Complete the Record Macro dialog box:
   a. In the *Macro name* box, key **personalfooter**.
   b. In the *Store macro in* box, select **Documents Based On [Your Name]** (your personal template).
   c. In the *Description* box, key **Personalized footer with name, filename, and path.**

4. Under *Assign macro to*, select **Keyboard**. The Customize Keyboard dialog box appears.

5. Assign the macro to a keyboard combination:
   a. With the insertion point in the *Press new shortcut key* box, press **Alt + 9**. If Word tells you that the **Alt + 9** key combination is already assigned, choose another similar combination.
   b. Click **Assign**.

c. In the *Save changes in* box, select your personal template.

Concept Builder

If you do not see your personal template listed under *Save changes in*, you did not attach your personal template to the document.

---

d. Click **Close**.

6. Note that **REC** is highlighted in the status bar and the Stop Recording toolbar appears (Figure 9-8). The mouse pointer changes to a pointer with a cassette tape.

FIGURE 9-8
Stop Recording
toolbar

(continued on next page)

7. Perform the actions to insert your path and file name in a footer:

Hot Tip

Remember that from here on every action is being recorded as part of the macro, so be sure you understand the instructions before performing each action.

a. Click the **Header and Footer** button on your custom toolbar.

b. Click the **Switch Between Header and Footer** button.

c. Key your name.

d. Press **Tab** twice.

e. Click **Insert AutoText** and then select **Filename and path**.

f. Click **Close** on the Header and Footer toolbar.

8. Click the **Stop Recording** button on the Stop Recording toolbar.

9. Close the document without saving the changes. When prompted to save the changes to your personal template, click **Yes**.

Concept Builder

If *Filename and path* was not available in Insert AutoText, you need to click AutoText on the Insert menu, click AutoText on the submenu, and change the *Look in* box of the AutoText tab to *All active templates*.

Running a Macro

Sometimes computer viruses are stored in macros, so Word 2000 offers security levels for running macros. When you open a template or load an add-in that was already installed when you installed Word 2000, macros within the file are automatically enabled. However, when you run a macro that you or someone else created, you may need to change the security level for running macros. Unless your network administrator enforces a security level, you can change the security level at any time as you work by choosing Macro on the Tools menu and selecting Security in the submenu. Then select the desired security level. When you set the security level to Medium, Word displays a warning whenever it encounters a macro from a source that is not on your list of trusted sources (see Figure 9-9). You can choose whether to enable or disable the macros in this warning box.

Concept Builder

You can maintain a list of trusted macro sources so Word will automatically enable macros from those sources. You can view the list by choosing **Macro** on the **Tools** menu, selecting **Security** in the submenu, and clicking on the **Trusted Sources** tab. You can add a source to the list when you attempt to open a document containing a macro from a source not on the list. Turn on *Always trust macros from this source* when the security warning is displayed.

FIGURE 9-9
Macro warning dialog box

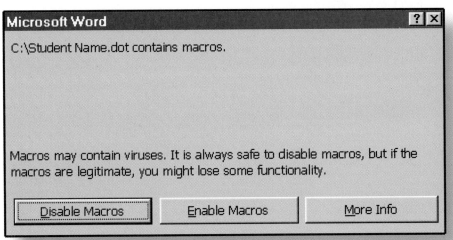

Microsoft Word

C:\Student Name.dot contains macros.

Macros may contain viruses. It is always safe to disable macros, but if the macros are legitimate, you might lose some functionality.

| Disable Macros | Enable Macros | More Info |

STEP-BY-STEP ▷ 9.5

1. Open the **Tools** menu, choose **Macro**, and then choose **Security**. Make a note of the setting before you change it so you can reset the security to its original setting at the end of the lesson.

2. If necessary, change the security setting to **Medium**. Click **OK**.

3. Click the **New** button to open a new document.

4. Attach your personal template.

5. A dialog box appears explaining that the template you attached contains macros.

6. Click **Enable Macros**.

7. Run the macro by pressing the shortcut keys **Alt + 9**.

8. Click the **Print Preview** button to view the footer you just inserted.

9. Close the document without saving the changes.

Concept Builder

If your macro did not run correctly, create the macro again using the same name. Answer *Yes* when asked if you want to replace the existing macro.

Creating a Toolbar Button to Run a Macro

An alternative to assigning a shortcut key combination is to create a toolbar button to run a macro. After naming the new macro, click Toolbar in the Record New Macro dialog box. Word opens the Customize dialog box. Click the Commands tab, as shown in Figure 9-10. The *Commands* list shows the name of the macro (it will be similar to *TemplateProject.NewMacros* plus your macro's name). Click the macro name and drag it onto the toolbar where you want it to display.

FIGURE 9-10
Commands tab in the Customize dialog box

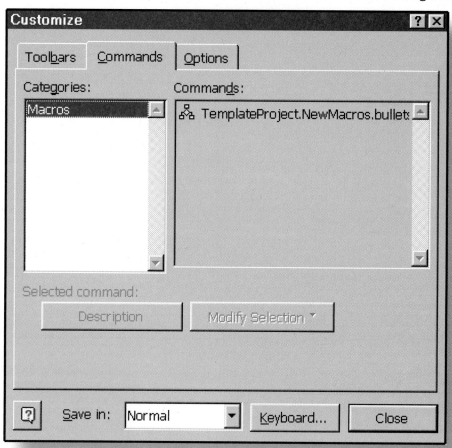

You can modify your toolbar button by clicking the Modify Selection button in the Customize dialog box. You must save your changes in your personal template. At any time, you can easily remove the toolbar button by holding down Alt while you drag the button off the toolbar.

STEP-BY-STEP ▷ 9.6

1. Click **New**, attach your personal template, and if prompted, enable macros.

2. Open the **Tools** menu, choose **Macro**, and then click **Record New Macro**.

3. Create a macro to customize a bullet symbol for bulleted lists:
   a. In the *Macro name* box, key **bullets**.

b. In the *Store macro in* box, select **Documents Based On** your personal template.

c. In the *Description* box, key **Bullets with customized font size and indents.**

d. Under *Assign macro to*, select **Toolbars**. The Customize dialog box opens. Click the **Toolbars** tab and select your custom toolbar. (When selected, the toolbar name should have a check mark.)

e. Click on the **Commands** tab. Click on the new toolbar button name (*TemplateProject.New-Macros.bullets*) in the *Commands* box and drag the name to position it on your custom toolbar.

f. Click **Modify Selection** and then select Default Style. The toolbar name changes to a button.

g. Select your personal template in the *Save in* box.

h. Click **Close** to close the Customize dialog box.

4. Record the macro:

a. Open the **Format** menu and choose **Bullets and Numbering**.

b. Click the first bullet option in the first row (to the right of *None*).

c. Click **Customize** to display the Customized Bulleted List dialog box.

d. Click **Font**.

e. Change the font size to **14** and then click **OK** in the Font dialog box.

f. Under *Bullet position*, change the *Indent at* setting to 1 inch.

g. Under *Text position*, change the *Indent at* setting to 1.5 inches.

h. Click **OK**.

i. Click the **Stop Recording** button on the Stop Recording toolbar. Close the document without saving. If prompted to save changes to your personal template, click **Yes**.

5. Open **AW Step9-6** from the student data files and save the document as **Recycling Paper** followed by your initials.

6. Attach your personal document and enable macros.

7. Select all the paragraphs except the last blank paragraph in the document.

8. Click the new toolbar button to run the macro.

9. Deselect the text. Print the document.

10. Reset the Bullets and Numbering dialog box: Open the **Format** menu and choose **Bullets and Numbering**. Click on the first bullet option in the first row (to the right of *None*) and then click **Reset**. Click **Yes** to reset the bullet to its original settings.

11. Save your changes and close the document.

 Hot Tip

The new button still displays on the Formatting toolbar, but the macro is not available unless your personal template is attached to a document.

12. Hold down **Alt** and drag the new icon off the Formatting toolbar to remove it.

 ## Editing a Macro

When you record a macro, Word stores the macro instructions in a programming language called Visual Basic. Each macro is stored in a module within the Visual Basic Editor. Generally when you want to change a macro, it will be easiest for you to re-record it. However, if the macro is complex and the changes you want to make are minor, such as changing the font size or font type, you might find it easier and quicker to edit the macro using the Microsoft Visual Basic Editor.

To edit a macro, open the Tools menu, choose Macro, and then click Macros. Click the macro you want to edit and then click Edit to open the Microsoft Visual Basic Editor, similar to Figure 9-11. Each instruction you recorded in the macro appears in Visual Basic code. You can make changes to the macro by changing the code. If desired, you can print the macro steps.

FIGURE 9-11
Microsoft Visual Basic Editor

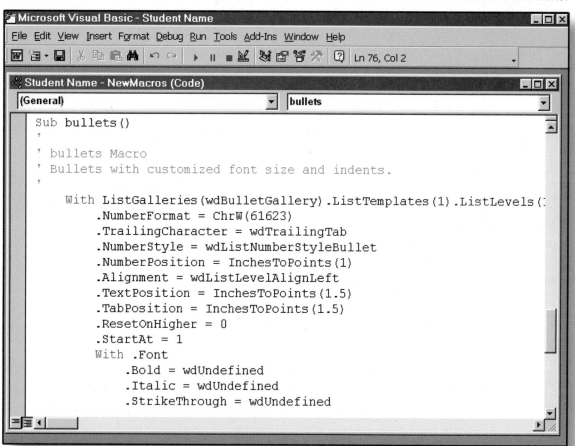

```
Microsoft Visual Basic - Student Name
File  Edit  View  Insert  Format  Debug  Run  Tools  Add-Ins  Window  Help

                                                        Ln 76, Col 2

Student Name - NewMacros (Code)
(General)                              bullets

Sub bullets()
'
' bullets Macro
' Bullets with customized font size and indents.
'
    With ListGalleries(wdBulletGallery).ListTemplates(1).ListLevels(
        .NumberFormat = ChrW(61623)
        .TrailingCharacter = wdTrailingTab
        .NumberStyle = wdListNumberStyleBullet
        .NumberPosition = InchesToPoints(1)
        .Alignment = wdListLevelAlignLeft
        .TextPosition = InchesToPoints(1.5)
        .TabPosition = InchesToPoints(1.5)
        .ResetOnHigher = 0
        .StartAt = 1
        With .Font
            .Bold = wdUndefined
            .Italic = wdUndefined
            .StrikeThrough = wdUndefined
```

S TEP-BY-STEP ▷ 9.7

SCANS

1. Click the **New** button to open a new document. Attach your personal template and enable macros.

2. Open the **Tools** menu, choose **Macro**, and then click **Macros**.

3. Even though you deleted the new button from the Formatting toolbar, the **bullets** macro is still stored in your personal template. In the *Macro name* box, select **bullets**.

4. Click **Edit** to display the Microsoft Visual Basic Editor and the new macros in your personal template.

Hot Tip

To maximize the view of the macro steps, close the Project - TemplateProject and the Properties - NewMacros panes.

5. Scroll down through the macro steps until you see the line *Size = 14*. (See Figure 9-12.)

FIGURE 9-12

```
    .AllCaps = wdUndefined
    .Hidden = wdUndefined
    .Underline = wdUndefined
    .Color = wdUndefined
    .Size = 14          Line speciying size
    .Animation = wdUndefined
    .DoubleStrikeThrough = wdUndefined
    .Name = "Symbol"
End With
```

6. Change 14 to **20**.

7. Click the close box to close the New-Macros(Code) dialog box.

8. Click the **Save** button to save the changes to your personal template and then close the Visual Basic window.

9. Key your first and last names and then select the text.

10. Open the **Tools** menu, choose **Macro**, and then select **Macros**.

11. If necessary, select **bullets** and then click **Run**. Notice that the bullet is now a larger font size.

12. Deselect the text. Leave the document on the screen for the next Step-by-Step.

Copying, Renaming, and Deleting a Macro

When you store macros in your personal template, the macros are stored as a collection in a macro project. The default name for the macro project is NewMacros. You can copy this macro project to the Normal template, or you can rename it. Copying the macro project to the Normal template makes the macros available to all documents associated with the Normal (the default) template. Renaming a macro project helps you to keep your macros organized. You can also delete a macro project when you know you no longer want to use the macros stored in it.

To copy, rename, or delete a macro project, open the Tools menu, choose Macro, and then click Macros. In the Macros dialog box, click Organizer to open the Organizer dialog box, shown in Figure 9-13. In the *Macro Project Items available in* drop-down list box, choose your personal template. The macro project for that template appears in the *In* list box. To copy all macros from your personal template to the Normal template, click Copy. To rename the macro project, click Rename and then key a new name for the project. Click Delete to remove all macros from your personal template.

You can delete a single macro from your personal template in the Macros dialog box. Simply click the macro name and then click Delete.

FIGURE 9-13
Organizer dialog box

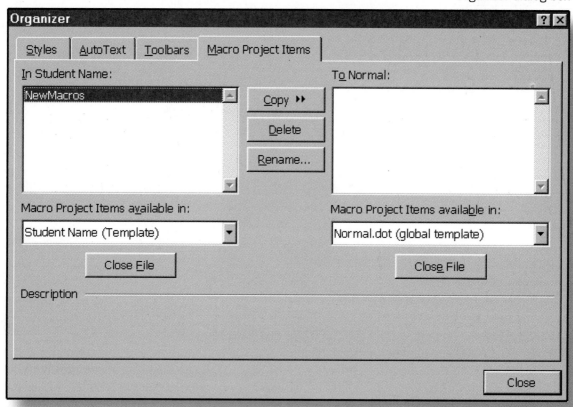

STEP-BY-STEP 9.8

SCANS

1. Open the **Tools** menu, choose **Macro**, and then select **Macros**.

2. Click **Organizer**. The Organizer dialog box opens.

3. If necessary, click the **Macro Project Items** tab.

4. On the left side of the dialog box, under *Macro Project Items available in*, click the down arrow and select your personal template. **NewMacros** is displayed in the list box on the left. Select **NewMacros** if necessary.

5. Click **Rename** and key **Macros**. Click **OK**.

6. Click **Close.**

7. Delete the bullets macro:
   a. Open the **Tools** menu, select **Macro**, and then select **Macros**.
   b. In the *Macro name* box, select **bullets**.
   c. Click **Delete**. Click **Yes** when asked if you want to delete the macro.
   d. Click **Close.**

8. Close the file without saving changes to the document. When prompted, do save changes to your personal template.

Using a Macro to Create a Template

The macros you have recorded so far have been simple, carrying out only a few instructions. You can, however, record macros that carry out a great many instructions. You can use a single macro, for example, to create a template to be applied to your documents.

In the next Step-by-Step, you will record a macro that sets up a document with formats common in reports. Each time you run the macro, it is as if you have applied a report template to your document.

S TEP-BY-STEP ▷ 9.9

SCANS

1. Click the **New** button, attach your personal template, and enable macros.

2. Create a macro to format a standard report:
   a. Open the **Tools** menu, choose **Macro**, and then choose **Record New Macro**.
   b. In the *Macro name* box, key **reportsetup**.
   c. In the *Store macro in* box, select **Documents Based On** your personal template.
   d. In the *Description* box, key **Standard report formats.**
   e. Under *Assign macro to*, select **Keyboard** and then key **Alt + 7**.
   f. Select your personal template in the *Save changes in* box.
   g. Click **Close**.

3. Record the macro:
   a. Open the **File** menu and choose **Page Setup**. Change the left and right margins to **1** inch.
   b. Press **Ctrl + 2** to change the line spacing to double.

   c. Open the **Format** menu and choose **Paragraph**. Format a first-line indent of 0.5 inch and set the paragraph spacing to **6** before and **0** after.
   d. Stop recording.

4. Close all open documents. Do not save the changes to the current document but do save the changes to your personal template.

5. Open a new document, attach your personal template, and enable macros.

6. Run the macro. Key a few lines of text to see if all your macro instructions are carried out. If the macro did not run successfully, make sure the steps you recorded are complete, and try again.

7. Close the document without saving the changes.

Customizing the AutoCorrect Feature

You already know AutoCorrect automatically corrects misspelled words immediately after an error is keyed. The words or text that will automatically be corrected are displayed in the AutoCorrect dialog box, shown in Figure 9-14. If you misspell the word as shown in the left column, Word will automatically replace the word with the correct spelling shown in the right column.

FIGURE 9-14
AutoCorrect dialog box

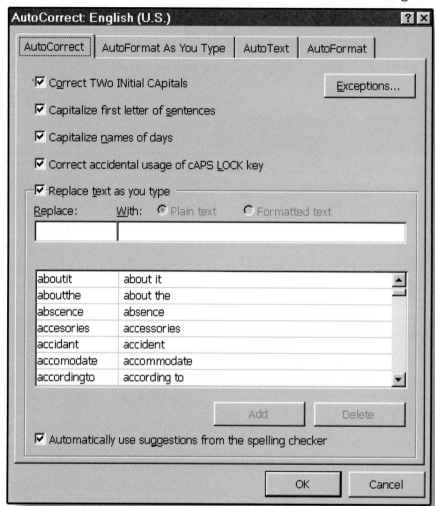

You can also use AutoCorrect to quickly insert text that you use over and over again. For example, you can create an AutoCorrect entry for your initials, so that every time you key your initials and a space, Word will automatically insert your full name.

If you know you frequently key certain words incorrectly, you can add the misspelling and the correct spelling to the AutoCorrect list. You can also set exceptions for the AutoCorrect feature so that it does not automatically correct certain words or spellings.

Adding an AutoCorrect Entry

To add words to the AutoCorrect list, open the Tools menu and choose AutoCorrect. Then key the AutoCorrect entry in the *Replace* box and the text you want Word to automatically insert in the *With* box. To remove an AutoCorrect entry, select it and then click the Delete button.

In the next Step-by-Step you will add a new word to the AutoCorrect list. However, because you may be sharing a computer, you will also delete the new word at the end of the Step-by-Step.

 Did You Know?

You can add words to the Auto-Correct list when using the spelling checker by clicking the AutoCorrect option in the Spelling and Grammar dialog box.

S TEP-BY-STEP ▷ 9.10

SCANS

1. In a new document window, open the **Tools** menu and choose **AutoCorrect**. The AutoCorrect dialog box displays the types of errors Word will automatically correct. If necessary, turn on all the options so your screen matches Figure 9-14.

2. Scroll through the list of frequently misspelled words until you see *agian* in the left column. Note that Word will automatically correct this misspelling to *again*.

3. Position the insertion point in the *Replace* box and key **wrd**. Tab to the *With* box and key **word**. Click **Add** and then click **OK**.

4. Key the following sentence exactly as shown with the misspelled words: **Sometimes we misspell the same wrd agian and agian.** As soon as you press the **spacebar** or end the sentence with a period, Word immediately corrects the misspelling.

5. Open the **Tools** menu and choose **AutoCorrect**. Key **wrd** in the *Replace* box. Word scrolls to that AutoCorrect entry in the list box.

6. Select the entry *wrd* in the left column, click **Delete**, and then click **OK**.

7. Leave the document open for the next Step-by-Step.

Setting AutoCorrect Exceptions

You can also customize AutoCorrect to *not* make specific types of corrections automatically. For example, personal, company, and product names often have unique spellings and/or capitalization. To store these names that you don't want Word to correct automatically, open the Tools menu, choose AutoCorrect, and then click Exceptions. The AutoCorrect Exceptions dialog box opens as shown in Figure 9-15.

FIGURE 9-15
AutoCorrect Exceptions dialog box

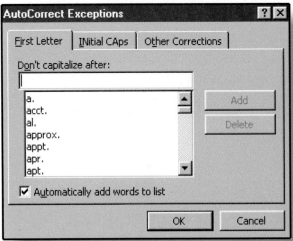

You can create a list of exceptions for three different categories: (1) words or text you don't want Word to capitalize after, (2) words or text in initial caps, and (3) other corrections that don't fall within the first two categories. To add an exception, key the exception in the text box on the appropriate tab and then click Add.

In the next Step-by-Step, you will create two AutoCorrect exceptions. However, because you may share your computer, you will delete the exceptions at the end of the Step-by-Step.

STEP-BY-STEP ▷ 9.11

SCANS

1. Open the **Tools** menu, choose **AutoCorrect**, and then click **Exceptions**. The AutoCorrect Exceptions dialog box opens. Notice that Word already provides a list of exceptions for first-letter capitalizations.

2. On the **First Letter** tab, key the abbreviation **Mfg.** in the *Don't capitalize after* box. Click **Add**. Normally, Word would capitalize after the period in *Mfg.*, but this exception will prevent Word from capitalizing the next word after *Mfg.*

3. Click the **INit CAps** tab. In the *Don't correct* box, key **EXcel** and then click **Add**. Normally, Word would lowercase the second capital letter in the

word *EXcel*, but this exception will prevent Word from making that AutoCorrect change.

4. Click **OK** twice. Key the following sentence: **The merger of EXcel and Durand Mfg. is almost complete.**

5. Open the **Tools** menu, choose **AutoCorrect**, and click **Exceptions**. Locate and select the **mfg.** entry and click **Delete**. On the **INitial CAps** tab, select the entry **EXcel** and click **Delete**. Click **OK** twice.

6. Close the screen without saving the changes.

Creating a Custom Dictionary

I f you frequently use proper names and acronyms that are not in Word's main dictionary, you will find it helpful to add those names to a custom dictionary. You can create several custom dictionaries. For example, you can create one for legal terms, one for medical terms, and another for engineering terms.

To create a custom dictionary, open the Tools menu, choose Options, and click the Spelling & Grammar tab. Click Dictionaries to open the Custom Dictionaries dialog box. Then click New to open the Create custom dictionary dialog box, shown in Figure 9-16. Specify a location for your new custom dictionary and then key a name for it. Click Save.

If the custom dictionary is active before you begin to use the spelling checker in a document, Word will check both the main dictionary and the custom dictionary before presenting unknown terms in the spelling checker. If desired, you can have up to 10 custom dictionaries active at the same time. To activate a custom dictionary, select the dictionary in the Custom Dictionaries dialog box.

If you select the custom dictionary before you use the spelling checker, you can quickly add a word to the dictionary while using the spelling checker. When Word presents a term as an unknown word, click Add. To add, delete, or edit words directly in the custom dictionary, select the dictionary in the Custom Dictionaries dialog box and then click Edit. Each word must be entered in a separate paragraph.

FIGURE 9-16
Create custom dictionary dialog box

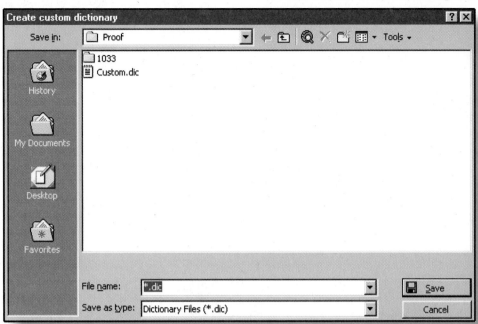

STEP-BY-STEP ▷ 9.12

SCANS

1. In a new document window, open the **Tools** menu, choose **Options**, and click the **Spelling & Grammar** tab.

2. Click **Dictionaries** to open the Custom Dictionaries dialog box.

3. Click **New** in the Custom Dictionaries dialog box to display the Create custom dictionary dialog box. In the *Save in* box, locate the folder where your data files are saved. In the *File name* box, key **UltraTech** followed by your initials. Click **Save**. Word will automatically add the .dic extension.

4. Select the dictionary **UltraTech** in the Custom Dictionaries dialog box and then click **Edit**. If you see a dialog box indicating that automatic spell check stops, click **OK**.

5. The dictionary file opens. Currently the dictionary contains no entries. Enter the following words exactly as shown, pressing **Enter** after each word:

   ```
   UltraTech
   coextrusion
   coextrusions
   ```

6. Save the custom dictionary document and then close the document.

7. Open **AW Step9-12** from the student data files and save the document as **Research Study** followed by your initials.

8. Open the **Tools** menu, choose **Options**, and click the **Spelling & Grammar** tab if necessary. Make sure *Check spelling as you type* is turned on. Click **Dictionaries** and select **UltraTech** if necessary. Click the *Custom dictionary* down

(continued on next page)

arrow and select the **UltraTech** custom dictionary. Click the **Check Document** button at the bottom of the dialog box and then click **Yes**. Click **OK**.

9. Right-click on the first unknown word *Lepri* and select **Add** in the pop-up menu. The word is added to the UltraTech dictionary. Right-click each of the remaining unknown words underlined in red and add them to the custom dictionary.

10. Save the changes to **Research Study**. Print and close the document.

11. Open the custom dictionary file, delete the word *Lepri*, and then save the changes and close the document.

Concept Builder

If prompted to save changes to the global Normal template upon exiting Word, click **No**.

Summary

In this lesson, you learned:

- There are two basic types of templates: global templates and document templates. *TOOLS > TEMPLT + ADD-IN*

- You can customize toolbars with buttons you use frequently. *TOOLS > CUSTOMIZE or VIEW > CUSTOMIZE*

- To create a macro, you record the sequence of actions required to complete a task. *TOOLS > MACRO > REC*

- Word 2000 enforces a security level for running macros. Depending on the security level, you may need to enable macros when you open a document. *TOOLS > MACRO > SECURITY*

- To run a macro saved in your personal template, your personal template must be attached to the document. *TOOLS > TEMPLT + ADD-INS > ATTACH*

- When you create a macro, you can assign a shortcut key or you can create a new toolbar button and add it to a toolbar.

- When you want to change a macro, you can re-record it or you can edit it in the Microsoft Visual Basic Editor.

- The Organizer enables you to copy and rename macros. *TOOLS > MACRO > MACROS > ORGANIZER*

- You can delete macros that you create.

- AutoCorrect entries can save you time entering frequently used or misspelled text.

- If you often key text that is not in the main dictionary, you can save time when using the spelling checker by creating a custom dictionary to store these terms. *TOOLS > OPTIONS > SPELLING + GRAMMAR > DICTIONARIES*

TOOLS MENU
Spelling + Grammar   Track Changes   Mail Merge   Macro
Language   Merge Docs   Envelopes + Labels   Templates
Word Count   Protect Docs.   Letter Wizard   Customize
Autosummarize   Online collaboration   Options
Autocorrect

LESSON 9 REVIEW QUESTIONS

TRUE/FALSE

Circle T if the statement is true or F if the statement is false.

T F 1. A macro groups commands and instructions together as a single command.

T F 2. When recording a macro, you cannot select text using the mouse.

T **F** 3. The formats created in a macro cannot be changed unless you record the macro again.

T **F** 4. Word automatically checks all custom dictionaries when the spelling checker is used.

T **F** 5. You must create all macros that you plan to use.

T **F** 6. You must know the keyboard shortcut to run a macro.

FILL IN THE BLANKS

Complete the following sentences by writing the correct word or words in the blanks provided.

1. To attach your personal template to a document, open the _____Tools_____ menu and choose _Templates + Add-Ins_

2. To record a macro, open the Tools menu, choose Macro, and then choose _Record New Macro_

3. To delete a macro, open the Tools menu, choose Macro, and then choose _Macros_____.

4. To remove a button that you added to a toolbar, hold down _____Alt_____ and drag the button off the toolbar.

LESSON 9 PROJECTS

PROJECT 9-1

1. Open a new document, attach your personal template, and enable macros.

2. Record a new macro that includes the following steps for formatting a table. Name the macro **tablesetup**. Store the macro in documents based on your personal template. Describe the macro as **Formatted table with 3 columns.** Assign the shortcut keys **Alt + 6** and save the changes in your personal template.
   - **A.** Create a table with 10 rows and 3 columns.
   - **B.** Center and key the following column headings in the first row: **Name**, **Title**, and **Date Hired**.
   - **C.** Center the table horizontally.
   - **D.** AutoFit the table to its contents.

3. Close the document without saving. When prompted, save the changes to your personal template.

4. Open a new document, attach your personal template, and enable macros.

5. Run the **tablesetup** macro.

6. Complete the table by entering the information illustrated in Figure 9-17. The table columns will automatically expand to accommodate the text you enter.

Hot Tip

Do not select the entire table or any cells within the table to apply the formats described. Use the menus and icons on the toolbars to apply the formats. For example, to center the column headings, click in each of the cells and then click Center.

FIGURE 9-17

Name	Title	Date Hired
Tuttle, Agnes	Sales Manager	8-30-86
Gibson, Ike	Sales Representative	7-7-96
Mercier, Karen	Office Manager	6-6-87
Swearingen, Pat	Manager	6-15-91
Cirsanti, Juanita	Director	6-15-90
Lee, Roger	Manager	4-5-88
Curran, Terry	Administrative Assistant	5-31-90
David, Brian	Manager	3-4-90

7. Run the macro for your **personalfooter**.

8. Save the document as **Staff** followed by your initials and clear the screen.

PROJECT 9-2

1. Open a new document, attach your personal template, and enable macros.

2. Edit the **tablesetup** macro to create a table with **20** rows (instead of 10).

3. Save the changes and clear the screen.

4. If you changed the security settings to enable macros, open the Tools menu, choose Macro, then choose Security, and reset the security level to its original setting.

CRITICAL THINKING

ACTIVITY 9-1

Celeste was recording a macro when she was interrupted by a co-worker who needed to get some information from a file that was stored on Celeste's computer. Naturally, Celeste didn't want to stop recording the macro and then have to start all over again. Was there any way Celeste could stop recording the macro and then finish recording the macro later?

Explain. Use the Help feature to find the answer.

ACTIVITY 9-2

Part of Celeste's macro involved selecting text. Since she cannot use the mouse to select text in a macro, how can she select the following parts of the document using the keyboard? Use the Help feature to find the answers.

- Select to the beginning of a line   *Home*
- Select one line up   ↑
- Select to the beginning of a word   *Control ← or →*
- Select to the beginning of the document   *Control + Home*
- Select to the end of the document   *Control + End*

LESSON 10

CREATING INDEXES AND TABLES OF CONTENTS

OBJECTIVES

Upon completion of this lesson, you should be able to:

- Identify index entries.
- Indicate a range of pages for an index entry.
- Create an index entry for a cross-reference.
- Compile an index.
- Update an index.
- Create and compile a table of contents using heading styles.
- Create and compile a table of contents using fields.
- Format a first page differently from subsequent pages.
- Update a table of contents.

⏱ **Estimated Time: 1 hour**

Creating and Modifying an Index

An index is a valuable tool when it includes the right choice of index entries. Index entries often include the main ideas and/or subjects of the document, various headings and subheadings, special terms, and cross-references to acronyms, synonyms, and other topics. The index is usually formatted with multiple levels of entries. The entries in the first level are called main entries. The entries in the second level are called subentries. Depending on the detail of the index, additional levels of subentries can be formatted.

Insert → Index + Table of Contents

Word makes it easy to create an ***index*** and a ***table of contents*** using the Index and Tables command. If you plan to include both an index and a table of contents in your final document, you should create the index first so that the page numbers for the index can be included in the table of contents.

Identifying Index Entries

To create an index, open the Insert menu and click Index and Tables. The Index and Tables dialog box opens, as shown in Figure 10-1. Click the Index tab, if necessary. You are now ready to identify (mark) the text in your document that you want to appear as entries in the index.

FIGURE 10-1
Index tab in the Index and Tables dialog box

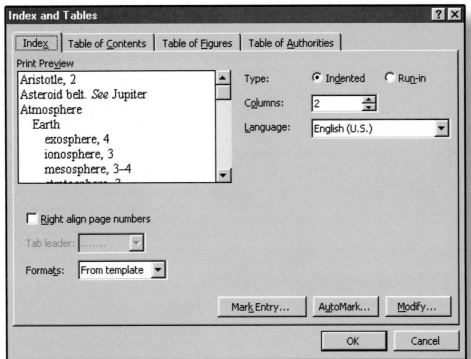

Click Mark Entry to open the Mark Index Entry dialog box, shown in Figure 10-2. You can mark index entries in this dialog box using either of two methods:

■ Select the text in the document window and then simply click Mark in the dialog box.

■ Position the insertion point at the end of the text to be indexed. (If the insertion point is placed before the text, during pagination a page break may be inserted between the index entry and the text.) After positioning the insertion point, key the index entry text in the dialog box and then click Mark.

To mark all occurrences of the same text throughout the document as index entries, click Mark All. To create a subentry that will print below

FIGURE 10-2
Mark Index Entry dialog box

a Level 1 index entry, first key the Level 1 entry in the *Main entry* box. Then key the subordinate (Level 2) entry in the *subentry* box. You can create a sub-subentry (Level 3) by keying first the Level 1 entry, then the Level 2 entry. In the *Subentry* box, add a colon after the subentry and key the Level 3 entry.

When you mark an index entry, Word inserts a *field* at the location of the insertion point, as shown in Figure 10-3. In order to display these fields, Show/Hide ¶ must be on. The XE in the field stands for *index entry*. The index entry text is enclosed in quotation marks. A backslash (\) within the field is known as a **switch**. The switch provides additional instructions such as bold and italic character formats.

FIGURE 10-3
Index entry field inserted in document

FINANCIAL·PERFORMANCE·AND·SOLVENCY{·XE·"FINANCIAL·
PERFORMANCE·AND·SOLVENCY"·\b·\i·}¶

STEP-BY-STEP ▷ 10.1

Once you begin creating index entries, do not close the Mark Index Entry dialog box until instructed to close it in Step-by-Step 10.3. The dialog box should remain open so you can mark multiple index entries.

1. Open **AW Step10-1** from the student data files and save the document as **Financial Review** followed by your initials.

2. Open the **Tools** menu and choose **Options** and click the **View** tab. Under *Formatting marks*, make sure that the **Hidden text** option is turned off. If necessary, click the check box to remove the check mark.

3. Identify a main (Level 1) index entry by selecting text:
   a. Select the words *FINANCIAL PERFORMANCE AND SOLVENCY* in the first heading (do not include the paragraph mark in your selection).
   b. Open the **Insert** menu and choose **Index and Tables**. The Index and Tables dialog box opens. If necessary, click the **Index** tab.
   c. Click **Mark Entry**. Word displays the Mark Index Entry dialog box. Notice that some of the selected text is displayed in the *Main entry* box.

 Hot Tip

The shortcut keys to open the Mark Index Entry dialog box are Alt + Shift + X.

   d. Turn on *Bold* and *Italic* near the bottom of the dialog box to format page number references in bold and italic in the index.
   e. Click **Mark**. If necessary, move the dialog box so you can see the field for the index entry.

4. Identify a main (Level 1) index entry without selecting text:
   a. Scroll down and position the insertion point at the end of the heading *ACCOUNTING SYSTEMS*.
   b. Click an insertion point in the *Main entry* box (the current entry will disappear). Click in the box again to position the insertion point in the box.
   c. Key **Accounting Systems**. Notice that it is not necessary to turn on Bold and Italic. They are already selected.
   d. Click **Mark**.

Hot Tip

Typographical errors can affect the accuracy of your index. Proofread each index entry for which you key the entry text. If you find an error after you click Mark, position the insertion point in the field text in your document and make the necessary correction.

5. Create a Level 2 subentry under a main entry:
   a. Position the insertion point at the end of the subheading *Chart of Accounts*.
   b. Position the insertion point in the *Main entry* box.
   c. Key the main entry **Accounting Systems**.
   d. Position the insertion point in the *Subentry* box and key the Level 2 subentry **chart of accounts**.
   e. Click **Mark**.

6. Create additional Level 2 subentries for *general ledger, board/finance committee minutes and reports, long-range plan, annual report, facility reports,* and *audits.* Use **Accounting Systems** each time as the main entry.

7. Create a Level 3 subentry under a main heading:
   a. Scroll up and position the insertion point at the end of the heading *Accounts Payable*.
   b. Position the insertion point in the *Main entry* box and key the main entry **Accounting Systems**.
   c. Position the insertion point in the *Subentry* box. Key the name of the Level 2 subentry, a colon, and the name of the Level 3 subentry as follows: **general ledger:accounts payable**.
   d. Click **Mark**.

8. Create additional Level 3 index subentries (use **Accounting Systems** as the main entry each time and **general ledger** for the Level 2 subentry) for *accounts receivable, cash accounts, investments, payroll,* and *payroll taxes.*

9. Save your changes and leave the document open for the next Step-by-Step. Also leave the Mark Index Entry dialog box open.

Hot Tip

Any word in the document can be identified as an index entry. Index entries do not have to be headings.

Using Bookmarks to Indicate a Range of Pages

The entries you have created constitute a basic index. If you want to indicate a range of pages for an index entry that spans several pages, you create a *bookmark*. A bookmark identifies a specific location in a document.

To reference a range of pages with a bookmark, first mark the index entry and select *Page range* under *Options* in the Mark Index Entry dialog box. Identify the page range by entering a bookmark name in the *Bookmark* text box. Then select the text in the document that is to be included in the page range. Open the Insert menu and choose Bookmark to display the Bookmark dialog box, similar to Figure 10-4. In the Bookmark dialog box, enter the same bookmark name that you used in the Mark Index Entry dialog box. Click Add to create the bookmark.

Concept Builder

A bookmark name can be up to 40 characters, and it must begin with a letter. The bookmark name can contain only letters, numbers, and the underscore character and can contain no spaces.

FIGURE 10-4
Bookmark dialog box

SCANS

1. Scroll to the heading *FINANCIAL MANAGEMENT* and position the insertion point at the end of the heading.

2. Position the insertion point in the *Main entry* box and key **Financial Management**.

3. Click **Page range** under *Options*.

4. Key **financial** in the *Bookmark* box.

5. Click **Mark**.

6. If necessary, scroll up slightly or move the dialog box. Notice that the index field contains a switch for a bookmark (\r *financial*).

7. Select the heading *FINANCIAL MANAGEMENT* and all the text below it (down to the end of the document).

8. Open the **Insert** menu and choose **Bookmark**. The Bookmark dialog box opens on top of the Mark Index Entry dialog box.

 **Hot Tip**

Ctrl + Shift + F5 is a shortcut for Insert Bookmark.

9. Key **financial** in the *Bookmark name* box.

10. Click **Add**. Then deselect the text.

11. Save your changes and leave the document open for the next Step-by-Step. Leave the Mark Index Entry dialog box open.

Creating a Cross-Reference

Creating Indexes and Tables of Contents

You can also follow an entry with text instead of a page number to create a ***cross-reference*** in the index. A cross-reference refers the reader to another index entry. When marking the index entry, select *Cross-reference* under *Options* in the Mark Index Entry dialog box. Then enter the text to be used as a cross-reference.

STEP-BY-STEP ▷ 10.3

SCANS

1. Go up to the subheading *Investments* on page 2 (under *General Ledger*) and position the insertion point at the end of the words *investment decisions* in the first sentence.

2. Position the insertion point in the *Main entry* box and key **investment decisions**.

3. Click *Cross-reference* under *Options* and key the text for the cross-reference, keying a space after each comma: **Accounting Systems, general ledger, investments**. (Word automatically places

the text you key to the right of *See* in the text box.) Word will print the word *See* in italic before the cross-reference text in your index.

4. Click **Mark**. Notice the cross-reference notation in the field in your document.

5. Click **Close** to close the Mark Index Entry dialog box.

6. Save your changes and leave the document open for the next Step-by-Step.

Compiling an Index

After all index entries have been marked, you can pull them together to create the index. This is known as *compiling* the index. It is important that you compile the index after you make all changes and revisions to your document. If you make changes to the document after the index is created, the page number references in the index may no longer be correct, and you will then need to update your index.

Show/Hide ¶ must be turned off before you compile the index. As Word compiles the index, the document is paginated. When hidden text characters (such as the fields for the index entries) are displayed, Word treats them as text rather than as hidden text, which may make the page numbers in the index inaccurate.

To compile the index, position the insertion point where you want to insert the index and then open the Insert menu, choose Index and Tables, and select the Index tab. Select either a normal or run-in type and specify the number of columns. Entries are arranged in alphabetical order with letters inserted as separators. The entry text is separated from the page number by a comma and a space.

A normal index displays all subentries indented below the main entry. To save space, a run-in index can be created, displaying subentries on the same line as the main entries. The index can also be divided into sections, with blank lines or letters separating each section. Generally, you will format the index on a page by itself at the end of the document.

STEP-BY-STEP ▷ 10.4

1. Move the insertion point to the end of the document and insert a page break.

2. If necessary, click the **Show/Hide ¶** button to turn off the display of nonprinting characters.

(continued on next page)

3. Open the **Insert** menu and choose **Index and Tables**. If necessary, click the **Index** tab.

4. Under *Type*, click **Run-in**.

5. Under *Formats*, select **Classic** from the drop-down list. Notice in the *Print Preview* box that subentries begin on the same line as the main entries and are separated by semicolons.

6. Click **Indented**. Notice in the *Print Preview* box that subentries are indented below the main entry.

7. Click **OK**.

8. If necessary, switch to Print Layout view and compare your screen to Figure 10-5. Line endings vary from printer to printer, so do not be concerned if your page numbers do not match exactly those shown in the illustration.

 Hot Tip

If your document does not run onto page 4 when hidden text is turned off, you will not see a page range for *Financial Management*.

9. Save your changes and leave the document open for the next Step-by-Step.

FIGURE 10-5
Displayed portion of compiled index

A

Accounting Systems, *1*
　annual report, *3*
　audits, *3*
　board/finance committee minutes and
　　reports, *2*
　chart of accounts, *1*
　facility reports, *3*
　general ledger, *1*
　　accounts payable, *1*
　　accounts receivable, *1*
　　cash accounts, *2*
　　investments, *2*

　payroll, *2*
　payroll taxes, *2*
　long-range plan, *3*

F

Financial Management, *3–4*
FINANCIAL PERFORMANCE AND
　SOLVENCY, *1*

I

investment decisions. *See* Accounting
　Systems, general ledger, investments

Updating an Index

Although the index should be created after editing is completed, there may be occasions when changes need to be made after the index is compiled. If any editing changes affecting page breaks are made to the document, index entries may move to different pages, and page breaks throughout the document may change. The page number references in the index may therefore no longer be accurate. When this happens, the index must be updated. Since the index entries are formatted as fields, you simply need to update the fields in the index. You can do this quickly by clicking in the index and pressing F9.

When you update the entire index, any text or formatting you added to the finished index is lost.

STEP-BY-STEP ▷ 10.5

1. Scroll up in the document and select the heading *Board/Finance Committee Minutes and Reports* and the paragraph below the heading. Move the text to just below *AC-COUNTING SYSTEMS.*

2. If necessary, turn off **Show/Hide ¶**.

3. Click in the index and press **F9** to update the index fields.

4. Scroll to the top of the index. Notice that the *board/finance committee minutes and reports* entry is now listed as appearing on page 1.

5. Switch to Normal view.

6. Position the insertion point in front of the *A* at the top of the index and insert a blank line.

7. Key **INDEX** in the new blank paragraph. Change the text to **12** pt.

8. Select the new heading (including the following paragraph mark), click the **Column** button on the Standard toolbar, and select one column.

9. Open the **Tools** menu, choose **Options**, and then select the **Print** tab. If necessary, turn off *Hidden text*, and then click **OK**.

10. Save your changes. Print only the page containing the index and close the document.

Creating and Modifying a Table of Contents

A table of contents provides an overview of the topics in a document. In Print Layout view, you can use the table of contents to quickly locate page numbers for specific information. In Web Layout view, the entries in the table of contents are formatted as hyperlinks. When you click on the hyperlink, the insertion point jumps to the topic.

A table of contents can be created based on heading styles already applied within the document. These heading styles may be custom styles that you applied, built-in heading styles supplied by Word, or outline-level styles assigned when you create a document in outline format. The alternative to using heading styles is to insert field codes to define the table of contents entries.

Show/Hide ¶ must be turned off when you compile or print the table of contents, or hidden text characters (such as your index fields) will be included when Word paginates. With hidden text included, page numbers in the table of contents may be inaccurate. As you did with the index, be sure to compile the table of contents after all editing is completed, or you may need to recompile the table of contents to ensure page numbers are accurate.

To create a table of contents, position the insertion point where you want the table to appear. Open the Insert menu and click Index and Tables. Click the Table of Contents tab (Figure 10-6) and select options for your table of contents.

When Word compiles the table of contents, it is inserted at the location of the insertion point. Each entry in the table of contents is formatted on a separate line. The entry name is separated from the page number by a tab character, and the page numbers are right aligned at the right margin.

Using Heading Styles to Create a Table of Contents

The easiest way to create a table of contents is to use Word's outline heading styles. Two levels of heading styles have already been applied in the document you will work with in Step-by-Step 10.6. If you work with a document with several heading style levels, you can specify the number of heading levels to be included in the table of contents.

FIGURE 10-6
Table of Contents tab in the Index and Tables dialog box

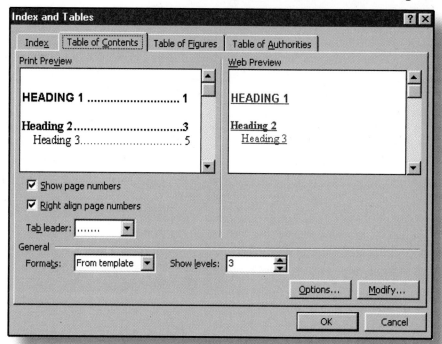

S TEP-BY-STEP ▷ 10.6

1. Open **AW Step10-6** from the student data files and save the document as **Cleanup** followed by your initials.

2. Position the insertion point at the beginning of the document and insert a page break.

3. Position the insertion point on the page break.

4. If necessary, turn off **Show/Hide ¶**.

5. Open the **Insert** menu and choose **Index and Tables**. The Index and Tables dialog box opens.

6. Click the **Table of Contents** tab. If necessary, click **Show page numbers** and **Right align page numbers**.

7. Select **Classic** under *Formats* and click **OK**.

8. Compare your screen to the illustration in Figure 10-7. (Page numbers may vary as a result of different printer settings.)

9. Move the insertion point to the top of the table of contents (the table of contents will be shaded) and press **Enter**.

10. Position the insertion point on the blank line and key **TABLE OF CONTENTS**.

11. Save your changes. Print the first two pages of the document. Close the document.

FIGURE 10-7
Compiled table of contents

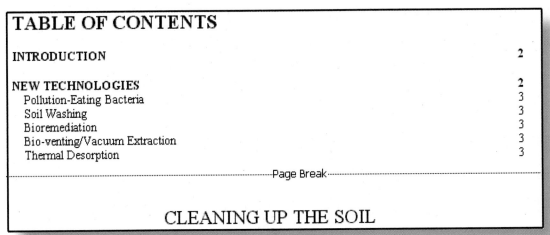

TABLE OF CONTENTS

INTRODUCTION	2
NEW TECHNOLOGIES	2
Pollution-Eating Bacteria	3
Soil Washing	3
Bioremediation	3
Bio-venting/Vacuum Extraction	3
Thermal Desorption	3

·······························Page Break·······························

CLEANING UP THE SOIL

Inserting Fields to Create a Table of Contents

FIGURE 10-8
Field dialog box

If your document does not have obvious headings for every table of contents entry (or if your headings are not formatted with heading styles), you can create the table of contents using fields. Position the insertion point where you want to reference a page number. Open the Insert menu and choose Field. The Field dialog box opens, similar to Figure 10-8.

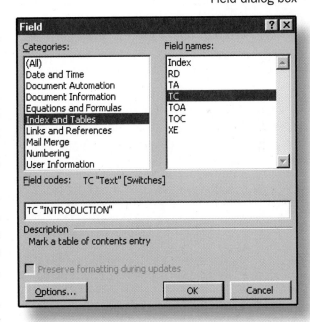

Select Index and Tables in the *Categories* list. In the *Field names* list, click the TC field. Then in the *Field codes* box, enter the text for the table of contents entry. If no level is specified for the entry, Level 1 is assumed. To specify a different level, click Options in the Insert Field dialog box, select the \l switch, and enter a level number.

By default, Word builds a table of contents by styles. If you insert fields to identify the table of contents entries, you must change this default before compiling the table of contents. In the Index and Tables dialog box, click Options to open the Table of Contents Options dialog box, shown in Figure 10-9. Click in the *Styles* check box to turn off this option and then turn on the *Table entry fields* option.

FIGURE 10-9
Table of Contents Options dialog box

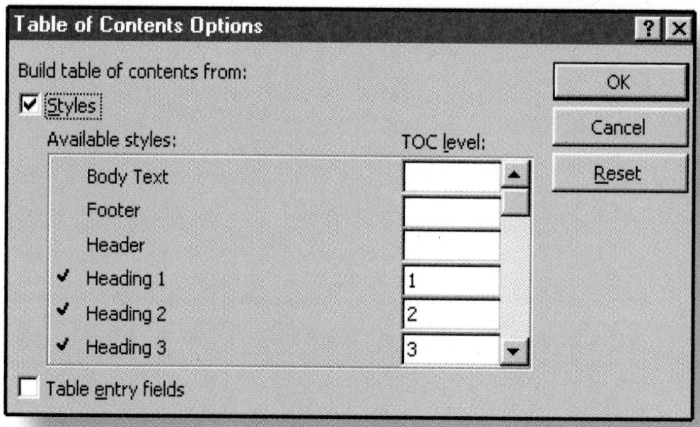

STEP-BY-STEP ▷ 10.7

1. Open **AW Step10-7** from the student data files and save the document as **Solid Waste** followed by your initials.

2. If necessary, turn on **Show/Hide ¶** so that you will see your table of contents field entries as you create them. (They will be formatted as hidden text.)

3. Add a Level 1 table of contents entry in a field:
   a. Position the insertion point before the tab symbol at the beginning of the first paragraph, which begins, *Solid waste . . . .* This is where the page number is to be referenced.
   b. Open the **Insert** menu and choose **Field**. The Field dialog box appears.
   c. Under *Categories*, click **Index and Tables**.
   d. Under *Field names*, click **TC** (not TOC).
   e. Position the insertion point in the *Field codes* box after the blank space that follows *TC*.
   f. Key **"INTRODUCTION"**. Be sure to key the quotation marks.
   g. Your dialog box should look like Figure 10-8. Click **OK**.

4. Position the insertion point before the tab at the beginning of the last paragraph, which begins, *Due to the critical shortage . . . .* Create a Level 1 table of contents entry called **"CONCLUSION"**.

5. Add a Level 2 table of contents entry in a field:
   a. Position the insertion point before the tab at the beginning of the second paragraph, which begins, *There are essentially . . . .* In the *Field codes* box in the Field dialog box, key **"Disposal of Garbage"**.
   b. Click **Options**. The Field Options dialog box opens.
   c. Under *Switches*, click **\l**. Then click **Add to Field**.
   d. Click in the *Field codes* box immediately to the right of \l and key **2**.
   e. When your dialog box looks like Figure 10-10, click **OK** twice.

6. Add additional Level 2 table of contents entries as shown in the following list. Position the insertion point at the indicated position and use the name shown in parentheses for the table of contents entry names.
   a. At the beginning of the fifth paragraph, which begins, *Much of the notion that . . .* (**Biodegradation**).

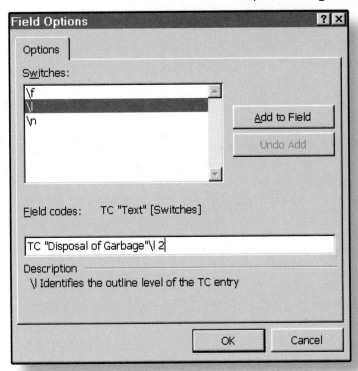

FIGURE 10-10
Field Options dialog box

b. At the beginning of the sixth paragraph, which begins, *Landfills also contain . . .* (**Hazardous Waste**).

c. At the beginning of the seventh paragraph, which begins, *Currently, there is . . .* (**Shortages of Landfills**).

d. At the beginning of the eighth paragraph, which begins, *Many landfills now . . .* (**Leachate**).

e. At the beginning of the eleventh paragraph, which begins, *The use of sanitary landfills . . .* (**Challenges**).

7. Compile the table of contents using the field entries:

a. Position the insertion point at the beginning of the document, insert a page break, and then position the insertion point at the beginning of the document again.

b. If necessary, turn off **Show/Hide ¶**.

c. Open the **Insert** menu and choose **Index and Tables**. If necessary, click the **Table of Contents** tab.

d. Select **Modern** under *Formats*.

e. Click **Options**. Word displays the Table of Contents Options dialog box.

f. Turn off *Styles* and turn on *Table entry fields*.

g. Click **OK** twice. Word compiles a table of contents.

8. Create a heading for the table of contents:

a. Move the insertion point to the top of the table of contents.

b. Press **Enter**.

c. Position the insertion point on the blank line and key **TABLE OF CONTENTS**.

d. Save your changes and leave the document open for the next Step-by-Step.

Format the First Page Differently from Subsequent Pages

The page on which the table of contents appears should be numbered separately from the rest of the document. Usually page numbers for front matter such as a table contents are formatted in lowercase Roman numerals. Therefore, when you format page numbers, you need to format the first page differently from subsequent pages in the document. You can format two different sets of page numbers in the same document by creating different sections for the page numbers.

STEP-BY-STEP ▷ 10.8

1. Split the document into two sections:
   a. Click the page break following the table of contents and press **Delete**.
   b. Open the **Insert** menu and choose **Break**. Then select **Next page** and click **OK**.

2. Format the page numbers in the report section:
   a. With the insertion point positioned in the section containing the heading *LANDFILLS*, open the **Insert** menu and choose **Page Numbers**.
   b. Change the *Position* to **Top of page (Header)** and leave the alignment set at *Right*. Turn off *Show number on first page*. — *leave this on, we are in a different section*
   c. Click **Format**. Click on **Start at** and select or key **1** in the *Start at* box. Then click **OK** twice.

3. Format the page numbers in the table of contents section:
   a. Move the insertion point to the table of contents heading and choose Insert Page Numbers. Leave the *Position* set for the top of the page and Alignment set at *right*. *Show number on first page* should be turned on.
   b. Click **Format** and change the number format to *i, ii, iii*.
   c. Click **OK** twice.

4. Save your changes and leave the document open for the next Step-by-Step.

Updating a Table of Contents

Generally, the table of contents is compiled after the document is finalized. If the document is subsequently revised, the changes could affect pagination, and the page numbers in the table of contents might no longer be correct. When this happens, the table of contents must be updated (recompiled). You can update a table of contents that was compiled from either outline headings or fields.

When you update the entire table of contents, any text or formatting you added to the finished table of contents is lost. Position the insertion point in the table of contents and press F9. Word will prompt you to update the page numbers or to update the entire table of contents.

STEP-BY-STEP ▷ 10.9

1. Turn on **Show/Hide ¶**.

2. Scroll down and select the paragraph beginning *Currently there is a critical shortage . . .* (include the table of contents entry and the ending paragraph mark).

3. Move the paragraph up so that it precedes the paragraph beginning *Landfills also contain . . . .* Be sure you position the text in front of the table of contents entry for that paragraph.

4. Update the table of contents:

  a. Turn off **Show/Hide ¶**.

  b. Move the insertion point to the top of the document and then press the down arrow once to select the table of contents.

  c. Press **F9**. When the Update Table of Contents dialog box is displayed, select **Update entire table** and click **OK**.

5. Save your changes. Print and close the document.

Summary 3/22/04, 917

In this lesson, you learned:

- It is important that you make all changes and revisions before creating an index so the page number references will be correct.

- To create an index, you must first identify the index entries.

- Word enables you to format bookmarks and cross-references to create more complex index entries.

- The easiest way to create a table of contents is to use Word's heading styles, but you can also create a table of contents using fields.

- If the document is revised, you can update the index and the table of contents.

LESSON 10 REVIEW QUESTIONS

TRUE/FALSE

Circle T if the statement is true or F if the statement is false.

T F **1.** If you plan to include both an index and a table of contents in your final document, you should create the index first.

T F **2.** If a document is outlined or is formatted with heading styles, it is quick and easy to create and compile a table of contents.

T **F** **3.** If you are keying an index entry, it does not matter whether you position the insertion point at the end or the beginning of the text to be indexed. *Should use beginning*

T F **4.** A cross-reference is an index entry followed by text instead of a page number.

FILL IN THE BLANKS

Complete the following sentences by writing the correct word or words in the blanks provided.

1. If any editing changes affecting page breaks are made to the document, the index and the table of contents should be ____*updated*____.

2. If you want to indicate a range of pages for an index entry that spans several pages, you mark the page range with a(n) ____*bookmark*____.

3. Pulling all the index entries together is called ____*compiling*____ the index.

4. A(n) _____normal_____ index displays all subentries below the main entry.

5. If your document does not have obvious headings for every table of contents entry, you will want to create the table of contents using _____fields_____.

6. To save space when subentries occur, a(n) _____run-in_____ index can be created displaying subentries on the same line as the main entries.

LESSON 10 PROJECTS

SCANS

PROJECT 10-1

1. Open **AW Project10-1** from the student data files and save the document as **Job Description** followed by your initials.

2. Mark Level 1 index entries for the first occurrence of each of the following terms found in headings. Use initial caps for the entries rather than all caps. Format the page numbers for the index entries in bold and italic.

   Title
   Purpose
   Term
   Attendance
   Responsible to
   Responsibilities
   Duties
   Resignation

3. Mark Level 2 index subentries for the following terms under the headings marked above. Mark the first occurrence of the term after the main level that is indicated below. For example, mark the first occurrence of *occasionally* after the main index entry *Attendance*. Key the subentries using lowercase. Format the page numbers for the index entries in bold and italic.

   Attendance/occasionally
   Attendance/regularly
   Responsibilities/administration
   Responsibilities/financial
   Responsibilities/membership
   Duties/attendance
   Duties/leadership
   Duties/participation

4. Mark Level 3 index subentries for the each of the following terms when they first occur after the main entry *Attendance* and the subentry *regularly*. Format the page number for the index entry in bold and italic.

   Attendance/regularly/monthly board meetings
   Attendance/regularly/standing committee
   Attendance/regularly/ad hoc committee
   Attendance/regularly/special events

5. Mark the word *POWERS* with a cross-reference to *Responsibilities*. (Key the index entry as **Powers**.)

6. Insert a page break at the end of the document and then compile an indented index. Use the *Classic* format.

7. Add the heading **INDEX** at the top of the index and then format the heading and paragraph mark for one column.

8. Save your changes and leave the document open for the next Step-by-Step.

PROJECT 10-2

1. Insert a next page section break at the beginning of the document.

2. Enter fields for table of contents entries for the following headings and the index. Because these headings are all the same level, there is no need to format a switch for the level of the entry.

TITLE
PURPOSE
TERM
MEETING ATTENDANCE
RESPONSIBLE TO
RESPONSIBILITIES
SPECIFIC DUTIES OF A MEMBER OF THE BOARD OF TRUSTEES
RESIGNATION
INDEX

3. Compile the table of contents and add the heading **TABLE OF CONTENTS** at the top of the table of contents page.

4. Format page numbers as follows:
   A. Format a lowercase roman numeral at the bottom center of the table of contents page.
   B. Format the 1,2,3 number format in the report section at the bottom center, but do not print a page number on the first page of the report.

5. Save your changes. Print and close the document.

CRITICAL THINKING

SCANS

ACTIVITY 10-1

Carmen is creating an index for a very long document. Specific text is repeated throughout the document, and she needs to mark each occurrence as an index entry. Is there a way Carmen can automatically mark each occurrence? Use the Help feature to find the answer. *Use a concordance file + Automark.*

ACTIVITY 10-2

Several individuals in Carmen's workgroup have contributed to the document, and all of the workgroup members reviewed the document before final copy was prepared. Carmen inserted a few bookmarks in the document to help team members locate information quickly. One of the team members asked Carmen to explain bookmarks and describe how they are created. Write one or two paragraphs describing what Carmen should say in her response to the team member.

Advanced Microsoft Word

COMMAND SUMMARY

FEATURE	MENU COMMAND	TOOLBAR BUTTON	LESSON
AutoFit a table	Table, AutoFit		2
Bookmark	Insert, Bookmark		10
Calculate	Table, Formula		1
Center a table horizontally	Table, Table Properties, Table		2
Chart	Insert, Picture, Chart		2
Columns, balance	Insert, Break, Continuous		4
Combine documents	Tools, Merge Documents		7
Comments	Insert, Comment		7
Compare documents	Tools, Track Changes, Compare Documents		7
Convert text to tables	Table, Convert, Text to Table		2
Drop caps	Format, Drop Cap		5
Embed object	Insert, Object		2
Endnotes	Insert, Footnote		6
Footnotes	Insert, Footnote		6
Graphic, size	Format, Picture		5
Hyperlink, create	Insert, Hyperlink		6
Index	Insert, Index and Tables, Index		10
Insert a file	Insert, File		6
Link object	Insert, Object		2
Macro, edit	Tools, Macro, Macros		9

FEATURE	MENU COMMAND	TOOLBAR BUTTON	LESSON
Macro, record	Tools, Macro, Record New Macro		9
Macro, run	Tools, Macro, Macros		9
Merge envelopes	Tools, Mail Merge		3
Merge form letters	Tools, Mail Merge		3
Merge mailing labels	Tools, Mail Merge		3
Merge table cells	Table, Merge Cells		2
Page border	Format, Borders and Shading, Page Border		5
Picture, insert	Insert, Picture, From File		5
Properties, changing file	File, Properties		7
Protect a document	Tools, Protect document		7
Routing documents	File, Send To, Routing Recipient		7
Shading	Format, Borders and Shading		5
Sort	Table, Sort		1
Split table cells	Table, Split Cells		2
Symbol, insert	Insert, Symbol		8
Table, delete rows	Table, Delete, Rows		2
Table, insert columns	Table, Insert		2
Table, insert rows	Table, Insert		2
Table of contents	Insert, Index and Tables, Table of Contents		10
Text flow	Format, Paragraph		6
Track changes	Tools, Track Changes		7
Version	File, Versions		7
Watermark	View, Header and Footer		5

MULTIPLE CHOICE

Select the best response for the following statements.

1. If you want to change a macro, you can _____ it.
   A. Edit
   B. Re-record
   C. Copy
   D. A or B

2. When preparing a mail merge, the document containing the variable text to be merged is called the _____.
   A. Merged document
   B. Main document
   C. Data source
   D. Merge field

3. Sorts can be based on _____.
   A. Any single column in a table
   B. As many as three criteria at a time
   C. The first word in a paragraph
   D. All of the above

4. Before performing a calculation in a table, _____.
   A. The insertion point should be positioned in the cell where the total (result) is to appear
   B. All blank rows should be deleted
   C. The row or column containing the figures for the calculation should be selected
   D. None of the above

5. A _____ restricts available choices in an online form.
   A. Check box form field
   B. Drop-down form field
   C. Text form field
   D. Help message

WRITTEN QUESTIONS

Key a brief answer to the following questions.

1. Distinguish between scaling a graphic and cropping a graphic.

2. Describe the advantages of using the versioning feature.

3. Explain why you would protect a document before distributing it within your workgroup.

4. Why are online forms created as a template?

5. Distinguish between linking and embedding an object.

APPLICATION 1

1. Open a new document, create a table, and key the expense report illustrated in Figure App-1.

FIGURE APP-1

CAREER SEMINAR SPONSORS
Donation Amounts

Sponsor	Donation	Date
AJ's Food Market	$545	March 4
Roma Warehouse	$1,000	March 4
Surgery Association	$650	April 6
Golden Time Jewelers	$500	May 9
Arts West	$435	May 23
Equipment Rental Depot	$650	April 6
Shear Management	$750	May 8
Whole Foods Market	$550	May 18
Commerce Bank	$1,500	May 19
Citizen's Professional, Inc.	$1,200	June 6
Furniture Supply	$1,000	June 8

2. Save the document as **Donations** followed by your initials.

3. Center the table horizontally and AutoFit the column widths to fit the cell contents.

4. Add shading to the row with the column headings and center the column headings.

5. Sort the table in ascending order based on the *Sponsor* column.

6. Move the *Donation* column to become the first column in the table.

7. Sort the table in descending order based on the *Donation* column.

8. Insert a row at the bottom of the table and then calculate the total for the *Donation* column.

9. Save your changes. Print and close the document.

APPLICATION 2

The Internet offers a dynamic means for obtaining information. A common question is how to cite Internet sources in an academic paper.

1. Use your search engine tools to find information and guidelines describing how to properly cite sources from the Internet. Include in your search topics for citing the following resources: Web page documents, pictures, video, and sound clips.

2. Compose a report explaining your findings. In the report, provide examples for each of the types of resources named in step 1.

3. Format the report as follows:
   A. Double-space the entire report.
   B. Create a title and subheadings. Format the text flow for each subheading to keep the subheading with the first paragraph that follows it.
   C. Format endnotes to cite your sources.
   D. Create an appropriate header or footer with the title and page number.

4. Save the report as **Citing Sources** followed by your initials. Print the document.

APPLICATION 3

SCANS

1. Create a new document template.

2. Key the online form illustrated in Figure App-2.

   A. Insert an appropriate symbol or graphic for the first line of the form and size the symbol or graphic as needed.
   B. Insert a drop-down form field for the location of the seminar and the date of the seminar using the following options:

   Location:

       Chicago
       Dallas
       New York
       San Francisco

   Date:

       January 15
       January 22
       January 29
       February 5

   C. Insert check box form fields for the title (*Mr.*, *Mrs.*, *Ms.*, or *Miss*).
   D. Insert text form fields for all remaining parts of the form. Limit the state field to two characters. All other text fields can be unlimited.

3. Protect the document for forms.

4. Save the template as **Sign Me Up** followed by your initials. Close the document.

5. Create a new document based on the solution **Sign Me Up**.

6. Fill in the form to register for the New York seminar on January 29. Use your name and address. Leave blank any form fields that do not apply (such as *Work phone*, *Fax*, or *E-mail*).

7. Save the document as **Registration** followed by your initials. Print the form and close the document.

APPLICATION 4

1. Open **AW App4** from the student data files and save the document as **Home Remedies** followed by your initials.

2. Create an index:
   A. Mark the following words or groups of words that occur in the paragraphs below the headings. Mark each word or group of words as main index entries with the bold and italic formats for the page numbers.
      1) Under *Minor Ills*, mark *sore throat* and *relax*.
      2) Under *Cure-Alls*, mark *bleeding gums*, *fever blister*, *eyestrain*, and *chicken pox*.
      3) Under *Insect Bites*, mark *mosquito bite*.
      4) Under *Poison Ivy/Poison Oak*, mark the first occurrence of *urushiol*, *poison ivy*, and *poison oak*.
      5) Under *Congestion*, mark *congestion*.
      6) Under *Tension Headaches*, mark *tension headache*.
      7) Under *Hiccups*, mark the first occurrence of *hiccups*.
   B. Insert a hard page break at the end of the document.
   C. Turn off **Show/Hide ¶** and compile an indented index using the *Classic* style.
   D. Add the heading **Index** at the top of the index. Format the heading for one column (including the paragraph mark) and then center the heading. Apply the Heading 1 style to the index heading so it will be included as an entry in the table of contents. Center the index heading.

3. Create a table of contents:
   A. Insert a next page section break at the top of the document.
   B. Position the insertion point on the section break, turn off **Show/Hide ¶**, and compile a table of contents using outline heading styles and leaders (the *Formats* box should show *Classic*).
   C. Add the heading **Table of Contents** at the top of the table of contents. Apply the Heading 1 style and center the heading.

4. Add page numbers to the table of contents and document sections:
   A. With the insertion point in the table of contents section, format a page number at the bottom center of the page including the first page. Change the number format to lowercase roman numerals (*i, ii, iii*).
   B. With the insertion point in the document section, format a page number at the bottom center to start at the number 1. Change the number to the 1,2,3 format and show the page number on the first page.

5. Save your changes. Print and close the document.

ON-THE-JOB SIMULATION

You are an office assistant for Charles Feenstra, the vice president of marketing for a distribution company. The sales figures for the first and second quarters are compiled, and Charles has asked you to draft a letter to be sent to each of the managers throughout the company's four regions.

JOB 1

1. Key the document illustrated in Figure J-1.

July 10, ----

xx
xx
xx
xx

Dear xx:

The national sales figures for the first and second quarters are summarized in the table below. As you can see, sales dropped during the second quarter.

Region	First Quarter	Second Quarter	Year to Date
Eastern Region	2,436,711	2,154,899	
Western Region	2,246,989	1,878,322	
Central Region	1,900,843	1,345,121	
Southern Region	1,500,676	1,321,449	
Total			

We must now focus on activities for the third quarter and carefully analyze our markets. We must make every effort to ensure that we meet our sales projections for the third quarter. When we meet next week in the national office, be prepared to describe your goals for the third quarter and how you will attain them.

Sincerely,

Charles Feenstra
National Marketing Manager

xx

2. Save the document as **Sales Figures** followed by your initials.

3. Format and sort the table:
   A. Center the column headings.
   B. Calculate row and column totals.
   C. Center the table horizontally and AutoFit the columns for contents.
   D. Sort the table in ascending alphabetical order based on the region names. Do not sort the Total row.
   E. Remove the table borders so they do not print.

4. Save your changes and print the document. Leave the document open for the next Job.

JOB 2

Mr. Feenstra has approved the letter and now asks you to prepare final copies to send to each of the regional managers.

1. Indicate the letter as the main document to be used for a form letter.

2. Open **AW Job2** from the student data files to merge with the form letter.

3. Complete the main document by substituting field names for the letters *xx* in the main document.
    A. The inside address should be formatted as follows:

        ```
        Title FirstName LastName
        JobTitle, Company
        Address
        City, State  PostalCode
        ```

    B. The *xx* in the salutation should be substituted with the FirstName field.

4. Merge the form letter to a new document and save the new document as **Merge 1** followed by your initials.

5. Close all documents, saving if prompted.

JOB 3

Mr. Feenstra recently hired three new district managers and he wants each of them to receive the form letter you created.

1. Open **AW Job2** from the student data files and save the document as **Managers**.

2. Edit the data source to include the individuals listed below.

    ```
    Ms. Heidi Baldridge      Mr. Mike Heitkamp        Ms. Marjorie Lashley
    District Manager         District Manager         District Manager
    Micro Innovations        Micro Innovations        Micro Innovations
    32 North Main Street     18 Lownes Lane           16610 SE 27 Street
    Lombard, IL 06148-2000   Springfield, PA 19064-5545   Bellevue, WA  98008-8856
    Region: Central          Region: Eastern          Region: Western
    ```

3. Sort the data source in ascending order by last name.

4. Save your changes. Close the document.

5. Open **Sales Figures** and use the Mail Merge Helper dialog box to specify **Managers** as the data source.

6. Filter the data source for district managers.

7. Merge the form letter to a new document and save the new document as **Merge 2** followed by your initials. Print the merged letters and close the document.

8. Save the **Sales Figures** document and leave it open for the next Job.

JOB 4

Mr. Feenstra is preparing for a meeting with his managers. He asks you to create a chart from the table you included in the letter to the managers.

1. Use the information in the table within the letter to create a column chart (do not chart the *Total* row). Word will automatically try to chart the blank row below your column headings. Select row 1 in the datasheet and click **Delete**. Delete any other sample data in the datasheet. Title the chart **Year to Date Sales** and place the legend at the bottom of the chart.

2. Copy the chart to the Clipboard and then close the **Sales Figures** document without saving the changes.

3. Open a new document window and paste the chart in a new document.

4. Change to landscape orientation, resize the chart to show all the data, and then center the chart horizontally.

5. Save the document as **Chart** followed by your initials. Print the chart and then close the document.

UNIT

ADVANCED MICROSOFT® EXCEL

Estimated Time for Unit: 15.5 hours

APPLYING ADVANCED FORMATS TO WORKSHEETS AND CHARTS

OBJECTIVES

Upon completion of this lesson, you should be able to:

- Apply accounting, fraction, and scientific formats.
- Create a custom format.
- Use AutoFormats.
- Apply conditional formats.
- Apply styles and data validation.
- Enhance the appearance of worksheet charts.

⏱ **Estimated Time: 1 .5 hours**

Introduction

M icrosoft Excel comes equipped with a number of advanced tools and features that empower you to create professional-looking spreadsheets that organize data and calculate complex formulas. In this lesson, you will learn how to apply advanced formatting features to data and charts on a worksheet.

Exploring Number Formats

F ormatting data changes the way it appears. For example, you can change the color of data in a cell, apply a border around a range of cells, or increase the type size of a worksheet title. You can also apply formats to give data more meaning. Excel has many formats available that you can apply to numbers, such as currency, percentage, and date and time. The more commonly used ones are explained in Table 1-1.

 Hot Tip

To select a range, simply click in the cell in the upper left corner of the range and drag to the cell in the lower right corner of the range. You also can select a range by clicking the cell in the upper-left corner, holding down the Shift key, and clicking the cell in the lower-right corner.

TABLE 1-1
Number formatting buttons

BUTTON	BUTTON NAME	WHAT THE BUTTON DOES
$	Currency Style	Applies a currency format with a dollar sign, commas between thousands, and two decimal places
%	Percent Style	Applies a percent sign with no decimal places
,	Comma Style	Displays commas between thousands and gives the cell entry two decimal places
+.0 .00	Increase Decimal	Adds one decimal place to the cell entry each time you click
.00 +.0	Decrease Decimal	Removes one decimal place from the cell entry each time you click

The Number tab in the Format Cells dialog box, shown in Figure 1-1, lists the other types of number formats you can apply. The left side of the Number tab shows the categories you can select from, such as Currency and Percentage. Options available for that category display in the right side of the dialog box. The *Sample* box shows an example of how the number will be displayed with the selected options.

Hot Tip

When you apply the currency style by clicking on the Currency Style button, the dollar signs are aligned at the left side of the cell(s). When you apply the format using the Currency option in the Format Cells dialog box, the dollar signs are flush against the numbers.

FIGURE 1-1
Number tab in the Format Cells dialog box

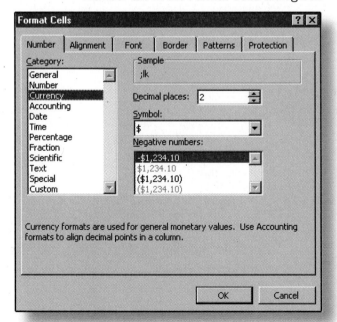

1. Open the **AE Step1-1** workbook from the student data files.

2. Save the file as **Budget** followed by your initials.

3. The data within the columns and rows should be displayed in a currency format. Select the range **B5:M11**.

4. Click the **Currency Style** button. Click outside the range to deselect it.

5. Select the range **B5:M11** again. Choose the **Format** menu and then select **Cells**.

6. Select the **Number** tab in the Format Cells dialog box, if it is not already selected.

7. Choose **Accounting** in the *Category* list box. This will ensure that the numbers in each column line up according to the decimal point and currency symbol.

8. From the *Symbol* drop-down list, select **$** and make sure the number of decimal places is **2**.

9. Click **OK**. Look at how your numbers are displayed. (Widen columns where necessary.)

10. Print the worksheet in landscape orientation and so the data fits on one page.

Concept Builder

To select landscape orientation and change other printing options, choose **Page Setup** on the **File** menu, and make appropriate changes in the Page Setup dialog box.

11. Close the workbook. Click **Yes** if you are asked if you want to save the file.

Scientific and Fraction Formats

Scientific calculations often dictate that numbers be displayed in exponential notation. Data is formatted using exponents, represented by the letter E within the format. A fraction format will display a decimal number as a fraction. For example, .25 would display as 1/4.

1. Open the **AE Step1-2** workbook from the data files.

2. Save the workbook as **Trends** followed by your initials.

3. Select the range **B5:G10**.

4. Choose the **Format** menu and then select **Cells**.

5. Select the **Number** tab, if it is not already selected.

6. Choose **Fraction** in the *Category* list box.

7. Select **Up to two digits** in the *Type* box. Change the number of decimal places to **1**.

8. Click **OK**. Look at how your numbers are displayed. (Widen columns where necessary.)

9. Open the Format Cells dialog box again, and in the *Type* box, select **Up to one digit**. Click **OK** and review how the numbers are formatted.

10. Now let's add a scientific format to the range B13:G17. Select the range **B13:G17**. Choose the **Format** menu and then select **Cells**.

11. Select the **Number** tab, if it is not already selected.

12. Choose **Scientific** in the *Category* list box and change the decimal places to **1**.

13. Click **OK** and review the scientific formatting of the range.

14. Print the worksheet in Portrait orientation and so it fits on one page. Then save and close the workbook.

Creating a Custom Format

There might be instances in which you need to apply a number format that is not already predefined. For example, the date format *Year-Month*, which would display a date in the format 2000-MARCH, is not one of the formats available in Excel. You can create your own format by selecting the *Custom* option in the *Category* list on the Number tab.

Formats are actually composed of codes. These codes are simply strings of characters that represent the actual data, such as *M* for *month*, *D* for *day*, and *Y* for *year*. You can easily create your own codes by assembling these characters in a certain order. Table 1-2 describes the various character codes you can select.

TABLE 1-2
Format codes

FORMAT CODE	WHAT IT MEANS
0	Placeholder for a digit. If there is not a digit to fill this place, a zero will hold the place.
#	Placeholder for a digit. If there is not a digit to fill this place, nothing will appear in the place.
; (semicolon)	Divides the parts of the format code.
$	Puts a dollar sign with the number at the same location it appears in the format code.
%	Puts a percent sign with the number at the same location it appears in the format code.
, (comma)	Puts a comma with the number at the same location it appears in the format code. *also used as multiplier*
. (decimal)	Puts a decimal with the number at the same location it appears in the format code.

(continued on next page)

A E - 5

TABLE 1-2
(continued)

FORMAT CODE	WHAT IT MEANS
M or m	Used for months in dates or minutes in time.
D or d	Used for days.
Y or y	Used for years.
H or h	Used for hours.
S or s	Used for seconds.

S TEP-BY-STEP ▷ 1.3

1. Open **AE Step1-3** from the student data files and save the workbook as **Personnel** followed by your initials.

2. Select the range **C5:C10**.

3. Choose the **Format** menu and select **Cells**.

4. Choose the **Number** tab, if necessary.

5. Select **Custom** in the *Category* list box.

6. Highlight the text in the **Type** text box and key **yyyy-d-mmmm**. (Entering four of the same format code tells Excel to enter the complete year number.)

7. Click **OK** and look at your dates.

8. Print the worksheet. Then save and close the workbook.

Using AutoFormat and Conditional Formatting

AutoFormat is a simple way to make your worksheet appear more professional. With AutoFormat, you can instantly format the entire worksheet at once. You don't need to select individual cells and apply individual formats; an AutoFormat is already designed for you. These formats include borders, cell shading, and data formatting. To apply an AutoFormat, select the range of cells you want to format and then select AutoFormat on the Format menu. The AutoFormat dialog box opens, as shown in Figure 1-2.

You may already be familiar with Excel's conditional formatting feature. With conditional formatting, you can apply certain formats to data that meets specified criteria. For example, if you wanted to highlight which products were your top sellers, you could specify that any product's sales that exceed a certain amount appear in red, boldface type.

FIGURE 1-2
AutoFormat dialog box

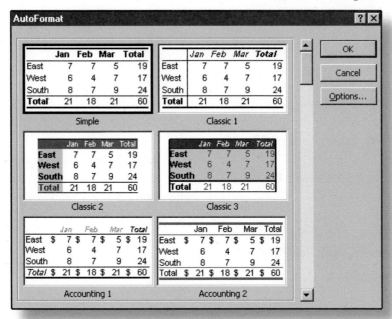

STEP-BY-STEP ▷ 1.4

1. Open **AE Step1-4** from the student data files, and save the workbook as **Formats**, followed by your initials.

2. You want to format the range **A4:M11**. Select any cell in the range.

3. Open the **Format** menu and then choose **Auto-Format**. The AutoFormat dialog box appears.

4. Choose the **3D Effects 2** selection from the AutoFormat list. Your worksheet should look similar to Figure 1-3

FIGURE 1-3
Applying an AutoFormat

	A	B	C	D	E	F	G	H	I	J	K	L	M
1	**The Future Company**												
2	*Annual Budget*												
3													
4		January	February	March	April	May	June	July	August	September	October	November	December
5	Stage 1	$53.50	$57.35	$61.20	$65.05	$68.90	$72.75	$76.60	$80.45	$84.30	$88.15	$92.00	$95.85
6	Stage 2	$65.00	$68.25	$71.50	$74.75	$78.00	$81.25	$84.50	$87.75	$91.00	$94.25	$97.50	$100.75
7	Stage 3	$99.00	$107.30	$115.60	$123.90	$132.20	$140.50	$148.80	$157.10	$165.40	$173.70	$182.00	$190.30
8	Stage 4	$45.50	$42.25	$39.00	$35.75	$32.50	$29.25	$26.00	$22.75	$19.50	$16.25	$13.00	$9.75
9	Stage 5	$45.00	$46.75	$48.50	$50.25	$52.00	$53.75	$55.50	$57.25	$59.00	$60.75	$62.50	$64.25
10	Stage 6	$67.00	$69.25	$71.50	$73.75	$76.00	$78.25	$80.50	$82.75	$85.00	$87.25	$89.50	$91.75
11		$375.00	$391.15	$407.30	$423.45	$439.60	$455.75	$471.90	$488.05	$504.20	$520.35	$536.50	$552.65
12													

(continued on next page)

5. Click **OK**. Look at your worksheet. Instant formatting!

6. Now, let's apply conditional formats to the data. You want to highlight budget figures that exceed $75,000 (75.00) in any given month for any department. Select the range **B5:M10**.

7. Open the **Format** menu and select **Conditional Formatting**.

8. Click the drop-down arrow for the second text box and click **greater than**. Key **75.00** in the third text box.

9. Click the **Format** button and on the Font tab, change the Font style to **Bold**, and the Color to a bright red.

10. Click **OK** and then click **OK** again to close the Conditional Formatting dialog box.

11. Print the worksheet in landscape orientation and so the data fits on one page. Then save and close the file.

Using Styles and Data Validation

You can use *styles* for formats that recur. If you want your worksheet to have a consistent appearance and you don't want the hassle of applying the formats over and over, you can use styles. The big advantage of using a style is that if you modify a style, each cell that is formatted using this style will change to reflect the new style.

Excel's data validation feature helps ensure that accurate data is being entered into a cell. For example, you can use the data validation feature to alert users if an incorrect entry, such as an invalid date, is entered into a cell. You can create messages that will display when a person enters incorrect data. The message alerts the user about the invalid entry, and normally explains what data is valid.

You can also create a message that will display whenever a cell is selected. This message prompts the user as to what type of data should be entered into the cell.

STEP-BY-STEP ➤ 1.5

1. Open **AE Step1-5** from the student data files and save it as **Style** followed by your initials.

2. Select cell **A3**.

3. Click the arrow on the **Fill Color** button and choose **Light Yellow**.

4. Click the arrow on the **Font Color** button and choose **Plum**. Click the **Bold** button.

5. Select **Style** on the **Format** menu.

6. Key **My Style** in the *Style name* box. The format options in the Style dialog box will change to reflect the new style as shown in Figure 1-4.

7. Click **OK**.

8. Select the range **B3:E3**.

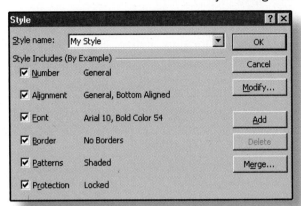

FIGURE 1-4
Style dialog box

9. Select **Style** on the **Format** menu. In the Style dialog box, click the **Style name** arrow and choose **My Style**.

10. Click **OK** and view the results.

Concept Builder

To remove a style, open the Style dialog box, select the style from the Style name drop-down list, and click **Delete**.

11. Select the range **B4:B15**.

12. With this range still selected, select the **Data** menu, click **Validation**, and select the **Settings** tab, if necessary.

13. Click the **Allow** drop-down list arrow and choose **Whole number**.

14. Click the **Data** drop-down list arrow and choose **between**, if necessary.

15. Enter **1** in the **Minimum** text box.

16. Enter **50** in the **Maximum** text box. This will only allow employee numbers between 1 and 50 to be entered.

17. Click the **Error Alert** tab and key **Data Entry Mistake** in the **Title** box.

18. In the Error message box, key **Employee Number must be between 1 and 50.**

19. Click the **Input Message** tab and key **Input Help** in the **Title** box.

20. In the Input message box, key **Please enter a number between 1 and 50.** Click **OK**.

21. In cell **A7**, enter the name **Brady Richardson**, and press **Tab**. Notice how the input message displays. Key **55** in cell **B7** and press **Enter**. The error message should display.

22. Click **Retry**. Then, key **4** and press **Enter**. Notice how the error message does not display when a correct number is entered.

23. In cell **C4**, key **Sales**; in cell **D4**, key **US**; and in cell **E4**, key **Sales**.

24. Print the current sheet, and then save and close the workbook.

Enhancing the Appearance of Charts

You've undoubtedly created charts in Excel files that illustrate the data on a worksheet. Charts are idea for adding graphic flare and punch to the presentation of data. You can enhance the appearance of a chart in many ways.

Adding a Drop Shadow and Changing Background Color

A drop shadow adds dimension to a chart and creates a professional appearance. An example of a chart with a drop shadow is shown in Figure 1-5.

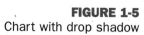

FIGURE 1-5
Chart with drop shadow

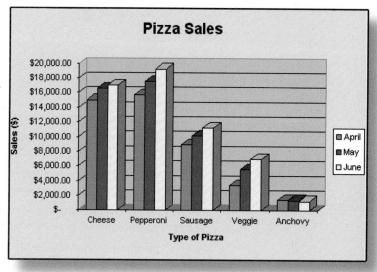

You can further customize the chart by changing the background color. The background color affects the chart area. The chart area is identified in Figure 1-5. Changes are made to the chart area in the Format Chart Area dialog box shown in Figure 1-6.

The options available on the tabs in the Format Chart Area dialog box are described below.

- **Patterns**. Lets you choose the border style for the chart. Attributes you can apply include border color, thickness of line (weight), shadow, or rounded corners. The *Sample* box will display a preview of the selected options.

- **Font**. Selected options in the Font tab affect selected text. You can change the font style and size, as well as the color of the font.

- **Properties**. Lets you select whether the chart will be printed with the worksheet. The default is set to allow the chart to be printed with worksheet data. You can also decide whether the chart can be sized or moved when worksheet cells are sized and moved.

FIGURE 1-6
Format Chart Area dialog box

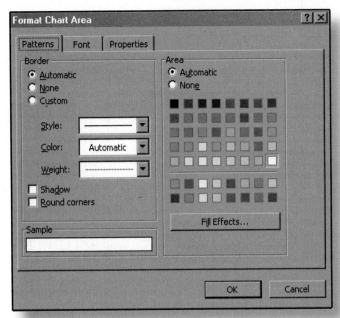

S TEP-BY-STEP ▷ 1.6

1. Open the **AE Step1-6** workbook from the data files and save it as **Bauer Pizza Chart** followed by your initials.

2. Click the chart to select it. If the Chart toolbar is not displayed, right-click on any toolbar and then select **Chart**. Make sure the chart is selected and choose **Chart Area** (if necessary) from the **Chart Objects** drop-down list on the Chart toolbar.

3. Click the **Format Chart Area** button on the Chart toolbar to display the Format Chart Area dialog box.

4. On the Patterns tab, click the **Shadow** option and the **Round corners** option.

5. Choose a light color or shade from the *Area* color palette.

6. Click **OK**. Your screen should look similar to Figure 1-7.

7. Print the worksheet. Remain in this screen for the next Step-by-Step.

 **Hot Tip**

You can also display the Format Chart Area dialog box by double-clicking on the chart area.

(continued on next page)

FIGURE 1-7

Chart with drop shadow and background color

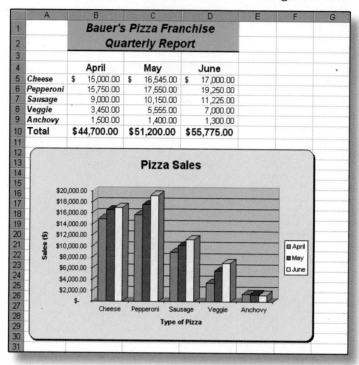

Formatting Chart Text

Formatting text in a chart is very similar to formatting text in the worksheet. You can change the format of any text in the chart by first selecting the text and then clicking the buttons on the Formatting toolbar. Or you can double-click the chart text to open its Format dialog box.

STEP-BY-STEP 1.7

1. Save the Bauer Pizza Chart file as **Bauer Pizza Chart 2** followed by your initials. Click on the chart title **Pizza Sales**.

2. Click the **Font Size** drop-down list arrow (on the formatting toolbar) and choose **18**.

3. Click the **Font** arrow and choose **Script12BT** (or a similar font).

4. Click the **Font Color** button and choose a color from the color palette. (Remember to select a different color from the chart background or the text will not be visible.)

5. On the Chart toolbar, click the **Chart Objects** drop-down list arrow and select **Category Axis**.

6. Click the **Angle Text Upward** button on the Chart toolbar. Notice how the text identifying the X axis is now displayed at an angle.

7. Your screen should look similar to Figure 1-8. Save and then print the worksheet. Remain in this screen for the next Step-by-Step.

FIGURE 1-8
Chart with font enhancements

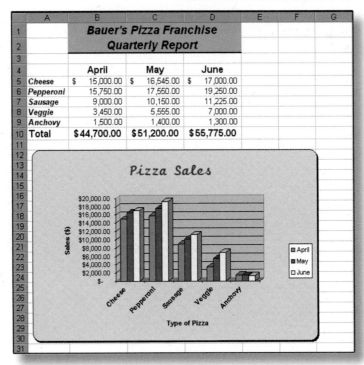

Adding a Data Table

A data table displays the worksheet data on the chart itself. This can be useful when your chart is on a separate sheet in the workbook, or for quickly referencing the worksheet data while viewing chart data series. To add a data table to a chart, click the Data Table button on the Chart toolbar.

STEP-BY-STEP ▷ 1.8

1. Save the Bauer Pizza Chart 2 file as **Bauer Pizza Chart 3**, followed by your initials. If necessary, click on the chart to select it.

2. Click the **Data Table** button on the Chart toolbar. Notice that the labels are no longer angled upward. When a data table is added to a chart, the axis labels return to a horizontal alignment.

3. Resize the chart so all the text is displayed. Click on the chart to select it, place your mouse

pointer over a selection handle, and drag it to the right, left, up, or down.

4. Select the **Legend** object on the chart, and press **Delete** to remove the legend.

5. Your screen should appear similar to Figure 1-9. Save and then print the worksheet in landscape orientation. Close the workbook.

(continued on next page)

FIGURE 1-9
Chart with data table

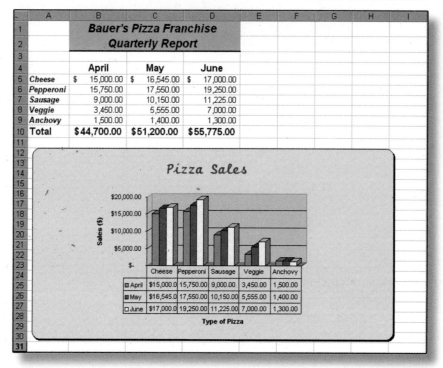

Summary

In this lesson, you learned:

- You can apply various number formats, such as accounting, fractions, and scientific formats.

- By creating a custom format, you can display the data in worksheet cells in any desired format.

- AutoFormats let you create instant worksheet formats.

- Conditional formatting enables you to highlight data that meets specified criteria.

- Styles let you apply the same formatting scheme over and over, thereby eliminating the time-consuming task of applying individual formats.

- Data validation can increase data entry accuracy.

- The appearance of worksheet charts can be enhanced by using the Chart toolbar and formatting techniques that you've also applied to worksheet data.

LESSON 1 REVIEW QUESTIONS

WRITTEN QUESTIONS

Write a brief answer to the following questions.

1. What is the difference between the following date codes: *dd-mmm-yy* and *dd-mmmm-yyyy*?

   dd-mmm-yy displays as 05-JAN-89

   dd-mmmm-yyyy displays as 05-JANUARY-1989

2. What are two methods for applying a currency format to numbers?

   format>cells> number>currency

   format>style> from drop down list select "currency"

3. How can AutoFormats save you time?

   The selected area will have various attributes set at one time. preferred formats can be used to create similar looking sheets.

4. If you applied the Percent Style with two decimal places to .0975, what would the number look like on the worksheet?

   10%

5. How would the number 1256777 appear if you selected the cell with this data and then clicked the Comma Style button?

1,256,777

6. Explain the difference between AutoFormats and styles.

AutoFormats are preset and selected from the Autoformat dialog. Which format items to apply can be selected also.

Styles can be modified as desired.

7. To apply a scientific format to a range of numbers, which category would you choose on the Numbers tab in the Format Cells dialog box?

Scientific

8. List the steps for creating a custom format.

Select cell/s to be formatted then Format > Style > type New Name in drop down list > Modify → set attributes as desired.

9. Which button on the Chart toolbar lets you select a chart object to modify?

Chart Object drop down list

10. When would you use a style?

Whenever a cell needs to stand out or for aesthetics. When you want to repeat the attributes in several other places.

LESSON 1 PROJECTS

PROJECT 1-1

1. Open **AE Project1-1** from the student data files and save the workbook as **Class Scores** followed by your initials.

2. Change the date format in column A so your dates appear in the format *March 14, 1998*.

3. Format the range **C12:G14** as percentages with no decimal places.

4. Save the workbook.

5. Print the worksheet in landscape orientation. Then close the file.

completed

PROJECT 1-2

1. Open **AE Project1-2** from the student data files and save the workbook as **Pizza** followed by your initials.

2. Add a currency format with two decimal places to the sales figures.

3. Change the alignment of the column headings to a –45 degree angle.

4. Center the title and subtitle across columns A through D.

5. Change the cell background color of the title and subtitle to a color of your choice.

6. Add a single top border and a double bottom border to the Total row.

7. Save the workbook and then print the range **A1:E11** in landscape orientation. Close the workbook.

Completed again 4-15-04

PROJECT 1-3

Continue from here 4-12-04   compl. 4-15

1. Open the **AE Project1-3** workbook and save it as **Sales Chart** followed by your initials.

2. Add a data table to the chart.

3. Resize the chart as you feel appropriate.

4. Change the border style of the chart to a rounded border.

5. Save the workbook and then print it in landscape orientation and so all the data fits on one page. Close the workbook.

CRITICAL THINKING

ACTIVITY 1-1

SCANS

You are the new manager of the New Internet Products Corporation. After reviewing workbooks created by the former manager, you decide to enhance the data contained in the files by applying different formatting features.

1. Open the **AE Activity1-1** workbook from the student data files and save it as **Trendy Resort Projected Sales** followed by your initials.

2. Format the worksheet using the formatting features you learned about in this lesson: apply an AutoFormat to the projected sales data and use conditional formatting to highlight those projected sales figures that exceed $60,000 for any month and any division.

3. Print the worksheet in landscape orientation and so all the data fits on one page. Then close the workbook.

ACTIVITY 1-2

SCANS

Using Excel's Help system, find information on the different types of Number formats. Write a brief explanation of each format and give an example of when you would apply it to worksheet data.

ADVANCED MICROSOFT EXCEL

PRINTING WORKBOOKS

OBJECTIVES

Upon completion of this lesson, you should be able to:

- Use Print Preview.
- Change page setup options.
- Create your own page breaks.
- Apply various printing features.
- Print formulas instead of totals.

Estimated Time: 1 hour

Print Preview

Before printing, you may want to view on the computer screen how the worksheet will look when it is printed on paper. Viewing the worksheet on-screen helps you identify problems before you print. This can save you time and effort. When you select Print Preview on the File menu or click the Print Preview button on the toolbar, a screen appears similar to the one shown in Figure 2-1.

An explanation of the buttons in the Print Preview screen are listed below.

- **Next.** Moves you to the next page of a multiple-page worksheet.
- **Previous.** Moves you to the previous page of a multiple-page worksheet.
- **Zoom.** Takes you back and forth between viewing your worksheet at 100% view and a view that fits the entire worksheet page on the screen. Your mouse pointer appears as a magnifying glass as you move it over the worksheet. You can move the magnifying glass over an area of the worksheet and click the mouse button to zoom in on that section of the worksheet. To zoom back out, click the mouse button again.
- **Print.** Prints the worksheet with the current settings.
- **Setup.** Opens the Page Setup dialog box.
- **Margins.** Click to display or hide dotted lines that indicate the current page margins.

FIGURE 2-1
Print Preview screen

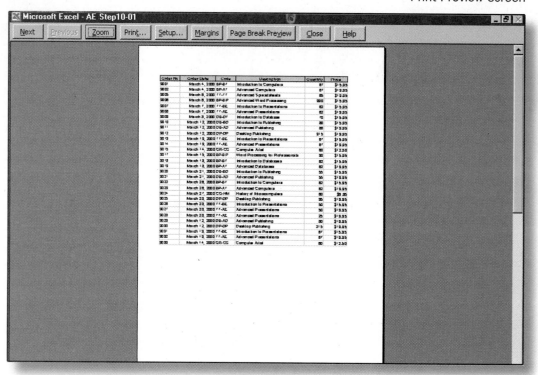

- **Page Break Preview.** Switches you to the Page Break Preview screen in which you can adjust the page breaks, resize the print area, and even edit the worksheet.

- **Close.** Closes the Print Preview screen.

- **Help.** Gives you additional information about each of the print features.

STEP-BY-STEP ▷ 2.1

1. Open the **AE Step2-1** workbook from the student data files and save it as **March Orders** followed by your initials.

2. Open the **File** menu and then select **Print Preview**, or click the **Print Preview** button.

3. Click the **Zoom** button. Note how the view has been increased to actual size.

4. Click **Zoom** again. The page of the worksheet should be returned to the previous view.

5. Click **Next** to see page 2 of the worksheet.

6. Click **Previous** to go back to page 1.

7. Click **Close** to close the Print Preview screen for now. Remain in this screen for the next Step-by-Step.

Choosing Sheet Preferences

You've probably opened the Page Setup dialog box to change the printing orientation and margins of a worksheet or to add a header or footer to a worksheet. The Sheet tab in the Page Setup dialog box, shown in Figure 2-2, contains additional settings for changing the way the worksheet will look when it is printed. For example, you can select to print the gridlines you see on the screen or you can print column letters across the top of the worksheet and row numbers down the left side of the worksheet. You can also choose to print column or row labels on all the pages of a worksheet, so that you don't have to keep referring back to the first page to see those headings.

FIGURE 2-2
Sheet tab in the Page Setup dialog box

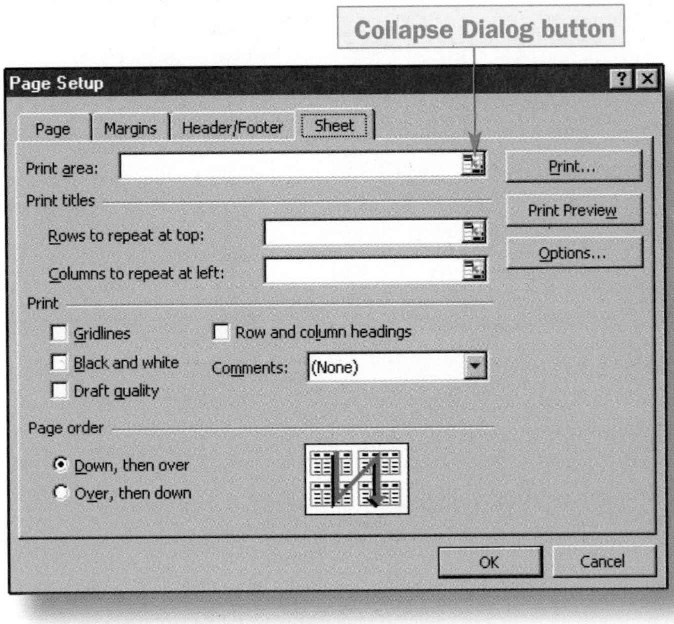

The options available on the Sheet tab are explained below.

■ **Print area.** If you don't want to print the entire worksheet, you can enter a range of cells to print in the Print area text box. If you want to print more than one range, enter a comma (,) between the ranges. You can also click the Collapse Dialog button at the end of the text box to select the print range directly on the sheet.

■ **Print titles.** You can specify a column or row of data to be printed at the left or top of every page.

■ **Print.** In this section, you can select whether or not you want gridlines to print. Selecting the *Black and white* option prints color items in black and white on a color printer. Selecting *Draft quality* prints the report in a lower print quality. As a general rule, draft quality prints much faster than a higher quality print. Selecting the *Row and column headings* option will print the actual column letters across the top of the worksheet data and row numbers to the left of the worksheet data. Selecting *Comments* will let you choose where you want to print any comments you've entered.

■ **Page order.** The Page order selections determine how the worksheet data will print if it extends to more than one page. The *Down, then over option* prints the data in order from top to bottom and then to the right. The *Over, then down* option prints the data from left to right and then down.

1. Open the **File** menu and then choose **Page Setup**.

2. Click the **Sheet** tab.

3. Click the **Collapse Dialog** button at the end of the *Print area* text box. You want to print the data for the Northwest Region only, so select **A1:F21**. Click the **Collapse Dialog** button again to return to the dialog box.

4. Next, let's remove the gridlines from the report. If the **Gridlines** option is checked, click it to deselect the option.

5. Click **OK**.

6. If necessary, widen column **F** to display the full column title.

7. Click the **Print Preview** button.

8. To print the worksheet directly from the Print Preview screen, click **Print** and then click **OK** in the Print dialog box.

9. Open the Page Setup dialog box again and click the **Sheet** tab, if necessary.

10. Delete the selection entered in the *Print area* text box.

11. Click the **Collapse Dialog** button in the *Rows to repeat at top* text box and select rows **1**, **2**, and **3** on the worksheet. Click the **Collapse Dialog** button again to return to the Page Setup dialog box.

12. Click the **Print Preview** button. Review both pages of the worksheet. The worksheet title, subtitle, and a blank row should appear on both pages.

13. Print the worksheet directly from the Print Preview screen. Then save and close the workbook.

Creating Page Breaks

When your worksheet data reaches the limits of the page, Excel determines where the data will be split between pages. However, as you preview a worksheet, you may notice page breaks in poor locations. For example, one page may end with Last Name data and the next page starts with First Name data. If changing the margins or paper size doesn't remedy the situation, you may need to modify the existing page breaks or insert your own.

To view page breaks, go to the Print Preview screen and then click the Page Break Preview button. Page breaks appear as blue dotted lines. You can move the page breaks by positioning the pointer on a page break line and dragging it to the new location. To insert a new page break, select the cell that you want to start on a new page and then select Page Break on the Insert menu.

To remove a page break, make sure you are in Page Break Preview. Then position the pointer on the page break line until it turns into a double-headed arrow and drag the line off the sheet.

STEP-BY-STEP ▷ 2.3

1. Open the **AE Step2-3** workbook from the student data files and save it as **P&K Regions** followed by your initials.

2. Click the **Print Preview** button.

3. Click the **Page Break Preview** button and then click **OK** if necessary to close the Welcome to Page Break Preview message box. Scroll down the worksheet and notice that there is a page break within the Southeast Region's data. It would be more useful to the reader if all of Southeast Region's data were on one page. Therefore, let's put a page break before the Southeast Region title. This will put all of this region's data on the second page of the worksheet.

4. Place the mouse pointer over the blue dotted line (page break) in the Southeast Region. The pointer turns into a two-headed arrow.

5. Drag the blue dotted line above the Southeast Region titles and release the mouse button. You have just moved the page break.

6. Click the **Print Preview** button again. (*Hint*: To return to the normal worksheet view, open the **View** menu and select **Normal**.)

7. Print the worksheet from the Print Preview screen. Then save the workbook and remain in this screen for the next Step-by-Step.

Applying Printing Features

When you click the Print button on the toolbar, Excel prints the worksheet with the default print settings. This may be fine for some of your worksheets. But, should you need to print more than one copy of the worksheet, for example, Excel offers a wide range of options in the Print dialog box, shown in Figure 2-3.

The options available in the Print dialog box are explained below.

FIGURE 2-3
Print dialog box

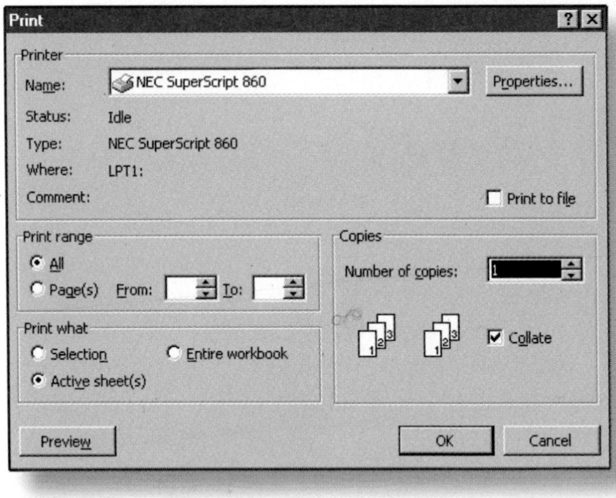

- **Name.** Displays the printer that is currently selected. If you want to change the selected printer, you can click the drop-down list arrow to display a list of printers. Below the *Name* text box is information on the status and printing location of the printer.

- **Properties.** Clicking this button lets you change various features such as the paper source or the printing resolution of graphics.

- **Print to file.** Selecting this option lets you print the document to a file instead of a printer.

- **Print range, All.** Prints all of the pages in the selection.

- **Print range, Page(s).** Enter the first and last pages of the worksheet you want printed in the *From* and *To* text boxes or click the arrows to select page numbers.

A E - 2 3

- **Print what, Selection.** Prints cells you selected before opening the Print dialog box. This can be the range selected on the worksheet or the range entered in the *Print area* text box in the Page Setup dialog box. To select more than one range on a worksheet for printing, select the first range and then hold down the Ctrl key as you select additional ranges. To indicate different ranges to print on the Sheet tab in the Page Setup dialog box, separate the ranges with a comma in the *Print area* text box. Excel prints each selected range on its own sheet.

- **Print what, Active sheet(s).** Prints only selected worksheet(s) in the workbook.

- **Print what, Entire workbook.** Prints the entire workbook.

- **Number of copies.** To print more than one copy, key the number of copies in the text box or click the up or down arrow.

- **Collate.** Organizes pages as you print more than one copy of a document. When this option is selected, a complete copy of the document is printed before the next copy is printed.

- **Preview**. Click Preview to open the Print Preview screen.

STEP-BY-STEP ▷ 2.4

1. Select the range **A1:E12**.

> ### Hot Tip
> You might want to include one row below and one column to the side of the selection you want printed. This helps eliminate the possibility of borders and text being cut off.

2. Open the **File** menu and then choose **Print**.

3. Click **Selection** from the *Print What* options.

4. In the Number of copies text box, enter **2** for the number of copies. Click **OK**.

5. Save and close the workbook.

Printing Formulas or Zeros

As you have learned, when you enter a formula in a cell, the result of the formula displays in the cell and the formula itself is shown in the Formula bar. But there are probably times when you'll want to see the actual formulas in the worksheet so that you can double-check a formula in case the result is erroneous. Excel lets you display and print formulas instead of results.

Excel also lets you decide whether or not a zero (0) will print as the only data in a cell. Since a zero is not a significant value, you may not want it displayed. If you choose not to display the zero, the cell appears blank.

You can apply these features by choosing Options on the Tools menu. In the Options dialog box, click the View tab, which is shown in Figure 2-4.

FIGURE 2-4
View tab in the Options dialog box

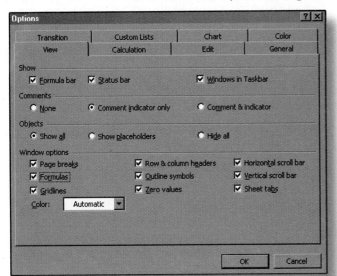

Hot Tip

A shortcut for viewing formulas is to press the Ctrl+` keys. Press these keys again to redisplay the totals. The ` key is normally to the left of the 1 key. Holding down the Shift key when pressing it creates the tilde (~) character.

STEP-BY-STEP ▷ 2.5

1. Open the **AE Step2-5** workbook from the student data files and save it as **Bauer Pizza** followed by your initials.

2. Open the **Tools** menu and then choose **Options**.

3. Select the **View** tab, if necessary.

4. In the Window options section, click the **Formulas** box. Then click **OK**. Look at your worksheet and notice how formulas are displayed where results appeared before.

5. Click the **Print Preview** button.

6. Click the **Setup** button, click the **Page** tab, and click **Landscape**. Then click the **Fit to** option and click **OK**.

7. Print the worksheet. Then save and close the workbook.

Summary

In this lesson, you learned:

■ You can preview a worksheet before it is printed. This helps you identify where margins may need to be adjusted, or page breaks inserted or deleted.

■ You can change page breaks in the Page Break Preview screen.

■ You can apply various printing options, such as printing specific selections of data, as well as printing multiple pages and collating.

- You can print formulas instead of the results of the formulas by opening the Options dialog box from the Tools menu. Options that affect what you see on the printed page appear on the View tab.

- Remove zero values. This is a great feature for the user who wants to see values greater than or less than zero, but not have the actual zeros displayed.

LESSON 2 REVIEW QUESTIONS

TRUE/FALSE

Circle T if the statement is true or F if the statement is false.

T F 1. The Next button in the Print Preview screen moves you to the next page of data.

T F 2. The Previous button in the Print Preview screen moves you to the previous page of a multiple page worksheet.

T F 3. The Zoom button in the Print Preview screen takes you back and forth between pages.

T F 4. The Print button in the Print Preview screen will only print the data range showing on the monitor

T F 5. The Close button in the Print Preview screen closes your workbook.

WRITTEN QUESTIONS

Write a brief answer to the following questions.

1. In the Page Setup dialog box, what tab should you select to print a specific range of cells?

    SHEET → PRINT AREA

2. Can you print more than one copy of a worksheet, or a selected range on a worksheet? If so, how?

    From Page Setup click OPTIONS > Copies
    From Print Preview → Setup > Options

3. What is meant by "printing a selection"?

first the area to be printed is selected then (highlighted) in the print dialog box select "SELECTION" radio button.

4. What are the steps for moving a page break to a location of your choice?

print preview > Page Break Preview > place cursor on Page Break Line When double headed arrow appears, drag page break to desired location.

5. What is the difference between landscape and portrait orientation?

long distance is horz in landscape vertical in portrait.

LESSON 2 PROJECTS

PROJECT 2-1

1. Open the **AE Project2-1** workbook from the student data files and save it as **Industry Inventory** followed by your initials.

2. Set up the worksheet so that the title prints at the top of each page.

3. Insert page breaks so that each region prints on its own page.

4. Print the worksheet. Then remove the page breaks you inserted and do not print the title at the top of each page.

5. Print the data for the Northeast and Northwest regions only. Make sure you include the worksheet title, as well as the headings for each region's data in the selection to print. Then print the worksheet.

6. Save and close the workbook.

PROJECT 2-2

1. Open the **AE Project2-2** workbook from the student data files and save it as **College Budget** followed by your initials.

2. Display formulas and remove the gridlines.

3. Preview the worksheet. Change the orientation to landscape and the scaling so the sheet prints on one page only.

4. Print the current sheet.

5. Save and then close the workbook.

Completed 4-19-04 1500

CRITICAL THINKING

SCANS

ACTIVITY 2-1

You are the Cruise Coordinator for the Tierra Travel Agency. You've just been asked to create a worksheet that contains the information shown Figure 2-5. Enter a formula for the *Trip Revenue* column that calculates the number of persons registered times the price per person. Apply any formats you think are appropriate. Save the workbook as **Tierra Travel**.

You need to print two copies of this workbook in landscape orientation with the formulas displayed. You will give one copy to the Cruise Captain and one copy to the Travel Director for them to review. Save and then close the workbook.

FIGURE 2-5

	A	B	C	D	E
1	*Tierra Travel Agency*				
2	*Fourteen-Day Cruises*				
3	*Information*				
4					
5	**Destination**	**Dates of Departure/Return**	**Price Per Person**	**Persons Registered**	**Trip Revenue**
6	Bahamas	April 1 - April 14	$ 549	17	
7	Barbados	May 14 - May 28	$ 768	26	
8	Alaska	June 22 - July 6	$ 999	41	
9	St. Thomas	July 17 - August 1	$ 479	7	
10	Jamaica	August 11 - August 25	$ 559	14	
11	Aruba	September 13 - September 27	$ 949	21	
12	Key West	October 1 - October 15	$ 329	5	

ACTIVITY 2-2

Using Excel's Help facility, find information on how to use the collate option in the Print dialog box. Explain how you might have used this option in printing files you worked on in this lesson.

SCANS

USING DATA LISTS

OBJECTIVES

Upon completion of this lesson, you will be able to:

- Create a data list.

- Add records to a list.

- Edit records in a list.

- Delete list records.

- Sort a list.

- Search for records that meet certain criteria.

⏱ **Estimated Time: 1 hour**

Introduction

You can sort and search data in a worksheet much like you do in a database. When data on a worksheet is set up as a data list, it can be manipulated in a variety of ways. In this lesson, you will learn how to create a list, and make changes to a list such as editing and adding records. Then, you will learn how to sort the list alphabetically and numerically and how to search for data that meets criteria you specify.

Understanding Lists

You can think of a *list* as a database table. Lists are used to organize, manage, and retrieve information. There are thousands of examples of lists in use today. For example, they are used to organize payroll information, keep track of inventories, and manage customer information.

A list consists of columns and rows of data—in fact, it looks similar to other worksheets you've created. Lists are made up of ***records***. A record is a collection of information about a particular object. The information could include a name, address, and telephone number. Records are further divided into ***fields***, a column of information that contains one type of data. For the previous example, you would have a name field, address field, and telephone number field. You enter information in fields. A list with records and fields is shown in Figure 3-1.

The data in a list can be manipulated in various ways. For example, you can sort the list alphabetically or numerically, by any column, or field. Or you can search the list for records that meet specific requirements (criteria). You can also print the list and display the data visually in a graph.

FIGURE 3-1

Data list

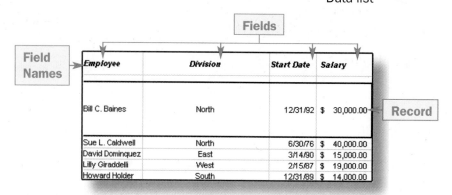

Creating a List

A list has to be set up according to a few simple guidelines which are explained below.

- The first row of the list (not including worksheet titles and subtitles) should contain the field names.

- You can have blank rows above the field names or below the last record. And you can have blank columns to the right or left of the list. However, you cannot have a blank row or column within the list.

- Every record must have the same fields.

- Each field does not have to contain data.

- You can use any of the usual formatting and editing techniques in a data list.

STEP-BY-STEP ▷ 3.1

1. Start a new workbook and enter the data shown in Figure 3-2. The list range is A4:H14. Worksheet titles and subtitles are not included in the list range, but field names are included.

2. Format the data so that it looks similar to the worksheet in Figure 3-2.

3. Save the workbook as **CTI Training** followed by your initials and remain in this screen for the next Step-by-Step.

FIGURE 3-2

Setting up a list

	A	B	C	D	E	F	G	H	I
1			**Computer Technology Institute**						
2			**Training Department**						
3									
4	**Last Name**	**First Name**	**Address**	**City**	**State**	**ZIP Code**	**Telephone**	**Area of Expertise**	
5	Arland	Ralph	27 Knight Street	Madison	Wisconsin	54347	608-555-3601	Word	
6	Crawford	Katie	1423 First Street	Madison	Wisconsin	53447	608-555-3199	Excel	
7	Gonzalez	Lisa	Rt. 3, Box 157	Madison	Wisconsin	54112	608-555-9987	Word	
8	Goodwin	Sallye	2563 Middle Rd.	Madison	Wisconsin	53446	608-555-8008	Word	
9	Keplinger	Joanne	P.O. Box 47654	Madison	Wisconsin	53447	608-555-6712	Access	
10	Khorjin	Fugi	P.O. Box 4225	Madison	Wisconsin	53447	608-555-9223	Access	
11	Pullis	Cheryl	10 North McDonald	Madison	Wisconsin	53329	608-555-3455	Powerpoint	
12	Rigola	Carol	386 Evergreen	Madison	Wisconsin	53238	608-555-6678	Word	
13	Thomsen	Barb	347 Edison Dr.	Madison	Wisconsin	53476	608-555-3345	Access	
14	Bretzke	Dee	4400 Lake Dr.	Madison	Wisconsin	54358	608-555-9938	Outlook	
15									
16									

Adding Records to a Data List

If you want to add a record to a list, you move to the row where you want to add the record, insert a row, and then key the data. You can also use the Data Form dialog box, shown in Figure 3-3, to enter your records.

The Data Form dialog box lets you view records one at a time. And you can perform other functions, such as editing, when you use the Data Form dialog box. Records are added to the bottom of the data list when you add records using this dialog box. You can also delete records and find records within the Data Form dialog box. The options available in it are as follows:

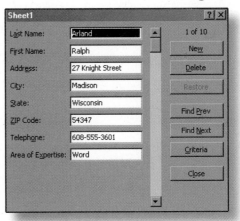

FIGURE 3-3
Data Form dialog box

- **New.** Lets you add a new record.

- **Delete.** Lets you delete the displayed record.

- **Restore.** Lets you undo changes to the displayed record.

- **Find Prev.** Goes to the record before the displayed record.

- **Find Next.** Goes to the record after the displayed record.

- **Criteria.** Lets you find records based on criteria you specify.

STEP-BY-STEP ▷ 3.2

1. Add a record to the list. Select cell **A5** and insert a row. Enter the following data in the appropriate fields:

   ```
   D.J. Mancini
   4212 Woodbridge Lane
   Madison, Wisconsin 54347
   608-555-4444
   Word
   ```

    **Hot Tip**

   If the inserted row assumes the same formatting as the preceding row, select the record by clicking on the row number and reformat it appropriately.

2. Let's try another method for adding records. Select any cell in the list range. (You must do this before you can get into the Data Form dialog box.) Open the **Data** menu and select **Form**. The Data Form dialog box appears. To move in the dialog box, click in the field's text box. Or, you can press **Tab** to move to the next field, and **Shift+Tab** to move to a previous field.

3. Click the **New** button. The fields should now be blank and ready for you to enter the new data.

4. Key the following data in the appropriate fields:

   ```
   Susan Fields
   19 Harbor Avenue
   Madison, Wisconsin 54358
   608-555-7788
   PowerPoint
   ```

5. Click the **Close** button. Make sure the new record appears at the end of the list.

6. Your screen should look similar to Figure 3-4. Save the file and remain in this screen for the next Step-by-Step.

(continued on next page)

FIGURE 3-4
Adding records to a list

	A	B	C	D	E	F	G	H
1			**Computer Technology Institute**					
2			**Training Department**					
3								
4	**Last Name**	**First Name**	**Address**	**City**	**State**	**ZIP Code**	**Telephone**	**Area of Expe**
5	Mancini	DJ	4212 Woodbridge Lane	Madison	Wisconsin	54347	608-555-4444	Word
6	Arland	Ralph	27 Knight Street	Madison	Wisconsin	54347	608-555-3601	Word
7	Crawford	Katie	1423 First Street	Madison	Wisconsin	53447	608-555-3199	Excel
8	Gonzalez	Lisa	Rt. 3, Box 157	Madison	Wisconsin	54112	608-555-9987	Word
9	Goodwin	Sallye	43 First St.	Madison	Wisconsin	53446	608-555-8008	Word
10	Keplinger	Joanne	P.O. Box 47654	Madison	Wisconsin	53447	608-555-6712	Access
11	Khorjin	Fugi	P.O. Box 4225	Madison	Wisconsin	53447	608-555-9223	Access
12	Pullis	Cheryl	10 North McDonald	Madison	Wisconsin	53329	608-555-3455	PowerPoint
13	Rigola	Carol	386 Evergreen	Madison	Wisconsin	53238	608-555-6678	Word
14	Thomsen	Barb	347 Edison Dr.	Madison	Wisconsin	53476	608-555-3345	Access
15	Bretzke	Dee	4400 Lake Dr.	Madison	Wisconsin	54358	608-555-9938	Outlook
16	Fields	Susan	19 Harbor Ave.	Madison	Wisconsin	54358	608-555-7788	PowerPoint
17								
18								

Sheet1 / Sheet2 / Sheet3 /

Editing Records in a List

You can edit a data list record the same way you edit worksheet data. First, you locate the cell you want to change and edit the data. You can also use the Data Form dialog box to make changes to a record.

STEP-BY-STEP 3.3

1. Select the cell containing the street address *2563 Middle Rd.* for Sallye Goodwin. Change the address to **43 First St.**

2. Now let's change a record using the Data Form dialog box. Open the **Data** menu and then select **Form**.

3. Click the **Find Next** button until you locate the record for Katie Crawford.

Hot Tip

If you move past a record in the Data Form dialog box, click the **Find Prev** button to go to the previous records.

4. Click in the **Telephone** field. The old telephone number is 608-555-3199. Change it to **608-555-4303**.

5. Click the **Close** button. Locate the record for Katie Crawford and view the change. Your screen should look similar to Figure 3-5.

6. Save the workbook and remain in this screen for the next Step-by-Step.

FIGURE 3-5
Editing records in a list

	A	B	C	D	E	F	G	H
1			**Computer Technology Institute**					
2			**Training Department**					
3								
4	Last Name	First Name	Address	City	State	ZIP Code	Telephone	Area of Expe
5	Mancini	DJ	4212 Woodbridge Lane	Madison	Wisconsin	54347	608-555-4444	Word
6	Arland	Ralph	27 Knight Street	Madison	Wisconsin	54347	608-555-3601	Word
7	Crawford	Katie	1423 First Street	Madison	Wisconsin	53447	608-555-4303	Excel
8	Gonzalez	Lisa	Rt. 3, Box 157	Madison	Wisconsin	54112	608-555-9987	Word
9	Goodwin	Sallye	43 First St.	Madison	Wisconsin	53446	608-555-8008	Word
10	Keplinger	Joanne	P.O. Box 47654	Madison	Wisconsin	53447	608-555-6712	Access
11	Khorjin	Fugi	P.O. Box 4225	Madison	Wisconsin	53447	608-555-9223	Access
12	Pullis	Cheryl	10 North McDonald	Madison	Wisconsin	53329	608-555-3455	PowerPoint
13	Rigola	Carol	386 Evergreen	Madison	Wisconsin	53238	608-555-6678	Word
14	Thomsen	Barb	347 Edison Dr.	Madison	Wisconsin	53476	608-555-3345	Access
15	Bretzke	Dee	4400 Lake Dr.	Madison	Wisconsin	54358	608-555-9938	Outlook
16	Fields	Susan	19 Harbor Ave.	Madison	Wisconsin	54358	608-555-7788	PowerPoint
17								
18								

Sheet1 / Sheet2 / Sheet3 /

Deleting Records

It is easy to delete a record in a list. You can delete a record by selecting a field in the record and deleting the entire row or by using the Data Form dialog box. If you mistakenly delete a record by deleting the row, you can click the Undo button to cancel the action.

If you are using the Data Form dialog box, Excel will display a message box that alerts you the record is about to be deleted permanently. You cannot use the Undo button to restore a record deleted in the Data Form dialog box.

STEP-BY-STEP ▷ 3.4

1. Select any field in the record for Carol Rigola.

2. Open the **Edit** menu and then select **Delete**.

3. Choose **Entire row** and then click **OK**. The record for Carol Rigola should be gone.

4. Let's delete another record. Open the **Data** menu and then select **Form**.

5. Click **Find Next** until the record for Fugi Khorjin is displayed.

 **Hot Tip**

You can also click the scroll arrows in the Data Form dialog box to move between records.

6. Click the **Delete** button. A message box appears.

7. Click **OK** to confirm that you want to delete the record.

8. Click **Close**. The record for Fugi Khorjin should be gone. The revised data list should look similar to Figure 3-6. Remain in this screen for the next Step-by-Step.

(continued on next page)

FIGURE 3-6
Deleting a record in a list

	A	B	C	D	E	F	G	H
1			**Computer Technology Institute**					
2			**Training Department**					
3								
4	**Last Name**	**First Name**	**Address**	**City**	**State**	**ZIP Code**	**Telephone**	**Area of Expe**
5	Mancini	DJ	4212 Woodbridge Lane	Madison	Wisconsin	54347	608-555-4444	Word
6	Arland	Ralph	27 Knight Street	Madison	Wisconsin	54347	608-555-3601	Word
7	Crawford	Katie	1423 First Street	Madison	Wisconsin	53447	608-555-4303	Excel
8	Gonzalez	Lisa	Rt. 3, Box 157	Madison	Wisconsin	54112	608-555-9987	Word
9	Goodwin	Sallye	43 First St.	Madison	Wisconsin	53446	608-555-8008	Word
10	Keplinger	Joanne	P.O. Box 47654	Madison	Wisconsin	53447	608-555-6712	Access
11	Pullis	Cheryl	10 North McDonald	Madison	Wisconsin	53329	608-555-3455	PowerPoint
12	Thomsen	Barb	347 Edison Dr.	Madison	Wisconsin	53476	608-555-3345	Access
13	Bretzke	Dee	4400 Lake Dr.	Madison	Wisconsin	54358	608-555-9938	Outlook
14	Fields	Susan	19 Harbor Ave.	Madison	Wisconsin	54358	608-555-7788	PowerPoint
15								
16								
17								
18								

Sheet1 / Sheet2 / Sheet3 /

Sorting a List

Sorting is used primarily in lists. You can quickly sort a list alphabetically or numerically using the Sort Ascending and Sort Descending buttons on the toolbar. Ascending order sorts alphabetically from A to Z and numerically from the lowest to the highest number. Descending order sorts alphabetically from Z to A and numerically from the highest to the lowest number. You can click the Undo button on the toolbar to undo a sort.

STEP-BY-STEP ⟹ 3.5

1. Click on any cell in the *Last Name* column.

2. Click the **Sort Descending** button. Your records should be sorted by Last Name in descending order from Z to A.

3. Save the workbook and remain in this screen for the next Step-by-Step.

Sorting a List with the Sort Dialog Box

The sort buttons provide a quick method for sorting a data list. But you may need more flexibility in your sort. The Sort dialog box provides you with numerous sorting options. You can specify by which field you want the data sorted. For example, maybe you want an address list to appear alphabetically by last name. You also can sort by more than one field. For example, you could sort by the Last Name field. Or you could sort by the Last Name and First Name fields. In this type of sort, Excel will first sort all the records by the Last Name field; then, if there are any records with the same last name, these records will be sorted alphabetically by first name.

To sort using the Sort dialog box, you choose Sort on the Data menu. The Sort dialog box appears, as shown in Figure 3-7.

You can designate up to three fields by which to sort in the dialog box. The header row options pertain to the row of column labels in a list. If the list has column labels as the top row, you'll want to select the

Header row option in order to exclude this data from being included in a sort. If the list does not have a row of column headings, then click the No header row option to indicate that the first row should be included in the sort. Clicking the Options button provides additional sort selections. The Sort Options dialog box appears, similar to Figure 3-8.

The options available in the Sort Options dialog box are described below.

■ **First key sort order.** Lets you specify a sort order other than ascending or descending. For example, you may want to sort the months of the year, "January, February, March."

■ **Case sensitive.** In a case-sensitive sort, records are sorted by capitalization. That is, records that begin with a capital letter appear first, followed by records that begin with the same letter in lowercase.

■ **Sort top to bottom.** Sorts the list from the top to the bottom rather than from left to right.

■ **Sort left to right.** Sorts the list from the left side to the right side rather than from top to bottom.

FIGURE 3-7
Sort dialog box

FIGURE 3-8
Sort Options dialog box

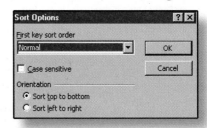

STEP-BY-STEP ▷ 3.6

1. Open the **Data** menu and then select **Sort**.

2. Click the **Sort by** drop-down list arrow and then select **Area of Expertise**. Choose **Ascending** as the sort order.

3. Click the **Then by** drop-down list arrow and select **Last Name**. If necessary, choose **Ascending** as the sort order.

4. Be sure the **Header row** option is selected. This instructs Excel to exclude the column labels from the sort.

5. Click **OK** to begin the sort. The records should be sorted alphabetically by area of expertise and then by last name.

6. Save the workbook and then print the sheet in portrait orientation and so all the data fits on one page. Close the workbook.

Searching for Records Meeting a Specific Criteria

Earlier in this lesson, you used the Data Form dialog box to find and edit records using very basic search procedures. With a large list, however, trying to find a record in this manner could take all day. To save time and increase your productivity, you can use the Criteria button in the Data Form dialog box to find one or more records that meet specific criteria.

1. Open the **AE Step3-7** workbook from the student data files and save it as **Arts & Crafts Data List** followed by your initials.

2. Select a cell in the field name row. (Excel starts the search from this point.) Open the **Data** menu and then select **Form**.

3. Click the **Criteria** button. Your screen should look similar to Figure 3-9. Notice the word Criteria in the upper right corner below the title bar. Also note the Form button has replaced the Criteria button. Clicking the Form button returns you to the Data Form dialog box.

FIGURE 3-9
Criteria dialog box

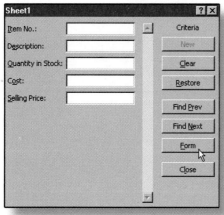

4. Click in the **Description** field and key **Varnish - Satin**.

5. Click the **Find Next** button. The record for Item No. 15-993 should be displayed. Notice that you are back in the Data Form where you can make changes to the record.

6. Click the **Find Next** button again. You should hear a beep or see a message when you choose the Find Next button, indicating that this is the only record that meets the criteria.

7. Click **Close** to close the Data Form.

8. Let's try to find another record. Open the Data Form.

9. Click the **Criteria** button.

10. Click in the **Item No.** field and key **12-295**.

11. Click the **Find Next** button. The record for Paint - White should be displayed.

12. Click the **Find Next** button. There should be no more records meeting the criteria.

13. Click **Close**. Then close the workbook.

Summary

In this lesson, you learned:

- A data list consists of records and fields of information. The list must be set up according to the following guidelines: no blank rows or columns within the list, and every record must have the same fields.

- You can add records to a list directly on the worksheet or in the Data Form dialog box.

- You can edit and delete records in a list directly on the worksheet or in the Data Form dialog box. When you delete records in the Data Form, they are deleted permanently.

- Lists are ideal for sorting worksheet data. You can sort data using the Sort Ascending and Sort Descending buttons or by selecting various options in the Sort dialog box.

LESSON 3 REVIEW QUESTIONS

WRITTEN QUESTIONS

Write a brief answer to the following questions.

1. What is a data list?

   a row of field names and rows which are records and columns which are fields   each record has the same fields

2. Not including titles and subtitles, what does the first row of a list normally contain?

   field names

3. What is a record?

   a row containing fields

4. What is a field?

   a location for specific data ie. LASTNAME

5. What are the guidelines for creating a list?

   *FIRST ROW IS FIELD NAMES
   NO BLANK ROWS WITHIN THE LIST.
   EACH RECORD HAS SAME FIELDS*

6. What are the two methods for adding a record to a list?

ADD BY EDITING THE CELLS
OR USE DATA > FORM

7. What is the advantage of using the Data Form dialog box to edit a record?

ONE RECORD SHOWN, SEARCH CAN BE PERFORMED

8. What are the two methods for deleting records?

DELETE ROW
USE DATA FORM

9. What is the difference between ascending order and descending order?

ASCENDING   A-Z or 1-10
DESCENDING Z-A or 10-1

10. Describe a case-sensitive sort.

Fields with same data only diff case will sort according to case — cap. first

LESSON 3 PROJECTS

PROJECT 3-1

1. Open the **AE Project3-1** workbook from the student data files and save it as **NL Corporation** followed by your initials.

2. Sort the list by **Division** and then by **Last Name**.

3. Print each division on a separate page and change the page setup to landscape orientation and so the data in rows 1 through 4 prints across the top of every page.

4. Save the workbook and then close it.

PROJECT 3-2

You are starting a home remodeling business. You realize the importance of keeping accurate information about your subcontractors. You decide to create a data list of your subcontractors that contains their mailing addresses and ID numbers. Start a new workbook and enter the information shown below.

ID No.	Company Name	Last Name	First Name	Address	City	State	ZIP	Phone
1005	At Home Decorating	Smith	George	516 Main St.	Houston	TX	73301	713-555-2341
3006	Carpets and More	Cartwrite	Zachary	8 Johnstown Road	Brazos	TX	77822	713-555-1928
9010	It's a Smash	Joshua	Daniel	Garden House Lane	Irving	TX	76221	214-555-1128
10005	Just a Little Touch	Anderson	Melissa	90 Maubel St.	Austin	TX	75377	512-555-0003
12330	Last Resort Furniture	Robinson	Pauline	67 Avenue Europe	El Paso	TX	73445	702-555-4435
14500	Never Say New	Martin	Jose	1 Lorraine	Houston	TX	73302	713-555-4423
14650	New and Improved	Johnson	Sally	1900 Oak St.	San Antonio	TX	75443	210-555-6558
14750	New Carpets	Kennedy	Rosa	12 Orchestra Trail	Riverside	TX	75234	214-555-6778
15665	One More Time	Levinson	Victor	7 Main St.	Lewisville	TX	76055	940-555-2108
16250	Paint, Paint, Paint	Fredrick	Helen	87 Polk St.	Southlake	TX	76056	940-555-2258
16400	Phil's Remodeling	Benntly	Lorna	52 Llano Largo	Shreveport	LA	75331	512-555-1926
17250	Redo Time	Davidson	Annabelle	Fifth Ave.	Bossier City	LA	71223	210-555-2276
17750	Roofs and More	Burke	Nathan	89 Chiaroscuro Rd.	Houston	TX	73303	713-555-4455
18500	Sinks and Such	Taylor	Beverly	12 East St.	Grapevine	TX	76055	940-555-6698
20550	Under Construction	Jameson	Marty	1924 Norton	Dallas	TX	76099	214-555-6600

1. Add the title **Subcontractor Mailing List**.

2. Format the data as you feel is appropriate.

3. Sort the list by **State** and then by **City** so that you can quickly glance at the subcontractors available in a specific area.

4. Save the workbook as **Mailing List** followed by your initials.

5. Print the worksheet in landscape orientation, and then close the file.

CRITICAL THINKING

ACTIVITY 3-1

Ms. Emily Smith, your boss at Lincoln College Fan-Fair, a sports apparel shop for Lincoln College, has just handed you the inventory list shown below. She asked you to key the items into a worksheet in a data list format with a title and subtitle.

Item No.	Item Description	Size	Cost	Selling Price
SS-LC1-S	Sweat Shirt - Lincoln College emblem	S	$10.99	$15.99
SS-LC1-M	Sweat Shirt - Lincoln College emblem	M	12.99	17.99
SS-LC1-L	Sweat Shirt - Lincoln College emblem	L	14.99	19.99
Cap-L	Baseball Cap	L	4.99	7.99
Cap-XL	Baseball Cap	XL	5.99	8.99
TS-LC-S	Tee Shirt - Lincoln College emblem	S	4.99	6.99
TS-LC-M	Tee Shirt - Lincoln College emblem	M	6.99	8.99
TS-LC-L	Tee Shirt - Lincoln College emblem	L	8.99	10.99
Shorts-S	Shorts	S	7.99	9.99
Shorts-M	Shorts	M	9.99	11.99
Shorts-L	Shorts	L	11.99	13.99
Shorts-XL	Shorts	XL	13.99	15.99
SP-LC-S	Sweat Pants - Lincoln College emblem	S	9.99	13.99
SP-LC-M	Sweat Pants - Lincoln College emblem	M	11.99	15.99
SP-LC-L	Sweat Pants - Lincoln College emblem	L	13.99	17.99
SP-LC-XL	Sweat Pants - Lincoln College emblem	XL	15.99	19.99

After you enter the data, apply an AutoFormat to quickly format the data list. Then add currency format to all dollar values. Save the file as **Lincoln FF Inventory**.

Ms. Smith has also asked that you sort the list by Item No. Finally, Ms. Smith would like a printout of this information

ACTIVITY 3-2

Use Excel's Help system to find information on databases in Excel as they relate to the topics covered in this lesson.

FILTERING AND EXTRACTING DATA

OBJECTIVES

Upon completion of this lesson, you should be able to:

■ Search a list using AutoFilter.

■ Search for records using the Top 10 feature.

■ Search a list using search operators.

■ Search for and extract records using advanced filters.

⏱ **Estimated Time: 1.5 hours**

Introduction

In the previous lesson, you learned how to create a list. Data was entered into a worksheet according to specific guidelines. When data is entered as a list, it can be manipulated in a variety of ways. In this lesson, you will learn how to *filter* (or find) records that meet certain criteria.

Displaying Records Using AutoFilter

AutoFilter is an Excel feature that lets you display only the records in a data list that meet specific criteria. When you apply the AutoFilter feature to your list, arrows appear in the cell for each column heading, as shown in Figure 4-1.

Click on these arrows to display a drop-down list for that field, similar to Figure 4-2. The drop-down list contains the different entries in that field, as well as other search options, such as Custom, which allows you to create your own search.

Select an entry, or one of the other search options, from the drop-down list, and Excel displays only records that meet the selected criteria. For example, if you selected the $2.99 entry in the Selling Price drop-down list shown in Figure 4-2, Excel would display only those records that had that value in the Selling Price field. The other records in the list are temporarily hidden from view. To redisplay them, click the AutoFilter button for the field you used to filter the records, and select the All option at the top of the drop-down list. You can tell which field (or column) is filtered because the filter arrow will be a different color from the other arrows. You can edit or modify records in a filtered list, and you can print the worksheet with only the filtered list displayed.

FIGURE 4-1
Applying AutoFilter

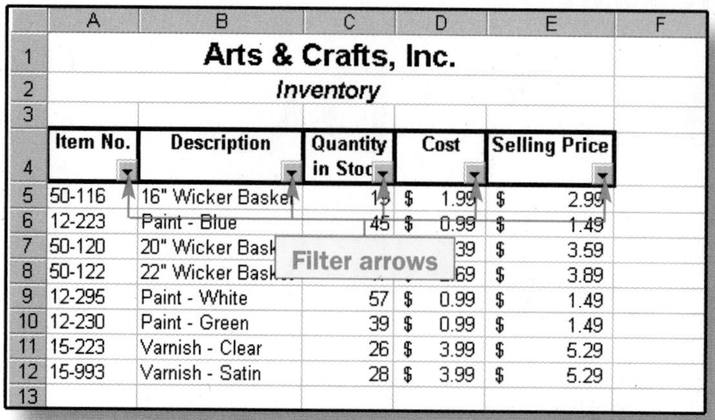

FIGURE 4-2
AutoFilter drop-down list

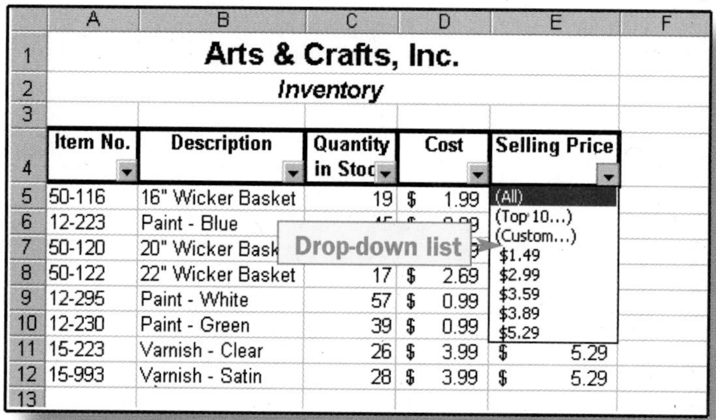

STEP-BY-STEP ▷ 4.1

1. Open the **AE Step4-1** workbook from the student data files and save it as **Filter1** followed by your initials.

2. Select a cell in the field name row. Open the **Data** menu, select **Filter,** and then select **AutoFilter.**

3. Click the **Cost** filter arrow.

4. Click **$0.99**. Notice how only the records that have a cost of $0.99 are displayed.

5. To redisplay all the records, click the **Cost** filter arrow and select **All.**

6. Let's try another filter. Click the **Selling Price** filter arrow.

7. Select **$5.29**. Note that only the records with a selling price of $5.29 are shown.

8. Print the filtered list. Then redisplay all records and remain in this screen for the next Step-by-Step.

Searching for Records Using Top 10

Excel's Top 10 feature offers you the ability to quickly display the highest or lowest values in a data list. For example, suppose you want to see the customers who have the highest account balances. You could quickly select these records using the Top 10 option from the AutoFilter list. Even though it's called the Top 10, you can display any number of records at the top or bottom of a list.

When you select the Top 10 feature, a dialog box appears, similar to Figure 4-3. The first option box in the Top 10 AutoFilter dialog box

FIGURE 4-3
Top 10 AutoFilter dialog box

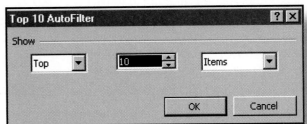

lets you choose the top or bottom of the list. The middle option box lets you select the number of records or the percentage of records to be displayed. The last option box lets you choose items or percent, meaning you can display a specific number of records to appear in the selected AutoFilter column or a percentage of records, such as the top 25%.

STEP-BY-STEP ▷ 4.2

1. Click the AutoFilter arrow for **Selling Price**.

2. Choose **Top 10**.

3. Click the down arrow next to the middle option box until **5** appears in the box.

4. Click **OK**. Five records with the highest selling prices should be displayed.

5. Let's try this again. Redisplay all records.

6. Click the **Quantity in Stock** AutoFilter arrow and choose **Top 10**.

7. Click the up arrow for the middle option box until **25** is displayed.

8. Click the drop-down list arrow for the last option box and choose **Percent**.

9. Click **OK**. You should see two records that make up the top 25% of records containing the highest quantities in stock.

10. Save the workbook as **Filter2** followed by your initial, and then print the filtered list.

11. Redisplay all records and remain in this screen for the next Step-by-Step.

Searching a List Using Search Operators

So far, you've located records meeting specific criteria, such as items that cost $0.99. In some cases though, you may need to find records that meet less-specific criteria or that fall into a range. For example, you may want to find all the records that have a cost of $1.49 *or greater*. To search in this manner, you will use **search operators.** Excel's search operators and their descriptions are explained in Table 4-1.

TABLE 4-1
Search operators

OPERATOR	EXAMPLE	THE FIELD VALUE IS
equals	equals 10	10
does not equal	does not equal 10	All values but 10
is greater than	is greater than 10	11 or greater
is greater than or equal to	is greater than or equal to 10	10 or greater
is less than	is less than 10	9 or less
is less than or equal to	is less than or equal to 10	10 or less
begins with	begins with C	any value that begins with C or c
does not begin with	does not begin with C	any value that does not begin with C or c
ends with	ends with 7	any value that ends with a 7
does not end with	does not end with 7	any value that does not end with a 7
contains	contains 1998 in them	any value that contains 1998 anywhere
does not contain	does not contain 1998 anywhere in them	any value that does not contain 1998

You select operators in the Custom AutoFilter dialog box, which is shown in Figure 4-4. Select an operator in the first text box by selecting from the drop-down list. Enter the search criteria in the text box to the right. We'll discuss the other options in the Custom AutoFilter dialog box later in this lesson.

FIGURE 4-4
Custom AutoFilter dialog box

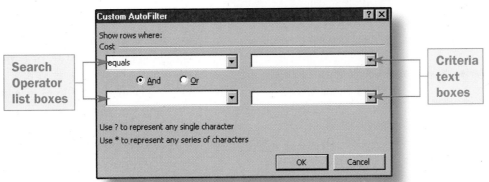

Search Operator list boxes

Criteria text boxes

STEP-BY-STEP 4.3

1. Click the **Cost** filter arrow.

2. Select **Custom**. The Custom AutoFilter dialog box appears, similar to Figure 4-4.

3. Click the drop-down list arrow next to the first text box and select **is greater than** from the list.

4. Click the drop-down list arrow in the box to the right and select **$0.99**. This tells Excel to find all records with costs greater than $0.99.

5. Click **OK**. You should see records that have costs greater than $0.99.

6. Display all records.

7. Let's try this again. Select the **Selling Price** filter arrow and select **Custom**.

8. Select **is less than** as the search operator.

9. Select **$5.29** as the criteria and click **OK**. You should see six records that have a selling price less than $5.29.

10. Display all the records and remain in this screen for the next Step-by-Step.

Searching a List Using AND

There may be times when you want to locate records that meet two criteria. For example, you may want to locate customers who have account balances over $200.00 *and* under $500.00. You can accomplish this by using *AND* in your search. You set up an AND search in the Custom AutoFilter dialog box, as shown in Figure 4-5.

FIGURE 4-5
Custom AutoFilter using AND

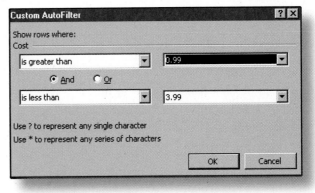

S TEP-BY-STEP ▷ 4.4

1. Click the **Cost** filter arrow and choose **Custom**.

2. Choose **is greater than** from the top search operator list box and select **$0.99** as the criteria.

3. Click **And** if it is not already selected.

4. Choose **is less than** from the bottom search operator list box and select **$3.99** as the criteria.

5. Click **OK**. You should see three records with costs greater than $0.99 and less than $3.99.

6. Save the workbook as **Filter3** followed by your initials and print the filtered list.

7. Display all records again and remain in this screen for the next Step-by-Step.

Searching a List Using OR

Excel also allows you to search for records in a single field that meet one set of criteria *or* another. For example, you may want to search for all customers based in *either* California or Texas. To search for more than one value, you use the *OR* search operator. You set up an OR search in the Custom AutoFilter dialog box, as shown in Figure 4-6.

FIGURE 4-6
Custom AutoFilter using OR

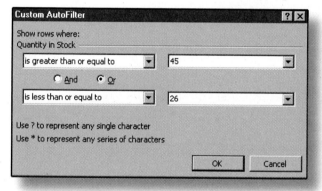

S TEP-BY-STEP ▷ 4.5

1. Click the **Quantity in Stock** filter arrow and choose **Custom**.

2. Select **is greater than or equal to** from the search operator list box and select **45** as the criteria.

3. Click **Or**.

4. Select **is less than or equal to** from the bottom search operator list box and select **26** as the criteria.

5. Click **OK**. You should see six records with a Quantity in Stock greater than or equal to 45 and less than or equal to 26.

6. Save the workbook as **Filter4**, followed by your initials, and then print the filtered list.

7. Display all the records again, and remain in the screen for the next Step-by-Step.

Searching a List Using Wildcards

So far, you've only searched for known values. But what if you don't know the exact value? This is where *wildcards* come in handy. Wildcards are used when you don't know the exact spelling of a word or name, or the exact value you're searching for. For example, you may want to find all the records for employees whose last names begin with A.

The wildcard symbols are an asterisk (*) and a question mark (?). A question mark (?) represents a single character and the asterisk (*) represents several characters. Table 4-2 lists examples of the wildcards and how you could use them.

TABLE 4-2
Wildcards

IF YOU ENTER . . .	EXCEL FINDS
A*	Apple, Alberdeen, Alabama
9??37	92237, 94537, 99937
J*n	June, January, Janet

STEP-BY-STEP 4.6

1. Click the **Item No.** filter arrow and choose **Custom**.

2. Key **50-*** in the top criteria text box and click **OK**. You should see three records with item numbers beginning with 50-.

3. Display all records.

4. Select the **Description** filter arrow and choose **Custom**.

5. Key **Paint - ?????** in the top criteria text box. This will find records that begin with Paint and have a five letter word following the -.

6. Click **OK**. You should see two records that meet the criteria.

7. Save the workbook as **Filter5** followed by your initials and then print the filtered list.

8. Display all records.

9. You are now finished using AutoFilter. Open the **Data** menu, select **Filter**, and then choose **AutoFilter**. The AutoFilter arrows should no longer be displayed. Remain in this screen for the next Step-by-Step.

Displaying Records Using Advanced Filters

In your previous searches, Excel would find records that met specific criteria and only display these records. Records not meeting this criteria would be temporarily removed from the screen. There may be instances, however, where you want to continue viewing all data list records and have records that meet a specific criteria copied to another location on the worksheet. This lets you view the list records and records that meet specific criteria at the same time. Excel lets you accomplish this with advanced filters.

The Advanced Filter feature searches for records meeting a criteria and copies the records to a specified range in the worksheet called the *copy to range*. The original records are left intact.

To specify the criteria using advanced filters, enter the search criteria in an area in the worksheet designated as the *criteria range*.

Each range will have field names. The field names must be the same for each range because Excel uses the field names as an indicator of what field should be searched. A sample worksheet using an advanced filter is shown in Figure 4-7.

After you enter search data in the criteria range, you select the Data menu, Filter, and then Advanced Filter. In order to have Excel copy records to the copy to range, select the *Copy to another location* option and enter this range in the *Copy to* text box. The *Unique records only* option prevents duplicate records from being copied to the copy to range.

FIGURE 4-7
Advanced filter worksheet setup

S TEP-BY-STEP ▷ 4.7

1. Create a criteria range. You will need to copy the data list field names to the criteria range. Select the range **A4:E4** (the field name row) and click the **Copy** button. When determining where the criteria range should be placed, try to allow enough blank rows below the list range so additional records could be added to the list in the future.

2. Select cell **A16** and click the **Paste** button.

3. Now let's create the copy to range. You will want to copy the list field names to this range as well. Select cell **A22** and click the **Paste** button.

4. Select cell **A17** in the criteria range and key **12-***. This tells Excel to search for all records with item numbers beginning with 12-.

5. Click anywhere in the list, open the **Data** menu, select **Filter**, and select **Advanced Filter**. The Advanced Filter dialog box appears, as shown in Figure 4-8.

FIGURE 4-8
Advanced Filter dialog box

6. Click the **Copy to another location** option. This instructs Excel to copy the filtered records to the copy to range.

7. Verify that the list range **$A$4:$E$12** is in the *List range* text box.

8. In the *Criteria range* text box, key **A16:E17**. You need to include the criteria range field

names and enough blank rows beneath the criteria field names to accommodate the criteria you are entering.

Hot Tip

You can use the Collapse Dialog button to select any of the ranges.

9. In the *Copy to* text box, key **A22:E35**. You need to include the field names and enough blank rows beneath the copy range field names to accommodate the records that Excel finds.

10. Click **OK**. Scroll to the copy to range. You should see three records with item numbers beginning with 12-. Remain in this screen for the next Step-by-Step.

Using Advanced Filters to Find Multiple Criteria

When you looked for records that met two criteria with AutoFilter, you used the AND search option. You can use this same search option with advanced filters. To find records that meet two criteria, you enter the criteria in the *same row* in the criteria range, as shown in Figure 4-9.

To find records that met one search criteria or another, you used the OR search option in AutoFilter. To search for records meeting one criteria or another in an advanced filter, you enter the criteria on *separate rows*.

 Hot Tip

Microsoft Query is an add-in program that lets you bring data into Excel from external sources. This eliminates the need to retype the information in an Excel list. You can retrieve data from several types of databases, including Microsoft Access, Microsoft SQL Server, and Microsoft SQL Server OLAP Services. You can also retrieve data from other Excel lists, from text files, and from the Web.

FIGURE 4-9
Using AND in an advanced filter

	A	B	C	D	E	F
1		Arts & Crafts, Inc.				
2		Inventory				
3						
4	Item No.	Description	Quantity in Stock	Cost	Selling Price	
5	50-116	16" Wicker Basket	19	$ 1.99	$ 2.99	
6	12-223	Paint - Blue	45	$ 0.99	$ 1.49	
7	50-120	20" Wicker Basket	21	$ 2.39	$ 3.59	
8	50-122	22" Wicker Basket	17	$ 2.69	$ 3.89	
9	12-295	Paint - White	57	$ 0.99	$ 1.49	
10	12-230	Paint - Green	39	$ 0.99	$ 1.49	
11	15-223	Varnish - Clear	26	$ 3.99	$ 5.29	
12	15-993	Varnish - Satin	28	$ 3.99	$ 5.29	
13						
14						
15						
16	Item No.	Description	Quantity in Stock	Cost	Selling Price	
17	50-*			>$2.00		
18						
19						
20						
21						
22	Item No.	Description	Quantity in Stock	Cost	Selling Price	
23	50-120	20" Wicker Basket	21	$ 2.39	$ 3.59	
24	50-122	22" Wicker Basket	17	$ 2.69	$ 3.89	

Data List

Criteria range

Copy to range

1. Select cell **A17** and clear the contents of the cell. You must remove criteria from a previous search before you can start a new search.

2. Enter **50-*** in cell **A17**.

3. Select cell **D17** and enter **>$2.00**. This will find all records that have an item number beginning with 50- and that have a cost greater than $2.00.

4. Click in any part of the data list, open the **Data** menu, select **Filter**, and select **Advanced Filter**.

5. Select **Copy to another location**.

6. Check the list, criteria, and copy to ranges. These ranges should still be entered correctly in the text boxes. If not, enter these ranges at this time.

7. Click **OK**. Look at the copy to range. You should see the records for item numbers beginning with 50- that have a cost greater than $2.00.

8. Let's try another advanced filter. Select the cells in the criteria range that you used in the previous search and clear the contents.

9. Select cell **D17** and enter **$.99**.

10. Select cell **D18** and enter **$3.99**. (This will find all records that have a cost of either $0.99 or $3.99.)

11. Click in any part of the list, open the **Data** menu, select **Filter**, and then select **Advanced Filter**.

12. Click **Copy to another location**.

13. In the *Criteria range* text box, delete the current range and key **A16:E18**. (You need to expand the range one row because you've entered criteria on two rows in the criteria range.)

14. In the *Copy to* text box, delete the current range and key **A22:E35**, if necessary.

15. Click **OK**. Look at the copy to range. You should see five records that have a cost of $0.99 or $3.99.

16. Save the workbook as **Filter6** followed by your initials.

17. Print the data, including the column headings, in the copy to range only.

18. Save and close the workbook.

Summary

In this lesson, you learned:

■ AutoFilter can be used to find records within a list that meet specific criteria. When you select AutoFilter on the Data menu, arrows are displayed in each field name's cell. You click the AutoFilter arrow for the field you want to search and select the entry or other search option from the drop-down list. Excel displays only those records containing the specified field criteria.

- Excel's search operators let you quickly create your search criteria. You use the AND search operator to find records that meet two criteria and the OR search operator to find records that meet one criteria or another.

- Wildcard characters can be used when you're not sure about the complete value for which you're searching. The asterisk (*) wildcard is used to represent any number of characters or numbers and the question mark (?) wildcard is used to represent a single character or number.

- Advanced filters can be used to find records that meet more complex criteria. The results of the search can then be copied to another location on the worksheet.

LESSON 4 REVIEW QUESTIONS

WRITTEN QUESTIONS

Write a brief answer to the following questions.

1. When would you use AND in a search? *When two conditions must be met for the search.*

2. When would you use OR in a search? *If either condition will suffice for search requirement.*

3. What is the difference between AutoFilter and Advanced Filter?
   * *auto filter shows only the records that meet search criteria and is more limited in the criteria*
   * *Advanced filter allows for viewing the complete list and the resulting search at the same time*

4. How do you indicate you want to find records meeting two criteria on different fields using advanced filters? *Use multiple fields on the same line*

5. How do you find records meeting one criteria or another using advanced filters.
Use multiple lines

TRUE/FALSE

Circle T if the statement is true or F if the statement is false.

T **F** 1. AutoFilter lets you copy records found in a search to another range on the worksheet.

T **F** 2. You can use the AND operator in an advanced filter, but not in an AutoFilter.

T **F** 3. If you wanted to find employees who worked in the Accounting department and the Marketing department, you would use the AND operator.

T **F** 4. If you selected the Top, 50, and Percent options in the Top 10 dialog box, the first 50% of records would be displayed.

T F 5. If you enter the search operator *begins with C*, the filter would find records that begin with C or c.

LESSON 4 PROJECTS

PROJECT 4-1

1. Open the **AE Project4-1** workbook from the student data files and save it as **Pet Store Inventory** followed by your initials.

2. Use AutoFilter to find products that cost less than $1.00. Print the filtered list in landscape orientation and so all the data fits on one page.

3. Use an advanced filter to find records for all Kitten products with a quantity in stock less than 100. Copy the found records to a range on the worksheet.

4. Print the copy to range, including column headings, in landscape orientation and so all the data fits on one page.

5. Save and close the workbook.

PROJECT 4-2

1. Open the **AE Project4-2** workbook from the student data files.

2. Use advanced filters to find records with the following criteria. Use a copy to range.
   A. Products that are available in a small size. Save the file as **Sports Store Sales – Small Size** followed by your initials. Print the results in portrait orientation.
   B. Products that have a sales price greater than $10.00 that are available in a large size. Save the file as Sports **Store Sales – Large Size** followed by your initials. Print the results in portrait orientation.

3. Save and then close the workbook.

CRITICAL THINKING

SCANS

ACTIVITY 4-1

You work in the personnel department at New Horizon Engine Corporation. You've set up a data list containing an extensive number of records. You decide to protect the worksheet to prevent changes. However, you've noticed that when you try to run an advanced filter on the list, you cannot redisplay the records afterward. Use Excel's Help system to determine why this is happening and how you can resolve the problem.

WORKING WITH ANALYSIS TOOLS AND PIVOTTABLES

OBJECTIVES

Upon completion of this lesson, you should be able to:

- Create scenarios.
- Use Excel's auditing feature.
- Create a PivotTable report, and an interactive PivotTable report.
- Create a PivotChart.
- Use Goal Seek.
- Use Solver.

⏱ Estimated Time: 2 hours

Introduction

Excel features a number of tools that give you the power to manipulate, analyze, and interpret worksheet data. Scenarios allow you to view what would happen to existing worksheet data if the value in one or more cells is changed. For example, if your company was expecting to receive increased revenue next year, you could use a scenario to see how your net income (bottom line) would be affected by this change. The auditing feature is designed to pinpoint errors in formulas. A PivotTable lets you rearrange how data in a list is organized. You can drag fields (or columns) to different locations in the PivotTable report in order to present the data in new way.

Creating Scenarios

A *scenario* is a group of values that produce different results when calculated. Scenarios are often used to develop budgets. For example, you may expect shipping or equipment expenses to increase next year. To find out how these increased expenses may affect your future budget, you can use the Scenario Manager to insert different values that generate different versions of the budget.

To create scenarios, you open the Scenario Manager dialog box, which is shown in Figure 5-1. Click Add to open the Add Scenario dialog box, shown in Figure 5-2. This is where you create a scenario. Enter a name for the scenario and then determine which cells contain the values that can be changed to produce a different result. Click OK to create the scenario. After you've created your scenarios, you can have the Scenario Manager save them in a preset report format on a separate sheet in the workbook. Excel automatically names the sheet "Scenario Summary" and applies formatting to the data.

You can combine scenarios into reports by using the Report Manager add-in. For example, if you have a "best case" scenario and a "worst case" scenario you can create a report that would print both of these scenarios. After a report is added, it is saved as a worksheet in the workbook.

FIGURE 5-1
Scenario Manager dialog box

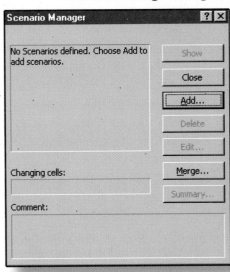

FIGURE 5-2
Add Scenario dialog box

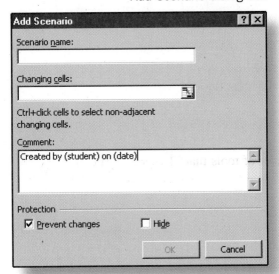

S TEP-BY-STEP ▷ 5.1

1. Open the **AE Step5-1** workbook from the student data files and save it as **International Income Statement** followed by your initials.

2. View the current budget.

3. Select the range **A5:B19**.

(continued on next page)

A E - 5 5

4. Open the **Tools** menu and then select **Scenarios**.

5. Click the **Add** button in the Scenario Manager dialog box.

6. In the Add Scenario dialog box, key **Current Budget** in the *Scenario name* text box.

7. Click the **Collapse Dialog** button in the *Changing cells* box, select the range **B10:B16**, and then press **Enter**.

8. Click **OK**. The scenario values appear in the Scenario Values dialog box.

9. Click **Add** in the Scenario Manager dialog box.

10. Key **Increased Equipment and Shipping** in the *Scenario name* text box and click **OK**.

11. In the Scenario Values dialog box, click in the **Equipment** text box (1:) and enter **90000**.

12. Click in the **Freight** text box (2:) and enter **9000**.

13. Click in the **Postage** text box (5:) and enter **8000**.

14. Click **OK**.

15. Click **Add** in the Scenario Manager dialog box.

16. Key **Increased Shipping and Office Supplies** in the *Scenario name* text box and click **OK**.

17. Click in the **Freight** text box and enter **10000**.

18. Click in the **Office Supplies** text box and enter **8500**.

19. Click in the **Postage** text box and enter **8000**.

20. Click **OK**.

21. In the Scenario Manager dialog box, click **Summary**.

22. In the Scenario Summary dialog box, make sure *Scenario summary* is selected and click **OK**. The scenarios are placed on a new Scenario Summary worksheet in the workbook.

23. Print the **Scenario Summary** worksheet in landscape orientation and so all the data fits on one page. Then save and close the workbook.

Using Excel's Auditing Feature

Excel's auditing feature identifies the cells that are referenced in a formula, thereby making it easier for you to determine where an error might occur in a formula. To use the auditing tools, you can select the Auditing commands on the Tools menu or display the Auditing toolbar to access the commands via toolbar buttons.

The auditing feature lets you trace *precedents* and *dependents*. A *precedent* refers to the cells that are referenced in a formula. If you select a cell containing a formula and then click the Trace Precedents button on the Auditing toolbar, Excel draws a line from the formula cell to each cell that is referenced in the formula.

A *dependent* refers to the cells that contain formulas that reference a selected cell. If you select a cell that contains a value and then click the Trace Dependents button on the Auditing toolbar, Excel draws a line to each cell that contains a formula that references the selected cell.

Figure 5-3 illustrates how Excel traces precedents and dependents. Cell F5 contains a formula that references cells B5, C5, D5, and E5. These are its precedents, as identified by the blue Trace Precedents

FIGURE 5-3
Tracing precedents and dependents

	A	B	C	D	E	F
1		Auto Parts, Inc.				
2		Number of Parts Sold				
3					Trace Precedents line	
4	Item	Spring	Summer	Fall	Winter	Total
5	Engines	2,000	1,977	2,133	2,204	8,314
6	Transmissions	3,321	3,194	2,988	3,087	12,590
7	Batteries	9,000	8,766	8,905	9,102	35,773
8	Brake Shoes	7,734	6,908			31,207
9	Tune-up Kits	10,988	9,788			42,981
10	Total	33,043	30,633	32,993	34,196	130,865
11						
12						
13						
14	Average Parts Sold	6,609	6,127	6,599	6,839	26,173

Trace Dependents line

Auditing toolbar

line through the cells. The value in cell B6 is used in formulas contained in cells F6, B10, and B14, as indicated by the arrows on the Trace Dependents lines.

Figure 5-3 also shows the Auditing toolbar. You can remove the precedents and dependents lines by clicking either the Remove Precedent Arrows or Remove Dependent Arrows buttons. Or you can click the Remove All Arrows button. If a cell contains a message like #DIV/0!, indicating an error in the formula, you can select it and click the Trace Error button on the Auditing toolbar. A red line is drawn to the cell(s) in which the problem occurs. The Circle Invalid Data and Clear Validation Circles buttons relate to finding cells that contain data that is outside the rules of validation that you've set.

STEP-BY-STEP ▷ 5.2

1. Open the **AE Step5-2** workbook from the student data files and save it as **Auto Parts** followed by your initials.

2. Open the **Tools** menu, select **Auditing**, and then choose **Show Auditing Toolbar**.

3. Click cell **F5**.

4. Click the **Trace Precedents** button. Your screen should look similar to Figure 5-4. Notice the line drawn through the cells contained in the formula. An arrow is displayed in the cell with the formula.

5. Click cell **B6**.

6. Click the **Trace Dependents** button. Notice that an arrow appears in each cell containing a formula that references cell B6. formula cells that contains cell B6 within the formula. You should have arrows in cells B10, B14, and F6. Your screen should look similar to Figure 5-5.

7. Notice that cell **G14** contains the #DIV/0! error message. Select the cell and then click the **Trace Error** button. A line from the cell extends to the cells G5:G9. This indicates that

(continued on next page)

A E - 5 7

FIGURE 5-4
Tracing precedents

	A	B	C	D	E	F
1		*Auto Parts, Inc.*				
2		*Number of Parts Sold*				
3						
4	**Item**	**Spring**	**Summer**	**Fall**	**Winter**	**Total**
5	*Engines*	2,000	1,977	2,133	2,204	**8,314**
6	*Transmissions*	3,321	3,194	2,988	3,087	**12,590**
7	*Batteries*	9,000	8,766	8,905	9,102	**35,773**
8	*Brake Shoes*	7,734	6,908	8,744	7,821	**31,207**
9	*Tune-up Kits*	10,988	9,788	10,223	11,982	**42,981**
10	**Total**	**33,043**	**30,633**	**32,993**	**34,196**	130,865
11						
12				▼ Auditing		
13						
14	**Average Parts Sold**	**6,609**	6,12			

Sheet1 / Sheet2 / Sheet3 /

FIGURE 5-5
Tracing dependents

	A	B	C	D	E	F
1		*Auto Parts, Inc.*				
2		*Number of Parts Sold*				
3						
4	**Item**	**Spring**	**Summer**	**Fall**	**Winter**	**Total**
5	*Engines*	2,000	1,977	2,133	2,204	**8,314**
6	*Transmissions*	3,321	3,194	2,988	3,087	**12,590**
7	*Batteries*	9,000	8,766	8,905	9,102	**35,773**
8	*Brake Shoes*	7,734	6,908	8,744	7,821	**31,207**
9	*Tune-up Kits*	10,988	9,788	10,223	11,982	**42,981**
10	**Total**	**33,043**	**30,633**	**32,993**	**34,196**	**130,865**
11						
12				▼ Auditing		
13						
14	**Average Parts Sold**	**6,609**	6,12			

Sheet1 / Sheet2 / Sheet3 /

the error is coming from Excel's inability to average cells with no data.

8. Click **Print Preview** to see how you could print this sheet with arrows displayed. Click **Close**.

9. Edit cell **G14** so that the formula finds the average of the values in cells **B14:F14**. The

error message is replaced by a correct value and the Trace Error arrows are removed.

10. Remove all arrows by clicking the **Remove All Arrows** button on the Auditing toolbar, and then print the worksheet in landscape orientation.

11. Save and close the workbook.

Creating a PivotTable Report

A ***PivotTable report*** is a unique Excel tool that lets you rearrange and summarize data in a list in order to analyze or interpret it in a different manner. It is an *interactive* feature, meaning you control how data is displayed by dragging items in the PivotTable window. For example, say you have a worksheet on employees that includes fields (or columns) for Last Name, First Name, Division, Starting Date, and Salary. You decide you want to see salary totals by division. You can use the PivotTable feature to quickly reorganize the data in an easy-to-read report format.

You can place the PivotTable report on a separate worksheet in the workbook or in another location within the same worksheet. You can also create a PivotChart from the report, which is discussed in the next section. Figure 5-6 shows a worksheet containing a data list and Figure 5-7 shows a PivotTable report created from the list. The PivotTable and PivotChart Wizard will take you step-by-step through the process of creating a PivotTable report. If you make changes to data in the worksheet you need to click the Refresh Data button on the PivotTable toolbar in order for the changes to be shown in the report.

FIGURE 5-6
Data list

	A	B	C	D	E
1	**Cellular Sales**				
2	*Employee List*				
3					
4					
5					
6	***Last Name***	***First Name***	***Division***	***Start Date***	***Salary***
7	Baines	Bill	Marketing	December 31, 2001	$30,000.00
8	Caldwell	Sue	Marketing	June 30, 1976	$40,000.00
9	Dominquez	David	Sales	March 14, 2000	$55,000.00
10	Giraddelli	Lilly	Accounting	February 15, 1987	$39,000.00
11	Holder	Howard	Sales	December 31, 1999	$34,000.00
12	Johnson	Jack	Accounting	May 24, 1990	$26,000.00
13	Tanquez	Trevor	Marketing	February 15, 1987	$52,000.00
14	Vegas	Vivala	Sales	July 27, 1987	$35,000.00
15	Crawford	Katie	Clerical	January 28, 1988	$29,000.00
16	Dominquez	Gary	Sales	July 31, 1988	$45,000.00
17	Gonzalez	Lisa	Accounting	February 1, 1989	$29,000.00
18	Goodwin	Sallye	Marketing	August 5, 1989	$34,000.00
19	Keplinger	JoAnne	Marketing	February 6, 1990	$30,000.00
20	Khorjin	Fugi	Marketing	August 10, 1990	$40,000.00

Sheet1 / Sheet2 / Sheet3

FIGURE 5-7
PivotTable report

	A	B	C
1	Drop Page Fields Here		
2			
3	Sum of Salary		
4	Division	Total	
5	Accounting	164000	
6	Clerical	105000	
7	Marketing	226000	
8	Sales	223000	
9	Grand Total	718000	
10			

STEP-BY-STEP 5.3

1. Open the **AE Step5-3** workbook from the student data files and save it as **Cellular Sales PivotTable** followed by your initials.

2. Click in any cell in the data list.

3. Open the **Data** menu and select **PivotTable and PivotChart Report**. The Step 1 of 3 PivotTable and PivotChart Wizard dialog box appears, as shown in Figure 5-8.

4. If necessary, select **Microsoft Excel list or database** and choose **PivotTable**.

5. Click **Next**. The Step 2 of 3 dialog box appears, as shown in Figure 5-9.

6. The range **A6:E28** should be displayed in the *Range* text box. Click **Next**. The Step 3 of 3 PivotTable and PivotChart Wizard dialog box appears, as shown in Figure 5-10.

7. Be sure that **New worksheet** is selected and click **Finish**. Your screen should appear similar to Figure 5-11.

(continued on next page)

FIGURE 5-8

PivotTable and PivotChart Wizard – Step 1 of 3 dialog box

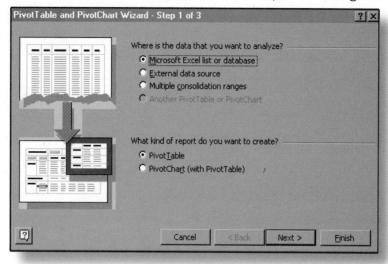

FIGURE 5-9

PivotTable and PivotChart Wizard – Step 2 of 3 dialog box

FIGURE 5-10

PivotTable and PivotChart Wizard – Step 3 of 3 dialog box

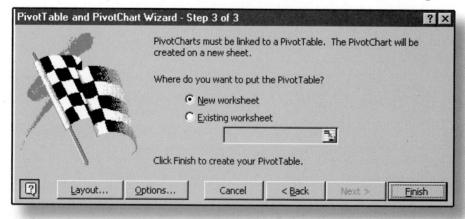

FIGURE 5-11
PivotTable report screen

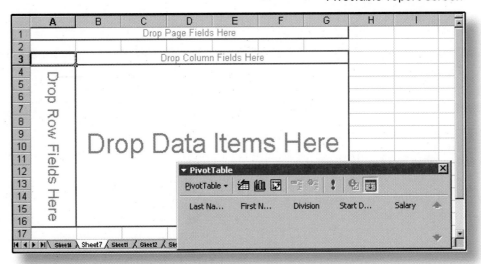

 Concept Builder

You can click the Layout button in the PivotTable and PivotChart Wizard - Step 3 of 3 dialog box to display the PivotTable structure that is shown in Figure 5-11.

8. Drag the **Division** field button on the PivotTable toolbar to the *Drop Row Fields Here* area.

9. Drag the **Salary** field button on the toolbar to the *Drop Data Items Here* area.

10. The PivotTable report should instantly appear, as shown in Figure 5-12. Notice that it is placed on a new worksheet, named *Sheet4*.

11. Let's rearrange the data for a different view. Click the **PivotTable Wizard** button on the toolbar. The Step 3 of 3 wizard dialog box opens.

FIGURE 5-12
Complete PivotTable

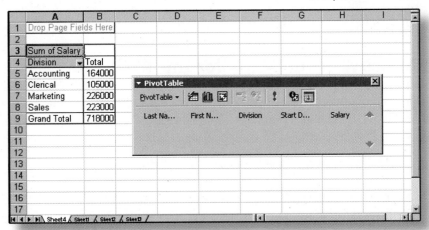

(continued on next page)

A E - 6 1

12. Click the **Layout** button. Drag the existing field buttons off the table diagram to clear it. Then, drag the **Division** field button to the Page section. Drag the **Last Name** field button to the Row section. Drag the **Salary** field button to the Data section.

13. Click **OK** to close the Layout dialog box, and then click **Finish** to close the wizard. Your PivotTable report should look like that shown in Figure 5-13.

14. Click the arrow in cell **B1**, select **Marketing**, and click **OK**. Notice how only the Marketing personnel salaries are now displayed.

15. Format the range **B5:B11** as **Currency** with no decimal places. Print **Sheet4** of the workbook. Save and then close the workbook.

Concept Builder

PivotTable reports can be formatted automatically using the Format Report button on the PivotTable toolbar. Click the button and an AutoFormat dialog box opens, displaying a number of preset formats from which you can choose.

4-22-04
1530

FIGURE 5-13
Rearranging data in the PivotTable

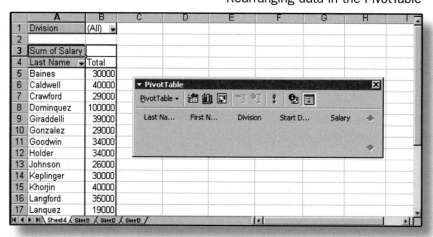

Start Here

Creating Interactive PivotTables for the Web

Excel's new interactive PivotTable feature lets users interact with the PivotTable data in Microsoft's browser program Internet Explorer. You can rearrange the data by dragging fields, just like you do in a regular PivotTable. You can also publish a PivotTable as a non-interactive Web page by simply saving it in HTML format. Others will not be able to change its layout or the way data is displayed.

S TEP-BY-STEP ▷ 5.4

1. Open the **AE Step5-4** workbook from the student files.

2. Save the workbook as an HTML file by opening the **File** menu and selecting **Save As Web Page**.

3. Enter **IAPivot** for the filename. Click the **Publish** button.

4. Choose **PivotTable** in the list box below the **Choose** text box.

5. Click the **Add interactivity with** option. Choose **PivotTable functionality** if necessary.

6. Click the **Open published web page in browser** option.

7. Click **Publish**. Microsoft Internet Explorer starts and the PivotTable appears in the Explorer window.

8. Since you requested that this PivotTable be interactive, you can make changes to it. Place your mouse pointer over the **Division** field in the upper left corner of the PivotTable. Your mouse pointer will turn into a four-headed arrow. Drag the **Division** field to the **Drop Column Fields Here** section in the PivotTable. The PivotTable now displays all of the Divisions at one time.

9. Close **Microsoft Internet Explorer**. Then close the **AE Step5-4** workbook. Remain in this screen for the next Step-by-Step.

Creating a PivotChart

Not only can you rearrange the data in worksheet by creating PivotTable reports, you can create a visual representation of this data in a PivotChart. A PivotChart report must be associated with a PivotTable report in the same workbook. Therefore, if a change is made to the PivotTable, the associated PivotChart changes as well.

You use the PivotTable and PivotChart Report Wizard to create the PivotChart. The wizard lets you specify the type of the data you want to use, set options for how the data is used, and lay out the chart elements.

When you create a PivotChart report that is based on an existing PivotTable report, the information in the chart is laid out like the data in the PivotTable report: row data in the table becomes category data (typically the X axis data) in the chart and column data in the table becomes series data (typically the Y axis) in the chart.

Before creating a PivotChart, let's review the parts of a chart as shown in Figure 5-14.

The parts of a chart are described below.

■ **Chart title.** Explains the purpose of the chart.

■ **X axis.** Typically the horizontal axis, which usually displays the categories of data.

■ **Y axis.** Typically the vertical axis, which usually displays the numeric chart data.

With the exception of the pie-type charts, each chart type has two axes: a horizontal and a vertical axis. The horizontal axis normally plots the categories along the bottom of the chart. The vertical axis normally plots values (such as dollar amounts) along the left side of the chart.

FIGURE 5-14
Parts of a chart

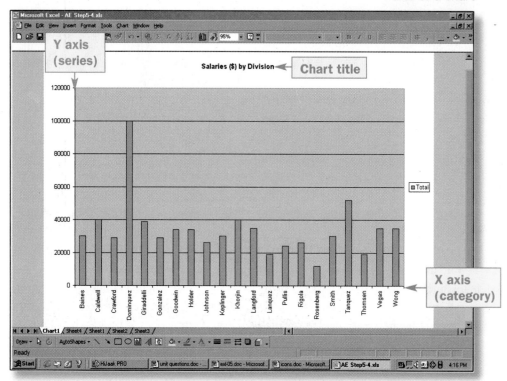

STEP-BY-STEP 5.5

1. Open the **AE Step5-5** workbook from the student data files and save it as **Cellular Sales PivotChart** followed by your initials.

2. Click any cell in the data list.

3. Open the **Data** menu and select **PivotTable and PivotChart Report**. The Step 1 of 3 PivotTable and PivotChart Wizard dialog box appears (see Figure 5-8).

4. If necessary, select **Microsoft Excel list or database** and choose **PivotChart (with PivotTable)**.

5. Click **Next**. The Step 2 of 3 dialog box appears (see Figure 5-9).

6. The range **A6:E28** should be displayed in the *Range* text box. Click **Next**. The Step 3 of 3

PivotTable and PivotChart Wizard dialog box appears (see Figure 5-10).

7. Be sure that **New worksheet** is selected and click **Finish**. Your screen should appear similar to Figure 5-15.

8. Drag the **Division** field button to the *Drop Page Fields Here* area.

9. Drag the **Last Name** field button to the *Drop More Category Fields Here* area. Your screen should look similar to Figure 5-16.

10. Drag the **Salary** field to the *Drop Data Items Here* area. The PivotChart should instantly appear, as shown in Figure 5-17.

11. Click the arrow next to the Division heading and select **Marketing**. Notice how only the

FIGURE 5-15
PivotChart screen

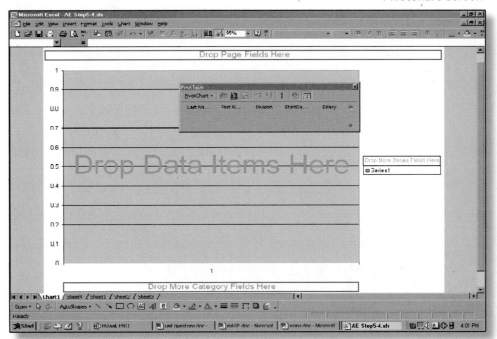

Marketing personnel salaries are now displayed, as shown in Figure 5-18.

12. Print the **Chart1** sheet. Then, save and close the workbook.

FIGURE 5-16
Adding fields to a PivotChart

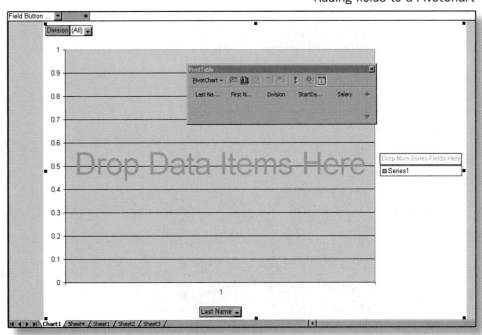

(continued on next page)

FIGURE 5-17
Complete PivotChart

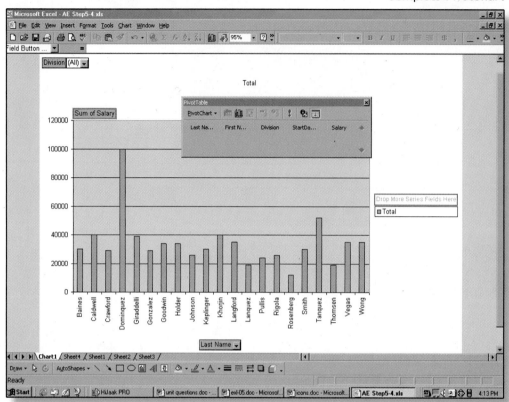

FIGURE 5-18
Salaries of marketing department employees

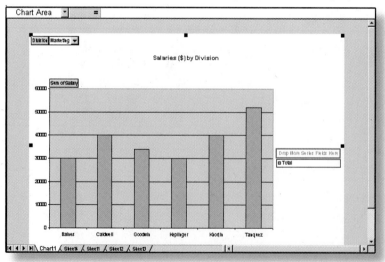

Using Goal Seek

FIGURE 5-19
Goal Seek dialog box

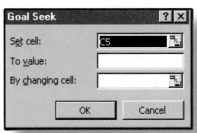

Formulas and functions usually perform mathematical calculations with known values to give you a result. Sometimes, however, you may know the result (goal), but you don't necessarily know the values needed to arrive at the goal. For example, you may want to save $15,000 for your first year of college five years from now. You need to know how much to save each month in order to meet this goal. The **Goal Seek** feature does this for you.

The Goal Seek dialog box is shown in Figure 5-19. In the *Set cell* box, you enter the cell that contains the formula. This lets Excel know what calculation to use when it is looking for the answer. You enter the desired goal in the *To value* box. In the *By changing cell* box, you enter the address for the cell in which you want the answer to be displayed.

STEP-BY-STEP ▷ 5.6

1. Click the **New** button to start a new workbook.

2. Select cell **C5**. (*Note:* You could select any cell to enter the formula in.)

3. Enter **=A5*12*5** (Using the above example with college funds, cell A5 will be the unknown monthly savings amount. Again, you can enter this information into any cell. This formula takes the unknown monthly amount in cell A5 and multiplies it by 12 payments per year for 5 years. You use Goal Seek to find the amount you need in cell A5 to come up with the result of $15,000. For simplicity's sake, let's ignore interest rate.)

4. Select cell **C5** (the cell with the formula).

5. From the **Tools** menu, choose **Goal Seek**. Cell C5 should appear in the *Set cell* text box.

6. In the *To value* box, enter **15000**. This is the goal value.

7. In the *By changing cell* box, enter **A5**. This is the cell address of the unknown value.

8. Click **OK**. The Goal Seek Status dialog box appears to let you know that it has found a value, as shown in Figure 5-20.

FIGURE 5-20
Goal Seek Status dialog box

9. Click **OK** in the Goal Seek Status dialog box and look at the value in cell A5. In this example, 250 should be in the cell. (To double-check if this is accurate, multiply $250 by 12 by 5 and, sure enough, you get $15,000.)

10. Save the file as **College Fund Goal** followed by your initials and close the workbook.

(continued on next page)

11. Now, let's try another example. You will determine what growth rate is necessary for your company to achieve a projected sales amount. Start a new workbook.

12. Select cell **A3** and enter **2001 Total Gross Sales**. Apply a bold format.

13. Select cell **A4** and enter **2001 Projected Growth Rate**. Apply a bold format.

14. Select cell **A5** and enter **2001 Projected Growth Sales**. Apply a bold format.

15. Choose cell **C3** and enter **850,000**. Apply the currency format.

16. Select cell **C5** and enter **=C3*C4**. (This will calculate the projected sales once Goal Seek calculates a growth rate for cell C4.) Format it as currency.

17. Select cell **C4** and give the cell a percentage format with two decimal places.

18. Select cell **C5**. This is the cell with the formula for projected sales.

19. Open the **Tools** menu and then select **Goal Seek**.

20. In the **To value** box, enter **1000000**. In the **By Changing** box, enter **C4**. (This tells Excel to change the amount in cell **C4** until the value is **C5** is $1,000,000.)

21. Click **OK**. The value in cell C4 should be **117.65%**. This indicates a 100% sales rate and a 17.65% growth rate necessary to achieve this projected sales total.

22. Save the workbook as **Projected Sales**. Print the sheet and then close the workbook.

Using Solver

Excel's Solver tool is used to determine two or more unknown values. For example, let's say you have a company that makes three sports products: baseball bats, footballs, and helmets. You need to sell $100,000 of sports equipment per year to break even. You want a general idea of how many of each item you need to sell. Solver can help you calculate how many of each item you need to sell to reach your goal.

STEP-BY-STEP ⇨ 5.7

1. Start a new workbook, and save it as **Solver**, followed by your initials.

2. Select cell **A1** and enter **15** (the sales price for the bat).

3. Select cell **A2** and enter **8** (the sales price for the football).

4. Select cell **A3** and enter **12** (the sales price for the helmet). Format cells **A1:A3** for currency.

5. Enter **0** in cells B1, B2, and B3. (Note: This is where Solver will enter the quantity that should be produced.)

6. Select cell **C1** and enter **=A1*B1** (this tells Excel to multiply the sales price by the quantity sold). Select cell **C2** and enter **=A2*B2**. Select cell **C3** and enter **=A3*B3**.

7. Select cell **C4** and enter **=SUM(C1:C3)**. This will total the dollar amount of sales. This is the cell you will set equal to the total dollar amount of sales you want.

8. For reference, let's enter the equipment item name in the row that contains data for the item. Select cell **D1** and key **Bat**, select cell **D2** and key **Football**, and select cell **D3** and key **Helmet**.

9. Select **C4**. Open the **Tools** menu and then select **Solver**.

 **Hot Tip**

> If the Solver Parameters dialog box does not appear, you will need to select **Add-ins** on the **Tools** menu and then add this feature from the Office 2000 CD.

10. Notice the Max, Min, and Value options in the dialog box. The Max option increases the goal cell to the largest possible value. The Min option increases the goal cell to the smallest possible value. The Value option sets the goal cell value to the value you specify in the Value of text box. Select **Value** and key **100,000** in the Value of text box.

11. In the **By Changing Cells** text box, enter **B1:B3** (these are the cells that will be adjusted to reach the desired solution).

12. Choose **Solve**. Look at the values.

13. Click **OK** when the Solver Results dialog box lets you know it found a solution.

14. You can round the numbers in column B by selecting these cells and clicking the **Decrease Decimal** button for each decimal place you want to remove.

15. Print the sheet. Then, save and close the workbook.

Summary

In this lesson, you learned:

■ Scenarios let you enter possible variations to values in a formula, and display in a Summary Sheet how the various values affect the outcome.

■ The auditing feature is ideal for identifying errors in formulas.

■ PivotTables let you easily and quickly rearrange and summarize data.

■ PivotCharts are ideal for graphically illustrating the data in a PivotTable report.

■ Goal Seek and Solver let you determine unknown values that would result in a specified goal or value.

TRUE/FALSE

Circle T if the statement is true or F if the statement is false.

(T) **F** 1. When you trace dependents of a cell, you are identifying the cells that contain formulas that reference the specified cell.

T **(F)** 2. You can only create one additional scenario for a set of values.

(T) **F** 3. You can change the layout of a PivotTable after it has been created in the PivotTable and PivotChart Wizard.

(T) **F** 4. Excel automatically creates a PivotTable report when you create a PivotChart

T **(F)** 5. You use Goal Seek in order to reorganize data to provide you with a different perspective on it.

WRITTEN QUESTIONS

Write a brief answer to the following questions.

1. Which analysis feature would you use if you wanted to predict how future changes in sales and expenses will affect your company's income?

    Scenarios

2. Which analysis feature would you use if you wanted to rearrange a data list in order to view another perspective of the data?

    Pivot table

3. Describe the purpose of a PivotTable report.

to display data in a desired arrange-ment or extract data in different ways.

4. Which tool would you use if you selected a cell containing a formula and you wanted Excel to draw a line to the cells that are referenced in the formula?

audit → trace precedents

5. Define precedents and dependents in Excel's auditing feature.

precedents - shows cells that are referenced by this cell (one with formula)

dependents - shows which cells reference this cell (one with data)

LESSON 5 PROJECTS

PROJECT 5-1

1. Open the **AE Project5-1** workbook from the student data files and save it as **International Sales** followed by your initials.

2. Select the range **A5:B19**. Create a scenario named **Increased Lease and Utilities Expense**. For the changing cells, enter the range **B10:B16**. Enter the following expenses into the scenario:
Cell B10 (Lease): **75000**
Cell B11 (Utilities): **9000**

3. Click the **Show** button and then click the **Close** button. This "shows" the scenario directly on the worksheet.

4. Print the **Income Statement** sheet and then save and close the workbook.

PROJECT 5-2

1. Open the **AE Project5-2** workbook from the student data files and save it as **Student List** followed by your initials.

2. Create a PivotTable with the following setup:
   PAGE: Class
   ROW: Last Name
   DATA: (Sum of) Grade Point Average

3. Modify the layout of the PivotTable so that a grand total Is not displayed. (Display the Step 3 of 3 wizard dialog box, click the **Options** button, and deselect the **Grand totals for columns** and **Grand totals for rows** options.)

4. Select the **Seniors** from the Page list.

5. Print **Sheet4**. Then save and close the workbook.

CRITICAL THINKING

SCANS

ACTIVITY 5-1

Excel's Solver tool is an add-in feature that you can install to perform additional analysis activities on your worksheet data. Solver lets you determine the maximum or minimum value of one cell by changing other cells. For example, you could determine the maximum sales you can achieve by changing the value of projected sales on a certain product. Use Excel's Help system to find more information on the Solver tool. Then write an essay explaining how a company might use Solver to determine the maximum profit it could obtain by changing various expenditures.

CREATING MACROS

Upon completion of this lesson, you should be able to:

- Discuss the purpose of macros.
- Create and record a macro.
- Run a macro.
- Edit a macro.
- Customize a toolbar by adding macro buttons.
- Assign a macro to a command button.

⏱ Estimated Time: 1.5 hours

Introduction

A *macro* is simply a way to automate some of the common, repetitive tasks you perform in Excel, thereby saving valuable time. In this lesson, you will learn how to create macros. When you create a macro, Excel converts the automated tasks you've entered into a *macro language*. An entire book could be devoted to macro programming. And if you'll be spending a considerable amount of time creating detailed macros, you'll find the study of macro language a rewarding experience. In this lesson, you'll focus on creating and editing a macro. In addition, you will learn how to add the macro as a button on a toolbar. Then you will add a macro to a button you create within a worksheet.

Understanding Macros

A *macro* is simply a way to record the actions necessary to complete a certain task. For example, you may need all the titles on your worksheets to be in a bold, large font, and centered across columns. It can be time consuming to do these same steps over and over each time you create a new worksheet. Macros can simplify these steps.

When you create a macro, Excel records the menu selections you make and keystrokes you use to complete a task. When you are ready to use the macro, you tell Excel to play back the macro by pressing a key combination (usually the Ctrl key plus another key) that you assign to the macro. As the macro is played back, the previously recorded steps are performed automatically before your eyes.

Creating, Recording, and Running a Macro

Creating a macro involves a few basic steps:

- Name the macro and assign any shortcut keys (keys that quickly start the macro).

- Turn on the recorder.

- Execute the sequence of actions you want recorded (you can choose commands from the menus, click on toolbar buttons, or use shortcut keys).

- Turn off the recorder.

- When you're ready to use the macro, press the shortcut keys assigned to the macro.

To create a new macro, select Record New Macro from the Macro submenu on the Tools menu. The Record Macro dialog box appears, like that shown in Figure 6-1. You can enter the name and description of the macro here. The options in the dialog box are explained below.

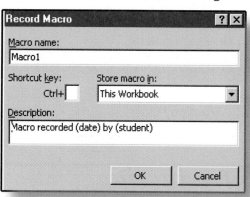

FIGURE 6-1
Record Macro dialog box

- **Macro name.** Enter an easily identifiable name for the macro.

- **Shortcut key**. Lets you assign a key combination that you can then press to start a macro.

- **Store macro in.** From the drop-down list, you can choose to store the macro in the Personal Macro Workbook. The macro is actually stored in Excel's PERSONAL.XLS workbook and is available for application in all workbooks. You can also select to store the macro in This Workbook, so it is only available when the current workbook is open; or your can store the macro in a New Workbook.

- **Description.** Key a brief description to use for future reference. This is optional.

STEP-BY-STEP ▷ 6.1

1. Open the **AE Step6-1** workbook from the student data files and save it as **Fonts** followed by your initials.

2. Open the **Tools** menu, select **Macro**, and then select **Record New Macro**.

3. In the Record Macro dialog box, key **Fonts** in the Macro name box.

4. Click in the **Description** text box to highlight the existing text and key **Applies bold, italic, large font with outline border**.

5. Click in the **Shortcut key** text box. This is where you enter the letter you use in combination with the Ctrl key to start your macro. You can use a single letter between A and Z as a shortcut key. Avoid using letters already assigned to shortcut keys, such as Ctrl+C (used for the Copy command on the Edit menu). You can glance through the menus to see what shortcut keys have already been assigned to commands.

6. Enter **t** in the text box next to *Ctrl+*.

7. Choose **This Workbook** from the *Store macro in* drop-down list, if necessary.

8. Click **OK**. Notice that the word *Recording* is displayed on the status bar. Also note the Stop Recording toolbar, shown in Figure 6-2, is displayed on the worksheet.

FIGURE 6-2
Stop Recording
toolbar

9. Open the **Format** menu and then select **Cells**.

10. Select the **Font** tab.

11. Choose the **Bold Italic** Font style and select a size of **14**.

12. Choose the **Border** tab. Select the fifth line *Style* option in the right column and then choose **Outline**.

13. Click **OK**.

14. Click the **Stop Recording** button (or open the **Tools** menu, select **Macro**, and then select **Stop Recording**). Notice that the formats were actually applied during the recording of the macro.

15. Let's see how this macro works. Select cell **A2**.

16. Press **Ctrl+t**. The subtitle should now be in a large, bold, italic font with an outline border. Adjust the column width, if necessary.

17. Let's create another macro. Select cell **A5**. Open the **Tools** menu, select **Macro**, and then select **Record New Macro**.

18. Key **Font2** in the *Macro name* box and key **Italic underlined font** in the *Description* text box.

19. Enter **r** in the *Shortcut key* text box next to *Ctrl+*.

20. Click **OK**.

21. Click the **Borders** button drop-down list arrow and choose the option to remove any borders. Click the **Underline** button and then the **Italic** button.

22. Click the **Stop Recording** button.

23. Now let's run the macro. Select the range **A6:A9** and press **Ctrl+r**. You should see the new macro features added to these cells.

24. Select the range **A13:A15** and press **Ctrl+r**.

25. Save the workbook and remain in this screen for the next Step-by-Step.

Editing a Macro

C

After you've created a macro, you can make changes to it if necessary. For example, you may have selected a dotted line as a cell border, and you decide that you really want a solid line.

Excel stores the macro in "macro code," called Visual Basic. To edit a macro, you open the Visual Basic Editor, as shown in Figure 6-3. The code in Visual Basic looks like and reads like actual text. You can make changes to the Visual Basic code just as you would edit text.

Hot Tip

You can delete a macro by selecting the **Tools** menu, **Macro**, and then **Macros**. In the Macro dialog box, click the macro's name and click **Delete**.

FIGURE 6-3
Visual Basic Editor

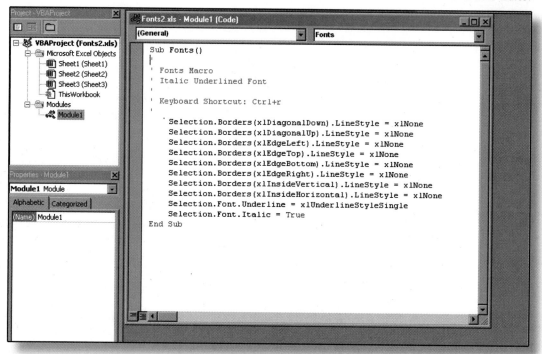

STEP-BY-STEP ▷ 6.2

1. Open the **Tools** menu, select **Macro**, and then click **Macros**.

2. Select the **Font2** macro and then click the **Edit** button.

3. Scroll down the Font2 code until you reach the *Selection.Font.Italic = True* line. Click at the end of the line and then press **Enter**.

4. Key **Selection.Font.Bold = True**.

5. Click the **Save** button.

6. Open the **File** menu and choose **Close and Return to Microsoft Excel**.

7. Select the range **A5:A9** and press **Ctrl+r**. Select the range **A13:A15** and press **Ctrl+r**.

You should see the new macro features added to these cells.

8. Print the worksheet. Then save and close the workbook.

Customize a Toolbar by Adding Macro Buttons

You may find that you use a macro so frequently that you would like it placed as a button on the toolbar. That way, all you have to do is click the macro button to run the macro. Plus, the macro will then be available in any Excel workbook you open. To add a button to a toolbar, you simply need to customize the toolbar.

STEP-BY-STEP ▷ 6.3

1. Open the **AE Step6-3** workbook from the student data files. A message box appears, asking if you want to disable or enable macros. Click the **Enable Macros** button and then save the file as **Macro1** followed by your initials.

2. Open the **View** menu, select **Toolbars**, and then select **Customize**.

3. Select the **Commands** tab. The Commands tab appears, similar to Figure 6-4.

4. Select **Macros** from the *Categories* list box.

5. Click **Custom Button** in the *Commands* list box and drag it from the dialog box to the Formatting toolbar, placing it between the Underline and Left Align buttons.

6. Place your mouse pointer over the Custom button on the toolbar and click the *right* mouse button. Choose **Assign Macro** on the shortcut menu. The Assign Macro dialog box appears, as shown in Figure 6-5.

FIGURE 6-4
The Commands tab in the Customize dialog box

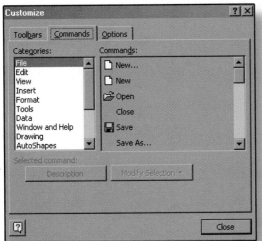

FIGURE 6-5
Assign Macro dialog box

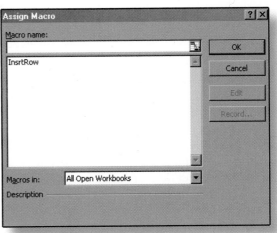

(continued on next page)

7. Click the **InsrtRow** macro and click **OK**. Click **Close** in the Customize dialog box. The new button should look similar to Figure 6-6.

8. To see how the button works, click cell **A8**.

9. Click the **Custom Button** button. You should see a new row inserted. Remain in this screen for the next Step-by-Step.

FIGURE 6-6
Macro button

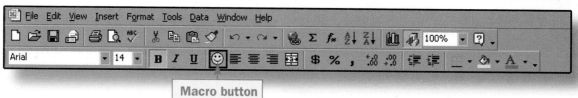

Macro button

Removing a Button from a Toolbar

You can easily remove a button from the toolbar. Open the Customize dialog box, select the Commands tab, and simply drag the button off the toolbar.

STEP-BY-STEP ⟫ 6.4

1. Open the **View** menu, select **Toolbars**, and then choose **Customize**.

2. If necessary, select the **Commands** tab.

3. Drag the **Custom Button** button to any spot off the toolbar. Look at the Formatting toolbar. The macro button should be gone.

4. Click **Close** in the Customize dialog box. Remain in this screen for the next Step-by-Step.

Assign a Macro to a Command Button

When you add a macro button to a toolbar, the button remains on the toolbar even as you work in different Excel files. You may, however, only need this macro for a specific workbook. A macro button placed directly on the worksheet provides easy access to a macro. The macro button only appears when the workbook is opened. Macro buttons also allow other users to run the macro without them having to know the macro's name.

A macro button can be created anywhere in a workbook. You can create a macro button in any shape, such as a rectangle or a circle. After creating the shape for the button, simply place the mouse pointer over the object, click the *right* mouse button, and choose Assign Macro.

Click the name of the macro you want to assign to the button and click OK. To add a name to a macro button, *right*-click the macro button again and choose Add Text on the shortcut menu. You will see an insertion point appear in the object where you can start typing the text. You will learn more about formatting objects on the worksheet in Lesson 12.

STEP-BY-STEP ▷ 6.5

1. Save the Macro1 workbook as **Macro2**.

2. Display the Drawing toolbar by opening the **View** menu, selecting **Toolbars**, and then **Drawing**.

3. Click the **Rectangle** button. Notice how the mouse pointer changes into a crosshair as you move the mouse pointer within the worksheet window.

4. Place your mouse pointer in the upper-left corner of cell **E2**, press and hold the left mouse button down, and drag to the lower-right corner of the cell. Release the mouse button. The rectangle should now be drawn in cell E2.

5. Place your mouse pointer over the rectangle object in cell **E2** and click the *right* mouse button.

6. Choose **Assign Macro** on the shortcut menu.

7. Click the **InsertRw** macro in the Assign Macro dialog box and click **OK**. The macro is now assigned to the rectangle object. This object is now considered a macro button.

8. Place your mouse pointer over the macro button, click the *right* mouse button, and choose **Add Text**. The insertion point should now be inside the macro button.

9. Key **New Row**.

10. With the macro button still selected, click on the **3-D** button on the Drawing toolbar and choose a 3-D shape of your choice.

11. Click anywhere outside the macro button to deselect it. The macro button should look similar to Figure 6-7.

12. To see how this macro button works, select cell **A3** and click the **New Row** macro button. You should see a newly inserted row.

13. Print the sheet. Then save and close the workbook.

(continued on next page)

FIGURE 6-7
Macro button within a worksheet

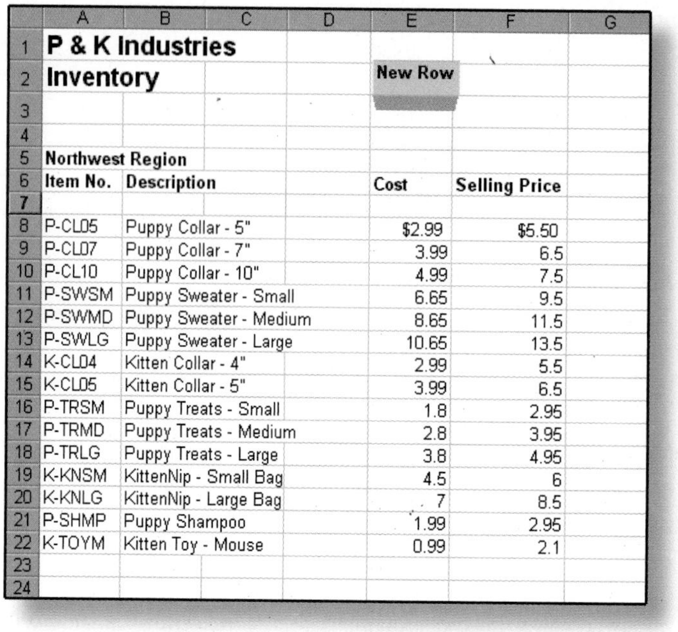

	A	B	C	D	E	F	G
1	**P & K Industries**						
2	**Inventory**				New Row		
3							
4							
5	Northwest Region						
6	Item No.	Description			Cost	Selling Price	
7							
8	P-CL05	Puppy Collar - 5"			$2.99	$5.50	
9	P-CL07	Puppy Collar - 7"			3.99	6.5	
10	P-CL10	Puppy Collar - 10"			4.99	7.5	
11	P-SWSM	Puppy Sweater - Small			6.65	9.5	
12	P-SWMD	Puppy Sweater - Medium			8.65	11.5	
13	P-SWLG	Puppy Sweater - Large			10.65	13.5	
14	K-CL04	Kitten Collar - 4"			2.99	5.5	
15	K-CL05	Kitten Collar - 5"			3.99	6.5	
16	P-TRSM	Puppy Treats - Small			1.8	2.95	
17	P-TRMD	Puppy Treats - Medium			2.8	3.95	
18	P-TRLG	Puppy Treats - Large			3.8	4.95	
19	K-KNSM	KittenNip - Small Bag			4.5	6	
20	K-KNLG	KittenNip - Large Bag			.7	8.5	
21	P-SHMP	Puppy Shampoo			1.99	2.95	
22	K-TOYM	Kitten Toy - Mouse			0.99	2.1	
23							
24							

Summary

In this lesson, you learned:

■ Macros are a method by which you can automate frequently used tasks.

■ Excel records macros in a code called Visual Basic. To edit a macro, you make changes to this code in the Visual Basic editing window. You edit the code as you would edit text.

■ You can run a macro by selecting it in the Macro dialog box or by pressing the shortcut keys (if a key was assigned). You can also run a macro if it is saved as a button on a toolbar or as a command button on a worksheet.

LESSON 6 REVIEW QUESTIONS

WRITTEN QUESTIONS

Write a brief answer to the following questions.

1. What is a macro?

   a set of instructions that will be executed when the assigned "Hot keys" are pressed or button clicked.

2. How do you delete a macro?

   Tools → Macro → Macros
   Highlight the macro to be deleted
   press delete button or "Alt-D"

3. What's the primary ~~different~~ difference between placing a macro button on a toolbar and placing it directly on a worksheet?

   ✶ On a toolbar the macro can be used in other worksheets
   ✶ if placed on a worksheet it is only accessable from that worksheet.

4. How do you edit a macro?

   Tools → Macro → Macros →
   Highlight macro to Edit → Press Edit

5. How do you return to your worksheet from the Visual Basic Editor window?

File → Close and Ret or Alt+Q

MATCHING

Determine the correct sequence of procedures in creating and running a macro by matching the letter of the step number in Column 2 with the procedure listed in Column 1.

Column 1	Column 2
_C_ 1. Execute the sequence of actions you want to record.	**A.** Step 1
_A_ 2. Turn the recorder on.	**B.** Step 2
_E_ 3. Use the macro by pressing the shortcut key assigned to the macro.	**C.** Step 3
	D. Step 4
_D_ 4. Turn the recorder off.	
	E. Step 5
_B_ 5. Name the macro and assign any shortcut keys.	

LESSON 6 PROJECTS

PROJECT 6-1

1. Open the **AE Project6-1** workbook from the student data files and save it as **Insert Column Macro** followed by your initials.

2. Create a macro that inserts a blank column. Name the macro **InsrtCol** and assign a shortcut key of your choice. Be sure to look at the shortcut keys on each menu before you assign a shortcut key to the macro.

3. Run the macro to be certain it works.

4. Print the current sheet in landscape orientation and then save and close the workbook.

4-27-04

Start Here 4-27-04

PROJECT 6-2

1. Open the **AE Project6-2** workbook from the student data files and save it as **Insert Row Macro**, followed by your initials.

2. Edit the **InsrtCol** macro to insert a row instead of a column.

3. Test the macro.

4. Print the current sheet. Then save and close the workbook.

CRITICAL THINKING

ACTIVITY 6-1

You are preparing an Excel worksheet for your company's month-end close. Open the **AE Activity6-1** workbook from the student data files and save it as **Month End**. Create a macro that totals each month's expenses and places them in the *Total* row. (*Hint*: When referencing cells for the formula, use the arrow keys on your keyboard to select them. Macros record your exact actions and do not adjust for relative cell references.) Print the sheet when you are done.

ACTIVITY 6-2

Use Excel's Help system to obtain more information on using Visual Basic to edit macros.

IMPORTING, EXPORTING, AND INTEGRATING DATA

OBJECTIVES

Upon completion of this lesson, you should be able to:

■ Import data from other applications to Excel.

■ Export Excel data to other applications.

■ Import and edit HTML files.

Estimated Time: 1 hour

Introduction

You can exchange data between Excel and other programs through the import and export/share features. In this lesson, you will learn how to import data from and export it to other applications.

Importing Data

Excel can open and read files created in other programs and saved in different formats. Following is a list of the types of files Excel can read:

■ Text

■ Query

■ Lotus 1-2-3

■ Quattro Pro and DOS

■ Microsoft Works 2.0

■ dBase

■ Data Interchange Format

■ SYLK

■ Web Pages

To import a file to an Excel workbook, you click the File menu and then select Open. From the *Files of type* drop-down list box, select the format of the file you want to import. Some files open directly into Excel, where you can then add and edit data, create charts, format the work-sheet, and print the data as you would any other Excel file.

Other file formats, such as text files, require additional for-matting that Excel's Import Wizard will apply. The Text Import Wizard, which starts auto-matically when you try to open a text file in Excel, is shown in Figure 7-1. The Wizard takes you step-by-step through the process

FIGURE 7-1
Text Import Wizard - Step 1 of 3

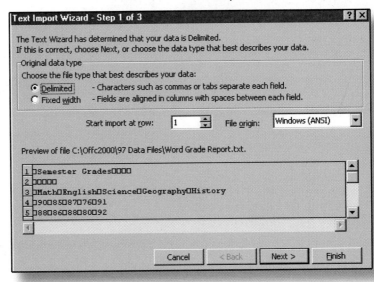

of importing a text file into Excel. You can also start the Wizard by opening the Data menu, choosing Get External Data, and then selecting Import Text File.

You can also save an Excel file in a different format so that it can be opened in a different program. Workbook files can be saved in any of the following formats:

- Web Page

- Template

- Text (Tab delimited)

- Formatted Text (space delimited)

- Text (MS DOS)

- Text (Macintosh)

- Unicode Text (for multilingual document creation)

- CSV (Comma delimited)

- WK*

- WQ1

- DBF

- Microsoft Excel 5.0/95 Workbook

To save a file for use in other programs, choose the File menu and select Save As. In the Save As dialog box, click the Save as type drop-down list arrow and choose the desired format. In the following Step-by-Step, you will import data from Word that has been saved as a text file.

1. Start Excel, if necessary, and click the **Open** button.

2. From the *Files of type* drop-down list in the Open dialog box, select **Text Files**.

Hot Tip

You can quickly import a text file by opening the **Data** menu, selecting **Get External Data**, and then selecting **Import Text File**.

3. Open the **AE Step7-1** text file from the student data files.

4. The Text Import Wizard - Step 1 of 3 dialog box appears. If necessary, click **Delimited** (the most common text type), and then click **Next**.

5. The Text Import Wizard - Step 2 of 3 dialog box appears, as shown in Figure 7-2. Make sure the **Tab** delimiter is selected. A sample of how the data will appear is displayed in the Data preview window. Click **Next**.

6. The Text Import Wizard - Step 3 of 3 dialog box appears, as shown in Figure 7-3. In this dialog box, you can change the data format. Notice the Advanced button in the Step 3 of 3 dialog box. Clicking the Advanced button opens the Advanced Text Import Settings dialog box shown in Figure 7-4. Here, you can add decimal places and a comma between thousands. Click **Finish** in the Step 3 of 3 dialog box.

7. The text file is placed in a new Excel workbook file that assumes the same name as the text file. Notice that the worksheet tab is also named according to the text file. Your worksheet should appear similar to Figure 7-5. Adjust the column widths as necessary.

8. Select **Save As** on the **File** menu, enter **Semester Grades** as the file name, and then click **Save**. This saves the file as an Excel workbook.

9. Print the active sheet and then close the workbook.

FIGURE 7-2
Text Import Wizard - Step 2 of 3

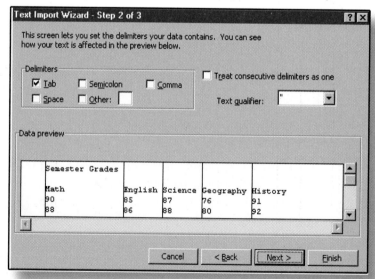

FIGURE 7-3

Text Import Wizard - Step 3 of 3

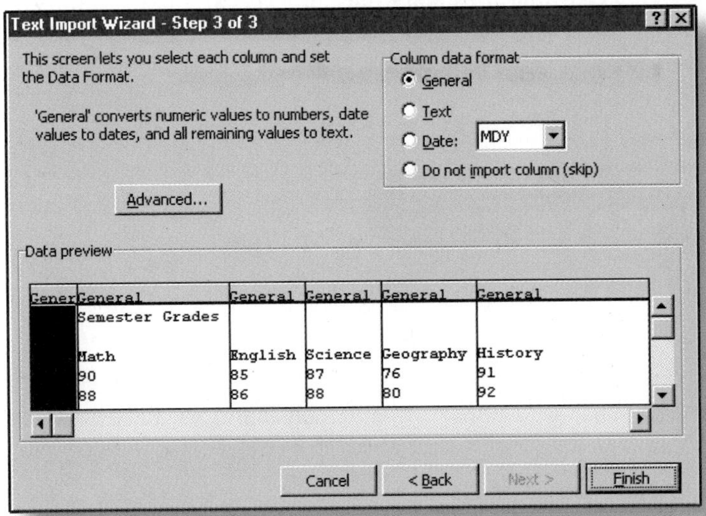

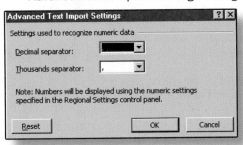

FIGURE 7-4

Advanced Text Import Settings dialog box

FIGURE 7-5

Imported text in Excel worksheet

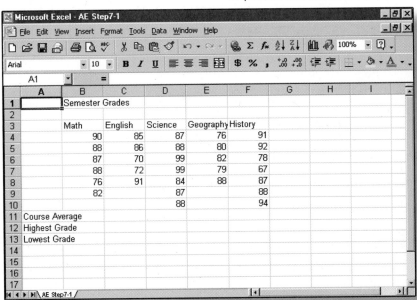

Working with Imported Text Files

One of the primary benefits of importing data into an Excel file is the ability to then use Excel's formula and data analysis tools on it. You can't create a PivotTable report on a table created in a Word document, for example, but you can if you import that table into Excel!

STEP-BY-STEP 7.2

1. Start a new workbook.

2. Open the **Data** menu, choose **Get External Data**, and then select **Import Text File**.

3. Select the **AE Step7-2** text file from the student data files and click **Import**.

4. Be sure **Delimited** is selected in the first dialog box and click **Next**.

5. Be sure **Tab** is selected in the second wizard dialog box and click **Next**.

6. In the third wizard dialog box, click **Finish**. An Import Data dialog box displays, asking you to verify where you want the data placed. Make sure cell A1 is designated and click **OK**. You'll

notice that an External Data toolbar displays on the worksheet. The toolbar contains buttons that let you modify and view properties of the original data. Click the toolbar's **Close** button to remove it from the screen.

7. Format the data in the **Cost** and **Selling Price** columns as **Currency**. Create a formula in column E for each product that finds the difference in selling price and cost. Format the column E data as **Currency**.

8. Save the file as **P&K Imported File**. Your screen should look similar to Figure 7-6.

9. Print the worksheet in portrait orientation and then close the workbook.

FIGURE 7-6
Imported text file with calculations

	A	B	C	D	E	F	G
1	P & K Industries						
2	Inventory						
3							
4	Northwest Region						
5	Item No.	Description	Cost	Selling Price			
6							
7	P-CL05	Puppy Collar - 5"	$ 2.99	$ 5.50	$ 2.51		
8	P-CL07	Puppy Collar - 7"	$ 3.99	$ 6.50	$ 2.51		
9	P-CL10	Puppy Collar - 10"	$ 4.99	$ 7.50	$ 2.51		
10	P-SWSM	Puppy Sweater - Small	$ 6.65	$ 9.50	$ 2.85		
11	P-SWMD	Puppy Sweater - Medium	$ 8.65	$ 11.50	$ 2.85		
12	P-SWLG	Puppy Sweater - Large	$10.65	$ 13.50	$ 2.85		
13	K-CL04	Kitten Collar - 4"	$ 2.99	$ 5.50	$ 2.51		
14	K-CL05	Kitten Collar - 5"	$ 3.99	$ 6.50	$ 2.51		
15	P-TRSM	Puppy Treats - Small	$ 1.80	$ 2.95	$ 1.15		
16	P-TRMD	Puppy Treats - Medium	$ 2.80	$ 3.95	$ 1.15		
17	P-TRLG	Puppy Treats - Large	$ 3.80	$ 4.95	$ 1.15		

Sheet1 / Sheet2 / Sheet3 /

Using Drag-and-Drop to Import Data

You can also insert a text file, or a different file type, such as a graphic object, by using the drag-and-drop method. To use drag-and-drop, you need to open the file from which you are importing, as well as the Excel workbook to which you want to import the data. Position the windows so you can see both programs on the screen by right-clicking an empty area on the taskbar, and choosing Tile Windows Vertically on the shortcut menu. Then, select the data you want to import, hold down the Ctrl key to copy the data, and drag it to the Excel worksheet.

STEP-BY-STEP ▷ 7.3

1. Open a new workbook in Excel.

2. Start the **Microsoft Word** program and open the **Table.doc** document from the student data files.

3. Right-click on an empty area on the taskbar, and choose **Tile Windows Vertically** on the shortcut menu. Make sure you can see cell **B5** in the Excel worksheet.

4. Click anywhere in the table in the Word document. Open the **Table** menu, choose **Select**, and then choose **Table**.

5. Place your mouse pointer over the table, press and hold down the mouse button, and hold

down the **Ctrl** key. Pressing the Ctrl key will copy the table instead of moving it.

6. Drag the data to cell **B5** in the Excel worksheet. Release the mouse button and the Ctrl key.

7. Use Excel's AutoFit option to change the column widths and row heights to accommodate the data.

8. Save the Excel workbook as **Addresses**, followed by your initials. Print the sheet in landscape orientation.

9. Close the Excel workbook file and then close the Word document without saving changes.

Using Drag-and-Drop to Import an HTML File

You probably know that files stored on the Web are saved in Hypertext Markup Language (HTML) format. You can easily import data in this format to a worksheet using the drag-and-drop method.

STEP-BY-STEP ▷ 7.4

1. Open a new workbook in Excel.

2. In Word, open the **Table.htm** file from the student data files.

3. Right-click an empty area on the taskbar and choose **Tile Windows Vertically** on the shortcut

menu. Make sure you can see cell **B5** on the Excel worksheet.

4. Place your mouse pointer in the left margin to the left of the table's first row, and click to select all the table data.

(continued on next page)

5. Hold down the mouse button, and then press and hold down the **Ctrl** key, and drag the table to cell **B5** in the Excel worksheet. Release the mouse button and **Ctrl** key.

6. Use Excel's AutoFit option to change the column widths and row heights to accommodate the data.

7. Save the Excel workbook as **Addresses2**, followed by your initials.

8. Close the Excel workbook file and then close the Word document without saving changes.

Inserting a Text or HTML File

You can also insert a text file, HTML file, or other file type into an Excel worksheet, as an object. Open the Insert menu, and choose Object. In the Insert Object dialog box, click the Create from File tab, and then click the Browse button to find the file you wish to insert. The file is treated as a separate object in the worksheet, similar to a chart.

STEP-BY-STEP ➡ 7.5

1. Open a new workbook in Excel.

2. Open the **Insert** menu, choose **Object**, and in the Object dialog box, click the **Create from File** tab.

3. Click the **Browse** button and select the **Table.doc** file from the student data files.

4. Click **Insert**. In the Object dialog box, click the **Display as icon** option, and then click **OK** to close the Object dialog box.

5. The Word file will be represented as an icon on the worksheet. Double-click the icon to view the table in Word.

6. Close Word without saving changes to the document.

7. Save the Excel workbook as **Inserted Table**, followed by your initials. Close the Excel workbook file.

 Extra Challenge

Insert the Table.htm file from the student data files as an icon in an Excel worksheet.

Exporting Excel Data

Data created in Excel can be saved in a different file format so that it can be opened in other applications. In addition, the compatibility features in Microsoft Office allow you to copy and drag information between Office programs.

STEP-BY-STEP ▷ 7.6

1. Open the **AE Step7-6** workbook from the student data files.

2. Start the **Microsoft Word** program.

3. Click the **Microsoft Excel** button on the taskbar to return to the AE Step7-3 workbook.

4. Select the range **A1:E19**.

5. Click the **Copy** button.

6. Click the **Microsoft Word** button on the taskbar.

7. Click in the Word document and click the **Paste** button. The student loan information is copied in a table format to the Word document. Now you could enter any text that explains the table and use your word processing tools to edit and format it.

8. Save the Word document as **Student Loan**. Print and then close the document. Then close the Excel workbook without saving changes.

Using Round-Tripping

Round-tripping is a new feature that lets you edit an HTML document. Perhaps you've published a worksheet to the Web, and you want to make modifications to you. Open the Internet Explorer browser program, open the file, and click the Edit button. The file will be "round-tripped" back to an Office 2000 application. This feature gives you the ability to edit an HTML document using the powerful features of the Office 2000 applications.

STEP-BY-STEP ▷ 7.7

1. Open the **AE Step7-7** workbook from the student files.

2. Save the workbook as an HTML file by clicking the **File** menu and selecting **Save As Web Page**.

3. Enter **RoundT** for the filename. Click the **Publish** button. Click the **Add interactivity with** option, and choose **Spreadsheet functionality** if necessary. Click the **Open published Web page in browser** option. Then, click **Publish**. The **Internet Explorer** program starts and the RoundT.htm file appears on screen.

4. Click the arrow on the **Edit** button on the Internet Explorer toolbar. You can select from among three Office 2000 programs in which to edit the file: Notepad, Microsoft Word, or Microsoft FrontPage. FrontPage is designed specifically for creating and editing Web pages, so select that option. After a minute, the spreadsheet data should open in FrontPage.

 Hot Tip

If FrontPage is not installed on your computer, select one of the other options on the Edit drop-down list.

5. Select cell **D5** and change the selling price for the sweatshirt to **$30.00**. Do the same for cells **D6** and **D7**.

(continued on next page)

6. Open the **File** menu and choose **Save**. Then, close the file.

7. Click the **Exploring** button on the taskbar to return to Internet Explorer.

8. Click the **Refresh** button on the toolbar to update the file.

9. Close **Internet Explorer**. Then, close the open workbook in Excel without saving changes.

Summary

In this lesson, you learned:

■ Data from another application, such as Microsoft Word, can be imported into Excel and set up in a tabular format. You can edit, format, and perform calculations and data analysis on imported data using any Excel tools or features.

■ You can save Excel files in different formats so that they can be exported to other applications.

■ Round-tripping is a new feature in Office 2000 that lets you edit HTML files using the features of the Office 2000 applications.

LESSON 7 REVIEW QUESTIONS

TRUE/FALSE

Circle T if the statement is true or F if the statement is false.

T **F** 1. Excel can only import and export between other Microsoft Office software applications.

T **F** 2. Once a file has been imported to Excel, you cannot make changes to it.

T **F** 3. Files in text (.txt) format are the only type of word processing file that can be imported to Excel.

T F 4. One of the benefits of importing data into Excel is the capability to use Excel's calculation and data analysis tools on the data.

T F 5. Excel data that is exported to another application can be edited and formatted using that application's tools and features.

WRITTEN QUESTIONS

Write a brief answer to the following questions.

1. Does the Text Import Wizard start when opening any file in Excel that was created in another program? Why or why not?

    No. only text (.txt) files cause the "Text Import Wizard" to open. the T.I.W, only formats .txt files

2. Why would you want to import a table with numbers from Word into Excel?

    to use Excel calculating features

3. List three file types that can be imported into Excel.

    Quatro Pro
    Word
    Lotus 123

4. List three file types that Excel files can be saved as before they are exported from Excel.

    HTML, WORD, Template

5. List the steps for copying information from Excel into a Word document.

    Select cell,range to copy the "control c" or Edit copy With word doc open switch to Word then Paste

A E - 9 3

Start here on 4-29-04

PROJECT 7-1

1. Import the **AE Project7-1** text file from the student data files into an Excel worksheet. Select **Delimited** as the file type that best describes the data. Choose the **Tab** delimiter and select the **General** column data format.

2. Adjust column widths where necessary. Apply any formats that you think are appropriate.

3. Save the workbook as **Address List** in Microsoft Excel Workbook file format.

4. Print the active sheet and then close the workbook.

PROJECT 7-2

1. Open the **AE Project7-2** workbook from the student data files.

2. Select all the data and copy this information to a new blank document in Microsoft Word.

3. Save the Word document as **NL Employee List**.

4. Insert four blank lines above the table. On the first line, key **NL Corporation**, and on the second line, key **Employee List**. Format the heading as you think is appropriate.

5. Modify the column widths and format the table as you feel is appropriate.

6. Print the document and then close it. Close the Excel workbook without saving changes.

CRITICAL THINKING

ACTIVITY 7-1

Import the text file **AE Activity7-1** into a new workbook. Save the workbook as **A&C Imported File**. Calculate totals in the worksheet as you feel necessary. Add any formats that you think will enhance the appearance of the worksheet. Print the sheet and then close the workbook.

ACTIVITY 7-2

You have imported a text file into Excel that contains the names, ID numbers, and salaries of all employees at your company. You know that you would like the imported data to change if any modifications are made to it in the original file. Use Excel's Help system to find information on updating or refreshing imported data. Write a brief essay on how you would proceed.

SCANS

USING TEMPLATES

OBJECTIVES

Upon completion of this lesson, you should be able to:

- Create a template.
- Save a template.
- Open and utilize a template.
- Edit a template.
- Use Excel's built-in templates.

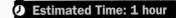

⏱ **Estimated Time: 1 hour**

Introduction

In this lesson, you will learn how to create and use templates. A ***template*** can be used over and over again to create new workbooks that follow the same format but that require different data. A template normally contains titles, subtitles, formats, and formulas, but *no* specific data values. Excel also provides preformatted templates, such as the Invoice template, that you can use to prepare customized workbooks.

Creating and Saving a Template

Let's consider an example of how a template can save you valuable time. Let's say you need to prepare a budget report each month. The budgetary items remain the same from month to month, but the actual numbers change on each report. Rather than entering the same text and formulas over and over, you can create a template and then "fill in the blanks" when you're ready to use it.

To create a template, you enter titles, subtitles, formats, and formulas. In other words, you enter everything but the data values. You then save the workbook as a template file. To create a new workbook using the template, simply open the template file and then save it as an Excel workbook with a new name. This maintains the template in its original form so that you can use it again.

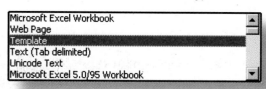
1. Start a new workbook.

2. Select cell **A1** and enter the title **Miss Bessie's Cookies**.

3. Select cell **A2** and enter the subtitle **Monthly Cookie Sales**.

4. Select cell **B5** and enter **Chocolate Chip**.

5. Select cell **B6** and enter **Oatmeal Raisin**.

6. Select cell **B7** and enter **Sugar**.

7. Select cell **B8** and enter **Peanut Blossom**.

8. Select cell **B9** and enter **Chocolate/ Macadamia**.

9. Select cell **B10** and enter **Total Sales**.

10. Select cell **C10** and enter a formula that will sum the range **C5:C9**.

11. For the format, bold all the text you have entered. Change the text size of the title to **16** and the size of the subtitle to **12**. Add italics to the subtitle. Widen column B to accommodate the data, if necessary.

12. Select **Save As** on the **File** menu.

13. Click the **Save as type** drop-down list arrow. The *Save as type* list displays, similar to Figure 8-1.

FIGURE 8-1
Save as type list box

| Microsoft Excel Workbook |
| Web Page |
| Template |
| Text (Tab delimited) |
| Unicode Text |
| Microsoft Excel 5.0/95 Workbook |

14. Select **Templates**.

15. Enter **Monthly Cookie Sales Template** as the file name.

Hot Tip

Excel typically saves templates in its Templates folder. For the purpose of this course, save the template in the folder with your exercise files.

16. Click **Save** and then close the workbook.

Opening and Using a Template

Now that you've created a template, it is ready to use. After you open a template and fill in the new data, you save the workbook as a regular Excel file. This leaves the original template intact so you can use it again. You will notice that the icon identifying a template file is different from that for a regular Excel workbook file. Figure 8-2 shows the icon for a template and the icon for an Excel file.

FIGURE 8-2
Workbook and template icons

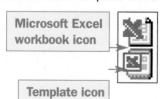

Microsoft Excel workbook icon

Template icon

S TEP-BY-STEP ▷ 8.2

1. Open the **Monthly Cookie Sales Template** file.

2. Enter the following data:

Cell	Enter
A3	January
C5	2544
C6	238
C7	878
C8	1433
C9	1052

Your worksheet should look similar to Figure 8-3.

3. Save the file as **January Cookie Sales**. Choose **Microsoft Excel Workbook** from the *Save as type* drop-down list.

4. Print the worksheet and then close the workbook.

FIGURE 8-3
Entering data in a template file

	A	B	C	D	E
1	**Miss Bessie's Cookies**				
2	*Monthly Cookie Sales*				
3	January				
4					
5		Chocolate Chip	2544		
6		Oatmeal Raisin	238		
7		Sugar	878		
8		Peanut Blossom	1433		
9		Chocolate/Macadamia	1052		
10		Total Sales	6145		
11					
12					
13					
14					

Editing a Template

You can quickly make changes to a template. Simply open the template, make changes, and save with the same filename. Make sure you select Template as the file type.

S TEP-BY-STEP ▷ 8.3

1. Open the **Monthly Cookie Sales Template** file.

2. Change the title font to a size of **18** and underline the subtitle.

3. Click the **File** menu, choose **Save As**, and select **Template** from the *Save as type* list box. When

the message box asks if you want to replace the existing file, simply click **Yes**.

4. Close the template file.

Using Excel's Built-in Templates

Excel provides a variety of preformatted templates to help you prepare workbooks quickly and efficiently. The templates provided typically include the Invoice, Loan Manager, and Purchase Order. The Invoice template guides you in preparing an invoice. The Loan Manager template lets you amortize a loan and determine the interest saved by refinancing or prepaying principal. A purchase order can be quickly prepared by using the Purchase Order template.

Hot Tip

The templates available on the Spreadsheet Solutions tab are determined by the options selected during installation.

To use the templates, select New on the File menu and then click the Spreadsheet Solutions tab or the tab where the templates are located. Select a template and a sample of it appears in the Preview box.

Double-click a template to open it. (You may see a message box about enabling macros. To continue, click Enable Macros.) If you select the Invoice template to open, your screen will look similar to Figure 8-4.

FIGURE 8-4
Invoice template

COMPANY NAME

Company Address
City, State ZIP Code
Phone Number fax Fax Number

Invoice No.

Customize...

INVOICE

Customer

Name		Date	1/9/99
Address		Order No.	
City	State	ZIP	Rep	
Phone		FOB	

Qty	Description	Unit Price	TOTAL

Payment Details
- ● Cash
- ○ Check
- ○ Credit Card

SubTotal	$0.00
Shipping & Handling	
Taxes State	
TOTAL	**$0.00**

Customize Your Invoice Invoice

Notice the shaded areas in the template. These areas contain formulas and other predefined calculations. Therefore, you do not enter any information into the shaded areas of a template.

Templates have a variety of helpful features that will guide you in entering the correct information. For example, notice the small triangle that appears in some cells. This indicates that a comment has been attached to the cell to provide you with more information on what data should be entered. Simply place the mouse pointer over the triangle to display the comment. An example of a comment is shown in Figure 8-5.

FIGURE 8-5
Displaying a comment in a template

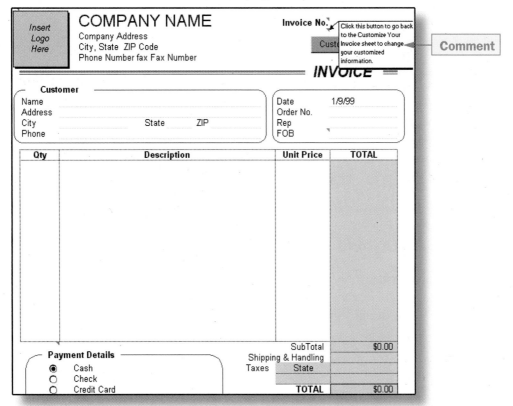

FIGURE 8-6
Invoice template toolbar

A toolbar specific to the template also is displayed, similar to the one shown in Figure 8-6. The buttons on the toolbar are described below.

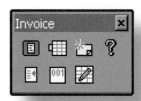

■ **Size to Screen/Return to Size.** Displays the template at a reduced size or returns the template to its full size.

■ **Hide Comments/Display Comments.** Turns the Comments on and off. When the Comments are turned on, a small triangle appears at the Comment locations.

■ **New Comment.** Lets you add your own Comment to a cell in the template.

■ **Template Help.** Displays a help topic for the current template. Describes the purpose and possible uses of the template.

■ **Display Example/Remove Example.** Fills in cells with an example showing how to use the sheet and then removes the example.

■ **Assign a Number.** Lets you assign an invoice number to the invoice.

■ **Capture Data in a Database.** Lets you create a database record of the invoice.

Excel's templates are set up as workbooks. They have various worksheets on which you will enter data and customize information. You will enter data in the same manner as you have been.

1. Open the **File** menu and select **New**.

2. Click the **Spreadsheet Solutions** tab or click the tab where the Invoice template is located.

3. Click the **Invoice** template icon. Notice how a sample of the template appears in the preview box. (If necessary, click the **Preview** button in this dialog box.)

4. Click **OK**. Save the workbook as **New World Invoice** followed by your initials. Make sure you save it as a Microsoft Excel Workbook file type.

5. Click the **Customize** button in the upper right corner of the template. You are now in the Customize Your Invoice worksheet.

6. Enter the following data into the appropriate categories in the template. To move in a template, simply click on the location in which you want to enter data or press the arrow keys. When you are done, the sheet should look similar to Figure 8-7.

Company Name	New World Imports
Address	17 Wall Street
City	Paris
State	New York
ZIP Code	00119
1st Tax Name	NY
1st Tax Rate	8.0%
Shipping Charge	7.00
Phone	610-555-8445
Fax	610-555-8766

7. Click the **Invoice** sheet tab to view the results. Your invoice worksheet should look similar to Figure 8-8.

FIGURE 8-7
Customing a template

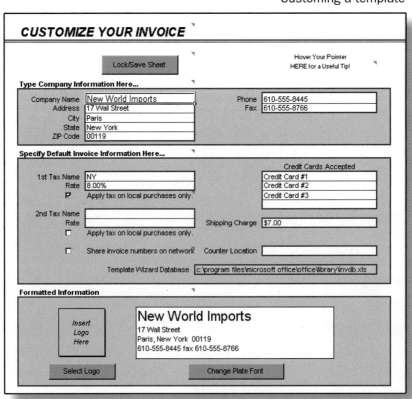

FIGURE 8-8
Invoice worksheet

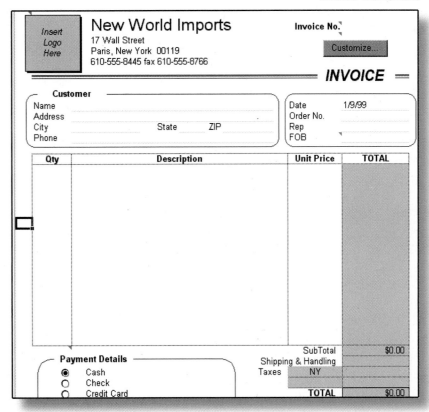

8. Enter the following information on the Invoice sheet.

Customer Name	Best Sales
Address	P.O. Box 555
City	West
State	TX
ZIP	78222
Date	1/9/99
Order No.	2330
Quantity	15
Description	20" Baskets
Unit Price	12.35
Taxes	None

9. Save the workbook. Print the **Invoice** worksheet and then close the workbook. If the Template File – Save to Database dialog box appears, click the **Continue without updating** option and then click **OK**.

10. Close the workbook.

 Extra Challenge

On the Invoice sheet in the New World Invoice workbook, insert text of your choosing for the **Insert Fine Print Here** cell and the **Insert Farewell Statement Here** cell. Click the **Insert Logo Here** button to add a graphic to the invoice.

 Hot Tip

If you need to get back to the Customize Your Invoice worksheet, click the **Customize** button or the worksheet tab.

Summary

In this lesson, you learned:

- Templates are a time-saving feature that can increase your productivity. You discovered how you can enter titles, subtitles, formats, and formulas into a workbook.

- When you open a template, you should save it immediately with a new file name. Then you can start entering data.

- Excel has a number of built-in templates. You can create your own individualized workbook using these templates as a basis.

LESSON 8 REVIEW QUESTIONS

TRUE/FALSE

Circle T if the statement is true or F if the statement is false.

T F 1. In one of Excel's existing templates, you would enter new data that is not part of the template structure on the Customize sheet.

T F 2. The red triangles on some cells in an existing Excel template indicate that a comment is attached to the cell.

T **F** 3. You cannot add comments to an existing Excel template.

T **F** 4. If you click the Display Example button on the template toolbar, Excel opens the Print Preview window in which it displays the template sheet.

T **F** 5. Once you create and save a new template in Excel, you cannot modify or edit the template workbook.

WRITTEN QUESTIONS

Write a brief answer to the following questions.

1. What is the purpose of a template? *allows for reuse of formats, formulas, and general layout of the workbook. Saves time.*

2. What information is typically entered when creating a template?

Text that doesn't change, heading labels, formulas, formatting

3. Would you enter data into a template when creating it? Why or why not?

NO. since data changes it is not part of the template. Some data could be entered if it rarely changes.

4. Why do you save a template with data entered into it as a workbook file instead of saving it as a template?

this is a unique version of the workbook so it is saved as a workbook

5. Describe two advantages of using templates.

Time Savings, Consistent Layout.

PROJECT 8-1

1. Create a template for the Lazy Dayse Pie Factory with the information below. You will use the template to create a new workbook that will contain three months of data.

Cell	Enter
A1	Lazy Dayse Pie Factory
A2	Quarterly Sales:
A4	Type of Pie
A6	Apple
A7	Cherry
A8	Lemon
A9	Pumpkin
A10	Blueberry

2. Add formatting to the text. You can add bold and change the size of the title and subtitle. Select the range **B6:D10** and apply currency formatting with no decimals.

3. Save the template as **Pie Sales**. Remember to save it in the same directory and folder as your course files.

4. Close the template.

5. Reopen the template and enter the data for the first quarter.

6. Enter **First Quarter** in cell **B2**.

7. Enter the months **January**, **February**, and **March** in the range **B4:D4**. Widen the columns as necessary.

8. Enter the following sales data:

Type of Pie	January	February	March
Apple	900	723	1056
Cherry	459	649	576
Lemon	341	376	471
Pumpkin	298	277	240
Blueberry	87	188	160

9. Save it as **First Quarter Pie Sales**. (Be sure you're saving this as a workbook.)

10. Print the worksheet and then close the workbook.

PROJECT 8-2

1. Open Excel's Loan Manager template (this is an add-in feature so you may need to install it from your Microsoft Office 2000 installation CD). Enter the following data on the Loan Data sheet:

Lender Name	Sierra International Bank
Amount	2500
Beginning of Loan	6/30/99
Annual Interest Rate	12
Length of Loan, Years	2

2. Customize the template by entering the following data into the appropriate categories.

Family Name	Sallye Goodwin
Street Address	4317 Lost Pines Drive
City	Oakland
State	CA
ZIP Code	93581
Phone Number	(510) 555-1234
Fax Number	(510) 555-5678

3. Save the workbook as **Line of Credit**. (Be sure to select Microsoft Excel Workbook from the *Save as type* drop-down list.)

4. Print the **Loan Data** worksheet. Then close the workbook.

CRITICAL THINKING

SCANS

ACTIVITY 8-1

Ms. Emily Smith, your boss at Lincoln College Fan-Fair, a sports apparel shop for Lincoln College, has just handed you the inventory list shown below. She wants you to create a workbook template file that contains the information and is formatted as you feel appropriate. Enter a formula in the Selling Price field that multiplies the value in the Quantity in Stock column by the Cost values. This will indicate the value of the inventory. Save the template as **Lincoln FF Inventory Template**.

Item No.	Item Description	Size	Quantity in Stock	Cost	Value
SS-LC1-S	Sweat Shirt - Lincoln College emblem	S			
SS-LC1-M	Sweat Shirt - Lincoln College emblem	M			
SS-LC1-L	Sweat Shirt - Lincoln College emblem	L			
Cap-L	Baseball Cap	L			
Cap-XL	Baseball Cap	XL			
TS-LC-S	Tee Shirt - Lincoln College emblem	S			
TS-LC-M	Tee Shirt - Lincoln College emblem	M			
TS-LC-L	Tee Shirt - Lincoln College emblem	L			

```
Shorts-S    Shorts                                              S
Shorts-M    Shorts                                              M
Shorts-L    Shorts                                              L
Shorts-XL   Shorts                                              XL


SP-LC-S     Sweat Pants - Lincoln College emblem    S
SP-LC-M     Sweat Pants - Lincoln College emblem    M
SP-LC-L     Sweat Pants - Lincoln College emblem    L
SP-LC-XL    Sweat Pants - Lincoln College emblem    XL
```

Create a new workbook from the *Lincoln FF Inventory Template* file for the January inventory data. Input the Cost and Quantity in Stock data, as shown below. Save the workbook as **Lincoln FF January Inventory**. Then print and close the workbook.

Item No.	Item Description	Size	Quantity in Stock	Cost	Value
SS-LC1-S	Sweat Shirt - Lincoln College emblem	S	45	$10.99	
SS-LC1-M	Sweat Shirt - Lincoln College emblem	M	62	12.99	
SS-LC1-L	Sweat Shirt - Lincoln College emblem	L	39	14.99	
Cap-L	Baseball Cap	L	489	4.99	
Cap-XL	Baseball Cap	XL	234	5.99	
TS-LC-S	Tee Shirt - Lincoln College emblem	S	65	4.99	
TS-LC-M	Tee Shirt - Lincoln College emblem	M	42	6.99	
TS-LC-L	Tee Shirt - Lincoln College emblem	L	97	8.99	
Shorts-S	Shorts	S	48	7.99	
Shorts-M	Shorts	M	22	9.99	
Shorts-L	Shorts	L	19	11.99	
Shorts-XL	Shorts	XL	7	13.99	
SP-LC-S	Sweat Pants - Lincoln College emblem	S	56	9.99	
SP-LC-M	Sweat Pants - Lincoln College emblem	M	31	11.99	
SP-LC-L	Sweat Pants - Lincoln College emblem	L	33	13.99	
SP-LC-XL	Sweat Pants - Lincoln College emblem	XL	21	15.99	

ACTIVITY 8-2

You've been using Excel templates for a variety of tasks at your office. However, you notice that one of the files you thought you had saved as a template is actually saved a regular Excel workbook. Use the Excel Help system to troubleshoot the problem and why it might have occurred. Write a short essay on how you should proceed.

WORKING WITH MULTIPLE WORKSHEETS AND WORKBOOKS

LESSON 9

OBJECTIVES

Upon completion of this lesson, you should be able to:

- Move between worksheets in a workbook.
- Add or delete a worksheet within a workbook.
- Copy and move data between worksheets.
- Copy an entire worksheet's data.
- Move between open workbooks.
- Save a workspace.
- Link workbooks.

⏱ Estimated Time: 2 hours

Introduction

Just as you copy and move data within a worksheet, you can copy and move data between different worksheets. In this lesson, you will learn how to move data among multiple worksheets. You will then learn how to add a worksheet to a workbook and how to delete a worksheet.

The lesson also covers working with multiple workbooks. You will find out how to save several workbooks together as a workspace. And you will learn how to total data from several workbooks into one workbook.

Moving Between Worksheets

Moving between worksheets is a quick and easy process. You've seen the worksheet tabs on your screen. By default, each new Excel workbook opens with three worksheets. To move between the worksheets, you simply click the worksheet tab.

Notice the *worksheet movement buttons* identified in Figure 9-1. If your workbook contains a number of sheets and you cannot see all of the worksheet tabs on your screen at one time, these buttons let you control your view of these worksheet tabs.

Clicking these buttons only displays the different worksheet tabs—they do not display a different worksheet. Once you have the tab of the sheet you want to work with in view, you simply click the sheet tab to display that worksheet.

FIGURE 9-1
Worksheet
movement buttons

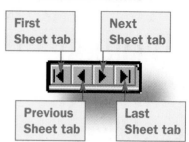

STEP-BY-STEP 9.1

1. Open the **AE Step9-1** workbook from the student data files.

2. Click the tab for **Sheet13** using the worksheet movement buttons to bring the tab into view.

3. Use the worksheet movement buttons to display **Sheet1**.

Hot Tip

You can press **Ctrl+PageDown** to go to the next worksheet in the workbook and **Ctrl+PageUp** to go to the previous worksheet.

4. Close the workbook without saving any changes.

Adding and Deleting a Worksheet

Frequently you'll find that you need more than three worksheets. You can add one or several worksheets to a workbook. Click the sheet that will *follow* the sheet you want to add, open the Insert menu, and select Worksheet. If the existing worksheets have not been named, Excel automatically labels the new worksheets Sheet4, Sheet5, and so on. If the worksheets are named, Excel assigns the Sheet1 and Sheet2 label names to the new sheets. You can rename the worksheets appropriately.

Hot Tip

You can also delete a worksheet by right-clicking the worksheet tab, and then selecting **Delete** on the shortcut menu.

You can easily delete worksheets. Click the tab for the sheet you want to delete, open the Edit menu, and then select Delete Sheet. The worksheet and all data on it will be deleted.

STEP-BY-STEP 9.2

1. Start a new, blank workbook. Click the worksheet tab for **Sheet3**. We'll now insert a new worksheet between Sheet2 and Sheet3.

2. Open the **Insert** menu and then select **Worksheet**. Notice the new sheet tab inserted before Sheet3.

3. Click the tab of the worksheet you just added, if necessary.

4. Open the **Edit** menu and select **Delete Sheet**. Click **OK**. The worksheet should now be deleted.

5. Close the workbook without saving any changes.

Copying Data Between Worksheets

Copying data between worksheets in a single workbook or between worksheets in different workbooks is similar to copying data within a worksheet. You select the cell or range of cells to be copied, click the Copy button or choose Copy on the Edit menu, click in the location to where you want to copy, and then paste.

In Excel, you can also copy data between worksheets by using the mouse in combination with the keyboard. First, you select the range you want to copy. Place the mouse pointer on the border of the selected cell or range until it turns into an arrow. Press the mouse button and then press the Ctrl and Alt keys simultaneously. Drag the selection to the tab of the worksheet you want to copy to. When you place your mouse pointer on the worksheet tab, that sheet becomes active. You can then position the range where you want the data copied to. The most important thing to remember is not to release the mouse button or the Ctrl and Alt keys until you are at the location in the worksheet where you want the data copied. Release the mouse button first and then release the other keys.

STEP-BY-STEP ▷ 9.3

1. Open the **AE Step9-3** workbook from the student data files and save it as **Complete College Budget** followed by your initials. You've just been informed, much to your dismay, that your meals, clothes, gas, and miscellaneous allowances will remain the same for all four years of college. Rather than retyping this data in each of the four worksheets, you can quickly copy the data. To do this, select the range **B8:M11** in the **First Year** worksheet.

2. Click the **Copy** button.

3. Select the **Second Year** worksheet. (If you were copying to another open workbook, you would select the workbook on the Window menu, and then select the sheet to which you wanted to copy the data.)

4. Select cell **B8**.

5. Click the **Paste** button. Notice how the data has been copied. Since Excel still retains the copied data in the Clipboard (and since nothing else has been placed in the Clipboard), you can copy the data again.

6. Select the **Third Year** worksheet.

7. Select cell **B8** and click the **Paste** button.

8. Now let's try using Excel's other method for copying data between worksheets. Click the **First Year** worksheet tab.

9. You will copy the expenses in two parts to get more practice using this method. Select the range **B8:G11**.

10. Place your mouse pointer over the border of the selected range until it turns into an arrow. When you see the arrow, press and hold the left mouse button down.

11. While still holding the left mouse button down, press the **Ctrl** and **Alt** keys. Drag down to the **Fourth Year** worksheet tab. Notice how the Fourth Year worksheet becomes active. Drag the range until you see a tip box display the range **B8:G11**. Release the mouse button and then release the Ctrl and Alt keys. Your data should now be copied.

(continued on next page)

12. When using this method of copying, the range you are copying to must be visible. In the Fourth Year worksheet scroll until columns H through M are visible.

13. Click the **First Year** worksheet tab.

14. Select the range **H8:M11**.

15. Place your mouse pointer over the border of the selected range until the pointer becomes an arrow. When you see the arrow, press and hold the left mouse button down.

16. While still holding the left mouse button down, press the **Ctrl** and **Alt** keys. Drag the range to the **Fourth Year** worksheet tab. In the Fourth Year worksheet drag until you see the range **H8:M11** displayed in the tip box. Release the mouse button and then release the Ctrl and Alt keys. Your data should now be copied.

17. Save the workbook and remain in this screen for the next Step-by-Step.

Copying an Entire Worksheet

Various worksheets in a workbook often follow a similar format. For example, some companies keep monthly budgets that summarize income and expenses. Each month's figures are entered on a separate worksheet using the same titles and row and column headings. Rather than re-entering this same information over and over again, you can simply copy the contents of one worksheet to another. This process is a little different than the copy and paste functions you've been using.

When you copy the entire worksheet, you copy not only the data, but all the formats as well. Excel actually inserts a new worksheet into the workbook to which this data is copied. The worksheet tab of the new worksheet contains the name of the copied worksheet, plus a (2) after the name to identify it as a duplicate. You can rename the worksheet tab to make it more easily identifiable and consistent with the other worksheet tabs by double-clicking on the worksheet tab, typing the new name, and pressing Enter.

STEP-BY-STEP 9.4

1. Click the **Fourth Year** tab.

2. Press and hold down the **Ctrl** key, place the mouse pointer over the **Fourth Year** sheet tab and drag the page icon to the right of the sheet tab. Release the mouse button and then release the Ctrl key.

3. Click the **Fourth Year (2)** tab. The worksheet should be identical to the Fourth Year sheet.

4. Double-click the **Fourth Year (2)** tab, key **Total College Expenses** as the new sheet name, and press **Enter**.

5. In the Total College Expenses worksheet, select cell **A2** and key **Total Expenses**.

6. Select the range **B8:M11** and press the **Delete** key.

7. Save the workbook and remain in this screen for the next Step-by-Step.

Moving Data Between Worksheets

You can move data between worksheets and workbooks just as easily as it can be copied. When you move data, you remove it from its original location and paste it to the new location. As with moving data within a worksheet, you can use the Cut and Paste tools to complete the function.

Excel also lets you move data between worksheets using the mouse and keyboard. This is similar to the method for copying data. You simply select the range you want to move, hold down the Alt key, and drag the selection to the worksheet tab and worksheet area where the data is to be pasted.

Previewing and Printing Multiple Worksheets

You can preview and print multiple worksheets in a workbook by **grouping** the sheets. Click the tab of the first sheet in the group, hold down the Shift key, and click the tab of the last worksheet in the group. You'll notice all the tabs of the sheets in the group are selected and the word *Group* appears in parentheses in the title bar. Click the Print Preview button to view the group of sheets. To print the group, make sure that the Active sheet(s) option is selected in the Print dialog box.

STEP-BY-STEP ▷ 9.5

1. Select the **Second Year** worksheet.

2. Look at the data in cells D15 through F17. This data relates to costs that should appear in the fourth year. Therefore, this data needs to be moved. Select the range **D15:F17**.

3. Click the **Cut** button.

4. Click the **Fourth Year** sheet tab.

5. Select cell **D15** and click the **Paste** button. Notice how the data is now where it should be. You can check the Second Year worksheet to see that the data you moved is gone.

6. Save the workbook.

7. You will now use Excel's other method for moving data. For practice, let's start by moving the range back to the Second Year worksheet. In the Fourth Year worksheet, select the range **D15:F17**, if necessary.

8. Place your mouse pointer on the border of the selected range until it turns into an arrow.

When you see the arrow, press and hold down the mouse button.

9. Press and hold down the **Alt** key and drag the range to the **Second Year** worksheet tab.

10. In the Second Year worksheet, drag to the range **D15:F17**. Release the mouse button and the Alt key.

11. For additional practice in this method of moving, let's move the range back to the Fourth Year sheet. In the **Second Year** worksheet, make sure the range **D15:F17** is selected.

12. Place your mouse pointer on the border of the selected range until it turns into an arrow. When you see the arrow, press and hold down the mouse button, press and hold down the **Alt** key, and drag the range to the **Fourth Year** worksheet tab.

13. In the **Fourth Year** worksheet, drag to the range **D15:F17**. Release the mouse button and the Alt key.

(continued on next page)

14. Set up each worksheet in landscape orientation and so it fits on one page, and then print the entire workbook. Save and close the workbook.

15. Let's compare the third and fourth year worksheets. Click the **Third Year** sheet tab, hold down the **Shift** key, and click the **Fourth Year** tab. Both sheet tabs should now be selected.

16. Click the **File** menu and select **Print**.

17. Choose the **Active sheet(s)** option in the Print dialog box and click **OK**.

18. Click any sheet tab that's not grouped to remove the grouped sheet feature.

19. Save and close the workbook.

Moving Between Workbooks

Just as you can move between worksheets within a workbook, you can also move between workbooks. You can use the Window menu or the keyboard to move between open workbooks. To move between open workbooks using the keyboard, you press Ctrl+F6. You'll learn later in this lesson how to copy and move data between workbooks.

STEP-BY-STEP ⟶ 9.6

1. Open the **AE Step9-6a** and **AE Step9-6b** workbooks from the student data files.

2. To move to the AE Step9-6a workbook, open the **Window** menu and then select the **AE Step9-6a** workbook, which should be listed near the bottom of the Window menu.

3. Press **Ctrl+F6** to move to the **AE Step9-6b** workbook.

4. Remain in this screen for the next Step-by-Step.

Saving a Workspace

Excel's *workspace* feature is designed to help you save time and work more efficiently. For example, you may have a workbook that contains the sales information for your company and another workbook that contains inventory information. You like to have both workbooks open at the same time to make changes. Rather than going through the steps to open one workbook at a time, you can group them as a workspace. Then when you want to open the workbooks, you only have to open the workspace file. All the workbooks grouped into that workspace open automatically. The workbooks still remain as separate files that you can open individually if you prefer.

Once a workspace is open, you can access each workbook by choosing its name from the Window menu or by pressing Ctrl+F6. Although they are part of the same workspace, they will need to be saved individually. To close multiple workbooks simultaneously, hold down the Shift key and open the File menu. The Close option changes to the Close All option. Select it to close any open workbooks.

STEP-BY-STEP ⟶ **9.7**

1. Open the **File** menu and then select **Save Workspace**.

2. The Save Workspace dialog box appears.

3. Key **College Workspace** in the *File name* text box and click **Save**.

4. Close both workbooks.

 **Hot Tip**

You can close all open workbooks at one time by holding down the **Shift** key while you click on the **File** menu. This menu should now display Close All rather than Close.

5. Let's open the workspace. Click the **Open** button and select **College Workspace**. Your screen should look similar to Figure 9-2.

6. Open the **Window** menu and check to see if both workbooks are open.

7. Close both workbooks.

FIGURE 9-2
College Workspace

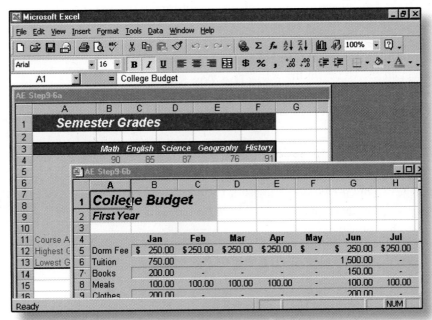

Summarizing Worksheets and Workbooks

A powerful feature of Excel is the ability to calculate data taken from several worksheets or from more than one workbook. For example, you may have separate worksheets for each month and you want to create a year-end worksheet that totals data from each monthly worksheet. *Linking* lets you enter formulas in a worksheet that reference cells in other worksheets or even other workbooks. References in other workbooks are referred to as *external references*.

When the data you are referencing is changed or modified, Excel automatically updates any formulas that contain the reference.

To enter a linking formula, select the cell in the worksheet where you want the formula to appear. If you want to perform a function, such as SUM or AVERAGE, on the data, then enter the function name. If you're referencing cell(s) in the same workbook, click the tab of the sheet containing the cell(s), and select the cell(s). Build the formula by clicking sheet tabs and selecting the appropriate cell(s).

If you are referencing data in the same cell or range on several consecutive sheets, then you can group the sheets in order to more efficiently select the desired cells. You also learned earlier in this lesson that you can preview and print multiple worksheets by first grouping them. Grouping also lets you perform the same action, whether it is selecting cells, formatting, or editing data, on all worksheets in the group at the same time. Remember that to group sheets, you click the tab of the first sheet in the group, hold down the Shift key, and click on the last sheet in the group. All the tabs of the sheets in the group appear selected, and the word *Group* appears in parentheses in the title bar.

You can also manually key in the names of cell references. To key in the reference to a cell on a different sheet within the same workbook, make sure you key the exact name of the sheet on which the cell is located. The sheet name is followed by an exclamation point and then the cell or range reference. An example of a linking formula that references cells on other sheets within the workbook is shown in Figure 9-3. The formula in cell B7 sums the values in cell E7 on the QTR 1, QTR 2, QTR 3, and QTR 4 worksheets.

Hot Tip

If the name of a worksheet or workbook referenced in a linking formula contains nonalphabetic characters, you must enclose the name in single quotation marks.

Concept Builder

You key in external references in two ways, depending on whether the workbook containing the reference is open or not. If the workbook is open, you key the exact name of the workbook in square brackets [ ], followed by the sheet name, an exclamation point, and the cells you are referencing. If the workbook containing the reference is not open, you must enter the full path name of the workbook, like the following: =SUM('C:\ABC Company\[Budget]1999'!A4:E12).

FIGURE 9-3
Linking worksheets

	A	B
1	**The Toy Store, Inc.**	
2	*Annual Sales*	
3		
4	*Year-End Totals Report*	
5		
6		**Year-End Totals**
7	**Dept 1**	=SUM('QTR 1:QTR 4'!E7)
8	**Dept 2**	=SUM('QTR 1:QTR 4'!E8)
9	**Dept 3**	=SUM('QTR 1:QTR 4'!E9)
10	**Dept 4**	=SUM('QTR 1:QTR 4'!E10)
11	**Dept 5**	=SUM('QTR 1:QTR 4'!E11)
12		

S TEP-BY-STEP ▷ 9.8

1. Open the **AE Step9-8** workbook from the student data files and save it as **Accounting Report** followed by your initials.

2. Look at the QTR 1, QTR 2, QTR 3, and QTR 4 worksheets. Notice the totals in E7:E11. These

are the totals that need to be combined on the Year-End Report worksheet. Select the **Year-End Report** worksheet.

3. Select cell **B7**. This cell will contain the linking formula.

4. Key the following: **=SUM(.**

5. Click the **QTR 1** worksheet tab.

6. Hold down the **Shift** key and click on the worksheet tab for **QTR 4**. This groups the four worksheets.

7. Click cell **E7** in the **QTR 1** worksheet. This cell contains the quarterly total for Department 1 in each worksheet.

8. Press **Enter**. The formula is completed on the Year-End Report worksheet.

9. In the **Year-End Report** worksheet, copy the formula in cell **B7** to the range **B8:B11**.

10. Print the **Year-End Report** worksheet. Then save and close the workbook.

Summary

In this lesson, you learned:

■ You can move among worksheets by clicking their tabs or by using the worksheet movement buttons to bring additional sheet tabs into view.

■ By default, a new Excel workbook includes three sheets. You can insert sheets by selecting Worksheet on the Insert menu. To delete a sheet, you click its tab and then select Delete Sheet on the Edit menu. Or you can right-click the sheet tab and select Delete on the shortcut menu.

■ You can copy and move data between worksheets and between workbooks using the Cut, Copy, and Paste commands.

■ By saving files as a workspace, you can open many files at one time by simply selecting the workspace name.

■ Linking formulas lets you summarize data on different worksheets within the same workbook or from different workbooks.

LESSON 9 REVIEW QUESTIONS

WRITTEN QUESTIONS

Write a brief answer to the following questions.

1. Explain two methods for copying data between worksheets.

   1. highlight cells to be copied, press cntrl c
   select the sheet tab where cells are going to be copied to.
   select upper left cell where cells are to be inserted
   press cntrl v

   2. highlight cells or range to be copied, move cursor to border of range
   hold cntrl+alt + pick button on mouse, drag to sheet tab
   then cell location where data should be. release the pick button
   then cntrl+alt.

AE-115

2. What is the difference between the sheet tabs and the worksheet movement buttons?

sheet tabs select the sheet.
worksheet movement buttons only move tabs so one can see it for picking

3. Which worksheet tab would you select if you want to insert a worksheet between Sheet2 and Sheet3?

sheet 3

4. Explain the purpose for using linking formulas.

to perform a calc. on cells from different sheets
references to other workbooks are external
references.

5. What is the purpose of a workspace?

allows opening all workbooks at once

6. Why would you want to group worksheets?

to use in linked formula. When the same cell
is used on different worksheels. = Sum(Marketing:Manufacturing!C5,

7. How do you group worksheets?

select first, hold shift and select last sheet of group.

8. Can you print grouped worksheets?

yes

9. When would you use worksheet movement buttons?

when more sheet ^tabs are available than will fit on the screen.

10. How would you key in a formula to sum the data in cell C3 on a sheet named Marketing and the data in cell E5 on a sheet named Manufacturing, when both sheets are in the same workbook?

= SUM(Marketing!C3, Manufacturing!E5)

LESSON 9 PROJECTS

PROJECT 9-1

1. Open the **AE Project9-1a** and **AE Project9-1b** workbooks.

2. In the **AE Project9-1a** workbook, select the range **C4:C12** and copy it to the same range in the **AE Project9-1b** workbook. Adjust the column width.

3. Delete the terminated employee **Trevor Tanquez** from the **AE Project9-1b** workbook.

4. Save AE Project9-1b as **2001 Payroll Master**, followed by your initials. Print a copy of the current sheet.

5. Save AE Project9-1a as **2000 Payroll Master**, followed by your initials.

6. Close both workbooks.

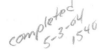

PROJECT 9-2

1. Create a workspace for the **2001 Payroll Master** and **2000 Payroll Master** workbooks created in the previous project. Name the workspace **Payroll Workspace**, followed by your initials.

2. Close all workbooks.

3. Open the **Payroll Workspace**.

4. Check to be certain both workbooks are open.

5. Close any open workbooks.

CRITICAL THINKING

ACTIVITY 9-1

Open the **AE Activity9-1** workbook. Use linking formulas to sum the Quarterly Totals figures for each department on the Year-End Report sheet. Save the workbook as **Sales Review** and print the **Year-End Report** worksheet.

ACTIVITY 9-2

As a manager in the personnel department of a major corporation, you are responsible for updating a number of Excel workbooks every week. You maintain workbooks on payroll, vacation schedules, health insurance benefits, time sheets, and expenses. Explain how you could use the Workspace feature in Excel to work more efficiently with these workbooks.

CREATING SHARED WORKBOOKS, DATA MAPS, AND WEB PAGES

OBJECTIVES

Upon completion of this lesson, you should be able to:

■ Create and use a shared workbook.

■ Insert and edit comments.

■ Track changes to a workbook.

■ Add protection properties to a workbook.

■ Create a data map for geographic regions.

■ Create a Web page for use on the Internet or an intranet.

⏱ **Estimated Time: 1 hours**

Introduction

This lesson introduces you to Excel features that give you even more control over how data is presented and used. You will learn how to share Excel workbooks with other users and incorporate modifications from more than one user. You can have Excel keep track of the changes over a period of time. In addition, you can add protection features to workbooks. This will help prevent unwanted changes in the workbooks.

Data maps are a handy way to illustrate geographical data in a worksheet, such as sales for particular states or countries. In addition, you will practice creating Web pages from Excel worksheets.

Creating a Shared Workbook

Excel lets you share files with other users so that you can review and modify the workbook as a group. If you want several people to work on a file at the same time, you save the file as a shared workbook and then make it available in a shared folder or on a shared network directory.

To create a shared workbook, open the Tools menu and select Share Workbook. In the Share Workbook dialog box, select the Editing tab, which appears similar to Figure 10-1.

In order for other users to work on this file simultaneously, select the *Allow changes by more than one user at the same time* option. This also allows a shared workbook to be merged. For example, you can open the shared workbook and then merge changes made by other users.

When you create a shared workbook, Excel lets you track the changes made to the workbook by individual users. You can choose to accept or reject changes that are made to the shared workbook when you merge the workbooks. Merging copies of a shared workbook combines the changes made by each user into a single file.

FIGURE 10-1
Editing tab of the Share Workbook dialog box

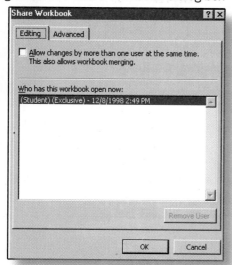

FIGURE 10-2
Advanced tab of the Share Workbook dialog box

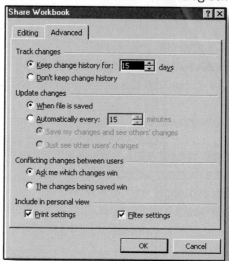

The Advanced tab in the Share Workbook dialog box (see Figure 10-2) gives you options for managing who makes what changes to the workbook. Those options are described below.

- **Track changes.** Maintains the history of changes made to the shared file based on the number of days selected. This option will need to be selected in order to merge changes from multiple copies of the same workbook.

- **Update changes.** Provides you with information about changes made to the file either when the file is saved or by the time specified in the minutes box.

Hot Tip

Whey using shared workbooks, you typically keep one copy of the shared workbook in a separate folder or drive. Changes are not made to this copy of the workbook; it is only used to merge changes. This helps eliminate confusion as to the location of the shared workbook that contains all of the recent changes.

- **Conflicting changes between users.** Displays the Resolve Conflict dialog box so you can see which changes conflicted and decide which changes to keep. The *Changes being saved win* option replaces any conflicting changes with your changes when the file is saved.

- **Include in personal view.** Lets you keep your personal print and filter options. Print options include page breaks, print areas, and changes made in the Print Preview screen.

STEP-BY-STEP ▷ 10.1

1. Open the **AE Step10-1** workbook from the student data files and save it as **Competition Real Estate** followed by your initials.

2. Open the **Tools** menu, select **Share Workbook**, and select the **Editing** tab in the **Share Workbook** dialog box.

3. Click the **Allow changes by more than one user at the same time** option.

4. Click the **Advanced** tab.

5. Under the *Track changes* options, make sure the **Keep change history for** option is selected and enter **15** for the number of days.

6. Click **OK**. A message box appears telling you the workbook will now be saved. Click **OK**. Notice that the title bar of the workbook now

displays [Shared] after the workbook name as shown in Figure 10-3.

7. To have Excel track the changes that are made in this workbook, open the **Tools** menu, select **Track Changes**, and then select **Highlight Changes**. The Highlight Changes dialog box appears, as shown in Figure 10-4. The dialog box contains options that let you determine which changes to a worksheet will be highlighted.

8. Select the **Track changes while editing** and **Highlight changes on screen** options.

9. Click **OK**. If a message box appears telling you that no changes were found, click **OK** to close the box.

10. Select cell **A2** and key **Home Listings – Residential**. Notice that a small black triangle appears in the upper-left corner of cell A2. This appears because you asked Excel to track the changes on screen. When a user of the worksheet places the mouse pointer over cell A2, a comment appears explaining the information that was in the cell prior to the change and the data entered into the cell after it was changed, as well as the name of the user who made the change and the date and time of the change (see Figure 10-5).

FIGURE 10-3
Shared workbook

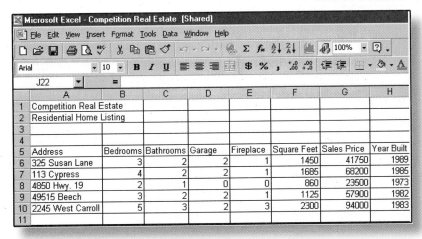

FIGURE 10-4
Highlight Changes dialog box

(continued on next page)

FIGURE 10-5
Comments outline the changes made

Microsoft Excel - Competition Real Estate.xls [Shared]

File Edit View Insert Format Tools Data Window Help

A3

	A	B	C	D	E	F	G	H	I	J	K	L	M	N
1	Competition Real Est													
2	Home Listings - Resi	Sandy Cable, 1/10/1999 11:17 PM: Changed cell A2 from 'Residential Home Listings' to 'Home Listings - Residential'.												
3														
4														
5	Address	B				Square Feet	Sales Price	Year Built						
6	325 Susan Lane	3	2	2	1	1450	41750	1989						
7	113 Cypress	4	2	2	1	1685	68200	1985						
8	4850 Hwy. 19	2	1	0	0	860	23500	1973						
9	49515 Beech	3	2	2	1	1125	57900	1982						
10	2245 West Carroll	5	3	2	3	2300	94000	1983						
11														
12														
13														

11. This comment will disappear after the workbook is saved. Click the **Save** button. Notice how the comment indicator in the upper left corner of cell A2 is gone.

12. Close the workbook.

To merge workbooks, you select the Tools menu and then choose Merge Workbooks. You can then save the workbook if prompted to do so. A list appears from which you can choose the copies of the shared workbooks to merge. After choosing the files you want to merge, click OK. If comments are attached to a cell by more than one user, Excel displays these comments, one after another, in the comment box.

Using Comments

In the previous Step-by-Step, you learned how Excel can track changes and place a comment in each cell in which a change was made. These comments display the name, date, and change information. As you probably know, a comment is simply a note that you can make about information in a cell. For example, if a salesperson's sales have increased dramatically over the past year and the reason for this increase is due to a territory reassignment, you may want to indicate this information in a comment.

To insert a comment, click in the cell where you want the comment to appear. Then select the Insert menu and choose Comment. A comment box opens, in which you simply key your comment.

If you need to change or edit your comment, simply click the cell containing the comment, open the Insert menu, and choose Edit Comment. The insertion point appears in the comment box, ready for you to make any necessary changes. To delete a comment, open the Edit menu, select Clear, and then select Comment. Or you can right-click in the cell and choose Delete Comment on the shortcut menu.

Hot Tip

You can also add a comment by right-clicking a cell and choosing Insert Comment on the shortcut menu. The shortcut menu also contains the Edit Comment and Delete Comment commands.

Exploring Workbook Properties

A workbook's properties can provide you with additional information on the file, like who created the workbook, where it's stored, when it was last modified or accessed, and the number of worksheets it contains. To view or modify workbook properties, select Properties on the File menu.

S TEP-BY-STEP ▷ 10.2

1. Open the **AE Step10-2** workbook from the student data files, and save it as **Property** followed by your initials.

2. Select cell **B9**. Open the **Insert** menu and then click **Comment**.

3. In the text box, enter **This cookie is a new product.**

4. Click anywhere outside the comment text box. Notice the red triangle in the upper right corner of the cell, indicating that it contains a comment. When you position the mouse pointer on cell B9, the comment displays.

5. Edit the comment by right-clicking cell **B9** and choosing **Edit Comment**. Key **First featured on March 1.** at the end of the comment.

6. Click anywhere outside the comment text box. Point to cell **B9** to view the comment.

7. Let's delete the comment: Right-click cell **B9** and click **Delete Comment** on the shortcut menu.

8. Now, let's change a workbook property. Open the **File** menu and choose **Properties**.

9. In the Properties dialog box, select the **Summary** tab, click in the **Author** box, and key your name to replace the existing name. Then, click in the **Subject** box and key **Cookie Sales**.

 Concept Builder

The Subject property is designed so you can group together files related to the same subject.

10. Click **OK**, and then close the workbook.

11. To view properties for a workbook that's not open, click the **Open** button. In the Open dialog box, select the **Property** file you just closed, click the drop-down arrow on the **Tools** button (on the dialog box's toolbar), and select **Properties**. The Properties dialog box opens.

12. Click the **Summary** tab, if necessary, to view the changes you made. Click **OK** to close the dialog box.

13. Double-click the **Property** workbook to open it, and remain in this screen for the next Step-by-Step.

Adding Protection Options

Although sharing workbooks is a practical way to update data and incorporate changes made by those who use the workbook, there are times when you won't want to share your data with anyone else.

With Excel's protection features, you can protect a single cell of data from being changed or deleted, or you can protect all the data on a worksheet, or even the entire workbook. After the data is protected, it cannot be altered. Excel refers to protected cells as *locked* cells. It may be easier to understand this concept if you visualize an imaginary lock on the cell that can't be opened to change data. You can remove the protection feature from a workbook as well. When you change a feature in a workbook, such as protection, you are actually changing the properties of the workbook. You can find the protection option on the Tools menu. After a worksheet is protected, you can remove the protection by choosing Unprotect Worksheet on the Tools menu.

You can also add a higher level of protection to a workbook. For example, when you protect a work-*sheet*, someone else can still open the workbook file. However, you may not want someone to view the information in your workbook. To prevent a workbook file from being opened by an unauthorized person, you can password-protect a workbook. If the person does not know the password, they cannot open the file.

Another protection option is Read-Only protection. This lets another user open the file, but if changes are made, the workbook must be saved with another name. The password and read-only features can be applied by clicking the Tools button in the Save As dialog box and then selecting General Options. You can add or remove password and read-only protections under General Options.

Passwords are case sensitive. In other words, if a password contains capital letters, you will need to enter the password using the same capital letters. For example, if you enter CAT as the password, CAT (not cat, or Cat, etc.) must be entered to open the workbook.

FIGURE 10-6
Protect Sheet dialog box

STEP-BY-STEP ▷ 10.3

1. The **Property** workbook should still be open. Open the **Tools** menu, and select **Protection**. Choose **Protect Sheet** on the submenu. The Protect Sheet dialog box appears, as shown in Figure 10-6. You could add a password to protect the worksheet in this dialog box.

2. Click **OK**. Your entire worksheet is now protected.

3. To see how this protection works, select cell **A11** and try to key **Sugar**. A warning box appears telling you that the cell is protected. Click **OK** to close the message box.

4. Save the workbook as **Protect** followed by your initials

5. To remove the protection, open the **Tools** menu, select **Protection**, and then click **Unprotect Sheet**.

6. To see how the worksheet is now unprotected, select cell **A11** and key **Sugar**. Remain in this screen for the next Step-by-Step.

In the preceding Step-by-Step, you protected a *worksheet*. In the next Step-by-Step, you will password-protect a *workbook*.

STEP-BY-STEP ▷ 10.4

1. To password-protect a workbook, open the **File** menu and choose **Save As**.

2. Click the arrow on the **Tools** button in the dialog box's toolbar, and choose **General Options**.

3. In the Save Options dialog box, key **CAT** for the password in the *Password to open* text box and click **OK**.

4. Key **CAT** again in the Confirm Password dialog box. Click **OK**.

5. Choose **Save** in the Save As dialog box. A message box appears asking if you want to replace the existing file named *Protect*. Click **Yes**.

6. Let's see how password protection works. Close the **Protect** workbook. Reopen the **Protect** workbook. The Password dialog box appears.

7. Key **CAT** and click **OK**.

8. Now, let's remove the workbook protection. Select **Save As** on the **File** menu.

9. Click the drop-down arrow on the **Tools** button and choose **General Options**. The highlight should be in the *Password to open* text box.

10. Press the **Delete** key to remove the password, and click **OK**.

11. Click **Save** to close the Save As dialog box. Click **Yes** when asked if you want to replace the existing file named *Protect*. Then, close the workbook.

Creating a Data Map

A data map can help you analyze sales and marketing data that is organized geographically. You can create map in Excel from columns of data within a worksheet. One column of data must contain geographic data, such as the names of states or countries.

To create a map, select the range of data you want to map. Then click the Insert menu, select Object, and then choose Microsoft Map on the Create New tab. Position the pointer on the worksheet where you want the map to appear and click. A map can then be edited and formatted in much the same way as a chart.

The data map feature is not installed with the standard Office 2000 installation. You can add it, though, from the installation CD.

Creating a Web Page

You can create a Web page from worksheet data or a chart and then publish the information on the World Wide Web. To create a Web page, you must save the data in HTML (HyperText Markup Language) file format.

Display the worksheet you want to save to the Web. Select Save as Web Page on the File menu. If you want to view the Web page you have created, simply select Web Page Preview on Excel's File menu. Or you can start your Internet browser and open the file from there.

STEP-BY-STEP ▷ 10.5

1. Open the **AE Step10-5** workbook from the student data files.

2. Open the **File** menu and select **Save as Web Page**.

3. Select the **Selection: Sheet** option. This will publish only the active worksheet as a Web page rather than the entire workbook.

4. In the *File name* box, type **Homes-for-Sale** and then click the **Save** button.

5. To view the Web page, select **Web Page Preview** on the **File** menu, or start Internet Explorer, or your Web browser. On the **File** menu, select **Open**, click the **Browse** button, and locate and open the **Homes-for-Sales** file. The worksheet data should be displayed as shown in Figure 10-7.

6. Close the Web page window and your Web browser. Then close any open files in Excel.

(continued on next page)

FIGURE 10-7
Web page

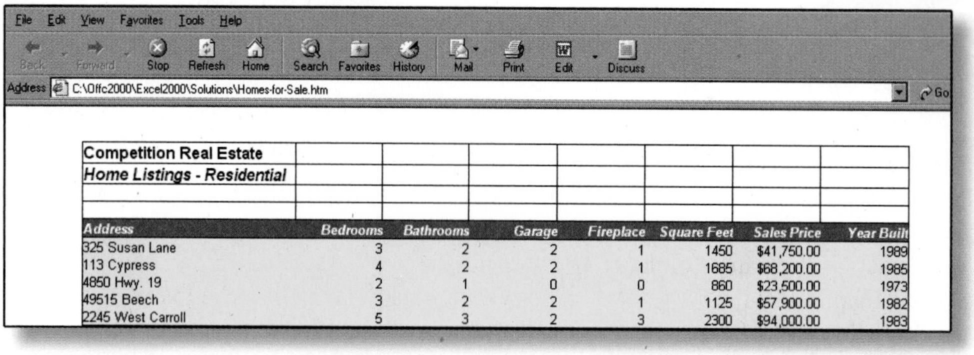

Competition Real Estate							
Home Listings - Residential							
Address	***Bedrooms***	***Bathrooms***	***Garage***	***Fireplace***	***Square Feet***	***Sales Price***	***Year Built***
325 Susan Lane	3	2	2	1	1450	$41,750.00	1989
113 Cypress	4	2	2	1	1685	$68,200.00	1985
4850 Hwy. 19	2	1	0	0	860	$23,500.00	1973
49515 Beech	3	2	2	1	1125	$57,900.00	1982
2245 West Carroll	5	3	2	3	2300	$94,000.00	1983

Summary

In this lesson, you learned:

- A shared workbook allows several users to make changes to a file at the same time. These changes can be tracked so you know who made the changes and when they were made. Workbooks can then be merged so that the changes made by individual users are combined and reflected in one file.
- Excel provides a number of options for protecting worksheet data from being viewed or changed by other users.
- Comments are notations that can be added to a worksheet.
- Data maps let you graphically illustrate geographic data.
- Excel lets you easily change workbook properties, such as the author of a workbook file.
- You can save a worksheet or an entire workbook in HTML format so that it can be viewed via the Web.

LESSON 10 REVIEW QUESTIONS

WRITTEN QUESTIONS

Write a brief answer to the following questions.

1. Explain what is meant by "shared workbook." a shared workbook can be edited by other users.

2. What option needs to be selected in order to allow multiple users to use a file at one time?

Tools > Share Workbook > Editing Tab >
Click Selection "Allow changes by
more than.., time.

3. Where is the above option located?

Tools > Share workbook > Editing Tab.

4. How many days will Excel keep a history of changes to a shared workbook?

whatever no. of days is set
on the Share workbook dialog
under Advanced Tab.

5. What File menu command needs to be selected in order to save workbook data or a chart as a Web page?

Save as Web Page

6. If changes to specific information in a workbook are suggested by more than one user, which option would you use to make changes?

Tools > Track Changes > Accept or Reject Changes

7. What type of data must at least one column of data contain in order for you to display it in a data map?

Geographical

8. How can you view a Web page after you've saved it in Excel?

Web Page Preview on File Menu or open from browser

9. Why would you want to save a worksheet as a Web page?

to publish on network or internet

10. In a shared workbook, what information does a comment display?

who made the change
Date and Time of change
Data before + after change

LESSON 10 PROJECTS

PROJECT 10-1

1. Open the **AE Project10-1** workbook from the student data files and save it as **GMRE Real Estate** followed by your initials.

2. Create a shared workbook. Keep track of changes for 60 days.

3. Save and close the workbook.

PROJECT 10-2

1. Start a new workbook and enter the following information:

   A1: MYO Oil Corporation
   A2: Oil Wells
   A4: State
   B4: Number of Wells

2. Enter the following three states in the State column, beginning in cell A5:

   Texas
   Louisiana
   Colorado

3. Enter the following data in the Number of Wells column, beginning in cell B5:

   52
   19
   64

4. Apply an AutoFormat of your choice to the data.

5. Save the workbook as MYO – Wells in HTML format.

6. View the page in Internet Explorer or the Web browser you are using. Then print the page.

7. Close your Web browser and then close any open Excel workbook.

SCANS

ACTIVITY 10-1

As the manager for Nationwide Retail Services, you decide to create a worksheet containing the names of your employees and their telephone numbers and publish it as a Web page. Create the worksheet using the names and phone numbers of 10 of your colleagues, friends, or other acquaintances. Format the worksheet as you feel is necessary. Save the workbook as **NRS Employees** and then publish the data to the Web.

SCANS

ACTIVITY 10-2

You created a Web page from an Excel spreadsheet. When you viewed the Web page in your Web browser, you noticed that the text in the cells appears to be cut off. Use Excel's Help system to troubleshoot the problem. Write a brief essay on how you would correct the problem.

USING OUTLINES, SUBTOTALS, AND LOOKUP FUNCTIONS

OBJECTIVES

Upon completion of this lesson, you should be able to:

- Create an outline from worksheet data.
- Remove an outline.
- Create subtotals from worksheet data.
- Remove subtotals.
- Work with named ranges.
- Use Lookup functions.

🕐 **Estimated Time: .5 hour**

Introduction

In this lesson, you will learn how to create outlines and subtotals in your worksheets. These features allow you to control which data in the worksheet is displayed or printed. An *outline* lets you view certain portions of worksheet detail. For example, you may only want to see row headings and row totals within a worksheet. The outline feature can do this for you in an instant.

Excel's subtotal feature lets you calculate totals and subtotals without having to enter formulas. Subtotals are often used with data lists.

Creating Outlines

An outline is especially helpful in large worksheets when you may want to view only parts of a worksheet. For example, you may want to view only column headings and the totals for those columns. By applying the outline feature, you can temporarily remove specified data from the display. You can then focus on the column totals.

Outlining can also help you organize and manage vast amounts of data. For example, without the outline feature, you would need to scroll from the top of a column all the way down to its bottom to see the results of a calculation performed on the column. In large worksheets, you can easily lose your place while doing this. When you display limited amounts of data in an outline, however, you can quickly view the tabulations completed at the end of a column or row.

Outlines are used only in worksheets that contain formulas. When you instruct Excel to create an outline, it looks for formulas within the worksheet data and displays that row or column of data and any data following the formulas. Column and row headings are retained as well for easy reference.

Figure 11-1 shows a worksheet for year-end sales. Formulas are entered in row 15 and column F.

FIGURE 11-1
Data before it is outlined

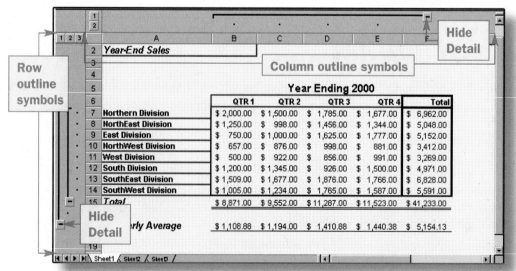

To apply an outline to the data, open the Data menu, select Group and Outline, and then choose Auto Outline. Figure 11-2 shows how the worksheet displays after Excel's Auto Outline feature is selected.

Notice the outline bars and symbols displayed to the left of rows and at the top of columns. These let you control the amount of detail displayed. The bars that appear are determined by where the formulas are located within a worksheet. For example, if there are formulas for columns and not for rows, bars will be displayed only for the columns. A Hide Detail symbol (the minus sign) indicates that all detail is showing; a Show Detail symbol (the plus sign) indicates that detail is hidden.

The column and row level symbols, located in the upper left corner of the outline area, let you display or hide details for the entire outline. Click on 1 to display the least amount of detail, such as the column and row headings and totals only, or click on 2 or 3 to see more detail.

FIGURE 11-2
Applying an Auto Outline

S TEP-BY-STEP ▷ 11.1

1. Open the **AE Step11-1** workbook from the student data files and save it as **Outline for Video Store** followed by your initials.

2. Open the **Data** menu, select **Group and Outline**, and then choose **Auto Outline** on the submenu. You should now see the outline symbols within the worksheet.

3. Click the **1** row level symbol. This hides all the row data except for the column headings and Quarterly Average row.

4. Click the **2** row level symbol. This displays two levels of row data—the Total row and the Quarterly Average row (see Figure 11-3). You can see

how outlines could be helpful in large worksheets because rather than scrolling from top to bottom in a column, you can simply click on an outline symbol to view the column totals.

5. Click the **Show Detail** symbol for the **Total** row. All the data should be displayed.

6. Click the **Hide Detail** symbol for the **Quarterly Average** row.

7. Save the workbook and then print the worksheet in landscape orientation. The worksheet should print as it appears on your screen. Remain in this screen for the next Step-by-Step.

FIGURE 11-3
Outlining data

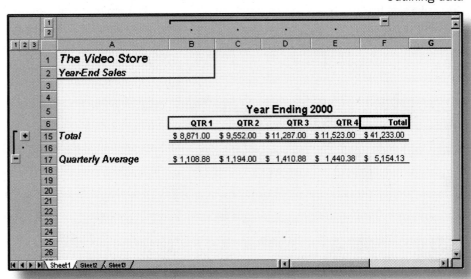

Removing an Outline

Just as quickly as an outline can be applied to worksheet data, it can be removed easily. When the outline is removed, worksheet data appears as it was before the outline was applied and the outline symbols are no longer displayed in the worksheet window.

1. Open the **Data** menu, select **Group and Outline**, and then choose **Clear Outline** on the submenu.

3. Close the workbook.

2. Save the workbook as **Outline for Video Store - Removed**.

Creating Subtotals

Excel can instantly calculate subtotals and averages within the worksheet data without your having to enter formulas. This feature is most useful when you want to view results of the worksheet data but you don't want formulas permanently entered into the worksheet. For example, in a very large worksheet containing formulas, it can take a while for the formulas to recalculate when worksheet data is changed. This can slow you down, not to mention test your patience. With Excel's Subtotals feature, you can group and sort data and then automatically insert a subtotal or grand total for the data. Data that is to be subtotaled should be set up as a list, and should be sorted.

When creating subtotals, you will notice buttons similar to the outline buttons. These allow you to view more or less data. Figure 11-4 shows a worksheet before subtotals are calculated. Figure 11-5 shows a worksheet in which the Subtotals feature has been applied. Notice how subtotals appear after each department.

To use the Subtotals feature, select the Subtotals option on the Data menu. The Subtotal dialog box opens, as shown in Figure 11-6.

FIGURE 11-4
Worksheet before subtotals

	A	B	C	D	E	F	G	H	I
1			Arts & Crafts, Inc.						
2			*Inventory*						
3									
4	Dept.	Item No.	Description	Quantity in Stock	Cost	Selling Price			
5	Basket	50-122	22" Wicker Basket	17	$ 2.69	$ 3.89			
6	Basket	50-116	16" Wicker Basket	19	$ 1.99	$ 2.99			
7	Basket	50-120	20" Wicker Basket	21	$ 2.39	$ 3.59			
8	Varnish	15-223	Varnish - Clear	26	$ 3.99	$ 5.29			
9	Varnish	15-993	Varnish - Satin	28	$ 3.99	$ 5.29			
10	Paint	12-230	Paint- Green	39	$ 0.99	$ 1.49			
11	Paint	12-223	Paint- Blue	45	$ 0.99	$ 1.49			
12	Paint	12-295	Paint- White	57	$ 0.99	$ 1.49			
13									
14									
15									
16									
17									

Sheet1 / Sheet2 / Sheet3 /

FIGURE 11-5
Applying subtotals

1 2 3		A	B	C	D	E		F		G	H
	1			**Arts & Crafts, Inc.**							
	2			*Inventory*							
	3										
	4	**Dept.**	**Item No.**	**Description**	**Quantity in Stock**	**Cost**		**Selling Price**			
	5	**Paint**	12-223	Paint - Blue	45	$	0.99	$	1.49		
	6	**Paint**	12-230	Paint - Green	39	$	0.99	$	1.49		
	7	**Paint**	12-295	Paint - White	57	$	0.99	$	1.49		
	8	**Paint Total**						$	4.47		
	9	**Varnish**	15-223	Varnish - Clear	26	$	3.99	$	5.29		
	10	**Varnish**	15-993	Varnish - Satin	28	$	3.99	$	5.29		
	11	**Varnish Total**						$	10.58		
	12	**Basket**	50-116	16" Wicker Basket	19	$	1.99	$	2.99		
	13	**Basket**	50-120	20" Wicker Basket	21	$	2.39	$	3.59		
	14	**Basket**	50-122	22" Wicker Basket	17	$	2.69	$	3.89		
	15	**Basket Total**						$	10.47		
	16	**Grand Total**						$	25.52		
	17										

Sheet1 / Sheet2 / Sheet3 /

The options available in the Subtotal dialog box are described below.

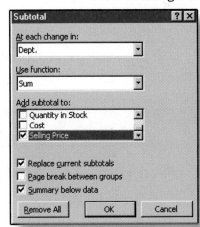

FIGURE 11-6
Subtotal dialog box

- **At each change in.** This option lets you select the column of data that will determine how data is grouped for subtotaling. At each change in the values appearing in the column, a subtotal is entered. For example, in Figure 11-5, the Dept. column was selected. There are three different values entered in the column, so Excel places a subtotal after each department's data.

- **Use function.** Lets you select the summary calculation to be performed. For example, you can choose Sum, Average, Min, Max, or Product.

- **Add subtotal to.** Determines in which column the subtotal will be placed.

- **Replace current subtotals.** If subtotals already exist, selecting this option will replace existing subtotals.

- **Page break between groups.** Creates a page break between each group subtotal.

- **Summary below data.** Places a summary—for example, a grand total—below the subtotals.

Hot Tip

You sort data in a list by using the Sort Ascending or Sort Descending buttons on the toolbar or by opening the Sort dialog box.

S TEP-BY-STEP ▷ 11.3

1. Open the **AE Step11-3** workbook from the student data files and save it as **A & C Subtotals** followed by your initials. Notice that the data is sorted by Quantity in Stock.

2. Select any cell in the **Item No.** column and click the **Sort Ascending** button.

3. Open the **Data** menu and then select **Subtotals**. In the Subtotal dialog box, notice that Dept. is entered in the *At each change in* text box. This means a subtotal will be calculated at each change in the Dept. column. We want to use the

Sum function to calculate the subtotals. If necessary, click on **Selling Price** in the *Add Subtotal to* list. This is where the subtotal values will appear. Click **OK**.

4. Click the **2** row level symbol to display only the subtotals and grand total.

5. Save the workbook and then print the worksheet. The worksheet should print as it appears on your screen. Remain in this screen for the next Step-by-Step.

Removing Subtotals

When you remove subtotals, the worksheet is displayed as it was before the subtotals were applied. If no changes have been made to the worksheet data, simply clicking the Undo button removes the subtotals. Or you can remove the subtotals by selecting the Subtotals option on the Data menu and then click Remove All in the Subtotal dialog box.

S TEP-BY-STEP ▷ 11.4

1. Click the **3** row level symbol to redisplay all of the data.

2. To remove the subtotals, open the **Data** menu, select **Subtotals**, and then select **Remove All**.

3. Save the workbook as **A & C Subtotals - Removed**. Then close the workbook.

Naming Ranges

Outlining and subtotaling are practical for organizing and viewing the data on a worksheet. Assigning names to specified ranges is another method for identifying and organizing data. Range names are especially useful in formulas. For example, you might have sales data for the month of April entered in the range B15:B20. To reference the data in a formula, as you've learned, you'd have to key in the range name, or select the range. By assigning a name, such as April, to the range, however, all you have to do is key in the range name in place of the range address. For most users, "April" is much easier to key in than "B15:B20."

Concept Builder

You can delete a range name by opening the Define Name dialog box, selecting the name, and clicking the **Delete** button.

You assign a range name by selecting the range, selecting Name on the Insert menu, and then defining the name in the Define Name dialog box.

Hot Tip

A shortcut for naming a range is to select the range you want to name, click the **Name Box** in the Formula bar, type the range name, and press **Enter**. Be sure to press **Enter** as your last step or the name will not be entered.

STEP-BY-STEP ▷ 11.5

1. Open the **AE Step11-5** workbook from the student data files, and save it as **FQBonus** followed by your initials.

2. Select the range **B6:B11**.

3. Open the **Insert** menu, click **Name**, and select **Define**.

4. In the Define Name dialog box, the name *January* may already appear in the *Names in workbook* text box. This is because Excel tries to find the name by looking at any word(s) that may be above the selected range. If the name does not appear, key **January** in the top box.

5. Click **Add** and then click **OK**.

6. Select the range **C6:C11** and follow steps 3-5 above to name this range **February**.

7. Select the range **D6:D11**, click the **Name Box** on the Formula bar, key **March**, and press **Enter**.

8. Select the range **E6:E11** and use either method to name this range **Total_Sales**.

9. Select the range **H6:I12** and name this range **Bonus_Table**.

10. Click in cell **B12** and enter the formula **=SUM (January)**.

11. Click in cell **C12** and enter the formula **=SUM (February)**.

12. Click in cell **D12** and enter the formula **=SUM (March)**. Remain in this screen for the next Step-by-Step.

Using Lookup Functions

You can use Excel's Lookup functions to look up existing values, rather than entering them yourself. Take a look at the worksheet in Figure 11-7.

To determine a salesperson's bonus, you need to compare their total sales to the bonus table. For example, Brenner's total sales for the first quarter were $74,766. When you compare this with the bonus table, you see that Brenner's sales are above $70,000, but below $75,000. Therefore, Brenner should get a bonus of $5,000. Rather than you having to determine the bonus amount for each total sales amount, you can have Excel's VLOOKUP function do this for you.

You use the VLOOKUP function when the data in your table is listed vertically from the top down. Use the HLOOKUP function when data is listed horizontally from left to right.

FIGURE 11-7
Looking up values

	A	B	C	D	E	F	G	H	I
1			PCI, Inc.						
2									
3									
4		First Quarter Sales						Bonus Table	
5	Last Name	January	February	March	Total Sales	Bonus		Sales	Bonus
6	Brenner	24,123	22,592	28,051	$ 74,766			-	-
7	Gutierrez	22,167	23,699	26,240	$ 72,106			$ 55,000	$ 2,000
8	Keplinger	27,834	28,399	28,976	$ 85,209			$ 60,000	$ 3,000
9	Larson	36,130	46,067	38,022	$ 120,219			$ 65,000	$ 4,000
10	Stein	21,667	24,137	26,657	$ 72,461			$ 70,000	$ 5,000
11	Yoshida	18,579	20,986	23,442	$ 63,007			$ 75,000	$ 6,000
12								$ 80,000	$ 7,000

STEP-BY-STEP 11.6

1. Select cell **F6**.

2. Click the **Paste Function** button.

3. In the Paste Function dialog box, select **Lookup & Reference** in the Function category box. Click **VLOOKUP** in the Function name list box and click **OK**.

4. In the Formula Palette, key **Total_Sales** in the Lookup_value box. This is the range containing the total sales value that you want Excel to look up.

5. Enter **Bonus_Table** in the Table_array box. This is where the amounts are that you want Excel to compare with the sales amount.

6. Enter **2** in the Col_index_num box. This represents the column number in the bonus table containing the data you want entered in cell **F6**. Click **OK**.

7. Copy the formula in cell **F6** to **F7:F11**.

8. Print the worksheet. Then, save and close the workbook.

Summary

In this lesson, you learned:

- An outline is one method of organizing vast amounts of data in a worksheet. You can display as much or as little of the worksheet data as necessary.

- Using the Subtotals feature is another way of handling large worksheets. Excel can quickly display totals, averages, and various other calculations without your having to enter any formulas.

- You can assign a name to a range of data to more easily reference it in a formula.

- Excel's Lookup functions allow you to "look up" existing data, rather than keying it in.

LESSON 11 REVIEW QUESTIONS

TRUE/FALSE

Circle T if the statement is true or F if the statement is false.

T F 1. It is most practical to outline a worksheet that contains a large amount of data and formulas that total or summarize portions of the data.

T **F** 2. You cannot print data that is outlined.

T **F** 3. An outline lets you hide rows of data, but not columns.

T F 4. You can total a group of data using the Subtotals feature.

T **F** 5. You cannot include a grand total on a list of data that has been subtotaled.

WRITTEN QUESTIONS

Write a brief answer to the following questions.

1. What must a worksheet contain in order for you to create an outline?

   formula

2. What is the purpose of an outline?

   To simplify the presentation of data

3. What is one advantage of the Subtotals feature?

   Quickly summarize categories of data without having to manual insert formulas.

4. What is one advantage of the Outline feature?

    Organizes a large amount of data very quickly & easily

5. Describe the purpose of the 1 level symbol in an outlined worksheet.

    minimizes the amount of data shown in either the columns or rows.

LESSON 11 PROJECTS

PROJECT 11-1

1. Open the **AE Project11-1** workbook from the student data files and save it as **Outline Review** followed by your initials.

2. Create an outline for the worksheet data that hides the Spring, Summer, Fall, and Winter data.

3. Print the worksheet and then close the workbook.

PROJECT 11-2

1. Open the **AE Project 11-2** workbook from the student data files and save it as **Subtotals Review** followed by your initials.

2. Set up the data for the four regions as a list. Insert a column before column A. In cell **A5**, key **Region**. Use the Format Painter to copy the format from cell **B5** to cell **A5**.

3. In cell **A6**, key **NW** for Northwest region. Copy the contents of cell **A6** to **A7:A20**. Do the same for the other three regions, using **SW** for Southwest, **SE** for Southeast, and **NE** for Northeast. Delete the rows containing the region name and column labels for each region, as well as any blank rows.

4. Delete blank columns within the data list.

5. If necessary, sort the data by the **Region** field. Then apply **average** subtotals that are based on changes in the **Region** field and added to the **Selling Price** field.

6. Hide the detail data so that only the regional averages and Grand Average are displayed. Print the worksheet and then close the workbook.

Completed
5-5-04
5:45U

CRITICAL THINKING

SCANS

ACTIVITY 11-1

In a new Excel workbook, create a data list of either household or office items that are, or should be, insured. Include columns for item categories, item names, the year purchased, and the estimated value of the item. Format the data as you feel is appropriate. Then use the outlining and subtotaling features to show and hide various levels of data. Display all the data and subtotals before printing the sheet.

WORKING WITH GRAPHICS AND EMBEDDED OBJECTS

OBJECTIVES

Upon completion of this lesson, you should be able to:

■ Identify the tools on the Drawing toolbar.

■ Draw objects and insert AutoShapes.

■ Add formatting and text to graphic objects.

■ Edit graphic objects.

■ Embed objects.

⏲ **Estimated Time: 1.5 hours**

Introduction

In this lesson, you will learn how to add graphic objects to worksheets. Just like the data you enter in a worksheet, you can format the graphic objects you create. This lesson discusses how to group several objects together so they can then be treated as a single object. In addition, you will learn how to select and move graphic objects.

Excel's embedding feature lets you ***embed*** or place objects into an Excel file. You can embed objects such as an Excel file into another Excel file or files and graphics from other applications. The embedded object becomes a part of the workbook in which it is embedded. You actually created an embedded object when you added a chart to a worksheet. You will now explore more embedding features.

Displaying the Drawing Toolbar

You already know how to enhance your worksheets by formatting data and creating charts to better illustrate the data. Using ***graphic objects*** provides further enhancements. For example, you may want to add an arrow to a worksheet to point out a significant item in the data. Or, you might want to box data to highlight it, or even add text within a text box to create a professional-looking document.

You will use the Drawing toolbar to create graphic objects. To display the Drawing toolbar, click the Drawing button on the Standard toolbar. The Drawing toolbar is displayed in Figure 12-1. The drawing toolbar buttons are described in Table 12-1.

FIGURE 12-1
Drawing toolbar

TABLE 12-1
Drawing tools

BUTTON	WHAT IT DOES
Draw	Clicking the arrow displays a menu from which you can choose options such as group, ungroup, flip, rotate, and align.
Select Objects	Lets you select an object.
Free Rotate	Applies rotation to objects.
AutoShapes	Clicking the arrow displays a list of predefined shapes from which you can select.
Line	Draws straight lines; press the Shift key to draw a straight line or a line at a 45-degree angle.
Arrow	Draws arrows; press the Shift key to draw arrows at a 45-degree angle.
Rectangle	Draws rectangles; press the Shift key to draw perfect squares.
Oval	Draws ovals; press the Shift key to draw circles.
Text Box	Draws a box in which you can enter word-wrapped text.
Insert WordArt	Displays a WordArt dialog box from which you can choose a style of WordArt and then type in your text.
Insert Clip Art	Lets you select from any clip art files you have.
Fill Color	Displays a color palette for filling the graphic object.
Line Color	Lets you choose a color for a selected line.
Font Color	Displays a palette from which you can a color for the selected text.
Line Style	Displays a menu of line style and width selections.
Dash Style	Lets you choose a dashed style for a line.
Arrow Style	Displays a menu of arrow styles from which you can choose.
Shadow	Lets you choose from a palette of shadows.
3D	Displays a palette of 3-D effects from which you can choose.

Drawing a Line

You can draw a line anywhere in your worksheet. If you want to draw a perfectly straight line, simply hold the Shift key down while drawing the line. To keep the Line tool active in order to draw several lines, double-click the Line button and then click once on it to turn it off.

Shift for Ortho

Hot Tip

Double-clicking a button on the Drawing toolbar will keep it active until you click once on the button to turn it off. For example, if you want to draw three lines, simply double-click the Line button, draw three lines, and then click the Line button once to turn it off.

STEP-BY-STEP ▷ 12.1

C

1. Open a new workbook. This workbook will be used for drawing practice.

2. Click the **Drawing** button on the Standard toolbar to display the Drawing toolbar. Click the **Line** button. The pointer should turn into a crosshair as you move it into the worksheet area.

3. Drag the crosshair pointer in a horizontal line starting in cell **B5** and ending in cell **E5**. When you release the mouse button, you will see selection handles on the line. If you make a

mistake, press Delete while the selection handles are still on the object and try again. You can remove the selection handles by clicking anywhere outside the line. To redisplay the selection handles, simply click on the object.

4. Let's try a line at a 45-degree angle. Click the **Line** button again. Hold down the **Shift** key while dragging from cell **B5** down to cell **C10** (release the mouse button before you release the Shift key). Remain in this screen for the next Step-by-Step.

Drawing a Rectangle or Square

You draw a rectangle or square by dragging from the upper-left corner to the lower-right corner of the object. If you want to create a square, hold down the Shift key while dragging. You can change the color or fill pattern of a rectangle or square by selecting the object and then clicking the Fill Color button.

STEP-BY-STEP ▷ 12.2

1. Click the **Rectangle** button.

2. Drag the crosshair pointer from the upper-left corner of cell **D7** to the lower-right corner of cell **F9**. Look at your rectangle. Note the selection handles around the rectangle.

3. To draw a square, click the **Rectangle** button.

4. Hold the **Shift** key and drag the crosshair pointer from cell **D10** to the lower-right corner of **D13**.

5. With this last object still selected, click the **Fill Color** button's arrow and click on a color of your choice. Remain in this screen for the next Step-by-Step.

Drawing an Oval or Circle

An oval is created in the same manner as a rectangle. Drag from the upper-left corner to the lower-right corner to create the object. Holding down the Shift key while dragging creates a circle.

STEP-BY-STEP ▷ 12.3

1. Click the **Oval** button.

2. Drag the crosshair pointer from the upper-left corner of cell **G1** to the lower-right corner of cell **G5**.

3. To draw a perfect circle, click the **Oval** button, hold down the **Shift** key, and drag the crosshair pointer from the upper-left corner of cell **H1** to the lower-right corner of cell **H3**.

4. With this last object still selected, click the **Fill Color** button's arrow and select a color of your choice.

5. Save the file as **Enhance Draw**.

6. Print the active sheet and then close the workbook.

Drawing AutoShapes and Text Boxes

AutoShapes represent a variety of ready-made shapes, such as arrows, stars, and banners. These shapes can be added to a worksheet by clicking the arrow on the AutoShapes button. A menu of various AutoShapes categories displays. Select an AutoShape category and then select a shape from the submenu. Position the pointer on the sheet where you want to begin the shape and drag to the lower right corner of where you want the shape to end. You can insert text into the AutoShape by clicking the Text Box button, drawing a text box within the AutoShape object, and then typing text. Figure 12-2 shows an AutoShape containing a text box. You can also use the Text Box tool to insert text anywhere else on the worksheet.

FIGURE 12-2
AutoShapes and text boxes

STEP-BY-STEP ▷ 12.4

1. Start a new workbook.

2. Click the **AutoShapes** button's arrow, select **Stars and Banners**, and choose a banner style of your choice.

3. Select a location within the worksheet and drag from the upper-left to the lower-right corner to create the banner.

(continued on next page)

4. To enter text within the AutoShape without inserting a text box at this point, simply start typing. Key **Attention: Employees**. Press **Enter** after *Attention:* so that the text appears on two lines. Format the text by selecting the **Font Size** button and clicking **16**. Click the **Bold** button and then the **Center** alignment button on the Formatting toolbar.

5. Click the **Text Box** button.

6. Draw a text box by dragging from the upper-left to the lower-right of the area where you want the text to appear.

7. Type the following information in the text box.

   ```
   Conference Information:

   Please note the place and time
   for the office relocation
   conference.

   Everyone must be present.
   ```

8. Then, with the text box selected, change the font style to bold, and center the text.

9. Save the workbook as **Conference**.

10. Print a copy of the active sheet and then close the workbook.

Creating WordArt

WordArt gives you various ways to display your text. The various WordArt styles are shown in Figure 12-3.

FIGURE 12-3
WordArt Gallery

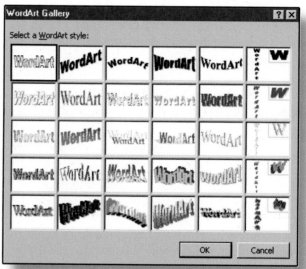

STEP-BY-STEP ⟩ 12.5

1. Start a new workbook.

2. Click the **Insert WordArt** button, choose a style of your choice, and click **OK**.

3. Type your name in the Edit WordArt Text dialog box and click **OK**. Remain in this screen for the next Step-by-Step.

Graphic Objects

Before you can make changes to a graphic object, it must be selected. An object is selected if it has selection handles around it. To select one object, simply point to the object and click. To select more than one object, hold down the **Shift** key while you select each object.

You can change the shape of a graphic object by dragging one of its selection handles. To proportionately change the shape of the object, hold down the Shift key while dragging one of the corner selection handles.

To move a graphic object, you must first select it. Then place the pointer over the object. When it turns into a four-headed arrow, press the mouse button and drag the object to its new location. You do not use the selection handles to move an object.

STEP-BY-STEP ▷ 12.6

1. Draw two circles on the same worksheet as the WordArt.

2. Practice selecting the different graphic objects you have created by clicking on them.

3. Practice selecting several objects by holding the **Shift** key while you select each object.

4. Deselect the objects by clicking on a blank area. Then, select any of the graphic objects on your worksheet.

5. Practice changing the shape by dragging the selection handles. Practice dragging the side selection handles as well as the corner selection handles.

6. Hold down the **Shift** key while dragging a corner selection handle of one of the graphic objects. Notice how the shape maintains its current proportions.

7. With the object still selected place the mouse pointer over the object until it turns into a four-headed arrow.

8. Drag the object to a new location.

9. Practice doing this with another object. Remain in this screen for the next Step-by-Step.

Formatting a Graphic Object

Colors, patterns, textures, and gradients can be added to any of the objects you have created. To add these enhancements, you must first select the object. Then use the Fill Color or Line Color tools to apply the format. You can also add and change 3-D effects by clicking the 3-D button.

STEP-BY-STEP ▷ 12.7

1. Click the **Oval** button and draw a circle. Remember to hold down the **Shift** key as you draw.

2. With the circle selected, click the **Fill Color** button's arrow.

(continued on next page)

3. Choose **Fill Effects**.

4. Click the **Gradient** tab and choose **Vertical** from the Shading styles.

5. Click the **Color 1** arrow and select a color of your choice.

6. Click **OK**.

7. Draw another circle.

8. With this circle selected, click the **Fill Color** button's arrow and choose **Fill Effects**.

9. Click the **Texture** tab.

10. Select a texture of your choice and click **OK**.

11. Experiment with the **3-D** and **Shadow** tools on the Drawing toolbar. The 3-D tool adds three-dimensional effects to the selected object.

12. Save the workbook as **3D Effects**. Print the active sheet and then close the workbook.

Embedded Objects

When you embed an object in a workbook, it becomes a part of that workbook. For example, if you embed one Excel file into another Excel file, the workbook and the embedded object become one file.

After an object is embedded in the worksheet, it can be resized or moved as any other graphic object. You click on the object and drag a selection handle to resize the object. Or you select the object and drag it to its new location.

Hot Tip

Always save any changes to your work before you try to embed an object. While embedding works most of the time, it takes a large amount of the computer's resources and memory, and it can, at times, give you unpredicted results.

STEP-BY-STEP ⟹ 12.8

1. Open the **Step-by-Step 12-13a** [8a] workbook from the student data files. You will embed an object into this file.

2. Open the **Step-by-Step 12-13b** [8b] workbook from the student data files. This is the file you will embed. Look it over briefly, and then close the workbook.

3. In the **Step-by-Step 12-13a** [8] workbook, select the range **H1:N30**. This is where you will embed the Excel file.

4. Open the **Insert** menu and then select **Object**. The Object dialog box appears. The Create New tab lets you run another Windows project so you can create an object to insert.

5. Select the **Create from File** tab. The Create from File tab, shown in Figure 12-4, lets you insert an existing file as an embedded object.

6. Click the **Browse** button and in the Browse dialog box, open the student data files, and choose the **Step-by-Step 12-13b** [8] workbook file.

Click **Insert**. In the Object dialog box, click **OK**. (This may take a few minutes.)

7. Save the workbook as **Embedded Object**. Remain in this screen for the next Step-by-Step.

Hot Tip

You can change the size and shape of the embedded object as you would a graphic object. This figure is displayed at 50%. You may need to change the Zoom percentage in order to view the worksheet with the embedded object on your screen.

FIGURE 12-4
Create from File tab

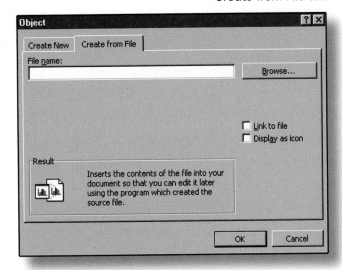

Editing an Embedded Object

To edit an embedded object, you simply double-click anywhere on the object. This will open the object in the application in which it was originally created. When you are finished editing the embedded object, return to the Excel worksheet by clicking the Close button of the editing window.

STEP-BY-STEP ▷ 12.9

1. Double-click the embedded file. The worksheet opens in an Excel window.

2. Select cell **B5** and change it to **$500,000**.

3. To close the embedded file's window, click on the window's **Close** button. Notice the changes in the embedded worksheet and its graph.

4. Save the workbook and then set up the page so that it breaks between the two sets of data. Print the worksheet in landscape orientation. Then close the workbook.

Summary

In this lesson, you learned:

- The Drawing toolbar contains tools for adding a variety of graphic objects and text to a worksheet.

- You can draw your own shapes using the Drawing tools, or you can insert AutoShapes.

- You can resize, move, format, and edit graphic objects on a worksheet, just like you would a chart or other worksheet object.

- You can embed objects in an Excel worksheet, and then move and resize them as you would other graphic objects. To edit an embedded object, double-click it to open the object in the application in which it was originally created.

LESSON 12 REVIEW QUESTIONS

MATCHING

Match the correct drawing tool in Column 2 to its name in Column 1.

Column 1		Column 2	
_D_	1. Line	A.	[icon]
_E_	2. Line Style	B.	[icon]
_A_	3. Text Box	C.	[icon]
_C_	4. Font Color	D.	[icon]
_B_	5. Insert WordArt	E.	[icon]

WRITTEN QUESTIONS

Write a brief answer to the following questions.

1. Briefly describe what an embedded object is.

object inserted is either created at time of insertion or from a file. the Object becomes part of the destination file. Changes made to the embedded object are also made in the destination.

2. How do you edit an embedded object?

double click on the object and the object will open in the program that created it.

3. How do you draw a perfect square?

use the rectangle command and hold down the shift key.

4. Which tab in the Object dialog box would you choose if you wanted to insert an existing file as an embedded object?

"Create from file."

5. What would you use the Text Box tool for?

to insert text as an object

LESSON 12 PROJECTS

PROJECT 12-1

1. Start a new workbook.

2. Draw a circle and fill the circle with a color of your choice.

3. Draw a rectangle and fill the rectangle with a color of your choice.

4. Draw a line connecting the circle to the rectangle. (*Hint*: Select the **Connectors** option on the AutoShapes menu).

5. Save the workbook as **Object 1**. Print the active sheet and then close the workbook.

PROJECT 12-2

1. Embed the Excel file **AE Project12-2a** in the student data files into the **AE Project12-2** file in the student data files. The file AE Project12-2a shows the auto parts sales for the second quarter of the year. The file AE Project12-2 shows the sales for the first quarter.

2. You may need to change the size of the range after you embed the file in order for the totals to be displayed.

3. Save the results as **Sams Auto Parts Semi-Annual Sales**.

4. Print the worksheet using the page setup options that you think are most apporpriate. Then close the workbook.

CRITICAL THINKING

SCANS

ACTIVITY 12-1

Using the file you created in Critical Thinking Activity 11-1, insert and/or embed graphic objects on the worksheet that enhance its appearance or help illustrate the data it contains. Format and edit the objects as you feel are necessary. Print the sheet when you are done

Advanced Microsoft Excel

COMMAND SUMMARY

FEATURE	MENU COMMAND	TOOLBAR BUTTON	LESSON
Align - Center	Format, Cells, Alignment, Center		
Align - Left	Format, Cells, Alignment, Left		
Align - Right	Format, Cells, Alignment, Right		
Bold	Format, Cells, Font, Bold		
Border	Format, Cells, Border		
Merge and Center	Format, Cells, Alignment, Center Across Selection		
Chart - Create	Insert, Chart		
Clear cell contents	Edit, Clear, Contents		
Column Width	Format, Column, Width		
Copy	Edit, Copy		
Currency format	Format, Cells, Number, Currency		
Cut	Edit, Cut		
Date Format	Format, Cells, Number, Date		
Delete Column	Edit, Delete, Entire column		
Delete Row	Edit, Delete, Entire row		
Drawing Toolbar	View, Toolbars, Drawing		
Font	Format, Cells, Font	Arial	

FEATURE	MENU COMMAND	TOOLBAR BUTTON	LESSON
Font Color	Format, Cells, Font		
Font Size	Format, Cells, Font		
Font Style	Format, Cells, Font		
Go To	Edit, Go To		
Hide - Column	Format, Column, Hide		
Hide - Row	Format, Row, Hide		
Insert Column	Insert, Columns		
Insert Hyperlink	Insert, Hyperlink		
Insert Row	Insert, Rows		
Italic	Format, Cells, Font, Italic		
Macro - Record	Tools, Macro, Record New Macro		
Macro - Run	Tools, Macro, Macros		
Macro - Stop Recording	Tools, Macro, Stop Recording		
New Workbook	File, New		
Open Workbook	File, Open		
Paste	Edit, Paste		
Paste Function	Insert, Function		
Percentage Format	Format, Cells, Number, Percentage		1
Print	File, Print		
Print Preview	File, Print Preview		2
Repeat last action	Edit, Repeat		
Row Height	Format, Row, Height		
Save Workbook	File, Save		

FEATURE	MENU COMMAND	TOOLBAR BUTTON	LESSON
Shade - Cell	Format, Cells, Patterns		
Sort - Ascending Order	Data, Sort, Ascending		3
Sort - Descending Order	Data, Sort, Descending		3
Toolbars - Display/Remove	View, Toolbars		
Underline	Format, Cells, Font, Underline		
Undo	Edit, Undo		
Zoom	View, Zoom	100%	

REVIEW QUESTIONS

TRUE/FALSE

Circle T if the statement is true or F if the statement is false.

T F 1. When you copy an entire worksheet, you copy the formats as well as the data.

T F 2. A data list is also referred to as a database.

T F 3. A chart can be created from a PivotTable report.

T **F** 4. Once you have created a chart from data on a worksheet, you cannot change it to a different type of chart.

T **F** 5. To publish an Excel worksheet as a Web page, you must first export the data to Microsoft Word and then save it as a text file.

WRITTEN QUESTIONS

Write a brief answer to the following questions.

1. Which Excel analysis tool would you use if you wanted to find an unknown value within a formula?

   Goal Seek or Solver

2. Which Excel feature would you use to automate repetitive tasks performed in Excel?

Record Macro

3. Explain what is meant by an "external reference" as it relates to linking workbook data.

references in other workbooks

4. Explain two methods for displaying the Drawing toolbar.

1. Click the "Drawing" button on the standard toolbar

2. Right Click any button on the standard toolbar and then click the Drawing Menu button

5. Explain the difference between tracing dependents and tracing precedents on a worksheet.

1. dependents are cells that are dependant on the chosen cell

2. precedents are cells the chosen cell is dependant on.

APPLICATIONS

APPLICATION 1

1. Open the **AE App1** workbook from the student data files

2. Group the worksheets and apply the AutoFormat feature of your choice.

3. Save the file as **THS Annual Sales**. Print the **Summary** sheet.

APPLICATION 2

1. The Invoice template can be used to enter data for a company's billing process. Open the Invoice template and enter the following information on the **Customize Your Invoice** sheet:

   Palm Tree Computer Sales
   P.O. Box 44577
   Las Vegas, NV 10665
   Phone: 555-2323
   Fax: 555-2333
   State Tax: 5.5%

2. Enter the following information on the Invoice sheet:

Customer Name	Harlingen Enterprises
Address	17 Gulf Road
City	Harlingen
State	TX
ZIP	70277
Date	6/30/2000
Order No.	25
Quantity	53
Description	686 Processors
Unit Price	$234.00

3. Customize the invoice further as you feel is necessary.

4. Save the invoice as **Invoice 25**. Print the invoice.

JOB 1

You are the owner of the Auto Parts Store, and you have just completed tallying sales for the first two quarters of the year. You decide to create workbooks for each quarter, first and second. Then, you will need a workbook that summarizes this data.

Using the following information, create a separate workbook for each quarter. Save the workbooks as **Auto 2000 – First Quarter** and **Auto 2000 – Second Quarter**. Save the summary workbook as **Auto 2000 – Annual Sales**.

Create an embedded chart to illustrate each quarter's data in the first and second quarter workbooks.

Print the annual sales summary workbook.

Auto 2000 Parts Sales
Quarterly Report

	January	February	March
Engines	$ 15,000.00	$ 16,545.00	$ 17,000.00
Transmissions	15,750.00	17,550.00	19,250.00
Batteries	9,000.00	10,150.00	11,225.00
Belts	3,450.00	5,555.00	7,000.00
Oil	1,500.00	1,400.00	1,300.00
Total	$ 44,700.00	$ 51,200.00	$ 55,775.00

Auto 2000 Parts Sales
Quarterly Report

	April	May	June
Engines	$ 14,000.00	$ 17,000.00	$ 17,240.00
Transmissions	16,000.00	16,550.00	17,880.00
Batteries	10,000.00	9,000.00	11,000.00
Belts	4,000.00	6,000.00	8,760.00
Oil	1,750.00	1,780.00	1,677.00
Total	$ 45,750.00	$ 50,330.00	$ 56,557.00

JOB 2

Mr. D.J. Mancini, your boss at Football 2000, a sports apparel shop, has just handed you the inventory list shown below. He would like you to enter the items into a worksheet.

1. Key the data. Insert a title and subtitle for the sheet. Format the data as you feel is appropriate. Be sure you include dollar signs and decimal places with the currency data. Save the workbook as **Football 2000**. When you are done, print the workbook.

Item No.	Item Description	Size	Cost	Selling Price
SS-LC1-S	Exercise Shirt—Football 2000 emblem	S	$10.99	$15.99
SS-LC1-M	Exercise Shirt—Football 2000 emblem	M	12.99	17.99
SS-LC1-L	Exercise Shirt—Football 2000 emblem	L	14.99	19.99
Cap-L	Cap	L	4.99	7.99
Cap-XL	Cap	XL	5.99	8.99
TS-LC-S	Polo Shirt—Football 2000 emblem	S	4.99	6.99
TS-LC-M	Polo Shirt—Football 2000 emblem	M	6.99	8.99
TS-LC-L	Polo Shirt—Football 2000 emblem	L	8.99	10.99
Shorts-S	Walking Shorts	S	7.99	9.99
Shorts-M	Walking Shorts	M	9.99	11.99
Shorts-L	Walking Shorts	L	11.99	13.99
Shorts-XL	Walking Shorts	XL	13.99	15.99
SP-LC-S	Exercise Pants—Football 2000 emblem	S	9.99	13.99
SP-LC-M	Exercise Pants—Football 2000 emblem	M	11.99	15.99
SP-LC-L	Exercise Pants—Football 2000 emblem	L	13.99	17.99
SP-LC-XL	Exercise Pants—Football 2000 emblem	XL	15.99	19.99

2. Now, Mr. Mancini would like a column inserted before the Cost column to contain the quantities of each item in stock. The title for this column will be **Quantity in Stock**. Enter the following information in the Quantity in Stock column.

Item No.	Quantity in Stock
SS-LC1-S	45
SS-LC1-M	62
SS-LC1-L	39
Cap-L	489
Cap-XL	234
TS-LC-S	65
TS-LC-M	42
TS-LC-L	97
Walking Shorts-S	48
Walking Shorts-M	22
Walking Shorts-L	19
Walking Shorts-XL	7
SP-LC-S	56
SP-LC-M	31
SP-LC-L	33
SP-LC-XL	21

3. Center the column headings. Center the data entered in the Quantity in Stock column.

4. Use Advanced Filtering to find all inventory items that are shirts. Display the results in a copy to range on the worksheet.

5. Print the worksheet. Then, save and close the workbook.

UNIT

ADVANCED MICROSOFT® ACCESS

Estimated Time for Unit: 12 hours

MODIFYING TABLE DESIGN

OBJECTIVES

Upon completion of this lesson, you should be able to:

■ Understand the use of input masks.

■ Select the correct input mask.

■ Enter data with input masks.

■ Use validation rules and text.

■ Set required properties.

■ Set lookup fields.

⏱ **Estimated Time: 1 hour**

Introduction

Microsoft Access is a powerful database application that lets you store, organize, and manipulate vast amounts of data. You should already be familiar with the primary objects that comprise a database: tables, forms, queries, reports, and macros. In the next 10 lessons, you'll learn more about each of these objects, plus other features that help you manage and control your database records.

In this lesson, you will learn more about the various data types you can apply when defining fields in a table. You will also explore the properties associated with particular fields. The lesson will discuss the use of input masks in setting up data types for fields. You will also learn about applying validation rules to data and how to create a lookup field.

Choosing an Input Mask

An **input mask** is a predetermined format for certain types of data entered in a field. For example, if you need to enter phone numbers in the format (XXX) XXX-XXXX, it might get tiresome typing both parentheses and the dash. Instead, you can apply Access's Phone Number input mask and then all you need to type is the numbers. The input mask inserts the parentheses and hyphen in the correct positions.

To create an input mask, you must be in the table's Design view. Select the field you want to create the input mask for and then click in the Input Mask text box in the Field Properties pane. The Build button (an ellipsis) appears at the end of the text box, as shown in Figure 1-1.

FIGURE 1-1
Applying an input mask

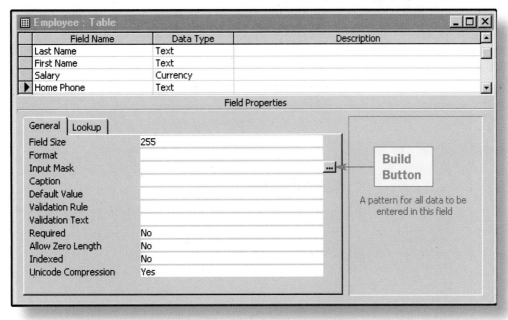

Click the Build button. A message box displays, requesting that you save the table before continuing. Click Yes to save the table. Access will then start the Input Mask Wizard, as shown in Figure 1-2. There are 10 common input mask formats from which you can choose.

FIGURE 1-2
Input Mask Wizard

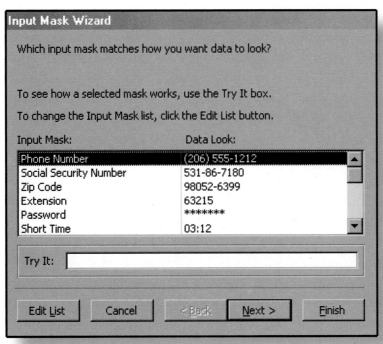

Select an input mask and then click in the Try It box to see an example of how your data will look. If you want to edit the mask, click the Edit List button to create a custom input mask. Once you select the mask you need, click the Next button to go to the next step in the Input Mask Wizard, as shown in Figure 1-3.

FIGURE 1-3
Second step in the Input Mask Wizard

Input Mask Wizard

Do you want to change the input mask?

Input Mask Name: Phone Number

Input Mask: !(999) 000-0000

What placeholder character do you want the field to display?

Placeholders are replaced as you enter data into the field.

Placeholder character: _

Try It:

| Cancel | < Back | Next > | Finish |

This step of the wizard asks you if you need to make changes to this mask. You may also select the placeholder for your number. The default is the underscore. The placeholder simply identifies in the table that there is an input mask assigned to the field. The place-holder is replaced by the data you enter in the field. Click the Next button and the Input Mask Wizard dialog box shown in Figure 1-4 appears.

In this step of the wizard, you decide how to store the data. For example, you may want a date field stored in the format *mm-dd-yy*. Just select this format and Access will store newly entered dates with this format. Most often, data will be stored with the symbols. Click the Next button and the final Input Mask Wizard dialog box appears, as shown in Figure 1-5. Clicking the Finish button will create your mask.

You can create an input mask when you define a field or after the field has been defined and data entered in it.

Hot Tip

When you apply an input mask to an existing field that already contains data, Access typically asks you to check the existing data with the new rules. Click **Yes** to apply the input mask. However, Microsoft Technical Support reports that there are some inconsistencies when the input mask formats actually change existing data.

FIGURE 1-4
Determining how to store data in the Input Mask Wizard

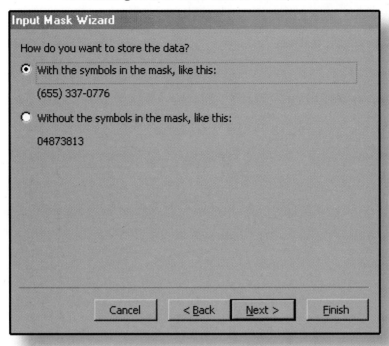

FIGURE 1-5
Final Input Mask Wizard dialog box

STEP-BY-STEP ▷ 1.1

1. Open the **AA Step1-1** database from the student data files.

2. Open the **Employees** table in Design view.

3. Select the **Home Phone** field name.

4. In the Field Properties pane, click in the **Input Mask** text box.

5. Click the **Build** button to start the Input Mask Wizard.

6. Select the **Phone Number** input mask, if necessary. Click **Next**.

7. You will not change the input mask. Click **Next**.

8. If necessary, select the **With the symbols in the mask, like this** option. Click **Next**.

9. Click **Finish** to apply your mask. Your screen should look similar to Figure 1-6. (After you save the table design, Access will add additional punctuation.)

FIGURE 1-6
Applying the phone number input mask

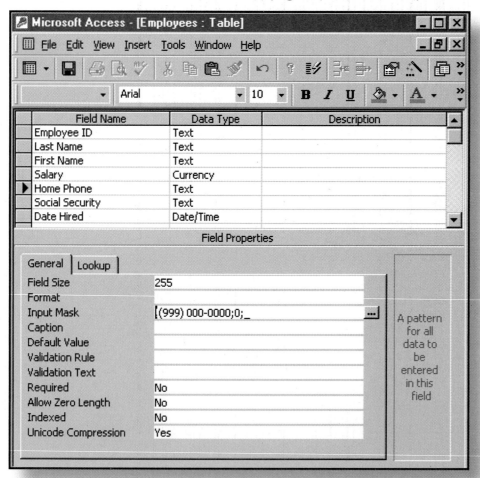

10. Let's create another input mask. Select the **Social Security** field name.

11. In the Field Properties pane, click in the **Input Mask** text box.

12. Click the **Build** button to start the Input Mask Wizard.

13. Click **Yes** to save the table.

14. Click the **Social Security Number** input mask. Click **Next**.

15. You will not change the input mask. Click **Next**.

16. If necessary, select the **With the symbols in the mask, like this** option. Click **Next**.

17. Click **Finish** to apply your mask. Click **Save**. Your screen should look like Figure 1-7.

18. Switch to Datasheet view. Remain in this screen for the next Step-by-Step.

FIGURE 1-7
Applying the Social Security input mask

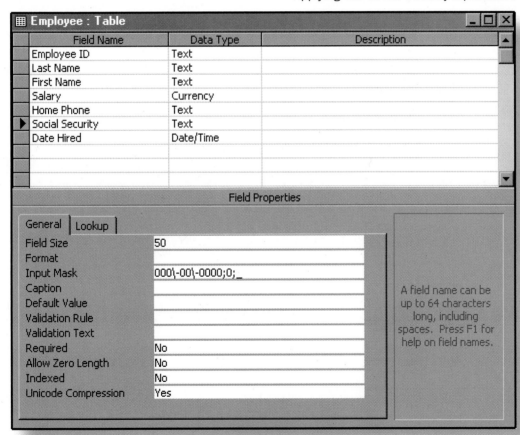

AA-7

Entering Data with Input Masks

After you have applied an input mask to a field, the format will be applied automatically as you enter new records.

S TEP-BY-STEP ▷ 1.2

1. Go to the **Home Phone** field of record **5** and select the value currently entered.

2. Type **8175557373**. When you start to type, underscores appear. This indicates that a mask has been applied to the field.

3. Press **Tab** to go to the **Social Security** field.

4. Type **000000005**. Notice how the input mask inserts the hyphens where appropriate.

5. Click in a different record to save the changes.

6. Adjust the column widths in the table as you feel appropriate. Then print the table in landscape orientation. Close the table and remain in this screen for the next Step-by-Step.

Setting Validation Rules

You can enhance the efficiency of data entry by setting validation rules. *Validation rules* are properties applied to a field that either require certain values to be entered or prevent them from being entered in a field. For example, validation rules can require that data entered in a salary field not exceed a certain dollar amount, such as $50,000. This can help prevent data entry errors and increase accuracy and conformity.

When you set a validation rule on a field, you are given the option to create a message that explains the validation rule to the data entry person. The validation text is displayed

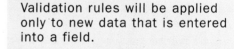

Hot Tip

Validation rules will be applied only to new data that is entered into a field.

in a message box that appears when data entered into the cell does not meet the validation rule. Using the above example, if a dollar amount greater than $50,000 is entered in the salary field, the validation message might be "Salary amounts cannot exceed $50,000."

S TEP-BY-STEP ▷ 1.3

1. Click **Tables** on the Objects bar and double-click **Create table in Design view**.

2. Define two fields for the table: The first field should be named **Product Description** and should be the **Text** data type. The second

field should be named **Product Price** and should be the **Currency** data type.

3. Click the **Save** button, enter **Product Sales** as the table name, and click **OK**.

4. Select **No** if asked to create a primary key field.

5. Select the **Product Price** field name.

6. In the Field Properties pane, click in the **Validation Rule** box and enter **<50**. This will restrict any product price that is equal to or more than $50 from being entered.

7. Click in the **Validation Text** box and enter **All product prices are less than $50**.

8. Click the **Save** button and then switch to Datasheet view.

9. Enter the following records:

Product Description	Product Price
Dog Carrier - Small	$27.50
Dog Carrier - Large	$500.00

10. When you press **Enter**, you should see a message box that displays the validation text as shown in Figure 1-8. Click **OK**.

FIGURE 1-8
Message box

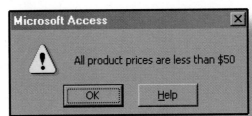

11. Enter **$47.50** for the Product Price and press **Enter**. Notice that Access accepts this amount since it is less than $50. Remain in this screen for the next Step-by-Step.

Setting Required Properties

For some fields, you may want to apply the Required property, which means that the field cannot be left blank when records are entered. For example, you might set up a table so that a customer's phone number must be entered in the phone number field. Access will not move to another record until data is entered in this field.

STEP-BY-STEP ▷ 1.4

1. Switch to Design view, if necessary.

2. Select the **Product Description** field and then click in the **Required** property text box.

3. Click the down arrow that appears at the end of the *Required* text box and click **Yes**.

4. Click the **Save** button. Access displays a dialog box that asks if you want to test the existing field information with the new required property selection. Click **Yes**.

5. Click the **View** button to switch to Datasheet view.

6. Go to the first empty **Product Price** field.

7. Key **$43.00** for the Product Price and press **Enter**.

8. You will see a warning box as shown in Figure 1-9 that explains that the Product Description field cannot contain a Null value. Click **OK** to close the warning box.

(continued on next page)

FIGURE 1-9
Warning box

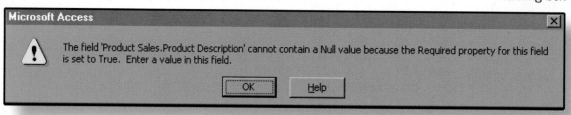

9. Click in the **Product Description** field for the record you are adding and enter **Cat Carrier - Medium**.

10. Close the table.

Creating Lookup Fields

You can define a *lookup field* in a table as a field that actually "looks up" and pulls data from a field in another table or query in the database. Looking up data from existing tables can help prevent data entry errors. You create a lookup field by using the Lookup Wizard. Or you can click the Lookup tab in the Field Properties pane and specify the table or query containing the data you want to look up.

In the following Step-by-Step, you will create a table that has only one field. This field will contain several shipping options. After this table is created, you will open an existing table and "look up" data in the new table in order to insert values in the existing table.

STEP-BY-STEP ⟹ 1.5

1. Create a new table in Design view.

2. Define a field named **Shipping Terms** of **Text** data type.

3. Click the **Save** button, enter **Shipping Terms** as the table name, and click **OK**.

4. Select **No** if asked to create a primary key field.

5. Click the **View** button to switch to Datasheet view.

6. Enter the following shipping terms as new records:

Record 1	Net 10th
Record 2	COD
Record 3	Cash Only
Record 4	1% in 10 Days

7. Close the **Shipping Terms** table.

8. Open the **Product Sales** table in Design view.

9. Define a new field named **Shipping Terms** with the **Text** data type.

10. With the **Shipping Terms** field selected, click the **Lookup** tab in the *Field Properties* pane.

11. Click in the **Display Control** box.

12. Click the down arrow at the end of the *Display Control* box and click **List Box**.

13. Click in the **Row Source** box.

14. Click the down arrow at the end of the Row Source text box and click **Shipping Terms**.

15. Click the **Save** button and switch to Datasheet view.

16. Add a new record: Enter Cat Carrier - Small in the Product Description field and **$23.50** in the Product Price field.

17. In the **Shipping Terms** field, click the down arrow. Your screen should look similar to Figure 1-10. Choose **1% in 10 Days**.

18. Enter **Net 10th** as the shipping term for the remaining records.

19. Adjust the column widths in the table, if necessary. Then print the table and close the database.

FIGURE 1-10
Lookup field

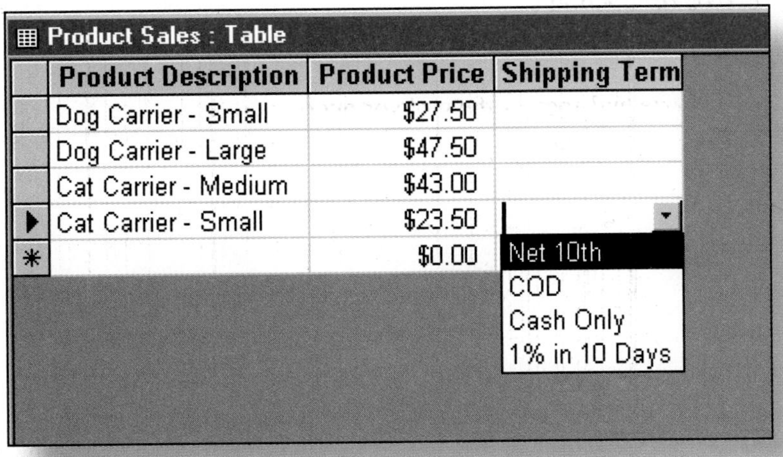

A A - 1 1

Summary

In this lesson, you learned:

- Input masks are used to save data entry time and improve accuracy of the data entered.

- After the input mask is created, data entered into the field will display the new format. In most instances, an input mask created on an existing field will apply the formatting changes to values already entered in the field.

- Validation rules can help prevent data entry errors by indicating when incorrect data is entered.

- When you apply the required property to a field, Access requires that a value be entered in the field before it lets you complete the record entry. Access will not allow another field to be selected until the field with required properties has data entered.

- A lookup field lets you pull or "look up" data from another table or query in the same database.

LESSON 1 REVIEW QUESTIONS

WRITTEN QUESTIONS

Write a brief answer to the following questions.

1. How many input masks are provided in the Input Mask Wizard?

   10 commonly used masks

2. To which data types can you add an input mask?

   text, currency, number, date/time,

3. What does the Input Mask Wizard do?

displays step by step instructions and entry of input mask parameters.

4. When you assign an input mask to a field that already contains data, what happens to that data?

a question is displayed asking you if you want to check existing data with the new mask. click YES to apply the mask. This may not work.

5. Why would you want to assign an input mask to a field?

Save time and prevent errors.

6. Explain the difference between a validation rule and validation text.

the rule is what data is allowed to be entered. Text is what is displayed if non-valid data is entered.

7. Explain the purpose of the Required field property.

prevents leaving a field blank.

8. What is the benefit of creating a lookup field? *only predetermined data can be entered*

9. Explain the steps for creating a lookup field. *1. a table with valid entries is created 2. the table where data will be entered is opened and the field properties where "lookup data" will be entered is selected. 3. look up table selected and type of control selected. 4. Where the data is located is selected.*

10. Explain the steps for setting a Required property field to Yes.

1. open table is design view and select field
2. click in "Required" box, on drop down select YES
3. click SAVE

LESSON 1 PROJECTS

PROJECT 1-1 *6-15-04*

1. Open the database **AA Project1-1** from the student data files.

2. Open the **Employees** table.

3. Enter an input mask for the Social Security field.

4. Make this field a Required field.

5. Print the table in landscape orientation.

6. Save and close the database.

PROJECT 1-2   6-15-04

1. Open the database **AA Project1-2** from the student data files.

2. Open the **Employees** table.

3. Make the **Employee ID** field a Required field and create an input mask for the **Phone Number** field.

4. Print the table.

5. Save and close the database.

CRITICAL THINKING

ACTIVITY 1-1

SCANS

You are the office manager for the Sadie Products Corporation. After viewing the company's existing database, **AA Activity1-1**, you realize that a new table needs to be created for recording sales information.

1. Define the following fields in the table:

   Customer ID
   Employee ID
   Product ID
   Quantity Sold

2. Save the table as **January Sales**.

3. For the Employee ID field, apply the lookup property so that you can pull data from the **Employees** table, using the **List Box** display control.

4. Create input masks for the fields that you think they would apply to.

ACTIVITY 1-2

SCANS

You should be familiar with how to change the Field Size property in a table. However, there are a number of different Field Size properties associated with fields that are defined as Number types. These include *byte*, *long integer*, *single*, and *double*. Use the Access Help system to find information on the different types of Number field size properties. Write a brief essay explaining the type of data to which you would apply these properties.

Determining the field length for a number field is a function of the data to be entered. each type requires different amounts of storage. It is best to select the smallest field that will contain the largest number that will be entered.

A A - 1 5

RELATIONSHIPS IN TABLES AND QUERIES

OBJECTIVES

Upon completion of this lesson, you should be able to:

- Understand relationships in tables.
- Create relationships among multiple tables.
- Enforce referential integrity.
- Create a query using related tables.

⏱ **Estimated Time: 1 hour**

Introduction

In this lesson, you will learn how to create relationships between tables. When tables are related, or joined, you have the ability to create forms, queries, and reports that pull fields and records from all tables in the relationship.

Understanding Table Relationships

Most databases contain more than one table. And more than likely, one or more of the tables contain identical data in at least one field. For example, a business might have a table containing customer names, customer ID numbers, and addresses, and another table that contains customer ID numbers and purchases or orders. If two or more tables contain a common field like the customer ID numbers in the preceding example, you can link these fields to create a relationship between the tables. Then you can create queries, forms, and reports using the data from the tables in the relationship.

There are three types of relationships that can be created in Access: a one-to-many relationship, a one-to-one relationship, and a many-to-many relationship. A *one-to-many relationship* exists when you relate a table whose common field is a primary key field to a table that does not have the common field as a primary key field. As you know, a *primary key* is a field that contains a value that uniquely identifies the record. Each value in this field must be unique. A *foreign key* is a field that refers to the primary key field in a related table.

Table 2-1 illustrates the one-to-many relationship. The Salesperson Number field in the Salesperson table is a primary key field. This field is a primary key field because you want only one ID number assigned to each salesperson. In the Invoice table, you would not want the Salesperson Number to be a primary key field because each salesperson will make many sales and you would need to enter the Saleperson Number for each sale.

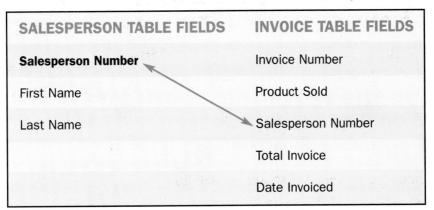

TABLE 2-1
One-to-many relationship

SALESPERSON TABLE FIELDS	INVOICE TABLE FIELDS
Salesperson Number	Invoice Number
First Name	Product Sold
Last Name	Salesperson Number
	Total Invoice
	Date Invoiced

It's important to remember that related fields are not required to have the same field name. However, related fields must be of the same data type.

When you set up a relationship between or among tables, you will be asked if you want to enforce referential integrity. *Referential integrity* simply refers to having Access check new data as it is entered into related fields. For example, as data is entered into the Salesperson Number field in the Salary table (shown in Table 2-1), Access will check to see if this is a correct number in the Salesperson Number field in the Salesperson table. If the Salesperson number that is being entered into the Salary table is not found in the Salesperson table, then Access will display an error message. This will alert the person entering the data to reenter the correct Salesperson ID number into the Salary table. This feature improves the accuracy and consistency of data entered.

Concept Builder

Remember, if a table has a primary key field, each record must have unique (nonmatching) information in this field.

STEP-BY-STEP ▷ 2.1

1. Open the database **AA Step2-1** from the student data files.

2. Click the **Relationships** button on the toolbar. Then select **Show Table** on the **Relationships** menu. The Show Table dialog box appears, as shown on Figure 2-1.

3. Select **Marketing Department** and then click **Add**. The Marketing Department table window is added to the Relationships window.

Hot Tip

You can also double-click on a table in the Show Table dialog box to add it to the Relationships window.

4. Select the **March Orders** table and click **Add**.

5. Click the **Close** button to close the Show Table dialog box. Your screen should look similar to Figure 2-2. Remain in this screen for the next Step-by-Step.

(continued on next page)

FIGURE 2-1
Show Table dialog box

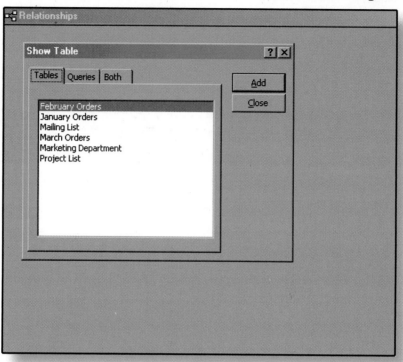

FIGURE 2-2
Relationships window with tables displayed

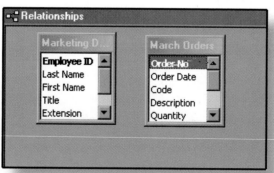

Defining Relationships Between Tables

To define a relationship between selected tables in the Relationships window, you drag a field from the primary table to the field in the related table that contains the same data. Once you release the mouse button, the Edit Relationships dialog box appears, as shown in Figure 2-3. The Edit Relationships dialog box displays options for enforcing referential integrity. Referential integrity can only be enforced between tables in the same database.

If you choose to enforce referential integrity, two options in the dialog box become available. The first option, *Cascade Update Related Fields*, allows for updates to occur between the primary table and the related table in the joined fields. For example, to change a salesperson's number, you would change it in the primary table and Access would automatically change that field information in the related table.

The second option, *Cascade Delete Related Records*, lets you delete a record in the primary table. Upon deleting the record in the primary table, Access will delete the record in the related table. Access finds the correct record or records by the joined field.

FIGURE 2-3
Edit Relationships dialog box

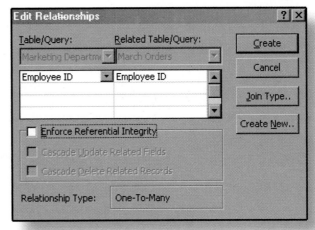

S TEP-BY-STEP ▷ 2.2

1. If necessary, scroll the March Orders table to display the **Employee ID** field.

2. Select the **Employee ID** field in the **Marketing Department** table. From the bold type, you can tell that this is the primary key.

   click on EMPLOYEE ID and hold then drag to 1 in March Orders

3. In the Edit Relationships dialog box, click the check box beside **Enforce Referential Integrity**.

4. Click **Create**. Your screen should look similar to Figure 2-4. Remain in this screen for the next Step-by-Step.

FIGURE 2-4
Relationship established

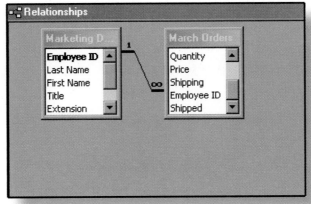

Notice the symbols on the relationship line connecting the two tables in Figure 2-4. The 1 indicates the primary table, and the infinity symbol (∞) indicates the related table. These symbols refer to the type of relationship that has been created. In this example, the 1 means that the Employee ID number can only appear one time in the Employee ID field in the Marketing Department table. However, since each employee can make many sales in March, the Employee ID can appear more than once in the March Orders table; thus, the infinity symbol. Therefore, this relationship is a one-to-many relationship.

S TEP-BY-STEP ▷ 2.3

1. Close the **Relationships** dialog box.

2. Click **Yes** to save the layout changes.

3. Open the **March Orders** table. This is the related table.

4. Click the **New Record** button. Enter the following information:

Field Name	Information
Order No.	3050
Order Date	3/15/00
Code	DB-BB
Description	Beginning Databases
Quantity	155
Price	$19.00
Shipping	$2.00
Employee ID	S555
Shipped	No

Hot Tip

You can press Ctrl+; to enter the current date.

5. Press **Enter**. Access cannot add the record to the table because there is no Employee ID *S555* in the primary table, Marketing Department. You should see a message box as shown in Figure 2-5.

6. Click **OK** to close the message box.

7. Click in the **Employee ID** field of the new record you just entered and key **N205**. Press **Enter**. Close the table.

8. Remain in this screen for the next Step-by-Step.

FIGURE 2-5
Message box

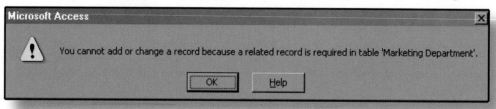

In the preceding Step-by-Step, it is important to understand why the message box appeared. If you need to enter a record in the March Orders table for an employee who is not yet recorded in the Marketing Department table, Access will display the message about adding or changing a record. A record for the employee must first be entered in the Marketing Department table.

STEP-BY-STEP ▷ 2.4

1. Open the **Marketing Department** table.

2. Click the **New Record** button and add the following record. Once you've entered the record, your screen should look similar to Figure 2-6.

Field Name	Information
Employee ID	S555
Last Name	Walters
First Name	William
Title	Marketing Rep
Extension	229
Date Hired	3/15/00
Salary	$62,000

 Hot Tip

If you close the table and reopen it, the records will be sorted according to the primary key field. In this Step-by-Step, records are sorted by Employee ID.

3. Close the **Marketing Department** table and remain in this screen for the next Step-by-Step.

FIGURE 2-6
Adding a record

	Employee ID	Last Name	First Name	Title	Extension	Date Hired	Salary
	N125	Loyal	Sally	Marketing Rep	338	10/12/97	$54,800.00
	N175	Limosine	John	Marketing Assistant	442	5/7/97	$32,000.00
	N205	Kemper	Bertha	Marketing Assistant	265	5/7/95	$46,000.00
	N440	Lopez	Karen	Marketing Manager	410	11/26/90	$45,200.00
	N445	Woodard	Katheryn	Marketing Assistant	932	12/3/97	$39,000.00
	N522	Robinson	Harold	Secretary	543	3/6/92	$30,000.00
	N550	Gordon	Kelly	Marketing Rep	435	5/2/97	$35,000.00
	N660	Anderson	David	Marketing Rep	876	2/27/95	$43,500.00
	N750	Joshua	John	Marketing Rep	564	4/20/95	$43,390.00
	S330	Martin	Annie	Secretary	912	1/5/94	$38,500.00
	S525	Taylor	Helen	Marketing Rep	234	8/9/89	$34,450.00
	S535	Williamson	Kori	Marketing Assistant	654	3/11/97	$29,000.00
	S555	Walters	William	Marketing Rep	229	3/15/00	$62,000.00
	S604	Smith	Jeff	Marketing Rep	411	4/7/90	$41,800.00
	S605	Johnson	Jennifer	Marketing Rep	287	1/25/89	$48,000.00
	S880	Davidson	Zach	Marketing Rep	581	7/10/89	$56,040.00

Marketing Department : Table

Now that the record for this employee is entered in the Marketing Department table, you enter any orders for him in the March Orders table.

S TEP-BY-STEP ▷ 2.5

1. Open the **March Orders** table.

2. Click the **New Record** button, and enter the following information:

Field Name	Information
Order No.	3051
Order Date	3/15/00
Code	DB-BD
Description	Beginning Publishing
Quantity	193
Price	$15.95
Shipping	$3.00
Employee ID	S555
Shipped	No

3. Adjust column widths in the table, if necessary. Print the table in landscape orientation and then close it. Remain in this screen for the next Step-by-Step.

Adding Tables to a Relationship

You can have more than two tables in a relationship. For example, in the previous Step-by-Steps, you created a relationship between the Marketing Department table and the March Orders table by joining their Employee ID fields. You can add another table to the relationship, as long as it contains a field that is also contained in either the Marketing Department or March Orders tables, or both.

Hot Tip

You can edit or delete relationships by *right*-clicking the join line between tables and choosing either the Edit or Delete options on the shortcut menu.

S TEP-BY-STEP ▷ 2.6

1. Click the **Relationships** button. The current table relationship is displayed in the Relationships window.

2. Click the **Show Table** button.

3. Select the **February Orders** table, click **Add**, and then select the **January Orders** table and click **Add**.

4. Click **Close** to close the dialog box.

5. In the **Marketing Department** table, drag the **Employee ID** field to the **Employee ID** field in the **February Orders** table, click the **Enforce Referential Integrity** check box, and click **Create**. Repeat this procedure for the **January Orders** table. Your screen should look similar to Figure 2-7.

6. Close the **Relationships** window.

7. Select **Yes** to save the relationships. Remain in this screen for the next Step-by-Step.

FIGURE 2-7
Multiple table relationship

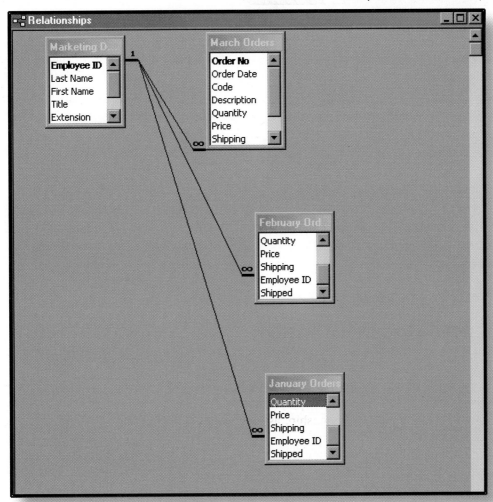

Setting and Removing Joins in a Query

After you've created a relationship between tables, you can pull information from the related tables in a query, form, or report. Using related tables in forms and reports is discussed in later lessons.

If your tables are not joined in a relationship, you can define the relationship in the query itself. As you probably remember, when you are in the query's Design view, a window containing the field names of the table you are querying appears in the top pane. When you select more than one table to query, a window for each table will appear in the top pane. To join tables, simply drag the field names as you did in the Relationships window.

If you need to remove the line joining the tables, thereby removing the relationship, simply click the line and then press Delete.

STEP-BY-STEP ▷ 2.7

1. In the Database window, click **Queries** on the Objects bar. Then double-click **Create query in Design view**.

2. Double-click the **Marketing Department** table and then double-click the **January Orders** table to add them to the query window.

3. Click **Close** to close the Show Table dialog box.

4. You will see a line appear between the **Marketing Department** and **January Orders** tables because you created a relationship between these tables in the previous Step-by-Step. Let's practice deleting a relationship in queries and then you'll reestablish the relationship.

5. To delete this relationship line, simply click on the line and press **Delete**.

6. Place the mouse pointer over the **Employee ID** field in the **Marketing Department** table and drag it to the **Employee ID** field in the **January Orders** table. You will see a line appear between the two tables, as shown in Figure 2-8. Notice how the 1 and ∞ symbols do not appear. You would need to open the Relationships window in order to select the one-to-many relationship. Access assumes this type of relationship in a query.

7. Double-click the **Order No** and **Quantity** fields from the **January Orders** table and the **Last Name** field from the **Marketing Department** table.

8. Sort the **Last Name** field in **Ascending** order.

9. Save the query as **Qry-January Orders by Rep** and then click the **Run** button to run the query.

10. Adjust the column widths and then print the results of the query. Close the query and then close the database.

FIGURE 2-8
Relationship created in a query

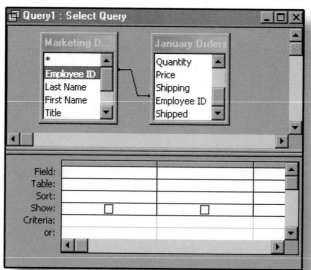

Establishing One-to-One Relationships

In a **one-to-one relationship**, each record in Table A can have only one matching record in Table B and each record in Table B can have only one matching record in Table A. This is because the common fields in these tables are both primary key fields. Table 2-2 illustrates the one-to-one relationship. Notice that in the Salesperson table, the Salesperson Number is a primary key field. This means that each salesperson is assigned his or her own individual number. In the Salary table, the Salesperson Number is also a primary key field for obvious reasons. You do not want a salesperson's number duplicated in this table or that individual will receive two paychecks!

TABLE 2-2
One-to-one relationship

SALESPERSON TABLE FIELDS	SALARY TABLE FIELDS
Salesperson Number	**Salesperson Number**
First Name	Position
Last Name	Salary

STEP-BY-STEP ▷ 2.8

1. Open the **AA Step2-8** database from the student data files.

2. Open each table to view the fields and records. Close the tables after viewing them.

3. Click the **Relationships** button.

4. Double-click the **Employee Information** table and the **Benefits Package** table to add them to the Relationships window.

5. Click the **Close** button to close the **Show Table** dialog box.

6. Place your mouse pointer over the **Employee Number** field in the **Employee Information** table.

Press and hold the mouse button down and drag to the **Employee Number** field in the **Benefits Package** table.

7. In the Edit Relationships dialog box, notice that the relationship is identified at the bottom as a *One-To-One*. Access recognizes that this is a one-to-one relationship.

8. Click **Create** to create the relationship. Then, click **Save** to save the relationship.

9. Close the Relationships window. Then, close the database.

Establishing Many-to-Many Relationships

A *many-to-many relationship* exists when a record in Table A has many matching records in Table B, and a record in Table B has many matching records in Table A, *and* a record in either Table A or Table B has many matching records in Table C.

Figure 2-9 shows an example of this type of relationship. Table A contains order information, with fields named Order Number (primary key), Customer Name, and Employee Number. Table B contains production information, with fields named Product ID (primary key), Product Name, and Selling Price. Table C contains different information on orders, with fields named Order Number (foreign key that refers to Table A), Product ID (foreign key that refers to Table B), and Selling Price.

FIGURE 2-9
Many-to-many relationship

Table A

Order Number	Customer Name	Employee Number
2000	Bill's Print Shop	1600
2001	Juarez Accounting	2300

Table C

Order Number	Product ID	Selling Price
2000	25	$ 14.95
2000	32	$ 17.95
2001	25	$ 14.95

Table B

Product ID	Product Name	Selling Price
25	Paper – Copy	$ 14.95
32	Paper - Laser	$ 17.95
37	Toner Cartridge	$ 32.45

STEP-BY-STEP ▷ 2.9

1. Open the **AA Step2-9** database from the student data files.

2. Open each table to view the fields and records. Close the tables after viewing them.

3. Click the **Relationships** button.

4. Double-click the **Orders**, **Order Details**, and **Products** tables to add them to the Relationships window.

5. Click the **Close** button to close the **Show Table** dialog box.

6. Place your mouse pointer over the **Product ID** field in the **Products** table. Press and hold the mouse button down and drag to the **Product ID** field in the **Order Details** table.

7. In the Edit Relationships dialog box, notice that the relationship is identified at the bottom as an *Indeterminate*. Access recognizes that this is *not* a one-to-one or one-to-many relationship.

8. Click **Create** to create the relationship. Then, click **Save** to save the relationship.

9. Place your mouse pointer over the **Order Number** field in the **Orders** table. Press and hold down the mouse button and drag to the **Order Number** field in the **Order Details** table.

10. Click **Create** to create the relationship. Then, click **Save** to save the relationship.

11. Close the Relationships window, and then close the database file.

Summary

In this lesson, you learned:

■ Creating a relationship between tables allows you to use information from both tables in forms, queries, and reports. In order to create a relationship, the tables must contain a common field of data.

■ There are three basic types of relationships: one-to-many, one-to-one, and many-to-many. A one-to-many relationship exists when you relate a table with a primary key field to a table where the common field is not a primary key field. Information in the primary table's key field will appear only once in the table, whereas information in the common field in the related table can appear many times because it is not a primary key field. A one-to-one relationship exists when the common field is a primary key field in both tables. A many-to-many relationship can exist between three or more tables.

■ Referential integrity refers to having Access check new data as it is entered into related fields. This feature helps the accuracy and consistency of data entered.

■ You can create relationships in a query's Design view. You can also delete relationships in the query window by clicking the join line and pressing Delete.

LESSON 2 REVIEW QUESTIONS

WRITTEN QUESTIONS

Write a brief answer to the following questions.

1. Why would you want to link tables together in a database? *1. so that information can be pulled from different tables 2. Easier maintenance of the database.*

2. In creating relationships, what is a primary table? *the table that has the primary key.*

3. Explain what referential integrity does.

verifies that new data entered matches what is in the related table.

4. What is a one-to-many relationship? *one record on the primary table relates to many on the related table*

5. List the steps for joining two tables in a query and explain why this feature is useful.

1. open the database 2. Select Query object 3. Create query in design view 4. double click the table to add to query in the show table dialog 5. click and drag the field in one table to the linked field in the related table.

MATCHING

Match the correct term in Column 2 to its description in Column 1.

	Column 1		**Column 2**
D 1.	Requires unique data to be entered into every record.	**A.**	Referential integrity
E 2.	Field whose data type is the same in each table in a relationship, but whose field name can vary.	**B.**	One-to-many relationship
A 3.	Checks data entry in a related table against data in the primary key table to be certain data exists in both tables.	**C.**	One-to-one relationship
		D.	Primary key field
B 4.	In this type of relationship, a table with a primary key field is related to a nonprimary key field in another table.	**E.**	Common field
C 5.	In this type of relationship, the common field in related tables is the primary key field in the tables.		

LESSON 2 PROJECT

PROJECT 2-1

6-16-04

1. Open the database **AA Project2-1** from the student data files.

2. Create a one-to-many relationship between the **Products** and **Transactions** tables by linking the common field.

3. Enforce referential integrity and save the relationship.

4. Create a query in Design view using the **Transactions** table and the **Customers** table. You will need to create a relationship between the tables using the Customer ID field in each table.

5. Add the **Transaction Number**, **Company Name**, **Quantity**, **Date Ordered**, and **Date Shipped** fields to the query in that order. The Company Name field is in the Customers table; the rest of the fields are in the Transactions table.

6. Save the query as **Qry-Transactions by Customer** and then run the query.

7. Adjust column widths, if necessary. Print the query results and then close the database.

CRITICAL THINKING

ACTIVITY 2-1   6-16

You are an Office Manager at Bayside Supplies. After a conversation with the owner of the company, you have determined that you need a printout of your customers and their transactions for the year. Using the **AA Activity2-1** database in the student data files, create and print a query with this information.

ACTIVITY 2-2

You have created a database that contains a number of tables. One of these tables is named Customers and another table is named Purchases. There is a Customer Number field in the Customers table that identifies each customer with an individual number. The Purchases table has a Customer Number field as well. You want to create a relationship between the two tables. Write a brief essay that explains which relationship you would choose for these tables and why. Use Access's Help system to find this information, if necessary.

Customers   *Purchases*

Cust ID   *Cust ID*

the primary key would be CUST ID in the customer table. The primary key would relate to the cust ID field (foreign key) in the Purchases table. This is a one to many relationship

AA-29

ADVANCED FORM FEATURES

OBJECTIVES

Upon completion of this lesson, you should be able to:

- Add a subform to a form.

- Add a record to a subform.

- Modify the properties of a subform.

- Create and modify a form in Design view.

> **Estimated Time: 1 hour**

A database form is a tool used primarily for data entry. You should already know how to create a basic form and modify its design. In this lesson, you will learn more about customizing and designing forms. You will also learn how to work with subforms.

Creating a Subform

As you know, you create a form from a database table or query. You can use any of the fields in the table or query to build your form. And you can create any number of forms using the same table or related tables. **Subforms** are useful when you want to show records from one table that are related to a specific record in the main form.

For example, say you have a table containing data on each of your customers. The fields in this table might include the customer's name, address, phone number, and a customer identification number. You have another table in the database that tracks orders. The fields in this table might include the product ordered, transaction amount, customer name, and the customer identification number. Now, as you go through your list of customers, you want to know how many orders they have put in over the past year. Since there is a common field between these two tables, the customer identification number, Access will allow you to view information from both tables at one time in a form that contains a subform. For example, your main form would include the information from the customers table and the subform would include information from the orders table. The main form and subform are displayed together on your screen. You can think of a subform as a form within a form. An example of a subform is shown in Figure 3-1.

You might also want to use subforms to simply combine information from separate forms. For example, let's say you've created a form from a table that contains personnel information. The fields are Employee ID, First Name, and Last Name. You've created a second form from a table that contains salary information. The fields are Employee ID, Department and Current Salary. Rather than creating a third form to combine this information, you can add the Department and Current Salary fields to the form

FIGURE 3-1

Lesson ③ Advanced Form Features

Main form with a subform

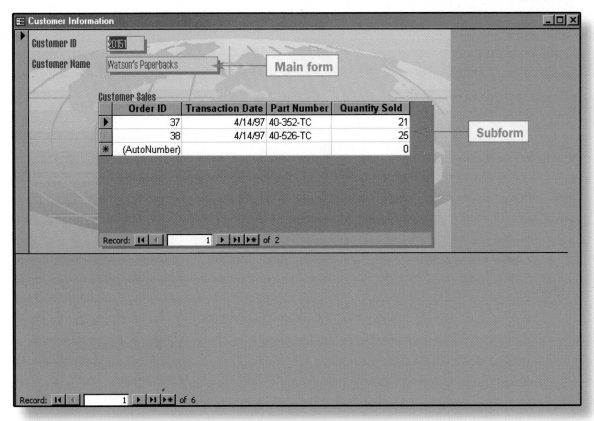

that contains personnel information. The form with the personnel information would be the main form. The subform shows the Department and Current Salary fields.

Main forms and subforms maintain the individual formats and styles you have applied to them. A subform has its own set of scroll bars and navigation buttons.

To add a subform to a main form, open the main form in Design view. Click the Subform/Subreport button in the Toolbox. Then click in the area of the main form where you want the subform to appear. Typically, you'll want the subform to appear in the Detail section of the form. Once you've clicked in the desired location, the Subform/Subreport Wizard starts, providing you with step-by-step instructions on how to create the subform.

Hot Tip

If the Toolbox is not displayed in Design view, select Toolbox on the View menu.

S TEP-BY-STEP ▷ 3.1

1. Open the **AA Step3-1** database from the student data files.

2. Click **Forms** on the Objects bar and then double-click the **Customer Information** form.

(continued on next page)

3. View the information in the form and then switch to Design view.

4. Enlarge the **Detail** section so that it's about 3" deep. If necessary, display the Toolbox.

5. Click the **Subform/Subreport** button in the Toolbox. Then, position the crosshair at the intersection of the 1" marks on the horizontal and vertical rulers and click. The SubForm Wizard displays, as shown in Figure 3-2.

6. Make sure that the **Use existing Tables and Queries** option is selected and then click

Hot Tip

If the SubForm Wizard does not start after clicking the Subform/Subreport button, make sure the **Control Wizards** button is selected in the Toolbox.

Next. The SubForm Wizard asks you which fields you want to include on the subform. See Figure 3-3.

7. Click the down arrow of the *Tables/Queries* box and choose the **Book Sales** table.

FIGURE 3-2
SubForm Wizard

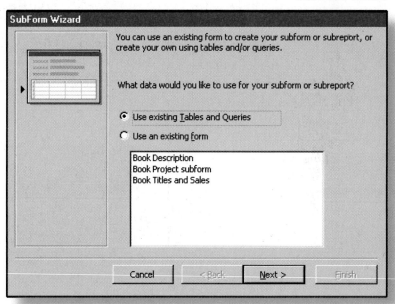

FIGURE 3-3
Selecting fields for the subform

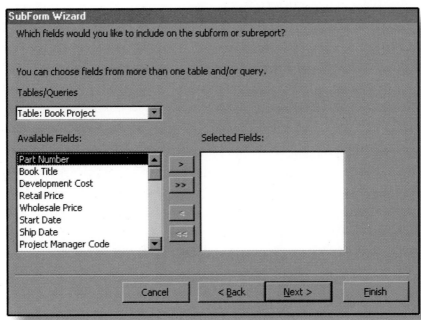

8. Double-click the **Order ID**, **Transaction Date**, **Part Number**, and **Quantity Sold** fields to place them in the *Selected Fields* box. Then click **Next**. The SubForm Wizard asks you to define which fields link the main form to the subform. See Figure 3-4.

9. The **Choose from a list** option should be selected. In the list, select **Show Book Sales for each record in Customer using Customer ID**. Then click **Next**. The final SubForm Wizard dialog box displays. Figure 3-5 shows the dialog box with a new name entered for the subform.

10. Enter **Customer Sales** for the Subform name and click **Finish**. The main form/subform should look similar to that shown in Figure 3-6. If a dialog box containing the fields for either table appears, click its **Close** button. Adjust the size of the subform by dragging one of its sizing handles, so you can see all the sections and controls.

11. Switch to Form view. Notice that the column widths in the subform are not wide enough to accommodate some of the field names. Adjust the widths as necessary by double-clicking the border between the field names.

12. Click the **Save** button. Scroll through the records in the main form and notice how the subform records change accordingly.

13. Print the form for record **1**. Remain in this screen for the next Step-by-Step.

(continued on next page)

FIGURE 3-4
Defining the linking field(s)

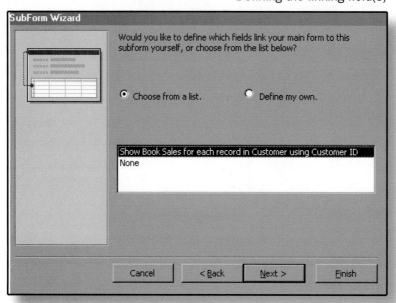

FIGURE 3-5
Naming the subform

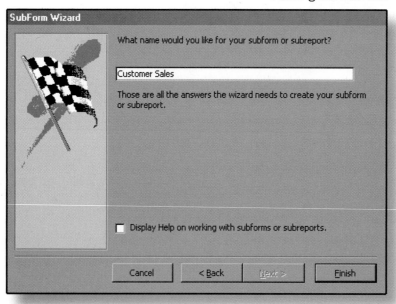

FIGURE 3-6
Main form and subform in Design view

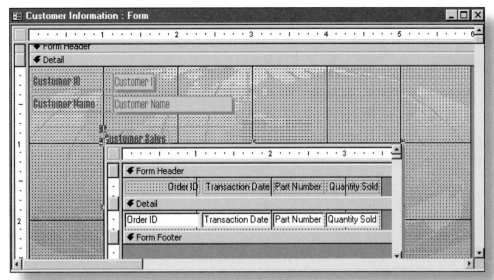

Let's review the parts of this main form and subform. The main form displays a customer record with the customer's ID and name. The subform displays the related records for this customer. When you select the navigation button to advance to the next record in the main form, you will see the orders related to that customer on the subform.

Adding a Record in the Subform

You can add a record to the subform. Access will also let you add records to the main form just as you can to any Access form.

STEP-BY-STEP ▷ 3.2

1. In the main form, go to the record for **Hector's Good Reading**.

2. In the subform, enter **2/5/2000** in the **Transaction Date** field.

   🖉 **Hot Tip**

   The Order ID field is an Auto-Number field, so Access will assign the number automatically for you.

3. Enter **41-241-TC** for the Part Number and then enter **75** for the Quantity.

4. If necessary switch to Design view and enlarge the subform so you can see all the records in the subform.

5. Switch to Form view and print the form for the **Hector's Good Reading** record only. Remain in this screen for the next Step-by-Step.

Modifying a Subform

You can control the basic appearance and operation of a form and a subform by changing its properties. For example, there are scroll bars and record navigation buttons that appear in both the main form and subform. You might decide to remove the scroll bars from the subform if all records in the subform can be viewed in the space provided.

STEP-BY-STEP ▷ 3.3

1. Switch to Design view. Click the gray box in the upper-left corner of the window, to the left of the horizontal ruler. (The color of this box may be different if you have chosen a color scheme other than Windows standard.) This selects the entire form.

2. Click the **Properties** button on the toolbar. Select the **All** tab.

3. Click in the **Scroll Bars** text box. This displays a drop-down arrow. Click the arrow and select **Neither**.

4. Click in the text box for **Navigation Buttons**. Click the drop-down arrow and select **No**. The Properties dialog box should look similar to Figure 3-7.

5. Close the **Properties** dialog box and then switch to Form view. Your screen should appear similar to Figure 3-8.

6. Save the form and then close it. Close the database.

FIGURE 3-7
Properties dialog box

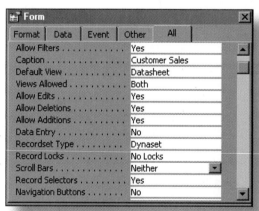

FIGURE 3-8
Adjusting form properties

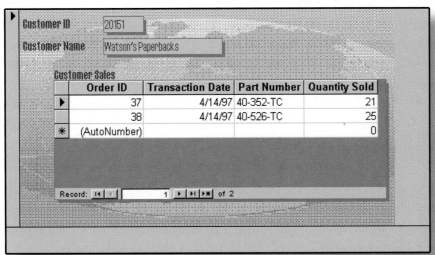

Creating and Modifying a Form in Design View

As you probably know, you can create a form using the Form Wizard, or by designing it from scratch in the Design view. Forms are developed primarily to streamline data entry. That's why Access provides you with a number of tools and options for designing forms that are user-friendly. You can re-arrange the order of fields, change field names, add and delete fields, and insert graphics and pictures, in order to customize the appearance of the form and maximize data entry time and effort.

Start here on 6-17-04

STEP-BY-STEP ▷ 3.4

1. Open the **AA Step3-4** database from the student data files.

2. Click **Forms** on the Objects bar.

3. Double-click **Create form in Design view**.

4. Place your mouse pointer in a blank area outside the Detail section of the form but within the Form window, and *right*-click. Choose **Properties** on the shortcut menu.

5. In the dialog box, select the **All** tab if necessary. Click in the **Record Source** text box, click the down arrow, and select **Orders**. You will use the Orders table to create the form.

6. Close the Form Properties dialog box. A window containing the fields in the Orders table should be displayed.

7. Place your mouse pointer over the **Order Number** field and drag it to the intersection of

(continued on next page)

the 1 inch marks on the horizontal and vertical rulers. Then, drag the **Customer Name** field and position it beneath the Order Number field. Finally, drag the **Employee Number** and position it below the Customer Name field.

8. Now, customize the form's header section. Open the **View** menu and then select **Form Header/Footer**. You should now see these sections in the Design view.

9. Click the **Label** button in the Toolbox and then click in the **Form Header** section.

10. Key **Orders** and press **Enter**. You should see selection handles around this box. If not, click on the label box to select it.

11. Click the **Bold** button on the Formatting toolbar. Then, click the down arrow on the **Font Size** button and choose **16**. To automatically increase the size of the label box, double-click on the middle right selection handle.

12. To insert a graphic, click the **Unbound Object Frame** button in the Toolbox and draw a box in

the upper left corner of the Detail section that's about 1 inch tall and 2 inches wide. The Insert Object dialog box should open.

13. Click **Microsoft Clip Gallery** in the Object Type list box and click **OK**.

14. Choose any piece of clip art you like and click **OK**.

15. To modify the graphic so it fits in the box you drew, *right*-click on it and choose **Properties** on the shortcut menu.

16. With the **All** tab selected, click in the **Size Mode** text box, click the down arrow, and choose **Zoom**. Close the Properties dialog box and view the results.

17. Save the form as **Orders**. Print the form for the first record.

18. Close the **Orders** form and then close the database.

Summary

In this lesson, you learned:

- A subform is simply a form within a form. This allows you to view, add, or make changes to information in more than one form at one time.

- After you create a subform, you can easily add or edit records within the subform as you would any form.

- You can create a form from scratch in Design view. Access provides you with great flexability in designing and modifying a form so that data entry time and effort are truly maximized.

- You can change properties of a form or a subform. For example, you may not want the scroll bars or record navigation buttons to appear in a subform. For some users, these features may be distracting since there are scroll bars and record navigation buttons on the main form. And since the subform will change to a related record if you select another record in the main form, having additional scroll bars and record navigation buttons may not be necessary.

LESSON 3 REVIEW QUESTIONS

WRITTEN QUESTIONS

Write a brief answer to the following questions.

1. What is a subform?

form within a form

2. Why would you want to use a subform?

show data on another table that is related to to main form.

3. How can you change the column width in a subform?

highlight the column and right click select column width

4. How can you add a new record to a subform?

Same as adding record is main form put cursor in cell and type

5. How do you open the Properties dialog box for the entire form?

In design view click in grey box in upper left corner of form. (at end of measuring bar) click on properties button

6. List three form properties that you can change with regard to navigation.

Scroll Bars, Record selectors, Navigation Buttons

7. Describe the differences between a main form and subform.

main form is created first then subform is overlaid.

8. Can a record be added to a main form even though it has a subform? If so, why is this possible?

yes the main form is just a different way of looking at data in the table.

9. If there are more records than can be displayed in the subform, how can you view the additional records?

use the scroll bars

10. How does Access recognize that there is a common field between a main form and a subform?

this is set in the subform wizard. the tables that are used for the main form and subform must be related. i.e. have a common field.

LESSON 3 PROJECT

PROJECT 3-1

1. Open the database **AA Project3-1** from the data files.

2. Create a one-to-many relationship between the **Marketing Department** table and the **January Orders** table using the **Employee ID** field as the common field.

3. Create a form using the Form Wizard for the **Marketing Department** table. Include the **Employee ID**, **Last Name**, and **First Name** fields on the form. Choose the Columnar layout and select a style of your choice. Name the form **Marketing Department Sales**.

4. Create a subform in the Marketing Department Sales form using the **January Orders** table. Include the **Order No**, **Order Date**, **Description**, **Quantity**, and **Price** fields in the subform. Accept the default name of **January Orders subform** for the subform.

5. Modify the main form to hide its scroll bars.

6. Make any other changes to the design of the forms that you think will make them more attractive.

7. Print the form for record **4**. Then close the form and the database.

CRITICAL THINKING

ACTIVITY 3-1

SCANS

You have just taken over as the database administrator for the Last Resort Sales Company. You view the existing database file, named **AA Activity3-1** on the student data files. You decide to create a main form/subform, using the **Employees** table for the main form and the **Personnel Information** table for the subform. You want a form that displays the employee's ID, last name, first name, and telephone number.

ACTIVITY 3-2

SCANS

As the personnel director for the New Cruise Line Company, you want to create a form that will display each employee's ID number, first name, and last name. You also want to display with this form salary information that is contained in another table. Use Access's Help system to find more information on creating subforms. Write a short essay that explains how you would proceed in setting up the main form and subform for the New Cruise Line Company.

Assuming no tables have been created. I would create a table with general employee infor. the another with a common field like employee ID.

A A - 4 1

ANALYZING DATA

OBJECTIVES

Upon completion of this lesson, you should be able to:

■ Calculate data using the Expression Builder.

■ Build summary queries.

■ Concatenate field values using a query.

■ Create AND and OR queries.

■ Apply filters.

🕐 **Estimated time: 1.5 hours**

Introduction

Queries are database objects that you use to search tables for records that meet certain criteria. You can design queries so that they display only selected fields and so that the results are sorted according to a certain field or fields. You can then generate reports that attractively present the query results.

In this lesson, you'll learn how to use queries to calculate and analyze records. Although databases are designed primarily to store and organize data, the query provides analytical capabilities that make database applications all the more powerful.

Using Queries to Calculate Data

Suppose you have a table of customer orders that contains fields for the quantity of a product purchased and the price per unit of the product. You'd like to be able to generate an invoice for the customer using the information in the table, but you realize that the invoice has to contain a total amount due. You can create a query that multiplies the quantity by the price per unit and then generates a total in a calculated field. This field is displayed in the query results, just like any other field in the table. You can rename the field as you desire, format it, and then include it on a form or report.

Using the Expression Builder

For many calculations, you'll want to use the *Expression Builder* to help you build the calculation or formula to be performed. The Expression Builder lets you select the type of operation or *function* you want to perform on selected fields. The commonly used types of operations are listed in Table 4-1.

TABLE 4-1
Types of operations

OPERATOR	WHAT IT DOES
+	Adds
–	Subtracts
*	Multiplies
/	Divides
=	Finds equal values or enters an equals sign
>	Finds values that are greater than the value entered
<	Finds values that are less than the value entered
<>	Finds values that are not equal to the value entered

A function, as you may know from working with spreadsheets, is a preset formula that comes with Access. For example, the SUM function lets you total the values in selected fields. Based on the selections you make, the Expression Builder "builds" the formula or expression for you.

To open the Expression Builder, click the Build button in the query Design window. The Expression Builder dialog box displays, as shown in Figure 4-1.

You build your formula or expression in the top portion of the dialog box. The list in the bottom-left pane of the Expression Builder includes the objects within the database file, as well as other elements you might want to use to build your expression. Double-click a folder icon to display a hierarchy

FIGURE 4-1
Expression Builder dialog box

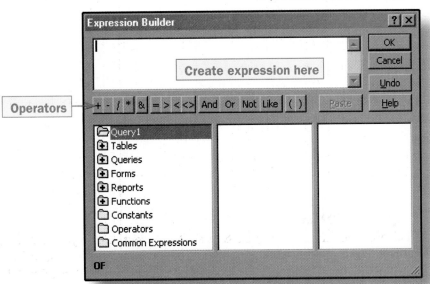

of subfolders that represent each of the objects or elements within the folder. Click the subfolder to display the object's fields (or expression's elements) in the middle pane. From the middle pane, you select the element that you want to add to the top portion of the dialog box by double-clicking the element. You can click an operator button or you can select the operator from the Operators folder in the lower left pane.

Figure 4-2 shows how a formula was built in the Expression Builder.

FIGURE 4-2
Building a formula

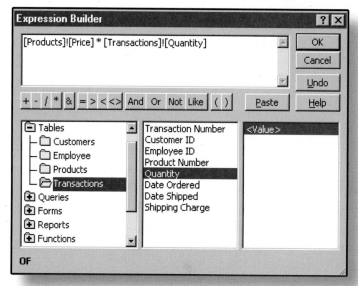

STEP-BY-STEP ▷ 4.1

1. Open the **AA Step4-1** database from the student data files.

2. Click **Queries** on the Objects bar.

3. Double-click **Create query in Design view**.

4. In the Show Table dialog box, double-click the **Products** table and then double-click the **Transactions** table to add them to the query. Click **Close**. Notice there is a one-to-many relationship between the two tables.

5. Double-click the **Transaction Number** and **Quantity** fields in the **Transactions** table to add them to the query grid. Double-click the **Price** field in the **Products** table to place it in the query grid.

6. Click in the **Field** cell of the fourth column in the grid and then click the **Build** button.

7. Double-click the **Tables** folder in the lower-left pane and then click the **Products** folder that displays beneath it. The fields in the Products table display in the middle pane.

8. Double-click the **Price** field to place it in the top box.

Concept Builder

If you place an incorrect field or element in the top Expression Builder box, simply highlight it and press **Delete**.

9. Click the * (asterisk) operator to add it to the expression.

10. Click the **Transactions** table folder to display its fields in the middle pane.

11. Double-click the **Quantity** field to place it in the top box. Your Expression Builder should look like Figure 4-2.

12. Click **OK** to close the Expression Builder.

13. Press **Enter** to enter this expression in the Field cell in the query grid.

14. Notice that Access has added *Expr1:* in front of the expression. This is the name that Access will automatically assign to the field in the query results. You can replace the heading with something more appropriate. Place your mouse pointer over **Expr1:** and double-click. Key **Order Total** and press **Enter**. Your screen should look similar to Figure 4-3.

Hot Tip

To increase the size of a column in the query grid, place the mouse pointer over the right border of the thin gray bar above the Field cell. When your mouse pointer turns into a two-headed arrow, simply double-click. The column width is automatically adjusted so you can see the full name entered in the Field cell.

15. Click the **Run** button to run the query. Notice how Order Total appears at the top of the calculated field. Next you will probably want to add a currency format to the data is this column.

16. Save the query as **Qry-Order Totals**. Remain in this screen for the next Step-by-Step.

FIGURE 4-3
Changing the name of the calculation field

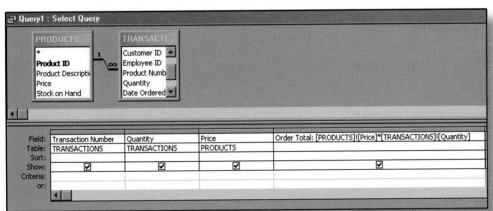

Modifying Query Properties

FIGURE 4-4
Field Properties dialog box

In the preceding Step-by-Step, you probably noticed that the values in the Order Total field were not formatted as currency. You can apply formats such as this to a field by changing the field's properties.

In the Design view, click the field name in the query grid and then click the Properties button. A Field Properties dialog box opens, like that shown in Figure 4-4.

To change the format to currency, click in the Format box, click the down arrow that appears, and choose Currency from the list.

Field Properties

General | Lookup

Description . . . .

Format . . . .

Decimal Places . . . .

Input Mask . . . .

Caption . . . .

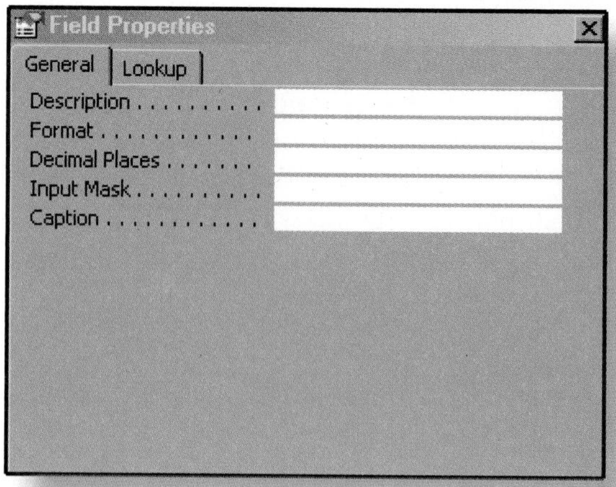

S TEP-BY-STEP ▷ 4.2

1. Switch to Design view. Click the **Order Total** Field cell in the query grid and the click the **Properties** button.

2. In the Field Properties dialog box, click the **Format** box, click the down arrow, and then select **Currency**.

3. Click the **Close** button to close the Field Properties dialog box.

4. In the query grid, click in the **Sort** cell for the **Transaction Number** field, and choose

Ascending. Switch to Datasheet view to run the query. You now have the fields you need in order to create a form or report that shows purchase totals.

5. Adjust the column widths, if necessary, and then print the query results.

6. Close the query and then close the database file.

Building Summary Queries

You can summarize values in a field by creating a summary query. Summary queries utilize functions, such as Sum, Avg, Min, and Max, to total or summarize values in a selected field. A list of some of Access's predefined functions is shown in Table 4-2.

In many instances, you'll want to group records for the summary. For example, you might want to know the total number of sales completed by each salesperson. You would group the records by the salesperson and then generate a summary of sales for each salesperson.

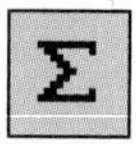

You create a summary query in Design view. In the query grid, you select the field by which you want to group the records (if there is one) and the field whose values you want to summarize. To do this, you must display the Total row in the query grid. Simply click the Totals button in the query design window. When you click in the Total cell for a field in the query grid, a drop-down arrow appears. Click the arrow to display the *Group By* option and the summary functions from which you can choose.

Σ

TABLE 4-2
Commonly used functions

FUNCTION	HOW IT IS USED
Sum	Totals the values in a field
Avg	Calculates the average of values in a field
Min	Finds the lowest value in the field
Max	Finds the highest value in the field
Count	Counts the number of items in a field
StDev	Finds the standard deviation of values within a field
Var	Finds the variance of values within a field
First	Locates the first value within a field
Last	Locates the last value within a field

STEP-BY-STEP ▷ 4.3

1. Open the **AA Step4-3** database from the student data files.

2. Click **Queries** on the Objects bar and then double-click **Create query in Design view**.

3. Double-click the **Sales Department** table and then double-click the **March Orders** table to add them to the query. Click **Close** to close the Show Table dialog box.

4. Double-click the **Last Name** field in the **Sales Department** table to place it in the query grid. Double-click the **Quantity** field in the **March Orders** table to add it to the query grid.

5. Click the **Totals** button. A Total row now appears in the query grid. Notice that the *Group By* option appears in the **Total** boxes for both fields.

6. You want the query to summarize orders for each salesperson, so leave the **Group By** designation in the **Last Name** column.

7. Click in the **Total** box of the **Quantity** column, click the down arrow, and then click **Sum**. This will apply the SUM function to the orders for each salesperson. Your screen should look similar to Figure 4-5.

8. Click the **Run** button to run the query. Notice how the total quantity sold by each salesperson is displayed. Also note that the column heading, *SumOfQuantity*, is automatically created for the field.

9. Save the query as **Qry-Quantity Sold**.

10. Adjust the column widths, if necessary. Print the query results and then close the query.

(continued on next page)

FIGURE 4-5
Summarizing sales

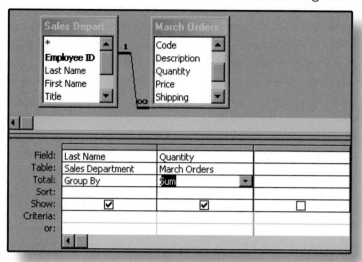

Using Concatenation

FIGURE 4-6
Concatenating field values

When a person's name is part of a record, it is best to put first names and last names in separate fields. But there may be times when you want the first name and last name combined as one value in a field. To join the values of fields, you can use the concatenation feature. *Concatenation* is defined as combining the text from two or more fields into one.

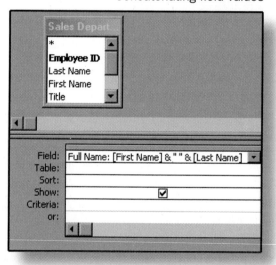

To concatenate fields you must be in the query Design view. In a Field cell of the query grid, first key the name you want to assign to the field followed by a colon (:). Then key in square brackets the complete name of the first field followed by an ampersand (&), opening quotation marks, followed by any other characters that you want to appear between the values, including spaces, the closing quotation marks, another ampersand, and the complete name of the second field in square brackets. So to concatenate a First Name and Last Name field and include a space between these names, you would enter:

```
Full Name: [First Name]&" "&[Last Name]
```

Figure 4-6 shows an example of the query criteria used to concatenate two fields.

When entering text in the Field cell, you might find it easier to view and edit the text by pressing Shift+F2. This opens a Zoom dialog box, shown in Figure 4-7, in which you can key the text. Click OK to close the box.

 **Hot Tip**

You can also use a + (plus sign) to concatenate text values.

FIGURE 4-7
Zoom dialog box

STEP-BY-STEP 4.4

1. Click **Queries** on the Objects bar and then double-click **Create query in Design view**.

2. Double-click the **Sales Department** table and then close the Show Table dialog box.

3. Click the first Field box of the query grid.

4. Key **Full Name: [First Name]&" "&[Last Name]**. Press **Enter** when you finish typing the concatenation.

5. In the second column of the query grid, choose

the **Extension** field to include in the query.

6. In the third column, select the **Last Name** field. Click in the **Sort** box and select the **Ascending** option. Click the **Show** box to remove the check mark so that this column does not display in the query results.

7. Run the query. Save the query as **Qry-Telephone List**.

8. Adjust the column widths and then print the query results. Close the query and the database.

Creating an AND Query

You can query a table or form for records that meet more than one set of criteria. This is referred to as an **And query**. For example, you might want to find records in an inventory database that have a cost of $.99 *and* a selling price of $1.99. To create an And query, you enter the search criteria for the appropriate fields in the same Criteria row in the query Design view.

STEP-BY-STEP ▷ 4.5

1. Open the **AA Step4-5** database from the student data files.

2. Open the **Transactions** table and view the records to familiarize yourself with them. Then close the table.

3. Click **Queries** on the Objects bar. Then double-click **Create query in Design view**.

4. Double-click the **Transactions** table in the Show Table dialog box. Then close the Show Table dialog box.

5. Double-click the **Transaction Number**, **Customer ID**, **Employee ID**, and **Quantity** fields to add them to the design grid.

6. Click the **Criteria** cell of the **Customer ID** field and key **5**. (This represents customer number 5.)

7. Click the Criteria cell of the **Employee ID** field and key **1**. (This represents employee number 1.)

8. Click the **View** button to run the query and view the results. You should see four records. Adjust the column widths so the complete field names display.

9. Save the query as **Qry-Cust#5 and Emp#1**.

10. Print the query results. Then, close the query and remain in this screen for the next Step-by-Step.

Creating an OR Query

You can query a table or form for records that meet one criteria or another. This is referred to as an *Or query*. For example, you may want to find records for customers who live in *either* Ohio *or* California. To create an Or query, you enter the first set of criteria in the first Criteria row in the Design view, and the second set of criteria in the or row. You can search for additional criteria by clicking in subsequent rows below the or row.

STEP-BY-STEP ▷ 4.6

1. If necessary, click **Queries** on the Objects bar. Then double-click **Create query in Design view**.

2. Double-click the **Transactions** table in the Show Table dialog box, and then close the dialog box.

3. Double-click the **Transaction Number**, **Customer ID**, **Employee ID**, and **Quantity** fields to add them to the grid.

4. Click the **Criteria** cell of the **Customer ID** field and enter **5**.

5. Click the **or** cell of the **Customer ID** field and enter **3**.

6. Sort the **Customer ID** field in **Ascending Order**.

7. Click the **View** button to run the query and view the results. You should see 26 records. Adjust

the column widths so the complete field names display.

8. Save the query as **Qry-Cust#5,#3**.

9. Print the query results. Then, close the query and remain in this screen for the next Step-by-Step.

Applying Filters to a Query

You can further define your query results by applying filters to them. A filter lets you temporarily "filter out" the records you don't want to see. You cannot save a filter like you do a query. And, once you close the filtered data, the original records redisplay when you open the table, form, or query.

You filter data in Datasheet view. Click in the field you want to filter on, open the Records menu, select Filter, and then select the type of filter you want to run from the submenu. Select Filter by Form to display a form containing only the field names. A drop-down arrow appears by the name of the field you've selected to run the filter on. When you click the arrow, a list displays showing the individual values entered in that field. Select one of the values, and Access filters out all records that do not contain that value in the field. You can also run a Filter by Form by clicking the Filter By Form button on the toolbar, clicking in the appropriate field and selecting the value you want to search for, and then clicking the Apply Filter button.

The Filter by Selection form works in a similar fashion. Select an existing value in the field you want to filter on, and then open the Records menu, select Filter, and then select Filter by Selection on the submenu. Or, you can click the Filter By Selection button on the toolbar.

To remove a filter, click the Remove Filter button on the toolbar, or select Remove Filter/Sort on the Records menu.

Filter By Form

Apply Filter

Filter By Selection

STEP-BY-STEP ▷ 4.7

1. If necessary, click **Queries** on the Objects bar. Then double-click **Qry-Cust#5,#3**.

2. Click in the first record's **Customer ID** field. It should be Customer ID number 3.

3. Click the **Filter By Selection** button. You should see 15 records.

4. Click the **Remove Filter** button.

5. Click the **Filter By Form** button. A form appears that lets you click in the field or fields that you want to filter.

6. Click in the **Customer ID** field, click the down arrow, and choose **5**.

7. Click the **Apply Filter** button. You should see 11 records that have a Customer ID number of 5.

8. Click the **Remove Filter** button. Close the query and close the database file.

Summary

In this lesson, you learned:

- The Expression Builder assists you in creating a formula to calculate values in a field.

- You can format fields by changing the field's properties. *in design view*

- You can summarize field values by creating a summary query. A summary query lets you summarize groups of records or all the records in a table.

- You can concatenate text values in two or more fields by entering the concatenation expression in the query Design view.

- An And query lets you search for records that meet more than one criteria. An Or query lets you search for records that meet one criteria or another.

- You can further refine query results by applying filters.

LESSON 4 REVIEW QUESTIONS

TRUE/FALSE

Circle T if the statement is true or F if the statement is false.

T **(F)** 1. You use the Expression Builder to modify the properties of a field.

(T) F 2. A concatenated expression can be created by using a plus sign or an ampersand.

T **(F)** 3. You click the Query Type button to add the Total row to the query grid.

T **(F)** 4. The MAX function will find the first value in a field.

(T) F 5. You normally use concatenation to combine text values.

WRITTEN QUESTIONS

Write a brief answer to the following questions.

1. What is the purpose of the Expression Builder?

   to build an expression for a calculated field that could be used on a form or report.

2. How do you display the Total row in the query grid?

Click on Sum symbol on query design menu.

3. List three of Access's predefined functions and give an example of how one of them might be used.

sum, avg., max — max could be used to find the largest quantity of an item that was ordered.

4. When would you use the Properties button in a query?

a field display change the format of

5. What is the purpose of the text and colon displayed before an expression?

names the field where the expression is used.

LESSON 4 PROJECTS

PROJECT 4-1

1. Open the **AA Project4-1** database from the student data files.

2. Create a query based on the **Customers**, **Transactions**, and **Products** tables.

3. If necessary, join the **Customer ID** fields in the **Customers** and **Transaction** tables, and join the **Product Number** and **Product ID** fields in the **Transactions** and **Products** tables.

4. In the query grid, add the **Customer ID** and **Company Name** fields from the **Customers** table, the **Price** field from the **Products** table, and the **Quantity** field from the **Transactions** table.

5. Create an expression that calculates price (from the **Products** table) times quantity (from the **Transactions** table). Rename the field **Total Price**.

6. Format the **Total Price** field as currency.

7. Save the query as **Qry-Sales Totals**.

8. Adjust column widths, if necessary. Print the results of the query. Then close the database file.

PROJECT 4-2

6-21-04

1. Open the **AA Project4-2** database from the student data files.

2. Create a query that groups the records by class and averages the grade point average of the class. Include only the Class and Grade Point Average fields in the query grid.

3. Format the summary field to display two decimal places. Adjust the column widths in the query results, if necessary. (*Hint*: You may need to set the number format to Standard.)

4. Save the query as **Qry-Class Averages**.

5. Print the results of your query. Then close the database file.

CRITICAL THINKING

ACTIVITY 4-1

SCANS

The pet supply company you work for has just been purchased by a larger supplier. The new owners want you to provide them with some information from the company database. They want to know the total cost of each transaction for the month of August and they also want to know the total transactions for the month. You decide to create queries to generate the information. Open the **AA Activity4-1** database from the student data files. Save your queries as **Qry-August Transactions** and **Qry-Total August Transactions**. Print the results of both queries.

ACTIVITY 4-2

SCANS

You maintain the corporate database for One Star Gas Company. You need to create a number of queries to generate information requested by other officers of the company. You want to present the data in the most attractive way possible. Use Access's Help system to find information on query format properties. Write a brief essay on the Help information you find and explain how you could apply these properties as you create your queries.

Query fields maintain the format of the field in the table unless changed in Query Design View. To change the format in the query without affecting the Table format do this. Place the cursor in the field you want to format and click properties to open the property sheet.

ADVANCED QUERIES

OBJECTIVES

Upon completion of this lesson, you should be able to:

■ Remove or change a field in a query.

■ Create a parameter query.

■ Understand action queries.

■ Create a delete query.

■ Create an update query.

■ Create a make-table query.

🕐 **Estimated Time: 1.5 hours**

In this lesson, you will explore further the different types of queries you can create in a database. You will learn how to set up a parameter query that lets you set parameters each time a query is run. You will also learn how to build action queries. These types of queries perform an action that changes what records appear in a table or form. The lesson will also review how to modify the design of a query.

Modifying a Query's Design

You can change a query's design by opening it in Design view. You can add or remove fields, change the order of fields, select a different field to sort by, or modify the search criteria.

To replace a field with another, click the Field name in the query grid, click the drop-down arrow at the end of the box, and select the new field you want included in the query. To delete a field, click on the thin gray bar above the field name in the query grid. This will select the entire column. Then press Delete to remove the field from the query grid.

To insert a field, select the field in the field list box and drag it to the Field name box in the query grid where you want it to appear. The existing field and all remaining fields will shift one column to the right. To move a field to a different spot in the query, click the gray bar above the field in the query grid to select the entire column. Then position the mouse pointer on the gray bar and drag the column to the new location. A dark vertical bar indicates where the field is going to be positioned when you release the mouse button.

1. Open the **AA Step5-1** database from the student data files.

2. Click **Queries** in the Object bar.

3. Double-click **Create query in Design view**.

4. Double-click the **Customers** table to add it to the query. Click **Close** to close the Show Table dialog box.

5. Double-click the **Last Name**, **First Name**, and **State** fields to enter them into the grid.

6. Click the **State** field in the query grid. Notice that a down arrow appears on the right side of this cell.

7. Click the down arrow and then click **Postal Code**. This changes the field from State to Postal Code.

8. Place your mouse pointer in the thin gray bar above the **First Name** field. You will see your mouse pointer turn into an arrow pointing downward. Click in this bar to select the field.

9. Press **Delete**. This removes the field from the query grid.

10. Place your mouse pointer over the **Phone Number** field in the field list.

11. Drag the **Phone Number** field to the first cell in the second column where **Postal Code** is currently located. Release the mouse button. Notice how the **Phone Number** field is now inserted in the second column, as shown in Figure 5-1.

12. Close the query without saving any changes. Remain in this screen for the next Step-by-Step.

FIGURE 5-1
Modifying a query's design

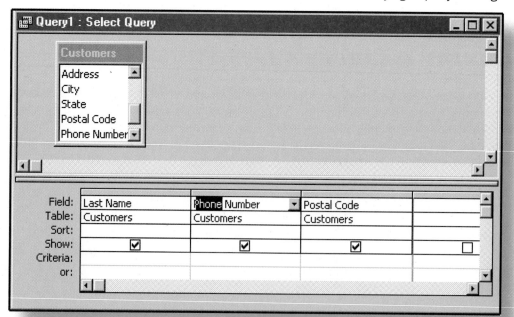

Creating a Parameter Query

Although you've just learned how easy it is to modify a query's design, there are instances when the search criteria changes frequently enough that it's easier and more efficient to create a *parameter query*. For example, suppose you have a large table of customer names and addresses. You want to provide your sales force with the information on customers in their individual sales territories only. Instead of creating half a dozen queries that find customers in each territory, you could create one query that asks you to enter the territory criteria each time it is run.

A parameter query lets you enter different criteria each time you use the query. To create a parameter query, you must enter a "prompt" in the field's Criteria cell in the query grid. A prompt tells the person running the query what criterion needs to be entered. It must be enclosed in brackets, as shown in Figure 5-2.

FIGURE 5-2
Entering a prompt for parameter query

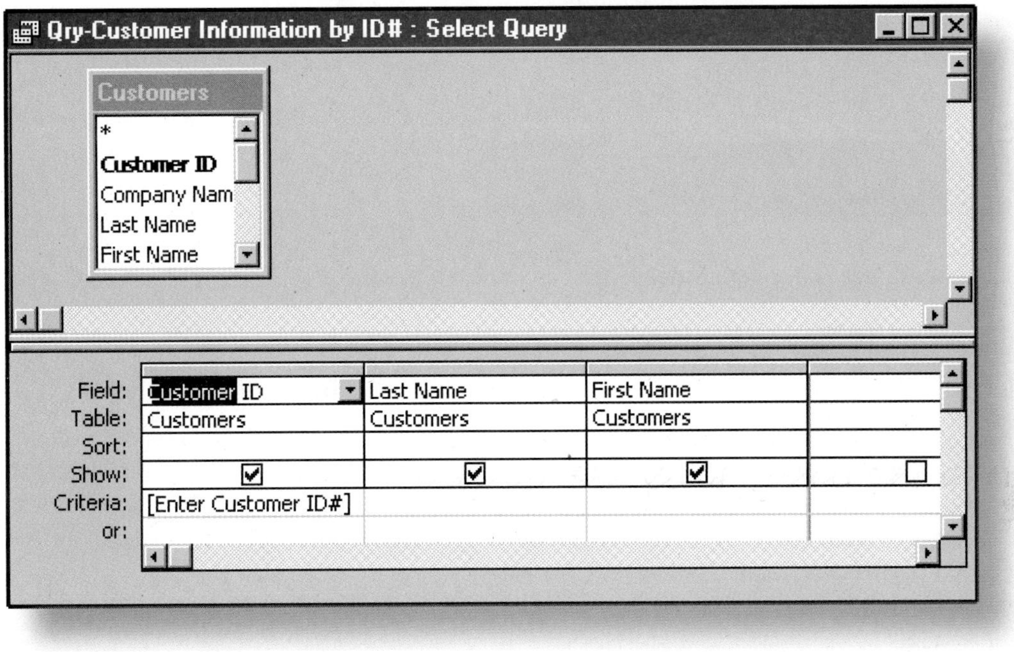

When you run the query, the Enter Parameter Value dialog box opens first, as shown in Figure 5-3. The prompt instructs you to enter the criterion or value for which you are searching. Click OK or press Enter to continue running the query.

Hot Tip

You can run a query by clicking the Run button in the Design view or by simply switching to Datasheet view.

FIGURE 5-3
Enter Parameter Value dialog box

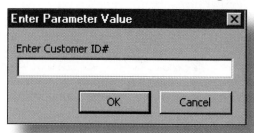

S TEP-BY-STEP ▷ 5.2

C

1. Click **Queries** in the Object bar, if necessary.

2. Double-click **Create query in Design view**.

3. Double-click the **Customers** table in the Show Table dialog box and then close the dialog box.

4. Double-click the **Customer ID**, **Last Name**, and **First Name** fields to add them to the grid.

5. Click in the **Criteria** cell of the **Customer ID#** field and key **[Enter Customer ID#]**. Press **Enter**.

6. Save the query as **Qry-Customer Information by ID#**.

7. Click the **Run** button to run the query.

8. In the Enter Parameter Value dialog box, key **9**. Click **OK** or press **Enter**. Your screen should look like Figure 5-4.

9. Close the query and remain in this screen for the next Step-by-Step.

FIGURE 5-4
Parameter query results

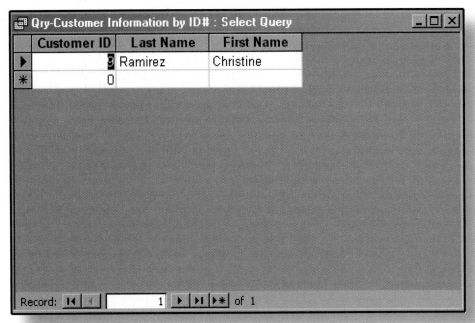

Understanding Action Queries

A query is considered an action query if it makes changes to a table. There are four types of action queries: append, delete, update, and make-table. An **append query** adds records from one table to another table. A **delete query** deletes records within a table. An **update query** changes the values in a field within a specified group of records. For example, if you wanted to give sales personnel a 6% raise, you could use an update query to find sales personnel within the table and increase their salary by 6%. The **make-table query** creates a new table using the records found from one or more other tables.

You design an action query in the Design window. Click the arrow next to the Query Type button and select the query you want to create. Action queries are identified in the Database window by an exclamation mark.

Concept Builder

You can speed up a query's run time by setting the Indexed property on the field by which you are searching. The primary key in a table is automatically indexed. To set the Indexed property on a field other than the primary key, open the table from which you will create the query in Design view, open the Properties dialog box for the field, click in the **Indexed** text box, and select **Yes** on the In-dexed property's drop-down list.

Creating a Delete Query

Access lets you delete records that meet specific criteria. However, be very careful when creating a delete query—once you delete records in this manner, they cannot be recovered. It is recommended that you make a copy of the table and run the query on the copied table. If you get the results you want, then you can perform the same query on the original table.

To create a delete query, open the query Design window. Click the Query Type arrow and select Delete Query. In the query grid, enter the criteria for the records you want to delete. For example, you might want to delete the records for all customers who haven't placed an order in two years. An example of a delete query is shown in Figure 5-5.

FIGURE 5-5
Designing a delete query

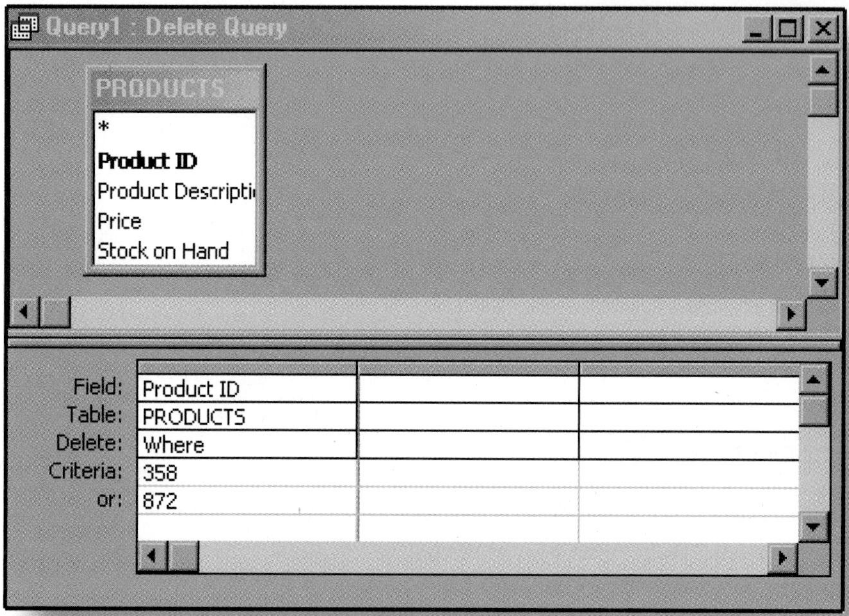

Click the Run button. A message box like that shown in Figure 5-6 appears, asking you to confirm that you want to delete the records that meet the criteria.

FIGURE 5-6
Delete query message box

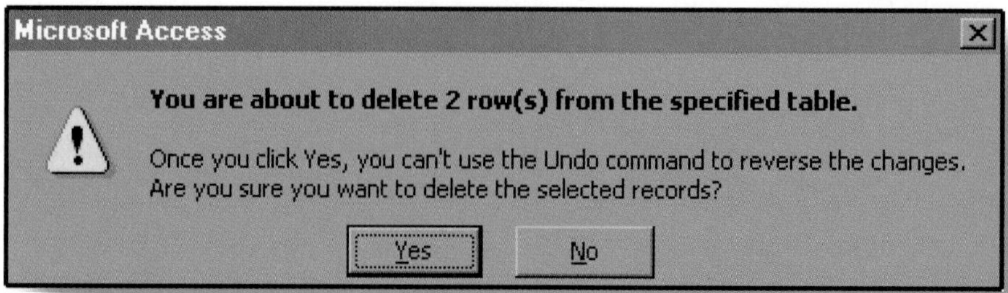

S TEP-BY-STEP ▷ 5.3

1. Click **Queries** in the Object bar, if necessary.

2. Double-click **Create query in Design view**.

3. Double-click the **Products** table in the Show Table dialog box and then close the dialog box.

4. Double-click the **Product ID** field to add it to the grid.

5. Click the arrow on the **Query Type** button and select **Delete Query**.

6. Click in the **Criteria** cell of the **Product ID** field and enter **358**. Then press the down arrow key to move to a second Criteria cell and enter **872**.

7. Click the **Run** button.

8. The message box opens, telling you that two records will be deleted. Click **Yes** to confirm the deletion.

9. Close the query without saving the changes.

10. Open the **Products** table and check to be sure the records you deleted are no longer in this table. Sort the records in ascending order by the **Product ID** field and then print the table.

11. Close the table and the database file.

Creating an Update Query

Update queries let you change field values in a table. Table records are permanently changed when the query is run. As with the Delete query, it is recommended that you make a copy of the table and run the query on the copied table. If you get the desired results, you can then run the query on the original table. To create an update query, click the Query Type button arrow in the Design view and select Update Query. Enter the criteria for the field in which you want to change the values. Then enter the value, or expression, that you want to update to. An example of an update query is shown in Figure 5-7.

Click the Run button. A message box like that shown in Figure 5-8 appears, asking you to confirm the update.

FIGURE 5-7
Designing an update query

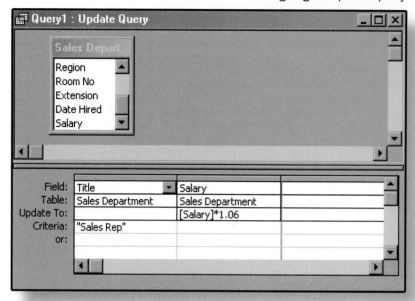

FIGURE 5-8
Update query message box

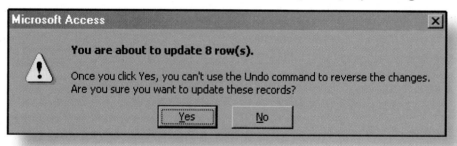

In the following Step-by-Step, you will create an update query in which you find the records for all sales reps and then update their salaries to reflect a 6% raise. Before you create the query, you might want to look at the Sales Department table and make a note of how many records will be changed. In this table, you have eight sales reps. The first sales rep listed is Rosa Navarro and she makes $42,440.00. After her raise, she should be making $44,986.40.

STEP-BY-STEP ▷ 5.4

1. Open the **AA Step5-4** database file.

2. Click **Queries** in the Objects bar, if necessary.

3. Double-click **Create query in Design view**.

4. Double-click the **Sales Department** table in the Show Table dialog box and then close the dialog box.

5. Double-click the **Title** and **Salary** fields to add them to the query grid.

6. Click the arrow on the **Query Type** button and then select **Update Query**.

7. Click in the **Criteria** cell of the **Title** field and enter **Sales Rep**.

8. Click in the **Update To** cell of the **Salary** field and enter **[Salary]*1.06**. This expression will calculate a 6% raise for each sales rep.

9. Click the **Run** button. You should see a message box showing that eight rows will be updated. Click **Yes** to confirm the update.

10. Close the query without saving.

11. Open the **Sales Department** table and check the salary amount for Rosa Navarro. Adjust the column widths if necessary. Print the table in landscape orientation and then close it. Remain in this screen for the next Step-by-Step.

 Hot Tip

Be careful to click the **Run** button only one time. Each time you run the query, it will calculate another 6% raise for the sales reps.

Creating a Make-Table Query

The make-table query is ideal for creating a new table that uses certain fields from one or more other tables. It's also commonly used to duplicate an existing table, minus a specified field or fields. For example, you might want to create a copy of a table containing employee records that does not include the field on 401(k) contributions.

When you select the Make-Table option from the Query Type list, you are asked to enter a name for the new table in the Make Table dialog box, as shown in Figure 5-9. You can also choose to create the table in another database file. Run the query and the new table is created automatically. The table is not linked to the existing table or tables. Therefore, if information in the original table changes, you will need to run the query again if you want to update this information in the new table. You can use the same table name as the previous table you made; simply choose Replace when asked to do so.

FIGURE 5-9
Make Table dialog box

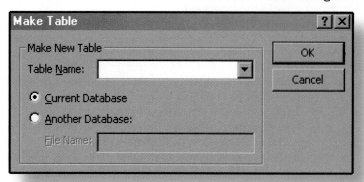

S TEP-BY-STEP ▷ **5.5**

1. Click **Queries** in the Objects bar, if necessary.

2. Double-click **Create query in Design view**.

3. Double-click the **Sales Department** table in the Show Table dialog box and then close the dialog box.

4. Double-click the **Last Name**, **First Name**, **Title**, and **Extension** fields to add them to the query grid. Sort the **Last Name** field in **Ascending** order.

5. Click the **Query Type** button and then select **Make-Table Query**.

6. The Make Table dialog box appears. Enter **Telephone List** for the new table name and click **OK**.

7. Click the **Run** button. A message box similar to that shown in Figure 5-10 opens.

8. Click **Yes** to confirm that you want to create a new table.

FIGURE 5-10
Make-Table query message box

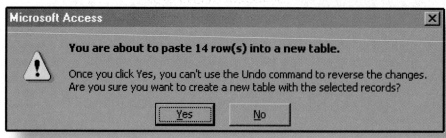

9. Save the query as **Qry-Make Telephone List Table**.

10. Close the query.

11. Open the **Telephone List** table and view the results. Print the table and then close it and the database.

Summary

In this lesson, you learned:

■ You make modifications to a query's design in the Design view. You can add or delete fields, change the order of fields, change the sort order, and modify the search criteria.

■ When the search criteria changes frequently enough, it's usually easier and more efficient to create a parameter query. A parameter query lets you enter different criteria each time you use the query. To create a parameter query, you must enter a "prompt" in the field's Criteria cell in the query grid.

■ The four types of action queries are: append, delete, update, and make-table. An append query adds records from one table to another table. A delete query deletes records within a table. An update query changes field values for a specified group of records. The make-table query creates a new table using the records from one or more tables.

LESSON 5 REVIEW QUESTIONS

TRUE/FALSE

Circle T if the statement is true or F if the statement is false.

T **F** 1. You can add fields and change the order of fields in a query, but you cannot delete fields in the query Design window.

T **F** 2. With a parameter query, you add records from one table to another table.

T F 3. The results of a delete action query are irreversible.

T **F** 4. Action queries are identified by an asterisk in the Database window.

T **F** 5. A make-table query can only create a new table in the database that contains the original table(s).

WRITTEN QUESTIONS

Write a brief answer to the following questions.

1. What is the purpose of a parameter query? *allows the query criteria to be changed each time the query is run.*

2. When would you use an update query? *to make the same change to several records*

3. What is the difference between an update query and a delete query? *update makes a change to a field of the queried records. Delete queries permanently delete records.*

4. Do you want to save update or delete queries? Why or why not?

   update yes – for future use if same type of change will be used again
   delete yes – may not be a good idea unless this is a complex query

5. Can you undelete records after they have been deleted in a delete query?

   No

PROJECT 5-1

1. Open the **AA Project5-1** database from the student data files.

2. Create an update query that finds the records in the **Inventory** table whose **Part Number** field begins with **44-**. Update the **On Order** field to **0**. (*Hint*: Use the criteria of **44-*** in the **Part Number** field.)

3. Save the query as **Qry-Discontinued Items**.

4. Sort the updated **Inventory** table by the **Part Number** field. Print the table.

5. Close the table and then close the database file.

PROJECT 5-2

1. Open the **AA Project5-2** database from the student data files.

2. Create a parameter query on the **Customers** table. In the Design window, add the **Company Name**, **Last Name**, **First Name**, **City**, **State**, and **Phone Number** fields to the query grid.

3. Key the following prompt in the **State** field: **Enter TX, OR, or CA**.

4. Sort the query in ascending order by the **Last Name** field.

5. Save the query as **Qry-Customers by State.**

6. Run the query using the **TX** parameter. Adjust the column widths, if necessary. Print the query results.

7. Run the query using the **OR** and **CA** parameters. Print the results of each query.

8. Close the query and the database file.

Completed 6-23-04

A A - 6 7

ACTIVITY 5-1

SCANS

You know that Access provides you with two tools for searching database tables: the filter and the query. But you're not clear about the differences between the two, and you've scheduled a training workshop with new employees that covers Access's search features. Use the Access Help system to find information on the types of filters and queries you can run on a database. Use one of the databases in the student data files provided with this lesson to experiment with the different filters and queries. Write a brief essay that lists the types of filters and queries, outlines the differences between filters and queries, and provides an example of when you would use each.

filters vs. query. filters and queries both select
subsets of records in a table or query. filters can
not be saved. filters will display all the fields in the
selected records whereas queries allow turning of selected
fields. Both filters and queries can be used for source
data for a report or form. queries allow calculations
to be made. One very useful tool is the ability to
save a filter as a query.

ADVANCED REPORT FEATURES

OBJECTIVES

Upon completion of this lesson, you should be able to:

- Understand bound, unbound, and calculated controls.
- Create a separate report header page.
- Customize footers in a report.
- Add a chart to a report.
- Create a report in the Design view.

Estimated time: 1.5 hours

A report is a database object that is used primarily for summarizing and printing data from tables and queries. You should already understand how to create a report using the Report Wizard. In this lesson, you will build on your knowledge of reports. You will learn how to add an unbound control to a report and how to create a cover page for a report. You will also learn how to modify the design of a report and add graphics, including charts, to a report.

Understanding Bound, Unbound, and Calculated Controls

A report's design is characterized by bound, unbound, and calculated controls. A **bound control** is linked to a field in a table or query. It will display information from this field in the report.

An **unbound control** displays information that is not found in a table or query. An example of an unbound control would be the report's title. The report title typically describes what information is found in a report. However, the report title does not represent a record or field data in the table or query.

A **calculated control** contains the result of a mathematical calculation. You learned in Lesson 4 how to use queries to calculate field data. You can calculate data in reports, too, by adding a calculated control to the report's design.

Adding Controls to a Report's Design

You use the Toolbox to add controls and modify the design of a report. You display the Toolbox in the report's Design view by clicking the Toolbox button. The Toolbox is shown in Figure 6-1. Your Toolbox may be displayed on the left side of your screen or with the other toolbars.

You can modify the format of the control in Design view. Use the Form/Report Formatting toolbar to change the font, font size, font style, alignment, and color of controls. To change other formats, select the control and then click the Properties button on the toolbar. A dialog box opens, listing all the properties associated with that control.

Hot Tip

You can also open a Properties dialog box by *right*-clicking the control and selecting **Properties** on the shortcut menu.

FIGURE 6-1
Toolbox

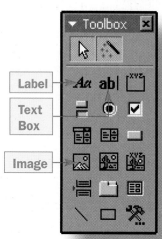

Label

Text Box

Image

S TEP-BY-STEP ▷ 6.1

1. Open the database **AA Step6-1** from the student data files.

2. Click **Reports** on the Objects bar.

3. Open the report **Wholesale versus Retail**.

4. Maximize the report.

5. Click the **View** button to switch to Design view.

6. If the Toolbox is not displayed, click the **Toolbox** button on the toolbar.

7. Click the **Text Box** button in the Toolbox.

8. Place your cursor in the **Detail** section of the report at about the 5" marker on the horizontal ruler and click. A text box should appear.

9. Click the label box of the control and press **Delete**. We only want to show the result of the calculation on the report. There's no need to assign a name to it.

10. Click the **Unbound** box to select it and then click in the box again to place the insertion point in the box.

11. Type **=[In-Stock Value]*1.25**. Press **Enter**. (Be sure to use the square brackets.)

12. *Right*-click the *Unbound* box and choose **Properties** on the shortcut menu.

13. Click the **All** tab and then click in the **Format** box. Click the drop-down arrow and choose **Currency**.

14. Close the Properties dialog box.

15. Click the **View** button to switch to Print Preview. Notice how the calculated control has multiplied the In-Stock Value by 1.25. Remain in this screen for the next Step-by-Step.

Concept Builder

You can move a control by selecting it and then dragging it to a new location. You can resize a control by selecting it and then dragging a selection handle. To select more than one control at a time, hold down the **Shift** key as you click each control.

Adding a Label to a Report

A label is an unbound control in which you can enter text, such as report titles, new names for fields, or other information that is not related to the table or query on which the report is based. Simply click the Label button in the Toolbox and then click in the report where you want to place the label.

STEP-BY-STEP 6.2

1. Switch to Design view and click the **Label** button in the Toolbox.

2. Position the crosshair in the **Page Header** section of the report at the 5" marker on the horizontal ruler and click.

3. Type **Retail Value** and press **Enter**. Your screen should look similar to Figure 6-2.

4. If needed, reposition the label to align properly with the other labels in the Page Header section of your report. Change the alignment of the

FIGURE 6-2
Adding a label

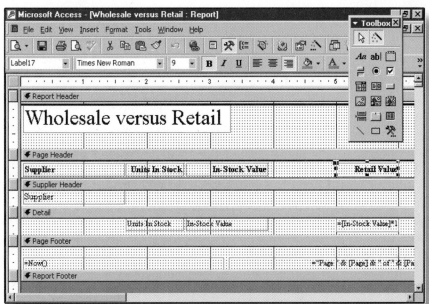

(continued on next page)

label to right-aligned. Reposition the calculated control you added to the Detail section to align with the other controls in the section.

5. Click the **Print Preview** button. Your report shows the added control.

6. Click the **Two Pages** button to see both pages. Your screen should look similar to Figure 6-3.

7. Click the **View** button to switch back to Design view. Remain in this screen for the next Step-by-Step.

FIGURE 6-3
Viewing two pages of the report

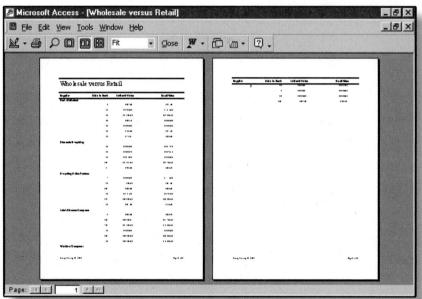

Creating a Title Page

As you are aware, there are several sections to a report. Anything that appears in the Report Header section will print only on the first page of the report and the Report Footer section will only print on the last page of the report. Anything that appears in the Page Header or Page Footer sections will print on every page.

You can place the Report Header section on a page of its own to create a title or cover page for the report. In the Design view, select the Report Header section and then click the Properties button. In the Properties dialog box, click in the *Force New Page* text box, click the down arrow, and select *After Section.* Access will place a page break between the Report Header and the Page Header sections of the report.

You can enhance a title page by using the various text formatting tools on the Formatting toolbar or by placing graphics or other images on it.

S TEP-BY-STEP ▷ 6.3

1. Click the gray bar for the **Report Header** section to select it and then click the **Properties** button.

2. In the Properties dialog box, click the **All** tab if necessary and then click in the **Force New Page** text box.

3. Click the arrow and choose **After Section**. Close the **Properties** dialog box.

4. Click **Print Preview** to view your report.

5. Click the **Multiple Pages** button and then select the **1X3 Pages** option.

6. Click **View** to return to Design view.

7. Delete the line above the report title. Click on the solid black horizontal line above the report title to select it. Press **Delete**.

8. Place the mouse pointer on the top border of the Page Header bar. When it turns into a double-headed vertical arrow, drag the Page Header section down approximately 4".

9. Click the **Wholesale versus Retail** label, click the arrow on the **Font/Fore Color** button, and select **Red**.

10. If necessary, display the Toolbox. Click the **Unbound Object Frame** button in the Toolbox.

11. Position the mouse pointer below the report title and click.

12. In the Insert Object dialog box, make sure the **Create New** option is selected. Double-click **Microsoft Clip Gallery** in the Object Type list box, click the **Pictures** tab, and select the **Business** category of pictures. Click a piece of art of your choosing and then click the **Insert clip** button.

13. Center and resize the report title and clip art on the page.

14. Preview your report and remain in this screen for the next Step-by-Step.

Customizing Report Footers

Footers in a report can be used to identify a number of things: the date the report was produced, the name of the report and the name of the person who created it, and the page number. To review, a report footer appears once on the last page of the report. A page footer appears on every page of the report.

But suppose your report has a title page on which you don't want a page footer to appear. You can remove a footer from the title page by changing the report's properties. Click the Select All button in the upper left corner of the report design window to select the entire report. See Figure 6-4. Click the Properties button to display the report's Properties dialog box, as shown in Figure 6-5.

In the Properties dialog box, click in the *Page Footer* box, click the down arrow, and choose *Not with Rpt Hdr*.

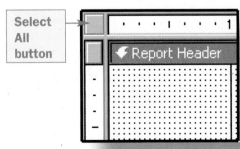

FIGURE 6-4
Selecting the entire report

FIGURE 6-5
Report's Properties dialog box

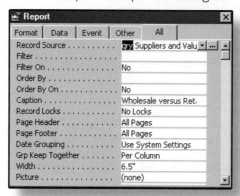

STEP-BY-STEP ▷ 6.4

1. Click the **View** button to switch to Design view. Display the Toolbox, if necessary.

2. Place the mouse pointer on the top border of the Report Footer section. When it turns into a double-headed arrow, drag down approximately $1/2$" to increase the size of the Page Footer section.

3. Click the **Label** button. Click in the **Page Footer** section below the field **=Now()**. The fields that are already in the Page Footer section are default footers assigned to the report by Access. You can delete them by selecting the controls and pressing Delete. Leave them intact for this Step-by-Step.

4. Type your first name and last name. Press **Enter**.

5. *Right*-click on the **Select All** button (located to the left of the horizontal ruler) and select **Properties** on the shortcut menu.

6. Click in the **Page Footer** text box, click the drop-down arrow, and select **Not with Rpt Hdr**. Close the Properties dialog box.

7. Preview the report. Notice how the footer is not displayed on the first page with the report header.

8. Notice how a little of the data in the report spills over to the last page. Switch back to Design view and adjust the size of the Supplier Header and Detail sections so that all the data fits on one page.

9. When you are happy with the appearance of the report, print it and then close it. Remain in this screen for the next Step-by-Step.

Adding a Chart to a Report

In many instances, a chart can help illustrate the data you present in a report. Access's Chart Wizard walks you through the steps for creating a chart. Once you place it in the report's Design view, you can format and customize it as you would any other object or control.

STEP-BY-STEP 6.5

1. Click **Reports** on the Objects bar and then double-click **Create report by using wizard**.

2. In the first Wizard dialog box, select **Query: qry Supplier Totals** from the Tables/Queries drop-down list. This is the query the report will be based on.

3. Add both the available fields to the Selected Fields list box. Click **Next**.

4. You will not add any grouping levels. Click **Next**.

5. In this Wizard dialog box, choose to sort by the **Supplier** field and click **Next**.

6. In this Wizard dialog box, choose the **Tabular** layout and click **Next**.

7. In this Wizard dialog box, select the **Corporate** style and click **Next**.

8. In the final dialog box, enter **Supplier Totals** for the report title. Click **Finish**. The report opens in the Preview window.

9. Switch to Design view. Enlarge the **Detail** section so it is about 3" deep.

10. To add a chart to the report open the **Insert** menu and select **Chart**. Place the mouse pointer in the **Detail** section beneath the Supplier label. Press and hold the mouse button down and draw a box about $3^1/_2$ inches wide and $2^1/_2$ inches tall. When you release the mouse button, the Chart Wizard opens, as shown in Figure 6-6.

11. Click the **Queries** button in the *View* options and then select **qry Supplier Totals**. Click **Next**.

FIGURE 6-6
Starting the Chart Wizard

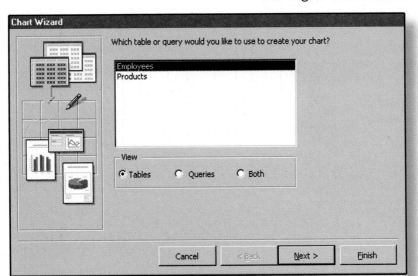

(continued on next page)

12. In this dialog box, the Chart Wizard asks you to select the fields containing the data you want to chart. See Figure 6-7. Add both available fields to the *Fields for Chart* list box. Click **Next**.

13. In this dialog box, the Chart Wizard asks you to determine the type of chart. See Figure 6-8. Select the **3-D Column Chart** (the second chart option in the first row). Click **Next**.

14. In this dialog box, the Chart Wizard asks you to place the fields on the appropriate parts of the chart. See Figure 6-9. Click **Next** to accept the layout proposed by the Chart Wizard.

15. In this dialog box, shown in Figure 6-10, accept the selections made by the wizard and click **Next**.

16. The final dialog box displays, as shown in Figure 6-11. Enter **Supplier Totals** as the title of the chart. Make sure the **Yes, display a legend** option is selected and click **Finish**.

17. Preview the report. Then print the report, close it, and close the database.

Concept Builder

You can modify the appearance of the chart just as you would any other object or control in the report's Design view. First, double-click the chart to make it active. A Chart menu appears on the Menu bar and a toolbar with buttons for formatting the chart displays. To format a specific part of the chart, such as its title or legend, right-click the part and then select the Format command on the shortcut menu. A dialog box containing formatting options specific to that part appears.

FIGURE 6-7
Selecting the fields to chart

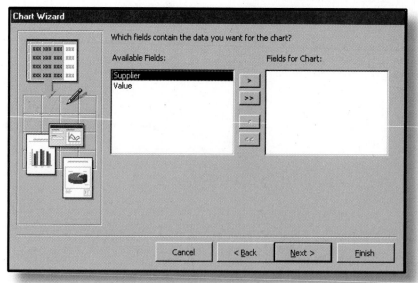

FIGURE 6-8
Selecting the chart type

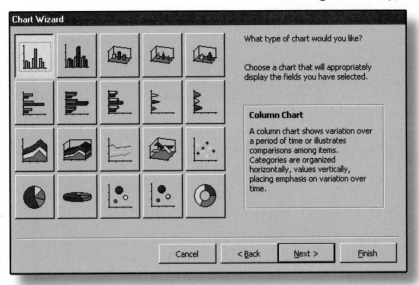

FIGURE 6-9
Determining the layout of the chart

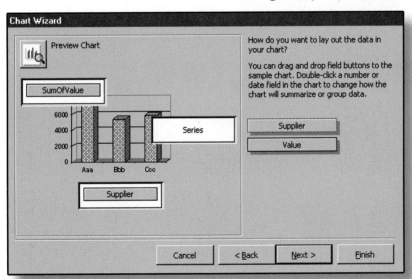

(continued on next page)

FIGURE 6-10
Linking chart data to field data

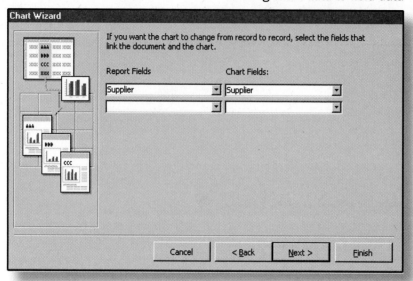

FIGURE 6-11
Entering a title for the chart

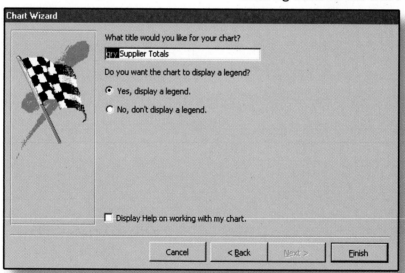

Creating and Modifying a Report in Design View

Instead of using the Report Wizard to create a report, you can design it from scratch in the Design view. Access provides you with a number of tools and options for designing reports that are attractive and easy to read and interpret. You can rearrange the order of fields, change field names, add and delete fields, insert graphics and text, and add title pages, headers, and footers.

You can also add a subreport to a main report. You learned in Lesson 3 how to insert a subform in a main form so that you could display related records from another table. The concept works the same in reports. When the main report and subreport are synchronized, selecting a record in the main report displays the corresponding record(s) in the subreport.

STEP-BY-STEP ▷ 6.6

1. Open the **AA Step6-6** database from the student data files.

2. Click **Reports** on the Objects bar, and then double-click **Create report in Design view**.

3. Place your mouse pointer in a blank area outside the Detail section of the report but within the Report window, and *right*-click. Choose **Properties** on the shortcut menu.

4. In the dialog box, select the **All** tab, if necessary. Click in the **Record Source** text box, click the down arrow, and select **Orders**. You will use the Orders table to create the report.

5. Close the Report Properties dialog box. A window containing the fields in the Orders table should be displayed.

6. Place your mouse pointer over the **Order Number** field and drag it to the intersection of the 1-inch marks on the horizontal and vertical rulers. Then, drag the **Customer Name** field and position it beneath the Order Number field.

Finally, position the **Employee Number** field below the Customer Name field.

7. Now, customize the report's header section. Open the **View** menu and select **Report Header/Footer**. You should now see these sections in the Design view.

8. Click the **Label** button in the Toolbox and then click in the **Report Header** section.

9. Key **Orders** and press **Enter**. You should see selection handles around this box. If not, click on the label box to select it.

10. Click the **Bold** button on the Formatting toolbar. Then, click the down arrow on the **Font Size** button and choose **16**. To automatically increase the size of the label box, double-click the middle right selection handle.

11. To insert a graphic, click the **Unbound Object Frame** button in the Toolbox and draw a box in the upper left corner of the Detail section that's about 1 inch tall and 2

(continued on next page)

inches wide. The Insert Object dialog box should open.

12. Click **Microsoft Clip Gallery** in the Object Type list box and click **OK**.

13. Choose any piece of clip art you like and click **OK**.

14. To modify the graphic so it fits in the box you drew, *right*-click on the box and choose **Properties** on the shortcut menu.

15. With the **All** tab selected, click in the **Size Mode** text box, click the down arrow, and choose **Zoom**. Close the Properties dialog box and view the results.

16. Save the report as **Orders**.

17. Place your mouse pointer on the top edge of the **Page Footer** band. When it becomes a two-headed arrow, drag the band down about 2 inches to increase the size of the Detail section.

18. Click the **Subform/Subreport** button in the Toolbox and draw a box below the field names in the Detail section that's about 2 inches tall and 3 inches wide. When you release the mouse button, the SubReport Wizard opens with step-by-step instructions for creating a subreport.

19. The **Use existing Tables and Queries** option should be selected. Click **Next**.

20. If necessary, click the down arrow on the **Tables/Queries** box and select **Order Details**.

21. Click the double arrow to add all the fields in the Available Fields list box to the Selected Fields box. Click **Next**.

22. Now you will *synchronize* your report. Click **Choose from a list** if necessary, and **Show Order Details for each record in Orders using Order Number**. This will display the corresponding record in the subreport when an order number is selected in the main report. Click **Next**.

23. The name **Order Details subreport** should appear as the name for the subreport. Click **Finish**.

24. Click on the **Order Details subreport** label box that appears above the subreport and then press the **Delete** key to delete this text box.

25. Click the **View** button to preview the report.

26. Save the report and then print it.

27. Close the report and the database file.

Summary

In this lesson, you learned:

■ Reports are characterized by bound, unbound, and calculated controls. Bound controls are tied to a field in the table or query on which the report is based. Unbound controls are not tied to a field. For example, a graphic inserted on a report is an example of an unbound field. A calculated control is an unbound control that contains the result of an expression or formula.

■ A report header appears once on the first page of the report. You can create a title page for a report by inserting a page break after the Report Header section of the report.

■ A report footer appears once on the last page of a report, and a page footer appears at the bottom of each page in a report. Footers typically contain information such as the name of the report, the author of the report, page numbers, and the date the report was created.

■ You can add a chart to a report to graphically illustrate data. You can modify a chart in the Design view. First double-click the chart to make it active. Then *right*-click the part you want to modify and select the Format command on the shortcut menu.

■ Creating a report from scratch in Design view gives you optimum flexibility in the design and appearance of the report.

LESSON 6 REVIEW QUESTIONS

TRUE/FALSE

Circle T if the statement is true or F if the statement is false.

T F 1. An unbound control displays information that is not tied to a table or query.

T F 2. You click the Label button in the Toolbox to add a field from an underlying table or query to a report.

T F 3. A calculated control is an example of an unbound control.

T F 4. You cannot change the properties of a bound control.

T F 5. A report footer appears at the bottom of every page in a report.

Write a brief answer to the following questions.

1. What is an unbound calculated control? What could it be used for?

   creates a text box that displays the result of a calculation using one or more field from tables

2. Where do you add the expression in an unbound calculated control?

   in the control box (text box) in design view

3. In a report, where will the page footer print?

   end of each page

4. In what view must you be to change the properties of a report? Explain two ways for displaying the properties of a control.

   design view

   1. design view - select the control box and right-click to display the context menu select properties.

   2. design view - select the control then from menu select properties. (formatting toolbar)

5. How would you select an entire report?

from design view click in upper left gray box and black dot in this box indicates the entire report is selected.

LESSON 6 PROJECT

Start here on 6-24-04

PROJECT 6-1

1. Open the **AA Project6-1** database from the student data files.

2. Create a report with the Report Wizard using **qry Customers by State**.

3. Include all four fields and group the data by state. Use the **Outline 1** layout with the **Formal** style.

4. Title the report **Customers by State**.

5. Create an unbound calculated control that multiplies the price by the stock on hand. (You may need to make room for the new control on your report.)

6. Format the new control for currency.

7. Label the unbound calculated control **Inventory Value**.

8. Delete the lines in the **State Header** section. Make any other modifications to the report's design that you think will enhance its appearance.

9. Print the report. Then close the database.

completed 6-24 1:40

SCANS

ACTIVITY 6-1

You are the manager for a pet supply company that is undergoing a merger. The owners of the company want you to give them some information about sales and product prices in a report. They ask you to create a report that shows the total transactions for the entire month. Use the **AA Activity6-1** database in the student data files. You will need to create a query that groups and sums the products sales. Then create the report from this query.

ACTIVITY 6-2

SCANS

Your company, the Make-It-Yourself Pizza Parlor, is experiencing an increase in sales due to the popularity of the make-it-yourself concept. You've kept track of the information for your company in an Access database. You decide that you would like to illustrate your sales data in a report that includes a chart. Use Access's Help system to find information on the different types of charts you can create in a report. Write a brief essay outlining how you would proceed in creating a sales report that included a chart.

Adding a chart to a report

1. open the report in Design View.
2. Click Chart on the insert menu.
3. click where the chart will go.
4. follow the Chart Wizard directions
5.

IMPORTING AND EXPORTING DATA

OBJECTIVES

Upon completion of this lesson, you should be able to:

- Explain importing and exporting.
- Import data from other applications.
- Export data to other applications.

⏱ **Estimated Time: 1 hour**

As part of the Microsoft Office suite of applications, Access is designed so that you can easily exchange data with other programs. In this lesson, you will learn how to import data from and export it to other applications. ***Importing*** refers to bringing information from another program into Access. You can also bring information from one Access database into another. Once this data is imported, you can treat it as any other Access data. ***Exporting*** refers to placing Access data into another program or another Access database file.

Importing Data

Access can import and read files created in other programs and saved in different formats. Table 7-1 lists the types of files Access can read.

You can import a file into a table that already exists in Access, or you can import a file and let Access create the table for you. If you have Access create the table, the file will need to be in a database table format with columns, or fields, of data. If the data you're importing is already set up with column names or titles, Access will automatically transfer these to the new table as field names. Otherwise Access will assign numbers for the field names; you simply modify the names in the table's Design view.

TABLE 7-1
Types of files Access can read

PROGRAM	TYPES OF FILES
Microsoft Access database	2.0, 7.0/95, 97, 2000
Microsoft Access project	2000
dBASE	III, III+, IV, and 5 7 (Linking [read/write] requires Borland Database Engine 4.x or later)
Paradox, Paradox for Windows	3.x, 4.x, and 5.0 8.0 (Linking [read/write] requires Borland Database Engine 4.x or later)
Microsoft Excel spreadsheets	3.0, 4.0, 5.0, 7.0/95, 97, and 2000
Lotus 1-2-3 spreadsheets (link is read-only)	.wks, .wk1, .wk3, and .wk4
Microsoft Exchange 　　Delimited text files 　　Fixed-width text files	 All character sets All character sets
HTML	1.0 (if a list); 2.0, 3.x (if a table or list)
SQL tables, Microsoft Visual FoxPro, and data from other programs and databases that support the ODBC protocol	Visual FoxPro 2.x, 3.0, 5.0, and 6.x (import only)

To import data into a database file, open the database file and select the Get External Data command on the File menu. From the submenu, choose Import. Access will take you step-by-step through importing a file.

STEP-BY-STEP ▷ 7.1

1. Open the **AA Step7-1** database from the student data files.

2. Click the **File** menu, choose **Get External Data**, and then select **Import**.

3. In the Import dialog box, click the **Files of type** drop-down arrow and select **Microsoft Excel**.

4. Select the **Sales Personnel** file and click the **Import** button. The Import Spreadsheet Wizard appears, as shown in Figure 7-1. Notice you have the option to import a specific worksheet or a range of data on a worksheet.

FIGURE 7-1

Starting the Import Spreadsheet Wizard

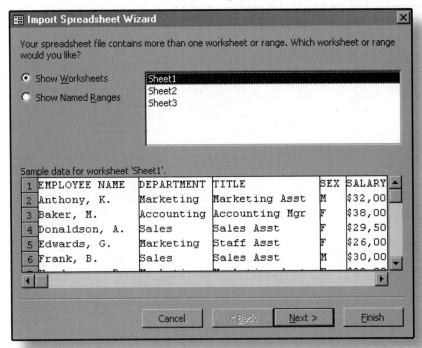

5. Click **Next**. The second dialog box of the Import Spreadsheet Wizard appears, as shown in Figure 7-2. Notice that the first row of the spreadsheet contains column headings (field names).

6. Select **First Row Contains Column Headings** and click **Next**.

7. The next dialog box of the Import Spreadsheet Wizard appears, as shown in Figure 7-3. If necessary, select the **In a New Table** option and click **Next**.

(continued on next page)

FIGURE 7-2
Specifying field names

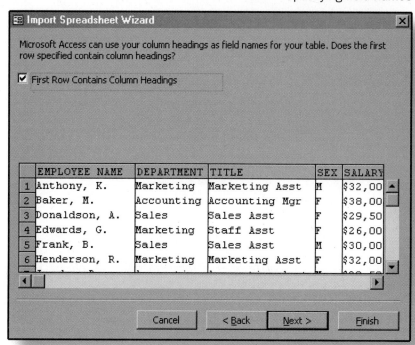

FIGURE 7-3
Placing data

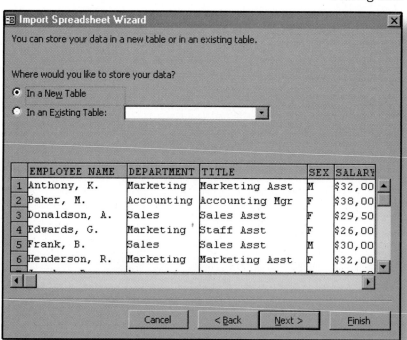

8. In this dialog box (see Figure 7-4), you can specify information about each field, such as its name and the data type. Typically, Access can determine the data type for each field. Click **Next**.

9. The fifth wizard dialog box appears, as shown in Figure 7-5. In this dialog box, you select whether you want Access to assign a primary key field. Choose **Let Access add primary key** and click **Next**.

10. The last dialog box appears, as shown in Figure 7-6. Key **New Sales Department** in the *Import to Table* box.

11. Click **Finish**.

12. You will see a message box letting you know that the import is complete. Click **OK**.

13. Open the **New Sales Department** table and view the results. Your screen should look similar to Figure 7-7.

14. Adjust the column widths in the table, if necessary, and then print it.

15. Close the table and then close the database.

FIGURE 7-4
Setting field names and options

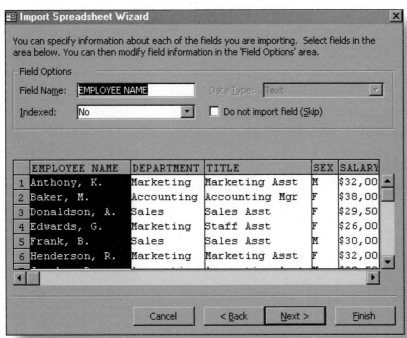

(continued on next page)

AA-89

FIGURE 7-5
Setting a primary key

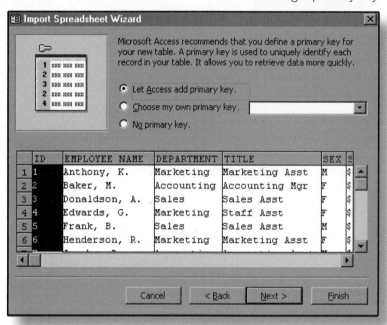

FIGURE 7-6
Identifying the table to contain the imported data

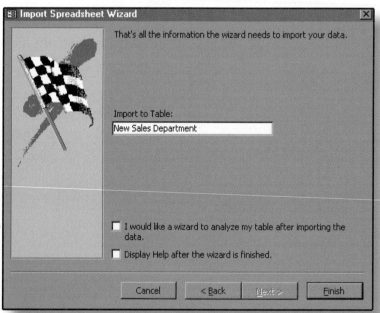

FIGURE 7-7
Excel data imported to a table

ID	EMPLOYEE NA	DEPARTMENT	TITLE	SEX	SALARY	DATE HIRED
1	Anthony, K.	Marketing	Marketing Asst	M	$32,000.00	2/1/89
2	Baker, M.	Accounting	Accounting Mgr	F	$38,000.00	5/26/84
3	Donaldson, A.	Sales	Sales Asst	F	$29,500.00	3/15/91
4	Edwards, G.	Marketing	Staff Asst	F	$26,000.00	8/17/90
5	Frank, B.	Sales	Sales Asst	M	$30,000.00	4/10/88
6	Henderson, R.	Marketing	Marketing Asst	F	$32,000.00	10/24/89
7	Jacobs, D.	Accounting	Accounting Ass	M	$28,500.00	1/20/91
8	Kilpatrick, S.	Legal	Attorney	M	$50,000.00	6/11/87
9	Matthew, H.	Marketing	Marketing Mgr	M	$35,000.00	5/5/90
10	Nicholson, P.	Sales	Staff Asst	F	$25,000.00	12/9/91
11	O'Hara, J.	Sales	Sales Mgr	M	$38,000.00	7/1/84
12	Rose, V.	Legal	Attorney	F	$45,000.00	9/16/88
13	Sanders, N.	Marketing	Marketing Asst	M	$31,500.00	2/10/90
14	Willis, E.	Accounting	Accounting Ass	M	$29,000.00	11/28/89
*	(AutoNumber)					

New Sales Department : Table

Exporting Data to Other Programs

You can also export Access data to other programs. For example, with the compatibility features in Office 2000, you can export an Access table, query, form, or report to Word or Excel.

STEP-BY-STEP 7.2

1. Open the **AA Step7-2** database from the student data files.

2. If necessary, click **Tables** on the Objects bar, and then select the **Employee Information** table.

3. Click the down arrow on the **Office Links** button and then select **Analyze It with MS Excel**. The Excel program opens and the records from the Employee Information table are automatically inserted in a new worksheet. The Excel file is automatically named **Employee Information.xls**.

Hot Tip

You can also use the OfficeLinks button to quickly export Access data to a Word document.

4. Close the **Employee Information.xls** file.

5. Click the **AA Step7-2** button on the taskbar to return to Access. Remain in this screen for the next Step-by-Step.

Linking to Existing Data

You can link data that's shared between Access and Excel, so that changes made to the records in the original application are reflected in the records in the destination application. In other words, if you import data from Excel into an Access table, and then make changes to the data in the Excel worksheet, these changes will automatically be reflected in the Access table.

To link data, select Get External Data on Access's File menu, and then choose **Link Tables** on the submenu. Select the file you want to link and click OK. The Link Spreadsheet Wizard will take you through the process of creating a link to existing data. Once the link is created, a special link icon precedes the table's name in the Access Database window.

Using Drag-and-Drop to Integrate Data

You can also insert records from Access into Excel by using the drag-and-drop method. Make sure both applications are open with the appropriate files opened between which you will share the records. Size and position the application windows so you can see both files on the screen. To do this, simply right-click an empty area on the taskbar, and choose Tile Windows Vertically on the shortcut menu. Select the data you want to move and drag it to the new location. If you want to copy the data rather than move it, make sure you hold down the Ctrl key as you drag and drop.

STEP-BY-STEP ▷ 7.3

1. Start the **Microsoft Excel** program.

2. Switch back to Access and open the **Employee Information** table in the AA Step7-2 database.

3. *Right*-click an empty area on the taskbar and choose **Tile Windows Vertically** on the shortcut menu.

4. Select all the records in the Access table by clicking the **Select All** button located to the left of the *Employee Number* field name.

5. Place your mouse pointer on the border of the selected records. When it turns into the standard arrow pointer shape, press the mouse button, hold down the **Ctrl** key, and drag to cell **A1** in the Excel worksheet. Release the mouse button and then release the **Ctrl** key.

6. Change the column widths in Excel to accommodate the data by placing your mouse pointer over the right border of the column heading (gray area with column letters) and

double-clicking when your mouse pointer turns into a two-headed arrow. You can also adjust row heights by double-clicking the border lines between the row numbers.

7. Save the Excel workbook as **Emp** followed by your initials. Then, click the **Print** button on the toolbar to print the worksheet.

8. Close the Excel workbook file. Then, click the **New** button to open a blank workbook.

9. Now you will use the drag-and-drop method to copy query result records. Switch to Access, close the **Employee Information** table, and then click **Queries** on the **Objects** bar.

10. Open the **Qry-Employee Data and Benefits** query.

11. Select all the records in the query by clicking the **Select All** button located to the left of the *Employee Number* field name.

12. Place your mouse pointer on the border of the selected records. When it turns into the standard arrow pointer shape, press the mouse button, hold down the **Ctrl** key, and drag to cell **A1** in the Excel worksheet. Release the mouse button and then release the **Ctrl** key.

13. Change the column widths in Excel to accommodate the data by placing your mouse pointer over the right border of the column heading (gray area with column letters) and double-clicking when your mouse pointer turns into a two-headed arrow. You can also adjust row heights by double-clicking the border lines between the row numbers.

14. Save the Excel workbook as **EmpDandB** followed by your initials. Click the **Print** button on the toolbar to print the worksheet.

15. Close the Excel workbook and exit Excel. Switch back to Access and maximize the window, close the query, and then close the database.

Summary

In this lesson, you learned:

■ Importing refers to bringing data from other Access databases or applications into Access. The Import Wizard takes you step-by-step through the process of importing data.

■ You can easily export Access data to another application, such as Microsoft Word or Excel, using the OfficeLinks button, or the drag-and-drop method.

LESSON 7 REVIEW QUESTIONS

TRUE/FALSE

Circle T if the statement is true or F if the statement is false.

T F **1.** You can import Lotus files into Access.

T F **2.** Importing refers to moving or copying Access information to another application, such as Microsoft Word.

T F **3.** You can import files that Access does not recognize, but you cannot use the Import Wizard to bring them into Access.

T F **4.** When you export a file, the file is placed in Windows Explorer until the export is complete.

T F **5.** When you import data into an Access table, the data being imported must already have column names.

OBDC - open database connectivity - protocol for accessing info from SQL servers!

WRITTEN QUESTIONS

Write a brief answer to the following questions.

1. When importing data into an Access table, what must you know about the first row of information in the imported data?

   if first row has column headings then access can use as field name. If this isn't the case then field names can be assigned.

2. When importing spreadsheet information, such as from Excel, can you specify which information you want to import, or do you have to import the entire spreadsheet?

   a specified part of the data can be imported

3. List two types of file formats that can be imported into Access.

   HTML, ODBC

4. Can you export Access data into a form letter in Word?

   yes

5. What applications does the OfficeLinks button allow you to quickly export Access data to?

   word + excel

PROJECT 7-1

1. Open the **AA Project7-1** database file.

2. Import the **Accounting Department** file into Access as a table. The Accounting Department file is a spreadsheet in Excel.

3. Let Access set the primary key field for you and name the table **Accounting Department**.

4. Adjust column widths in the table, if necessary. Then print the table.

5. Close the database file.

completed 6-28-04

CRITICAL THINKING

SCANS

ACTIVITY 7-1

You are the database administrator for the Last Resort Sales Company. You want to import a file from Excel into Access. Once this spreadsheet is imported into Access, you will create a report from the new table. Open the **AA Activity7-1** database from the student data files. Import the **Addresses** workbook. Let Access set the primary key field for you and name the table **Addresses**. Name the report you create appropriately. Modify the design of the report as you think is necessary. Then print the report.

ACTIVITY 7-2

Use the Access Help system to find out what types of graphics files you can import into Access. Write a brief essay explaining how the procedure works and give a couple of examples of when you would want to import a graphics file.

CREATING MACROS AND SWITCHBOARDS

OBJECTIVES

Upon completion of this lesson, you should be able to:

- Discuss the purpose of macros.

- Create and run a macro.

- Edit a macro.

- Add macro buttons to a form.

- Create a switchboard.

- Create a conditional macro.

- Add macro actions to a single condition.

- Use the Macro Builder.

⏱ Estimated Time: 1.5 hours

A macro is a handy tool you use to automate tasks you perform in Access. You may have used macros in other computer programs, and you'll find that they work in basically the same way: You record a set of commands in a macro; then to complete the task, you simply run the macro instead of executing the individual commands. In this lesson, you will learn how to create macros using the predesigned macros available in Access. You will also learn how to set up a switchboard. A switchboard utilizes macros to make moving around and working in a database a simple operation, even for the novice user.

Creating a Basic Macro

A *macro* is a set of actions necessary to complete a certain task. For example, you may use a form frequently, and every time you open this form, you need to go to a new record to begin entering record information. It can be time consuming to do these same steps over and over each time you need to enter new records. With a macro, these steps are recorded as a single operation. All you have to do is run the macro to automatically open the form and go to a new record.

You create a macro in the Macro Design window. See Figure 8-1. In the Action column, you determine the "actions" that you want the macro to perform. If you want to make a note as to why you selected a certain action or what you intend for this action to do, you can enter this information in the Comment column. In the Action Arguments section, you can apply more specific directions for each action.

After you create and save the macro, you run it by clicking the Run button in the Design window. You can also run a macro directly from the Database window by selecting it and then clicking the Run button. Or you can simply double-click the macro's name in the Database window. Let's review how to create and run a macro.

FIGURE 8-1
Macro Design window

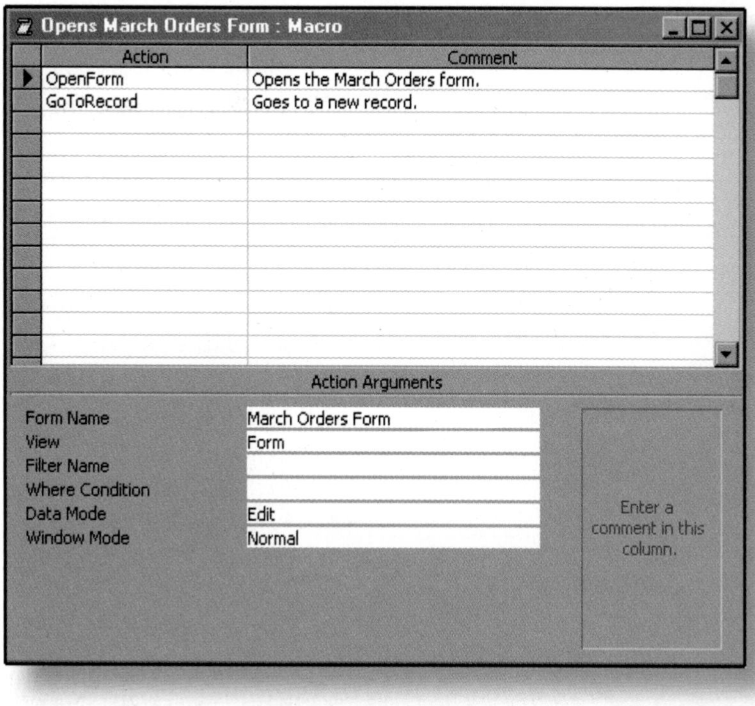

STEP-BY-STEP ▷ 8.1

1. Open the **AA Step8-1** database from the student data files.

2. Click **Macros** in the Objects bar.

3. Click the **New** button.

4. If necessary, click in the first row of the **Action** column, click the down arrow, and then select **OpenForm** from the *Action* list.

5. Click in the **Comment** box for this action and key **Opens the March Orders form**.

6. Click in the **Form Name** box in the *Action Arguments* section, click the down arrow, and then select **March Orders Form** from the list.

7. Click in the **Data Mode** box, click the down arrow, and then select **Edit**. This allows you to edit or add new records to the form after it is opened. You will not change the other Action Arguments.

8. In the second row of the *Action* column, click the down arrow and select **GoToRecord** from the *Action* list.

(continued on next page)

9. For the comment, key **Goes to a new record**.

10. Click the **Object Type** box in the *Action Arguments* section and click the down arrow.

11. Select **Form** from the list.

12. For the **Object Name** action argument, click the down arrow, and select **March Orders Form** from the list.

13. For the **Record** action argument, click the down arrow and select **New** from the list.

14. Click the **Save** button, enter **Open March Orders Form** for the macro name, and click **OK**. You have just created a macro that will open the March Orders Form and go to a new record. Your screen should look similar to Figure 8-1.

15. Click the **Run** button. The form should open automatically and a new record data should be displayed, as shown in Figure 8-2.

16. Close the form.

17. The next two macros you create will be used in the switchboard you create at the end of this lesson. Do not try to run these macros at this time. First create a macro that will close **March Orders Form**. Click **Macros** in the Objects bar, and then click the **New** button.

18. If necessary, click in the first row of the **Action** column, click the down arrow, and then select **Close** from the *Action* list.

19. Click in the **Comment** box for this action and key **Closes an object**.

20. Click the **Save** button and enter **Close** for the macro name. Close the Macro Design window.

21. Select **Macros** in the Objects bar, if necessary, and click the **New** button.

FIGURE 8-2
Opening the March Orders Form with a macro

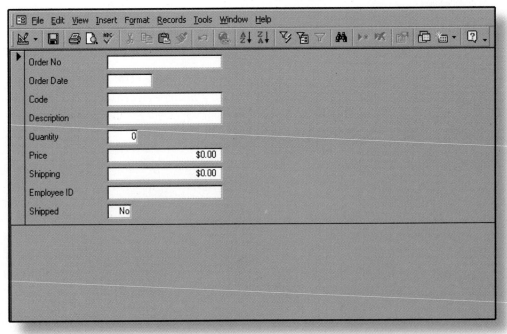

22. If necessary, click in the first row of the **Action** column, click the down arrow, and then select **Quit** from the Action list.

23. Click in the **Comment** box for this action and key **Closes the Access program**.

24. Click the **Save** button and enter **Exit Access** for the macro name. Close the Macro Design window and remain in this screen for the next Step-by-Step.

Editing a Macro

You can easily modify a macro in the Macro Design window. Simply add or delete actions and change the Action Arguments as necessary. Then make sure you save the changes to the macro.

STEP-BY-STEP ▷ 8.2

1. Display the **Open March Orders Form** macro in the Macro Design window. Let's add a third action.

2. Click in the third Action row, click the down arrow, and choose **Maximize**. This action will maximize the form when you open it. Your macro design should look similar to Figure 8-3.

3. Click **Save** and close the Macro Design window.

4. Run the macro from the Database window.

5. Close **March Orders Form** and remain in this screen for the next Step-by-Step. If necessary, click the **Restore** button in the Database window.

FIGURE 8-3
Modifying a macro

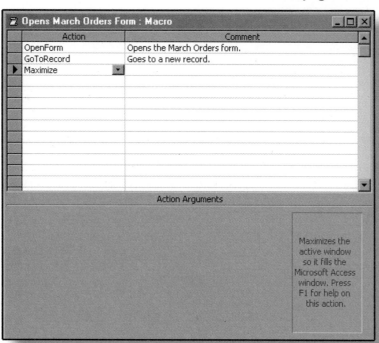

Creating a Macro Button in a Form

You can represent a macro as a button in a database form or report. For example, you might create a macro that prints and closes a report. You could insert a button for this macro directly in the report's Design view. All you have to do is click the button and the report will print and then close.

To create a button, simply drag the macro from the Database window to the object in which you want to place it. The button is named according to the macro name.

Hot Tip

If you cannot see the full name of the macro in the button, simply place your mouse pointer over the right-middle selection handle until it turns into a double-headed arrow. Then double-click.

S TEP-BY-STEP ▷ 8.3

1. You will now add a macro button for the **Close** macro in March Orders Form. Open **March Orders Form** in Design view. If necessary, widen the **Details** section by about an inch.

2. Redisplay the Database window and make sure **Macros** is selected in the Objects bar. Resize the March Orders Form window and the Database window so they are side by side, as shown in Figure 8-4.

FIGURE 8-4
Creating a macro button

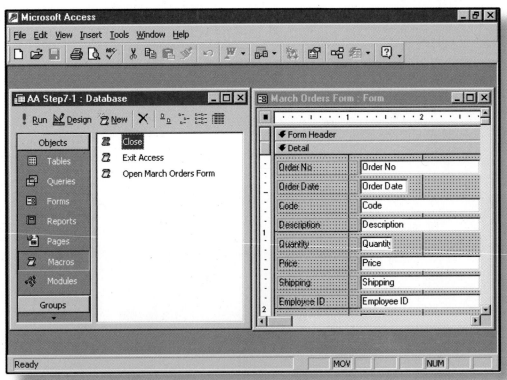

3. In the Database window, press and hold down your mouse button and drag the **Close** macro to the right of the field names in the **Detail** section of March Orders Form. See Figure 8-5.

4. Maximize the **March Orders Form** window and then switch to **Form** view. Navigate through various forms. The Close button should appear on each form.

5. Go to record **4** and print it. Then click the **Close** button to close the form. If you are asked if you want to save changes to the design of the form, click **Yes**. Remain in this screen for the next Step-by-Step.

FIGURE 8-5
Form with macro button

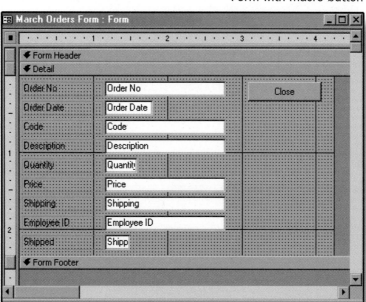

Creating a Switchboard

A switchboard is a powerful feature in Access in that it serves as the "command center" for working with your database objects. It's different from the Database window in that it generally contains macro buttons that let you open, close, and perform various other actions on database objects simply by clicking a single button.

You set up a switchboard on a form. Create a new form in Design view and move macros from the Database window to the switchboard, just as you did in the previous Step-by-Step. As you can imagine, a switchboard is a useful tool for novice users of a database who aren't familiar with the various database objects or how to work with them.

C

1. Open a new form in Design view.

2. Select **Macros** in the Objects bar in the Database window and then adjust the Form window and the Database window until they are side-by-side as shown in Figure 8-6.

3. Drag the **Open March Orders Form** macro to the form's **Detail** section.

4. Drag the **Exit Access** macro to the form's **Detail** section.

5. Maximize the Form window. Then adjust the size of the macro buttons on the form so you can see the full name of each.

6. Save the form as **Switchboard**. Your screen should look similar to Figure 8-7.

7. Switch to Form view and click the **Open March Orders Form** macro button.

8. Close **March Orders Form** and the **Switchboard** form. Remain in this screen for the next Step-by-Step.

FIGURE 8-6
Creating a switchboard

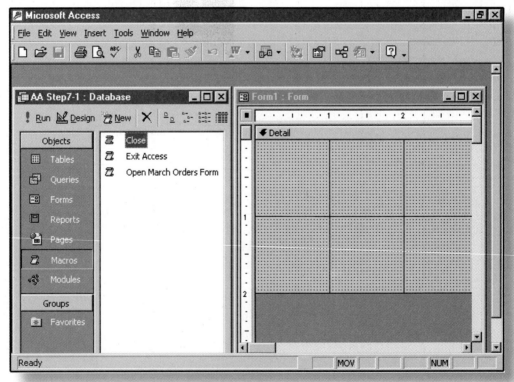

ADVANCED MICROSOFT ACCESS

FIGURE 8-7
Switchboard form

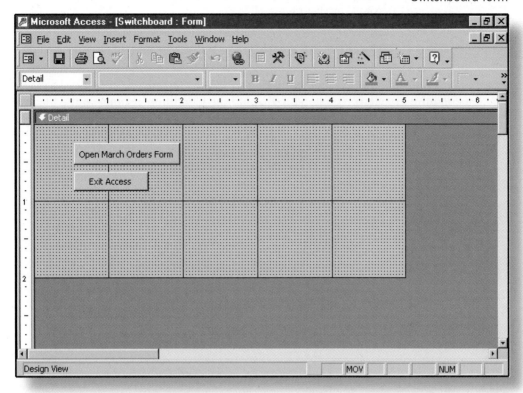

Creating an Autoexec Macro

You can create a macro that automatically opens the switchboard form when you open the database. To create such a macro, you select the object you want to open in the macro Design window, and you save it using the name "autoexec."

Hot Tip

Each database file can have only one autoexec macro.

S TEP-BY-STEP ▷ 8.5

1. In the Objects bar, click **Macros** and then click **New**.

2. Click in the first Action cell and select **OpenForm**.

3. In the argument section, select **Switchboard** from the *Form Name* drop-down list.

4. Click in the second Action cell, click the down arrow, and choose **Maximize**.

5. Save the macro as **autoexec**.

6. Close the macro and then close the database file.

7. Open the database file. The Switchboard form should open automatically.

8. Click the **Exit Access** button to exit Access.

A A - 1 0 3

Creating Conditional Macros

You can design a macro that will run only if a condition is true. If the condition tests false, the action will not take place. This is called a *conditional macro*. For example, you could create a macro in which a message box displays if a certain value is entered in a specified field. Suppose you want to remind employees to mail out a new products brochure to any customer placing an order for a new product.

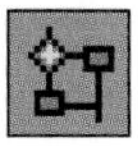

To create a conditional macro, you need to display the Condition column in the macro Design window. Click the Conditions button in the Design view. A Condition column now appears to the left of the Action column in the upper pane. Enter an expression that you want Access to test as either true or false in the Condition column. Select the action you want the macro to execute if the condition is true, and enter a comment describing the action, if desired. An example of a conditional macro is shown in Figure 8-8.

FIGURE 8-8
Conditional macro

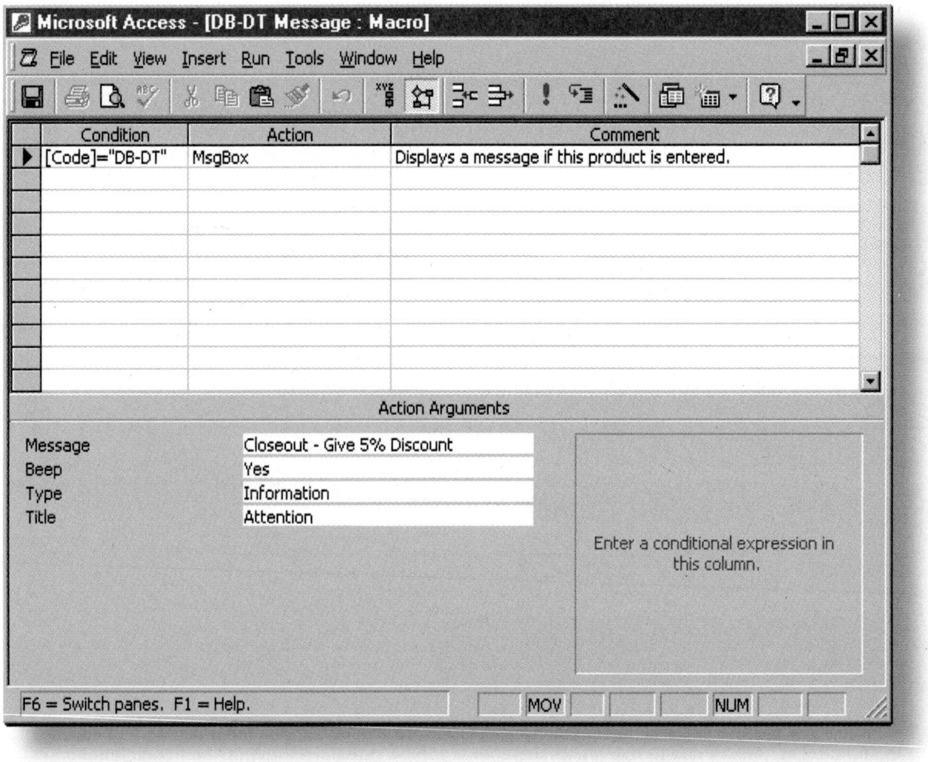

In this example, if the data entered in the field named "Code" is *DB-DT*, then a message box will be displayed to indicate that this is a closeout product and the customer is entitled to a discount.

Once you've created a conditional macro, you attach it to a field in a form by entering it in one of the field's *event properties*. Every time an action occurs, such as selecting the field, entering data into the field, or exiting the field, Access will look to see if there is a conditional macro action associated with the field. For example, if you want the macro to run after you have entered data into the field and before you exit the field, you would select the On Exit event. The macro would run as you leave this field if the condition of the macro is met. Event properties are described in Table 8-1.

TABLE 8-1
Event properties

Lesson ⑧ Creating Macros and Switchboards

EVENT	DESCRIPTION OF EVENT
Before Update	Occurs after information in a record is changed but before saving it
After Update	Occurs after information in a record is changed and saved
On Change	Occurs when a value is changed
On Enter	Occurs as you select a field
On Exit	Occurs before leaving a field
On Got Focus	Occurs when a field is selected
On Lost Focus	Occurs when a field is exited or another field is selected
On Click	Occurs when a mouse button is clicked over the object
On Dbl Click	Occurs when a mouse button is clicked twice over the object
On Mouse Down	Occurs when a mouse button is pressed
On Mouse Move	Occurs whenever a mouse is moved over the object
On Mouse Up	Occurs when a mouse button is released
On Key Down	Occurs when a key is pressed in a field
On Key Press	Occurs when a key is pressed and released in a field

S TEP-BY-STEP ▷ 8.6

1. Open the **AA Step8-6** database from the student data files.

2. Click **Macros** in the Objects bar, if necessary, and then click the **New** button.

3. Click the **Conditions** button to add the Condition column.

4. Click the first **Condition** cell and key **[Code]= "DB-DT"**.

5. Click the first **Action** cell, click the down arrow, and select **MsgBox**.

6. Click the first **Comment** cell and enter **Displays a message if this product is entered**.

7. Click in the **Message** argument box and key **Closeout - Give 5% Discount**.

(continued on next page)

8. In the **Beep** argument box, click the down arrow and select **Yes**. This means a beep will sound if the condition is met.

9. In the **Type** argument box, click the down arrow and select **Information**. This indicates the type of message box that will display when the condition is met.

10. In the **Title** argument box, key **Attention**. This will display in the title bar of the message box.

11. Save the macro as **DB-DT Message**. Your screen should look similar to Figure 8-8. Close the macro Design window.

12. To attach this macro to a form, click **Forms** in the Object bar.

13. Click the **February Orders Entry Form** and click the **Design** button.

14. *Right*-click the text box (this is the box on the right of the control) for the **Code** field to display the shortcut menu. Select **Properties**.

15. Click the **Event** tab, click the **On Exit** box, and click the down arrow.

16. Click the **DB-DT Message** macro. This attaches the conditional macro to the **Code** field. Now, if the conditions of the macro are met as a person leaves the **Code** field, the macro action will be performed. Your screen should look similar to Figure 8-9.

17. Close the Properties dialog box. Click the **Save** button.

18. To test the macro, switch to Form view.

FIGURE 8-9
Attaching the conditional macro to a field

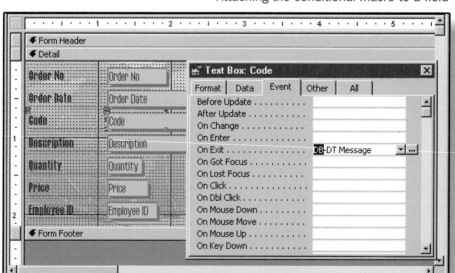

19. Enter the following record. The message box shown in Figure 8-10 will be displayed when you attempt to exit the Code field. Click **OK** to close the message box.

Order No.: 3090
Order Date: 3/14/2000
Code: DB-DT
Description: Introduction to Databases
Quantity: 200
Price: $15.95
Employee ID: N175

20. Print the form for the new record. Close the form. Remain in this screen for the next Step-by-Step.

FIGURE 8-10
Conditional macro message box

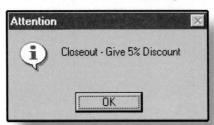

Attention

 Closeout - Give 5% Discount

OK

Extra Challenge

For the preceding Step-by-Step, create a calculated field in the **February Orders Entry Form** that calculates a 5% discount on the **Price** field. This way, when the message box appears, the data entry person will know to invoice the customer for the discounted price rather than the regular price.

Adding Actions to a Condition

You can design a conditional macro so that more than one action takes place if the condition tests true. For example, using the example you have been working with in this section, you might want the message box to display for items to be discounted *and* you might want the price automatically adjusted for the discount. You can easily link a series of actions to a single condition in the macro Design window. In the row directly beneath the existing condition, type an ellipsis (...) in the *Condition* column. Then specify the subsequent action in the *Action* column. Enter a comment for the action, if desired, and specify its arguments. Figure 8-11 shows an example of two actions applied to a single condition. You can add as many actions as you want to a condition.

In this example, if the item code entered is *DB-DT*, then the first message box will be displayed, explaining that this item is discontinued. When you click on OK in this message box, another message box then will be displayed, indicating that the item code for the replacement item is *BP-RR*.

FIGURE 8-11
Two actions for a condition

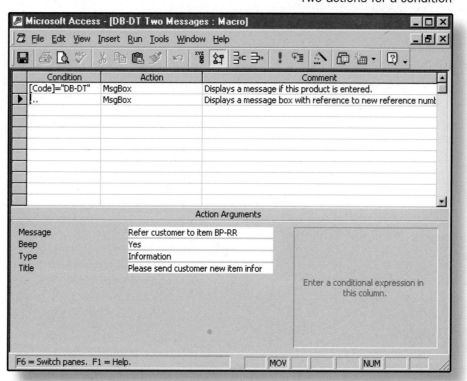

STEP-BY-STEP ▷ 8.7

1. Click **Macros** on the Object bar, if necessary.

2. Click the **DB-DT Message** macro and then click the **Design** button.

3. In the second **Condition** cell, key **...** (an ellipsis).

4. In its **Action** cell, click the down arrow and select **MsgBox**.

5. For its comment, key **Displays a message box with reference to new reference number**.

6. Click the **Message** argument box and key **Refer customer to item BP-RR**.

7. In the **Beep** argument box, click the down arrow and select **Yes**.

8. In the **Type** argument box, click the down arrow and select **Information**.

9. In the **Title** argument box, key **Please send customer new item information**.

10. Save the macro as **DB-DT Two Messages**. Then close the macro.

11. Open **January Orders Entry Form** and attach the **DB-DT Two Messages** macro to the **On Exit** event property for the **Code** field just as you did in the preceding Step-by-Step in *February Orders Entry Form*.

12. Switch to Form view and enter the following new record. When you press Enter after entering the code, the first message box is displayed. When you click **OK**, the second message box will display. Click **OK**.

Order No.: 3091
Order Date: 1/15/2000
Code: DB-DT
Description: Introduction to Databases
Quantity: 19
Price: $15.95
Employee ID: N175

13. Print the form for the new record. Then close the form and the database.

Using the Macro Builder

Access has a helpful feature called the Macro Builder that lets you create a macro as you work with a form or other object. In the object's Design view, open the Properties dialog box for the field to which you want to apply the macro. Select the Event tab in the dialog box, and then click the Build button at the end of the event text box. Once you open the Macro Builder, you will notice that it looks identical to the macro design window. When you have "built" the macro, you are returned to the object's Design view.

S TEP-BY-STEP ▷ 8.8

1. Open the **AA Step8-8** database from the student data files. Then, open the **Order Details** form in Design view.

2. *Right*-click the **Product ID** text box, and select **Properties** on the shortcut menu.

3. Click the **Event** tab and then click in the **On Exit** box. Click the **Build** button (…), select **Macro Builder**, and click **OK**.

4. Save the macro as **New Product** and click **OK**.

5. Click the **Conditions** button to add the Condition column.

6. Click in the first cell of the **Condition** column and type **[Product ID]="32"**

7. Click in the first **Action** cell and choose **MsgBox**.

8. Click in the **Message** text box in the Action Arguments pane, and key **Please send new product information!**

(continued on next page)

9. Click in the **Type** Action Arguments box, click the down arrow, and choose **Information**.

10. Click in the **Title** Action Arguments box and key **New Product**.

11. Click the **Save** button, and then close the macro design window. You are returned to the form Design view. Close the Text Box Properties dialog box.

12. To see how this macro works, click the **Save** button and then click the **View** button.

13. Click the **New Record** button and enter the following data:

    Order Number   2005
    Product ID   32 (The message box should display when you attempt to exit the field. Click **OK**.)
    Selling Price $17.95

14. Close the form and then close the database.

Summary

In this lesson, you learned:

■ A macro lets you automate frequently performed tasks. To create a macro, simply select the actions you want the macro to perform and then save the macro.

■ You can modify the actions in a macro by opening it in the Design window. Make sure you save the macro after you've modified it.

■ Macros can be displayed as a button placed on a form or report. Simply drag the macro from the Database window to the Design view of the object in which you want the button to appear.

■ A switchboard serves as the "command center" for a database. It is typically set up as a form that contains macro buttons allowing the user of the database to execute certain actions at the click of a button.

■ A conditional macro will run only if a condition tests true. You can apply a number of actions to a single condition.

LESSON 8 REVIEW QUESTIONS

TRUE/FALSE

Circle T if the statement is true or F if the statement is false.

T F 1. You can only create macros to perform actions on database forms and reports.

T **F** 2. You would use the OpenForm macro action to automatically open any database object.

T F 3. You can run a macro directly from the Database window.

T F 4. You can represent a macro with a button in forms and reports.

T F 5. A database file can have only one macro named "autoexec."

WRITTEN QUESTIONS

Write a brief answer to the following questions.

1. What is a macro?

   a set of instructions that will run when a condition is met on a form or report or when Run Macro is clicked. Can also run by double-clicking the macro name.

2. Why would you want to enter comments for an action in the macro Design window?

   to help document why & what this action.

3. List the steps for creating a macro.

   Select Macro Object, New, Select Action, Comment, Specify Arguments

4. Describe two methods for running a macro.

1. from database view click "Tools", "Macro", "Run Macro" select the macro, click "OK"

2. Create a Macro Object for a form button. click the button,

5. After a macro is created and saved, can changes be made to the macro? Explain.

yes, highlight the name of the macro select design view

LESSON 8 PROJECTS

PROJECT 8-1

1. Open the **AA Project8-1** database from the student data files.

2. View the **Dairy and Grains** form and the **Discontinued Items** form.

3. Create a macro that opens each form in Form view and maximizes the form window.

4. Save the macros as **Open Dairy Form and Maximize** and **Open Discontinued Form and Maximize**.

5. Run the macros.

6. Close the forms. Remain in this screen for Project 8-2.

PROJECT 8-2

1. In the **AA Project8-1** database file, create a **Close** macro and place it as a button on both the **Dairy and Grains** form and the **Discontinued Items** form.

2. Create another new macro using the GoToRecord action and save it as **New Record**. Place the macro as a button on both the **Dairy and Grains** form and the **Discontinued Items** form.

3. Print the **Dairy and Grains** form. Then close it.

4. Create a switchboard that contains buttons for the **Open Dairy Form and Maximize** macro and the **Open Discontinued Form and Maximize** macro. Save the form as **Switchboard**.

5. Create a macro to exit the Access program. Save it as **Exit Access** and place it as a button on the Switchboard form.

6. Make any modifications you feel are necessary to the **Switchboard** form's design.

7. Create an **autoexec** macro that displays the Switchboard form and maximizes it when the database is opened.

8. Close the database.

PROJECT 8-3

1. Open the **AA Project8-3** database from the student data files.

2. Create a conditional macro that displays an **information** box when the state of **CA** is entered into the **State** field. Enter an appropriate title and message informing the person entering data that a promotional gift should be sent to California customers.

3. Save the macro as **California Promotion.**

4. Attach this macro to the **State** field in the **Promotion List** form and have the macro run as the field is exited.

5. Save the form.

6. Enter a record in the form to test the macro. Make sure you key **CA** in the State field.

7. Print the form. Then close the form and the database file.

Completed 6-30-04

ACTIVITY 8-1

SCANS

As the database administrator for a pet store, you want to provide quick and easy access to the product and transaction information stored in the **AA Activity8-1** database in the student data files. You want people in the company to be able to find a price of a product and to be able to view transactions. Your first task will be to create a form using the **Products** table. Design the form in any manner you feel appropriate. Then create a switchboard in the database file. Be creative in the types of macros you create and the design of the switchboard form.

ACTIVITY 8-2

SCANS

You've been designated to create a database switchboard for your company, One Star Gas Company. Use what you've learned in this lesson and the Access Help system to write a brief essay that explains to novice users of the database how a switchboard works.

WORKING WITH WEB FEATURES

OBJECTIVES

Upon completion of this lesson, you should be able to:

■ Create a hyperlink in a database object.

■ Build data access pages
for use on the Internet.

Estimated Time: 1 hour

Like other Microsoft Office 2000 applications, Access is designed with a number of Web-related features that make it easy for you and other users to work with database information. This lesson focuses on hyperlinks and data access pages.

Creating a Hyperlink

A *hyperlink* represents a direct link between one file and another stored on the same computer, on another computer in a network, or on the Internet. If you've spent any time browsing the Web, you've clicked hyperlinks to jump to different Web sites or pages. The hyperlink actually contains the address of the Web page to which you are jumping. Hyperlinks are easily identified because they normally appear in a different color and are underlined, or the mouse pointer takes on a different shape, like a pointing finger, when you place it on the hyperlink.

You can insert hyperlinks in database objects that link the object to another file. The concept works the same as it does on Web pages. The address contained in the hyperlink might be the URL (Uniform Resource Locator) for a Web page or it might be the path name for another computer file.

1. Open the **AA Step9-1** database from the student data files.

2. Click **Forms** in the Objects bar and then open **March Orders Form** in Design view.

3. Click the **Insert Hyperlink** button on the toolbar. The Insert Hyperlink  dialog box opens, as shown in Figure 9-1. (Your screen may alredy contain links depending on the setup options and the computer you are using.)

4. Click the **File** button to "browse" for the file you want the hyperlink to jump to.

5. Double-click the file **New Products** in the student data files. This is an Excel file that you will jump to when you click the hyperlink.

6. Click **OK**. The hyperlink should be selected in your form.

7. Move the hyperlink to the Form Header section.

8. If necessary, edit the text of the hyperlink so it reads **New Products**. Change the font size of the hyperlink to **18** and change the font color to white. Your screen should look similar to Figure 9-2.

9. Switch to Form view.

10. Place the mouse pointer on the hyperlink in the form. Your cursor should turn into the shape of a pointing hand. Then click. This will open the Microsoft Excel program if it's not already open, and the New Products work-

FIGURE 9-1
Insert Hyperlink dialog box

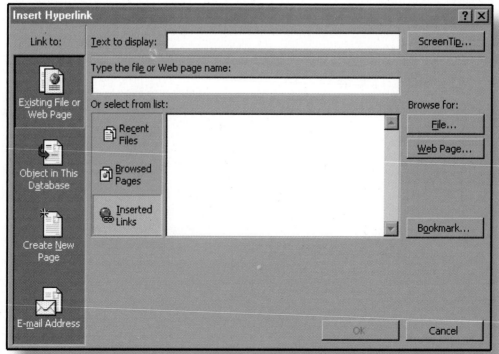

FIGURE 9-2
Formatting the hyperlink

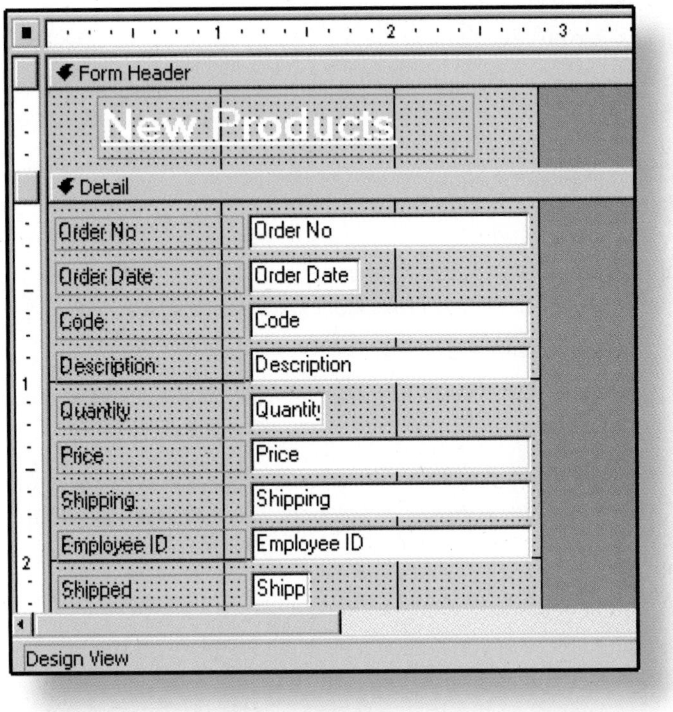

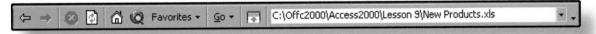

FIGURE 9-3
Web toolbar

C:\Offc2000\Access2000\Lesson 9\New Products.xls

sheet will be displayed. The Web toolbar, shown in Figure 9-3, also displays.

11. Click the **Back** button on the Web toolbar to return to your form.

12. If necessary, display the **Web** toolbar in Access. Click the **Forward** button on the Web toolbar to return to Excel spreadsheet.

13. Close the New Products file and exit Excel.

14. Maximize **March Orders Form** if necessary. Close the **Web** toolbar. Print the first record in **March Orders Form** and then close the database.

> ### Hot Tip
>
> To modify a hyperlink, *right*-click the hyperlink and select **Hyperlink**, **Edit Hyperlink** on the shortcut menu.

Understanding Data Access Pages

Data access pages are a new feature in Access 2000. A ***data access page*** is an object in the database that lets you set up other objects, such as tables, forms, and reports, so that they can be published to the Web. Then Web users can view and work with the data.

Creating Pages

You create a data access page in much the same manner as you create a form or report. You work in the page's Design view to add and manipulate fields and other controls. You can also group and sort the information that appears in a data access page.

There are three methods for creating a data access page:

■ You can use the AutoPage feature. With AutoPage, all you have to do is select a record source, such as a table or query, and then AutoPage automatically creates a data access page using all the fields from this record source.

■ You can use the Page Wizard to design a data access page. The wizard asks you questions about the record source, fields, layout, styles, and formats you want to use and then creates a page based on your selections.

■ You can also convert an existing Web page into a data access page.

Once you've created a page, you can select Web Page Preview on the File menu to start your browser and view the page. In the following Step-by-Step, you'll create a data access page using AutoPage.

S TEP-BY-STEP ▷ 9.2

1. Open the **AA Step9-2** database from the student files.

2. Click **Pages** on the Objects bar and then click **New**.

3. Click the down arrow in the *Choose the table or query* box. Choose the **Book Sales** table.

4. Click **AutoPage: Columnar**. Your screen should look similar to Figure 9-4.

5. Click **OK**. Your screen should look similar to Figure 9-5. Notice the toolbar that displays.

In addition to navigation buttons, the toolbar contains other Access buttons for sorting and filtering data. AutoPage automatically names the page using the table name from which it was created.

6. Close the page. If a message box appears asking if you want to save changes to the page, click **Yes**. Remain in this screen for the next Step-by-Step.

FIGURE 9-4

New Data Access Page dialog box

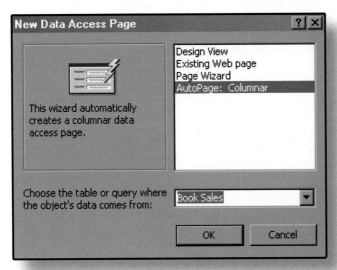

FIGURE 9-5

Data access page

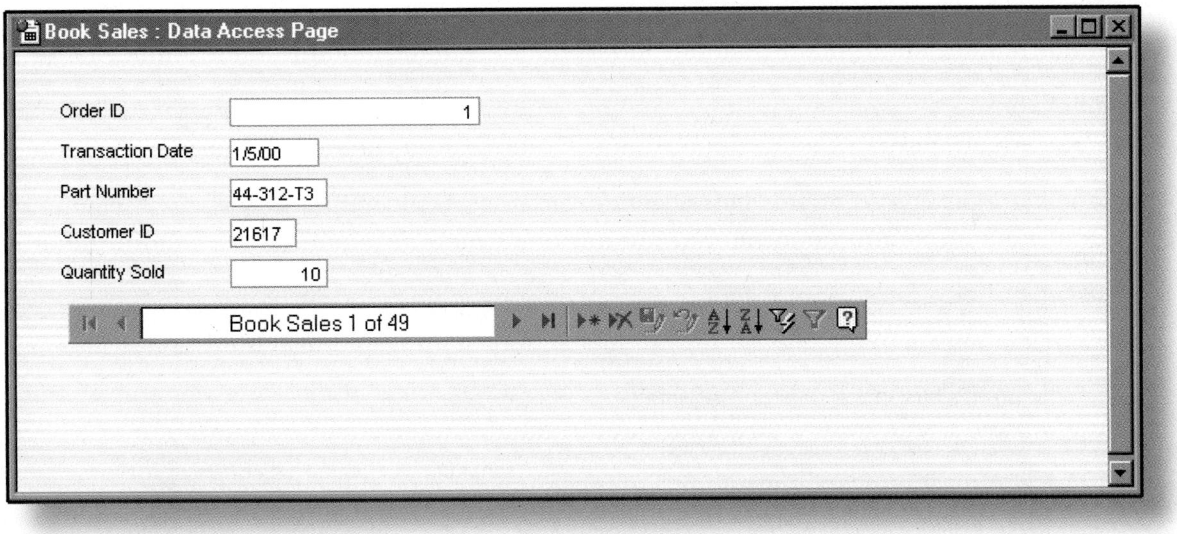

CREATING PAGES WITH THE WIZARD

AutoPage is a suitable tool for quickly creating a data access page using all the fields in the record source. However, you may want a little more flexibility in choosing the fields you want on the page, and you might want to group or sort the page data. The Page Wizard lets you choose the desired fields, the field you would like the page to be grouped by, and how you want the records sorted.

STEP-BY-STEP ▷ 9.3

1. If necessary, click **Pages** on the Objects bar.

2. Double-click **Create data access page by using wizard**. The Page Wizard opens.

3. Click the down arrow in the *Table/Queries* box and select the **Inventory** table.

4. Click the right-pointing double-arrow button to place all the fields in the table in the *Select Fields* box. Your screen should look similar to Figure 9-6.

5. Click **Next**. The Page Wizard asks if you want grouping levels applied. Click the **Part Number** field and click the single right-pointing arrow to group the records by part number. Your screen should look similar to Figure 9-7.

6. Click **Next**. The Page Wizard asks if you want to sort the records. Click the arrow in the first text box and choose **In Stock**. Your screen should look like Figure 9-8.

FIGURE 9-6
Selecting fields to add to the page

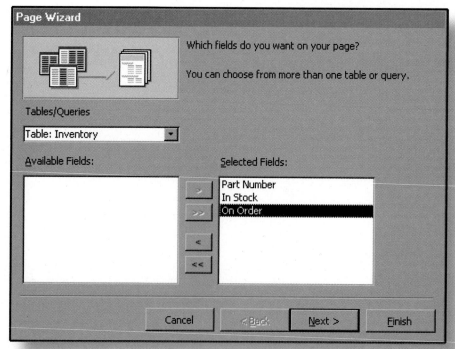

FIGURE 9-7
Choosing a field to group by

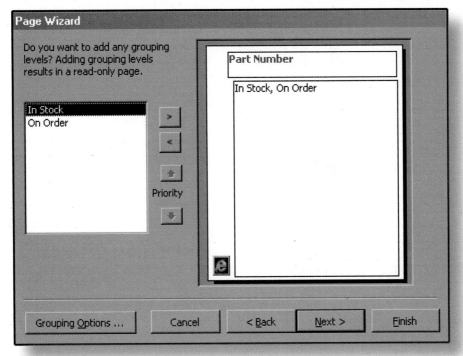

FIGURE 9-8
Choosing a field to sort by

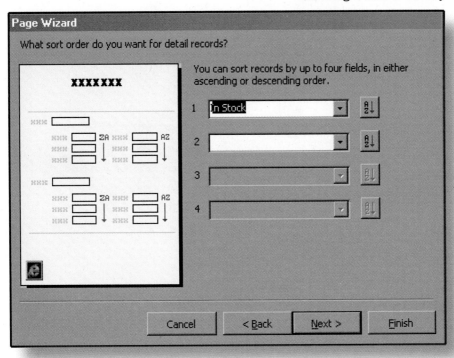

(continued on next page)

7. Click **Next**. The Page Wizard asks you to name the page. Key **In Stock Inventory** in the title box and select the **Open the page** option, if necessary. Your screen should look similar to Figure 9-9.

8. Click **Finish**. Click the **+** button next to *GroupOfInventory-Part Number* to display the field information on the part. Your screen should look similar to Figure 9-10.

9. Use the record movement buttons to move to other records. You can click the **+** button in each record to display the In Stock and On Order information.

10. Close the page. Click **Yes** if you are asked if you want to save design changes and remain in this screen for the next Step-by-Step.

FIGURE 9-9
Naming the data access page

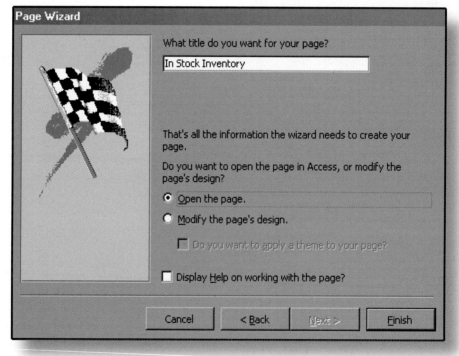

FIGURE 9-10
Completed page

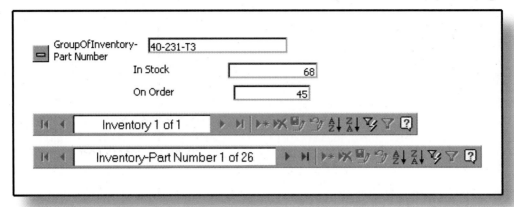

Making Changes to Page Design

You can change a page's design much like you modify the design of a form or report. You can add or remove fields. Fields and controls can be sized and moved and data can be formatted in the same manner. When you place the mouse pointer over a field in the Page Design view, your mouse pointer turns into a four-headed arrow, instead of the two-headed arrow you saw in forms and reports.

STEP-BY-STEP ▷ 9.4

1. If necessary, click **Pages** on the Objects bar, select the **In Stock Inventory**, and then click the **Design** button.

2. Click the **Click here and type title text** and key **Inventory**. Click outside the text area to deselect it.

3. Place your mouse pointer over the right side of the In Stock field and click. Notice how your mouse pointer turns into a four-headed arrow as you move it over the selection handles.

4. Place your mouse pointer over the middle right selection handle. When you see the _two-_ four-headed arrow, press and hold the mouse button down and drag to the right about $1/2$ inch. The In Stock field should be about $1/2$ inch wider than it was before you resized it.

5. You will now move the On Order field. Place your mouse pointer over the right side of the **On Order** field. Press and hold the mouse button down and drag to the right. Notice how both sides of the field control move. Position

(continued on next page)

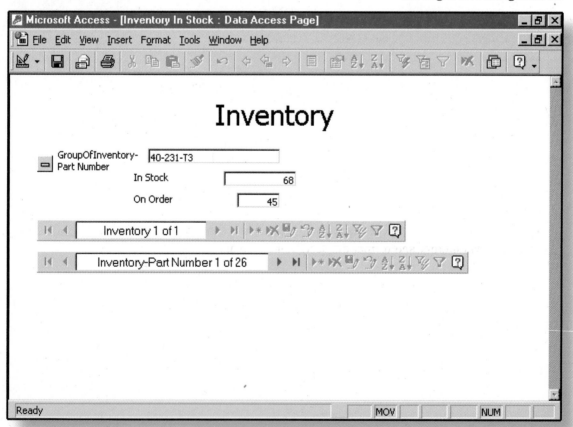

the right box of the control so it is centered under the right box of the In Stock field.

6. Now let's move the left side of the On Order field. Place your mouse pointer over the left side of the **On Order** field, press and hold the mouse button down, and drag until the left side of the On Order box is aligned with the left side of *In Stock*.

7. Click the **View** button to see how your modifications look. If necessary, click the **+** sign. Your screen should look similar to Figure 9-11.

8. Click the **Save** button to save the page. Then select **Web Page Preview** on the **File** menu. This will start Internet Explorer and display the page as it will appear to other users on the Web.

9. Close Internet Explorer. In Access, close the **In Stock Inventory** page and then close the database.

FIGURE 9-11
Moving and resizing controls

Summary

In this lesson, you learned:

■ You can insert hyperlinks in database objects that link the object to another file. The concept works the same as it does on Web pages. The address contained in the hyperlink might be the URL (Uniform Resource Locator) for a Web page or it might be the path name for another computer file.

■ A data access page is an object in the database that lets you set up other objects, such as tables, forms, and reports, so that they can be published to the Web. Other Web users can then view and work with the data. You design and modify data access pages in much the same manner as you would a form or report.

LESSON 9 REVIEW QUESTIONS

TRUE/FALSE

Circle T if the statement is true or F if the statement is false.

T **(F)** 1. A hyperlink in a database object can only link the object to another file on the same computer.

(T) F 2. To insert a hyperlink, you click the Insert Hyperlink button on the Web toolbar.

(T) F 3. You can edit and format a hyperlink once it has been inserted in the object's Design view.

(T) F 4. You can modify and format the design of a data access page just as you would a form or report.

T **(F)** 5. You cannot add fields to a page after it has been created using the Page Wizard.

WRITTEN QUESTIONS

Write a brief answer to the following questions.

1. What is a hyperlink? Why might you want to create one?

   1. An area or text that when clicked will navigate to another file, URL, bookmark.
   2. For easy navigation to other information

2. How do you create a hyperlink?

   from design view select insert hyperlink then complete the information in the "insert hyperlink" dialog box.

3. How can you identify a hyperlink in a file?

   different color and underlined. When cursor goes over it changes to pointing hand.

4. What is the purpose of a page?

   for publishing so that others may use. could be on internet of network,

5. What are the three methods for creating a page?

   Autopage, Page Wizard, convert existing Web Page.

LESSON 9 PROJECTS

PROJECT 9-1

1. Open the **AA Project9-1** database from the student data files.

2. Open the **Products Purchased by Customer** form in Design view.

3. Insert a hyperlink in the Form Header section that jumps to the **Product List** Excel file in the student data files. Edit the label for the hyperlink, if desired.

4. Change the name of the hyperlink label, if desired. Test the hyperlink by moving forward and back between programs.

5. Close the **Product List** file and Excel.

6. Print the first page of the form. Then close the form and the database.

PROJECT 9-2

1. Open the **AA Project9-2** database from the student data files.

2. Create a data access page for the **Products** table. Use the **Product ID**, **Product Name**, **English Name**, and **Units in Stock** fields. Sort by the **English Name** field.

3. Save the page as **Available Products**. View the page on the Web, if desired.

4. Key a title in the page's Design view of **Available Products**.

5. Close the database.

Completed 6-30-04

CRITICAL THINKING

SCANS

ACTIVITY 9-1

You want to create a data access page for your company's intranet that your sales force can access to review transactions. You also want a page that alphabetically lists employees by their last names (and then first names) and their telephone numbers. Use the **AA Activity9-1** database in the student data files to create the pages.

SCANS

ACTIVITY 9-2

Several months ago, you inserted a hyperlink in a database report that jumps to the Web site for one of your company's distributors. Today, you click the hyperlink and you get a message telling you the Web site cannot be found. Write a brief essay that explains what the problem might be.

USING ADVANCED ACCESS TOOLS

OBJECTIVES

Upon completion of this lesson, you should be able to:

- Compact a database.
- Distinguish between encrypting and decrypting a database.
- Secure a database.
- Set a password for a database.
- Set startup options.
- Understand the use of add-ins.

⏱ Estimated Time: 1 hour

Access offers a variety of features that can assist you in managing your database files. In this lesson, you will learn how to compact a fragmented database so that it is stored most efficiently on disk. You will also learn about the various security features you can apply to the information contained in a database. Databases often contain sensitive information, such as employee salaries, so it is important for you to understand how to protect them. Access also comes with a number of "add-in" applications that are designed to give you more control over the objects in the database. These applications are called add-ins because they typically are not included in the standard installation of Access.

Compacting a Database

When you use a database over time or if you delete database objects, your database can become fragmented. *Fragmentation* occurs when parts of the database file become scattered over an area of the disk where the file is stored. This can cause the database to run slower and less efficiently.

Compacting or *defragmenting* a database removes the unused or wasted space within the database file. A database should be compacted on a regular basis. Compacting is also a great method for making a copy of your database. For example, if your database is saved to a shared location, you may want to make a copy of it and store it on your computer's hard drive. This procedure will create a backup of the database on your hard drive.

 Concept Builder

You can convert a database file to a previous version of Access. To convert an opened database file, open the **Tools** menu, choose **Database Utilities**, choose **Convert Database**, and then select **To Prior Access Database Version**. A dialog box opens that asks you to enter a filename for the converted file. Click **Save**.

S TEP-BY-STEP ▷ 10.1

1. Open the **AA Step10-1** database from the student files.

2. Open the **Tools** menu and select **Database Utilities**.

3. Click **Compact and Repair Database**. Your database is now compacted. Close the database.

Hot Tip

To compact a database that isn't open, open the Tools menu in Microsoft Access select Database Utilities. Click Compact Database and Repair Database. In the Database To Compact From dialog box, select the database you want to compact. Click Compact. In the Compact Database Into dialog box, enter a file name for the new compacted file.

Encrypting and Decrypting a Database

E*ncrypting* means to take meaningful information and turn in into scrambled code of some sort. When you encrypt a database, Access compacts the database file and then makes it indecipherable.

Decrypting refers to removing the encryption. The decryption process unscrambles the encryption code so that your database file once again displays meaningful information.

To encrypt or decrypt a database file, open the Tools menu, select Security, and then select Encrypt/Decrypt Database. Then simply follow the directions provided for using this feature.

Hot Tip

Do not encrypt or decrypt a database when it is open. In a multiuser environment, everyone must close the database file before either of these procedures will work.

Securing a Database

M icrosoft Access gives you two methods of securing a database. You can set a password for the database or you can limit what parts of a database can be viewed or changed by setting user-level protection.

Setting a Password

The easiest way to secure a database is to assign a password to the database file. Then when someone tries to open the database file, he or she will need to know the password before it can be opened. You can remove and change a password as well. Open the database using the *Open Exclusive* option in the Open dialog box. Open the Tools menu, select Security, and then select Unset Database Password.

Hot Tip

A password is case sensitive. For example, if you entered **Cat** as your password, you will need to enter **Cat** for the password every time. You could not use **cat**, **CAT**, **cAT**, or any other uppercase/lowercase combination.

C

1. Open the **File** menu, select **Open**, and select the **AA Step10-2** database in the student data files. Click the down arrow on the **Open** button in the lower-right corner and select **Open Exclusive** from the list box.

2. Open the **Tools** menu, select **Security**, and then click **Set Database Password**.

3. In the **Password** box, type **CAT**.

4. In the **Verify** box, type **CAT** again. Your screen should look similar to Figure 10-1.

FIGURE 10-1
Password dialog box

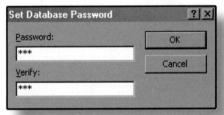

5. Click **OK**. The password is now set. The next time you or anyone else tries to open the database, a password will be required before it will open. Let's try closing and opening this database file.

6. Close the database file.

7. Open the **AA Step 10-2** database file using the **Open Exclusive** option in the Open dialog box. You should see a message box like that shown in Figure 10-2. Key the password and press **OK**.

FIGURE 10-2
Password Required message box

8. Change the database password: Open the **Tools** menu, select **Security**, and then select **Unset Database Password**.

9. Key **CAT** in the Unset Database Password dialog box, and then click **OK**.

10. Close the database and then reopen it. You do not need to enter a password now. Close the data base again.

 **Hot Tip**

If you lose or forget your password, it can't be recovered. You will not be able to open the database file again.

Applying User-Level Security

Another method for securing a database is to set user-level security. Then any individual who wants to use the database is required to enter his or her name and a password when the Access program is started. You typically designate security levels for "users" and "admins." Users are restricted to the information that they can view or change, whereas admins have permission to use all the database objects.

The easiest method for applying user-level security is with the Security Wizard. Open the Tools menu, select Security, and then select User-Level Security Wizard. The first dialog box of the Security Wizard is shown in Figure 10-3. Simply follow the directions in the wizard dialog boxes to set the security options on the file.

FIGURE 10-3
Security Wizard

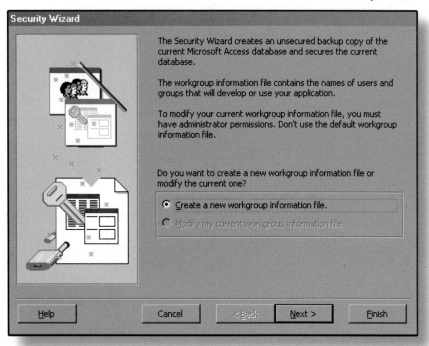

Security Wizard

The Security Wizard creates an unsecured backup copy of the current Microsoft Access database and secures the current database.

The workgroup information file contains the names of users and groups that will develop or use your application.

To modify your current workgroup information file, you must have administrator permissions. Don't use the default workgroup information file.

Do you want to create a new workgroup information file or modify the current one?

⊙ Create a new workgroup information file.

○ Modify my current workgroup information file.

| Help | | Cancel | < Back | Next > | Finish |

Setting Startup Options

As you've worked through this course, you've probably become used to seeing certain screens each time you start Access and a database file. For example, you always see the Menu bar and the Database window when you first start Access and select a database file to open. You can control what you see when you start the program by modifying the program's startup options. The startup options determine how your screen will look when Access is started. These options also let you control which add-ins need to be loaded (you'll learn about these later in this lesson) and various other features, such as whether shortcut menus will be available. To view or change the startup options, select Startup on the Tools menu. The Startup dialog box opens, as shown in Figure 10-4.

Clicking the Advanced button in the Startup dialog box displays the options shown in Figure 10-5. Any changes you make to the startup options will take effect the next time you start Access.

Did You Know?

Replication of a database enables users at different locations to work with the database and make modifications to it. For example, if you're a salesperson, you can maintain a replica of your company's database on your laptop computer. When you connect to the company's network, you can incorporate the changes you made into the company's existing file. The Replication feature can be found on the Tools menu. This feature is typically not included in the standard Access installation.

FIGURE 10-4
Startup dialog box

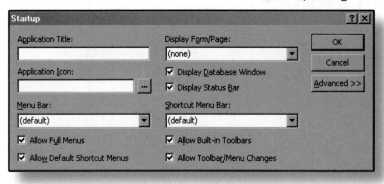

FIGURE 10-5
Advanced startup options

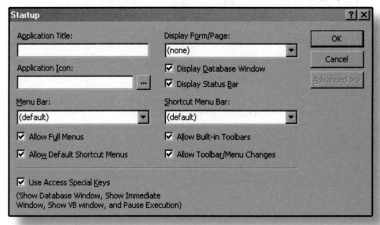

STEP-BY-STEP ▷ 10.3

1. Open the **AA Step10-3** database from the student data files.

2. Open the **Tools** menu and select **Startup**.

3. Deselect the **Allow Default Shortcut Menus** option, and click **OK**.

4. Close the database file. Then, reopen it.

5. Place your mouse pointer on a table name in the Database window and *right*-click. Notice that a shortcut menu does not appear.

6. Close the database file.

Using Add-Ins

Add-ins are programs, procedures, or objects that can be added to increase the available features in Access. To add an add-in, you can use the Add-in feature. Open the Tools menu, choose Add-Ins, and then select Add-In Manager.

Some of the add-ins that are available in Access are the Database Splitter, Analyzer, and the Link Table Manager. The Database Splitter splits a database file into two files. One file contains the tables and the other file contains the queries, forms, reports, data access pages, macros, and modules. By splitting the database into two files, users can access the data but create their own queries, forms, reports, and so on. This allows for a single source of data on a network. The Database Splitter can be found under Database Utilities on the Tools menu. The first screen of the Database Splitter Wizard is shown in Figure 10-6.

FIGURE 10-6
Database Splitter Wizard

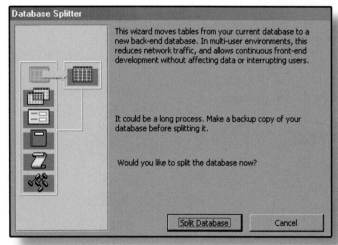

The Table Analyzer Wizard can be used to find a table that contains duplicate information in one or more fields. The Analyzer will locate this data and store it in a related table. This stores your data more efficiently. The Analyzer process is called *normalization*. The first dialog box of the Table Analyzer Wizard is shown in Figure 10-7. This dialog box explains the problems that the Table Analyzer will be looking for. Figure 10-8 shows the second dialog box of the Table Analyzer Wizard. In this dialog box, Access explains how it will take care of the problems it finds. You can find the Table Analyzer under Analyze on the Tools menu. The Linked Table Manager assists you with the process of linking tables located outside the current database.

FIGURE 10-7
Table Analyzer Wizard explains problems it will be looking for

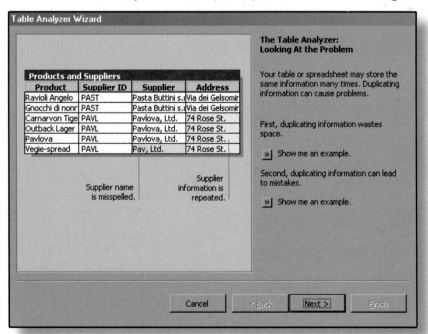

FIGURE 10-8

Table Analyzer Wizard explains how it will solve the problems

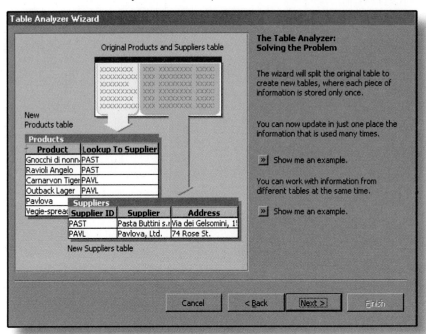

In the following Step-by-Step, you will use the Table Analyzer feature to look for problems in a database table within a database. If Table Analyzer Wizard does not find any problems, Access will display a message to let you know.

STEP-BY-STEP ▷ 10.4

1. Open the **AA Step10-4** database from the student data files.

2. Click once on the **Transactions** table to highlight the table name in the Database window.

3. Open the **Tools** menu, choose **Analyze**, and then select **Table**.

4. Read the information in the first dialog box of the Table Analyzer Wizard. Then, click **Next**.

5. Read the information in the second dialog box of the Table Analyzer Wizard and click **Next**.

6. Read the information in the next dialog box and then click **Next**.

7. If necessary, click the **Yes, let the wizard decide** option and then click **Next**.

8. A message should appear stating that the wizard does not recommend splitting your table. To close the Table Analyzer Wizard, click **Cancel**.

9. Close the database file.

Summary

In this lesson, you learned:

- Compacting a database compresses the database and removes any wasted space within the file. This will increase the efficiency of the database.

- Encrypting scrambles database information so that it cannot be read; decrypting unscrambles the encryption.

- A database can be secured by creating a password for it or by applying user-level security. If a password is set for a database file, it cannot be opened unless the user enters the password. Database security can be set on an individual basis by giving each user specific permission to view or change data in tables, forms, reports, and so on.

- You can control the way your screen looks when you start Access by modifying the startup options.

- Add-ins are additional programs, procedures, and objects that expand the capabilities of Access. Some of the add-ins that are available are the Database Splitter, Analyzer, and the Link Table Manager.

LESSON 10 REVIEW QUESTIONS

WRITTEN QUESTIONS

Write a brief answer to the following questions.

1. Describe what happens to a database file once you encrypt the file.

   information is encrypted after the database is compacted.

2. If you wanted to prevent unauthorized personnel from opening a database file, which feature could you use?

   password protection

3. Which feature would you use to give certain persons access to specific information within a database file?

user level security

4. Give a brief description of the Table Analyzer feature.

looks for duplicate information and creates multiple tables so that data is better organized and less chance for errors.

5. List two ~~two~~ startup options you can modify.

Application Title, Form or Page to open on startup.

6. Over time, a database becomes fragmented. Describe what you could do to fix this problem.

Compact

7. Define fragmentation.

database information that is physically stored in various locations on the harddisk in a non-contiguous fashion.

8. What is meant by defragmentation?

to make the database info contiguous on the hard drive

9. If you wanted to prevent an individual from having any access to database information, would you set password protection or user-level security? Why?

user level, so that others could use without having to issue a password.

10. Describe how the Database Splitter works.

separates the forms, reports, pages queries, macros from Tables so that users can use common data in a custom way.

LESSON 10 PROJECT

PROJECT 10-1

1. Assign a password of DOG to the **AA Project10-1** database in the student data files.

2. Close the file and reopen it to test the password.

*Tools
Security
Set D.B. Password*

CRITICAL THINKING

ACTIVITY 10-1

As the new systems manager for a small business, you want to know how to secure the information contained in the company's database. Specifically, you need to know how to apply user-level security to a new workgroup. Use Access's Help system and resources on the Internet to find information. Write a brief essay that describes how you would go about adding a new workgroup and securing the database file.

COMMAND SUMMARY

FEATURE	MENU COMMAND	TOOLBAR BUTTON	LESSON
Build expression			4
Condition, add to macro action			8
Datasheet View	View, Datasheet View		
Deletes selected record	Edit, Delete Record		
Field List	View, Field List		
Find Record	Edit, Find		
Form View	View, Form View		
Hyperlink	Insert, Hyperlink		9
Macro, run			8
Merge table with Word or Excel			7
Moves to the first record	Edit, Go To, First		
Moves to the last record	Edit, Go To, Last		
Moves to the next record	Edit, Go To, Next		
Moves to the previous record	Edit, Go To, Previous		
New Record	Insert, New Record		
Properties	View, Properties		3
Query, create			4
Query, run			2
Relationship, create			2
Toolbox	View, Toolbox		6
Totals			4
Undo	Edit, Undo		

TRUE/FALSE

Circle T if the statement is true or F if the statement is false.

T F 1. Before you can add a subform to a form, both the main form and subform must already be created.

T F 2. You must use the Expression Builder to calculate values in fields.

T F 3. You do not have to enforce referential integrity in a table.

T F 4. A data access page allows Web users to interact with selected database objects.

T F 5. A lookup field is created automatically by the Input Mask Wizard.

MULTIPLE CHOICE

Select the best response for the following statements.

1. To create a subform you must open the main form and switch to
   A. Form view
   B. Print Preview
   C. Form Design view
   D. Table Design view
   E. None of the above

2. A hyperlink allows you to
   A. jump from one document to another
   B. jump from a subform to Web sites
   C. jump to an intranet site
   D. all of the above
   E. none of the above

3. In the Query Design screen, the primary field is
   A. indicated on the status bar
   B. bolded
   C. the field that is linked
   D. all of the above
   E. none of the above

4. On the relationship line connecting two tables, a *1* indicates
   - A. the primary table
   - B. the related table
   - C. the related field
   - D. the primary key of the related table
   - E. none of the above

5. Setting required properties in a table field to *Yes*
   - A. forces data to be entered into the field
   - B. prohibits you from moving to the next record until data is entered into the field
   - C. forces you to use an input mask for the field
   - D. both A and B are correct
   - E. both B and C are correct

APPLICATIONS

APPLICATION 1

SCANS

1. Open the **AA App1** database from the student data files.

2. Create a query using the **Employees** table that displays only those employees who work in the Sales Department. Show all the fields in the query and name the query **Sales Department**. Print the query results in landscape orientation.

3. Create a query using both the **Employees** and **Personnel Information** tables that displays the last name, first name, department, and telephone number for each employee and name the query **Telephone List**. Print the query results.

4. Create a report from the **Telephone List** query with the employee information grouped by **Department** and sorted by **Last Name** and then **First Name** within the department. Use a layout and style of your choice. Name the report **Telephone List**. Make any modifications to the design of the report that you feel are necessary. Print the report.

APPLICATION 2

SCANS

1. Open the **AA App2** database from the student data files.

2. Create a query from the **Products** table that displays Dairy products (Category ID 4) and Grains/Cereals products (Category ID 5) only. Display all the fields. Name the query **Dairy and Grains/Cereals**. Print the query results in landscape orientation.

3. Create a query from the **Products** table that displays Discontinued items only. Display all the fields. Name the query **Discontinued Products**. Print the query results in landscape orientation.

4. Create a form for each of the above queries. The forms should be in a <u>tabular format</u> using a <u>style of your choice</u>. Name the forms using the <u>same names as the queries</u> from which you created them. Modify the <u>design of each form as you feel necessary</u>. Then <u>print each form</u>.

5. Create a switchboard form that automatically appears maximized when the database file is opened. The switchboard form should include macro buttons that open and maximize the **Discontinued Products** form and the **Dairy and Grains/Cereals** form.

6. Test the macros and then close the database file.

ON-THE-JOB SIMULATION

JOB 1

SCANS

You are the new administrative assistant for the Registrar's Office at WUC University. The employees in the Registrar's Office are challenged by the current database and they want you to make it easier for them to use. Open the **AA Job1** database from the student data files. In reviewing the objects in the database, you realize that in order to make it more user friendly, you need to create the following information.

1. Forms that display each level of student Class status. (*Hint*: Create the forms from queries that display students from each class.) Name each form according to the class.

2. A form that displays students who are at risk for scholastic probation with grade point averages lower than 2.25. (*Hint*: Create the form from a query that finds students with the lower GPAs.) Name the form **Probation Possibles**.

3. A form that displays students who will appear on the Dean's List with grade point averages of 3.5 or higher. (*Hint*: Create the form from a query that finds students with the higher GPAs.) Name the form **Dean's List**.

4. To make these forms user-friendly, you decide to include a Close macro button in each form. After you have added the macro button, print the forms.

5. Finally, you decide that you would like a switchboard form to appear when a user opens the database file. The form will contain macro buttons to display the forms. Name the form **Switchboard**.

SCANS

JOB 2

You are the owner of the Best Bet Products Distribution Center. You've created an Access database that contains the names and addresses of your customers, the products your company sells, and the costs of the products. Sales are excellent this year and you want to show appreciation to your customers for their loyalty. Therefore, you create a query that calculates total sales by customer using the **Customers**, **Products**, and **Transactions** tables. Then you need to create mailing labels for the customers whose sales were greater than $100. These mailing labels will be used to send out discount coupons to each customer. Use the **AA Job2** database in the student data files for this job.

UNIT

ADVANCED MICROSOFT® POWERPOINT

Estimated Time for Unit: 13 hours

USING ADVANCED TEXT FEATURES

OBJECTIVES

Upon completion of this lesson, you should be able to:

- Find and replace text in a slide show.
- Adjust text spacing using tabs and indents.
- Insert symbols.
- Number paragraphs automatically.
- Modify fonts for an entire presentation.
- Add a text box.
- Create and modify a macro.
- Insert a hyperlink.
- Create a summary slide.

⏱ Estimated Time: 2 hours

Your first impression of a PowerPoint slide will probably be of the graphical elements of the slide: its colors, background pattern, and layout. But presentations make their points largely through the use of text. In this lesson, you will learn more about how to edit and manipulate text in a slide show.

Finding and Replacing Text

If your slide show consists of only a few slides, you can easily find text you want to change by displaying each slide and making the necessary changes. In a slide show containing many slides, this process could take a lot of time. You can use PowerPoint's Find and Replace commands to make the editing process quicker.

The Find and Replace commands work the same way in PowerPoint as in other Office 2000 applications. You can use the Find and Replace commands in Slide view or Outline view (as well as in Normal view). PowerPoint automatically opens each placeholder that contains text you want to find. Found text is highlighted on the slide or in the outline, as shown in Figure 1-1.

If you just want to locate a word or phrase, use the Find command. The Find dialog box also gives you the option to replace text you are searching for. If you know you want to replace existing text with new text, use the Replace command.

Hot Tip

If no one has used the Replace command since PowerPoint was installed, you will find it by clicking the arrows at the bottom of the Edit menu.

FIGURE 1-1
Found text is highlighted on a slide

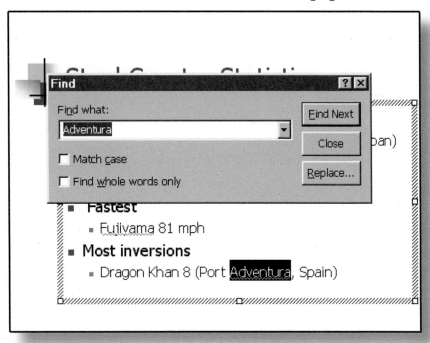

STEP-BY-STEP 1.1

You have recently begun work for ExperTech, Inc., a company that provides computer training, technical support, and computer repair services. Every Friday at noon, employees are encouraged to share work-related or personal enthusiasm with other employees in an informal Brown Bag Forum. A friend wants to share her interest in roller coasters at the Brown Bag Forum, and she has asked you to help her prepare a presentation on the subject.

1. Open **AP Step1-1** from the student data files. This file contains a draft of the final presentation. Change to Slide view.

2. Save the file as **Coasting** followed by your initials. Take a moment to scroll through the slides and become familiar with their content.

3. Your friend thinks she made an error in identifying the location of a particular roller coaster. She believes she keyed *Adventura* rather than *Aventura*. You're not sure where this information is located in the slide show. You can use the Find command to check. Open the **Edit** menu and click **Find**.

4. In the *Find what* box, key **Adventura**. Click **Find Next**. PowerPoint finds the word on slide 7. (You might have to move the Find dialog box to see the highlighted word.)

5. Click the highlighted word on the slide to remove the highlight. Remove the letter *d* from the word so that it reads *Aventura*.

(continued on next page)

6. Click **Close** in the Find dialog box.

7. *Roller coaster* is currently spelled as one word throughout the slide show. Your friend has changed her mind about this spelling because the dictionary spelling is two words. You need to change the spelling throughout the slide show. Switch to Outline view.

8. Open the **Edit** menu and click **Replace**. (You might need to click the arrows at the bottom of the menu to locate the Replace command.)

9. In the *Find what* box, key **rollercoaster**. Press **Tab** to move to the *Replace with* box and key **roller coaster**. Click **Find Next**. When PowerPoint highlights the first instance of *rollercoaster*, click **Replace**. PowerPoint then moves to the next instance.

10. Replace each instance of *rollercoaster* with *roller coaster*. Notice that PowerPoint automatically returns to the beginning of the

slide show to locate instances on slides before the current slide. When PowerPoint completes the search, click **OK** and then close the Replace dialog box.

11. Switch to Slide view and return to slide 1.

12. Save your changes and leave the presentation open for the next Step-by-Step.

Concept Builder

Be careful when using Replace All. You might replace text that does not relate to your current search. Unless you know your slide text very well, use the Replace button so you can check each instance before replacing it.

Adjusting Text Using Tabs and Indents

In most cases, text you insert on a slide will be aligned according to the design template. But on some occasions, you might want to make groups of words more readable by aligning them precisely with tabs. You can use PowerPoint's horizontal ruler to set and adjust tabs and indents just as you do in Word.

Clicking on a text placeholder displays the current indent and tab options for that text. If the placeholder contains more than one level of bullet or text, indents are displayed for all levels of text, as shown in Figure 1-2. To adjust an indent, simply drag the indent marker on the ruler. To place a tab, click the tab box at the left of the horizontal ruler to select a tab type, and then

FIGURE 1-2

Notice two sets of indent markers for the two text levels

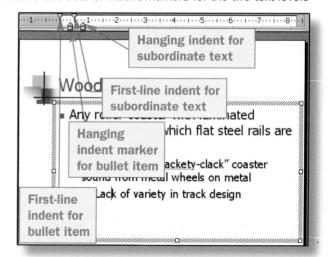

click on the ruler where you want the tab stop. Indents and tabs you set in the first line of a particular text level apply to all other entries at that same text level.

S TEP-BY-STEP ▷ 1.2

1. In your quick read through the slides, you noticed several places where tabs and indents might be used to make the text easier to read. Advance to slide 4 and click the placeholder for the bullet and text items. If necessary, click **Ruler** on the **View** menu to display the current indent and tab options for the text.

2. The second line of the Pro item would look better if it were aligned with the other text. A hanging indent would also help. Click anywhere in the Pro item.

3. Locate the hanging indent marker for the Pro text. It is the *second* upward-pointing marker from the left on the ruler. Drag this hanging indent marker to the 1.25-inch mark on the horizontal ruler. The second line of the Pro text should move to the right to align with the word *That* in the first line of the Pro text.

> ### Hot Tip
>
> If the whole Pro and Con section moves to the right, you are dragging the hanging indent marker for the bullet item. Choose the *second* hanging indent marker from the left side of the ruler.

`4. Make sure a left tab symbol is displayed in the tab box at the left of the ruler. Click anywhere on the ruler to insert the left tab, and then drag the tab symbol to the 1.25-inch mark, right on top of the hanging indent marker. Your ruler should look like the one shown in Figure 1-3.

`5. To align the text on the new tab stop, position the insertion point to the right of the red word

Pro. Press **Delete** to remove the existing space. Then press **Tab** to align the first line of the Pro text on the 1.25-inch tab stop. Remove the space and insert the tab for the Con item in the same way.

6. Align the Pro and Con text on slide 6 using the information in steps 3–5.

7. The glossary items on slide 11 would be easier to read if the definitions were aligned and indented.
   a. Click in any glossary item. Notice on the ruler that you have only one set of indent markers this time.
   b. Drag the hanging indent marker to the 2-inch mark on the ruler.
   c. Drag the left tab mark already on the ruler to the 2-inch mark, on top of the hanging indent marker.
   d. Remove the space following each glossary item and press **Tab** to align the first line of each definition on the 2-inch tab stop.

FIGURE 1-3
Position the hanging indent marker and the left tab as shown here

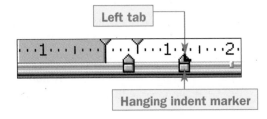

8. Save your changes and leave the presentation open for the next Step-by-Step.

Inserting Symbols

Another way to improve the readability and accuracy of your text is to insert special characters and symbols where appropriate. Clicking the Symbol command on the Insert menu displays the symbols available for the font you are currently using, as shown in Figure 1-4.

You are not limited to the symbols shown for the current font (called Normal Text in the dialog box). Click the down arrow in the Font box to see other fonts that contain symbols you can use on your slides. Fonts such as Webdings, Wingdings, and Dingbats supply many different types of symbols, shapes, arrows, and numbers that can add interest to your slide text.

To insert a symbol from the Symbol dialog box, click the symbol. PowerPoint displays it at an enlarged size so that you can make sure it is the correct symbol. Click Insert to insert the symbol. When you have finished with the Symbol dialog box, click Close.

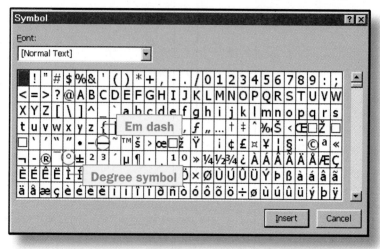

FIGURE 1-4
The Symbol dialog box

Concept Builder

In Word, you can leave the Symbol dialog box open between insertions. In PowerPoint, you must close the dialog box after each use.

S TEP-BY-STEP ▷ 1.3

1. You can improve readability of the text on slide 2 by inserting em dashes (—) between the dates and the text that follows. Open the text placeholder and position the insertion point immediately after the word *1400s*.

2. Open the **Insert** menu and click **Symbol**. Click the em dash, the eighth symbol from the left in the fifth row.

3. Click **Insert** and then **Close**. Press **Delete** once to remove the existing space between the em dash and the text.

4. To save time in inserting the em dash after the other dates, highlight the em dash and click the **Copy** button. Position the insertion point immediately after the word *1700s*. Click the **Paste** button. Remove the extra spaces before and after the em dash. Insert dashes for the other items in the text placeholder.

5. The "steepest drops" on slides 5 and 7 are measured in degrees. Move to slide 5 and position the insertion point immediately after the phrase *Cyclone 58.6*.

6. Open the **Insert** menu and click **Symbol**. Locate the degree symbol (fifth from the left in the sixth row) and click it. Click **Insert** and **Close**.

7. Insert a degree symbol on slide 7 following the phrase *Oblivion 88*. Insert a degree symbol after the number *360* on slide 11.

8. Save your changes and leave the presentation open for the next Step-by-Step.

 Did You Know?

The 88° drop of the Oblivion roller coaster is practically straight down!

Numbering Paragraphs

By default, PowerPoint organizes text data into bullet items. Sometimes, however, you might want to show how items of text fall in a particular order. To do so, you can use PowerPoint's automatic paragraph numbering feature.

The feature is simple to use: Select the text items you want to number and click Numbering on the toolbar. The items are automatically numbered starting with 1.

You can adjust the color and size of the number by opening the Format menu and clicking Bullets and Numbering. In the Bullets and Numbering dialog box (Figure 1-5), click the Numbered tab. Notice the numbering styles available and the settings at the bottom of the dialog box. To modify the size of the number, insert or change the number in the *% of text* spin box. Change the number color by clicking the *Color* box to choose a color from the current color scheme (or any other available color).

FIGURE 1-5
Bullets and Numbering dialog box

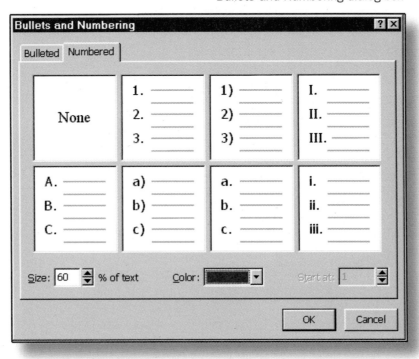

1. The data on slide 8 is a list of the most popular coasters, as decided by coaster enthusiasts voting online. This kind of data could be organized as a numbered list. Select all the bulleted items in the placeholder. Click **Numbering** on the toolbar.

2. The numbers look a little small. With the numbered items still selected, open the **Format** menu and click **Bullets and Numbering**. Click the **Numbered** tab. Change the *% of text* number to **75**. Click **OK**.

3. Save your changes and leave the presentation open for the next Step-by-Step.

Replacing Fonts in a Presentation

The current design template controls fonts, font styles, and font sizes for various text objects in a presentation. If you do not like one of the fonts in your presentation, you can quickly change it using the Replace Fonts command on the Format menu.

Clicking this command opens the Replace Font dialog box shown in Figure 1-6. The fonts used in the current presentation are shown in the *Replace* drop-down list. To select a replacement font, click the font you want to replace and then click the down arrow in the *With* list box. Choose a new font on the list. Then click the Replace button.

FIGURE 1-6
Replace Font dialog box

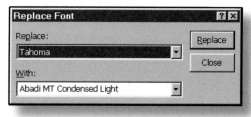

Note that when you replace fonts in this fashion, you replace *all* instances of the font in the presentation. The Replace Font dialog box remains open after you click Replace, so if you don't like the result of your change, you can choose another font to replace or replace the one you just changed with a different font.

1. You are not very fond of the default font for the current design template and would like to change it throughout the presentation. Open the **Format** menu and click **Replace Fonts**.

2. In the Replace Font dialog box, the font *Tahoma* should be highlighted. Click the down arrow in the *With* list box to display a list of fonts.

3. Scroll to and click **Times New Roman**. Click **Replace**. All instances of the Tahoma font change to Times New Roman. Close the dialog box and scroll through the slides to see the new font in place.

4. Save your changes and leave the presentation open for the next Step-by-Step.

Adding Text Boxes

Placeholders are positioned on slides according to the current design template. You can, however, move any placeholder on a slide to achieve a particular effect. You can also add a ***text box*** to a slide to insert text for which no placeholder has been provided. Text boxes are also useful to add comments or other information to a slide.

FIGURE 1-7
The Text Box tool on the Drawing toolbar

Text Box tool

The easiest way to add a text box is to click the Text Box tool on the Drawing toolbar, part of which is shown in Figure 1-7. When you click the Text Box tool, your insertion point changes to a cross shape.

You have two options for creating a text box. You can simply click the location on the slide where you want to insert the text box. A hatched box appears, as shown in Figure 1-8, with an insertion point indicating where text will appear when keyed. When you insert a text box this way, the text box expands to hold all the text you key without wrapping any text. To limit the text box to a particular size, position the cross-shaped pointer where you want the text box to begin, press the left mouse button, and hold it down while you drag the pointer to the place you want the text box to end. (See Figure 1-9.) As you key text in a box you have defined this way, text wraps at the end of the box and the box's depth increases to hold all the text.

FIGURE 1-8
Clicking on the slide to insert a text box

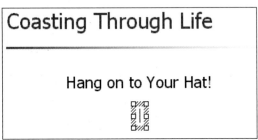

FIGURE 1-9
Dragging a text box on the slide

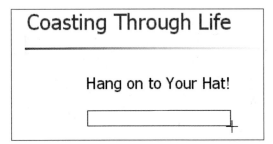

Use the ruler to help you position your text box. As you move the pointer on the slide, a vertical dashed line shows your current position on the ruler.

Text boxes are controlled to some extent by the design template currently in place. For example, in some design templates the text in a text box automatically centers. Font may also be specified by the design template. If the alignment or font is not to your liking after you create the text box, you can reformat the text using PowerPoint's formatting features.

You can also move a text box, or any placeholder, to position it exactly where you want it on the slide. Click the text box or placeholder so that it displays a hatched-line border. Position the pointer anywhere on the border so that it takes the shape of a four-headed arrow. Hold down the left mouse button and drag the text box or placeholder where you want it.

Hot Tip

If the Drawing toolbar is not displayed on your screen, right-click the Standard toolbar and click next to *Drawing*.

Concept Builder

To delete a text box or placeholder, click the hatched-line border until it turns into a thick border of small dots. Then press Delete.

1. You remind your friend that she should put her name on the presentation. Adding a text box to slide 1, you both agree, will take care of this.

2. Move to slide 1. Display the Drawing toolbar if necessary and click the **Text Box** tool.

3. Move the pointer on the slide until the vertical dashed guide on the ruler is centered on 0. About half an inch below the slide's subtitle,

click the pointer to create a new text box. Your text box should look similar to the one in Figure 1-8.

4. Key the following text at the insertion point in the text box: **A presentation by Claire Minihan**.

5. Save your changes and leave the presentation open for the next Step-by-Step.

Creating and Modifying a Macro

If you find you are performing the same task over and over as you create and modify presentations, you might find it worthwhile to create a macro to handle the chores. *Macros* store all the steps required to complete a task and then perform those steps for you at your request.

To tell PowerPoint you want to create a new macro, open the Tools menu and click the Macro command. On the submenu, click Record New Macro. The Record Macro dialog box opens, similar to the one shown in Figure 1-10. The default macro name will depend on how many macros you have created in your current PowerPoint session. Change the name by highlighting the default name, if necessary, and keying a new one. By default, the macro is stored in the current presentation, but if you have several presentations open, you can also choose to store the macro in all of them by clicking the down arrow in the *Store macro in* list box and choosing *All open presentations*.

After you click OK in the dialog box, you can begin performing the actions you want the macro to store. The Stop Recording toolbar displays while you are recording. When you have finished the task you are recording, click the Stop Recording button on the Stop Recording toolbar. Your macro is then stored in a macro module in your presentation.

FIGURE 1-10
Record Macro dialog box

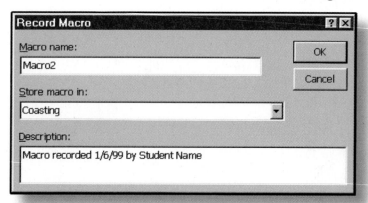

STEP-BY-STEP ▷ 1.7

1. Claire is an enthusiastic supporter of the Brown Bag Forums and knows she will be creating more presentations for the Forums. She would like to insert a text box on her first slide indicating that the presentation was created specifically for the Brown Bag Forums. You can create a macro for this task. Move to slide 1.

2. Open the **Tools** menu and click **Macro**. Then click **Record New Macro** on the submenu.

3. Key the macro name **forum** and then click **OK**. The Stop Recording toolbar should display in your PowerPoint window.

4. Click the **Text Box** tool on the Drawing toolbar. Click near the top of the slide at the 4.5-inch mark. Click the **Align Right** button on the toolbar. Key **Forums**.

5. Click the **Stop Recording** button on the Stop Recording toolbar. If the Stop Recording toolbar is not visible on your screen, open the **Tools** menu, click **Macro**, and click **Stop Recording** on the submenu.

6. Save your changes and leave the presentation open for the next Step-by-Step.

To play a macro you have already recorded, open the Tools menu, click Macro, and then click Macros on the submenu. In the Macro dialog box, click the name of the macro you want to run and then click the Run button. In this dialog box, you also have the option of deleting a macro or editing it.

When you click the Edit button to edit a macro, the Microsoft Visual Basic Editor opens, as shown in Figure 1-11. The Project Viewer pane at the left of the window shows all presentations currently open (in this case, only *Coasting* is open) and displays the macro modules stored in that presentation. The Visual Basic code for the macro you recorded displays in the larger pane. You can modify a macro by making changes to its code in this pane.

PowerPoint stores macros by default in a single presentation. You can easily copy a macro to another presentation, however, using the Visual Basic window. Open the presentation containing the macro you want to copy as well as the presentation to which you want to copy the macro. If you do not have the Visual Basic window open, you can open it by clicking Visual Basic Editor on the Macro submenu. You should see both open presentations in the Project viewer. To copy a macro module from one presentation to another, simply click on the module and drag it to the other presentation.

FIGURE 1-11
Visual Basic Editor

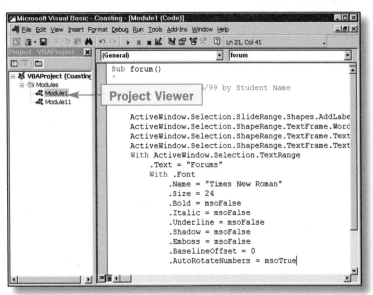

1. You realize you have keyed only *Forums* for your macro when you intended to key *Brown Bag Forums*. You need to edit your macro. Click the outside border of the text box you created when recording the macro and press **Delete** to remove it from the slide.

2. Open the **Tools** menu and click **Macro**. Click **Macros** on the submenu to open the Macros dialog box. You should see your *forum* macro in the macro list. Select it if necessary and click **Edit**.

3. In the Visual Basic Editor, locate the line in the code pane about one-third of the way down that reads *.Text = "Forums"*. This is the text you actually keyed in the text box.

4. Position the insertion point in front of the *F* in the word *Forums* in this line and key **Brown Bag** and a space. All three words must be contained within the open and close quotation marks, like this: "Brown Bag Forums".

5. Close the Visual Basic Editor by clicking its close box. In PowerPoint, open the **Tools** menu again, click **Macro**, and then click **Macros** to open the Macros dialog box. Select the *forum* macro if necessary and click **Run**. The modified macro displays at the top of your slide.

6. Save your changes and leave the presentation open for the next Step-by-Step.

Inserting Hyperlinks on Slides

Hyperlinks can serve many useful functions on slides. You can use a hyperlink to jump to a particular slide in the presentation. A hyperlink can take you directly to another document on your computer or on a network. A hyperlink can also take you to a specified Web site.

The easiest way to insert a hyperlink is to key or highlight the hyperlink text and then click the Insert Hyperlink button on the Standard toolbar. When you do so, the Insert Hyperlink dialog box opens, similar to the one shown in Figure 1-12.

The Insert Hyperlink dialog box is packed with options for creating a hyperlink. The *Link to* area of the dialog box lets you choose the location of the item you want to link to. By default, the Existing File or Web Page option is active. You have three other choices:

■ Choose *Place in This Document* to link to a slide in the current presentation.

■ Choose *Create New Document* to start a new document that your hyperlink will then jump to.

■ Choose *E-mail Address* to create a hyperlink to someone's e-mail address.

The *Text to display* box lets you change the wording of the hyperlink text. Click the ScreenTip button if you want to create a ScreenTip that will display when you place the pointer on the hyperlink.

In the *Type the file or Web page name* box, key the name of the file or Web page that the hyperlink will jump to. If you do not know the file name or the site address, you can select from three handy lists: *Recent Files* (files you have recently opened), *Browsed Pages* (Web or other HTML pages you have recently read), or *Inserted Links* (Web addresses you have recently keyed).

If you cannot locate the file or address you want on one of these lists, you have three other options for locating the item you want to link to:

FIGURE 1-12
The Insert Hyperlink dialog box

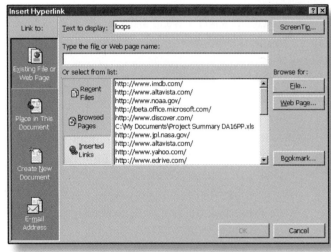

- Click the File button to open the Link to File dialog box. In this dialog box, you can locate any file on your computer or network.

- Click the Web Page button to open your Web browser. You can use your Web browser to locate the page you want to link to.

- Click the Bookmark button to see a list of "places" in the current document you might want to link to, such as First Slide, Last Slide, or a specific slide number. This is the same list you see when you click *Place in This Document.*

After you have located the file, Web page, or slide you want to link to, click OK. PowerPoint then creates the hyperlink you have specified. The hyperlink appears underlined and in a different color. Although you can see the hyperlink in all views, you can only activate it in Slide Show view.

Web Sites

The many roller coaster enthusiasts in this country have created a number of excellent Web sites relating to roller coasters. Some have pictures or even videos of popular roller coasters. Use your Web browser to search for *rollercoasters* or *roller coasters.*

STEP-BY-STEP ▷ 1.9

1. Your friend Claire suggests that it might be useful to create hyperlinks for the glossary terms so that she can jump to the glossary slide as she is presenting her material. Move to slide 2, where the first glossary term appears.

2. Highlight the word *loops* in the last bulleted item. Click the **Insert Hyperlink** button on the Standard toolbar.

3. In the Insert Hyperlink dialog box, click the **Place in This Document** icon. Scroll down the list of slide titles and click slide 11. A preview of the slide displays. Click **OK**. Notice that the word *loops* is now red and underlined.

4. Use the same procedure to create hyperlinks for the following glossary terms: *corkscrew* on slide 2, *inversions* on slide 7, and *Lift hill* on slide 9.

(continued on next page)

5. Save your changes and move to slide 1.

6. Check the slides and the hyperlinks by running the slide show:
  a. Click the **Slide Show** view button at the bottom of the screen. Use the mouse to advance to slide 2.
  b. Click the first hyperlink on slide 2 to jump to slide 11, *Coaster Glossary*. After you have read the definition of *loop*, right-click on the slide, click **Go**, and click **Previously Viewed** to return to slide 2.
  c. Try the other hyperlinks to make sure they link properly to slide 11. Return each time to the previously viewed slide. You will learn additional ways to navigate among slides in Lesson 6 of this unit.

7. After you have viewed all the slides, save your changes. Leave the presentation open for the next Step-by-step.

Extra Challenge

If you live near an amusement park with a roller coaster, find information about the roller coaster similar to the statistics in this presentation. Add a slide to the presentation that gives the name and any other facts about the roller coaster you have been able to find.

Creating a Summary Slide

After you have completed work on a presentation, you might want to prepare a "table of contents" slide that will introduce the topics in your presentation. You can create a *summary* slide automatically from the titles of slides in a presentation.

To create a summary slide, you must be in Slide Sorter view. Click the first slide whose title you want to include on the summary slide. Then, hold down Ctrl and click the other slides. Click the Summary Slide button on the Slide Sorter toolbar. PowerPoint automatically creates a slide with the title Summary Slide and positions the slide after the presentations Title slide. The titles of the slides you selected appear as bullet items on the summary slide. You can then change the slide's title if desired.

STEP-BY-STEP ▷ 1.10

1. To create a summary slide for your presentation, switch to Slide Sorter view. Click slide 2.

2. Hold down **Ctrl** and click slides 4, 6, 8, 9, 10, and 11.

3. Click the **Summary Slide** button on the Slide Sorter toolbar. PowerPoint creates the summary slide and positions it as a new slide 2.

4. With slide 2 selected, switch to Slide view. Change the slide title to **Contents**.

5. Save your changes. Print the presentation as handouts with 6 slides per page. Close the presentation.

Summary

In this lesson, you learned:

- The Find command can help you locate specific text in your presentation. The Replace command makes it easy to substitute one word or phrase for another throughout the presentation. Find and Replace are easiest to use in Slide view and Outline view.

- To align text more precisely on a slide, you can use tabs and change indents.

- You can use the Symbol command to display a palette of special characters and symbols that make your text more accurate and readable.

- Numbering paragraphs is another way to organize text in a placeholder.

- The Replace Fonts command allows you to replace all instances of one font with another font throughout a presentation.

- Text boxes can be used to add information or comments to slides.

- Macros can automate the process of performing repetitive tasks. You can modify or copy a macro in the Visual Basic Editor.

- You can link text on your slides to a number of different types of resources, such as files on your computer or server, other slides in your presentation, Web pages, or even e-mail addresses.

- You can create a summary slide from the titles of slides in a presentation.

LESSON 1 REVIEW QUESTIONS

TRUE/FALSE

Circle T if the statement is true or F if the statement is false.

T **F** 1. When replacing text, the best option to choose is Replace All.

T F 2. Setting a tab in the first line of a text level sets the same tab in all other lines at that level.

T **F** 3. You can leave the Symbol dialog box open to insert a number of symbols on several slides.

T F 4. By default, a macro stores only in the current presentation.

T **F** 5. Text boxes always format text as left-aligned in Times New Roman.

WRITTEN QUESTIONS

Write a brief answer to the following questions.

1. Why would you use the Replace command instead of the Find command when making changes to a presentation?

   to make changes on several slides

2. A presentation you are currently working on contains the proper name *Halvørsen*. How would you insert the proper foreign-language character ø?

   click inside text placeholder and insert symbol click on symbol, insert, close. add text to create Halvørsen

3. What two ways can you insert a text box on a slide, and what happens to text in each kind of text box?

   clicking in one location creates a box that expands as text is added.

   clicking and dragging a box causes text to wrap in a fixed size box.

4. In the Insert Hyperlink dialog box, what option would you choose to create a hyperlink to a file you have recently opened?

   existing file or web page.

5. How does a hyperlink appear on a slide?

LESSON 1 PROJECTS

PROJECT 1-1

SCANS

ExperTech, Inc., is in the process of converting its written employee manual to an online format. The online manual will be used as both an orientation tool for new employees and a reference tool for current employees. You are a member of the team preparing the final version. Use what you have learned in this lesson to improve the manual.

1. Open **AP Project1-1** from the student data files. Save the file as **ET Manual** followed by your initials.

2. Switch to Slide view and scroll through the slides to review the information in the manual.

3. The person who created this draft presentation was in such a hurry he neglected to capitalize the *T* in *ExperTech*. Use Replace to correct the spelling of the company name throughout the presentation.

4. The company name, *ExperTech*, is registered. Use the Symbol command to insert the registered symbol (®) after the name on the first slide only. Use the Font command to format the symbol as a superscript.

5. On slide 4, use a tab to right align the numbers of full-time and part-time employees.

6. On slide 6, highlight the phrase *9-on-1-off schedule* and create a hyperlink to the data file **Nine-On Schedule**.

7. Add a text box on slide 1 about two inches below *Employee Manual* and insert the text **Last Revision:**. Insert the current date following the colon.

8. Create a summary slide using slides 2, 3, 5, and 9. Change the title of the summary slide to **Contents**.

9. Save your changes. Run the slide show and test the hyperlink. (*Hint:* You can use the Back arrow on Word's Web toolbar to return from the document to the slide show.)

10. Print the slide show as handouts with 9 slides per page. Save and close the presentation.

PROJECT 1-2

You are a meteorologist with a local television station. You have been asked to donate your time by giving a presentation at a fundraising event for a worthy charity. The person who recruited you suggested, "Why don't you do a presentation on, oh, how about the weather?" You have gathered some interesting facts about "the weather" and now need to refine your slides for the presentation.

1. Open **AP Project1-2** from the student data files. Save the file as **Lightning** followed by your initials.

2. The third bulleted item on slide 4 gives the Fahrenheit temperature of air heated by lightning. After the number *40,000*, insert a degree symbol and the letter **F**.

3. On slide 6, use tabs to align the two columns of lightning after effects.

4. On slide 2, create a wrapping text box with right alignment and insert the following epigraph:

> It is vain to look for a defense against lightning.
> —*Publius Sirius*

5. Replace the Times New Roman font in the presentation with the Tahoma font.

6. Save your changes. Run the slide show.

7. Print the slides as handouts with 9 slides per page. Close the presentation.

PROJECT 1-3

You own a home in a historic neighborhood. Recently, you and your neighbors have begun to wonder whether the homes in this area contain lead paint. And if they do, what are the likely hazards? As the chair of the Richmond Heights Community Council (RHCC), you have contacted your city's Health Department for information. In return, the Health Department has sent you slides you can present to other members of the RHCC. You notice that the presentation needs some tweaking before you can present it to your neighbors.

1. Open **AP Project1-3** from the student data files. Save the presentation as **Lead** followed by your initials.

2. Scroll through the slides to become familiar with their content.

3. Change the bulleted items on slide 4 to numbered items.

4. Slide 9 needs some work to make the blood lead levels easier to read and understand. Follow these steps:
   A. Whoever keyed the data on this slide used a letter *u* instead of the μ symbol that stands for *micro*. Replace the each letter *u* with a μ symbol.
   B. To reduce wordiness, replace the words *Less than* with the < symbol.
   C. Evidently, the numbers *10 19, 20 44*, and *45 69* are ranges. Number ranges are usually indicated using en dashes (–). Insert an en dash (to the left of the em dash in the Symbol dialog box) for the number ranges.
   D. Use tabs to align the descriptions of each blood lead level.

5. If your own community's health department has a Web site or e-mail address, add a hyperlink at the bottom of slide 1 to that address.

6. Save your changes. Run the slide show as practice before your neighborhood presentation.

7. Print the slide show as handouts with 9 slides per page. Close the presentation.

CRITICAL THINKING ACTIVITY

SCANS

ACTIVITY 1-1

Your small company is considering moving to another, much larger city in the state. You have been assigned to do Internet research on the cultural and recreational options available in the new city and then to prepare a presentation summarizing your findings. You would like to be able to display some of the sites you found on the Web.

Write a brief description of the research you would undertake and how you would display information from the new city as you are running the presentation.

ACTIVITY 1-2

You created a presentation containing a number of hyperlinks to documents on your intranet. During a cleanup operation, you moved some of the documents to new folders. Now your hyperlinks don't work. What happened and how can you fix the problem?

Use the PowerPoint Help files to try to locate the cause of your problem and how to fix it. Write a brief summary of your findings.

LESSON

2

CREATING TABLES AND CHARTS

OBJECTIVES

Upon completion of this lesson, you should be able to:

- Insert a table on a slide.

- Modify the table format.

- Insert an Excel worksheet on a slide.

- Create and modify data charts.

- Create and modify an organization chart.

⏱ **Estimated Time: 2 hours**

As you have seen, PowerPoint offers many different ways to place and arrange text on a slide. You saw in the previous lesson how to use tabs to organize information in columns and rows. Tabs work fine if you have only a few items to arrange. To organize a larger collection of text or number information, you can use PowerPoint's table feature.

If you want to present a lot of number data, you can insert an Excel worksheet on your slide. The Excel worksheet is an embedded object that functions just like any worksheet in Excel.

You can display a visual representation of number data by creating a chart of the data. PowerPoint offers a number of chart types and several slide layouts specifically for creating charts.

PowerPoint also enables you to create and modify organization charts. An organization chart shows how persons or items relate to each other.

This lesson explores all of these ways to organize text and number data on your slides. By the time you finish this lesson, you will know how to create simple and sophisticated tables and create several different kinds of charts.

Working with Text Tables

To arrange text in columns and rows for easy reading, you can create a table. You have three options for creating a table:

- You can use the Table slide layout and then double-click the table placeholder to create the table.

- You can click the Insert Table button on the toolbar or click Insert Table on the Insert menu, to create a table on any slide.

- You can use the Draw Table tool to "draw" a table, placing rows and columns right where you want them.

Use tables if the data you want to organize consists of text or numbers that do not need to be calculated. If you want to perform calculations on numbers, use an Excel worksheet. You will learn how to embed a worksheet later in this lesson.

Creating a Table Using the Table Slide Layout

Creating a table using the Table slide layout is the easiest way to set up a table on a slide. PowerPoint guides you through the process and places the table you specify in a frame on the slide. You are then ready to enter the data.

To begin, select the Table layout in the New Slide dialog box, as shown in Figure 2-1. After you click OK, PowerPoint displays the Table slide on your screen (Figure 2-2). Note the placeholders for the title and the table.

Concept Builder

You can also add a Microsoft Word table on a slide by opening the **Insert** menu, clicking **Picture**, and then choosing **Microsoft Word Table**.

FIGURE 2-1
Click the Table layout in the New Slide dialog box

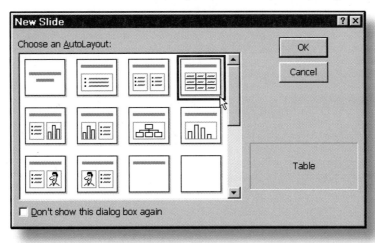

FIGURE 2-2
A new slide with the Table layout

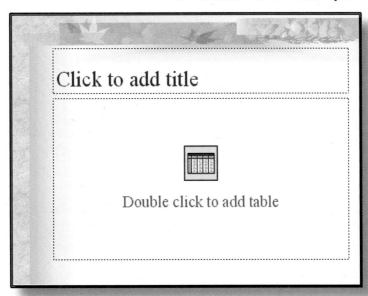

To set up the table, double-click as instructed in the table placeholder. PowerPoint opens the Insert Table dialog box (Figure 2-3). Here you can specify the number of rows and columns for the new table. After you click OK, Power-Point displays the table structure on your slide, as shown in Figure 2-4. PowerPoint also displays the Tables and Borders toolbar. This toolbar offers a number of tools and commands to help you adjust and format your table.

Notice that the Draw Table tool on the Tables and Borders toolbar is active. When this tool is active, your pointer takes the shape of a pencil. If you want to add additional columns and rows at this time, you can do so by drawing them with the pointer. You will learn more about using this tool later in this lesson. To turn off the Draw Table tool, click the tool in the toolbar to deselect it.

Concept Builder

If you want to change a slide from its current layout to the Table layout, open the Format menu, click Slide Layout, and then in the Slide Layout dialog box, choose the Table layout.

Hot Tip

You can also insert a table on any slide by opening the Insert menu and clicking Table.

FIGURE 2-3
Specify rows and columns in the Insert Table dialog box

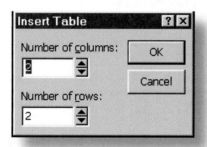

FIGURE 2-4
The table structure on the slide

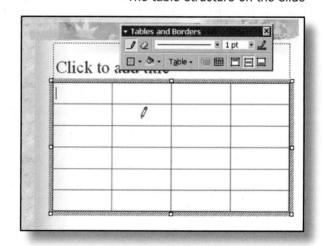

STEP-BY-STEP ▷ 2.1

SCANS

Three years ago, you and your partner purchased the Deer Creek Inn, a relatively small resort lodge located in the Midwest. You are ready to turn your attention to some organized strategic planning. You want to review the previous year and use the information you have gathered to plan for the next year.

1. Open **AP Step2-1** from the student data files. Save the file as **Deer Creek Review** followed by your initials.

2. Scroll through the slides to familiarize yourself with their content. You have gathered data on the conveniences offered by each type of

room at the Inn. This information can best be presented in a table.

3. Move to slide 3 and click the **New Slide** button on the toolbar. In the New Slide dialog box, click the **Table** layout (the last layout in the first row). Click **OK**.

4. In the new slide, key the title **Guest Room Amenities**.

5. Double-click the table placeholder. In the Insert Table dialog box, replace the default values with **4** columns and **5** rows. Click **OK**.

6. The new table displays on the slide. If necessary, turn off the Draw Table tool by clicking the Draw Table button on the Tables and Borders toolbar.

7. Save your changes and leave the presentation open for the next Step-by-Step.

 Web Sites

Many hotels, resorts, and bed and breakfasts have their own Web sites. Use a directory such as Yahoo and follow Travel and Lodging links to find lodgings online.

Entering text in a PowerPoint table is much the same as entering text in a Word table. Use Tab to move from cell to cell. Use Enter only if you want to create a new line in that cell. Remember that slides use large font sizes for ease of reading. Text you enter in a table is also a large font size. If the text you enter runs into the next cell, you can adjust font size or column width after you have completed the table.

When you have finished keying text in a table, click outside the table on the slide. You will then see the table in place on the slide.

S TEP-BY-STEP ▷ 2.2

1. Key the text shown below in the table. Use **Tab** to move from cell to cell in the table.

	Lodge	Cabins	Suites
Data port	Some	Some	Yes
Microwave	No	Yes	Yes
Whirlpool/spa	Some	No	Yes
VCR .	Some	Some	Yes

2. Click outside the table to see it in place on the slide.

3. Save your changes and leave the presentation open for the next Step-by-Step.

Modifying a Table

Tables are rarely perfect the first time around. Even if everything fits as you planned, you might want to change some formatting options to make the table more interesting. You can use text formatting options to change the look of the text. Use the tools on the Tables and Borders toolbar or the Table command on the Format menu to modify the table's structure and format.

Concept Builder

If your table includes decimal numbers, you can align them by setting a tab in a table cell. Use Ctrl+Tab to move to a tab stop in a table cell.

The Tables and Borders toolbar, shown in Figure 2-5, provides enough tools to restructure or reformat almost any table. The tools on this toolbar work the same way as the tools on Word's Tables and Borders toolbar.

FIGURE 2-5
Tools on the Tables and Borders toolbar

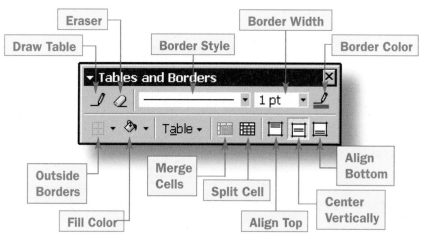

Using the tools on the Tables and Borders toolbar obviously requires you to make one formatting decision at a time. To modify a number of formatting options at one time, open the Format menu and click the Table command. The Format Table dialog box displays, as shown in Figure 2-6. The three tabs in this dialog box let you select a number of formatting options that all take effect when you click OK.

To modify text and table structure, you must select text or the part of the table you want to change. You can select text by simply dragging over it. Select a row or column by dragging all cells in that row or column, or use a command on the Table menu. Changing column width and row height is as easy as dragging a gridline to a new position.

FIGURE 2-6
The Format Table dialog box

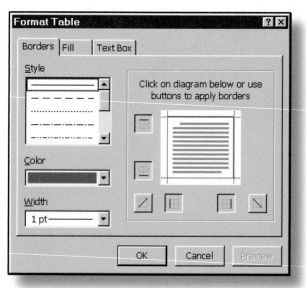

STEP-BY-STEP ▷ 2.3

1. Your table needs some modification to present the data attractively. Start from the top by adding interest to the column header row:

   a. Select all cells in the first row by dragging across the row.

   b. To add a fill color, click the down arrow next to the **Fill Color** tool on the Tables and Borders toolbar. Select the dark yellow color from the line of color samples available for the current design template. (The ScreenTip will read *Follow Accent Scheme Color*.) Click anywhere in the table to see how the fill color looks.

   c. Select the cells in the first row that contain text and boldface and center them using toolbar buttons.

2. Now adjust the column widths to display all text. Follow these steps:

   a. To display all text in the first column, position the pointer over the gridline at the right of the first column. The pointer becomes a double-pointed vertical line.

   b. Drag the gridline to the right to about the 2.5-inch mark on the horizontal ruler.

   c. The second column of the table is now smaller than it was. Adjust the gridlines of the last three columns so that the columns are all approximately the same width.

3. You realize you left out a row. Every guest room at Deer Creek has in-room coffee. Follow these steps to insert the data:

   a. Position the insertion point in the *Microwave* cell.

   b. Click **Table** on the Tables and Borders toolbar. On the menu, click **Insert Rows Below**.

   c. In the new row, key **Coffee** in the first cell and then **Yes** in the remaining three cells.

   d. Center the data in the last three columns.

4. Your data is easy enough to read that you decide you don't need gridlines. Remove them as follows:

   a. First select the entire table by clicking the **Table** button on the Tables and Borders toolbar. On the drop-down menu, click **Select Table**.

   b. Click the down arrow next to the **Outside Borders** tool on the Tables and Borders toolbar. Click the **No Border** option (it shows only a dashed outline, no solid lines).

5. Click outside the table on the slide to see your modifications.

6. Save your changes and leave the presentation open for the next Step-by-Step.

Creating a Table Using the Draw Table Tool

The Draw Table tool gives you considerable flexibility in creating a table. If, for example, you want some rows of the table to be a different height, or want some rows to contain more columns than others, the Draw Table tool is the best option.

To use the Draw Table tool, click the Tables and Borders button to open the toolbar with the Draw Table tool active. First use the tool to draw the outside border of your table. You do this by dragging from the top left corner to the bottom right corner, as if you were using a drawing tool to create a rectangle. Then, to indicate where you want rows and columns, drag the pointer from left to right or top to bottom of the table. The Draw Table feature automatically creates straight lines where you indicate. If they are not precisely where you want them, you can move them by dragging as you did in Step-by-Step 2.3. If you decide you don't want a gridline after all where you have placed one, click the Eraser tool and drag it over the line until the line disappears.

The Draw Table tool makes it possible to split table cells diagonally, as shown in Figure 2-7. Simply draw the line from the upper right corner of the table cell to the lower left corner. To insert text in a split cell, use the Align Top alignment for the top half of the diagonal cell. Key your text (don't worry if a portion of the diagonal line disappears while you are doing so). Press Enter to insert a new line. Use the spacebar to move into the bottom half of the diagonal cell and key the text for this portion of the cell. To control the location of text more precisely in the bottom portion of the cell, space over to the right border of the cell. Then, set a tab in the white portion of the ruler, which shows the cell width. Backspace to remove your spaces. To move to a tab in a table cell, hold the Ctrl key while pressing Tab.

FIGURE 2-7
Split cells diagonally using the Draw Table tool

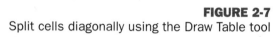

The Draw Table tool stays active until you click the Draw Table button to turn it off. If you want to change the style, width, or color of the gridlines, you can save time by making your choices before you start drawing the gridlines.

STEP-BY-STEP ▷ 2.4

1. You want to add a table showing landscaping that will be done in phase 3 of your master plan. Add a new slide following slide 10 using the Title Only layout. Key the title **Landscape Plan—Phase 3**.

2. Click the **Tables and Borders** button on the toolbar (you might find this button on the More Buttons palette). Using the pencil pointer, begin about an inch below the title and draw an outside border for the table that stops about an inch from the left, bottom, and right sides of the slide.

3. You need four columns for your table, with the first column wider than the other three.

Position the pencil pointer about a third of the way across the table at the top border and then drag downward. After you have dragged about halfway down the table, Power-Point fills in a dotted line as shown in Figure 2-8. Add two additional lines to mark the other three columns.

4. You need seven rows for your data. Using the procedure above, insert six gridlines to mark the seven rows. Notice that PowerPoint automatically distributes the space evenly so that all your rows are the same height.

FIGURE 2-8
Drawing the first line

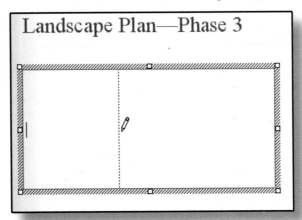

5. Insert the following information in the table:

	Spring	Summer	Fall
Create new beds	X		X
Plant bulbs			X
Plant maples/oaks	X		X
New stone edging		X	
Clear woods	X		
Terracing		X	

6. Adjust columns as necessary to display all the information. Format the table to match the previous table or format as desired.

7. Save your changes and leave the presentation open for the next Step-by-Step.

Concept Builder

You do not have to click the Draw Table tool to deselect it. Once you begin keying text, the tool is automatically deselected.

Integration: Inserting Worksheet Data on a Slide

If you want to include numerical data on a slide, you can use an Excel worksheet to handle the data. You have several options for placing a worksheet on a slide:

■ You can copy data from an existing worksheet and insert it on the slide using the Paste Special command. If you choose Paste in the Paste Special dialog box, you create an ***embedded object***. If you choose Paste Link in the Paste Special dialog box, you create a ***linked object***. You edit an embedded worksheet from PowerPoint by double-clicking the worksheet object. You edit a linked worksheet in Excel. Any changes you make in Excel are then also made in the linked worksheet on the slide.

■ You can also insert an Excel worksheet directly on a slide by using the Object command on the Insert menu. <u>A worksheet inserted this way is an embedded object</u>. When you edit the worksheet, you do so from PowerPoint using Excel's menus and tools.

Using an Excel worksheet to organize data makes sense if you want to calculate the data or format it easily using Excel's cell formatting options. The linking option is a good way to share data between applications. For example, you can maintain data in a worksheet, paste link that data to a PowerPoint slide, and automatically update the slide every time you modify the worksheet data.

In the next Step-by-Step, you will insert an Excel worksheet using the second option above. To start this process, open the Insert menu and click Object. The Insert Object dialog box opens as shown in Figure 2-9. The list of available object types will vary according to the applications on your computer.

FIGURE 2-9
The Insert Object dialog box

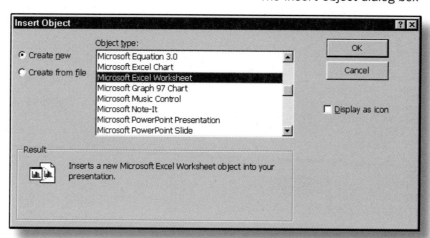

To create a new object, make sure the *Create new* option is selected. Then choose the type of object you want to create from the *Object type* list. Note that you can choose to display the object as an icon rather than full size. When you click OK, the object appears on your slide in a frame with the menus and toolbars of the object's application available for your use.

You can also insert an object that has already been created by another application. Click the *Create from file* option and then key the path to the object or click the Browse button to locate the file on your computer or network. When you choose this option, you can specify that the object be displayed as an icon, as well as specify that it will be a linked object rather than embedded. When you click OK, the object appears on your slide.

When an embedded object is active on a slide, it is surrounded by a hatched border, as shown in Figure 2-10. To see the embedded object in place on the slide, click outside the hatched border. To move or resize the embedded object, click on it once. Eight white handles appear at the borders of the object to indicate it is selected. You can then move the object by dragging or resize it by dragging one of the white handles.

FIGURE 2-10
An embedded object on a slide

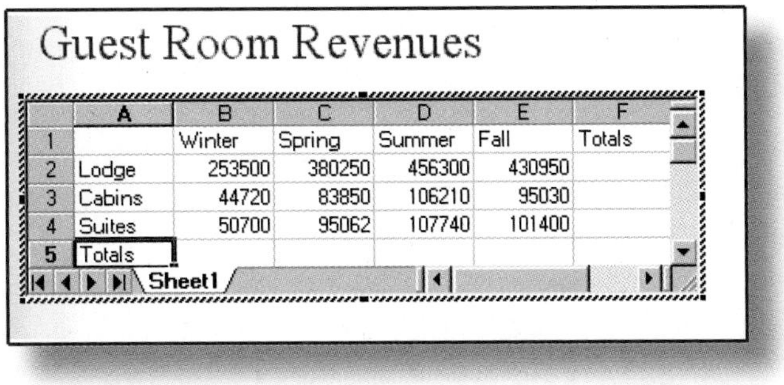

STEP-BY-STEP ▷ 2.5

1. You are now ready to organize some occupancy statistics you have gathered. Because you want to format and calculate these numbers, you decide to insert an Excel worksheet on your slide to handle the data. First, insert a Title Only slide following slide 11. Key the title **Annual Statistics**.

2. Next, insert a Title Only slide following the new slide 12 and title it **Guest Room Revenues**. Click anywhere on the slide to close the placeholder.

3. Open the **Insert** menu and click **Object**. In the Insert Object dialog box, scroll in the *Object type* list to locate **Microsoft Excel Worksheet** and select it. Click **OK**.

4. The worksheet object appears on your slide. Don't worry if the cells appear very small. You will fix that later in this Step-by-Step. Key the information below in the worksheet cells. Remember that you can check the contents of each cell by looking at the formula bar located above the ruler.

	Winter	Spring	Summer	Fall	Totals
Lodge	253500	380250	456300	430950	
Cabins	44720	83850	106210	95030	
Suites	50700	95062	107740	101400	
Totals					

5. Limit the area of the worksheet that displays on the slide:
   a. Position the pointer on the small black rectangle (the sizing handle) in the right hatched border of the object.
   b. When the pointer turns into a double-pointed arrow, carefully drag the hatched border to the left. Release the mouse button when the border is in the middle of column G. The border should then snap to the boundary between columns F and G. You might have to repeat this step to position the border.
   c. Position the pointer on the sizing handle in the middle of the bottom hatched border. When the pointer turns into a double-pointed arrow, drag the bottom border up until it is just below row 5. You might need to repeat this step to move the border just below the data you entered.

6. Click outside the object to see it in place on the slide. Of course, the cell data is much too small. To remedy this, click once on the worksheet object to select it. Drag the right bottom corner handle down and to the right until the edge of the object is about an inch from the right edge of the slide. Notice that the object maintains its original width–height proportions as you resize it.

(continued on next page)

7. Now calculate and format the data as follows:
   a. Double-click the worksheet object to open it in Excel.
   b. Boldface and center the column heads. Boldface the word *Totals* in cell A5.
   c. Format the cell ranges **B2:F2** and **B5:F5** for currency with a dollar sign and no decimals. Format the cell range **B3:F4** for currency with no dollar sign or decimals.
   d. Use the SUM function to total the revenues for each season of the year and each lodging type.
   e. Boldface the totals. After you take this step, you will probably have to widen columns to display all the data. Resize the object as needed to display the data.

8. Click outside the worksheet object to return to PowerPoint. Adjust the position and size of the object if necessary to display it as large as possible.

9. Save your changes and leave the presentation open for the next Step-by-Step.

Working with Data Charts

Numbers can be a step beyond text in terms of conveying information. To go a step beyond numbers, you can use a chart to display number values visually.

PowerPoint offers 14 different types of charts, from the familiar line and pie charts to specialized charts such as bubble charts and pyramid charts. PowerPoint also has a long list of specialized charts that you can customize for your use. The process for inserting a chart, however, is the same no matter what type of chart you want to end up with.

Inserting a Data Chart

PowerPoint offers several slide layouts preformatted to contain charts. The Chart layout lets you insert a chart on the entire lower half of the slide. The Text & Chart and Chart & Text layouts let you insert a chart on a quarter of the slide, with text opposite the chart. You can also insert a chart on any slide by clicking the Chart command on the Insert menu or by clicking the Insert Chart button on the toolbar.

Each chart layout has a chart placeholder. When you double-click the placeholder, PowerPoint displays a sample chart on the slide and the chart *datasheet*, as shown in Figure 2-11. The datasheet is a worksheet-like grid in which you enter text and numbers that will be used to create the chart.

The datasheet contains sample data to guide you in keying your own information. To replace the datasheet data, simply highlight it and key new data. You can also remove sample data by highlighting it and pressing Delete. As you enter your own information, the sample chart on the slide changes to show your data. When you have finished keying your data, you can either close the datasheet by clicking its close box or click outside the chart on the slide to close the datasheet and see the chart in place.

FIGURE 2-11

PowerPoint displays a sample chart when you double-click the placeholder

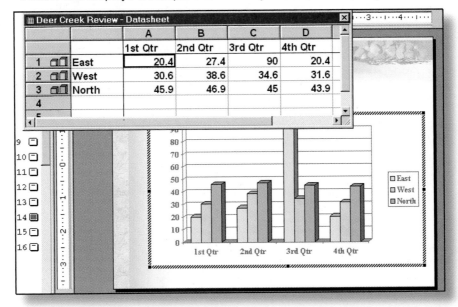

By default, PowerPoint creates a 3-D column chart. You can stick with this default choice or request a different type of chart before you begin entering data in the datasheet. You will learn more about choosing different types of charts in the next section.

Concept Builder

If the data you want to chart is currently located in an Excel worksheet, you can quickly import that data using the Import File command on the Edit menu (or the Import File button on the toolbar). This option lets you find the Excel file, specify which worksheet the data may be found on, and insert the entire file or only a selected range.

STEP-BY-STEP ▷ 2.6

1. Add a new slide after slide 13. Use the Chart layout in the New Slide dialog box. Key the title **Seasonal Lodging Revenues**.

2. Double-click the chart placeholder. Key the information below in the datasheet:

	Winter	Spring	Summer	Fall
Lodge	$253,500	$380,250	$456,300	$430,950
Cabins	44,720	83,850	106,210	95,030
Suites	50,700	95,062	107,740	101,400

3. Click outside the chart to close the datasheet and see the chart in place.

4. Save your changes and leave the presentation open for the next Step-by-Step.

Modifying a Data Chart

Figure 2-12 shows the chart you just created, with parts of the chart labeled. Each of these chart features can be modified to customize the chart. You can also redisplay the datasheet and change the data used to plot the chart. You can even choose a new chart type that you think might display your data better. Before you can modify a chart, you must double-click it to make it active. When active, the chart has a hatched-line border around it.

FIGURE 2-12
The completed data chart

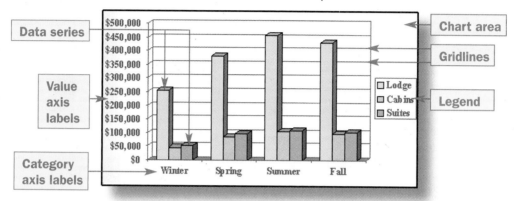

The easiest way to modify a part of a chart is to double-click on the item you want to edit. PowerPoint will then open a dialog box specific to that area. Double-clicking on the legend, for example, opens the Format Legend dialog box. Each of these specific dialog boxes gives you several tabs where you can select from among a number of options. You can change fonts, styles, colors, alignment, number formats, and many other options.

When a chart is active, you also have access to commands on the Chart menu. These commands will vary according to the type of chart, but two commands are always available: Chart Type and Chart Options.

Clicking the Chart Type command opens the dialog box shown in Figure 2-13. Here you can choose a specific kind of chart to create. Each chart type has several variations shown in the *Chart sub-type* area. To choose one of these charts, simply click the example. To see how the data currently entered in the datasheet will look as a particular chart type, press the Press and Hold to View Sample button.

Clicking the Chart Options command opens the dialog box shown in Figure 2-14. The tabs in the Chart Options dialog box let you make a number of alterations to your chart at one time and then put them all into effect by clicking the OK button. Here, for example, you can add titles for the chart and for each axis, specify gridline settings, position the legend, and choose data labels, among other options.

 **Hot Tip**

By default, font sizes of chart elements will change as you resize the chart. This is called Auto scale. To set a fixed size for fonts, remove the check from the *Auto scale* check box on the Font tab.

 **Hot Tip**

Be careful when deciding to change a chart type. Some chart data is not suitable for other chart types.

FIGURE 2-13
The Chart Type dialog box

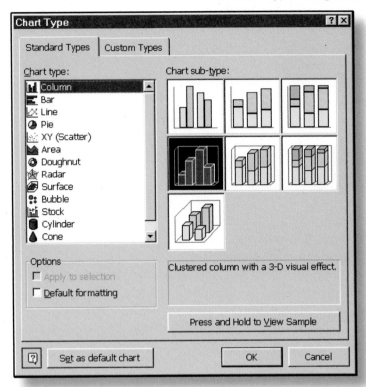

FIGURE 2-14
The Chart Options dialog box

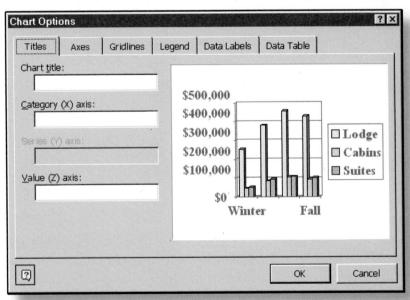

There is one more way to speedily modify the look of your chart. The buttons on the More Buttons palette let you display or remove gridlines or the legend, change the direction of the data series, change fill color for a data series, change the chart type, and even change the size of the chart area. As for all Office 2000 toolbars, these buttons will move off the palette and onto the Standard toolbar as you use them.

You can move and resize a chart in the same way you move and resize a table. Click once on the chart to select it (the white selection handles appear around the chart area). You can then drag the chart where you want it or drag any handle to resize it.

STEP-BY-STEP ▷ 2.7

1. After examining your chart critically, you decide that should have plotted the totals for each season so that you can compare the figures for all types of lodging over the year. You'd also like to make a few other cosmetic changes to the chart. Double-click the chart to open it.

2. If the datasheet does not display, open the **View** menu and click **Datasheet**. In the datasheet, delete all but the column headings of *Winter*, *Spring*, *Summer*, and *Fall*. Insert the following values for these seasons:

   ```
   Winter    Spring    Summer    Fall
   348,920   559,162   670,250   627,380
   ```

3. Close the datasheet. You now have no need for the legend. Remove it by clicking once to select it and then pressing **Delete**. Note that your columns now expand to fill the whole chart area.

4. You'd like to change the look of the category axis labels. Double-click *Winter* to display the Format Axis dialog box. Click the **Font** tab if

necessary and choose **Bold Italic** style. Click **OK** to close the dialog box.

5. You'd like to change the color of the columns. Double-click any column to display the Format Data Series dialog box. Click the **Patterns** tab if necessary. Notice that the design template's default colors appear in the bottom color palette in the *Area* area. Click the dark yellow color and then click **OK**.

6. Click outside the chart to see your changes. You notice that revenues in the winter are significantly lower than those in the other seasons. You and your partner decide to brainstorm some strategies for getting more guests into the Inn during winter. Move to slide 15 and add a bullet point: **Consider ways to improve winter occupancy**.

7. Save your changes and leave the presentation open for the next Step-by-Step.

Creating and Modifying a Pie Chart

Although all charts start with a datasheet, the datasheets for some chart types require you to enter data in a specific way. When creating a pie chart, for example, the sample datasheet looks like the one in Figure 2-15. Pie charts have only one series, despite the data shown in the sample. In order to display each data point as a separate pie slice, you must enter them in the first row under the headings across the datasheet rather than down the first column.

FIGURE 2-15

A sample pie chart datasheet

		A	B	C	D
		1st Qtr	2nd Qtr	3rd Qtr	4th Qtr
1	East	20.4	27.4	90	20.4
2	West	30.6	38.6	34.6	31.6
3	North	45.9	46.9	45	43.9
4					

Deer Creek Review - Datasheet

Pie charts give you some unique opportunities for display. You can create an *exploded slice* on a pie chart to make it more obvious simply by selecting the slice and dragging it away from the pie. You can adjust the location of the various slices by rotating the pie. If you have chosen a 3-D pie chart, you can control the angle at which the pie displays. And, of course, you can also perform any of the modifications you learned about in the previous section.

Concept Builder

If you want to use a column of data for a pie chart, rather than a row of data, click the By Column button on the toolbar. You can then paste or key data down the first column rather than across the first row.

STEP-BY-STEP ▷ 2.8

1. You would like to see a chart showing what percent each lodging option contributes to the overall lodging revenue. Add a new slide following slide 14 using the Chart layout. Key the title **Revenue by Lodging Type**.

2. Double-click the chart placeholder to open the datasheet. Open the **Chart** menu and click **Chart Type**. Click the **Pie** chart type and then click the second pie example in the top row of sub-types, a 3-D pie chart. Click **OK**. Notice that the datasheet changes to the proper format for pie chart data.

3. Delete the sample data (you might need to select a whole column and press **Delete** to remove data) and insert the following information, beginning in column A. Widen the columns by

dragging as you would in a spreadsheet so you can see all values.

Lodge	Cabin	Suites
$1,521,000	$329,810	$354,902

Concept Builder

You can also enter numbers without formatting and then format them using the Number command on the Format menu.

4. Close the datasheet. You want to make a few more cosmetic changes to your pie chart while it is still active.

   a. The legend might look better at the bottom of the chart, and the text in the legend should be larger. Double-click the legend

(continued on next page)

and click the **Placement** tab in the Format Legend dialog box. Then choose the **Bottom** option. Click the **Font** tab and change the font size to **22**. Then click **OK**.

b. To show what percent each pie slice is of the whole, you can add data labels. Double-click on the outside edge of any pie slice to open the Format Data Series dialog box. Click the **Data Labels** tab and choose the **Show percent** option. While you're in this dialog box, you'd like to rotate the first slice so that the Cabins and Suites slices appear at the right side of the pie. Click the **Options** tab. In the *Angle of first slice* text box, click the up arrow until a value of **120** degrees appears. Click **OK**.

c. The impact of the chart would be greater if it weren't so flat. Adjust the angle of the chart: Open the **Chart** menu and click **3-D View**. Change the Elevation of the chart to **25** degrees and then click **OK**.

d. Changing the elevation reduced the size of the pie. You can increase it by adjusting the plot area: Click once on the border around the pie (you will see a ScreenTip identifying it as the Plot Area). Drag a corner handle to increase the pie size. Then click again on the border and drag the pie to center it in the chart area. Remove the border around the pie by selecting it again and pressing **Delete**.

e. You want to point out the interesting fact that even though there are only half as many suites as cabins, the suites still account for more revenue than the cabins. Explode the Suites slice to emphasize this: Click in the middle of the Suites slice so that selection handles appear all the way around the slice. Drag the slice to the right about half an inch.

5. Click outside the chart to see it on the slide. Save your changes. Run the presentation to check your work.

6. Print the presentation as handouts with 9 slides per page. Close the presentation.

Extra Challenge

Insert a text box next to the exploded pie slice and insert a few words to point out that the revenues for the suites are even greater than those for cabins.

Working with Organization Charts

An **organization chart** shows how members of a group are organized. Although organization charts can be used to show the organization of things as well as people, such charts are most commonly used to show the structure of personnel in a company. The head of the company is shown at the top of the chart, with subordinates in levels below the top position.

Figure 2-16 shows an organization chart. Each box holds the name and usually the title of a person in the organization. Notice that the executive director of the organization, Mr. Yarrow, is in the box at the top of the chart. Persons who report to him are listed in the next level. His assistant, Shari, has a box between Mr. Yarrow's box and those of the persons reporting to him. This position indicates that she assists Mr. Yarrow and no other member of the organization.

Persons who report to another person are called *subordinates*. Persons on the same level of an organization chart are called *co-workers*. Persons who supply support services or assist only one member of the staff are called *assistants*. It is possible to have many levels in an organization chart if the organization is a complex one.

FIGURE 2-16

A sample organization chart

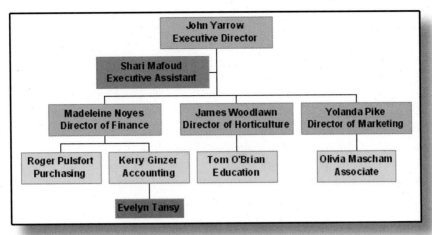

Inserting an Organization Chart on a Slide

PowerPoint supplies a layout specifically for creating an organization chart. As for table and chart layouts, you click the organization chart placeholder to begin creating the chart. PowerPoint then opens the Microsoft Organization Chart application to allow you to create the chart. As shown in Figure 2-17, a sample organization chart opens with the first box active for you to key the information for the top level of the chart.

FIGURE 2-17

Create an organization chart in this application

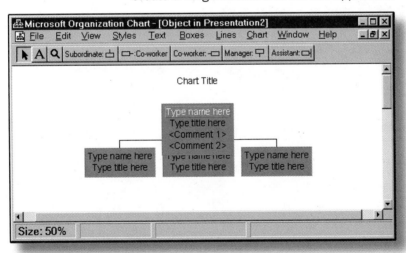

To insert the first name or item, simply start keying in the highlighted *Type name here* line. To add a title for the person, press Enter or Tab to move to the *Type title here* line. You can add additional comments on the *Comment* lines provided in the box. As you key text, the box expands to hold it. When finished, click outside the box. You can then key text in another box by clicking it to select it. The chart adjusts to display all text in all boxes.

After you have entered the information you want in your chart, update the presentation by opening the File menu and clicking Update. (The Update command will also include the title of the current presentation.) Then open the File menu again and click Close and Return to the presentation. The organization chart will be in place on the slide.

Adding Boxes to an Organization Chart

The sample chart that appears when you create a new organization chart has a top level box and three subordinate boxes. Most organizations are more complex than this, however, so you often need to add boxes for assistants, subordinates, and co-workers.

You add boxes using the box tools at the top of the chart window (Figure 2-18). You can use these tools to add a subordinate, a co-worker, a manager, or an assistant. To add a box, click the box tool for the type of box you want to create, then click the box to which you want to attach the new box. Notice that you can add a new co-worker either to the right or the left of a box.

FIGURE 2-18
Box tools

Hot Tip

To add more than one box at a time click the box tool multiple times, and then click the box you want to attach the new boxes to.

STEP-BY-STEP 2.9

You work for the Civic Garden Center in your town. The Civic Garden Center is in the process of reorganizing under a new director. You have been asked to prepare a presentation explaining the new changes. Your first priority is to create an organization chart to show the new structure.

1. Open a new, blank presentation. Accept the Title Slide layout and switch to Slide view. Save the presentation as **Garden Center Reorganization** followed by your initials.

2. Apply a new design template: click the **Common Tasks** button on the toolbar, select **Apply Design Template** on the menu, and locate the **Sandstone** design template. Click **Apply**.

3. Key the title **Civic Garden Center** and the subtitle **Reorganization Issues**. Add a new slide with the Organization Chart layout. (It is

the second layout from the right in the second row.)

4. Key the title **New Organization**. Then double-click the organization chart placeholder. Microsoft Organization Chart opens.

5. Insert names and titles in the chart as follows:
   a. In the top level box, the line *Type name here* is already highlighted for you. Key **Ben Goldman**. Press **Enter** and key **Director**. Click outside the box to close it.
   b. Click in the first subordinate box to the left and key your name. Press **Enter** and key **Special Projects**.
   c. Click in the middle subordinate box and key the name **June Halliday** and the title **Gift Shop Coordinator**.
   d. Click in the rightmost subordinate box and key the name **Larry Bowes** and the title **Operations**.

6. Mr. Goldman has acquired an assistant as a result of the reorganization. Add her box to the chart:

   a. Click the **Assistant** box tool and then click Mr. Goldman's box. The assistant box appears below and to the left of Mr. Goldman's box.

   b. Key the name **Roz Pargeter** and the title **Executive Assistant**.

7. Another result of the reorganization is that subordinates at your level have received salaried assistants, rather than part-time volunteers. Add subordinates as follows:

   a. To add a subordinate to your position, click the **Subordinate** box tool and then click on your box. Key the name **Pat Tomita**.

   b. June Halliday has two new assistants. Click the **Subordinate** box tool *twice* and then click June Halliday's box. Key the names **Teri Ogama** and **Shelley Martin**.

c. Add a subordinate to Larry Bowes named **Jean Suget**. Then add a subordinate to Jean Suget named **Liz Grantham**.

 Did You Know?

You can resize the Microsoft Organization Chart window to see more of the chart area by dragging the bottom right corner down and to the right. Or you can maximize the window.

8. Open the **File** menu in the chart window and click **Update Garden Center Reorganization**. Then open the **File** menu again and click **Close and Return to Garden Center Reorganization**. The organization chart appears on your slide.

9. Save your changes and leave the presentation open for the next Step-by-Step.

Modifying an Organization Chart

You can modify an organization chart in a number of ways to make it more attractive and useful. Menus on the menu bar in the organization chart window give you options to change the style of the chart (how the boxes are displayed), the text in the boxes, box color and border, the lines between boxes, and the background of the chart. An organization chart is embedded on your slide just as is a chart or a table. To edit the chart, you double-click it to open the Microsoft Organization Chart application.

Before you can make modifications to a box, you must select it by clicking on it. If you want to make changes to a number of boxes, you can use the selection commands on the Edit menu. Click Select on the Edit menu to see a submenu of options you can select, such as All Managers or Connecting Lines. Click Select Levels to select specific levels in the chart. The top level is 1, and each level below that level has the next higher number. Your current chart, for instance, has four levels (the assistant is grouped with the first subordinate level). You can also select specific boxes by clicking the first, holding down the Shift key, and then selecting additional boxes.

You have many options for formatting the boxes in the chart. You can:

■ Change the way boxes are presented in the chart using the options on the Styles menu.

■ Change the font, font style, font size, color, and alignment of text using commands on the Text menu.

■ Change the color of the boxes using the Color command on the Boxes menu. This menu also allows you to select a shadow option for the boxes and change the border style, border color, and border line style for the boxes.

- Change the thickness, style, and color of the lines that connect the boxes using commands on the Lines menu.

- Change the background color of the chart using the Chart menu.

After you have created a chart, it is easy to restructure the chart. To change the level of a box, select it and drag it to attach it to a box at the new level. To remove a box, select the box and press Delete.

You can also make size modifications to the chart on the slide. Click the chart once to display handles, and drag the handles to increase or reduce the size of the chart. Drag the chart itself to relocate it on the slide.

S TEP-BY-STEP ▷ 2.10

1. You think the text in the chart would be easier to read if it were bold. Double-click the chart to edit it. Change the text in all boxes to bold as follows:
   a. Open the **Edit** menu and click **Select**. On the submenu, click **All**.
   b. Open the **Text** menu and click **Font**. Choose the **Bold** font style and click **OK**.

2. You'd like to add a shadow border to the boxes. With the boxes still selected, open the **Boxes** menu and click **Shadow**. On the submenu, choose the second shadow option in the second column. Click anywhere in the window to remove the highlight.

3. The connecting lines now look too thin. Open the **Edit** menu, click **Select**, and then click **Connecting Lines** on the submenu. Open the **Lines** menu and click **Thickness**. Choose the second line on the submenu (the one below the currently checked line). Click in the window to remove the highlight.

4. You have made a mistake in showing Liz Grantham as subordinate to Jean Suget. Liz and Jean are co-workers. To make this clear, click Liz's box to select it and drag it up until Jean Suget's box becomes highlighted. Release the mouse button. Both boxes should now be subordinate to Larry Bowes.

5. You'd like to emphasize the new staff positions by making their boxes a different color:
   a. Click in Roz Pargeter's box. Hold the **Shift** key and click each of the boxes in the last level of the chart.
   b. Open the **Boxes** menu and click **Color**. Choose the white color on the palette and click **OK**.

6. Click **Update Garden Center Reorganization** on the **File** menu. Then click **Close and Return to Garden Center Reorganization** on the **File** menu.

7. The organization chart is much too small at its current size. White selection handles should still be showing around the chart (if they aren't, click once on the chart to select it). Drag bottom corner handles to increase the size of the chart as much as possible. Then center it in the text area.

8. Run the slide show to see your organization chart at full size.

9. Save your changes. Print the presentation as handouts with 2 slides per page. Close the presentation.

SCANS

✳ PROJECT 2-1

You are an employee of the Madison County Park System. In the upcoming fall elections, citizens of Madison County will have the opportunity to vote on a tax levy that will supply funds to the park system, among other causes. The park system intends to use some of the levied monies to restore wetlands areas in several parks. As you have been trying to persuade friends and neighbors to vote for the levy, you have been asked over and over what a wetland actually is, and why would anyone want more of them. You decided to prepare a presentation on the subject that can be used in park centers to educate visitors. Your presentation is almost done, but you think it could benefit from some additional slides giving facts and figures about wetlands.

1. Open **AP Project2-1** from the student data files. Save the file as **Wetlands** followed by your initials. Scroll through the slides to become familiar with their content.

2. You think a table might be helpful to describe some of the different types of wetlands. Insert a new Table layout slide following slide 3. Title the slide **Wetland Characteristics**. Insert the following information in the table:

Name	Locations	Habitat for . . .
Freshwater marsh	Widespread	Grasses, frogs
Tidal marsh	Intertidal zones	Grasses, crabs, clams
Fen	Areas of mineral-rich water	Grasses, shrubs, trees
Bog	Glaciated areas	Sphagnum moss, shrubs, trees
Swamp	Saturated or flooded areas	Cypresses, gums, maples
Mangrove flat	Subtropical areas	Mangroves

3. Modify the table as necessary to fit all the information on the slide without overcrowding. Format the table as desired.

4. Visitors come to the Madison County Parks from two states other than the state in which the parks are located (Ohio). You decide a chart might help to show how many acres of wetlands have been lost since the first surveys of the country in 1780. Follow these steps:

   A. Add a new slide following slide 10 with the Chart layout. Key the title **Local Wetland Losses**. Create a column chart for the data below:

	Ohio	Indiana	Michigan
1780	5,000	5,600	11,200
1980	483	751	5,583

   B. Format the chart as desired. Insert the following value axis label: **In 1,000s of Acres**. (*Hint:* To add an axis label, open the **Chart** menu and click **Chart Options**. Insert the title on the **Titles** tab).

Summary

In this lesson, you learned:

■ You can use a table to organize text on a slide. To handle numerical data that you want to be able to format and calculate easily, use an Excel worksheet.

■ You can either embed or link an object on a slide. An embedded object is edited in PowerPoint using the menus and tools of its source application. A linked object is edited in the source application and the edits then appear in the linked object.

■ To show a visual representation of numerical data, use a data chart. PowerPoint offers 14 different types of charts, plus custom charts. To create a chart, insert the data in the chart's datasheet. You can then modify many parts of the chart to present the data just as you want.

■ You can use an organization chart to show how the members of a group relate to one another.

LESSON 2 REVIEW QUESTIONS

TRUE/FALSE

Circle T if the statement is true or F if the statement is false.

T **F** 1. You can create a table only on a Table layout slide. *Table Slide Layout / Insert Table / Draw Table*

T F 2. You can change a table column's width simply by dragging the gridline.

T **F** 3. You must use a worksheet for any table that contains numbers.

T **F** 4. By default, PowerPoint creates a line chart. *3D Column*

T **F** 5. To create an organization chart, you draw boxes right on your slide.

FILL IN THE BLANKS

Complete the following sentences by writing the correct word or words in the blanks provided.

1. Use the ___*pen*___ tool to place gridlines in a table right where you want them.

2. You can find a number of tools useful for creating and modifying tables on the *Tables + Borders* toolbar.

3. You edit an embedded worksheet from PowerPoint by *double clicking* the worksheet object.

4. You key information you want to use in a chart in the *datasheet*.

5. To emphasize a slice of a pie chart, you *explode* the slice.

5. One of the most alarming facts about wetland loss is the rate of loss in this century. You have some data ending in 1985 that shows how the rate of loss has increased. Although not right up to the minute, it shows the trend of loss over the century. A line chart would be perfect to display this data. Follow these steps:

   A. Add a new slide following slide 11 with the Chart layout. Title the slide **Rate of Wetland Loss**. Create a line chart using the following data:

	1913	1946	1967	1980	1985
Coastal areas	8.5	20.1	35.7	50.1	55.0
Other areas	6.7	15.8	28.1	39.4	45.0

   B. Format the lines and the legend as desired. Insert the following value axis label: **Land Loss in Sq Mi/Yr**

6. Save your changes. Run the slide show.

7. Print the presentation as handouts with 6 slides per page. Close the presentation.

✳ PROJECT 2-2

You (the meteorologist) have been refining your weather presentation. You have added information about hurricanes. You now want to add some interesting (and frightening) data about weather-related disasters.

1. Open **AP Project2-2** from the student data files. Save the file as **Weather** followed by your initials. Scroll through the slides to become familiar with the new material.

2. As a general introduction to the costly side of weather, you want to add a table listing various kinds of weather disasters and their costs in dollars and lives. Add a new slide following slide 2 with the title **Costs of Weather Disasters**. Insert a table to present the following information. Then format the table as desired.

Disaster	Economic Costs	Deaths
Floods	$31 billion	171
Drought	$5 billion	Unknown
Hurricanes	$40 billion	159
Other storms	$15 billion	517

3. Insert a text box below the table to contain the following information: **Billion-dollar weather-related disasters in the U.S. during the 1990s.**

4. People are always asking you how hurricane categories are determined. Why not include a table showing the characteristics of each category of hurricane? Add a slide following slide 5 with the title **The Saffir-Simpson Scale**. Draw a table to present the following information and then format the table as desired. (*Hints:* Don't forget to use the en dash for ranges of numbers. Use

A P - 4 3

the Symbol command to insert the straight quotation marks ["] that stand for inches in the barometric pressures.)

Scale	Central Pressure	Winds mph	Damage
1	>28.94"	74–95	Minimal
2	28.91–28.50"	96–110	Moderate
3	28.47–27.91"	111–130	Extensive
4	27.88–27.17"	131–155	Extreme
5	<27.17"	>155	Catastrophic

5. Save your changes. Print the first eight slides in the presentation as handouts with 9 slides per page.

6. Close the presentation.

PROJECT 2-3

SCANS

Create a presentation to summarize information about a company or organization with which you are familiar. Start with a title slide giving the name of the company or organization. Add a bulleted list of general information. Then insert an organization chart to show the structure of the company or organization. Give the presentation an appropriate name and print it as handouts.

CRITICAL THINKING

ACTIVITY 2-1

SCANS

You work for a company whose stock is traded on a local exchange. Your boss has asked you to prepare a chart showing the stock's performance over the past month. What kind of information do you need to gather to create such a chart? What kind of chart would you use for this task? Create some hypothetical data and create the necessary chart.

ACTIVITY 2-2

SCANS

You are in charge of maintaining data in Excel for your company's local sales. For an upcoming sales meeting, you have been asked to prepare a number of Excel charts detailing performance by each salesperson as well as total sales, sales by quarter, and sales by client. At the last moment, the Sales Manager asks if you can supply slides showing those charts. Can you insert the chart data on a slide without having to recreate each chart?

Use PowerPoint's Help system to explore your options for transferring data and charts from Excel to PowerPoint. Using Word, write a brief summary of your best option.

WORKING WITH VISUAL AND SOUND OBJECTS

OBJECTIVES

Upon completion of this lesson, you should be able to:

- Insert and modify clip art.

- Use the drawing tools to create simple drawings.

- Insert pictures and scanned images on slides.

- Insert sound objects on slides.

- Insert video clips on slides.

🕐 **Estimated Time: 2 hours**

Tables and charts are a great way to organize data as well as add further interest to your slides. In this lesson, you learn about a number of other objects you can add to slides to make them even more appealing to your audience. You probably already know how to insert clip art onto a slide. In this lesson, you'll learn how to modify clip art in several ways. You'll also learn the basics of using PowerPoint's drawing tools. To add further interest to your slides, you'll learn how to insert sound, picture, and video objects.

Working with Clip Art

Although Office 2000 gives you access to many clip art images (and even more on the Clip Gallery's Web site), you might find that the graphic you pick isn't *quite* right for your slide. Perhaps the colors in the graphic don't go well with your current design template. Or perhaps you need only part of the graphic. Or perhaps it's not the right size for the location you've chosen.

Fortunately, you can modify clip art graphics to solve these problems. You can resize and move a piece of clip art, use a cropping tool to remove parts of the graphic you don't want, and recolor parts of the graphic to match your current design template colors.

FIGURE 3-1
The Picture toolbar

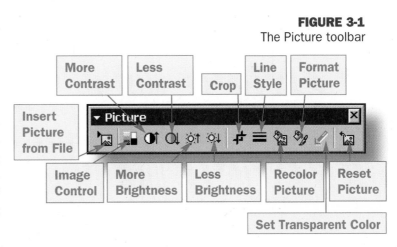

The Picture toolbar (Figure 3-1) contains a number of tools you can use to modify clip art. The Picture toolbar displays each time you select a graphic. If the toolbar does not display, you can turn it back on by right-clicking any toolbar and then selecting Picture.

Resizing and Moving Clip Art

Resizing and moving clip art graphics are very simple procedures. Once you have inserted the graphic, click it once to select it. The white selection handles appear to let you know the object is selected.

To move the graphic, drag it to the place you want it. Or to move it to another slide, click the Cut command, move to the slide where you want the graphic, and then click the Paste command.

You have several options for resizing a graphic. The simplest way is to drag one of the selection handles in the direction you want to resize. When resized this way, the graphic does not necessarily maintain its original proportions. It is possible to distort the graphic this way—and you might want to do so to make a particular point.

To size a graphic more exactly, open the Format menu and choose Picture. The Format Picture dialog box opens. Click the Size tab to see options for sizing a picture, as shown in Figure 3-2. You can enter a specific height or width for the picture. Or you can specify a percentage reduction or enlargement for the picture. The check mark in the *Lock aspect ratio* check box makes sure that the picture's height-to-width ratio remain the same as you resize.

 **Hot Tip**

You can also open the Format Picture dialog box by clicking the Format Picture button on the Picture toolbar. (The dialog box and the button change their names depending on what kind of graphic object you have selected.)

FIGURE 3-2
Use options on the Size tab to resize a graphic

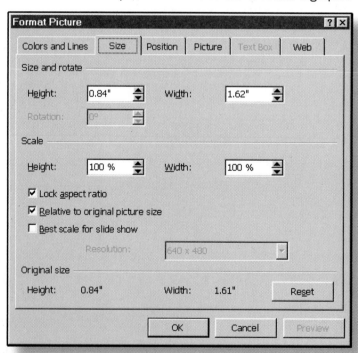

Cropping Clip Art

If you want to display only a portion of the clip art graphic on your slide, you can **crop** the graphic using the Crop tool on the Picture toolbar. To use the Crop tool, click the tool and then position the cropping pointer over a selection handle. Drag the handle upward or inward to remove a portion of the graphic. Dragging upward on the Crop tool shown in Figure 3-3, for example, will "erase" the bottom portion of the mountain. Click the Crop tool again when you have finished cropping.

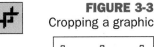

FIGURE 3-3
Cropping a graphic

Cropping tool

Recoloring Clip Art

You are not limited to the original colors of a clip art graphic. The Recolor Picture tool lets you customize a graphic by changing its colors to match those of your current design template. Or you can pick from a large palette of colors or even create your own custom color.

Clicking the Recolor Picture tool opens a Recolor Picture dialog box, such as the one shown in Figure 3-4. All colors used to create the graphic are shown. To change one of the colors, click the down arrow next to the color in the New column. PowerPoint displays a palette of colors for the current design template. To see other colors, click the More Colors button. You can then choose from a palette of colors on the Standard tab or choose to create your own color on the Custom tab. You can see the result of your changes in the preview window.

FIGURE 3-4
Change graphic colors in the Recolor Picture dialog box

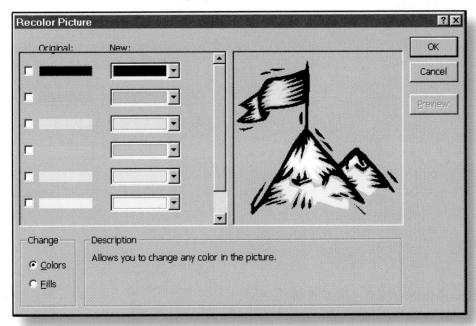

After you choose a new color, PowerPoint checks the check box next to that color to indicate it has been changed from the original. The original color is still displayed. To return to the original color, simply click the original color.

SCANS

One of your friends at ExperTech is so impressed by your work on Claire's roller coaster presentation that he asks for your help in preparing his own Brown Bag Forum lecture on exploration in the solar system. You have agreed to help him tweak the presentation into shape. (You have to learn to say no!)

1. Open data file **AP Step3-1**. Save the file as **Solar System** followed by your initials. Scroll through the slides to become familiar with their content.

2. Your friend has suggested that some kind of clip art might liven up the first slide. To insert the clip art, follow these steps:
   a. With slide 1 on the screen, click the **Insert Clip Art** button on the Drawing toolbar (*not* the Picture toolbar). After a few ~~minutes,~~ *seconds,* the Insert ClipArt dialog box opens.
   b. Scroll to locate the Science & Technology category and click it. Scroll through the images to find one that looks like the solar system. The ScreenTip reads SCIENCE MEDICINE ORBIT WMF. If you do not find clip art that matches this description, locate another clip art graphic that seems related to the subject.
   c. Click the clip art, and then choose **Insert Clip** from the pop-out menu. Close the Insert ClipArt dialog box.

3. The clip art has been inserted in the middle of the slide. To move it, click on it once to select it, if necessary, and drag it above the title.

4. Resize the graphic by clicking the bottom right corner handle and dragging downward and to the right until the graphic is about as wide as the title. Center the graphic in the space above the title.

5. The primary color scheme doesn't exactly match the colors in your current design scheme (much less nature). Recolor the planets in the solar system as follows:
   a. With the graphic still selected, click **Recolor Picture** on the Picture toolbar.
   b. In your estimation, the sun ought to be more yellow than red. Click the down arrow next to the red color in the Recolor Picture dialog box. None of the colors in the current design template palette are appropriate, so click **More Colors**. On the **Standard** tab, choose a bright yellow color for the sun. Click **OK**.
   c. You might now have both a yellow sun and a yellow planet. To change the color of the yellow planet (which might be Mercury), click the down arrow next to the yellow that does not have a check mark. Choose the dark red from the design template color palette.
   d. Using the procedure above, recolor the green planet and the blue planet as desired. When you are satisfied with your choices, click **OK**.

6. Save your changes and leave the presentation open for the next Step-by-Step.

Inserting Animated Clip Art

PowerPoint 2000 supports animated GIF (Graphics Interchange Format) clip art files. Animated GIFs will play during a presentation but not in Slide view. The best location to find animated clip art is on Microsoft's Clip Gallery Live Web site. You can easily jump to the Web site by clicking Clips Online in the Insert ClipArt dialog box.

Clip Gallery Live gives you access to many more clip art pictures than are installed with Office 2000. You can choose to download clip art graphics, pictures, sounds, or motion clips. A search feature lets you find clip art relating to a keyword or you can browse by category as in the Insert ClipArt dialog box. After you download a clip, it appears in the proper category in Office 2000's Clip Gallery so that you can use it again in the future.

You can also easily insert clip art of any type (graphics or animated GIFs) stored as a file on your computer (rather than in the Clip Gallery). To insert a clip art file, open the Insert menu, choose Picture, and then click From File. In the Insert Picture dialog box, locate the file and then click Insert.

Once an animated clip art graphic has been inserted, you can resize it and move it as desired, but you cannot edit the picture as you would any other clip art graphic. To modify an animated graphic, you need to use a program designed especially for creating animated bitmaps.

S TEP-BY-STEP ▷ 3.2

Complete this Step-by-Step if you can access the Clip Gallery Live Web site or if your instructor has provided an animated clip art file for you. To insert an animated clip art graphic supplied by your instructor, skip to step 7.

1. Scroll to the last slide in the show and then add a new slide with the **Blank** layout.

2. Click the **Insert Clip Art** button on the Drawing toolbar. The Insert ClipArt dialog box opens.

3. Click **Clips Online** in the Insert ClipArt dialog box. Then click **OK** to jump to the Web site. At the Clip Gallery Live Web site, click the **Accept** button to accept the terms and conditions for using clip art.

4. On the Clip Gallery Live Web page, click the **Motion** tab. (You might receive an error message. Click **OK**.) In the *Search Clips by Keyword* box, key **orbit**. Then click **go**. At least one animated clip art file should appear for downloading.

5. Click the **Download This Clip Now!** down arrow below the clip art. After a few moments, the downloaded clip will appear in the Insert ClipArt dialog box on the Motion Clips tab.

6. Click the clip art and choose to insert it on your slide. Go on to step 8.

7. To insert an animated clip art file from another source, open the **Insert** menu and click **Picture**. Then click **From File** on the submenu. In the Insert Picture dialog box, locate the data files for this lesson and click the name of the animated clip art file. Click **Insert**.

8. Resize the graphic by dragging a corner handle until it is about half again as big. Center the graphic in the lower portion of the slide.

9. Note that the graphic does not move in this view. You will see the animation later, when you run the slide show.

10. Save your changes and leave the presentation open for the next Step-by-Step.

Using Drawing Tools

PowerPoint's Drawing toolbar contains a number of useful tools (see Figure 3-5) almost identical to those you have already studied in Word. While you cannot create a complex illustration with these tools (for that you need a dedicated drawing program), you can easily create simple graphics to help illustrate your slides.

You can tell what many of the tools on the toolbar do just by looking at them. The Line tool, for example, draws straight lines. Some of the other tools and menus require more explanation.

FIGURE 3-5
The Drawing toolbar tools

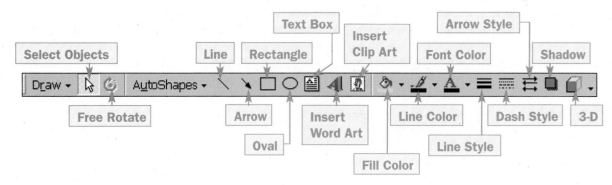

- The Draw pop-up menu contains a number of commands useful for working with the objects in a drawing, such as Group, Rotate or Flip, and Order.

- The AutoShapes pop-up menu displays five categories of predrawn shapes that you can use by themselves or as part of a drawing. AutoShapes can be inserted and resized easily. You can add text to an AutoShape by right-clicking the shape and selecting Add Text from the shortcut menu. Then, begin keying your text. When you add text this way, it does not automatically wrap in the AutoShape. To force the text to wrap, select the AutoShape if necessary, open the Format menu, choose AutoShape, and click on the Text box tab in the Format AutoShape dialog box. Click in the *Word wrap text in AutoShape* check box. To resize the AutoShape to accommodate text, click in the *Resize Autoshape to fit text* check box.

- You will use the coloring tools (Fill Color, Line Color, and Font Color) very often to change the color of filled objects, change the color of lines in the drawing, and change the color of text in text boxes.

- The Shadow tool adds a shadow to any selected object and the 3-D tool transforms a shape into the 3-D version of your choice.

If you are having trouble positioning an object, you can turn off the Snap command on the Draw pop-up menu. The Snap feature automatically aligns objects to an invisible grid. Another helpful command is Nudge, which will let you move an object by very small amounts in any direction.

To line up more than one object in a drawing, use the Align or Distribute command on the Draw menu. This command gives you a number of ways to align objects. You can align them at the left, center, right, top, middle, or bottom. You can also choose to distribute a number of objects evenly across the slide.

Before you can work with more than one object, you must select all the objects so they can be modified at the same time. You select more than one object by clicking the first one, then holding the Shift key and clicking each additional object.

To make it easier to copy or move a drawing that contains a number of objects, use the Group command on the Draw menu. Select all the objects that make up the drawing and then click the Group command. To modify one of the objects in the group, you must first Ungroup the objects.

Remember that drawing tools layer objects as you draw them. The first object is drawn in the top layer, but as you continue to draw objects, the first object is pushed down to the bottom. You can control the layering process using the Order command on the Draw menu. Select an object whose layer you want to adjust and then click the Order command and tell PowerPoint what layer to move the object to.

S TEP-BY-STEP ▷ 3.3

In this Step-by-Step, you create a simple drawing of one of the spacecraft used to explore our solar system. Don't worry about matching the sample drawing exactly. The important point to this exercise is to become familiar with the drawing tools and commands.

1. Your friend has given you a simple sketch of an exploration spacecraft to use as an illustration for his presentation. It is shown in Figure 3-6 and labeled according to his scrawled notes. You think you can re-create this drawing on a slide using PowerPoint's drawing tools.

FIGURE 3-6
The sample illustration

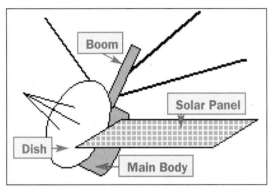

 Did You Know?

The Voyager spacecraft that surveyed planets at the far end of the solar system are still in flight and collecting data.

2. Move to slide 2. To free up space for the drawing, select the bulleted text placeholder, click the right middle selection handle, and drag the placeholder border about halfway across the slide.

3. First, create the main body of the craft using an AutoShape:
   a. Click **AutoShapes** on the Drawing toolbar, and then choose **Flowchart**. A palette of flowchart shapes displays. Click the second shape from the right in the last row, a 3-D cylinder.
   b. Drag the cross-shaped pointer to draw a shape about 1 inch tall and 1 inch wide. If the object does not automatically fill with a tan color, click the down arrow next to the **Fill Color** tool on the Drawing toolbar and choose the tan color from the palette.
   c. The cylinder is currently "facing" the wrong direction. To flip it, click **Draw** on the Drawing toolbar, and then choose **Rotate or Flip**. Click **Flip Horizontal**. The cylinder is now facing the right direction.
   d. The cylinder must be rotated to match the drawing. To rotate it, click the **Free Rotate** tool on the Drawing toolbar. Notice that the object is now surrounded by four green dots. Position the Rotate pointer on the lower left dot and drag to the left to rotate the cylinder about 45 degrees. Click the **Free Rotate** tool again to turn it off.

4. Create the dish next:
   a. Click the **Oval** tool on the Drawing toolbar. Draw an oval to match the size of the dish in the sample drawing.
   b. Rotate the oval about the same amount as the cylinder. Drag it into position over the cylinder.
   c. With the oval still selected, click the **Fill Color** tool on the Drawing toolbar. Select the white color from the palette.

5. Use the **Line** tool on the Drawing toolbar to draw the three lines in the dish to match those in the sample.

 Concept Builder

To draw exactly straight horizontal, vertical, and 45-degree lines, hold down the Shift key as you draw.

(continued on next page)

6. The boom is a long, thin rectangle. Use the **Rectangle** tool on the Drawing toolbar to draw the boom. Then rotate it to match the rotation of the cylinder and drag it into position. It will probably cover a portion of the oval. To solve this problem, with the rectangle still selected, click **Draw** on the Drawing toolbar, click **Order**, and then choose **Send to Back**.

7. Now draw the three lines extending from the boom and the main body (who knows what they are!). To make these lines heavier, with each line selected, click the **Line Style** tool on the Drawing toolbar and choose heavier weights for the lines (at least $1\frac{1}{2}$ pt).

8. Finally, you are ready to draw the solar panel:
   a. Click **AutoShapes** on the Drawing toolbar, choose **Basic Shapes**, and click the second AutoShape in the top row. Draw a slanted rectangle to match the size in the sample.
   b. Change the line style to $\frac{1}{2}$ **pt**.
   c. To insert the patterned fill, click the **Fill Color** tool on the Drawing toolbar and click **Fill Effects** at the bottom of the palette. The Fill Effects dialog box opens. Click the **Pattern** tab. Click the small grid pattern at the far right of the first row. Change the colors of the pattern by first clicking the **Foreground** color and choosing white. Then click the **Background** color and choose the tan color. Click **OK**.
   d. Move the solar panel into place if necessary.

9. Make any adjustments desired to shapes, positions, and colors. Then, to make it easy to move the drawing, click first the solar panel, then hold **Shift** and click all other objects. Click **Draw** on the Drawing toolbar and choose **Group**. Selection handles now surround the entire drawing. If your bulleted list placeholder gets in the way while you are trying to group objects, click away from the drawing and move the bulleted list placeholder further out of the way. Then try grouping again.

10. Drag the drawing to center it in the right half of the slide. Then drag the bulleted text placeholder back to its original position.

11. Save your changes and leave the presentation open for the next Step-by-Step.

Inserting Pictures and Scanned Images

You can add considerably more interest to a presentation by inserting pictures. You can find pictures in a number of locations: on the Web and on CD-ROM collections of line drawings and photographs, to name just two.

Pictures can be saved to file in many different formats. Images on the Internet are usually in JPG (called JPEGs) or GIF format. Pictures from other sources may be in BMP or TIFF format. The size of a picture in kilobytes (or even megabytes) depends on its resolution and the format used to save it. JPEG images, for example, tend to take up fewer bytes than TIFF images.

Hot Tip

To find out more about graphic file formats, consult PowerPoint's Office Assistant.

Inserting a picture is as easy as inserting clip art. Open the Insert menu, click Picture, and then click From File. Locate the picture file in the Insert Picture dialog box, shown in Figure 3-7. Once you have inserted the picture, you can resize and position it just as you would a clip art graphic.

FIGURE 3-7

Locate a picture in the Insert Picture dialog box

You can use options on the Picture toolbar to adjust the way the picture looks. The Image Control tool lets you display a picture as grayscale, black and white, or a watermark. The Contrast controls let you change the current contrast of the picture to make elements more clear. The Brightness controls let you lighten or darken the image.

You can also create a picture for a presentation by scanning a picture directly onto your slide. With your scanner connected to your computer, open the Insert menu, click Picture, and then choose From Scanner or Camera. You can select the quality of the scan according to how you intend to use it. After the scanned image appears on the slide, you can use the tools on the Picture toolbar to modify the image.

S TEP-BY-STEP ▷ 3.4

1. You have a good picture of Jupiter that would liven up the Jupiter slide. Insert the picture following these steps:

a. Move to slide 7. Open the **Insert** menu, click **Picture**, and then **From File**. In the Insert Picture dialog box, locate the data

files for this lesson. Click **Jupiter** and then click **Insert**.

b. Move the inserted picture to the lower right corner of the slide. Enlarge it to fill the corner without covering any text.

(continued on next page)

2. The picture is a little dark as it is. With the picture selected, click **More Brightness** on the Picture toolbar several times to lighten up the picture.

3. Save your changes and leave the presentation open for the next Step-by-Step.

Concept Builder

You can find pictures and other multimedia objects available for downloading from the Internet. But be careful when downloading or copying files from the Internet! To avoid serious problems, check downloaded files immediately for viruses. And remember—many collections of video and audio clips contain material obtained without proper copyright permission. Don't make the same mistake yourself!

Inserting Sound Objects

Sound objects can add interesting effects to your slides. You will learn later in this unit how to add sound effects to slide transitions and animations so that slides and objects "make noise" as they appear. But you can also add specific sound objects to individual slides that help illustrate the point of the slide.

Adding a sound object is as easy as adding clip art or a picture. Open the Insert menu, choose Movies and Sounds, and then choose either Sound from Gallery or Sound from File. If you have downloaded sounds from Clip Gallery Live, they will appear in the Insert Sound dialog box in the proper category. If you have a sound file elsewhere on your computer, use the Sound from File command to locate and insert the sound. A sound file is inserted on the current slide as an icon, as shown in Figure 3-8.

If you want to record your own sound, you can do so by clicking Record Sound on the Movies and Sounds submenu. Click the Record button to begin recording and the Stop button to stop recording. When you click OK, the sound you just recorded is inserted on the current slide as an icon.

The Play CD Audio Track option on the Movies and Sounds submenu lets you link an audio CD to your slides. You can choose the track from the CD to play and even control how much of that track to play. A loop option lets you repeat a track or portion of a track.

When inserting a sound object, PowerPoint will ask you whether you want the sound to play automatically when the slide appears. If you click Yes, the sound will play each time the slide displays in Slide Show view. If you choose No, you can play the sound during the presentation by clicking on it. (You will learn some other ways to control objects such as sound clips in future lessons.) You can test a sound without running the presentation by double-clicking the sound object in Normal view.

FIGURE 3-8
A sound object on a slide

Hot Tip

Windows 98 contains a number of sound files you can use in presentations. In the Windows folder, locate the Media folder and open it to see available sound files.

STEP-BY-STEP ▷ 3.5

1. To really get the audience in the mood for space, you'd like to add the sound of a rocket taking off. Move to slide 1.

2. Open the **Insert** menu, choose **Movies and Sounds**, and then click **Sound from File**. In the Insert Sound dialog box, locate the data files for this lesson. Click **liftoff** and then click **OK**.

3. When asked if you want the sound to play automatically, click **No**.

4. Move the sound object to the lower right corner of the slide.

5. To test the sound, change to Normal view, if necessary, and double-click the sound object.

6. Save your changes and leave the presentation open for the next Step-by-Step.

Inserting Movie Clips

Movie or video clips can add an extra dimension to a presentation. Most slides are rather static, so you can make your audience really sit up and take notice by including a video clip.

Video clips are inserted the same way any other object is inserted on a slide. Open the Insert menu and choose Movies and Sounds and then Movie from Gallery or Movie from File. If you have previously downloaded movies to the Clip Gallery, you can locate them by clicking the appropriate category. Use Movie from File to locate a video clip elsewhere on your computer.

As for sounds, you will be asked if you want the clip to play automatically when the slide displays. Click No if you want to control when to play the video. The inserted clip resembles a picture and can be resized and moved in the same way as a picture.

Web Sites

Web sites supported by various branches of the U.S. government are good sources of images, sounds, and video clips. Most such sites will allow you to use their multimedia materials in any nonprofit application, such as a personal Web page.

STEP-BY-STEP ▷ 3.6

1. The final object your friend wants you to add to his presentation is a video clip showing more information about the Mars Pathfinder mission. The video clip should go on slide 6. To make room for it, change the slide layout to Text & Media Clip.

2. Open the **Insert** menu, click **Movies and Sounds**, and then choose **Movie from File**. In the Insert

Movie dialog box, locate the data files for this lesson. Click **Mars video** and then click **OK**. When asked if you want the video to play automatically, click **No**.

3. The video clip displays in the media clip placeholder. To resize the clip, select it if necessary and access the Format Picture dialog box. Click the

(continued on next page)

Size tab and change the width of the picture to 3.75 inches. Click **OK**. Center the video clip in the space allotted for it at the right side of the slide.

4. You have now completed the slides for the presentation. Save your changes and run the presentation. Test the sound object and the video clip by clicking them once after you have read the text on those slides.

5. Print the slide show as handouts with 6 slides per page. Close the presentation.

Extra Challenge

Search the Web for pictures of the other planets discussed in this presentation and add them to the appropriate slides.

Summary

In this lesson, you learned:

■ Clip art graphics can be easily modified to fit the design scheme of your slide show. You can resize and move, recolor, and crop clip art to achieve just the look you want. You can also insert animated clip art images that move when displayed in a slide show.

■ PowerPoint's drawing tools can be used to create simple drawings to enhance a slide. PowerPoint provides a number of tools and commands to help you position and modify objects in a drawing.

■ Pictures can be used to add even more visual interest to a slide. Pictures can include photographs or line drawings. If you have a scanner attached to your computer, you can scan a picture right into place on a slide.

■ Sound and video clips provide other multimedia interest to a slide show. Sounds and video clips are added as easily as clip art and pictures. You can instruct PowerPoint to play them automatically when displaying them in the slide show or you can control when they play.

■ Clip Gallery Live is a Web site you can reach easily from the Insert ClipArt dialog box. Clip Gallery Live gives you access to numerous clip art graphics, pictures, sounds, and animated GIFs. Clips are added frequently and seasonal clips are spotlighted. When you download a clip from Clip Gallery Live, it is placed in the appropriate category in the Clip Gallery.

LESSON 3 REVIEW QUESTIONS

TRUE/FALSE

Circle T if the statement is true or F if the statement is false.

T **F** 1. Use the Resize tool to remove part of a clip art graphic you don't want.

T F 2. Before you modify any graphic object, you must select it.

T **F** 3. You can see an animated GIF in action in Normal view.

(T) F   4.   You can record a sound to insert on a slide.

T (F)   5.   You can view a video clip only in Slide Show view.

FILL IN THE BLANKS

Complete the following sentences by writing the correct word or words in the blanks provided.

1.   To specify an exact size for a graphic, click the _format picture_ tool on the Picture toolbar.

2.   To change the weight of a line in a drawing, click the _line style_ tool on the Drawing toolbar.

3.   Use the _order_ command to change the layer of a particular object.

4.   A predrawn object you can use in your drawings is called a(n) _drawing or graphic_

5.   Images on the Internet are usually in _tif & gif_ or _jpeg_ format.

LESSON 3 PROJECTS

✳ PROJECT 3-1

SCANS

1.   Open the **Wetlands** presentation you worked on in Lesson 2. Save the presentation as **Wetlands 2** followed by your initials.

2.   Insert the sound clip **loon** from your data files on slide 1. Choose to have the clip play automatically when the slide is displayed. Move the sound object to a corner of your slide away from text.

3.   On slide 3 insert the clip art graphic of the heron-like bird from the Clip Gallery's Animals category. Recolor the grass in the graphic using a green from the design template color palette.

4.   Search for other appropriate clip art graphics to place on your slides using keywords in the Insert ClipArt dialog box (for example, *bird, fish, lake*).

5.   If you have access to the Internet, locate a picture on Clip Gallery Live to place on slide 1. Move and resize the subtitle placeholder if necessary to position the picture. Modify the picture and/or clip art as desired.

6.   Run the slide show. Save your changes. Print the first six slides of the presentation as handouts with 6 slides per page. Close the presentation.

✳ PROJECT 3-2

1.   Open the **Weather** presentation you worked with in Lesson 2. Save the presentation as **Weather 2** followed by your initials.

2. You have obtained a satellite picture of Hurricane Fran before it came ashore. On slide 4, insert the picture **Fran** from the data files for this lesson. Resize and position the picture as desired. Crop the picture at the bottom to remove the color scale.

3. Slide 9 needs a corresponding illustration, but you don't have an appropriate picture. Use the Lightning Bolt AutoShape from the Basic Shapes palette. To form clouds, use one of the freehand drawing tools from the AutoShapes Lines palette or use the cloud shape from the Callouts palette. If desired, copy the cloud shape and paste several duplicates. Resize the duplicates to give the effect of a group of clouds. Flip or rotate the duplicates so they don't look exactly the same as the original. Color the clouds and lightning bolt as desired. (*Hint:* To give the illusion of depth to the clouds, use the Gradient fill effect and choose a darker color for the bottoms of the clouds.)

4. Group the objects in the drawing and position the drawing as desired.

5. Add the sound clip **lightning** from the data files for this lesson. Specify that the clip will play automatically when the slide is displayed. Move the sound icon to one corner of the slide.

6. Run the slide show. Save your changes and print the first nine slides as handouts with 9 slides per page. Close the presentation.

PROJECT 3-3

Choose one other slide show you have worked on in the previous two lessons and add appropriate clip art. If you have access to the Internet, search Clip Gallery Live for appropriate pictures, graphics, and sounds to liven up the presentation.

CRITICAL THINKING ACTIVITY

ACTIVITY 3-1

You are preparing a presentation and would like to illustrate it using drawings that were prepared for another use. These drawings have been saved in EPS (Encapsulated PostScript) format. Will you be able to use them in PowerPoint?

Use the Help files to find out if you can use them, any special steps you might have to take to do so, and what kind of printer you would have to have to print the drawings. Write a brief report about your findings.

ACTIVITY 3-2

You are working with a colleague, Jenna, to prepare a presentation for your company that will be used at a trade show and online. Jenna e-mails you a picture that she says will be just perfect for the presentation, but doesn't say where she got it.

What questions should you ask her before you use the file? What precautions should you take before you open the file? Write a brief report that answers these questions.

CUSTOMIZING OPTIONS

OBJECTIVES

Upon completion of this lesson, you should be able to:

- Customize a color scheme.
- Modify the slide background.
- Create custom slide masters.
- Create a custom show.
- Customize toolbars.
- Customize animation options.
- Create a new design template.
- Customize a Web presentation.

⏱ Estimated Time: 2.5 hours

So far in this unit, you have worked with presentations formatted with the standard design templates installed with PowerPoint 2000. As you begin to create your own presentations, however, you might find that none of the design templates is exactly right for the slides you want to create. Perhaps you don't like one color in the template, or you like the colors but the font is weird.

Good news! You can change many aspects of a design template to customize it for your use. You can apply a new color scheme; create a new background; change the fonts, color, style, and alignment of text; and even remove graphic elements from the slide masters. You can create your own design template if you don't find one among PowerPoint's standards that meets all your needs.

PowerPoint offers you many other ways to customize a presentation. Besides changing color schemes, backgrounds, and master items, you can create custom shows, which are like presentations within presentations, and custom animation effects for a particular presentation. You can create a toolbar for a specific use and modify existing toolbars. You can customize a Web presentation to show only specific slides or use only a specific browser.

Customizing the Color Scheme

A *color scheme* is a palette of eight colors that work well together. These eight colors are used for all color choices on the slides in a presentation. You can use them for text, charts, tables, and to recolor pictures. They are also used for slide master items such as rules and other graphics.

Each of PowerPoint's design templates comes with a set of color schemes. The number of color schemes available depends on the design template. Changing the color scheme is a quick way to give a slide show a new look.

You change the color scheme by opening the Format menu and clicking Slide Color Scheme. The Color Scheme dialog box opens, similar to Figure 4-1. Available color schemes are shown in the *Color schemes* area. To select a new color scheme, simply click the scheme you want to try. You have the option of applying the new color scheme to the current slide only (click Apply) or to all slides in the presentation (click Apply to All). After you apply the new color scheme, your slides will automatically display the new colors. If your presentation contains a chart, you might see a message telling you the chart is being reformatted with the new colors.

FIGURE 4-1
Choose a new color scheme in the Color Scheme dialog box

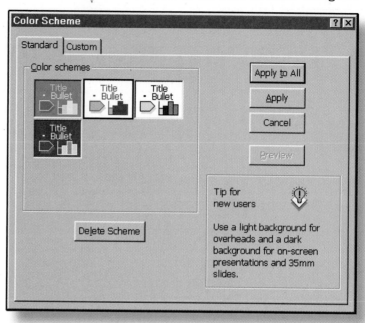

If you want to change only certain elements of the current color scheme, you can create a custom color scheme. Click the Custom tab in the Color Scheme dialog box to see options similar to those in Figure 4-2. The eight colors of the current color scheme are listed along with the slide elements that use those colors. This listing helps you decide how to change colors. If your background is white, for example, you do not want to choose white for your title text!

Choosing a new color for the color scheme is easy. Click the scheme color you want to change, and then click the Change Color button. PowerPoint opens the Fill Color dialog box, similar to Figure 4-3. The Standard tab shows the palette of all available colors. To choose a new color, simply click one of the hexagons in the color palette. In the lower right corner of the dialog box, PowerPoint shows you both the current color and the new color. Click OK when you're satisfied with your choice.

If you don't like any of the colors available on this tab, you can create your own color on the Custom tab. Drag the pointers over the color ranges until you achieve the color you want. Then click OK to add the color to the color scheme.

FIGURE 4-2
Create a custom color scheme on this tab

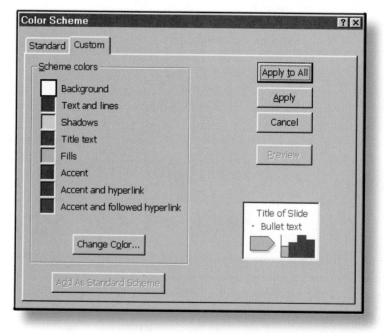

FIGURE 4-3
Choose a new color in this dialog box

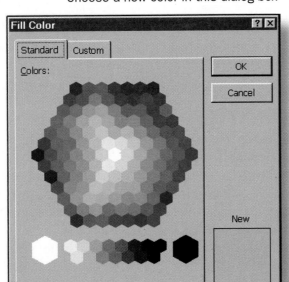

You can add your custom color scheme to the schemes available in the Color Scheme dialog box. Just click Add As Standard Scheme on the Custom tab after you have finished customizing a color scheme.

STEP-BY-STEP ▷ 4.1

You have been working with ExperTech's electronic manual to add information. You are now ready to consider the overall look of the presentation. You decide you have never been very happy with some of the colors in the current color scheme.

1. Open **AP Step4-1** from the student data files. Save the file as **ET Manual 2** followed by your initials. Scroll through the slides to remind yourself of their content. Notice in the charts on slides 5 and 6 that two of the data series colors are exactly the same. This could certainly be improved!

2. To see what other color schemes are available, open the **Format** menu and click **Slide Color**

Scheme. Four schemes are available in the Color Scheme dialog box.

3. Click the scheme with the dark blue background in the second row. Click **Apply to All**. Scroll through the slides to see how the color scheme has changed the look of the slides and the charts.

4. You decide to return to the original color scheme and make a few changes to the colors. Follow these steps:
   a. Open the Color Scheme dialog box again and click the original color scheme (the second in the first row).

(continued on next page)

A P - 6 1

b. Click the **Custom** tab and look at the list of colors provided in the color scheme. You see two problems here: First, that tan color is boring. Second, two of the accent colors are the same dark blue.

c. To change the tan *Fills* color, click it in the color list. Click **Change Color** to open the Fill Color dialog box. Click the **Standard** tab if necessary. Click the golden yellow hexagon that is fourth from the left in the third row from the bottom. Click **OK**.

d. The *Shadows* color should also be changed to a golden yellow so it doesn't look sickening next to your current *Fills* color. Click the **Shadows** color and then **Change Color**. On the **Standard** tab, click the golden yellow diagonally to the right and above the color you chose for *Fills* (it is the fifth hexagon from the left in the fourth row from the bottom). Click **OK**.

e. Now you can solve the problem with the accent colors. Click the first *Accent* color in the list and then click **Change Color**. On the **Standard** tab, click the last color on the right in the bottom row. Click **OK**.

f. If desired, change the color for *Accent and followed hyperlink*. You might want to create your own color for this item on the **Custom** tab in the Fill Color dialog box.

5. When you're satisfied with your new color palette, click **Apply to All**. Scroll through the slides again to see your new colors in action.

6. Save your changes and leave the presentation open for the next Step-by-Step.

Customizing the Slide Background

The ***slide background*** is the bottom "layer" of the slide. Depending on the design template, the background might be a plain color, a shaded color, or a texture. The graphic elements associated with a design template, such as the horizontal lines and blocks of color on the slides you're currently working with, are also part of the slide background, but they are located on the slide masters. You will learn more about changing master elements in the next section of this lesson.

You can change the slide background to a new color from your current color scheme, or any other color on the standard palette. Or you can change it to a color gradient made up of one or two colors. You can also apply a texture as a background or choose one of a large selection of patterns. If you want, you can apply different backgrounds to each slide in a presentation, but you can apply only one background at a time to an individual slide.

To change the background of slides in a presentation, open the Format menu and choose Background. The Background dialog box opens, similar to the one in Figure 4-4. The current background color displays in the list box in the *Background fill* area. Click the down arrow next to the background color to see the other color choices for the current color scheme.

If you don't want to use one of the colors from the current color scheme, you can click More Colors to see the standard palette. Choose one and click OK to make it the background color.

To create a more sophisticated background, click Fill Effects. PowerPoint opens the Fill Effect dialog box, similar to Figure 4-5. The Fill Effects dialog box contains four tabs of options for backgrounds: Gradient, Texture, Pattern, and Picture.

FIGURE 4-4
Background dialog box

FIGURE 4-5
The Gradient tab in the Fill Effects dialog box

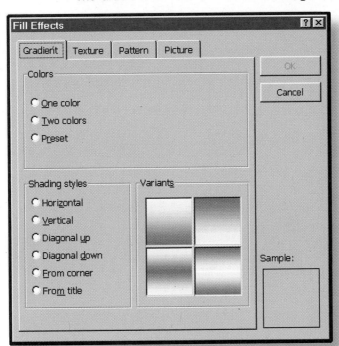

The Gradient tab lets you create special color effects using one or two colors. The colors are shaded in various directions and styles. The *One color* option lets you specify the color and choose how dark the shading becomes. The *Two colors* option lets you specify two colors that will be used to create the gradient. The *Preset* option offers a list of gradients that have already been created for you, with names such as Early Sunset, Desert, and Chrome.

FIGURE 4-6
The Texture tab

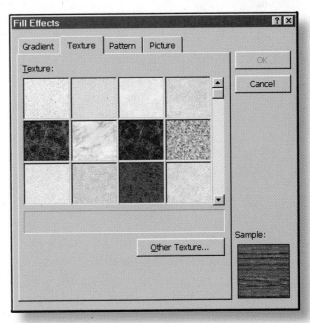

The Texture tab (Figure 4-6) offers you 24 different textures you can use as backgrounds. Textures range from natural items such as wood and marble to cloth and various papers. To select a texture, simply click on the sample.

The Pattern tab (Figure 4-7) offers numerous patterns you can use to jazz up a plain background. You can choose the colors for the Foreground (the actual pattern) and Background (the color behind the pattern).

The Picture tab shows nothing, if no pictures have been selected previously. Click Select Picture to browse for pictures you can use as backgrounds. When you have located the picture, click Insert.

FIGURE 4-7
The Pattern tab

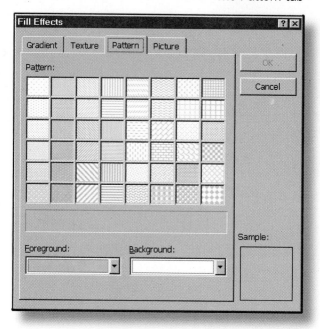

The Background dialog box contains a check box that deserves mention. If your design template contains graphics on the slide masters that you do not want on your slides, you can click in the *Omit background graphics from master* check box. Checking this box will remove master graphic elements from your slides. But be careful! This option also removes master items such as headers, footers, slide numbers, and dates. If you want to remove master graphics, you are better off doing so on the masters themselves.

S TEP-BY-STEP ▷ 4.2

1. You decide to customize your plain white background for this presentation. Open the **Format** menu and click **Background**. The Background dialog box opens.

2. Click the down arrow next to the current background color. None of the current color scheme colors look suitable for a background. Click **Fill Effects**.

3. Click the **Texture** tab and scroll down to see all the choices. Click the **Papyrus** choice and then click **OK**. In the Background dialog box, click **Apply** to apply the background to slide currently on your screen.

4. Papyrus just isn't right. How about a gradient? Follow these steps:

   a. Open the Background dialog box and access the Fill Effects dialog box. Click the **Gradient** tab.

   b. Click the **Two colors** option. In the *Color 1* list box, choose the white color. In the *Color 2* list box, choose the first golden yellow color.

   c. Click the **Diagonal up** shading style and click the first variant. Click **OK**.

   d. Apply the gradient to all slides in the presentation.

5. Scroll through the slides to see how the new background looks on the different slides in the presentation.

6. Save your changes and leave the presentation open for the next Step-by-Step.

Customizing Masters

Each design template comes with its own set of masters: a slide master, a title master (usually), a handout master, and a notes master. The masters in a presentation control most items that appear on a slide or handout:

■ The slide master specifies what font is used for the title, how it is aligned, what color it is, and what style it is. The slide master also specifies fonts and bullet styles for all levels of bulleted text on a slide.

■ The title master specifies text formatting for the title and subtitle on a Title layout slide.

■ The handout master specifies how the thumbnails will be arranged when you print handouts.

■ The notes master lets you specify items you want to appear on the notes pages you print.

Masters may also contain graphics that appear on every slide in the presentation. In addition, masters contain placeholders for text you might want to include on every slide or handout, such as headers, footers, slide or page numbers, and dates.

Changes you make to the masters appear on all slides controlled by that master. For example, if you change the font of bulleted items on the slide master, all bulleted items will show that changed font. Some changes you make on the slide master, such as changes to the title placeholder, will also appear on the title master.

Note that changes you make to the masters apply only to the current presentation. You do not have to worry that changes you make to a design template's masters will appear the next time you use that template.

To view a master, open the View menu and click Master. Then click the master you want to view from the submenu. Figure 4-8 shows the slide master for the current presentation. Notice the placeholders for the

FIGURE 4-8
The slide master

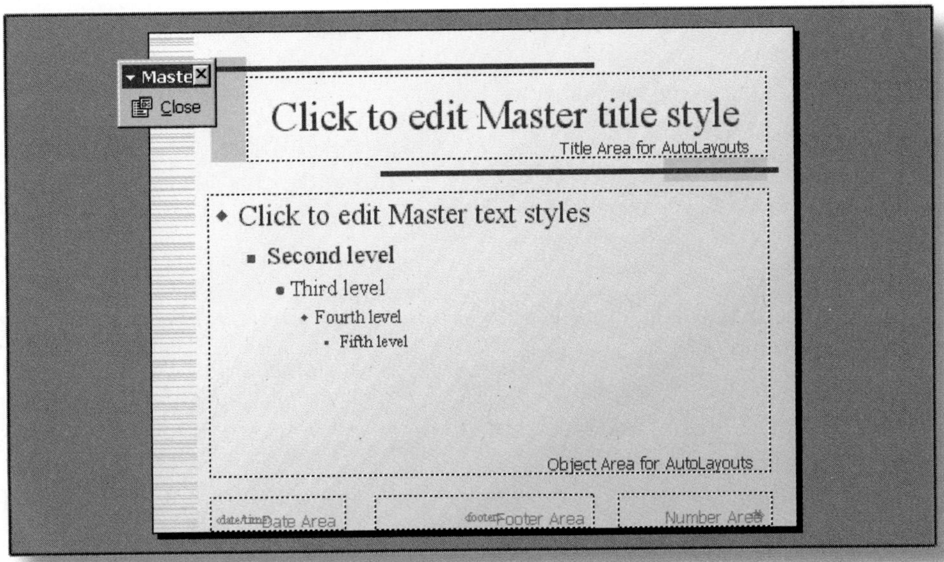

title, text, date, footer, and number. To change title or text styles, select the item you want to change and then apply the new formats to it. To change the location of a placeholder, click and drag it.

To insert a date, footer, or number that will appear on all slides, you must use the Header and Footer command on the View menu. In the Header and Footer dialog box, click the items you want to appear on the slide and specify any further information, such as footer text or a date.

You can also insert your own text boxes on masters to add information such as a company name or logo that you want to appear on every slide.

STEP-BY-STEP ▷ 4.3

1. To further customize your presentation, you want to make some changes to the masters. First, begin with changes to the slide master. Follow these steps:

   a. Open the **View** menu and click **Master**. Choose **Slide Master** on the submenu.

   b. Change the alignment of title text by clicking the **Align Left** button on the toolbar.

   c. You like the series of horizontal lines at the left border of the title slide, but you don't like them on subsequent slides. Click on the horizontal lines at the left edge of the slide. Note the selection handles that appear all the way around the slide, indicating that the graphic elements on the slide have been grouped. Click **Draw** on the Drawing menu and choose **Ungroup**. Click anywhere on the slide to deselect all items and then click again on the horizontal lines. Click **Delete** to remove them.

   d. You'd like to add the company name to every slide. Draw a text box in the top right corner of the slide and key © **ExperTech, Inc.** Copy this text box so you can use it on the title slide also.

2. Now move to the title master: Open the **View** menu, click **Master**, and click **Title Master**. Notice that the title has become left-aligned to match the new alignment on the slide master. Make these additional changes:

   a. Right align the subtitle.

   b. Paste the text box from the slide master. Position it in the top right corner of the slide.

   c. Add the current date and slide numbers: Open the **View** menu and click **Header and Footer**. Specify the current date in the *Fixed* text box and click in the **Slide number** check box. While you are in this dialog box, click the **Notes and Handouts** tab. Click the **Date and time** check box and key the same date in the *Fixed* text box. Click the **Header** check box and key the presentation name, **ET Manual 2**, in the header text box. Click in the **Page number** check box. Click **Apply to All**.

3. View the handout master. Notice that the placeholders for header and date are not aligned. Drag the Date Area placeholder down to align with the Header Area placeholder. Center the header and date in their placeholders by selecting each placeholder and clicking the **Center** button.

4. Change to Slide view. Scroll through the slides to see the changes you have made. You might have to move the sound object on slide 1 to keep it from blocking the view of the company name.

5. Save your changes and leave the presentation open for the next Step-by-Step.

Creating Custom Shows

A *custom show* is a group of related slides in a presentation that you gather and name. They are actually presentations within a presentation. Creating custom shows gives you flexibility when presenting a large number of slides. You can group related topics in the presentation and then jump over the groups that are not applicable to a particular audience.

You create a custom show by first opening the Slide Show menu and clicking Custom Shows. The Custom Shows dialog box opens, as shown in Figure 4-9. Click New to start the process.

The Define Custom Show dialog box opens. Here you name the custom show and select the slides that belong in it. Select a slide by clicking it in the list on the left and then clicking

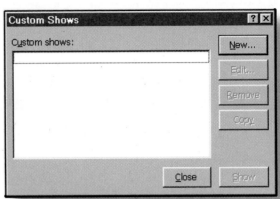

FIGURE 4-9
Starting a new custom show

the Add >> button. If you add a slide by mistake, click it in the right-hand list and click Remove. Figure 4-10 shows a new custom show named Introduction that contains five slides. Notice that you can reorder the slides in your custom show list using the up and down arrows to the right of the list. When you have finished adding slides and arranging them, click OK.

FIGURE 4-10
Slides have been added to a custom show

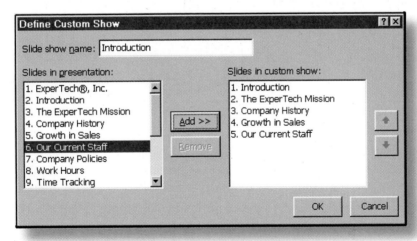

After you have created one show, you can create others from the same presentation, edit an existing show, remove a show, or make a copy of a show. Click the Show button in the Custom Shows dialog box to immediately run a slide show of the slides in the selected custom show.

Once you have created custom shows, you can create an *agenda slide* that displays the names of the custom shows. An agenda slide acts like a table of contents for the presentation. In Lesson 6, you will learn how to add action settings to the items on an agenda slide to let you easily jump back and forth in a presentation from one section to another.

Create an agenda slide in Slide Sorter view by clicking the first slide of each custom show and then clicking Summary Slide on the toolbar. A new slide appears with the titles of the slides you selected as bullet items.

Hot Tip

To select more than one slide in Slide Sorter view, click the first and then hold Ctrl and click the others.

STEP-BY-STEP ▷ 4.4

1. Your current presentation has several neat and obvious sections that could become custom shows. Create the first custom show following these steps:

   a. Open the **Slide Show** menu and click **Custom Shows**. In the Custom Shows dialog box, click **New**.

   b. In the Define Custom Show dialog box, key the name for the first custom show: **Introduction**.

   c. In the left-hand list, click slide 2, **Introduction**. Click **Add >>**. Then click slides 3, 4, 5, and 6 and add each to the list on the right. Your dialog box should look like the one in Figure 4-10.

   d. Click **OK**.

2. Create a second custom show named **Company Policies**. It should contain slides 7–10. Create a third custom show named **Benefits** that contains the remaining slides. Click **Close**.

3. Create an agenda slide for the sections in your presentation by following these steps:

   a. Switch to Slide Sorter view. Click slide 2, then hold **Ctrl** and click slides 7 and 11.

   b. Click **Summary Slide** on the toolbar. The new summary slide appears as slide 2.

   c. Switch to Slide view. Change the title on slide 2 to **Contents**.

4. Save your changes and leave the presentation open for the next Step-by-Step.

Customizing Toolbars

As you spend more time working with PowerPoint, you might find yourself wishing that you could add tools to the toolbars you use regularly, to avoid having to use menu commands. Or you might wish you could create your own toolbar to hold a selection of tools you use often. If so, you will be happy to know that you *can* customize toolbars to show only the tools you want. You can also create your own toolbar.

When creating or customizing a toolbar, you use options in the Customize dialog box. Open the Tools menu and click Customize. To create a new toolbar, click the Toolbars tab. All available toolbars are listed, as shown in Figure 4-11. Those toolbars that are currently active are checked. Create a new toolbar by clicking the New button. You will then be asked to name the toolbar. After you key a name and click OK, the new toolbar appears in the toolbar list and is checked by default.

Notice the Reset button on the Toolbars tab. If you have changed a toolbar in a way you didn't want to, select the toolbar in the list and then click Reset. Original settings are restored for that toolbar.

To remove tools from a toolbar, click the tool, hold down the Alt key, and drag the tool off the toolbar. Note that you cannot use Undo to reverse this action. To restore a tool you have removed from a toolbar, you must use the Reset button in the Customize dialog box.

To add tools to a toolbar, click the Commands tab in the Customize dialog box (Figure 4-12). To the left on this tab is a list of general categories. To the right are the commands available for the selected category. Select a category, scroll through the list of commands, and drag any command you want onto a toolbar. If you are not sure what a particular command does, select it and then click the Description button. After you place a tool on a toolbar, you may modify it while it is still active by clicking the Modify Selection button. A pop-up list gives you options for changing the look of the new tool.

FIGURE 4-11

Create or modify a toolbar in the Customize dialog box

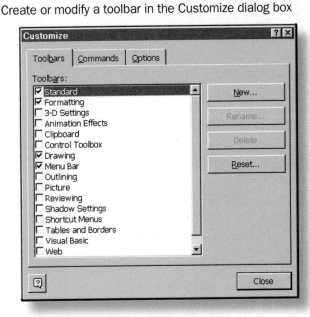

 **Hot Tip**

You can use the Commands tab to add commands to menus, too. Display the menu you want to add a command to and then drag the command to any location on the menu.

FIGURE 4-12

Add tools or menu commands from this tab

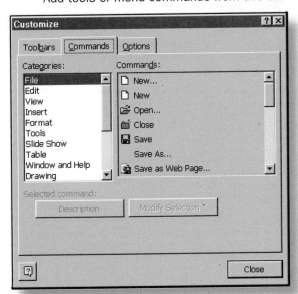

S TEP·BY·STEP ▷ 4.5

Create a custom toolbar to hold some of the tools you use frequently.

1. Open the **Tools** menu and click **Customize**. The Customize dialog box opens.

2. Click the **Toolbars** tab. Click **New**. Key your first name as the toolbar name and click **OK**. The new toolbar should appear somewhere in your PowerPoint window (it will be floating over the slide, not docked with the other toolbars).

3. Click the **Commands** tab. If necessary, select the **File** category. You are always having to save presentations with new names, so add the Save As command to your toolbar: click **Save As** in the *Commands* list and drag it to your floating toolbar.

4. Change the look of the new Save As tool: click **Modify Selection**. On the pop-up menu, click **Image and Text**. Then click **Change Button Image** on the same menu. On the pop-out palette, click the last icon in the first row.

5. Click the **Slide Show** category in the *Categories* list. Scroll to locate the **Custom Animation** command and drag it to your toolbar.

6. Browse through the commands in categories that interest you and add additional commands to your toolbar as desired. When you are finished, click **Close** to close the Customize dialog box.

7. Leave the presentation open for the next Step-by-Step.

Creating Custom Animation

PowerPoint offers a multitude of ways to animate objects on your slides. *Animation* in this case means that your titles fly into position as a slide displays, or that your bulleted lists appear one item at a time. You can animate any object on a slide, including sounds, videos, and the data series in your charts. You can even animate graphics such as clip art pictures. For example, you can animate a cloud graphic so that it appears to float into place on your slide.

Animating the objects on a slide gives you greater control over the slide's content when giving a presentation. For example, you can control the display of key information—the all-important year-end sales figures in a chart, say—until you know your audience is ready to receive the information.

Many design templates offer built-in animation for graphic objects. The template you are currently working with, for example, specifies that the horizontal lines above and below the title will fly in from right and left. It's up to you to animate the other objects on each slide.

The place to start animating objects on your slides is the Custom Animation dialog box. Open the Slide Show menu and choose Custom Animation. The Custom Animation dialog box opens, similar to Figure 4-13. Notice that the objects that can be animated are listed next to check boxes. Click the check box of the object you want to animate. Then make selections on the tabs at the bottom of the dialog box, as follows:

■ On the Order & Timing tab, specify the order in which the selected object will be animated. Then indicate how to start the animation. You can choose to start the animation by clicking the mouse or you can have PowerPoint start it for you automatically after a specified time delay.

■ On the Effects tab, choose an animation effect. You also must specify the direction from which the object will appear and if it will have an accompanying sound effect. If you are animating text in a bulleted list placeholder, you can choose to have bulleted items appear all at once, one by one, in groups according to text level, or in reverse order.

FIGURE 4-13
Specify animation settings for objects in this dialog box

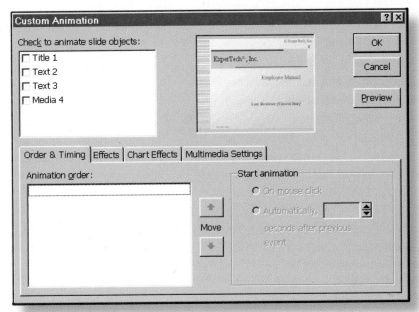

■ On the Chart Effects tab, choose an animation effect and accompanying sound effect. You can also choose how to introduce each chart element.

■ On the Multimedia Settings tab, choose settings for a media object. You can hide the object when it is not playing, have it play for a specific number of slides, and pause the slide show while the object is playing. This is an important setting if your slide show is set up to play with automatic timings.

You can see how your animation is going to look by clicking Preview in the Custom Animation dialog box. Another way to see how your animations are going to look without running the slide show is to click Preview Animation on the Slide Show menu. PowerPoint shows you the animation effects for the current slide.

STEP-BY-STEP ▷ 4.6

1. Add some animation effects to your slides to keep readers alert. With slide 1 on the screen, click the **Custom Animation** button on your custom toolbar (or open the **Slide Show** menu and click **Custom Animation**).

2. Animate the objects on this slide as follows:
   a. Click in the check box next to **Title 1**. On the Order & Timing tab, click the **Automatically**

option and specify a timing of 3 seconds after the previous event. On the Effects tab, if necessary, choose the **Fly** effect in the first list box and specify the direction as **From Right**. If it is not already selected, set the sound effect to **[No sound]**. In the *Introduce text* area, choose to introduce the text **By Word**.

(continued on next page)

b. Click in the check box next to **Text 2.** On the Order & Timing tab, make sure the automatic settings are the same as for the title object. On the Effects tab, specify that the object fly in from the left, with no sound effect. Choose to introduce the text **All at once.**

c. Click in the check box next to **Media 4**. On the Order & Timing tab, set an automatic timing of 0 seconds to have the sound play almost as soon as the subtitle appears. On the Effects tab, specify that the sound object zoom in, with no sound effect. On the Multimedia Effects tab, click in the **Play using animation order** check box.

d. Click **Preview** to check your animations for this slide. Click **OK** to close the dialog box.

3. Now try your hand at animating a chart. Move to slide 6 and open the Custom Animation dialog box. Follow these steps to animate the objects on this slide:

a. Animate the title using timings and settings as desired.

b. Click in the **Chart 2** check box. Set an automatic timing for the chart and then click the **Chart Effects** tab. Choose to introduce the chart elements **by Category**. Use the **Dissolve** effect and use the **Applause** sound effect.

c. Click **OK** to close the dialog box.

4. With slide 6 on the screen in Slide view, open the **Slide Show** menu and click **Animation Preview** to see the animation for this slide. Close the Animation Preview window.

5. Add custom animations to other slides if desired. When you have finished adding the animations, run the slide show to see your effects on the big screen.

6. Save your changes. Print the first six slides of the presentation as handouts with 6 slides per page. Notice the header and the date you specified in the handout master. Close the presentation.

Extra Challenge

Add preset animations to objects you did not animate in Step-by-Step 4.6.

PowerPoint gives you another quick way to add animation to an object on a slide using the Preset Animation command on the Slide Show menu. When you choose this command, a submenu gives you a choice of 14 animation effects with accompanying sound effects. To use one of these animation effects, click in the object you want to animate and then open the Slide Show menu, click Preset Animation, and choose the effect you want from the submenu.

Creating a Design Template

You now have all the information you need to create your own design template. Creating a design template is a good way to lend a uniform appearance to presentations generated for specific purposes or by particular persons. A business, for example, might want to standardize all the presentations created for its use.

You have two options when creating a design template. If you like the look of one of PowerPoint's design templates, you can start with that template and add to it or modify it until you are happy with your changes. Or you can start from a blank presentation and add everything from the background up. In either case, once you have completed your design, save it as a template by clicking Save As on the File menu. In the Save as Type list box, choose Design Template.

You can save your template with your own files or you can let PowerPoint place it in the Templates folder where you can easily choose it for other presentations. If you save the template somewhere besides the Templates folder, you can still apply its formats to a new slide show. To do so, click Apply Design Template and then in the Apply Design Template dialog box, change the file type from Design Templates to All Files or All PowerPoint Presentations. Then use the *Look in* box to locate the folder where you saved your own template. Click its name and then click Apply.

STEP-BY-STEP ▷ 4.7

The Madison County Park Board would like you to create a new design template to use for any future presentations.

1. Start a new, blank presentation and accept the Title slide layout.

2. If desired, change the color scheme to one of the available schemes. Then, using what you have learned in this lesson, modify or create a design template suitable for the kinds of presentations the park system is likely to make.

3. Make sure the words **Madison County Park System** will print on each slide of every presentation.

4. If desired, insert a park-related clip art graphic on at least the title master. Specify that slide numbers will print on all slides.

5. When you have finished setting up your design template, save it as a **Design Template** with the name **Custom Template** followed by your initials.

6. On the title slide, key the title **A Presentation of . . .** and the subtitle **The Madison County Park System**. Create two or three more sample slides, including one with a chart, to show the features of your design. Save the presentation as **Madison Parks**. (Don't forget to use your custom toolbar button for Save As!)

7. Print the sample presentation as handouts with 4 slides per page. Leave the document open for the next Step-by-Step.

Customizing Web Pages

PowerPoint 2000 is designed so that you can easily transform a presentation into Web pages. You can then make your presentation available on the Internet for others to browse through. PowerPoint gives you a number of options for formatting your Web pages. After you have published a presentation for Web use, you can use the Microsoft Script Editor to make changes to the HTML code to fine-tune your presentation.

You can easily save any slide as a Web page by opening the File menu and clicking the Save as Web Page command. The Save As dialog box opens as shown in Figure 4-14. You can select a location to save the Web page (such as on a Web server or intranet). Notice at the bottom of the dialog box PowerPoint shows you the title it will use for the Web page (usually the slide title). You can change the page title by clicking the Change Title button and keying a new title in the Set Page Title dialog box. Slides saved this way as Web pages can be edited by members of a workgroup.

FIGURE 4-14
Save or publish a Web page in this dialog box

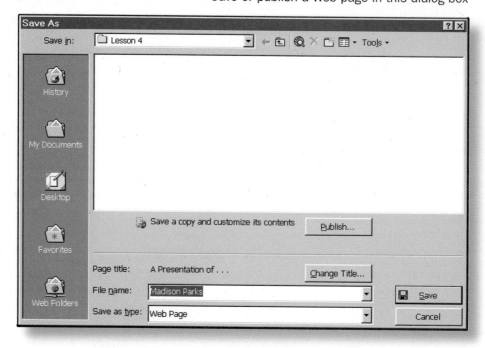

To exercise more control over your presentation as it will appear on the Web, click the Publish button in the Save As dialog box. You will learn more about publishing a presentation in the next section.

Publishing a Presentation

Publish a presentation when you want to choose particular slides from a presentation to appear on the Web, when you want control over how the slides appear on the Web, or when you want to be the only one to edit the presentation. Publishing allows you to place your presentations in various locations on the Web. When you publish a presentation, you can also specify browsers that will be able to open your presentation.

To publish a presentation, open the File menu and choose the Save as Web Page command. In the Save As dialog box, specify a location for the published files and a file name. If necessary, change the page title. Then click the Publish button. PowerPoint opens the Publish as Web Page dialog box shown in Figure 4-15.

FIGURE 4-15
Publish as Web Page dialog box

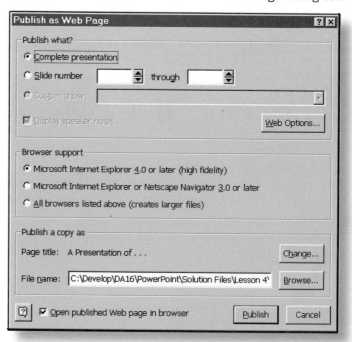

In the *Publish what?* area of this dialog box, you can choose whether to publish the entire presentation, only selected slides, or a particular custom show. You can also decide whether to display any speaker notes associated with your slides.

In the *Browser support* area of the dialog box, you can choose a specific target browser for your presentation. Note that you can select all browsers to ensure that all viewers will be able to see your presentation properly, but this option makes your Web files larger.

In the *Publish a copy as* area, you can change your page title and specify a location for the published files. To see your Web pages right away in your browser, click in the *Open published Web page in browser* check box.

To see additional formatting options for your Web pages, click the Web Options button. Power-Point opens the Web Options dialog box shown in Figure 4-16. Four tabs contain options for formatting appearance, controlling files and pictures, and specifying encoding options.

FIGURE 4-16
Web Options dialog box

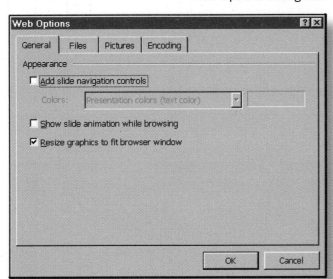

STEP-BY-STEP ▷ 4.8

Publish the current presentation for Web use.

1. Open the **File** menu and click **Save as Web Page**. The Save As dialog box opens. If necessary, move to the location where you have saved other files for this lesson.

2. The default title for the Web presentation is your slide title, *A Presentation of . . . .* Click

Change Title and key the title **Madison County Parks** in the Set Page Title dialog box. Click **OK**.

3. In the Save As dialog box, click **Publish**. The Publish as Web Page dialog box opens.

4. Click **Web Options** to open the Web Options dialog box. If necessary, on the General tab

(continued on next page)

click the **Add slide navigation controls** check box. Click **OK**.

5. Make sure the *File name* box shows the folder where you want to store your Web files. Click the **Open published Web page in browser** check box if necessary.

6. Click **Publish**. PowerPoint saves your presentation in HTML format for the Web and opens it

in your browser. Notice the outline to the left of the first slide, showing the titles of your slides. To move from slide to slide, you can click a title in the outline, or you can click the navigation buttons at the bottom of the slide.

7. Close your browser. Leave the presentation open for the next Step-by-Step.

Modifying Web Pages

If you want to modify the HTML code for a presentation you have published, you should do so in your original presentation. That way, you can make sure that your source presentation is always the most up-to-date version. To modify the presentation, open the Tools menu, click Macro, and then click Microsoft Script Editor on the submenu. The Microsoft Development Environment opens as shown in Figure 4-17.

Script Editing not installed.

FIGURE 4-17
Microsoft Development Environment

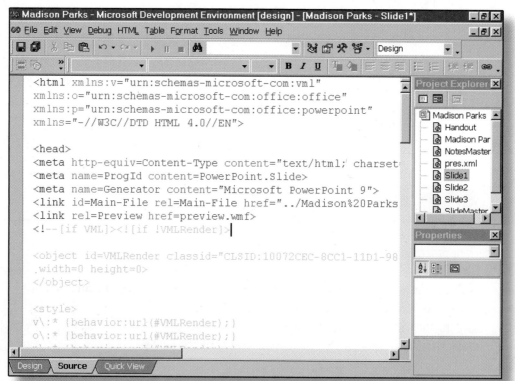

Making substantial changes in this view requires some knowledge of HTML code. You can edit the code directly in the window and then click the Quick View tab at the bottom of the window to see the result of your changes. When you have completed your changes, return to your PowerPoint presentation. The Refresh toolbar is open in PowerPoint. Click the Refresh button to update the presentation with your changes or click Do Not Refresh if you have changed your mind.

Each time you make changes to a Web presentation, you must republish it. When you do so, you can either change the name of the Web presentation to maintain control over various versions or you can save the presentation with the same name and overwrite existing files.

STEP-BY-STEP ▷ 4.9

1. You realize the subtitle of your presentation would look better without that *The*. You can make this simple change to the HTML code using the Microsoft Script Editor. Open the **Tools** menu and click **Macro**. On the submenu, click **Microsoft Script Editor**.

2. The Microsoft Development Environment opens. (Your screen might not exactly match the one shown in Figure 4-17.) If desired, close all the panes except the one in the center that shows the HTML code.

3. Scroll all the way to the bottom of the HTML code pane. You should see the slide title and subtitle in black text amid the multicolored coding. Click just to the left of the word *Madison* and backspace four times to remove the word *The* and the space.

4. On the taskbar, click the button for the *Madison Parks* presentation. On the Refresh toolbar, click the **Refresh** button. Your slide subtitle should change to show the removal of the word *The*.

5. To save changes to your Web presentation, click the **Save** button on the Standard toolbar. The Save As dialog box opens. Change the file name back to **Madison Parks**. Click **Publish**. In the Publish as Web Page, click **Publish** again. You will receive a message asking if you want to overwrite your existing Web files. Click **Yes**. View the revised Web page in your browser.

6. Close your browser. Close Microsoft Development Environment. Close the *Madison Parks* presentation without saving changes.

Summary

In this lesson, you learned:

■ Changing the color scheme is a quick way to give slides a fresh new look. To fine-tune the look of a presentation, you can change individual colors in the color scheme.

■ You have many options for changing the background of a slide. You can change the color, create a gradient of one or more colors, add a texture, or use a pattern. You can use multiple backgrounds in a presentation, but only one at a time on a slide.

■ PowerPoint's masters control the placement of text and other items on a slide, as well as color, font, style, and size of text. Masters also provide placeholders for text you might want to display on every slide, such as a footer, a slide number, or a date. You can modify master elements to customize your presentation.

- Custom shows are like presentations within presentations. Gathering slides into a custom show allows you to control groups of slides during a presentation.

- Customizing toolbars allows you to emphasize tools you use frequently. You can also create new toolbars to hold tools for a specific application.

- PowerPoint offers many different animation effects you can use to help control information during a presentation, as well as add visual interest to your slides. Special effects are included for charts and media objects.

- You can easily create your own design template. Customized design templates help you to maintain a consistent look in your presentations.

- PowerPoint allows you to publish presentations to the Web so that a wide audience can access them. You can choose to publish the entire presentation or only selected slides, and you can specify browser support for your presentation. You can format Web pages to present them just as you want them. Use the Microsoft Script Editor to modify HTML code for your Web pages.

LESSON 4 REVIEW QUESTIONS

TRUE/FALSE

Circle T if the statement is true or F if the statement is false.

T **F** 1. All design templates have at least six different color schemes.

T F 2. You can use any picture as a slide background.

T F 3. If you change the alignment of a title on a title master, you will see that same change every time you use a Title layout slide.

T F 4. An agenda slide is like a table of contents for the sections in your presentation.

T F 5. Select a sound effect to accompany an animation effect on the Multimedia Effects tab in the Custom Animation dialog box.

FILL IN THE BLANKS

Complete the following sentences by writing the correct word or words in the blanks provided.

1. A(n) _color scheme_ is a palette of eight colors that work well together.

2. The _notes master_ master lets you specify items you want to appear on notes pages you print.

3. _custom shows_ are groups of related slides in a presentation.

4. To create a new toolbar, open the Tools menu and click _customize_.

5. To have the most control over a presentation you want to make available on the Web, you should _publish_ it.

LESSON 4 PROJECTS

✴ PROJECT 4-1

1. Open **Deer Creek Review**, which you worked on in Lesson 2. Save the presentation as **Deer Creek 2** followed by your initials.

2. Change the color scheme to the last in the list of available schemes. Since you don't like the silver blue color used for *Fills* in this scheme, change that blue to a slate or gray blue. Change the color for *Text and lines* to a dark blue similar to the color for *Title* text.

3. On the title master, insert clip art of a deer (look in the Insert ClipArt dialog box or on the Clip Gallery Live Web site for suitable deer clip art). Recolor the image if necessary so that the deer is a color from the current color palette. Resize the graphic to a small size and place it somewhere on the master. (*Hint:* Run through each slide to make certain the graphic is not hiding any text.) Copy the graphic for use in the next step.

4. On the slide master, remove the vertical texture at the left of the slide and extend the "curved page" look all the way to the left edge of the slide. Move the page number placeholder to the left to make room for the deer graphic. Paste the deer graphic in the lower right corner of the slide. Make any other changes to the master that you want.

5. Create custom shows for the slides in the presentation. Create an agenda slide and title it **Agenda**. *summary*

6. Animate the charts in the presentation as desired. Run the presentation to see your changes in action.

7. Print only the first two slides of the presentation as handouts with 2 slides per page. Save your changes and close the presentation.

✴ PROJECT 4-2

1. Open **Weather 2** that you worked with in the previous lesson. Save it as **Weather 3** followed by your initials.

2. Choose a new color scheme for the presentation. Modify any individual colors in the scheme that you don't like (or don't think suitable to the subject matter).

3. Add slide numbers and a date that will change each time the presentation is opened. For printed handouts, insert a date that will automatically update and the header **Talking About the Weather**.

4. On the handout master, move the header and date placeholders down a bit so they will not print right at the top of the page. Center the contents of each placeholder.

5. On slide 9, animate the drawing so that it flies in the from the left automatically. Specify that the sound object fly in the from left and play automatically immediately after the clouds appear.

6. Print only the first two slides of the presentation as handouts with 2 slides per page. Check that your handout master settings are correct.

7. Save your changes and close the presentation.

PROJECT 4-3

1. Open the **Lead** presentation you worked on in Lesson 1. Save it as **Lead 2** followed by your initials.

2. You are about to deliver this presentation to your concerned neighbors. As you review the slides, the design and color strike you as being a bit too bright and festive for the subject at hand. Rework the design and colors as desired to create a design you think more suitable. You can change master items, the background, colors, fonts, and anything else you want.

3. Slide 9 has a speaker's note attached to it. Format the notes master as follows: remove the header placeholder and center the date placeholder above the slide sample. Center the date in the date placeholder. Change the font of the note text to 10 pt.Arial.

4. Add slide numbers. Add an automatically updating date for handouts and notes only.

5. Animate the slides as desired. On at least one slide, animate the bulleted items so they appear one item at a time (on mouse click). Then run the presentation to see your animations.

6. Print only the slide containing the speaker's note. Save your changes and close the presentation.

7. To delete your custom toolbar, open the **Tools** menu and click **Customize**. Click the **Toolbars** tab. Select your toolbar and click **Delete**. Click **Close**.

CRITICAL THINKING

ACTIVITY 4-1

While on vacation, you took a very fine picture of a golden sunset over a lake (okay, sunset pictures are a dime a dozen, but this is one *you* took). You'd like to use the sunset picture as a background for a slide show you have to present on travel options for the company's yearly sales conference.

How would you go about transforming the picture from the photograph you have in your hand to the background on a PowerPoint slide? Use Word to write a step-by-step solution.

ACTIVITY 4-2

You have prepared a presentation for your company's annual review. Several of the slides relate to some new policies the board wants to put in place for next year. These policies are important, and you wish you had some way to set them off from the other slides in the presentation. Could you apply a different color scheme to just a few slides in a presentation?

Use PowerPoint's Help system to research the answer to this question. Using Word, write a summary of what you find out.

IMPORTING AND EXPORTING INFORMATION

OBJECTIVES

Upon completion of this lesson, you should be able to:

- Create slides from a Word outline.

- Import slides into a presentation from another presention.

- Share data among the Office 2000 applications.

- Export an outline to Word.

- Send PowerPoint presentations to others.

- Specify output options.

⏱ **Estimated Time: 2.5 hours**

So far in this unit, most of the data in your presentations has been created in PowerPoint. Power-Point has so many tools and features that you can easily create almost any kind of information you want to display, from text to tables to charts.

When you are using PowerPoint as a part of the Office 2000 suite of applications, however, you have many more options for getting data onto your slides. If data you need already exists in an Excel worksheet, you can simply embed or link that data on a slide—no need to rekey it. If you have already organized data in an Access database, you can copy portions of that data to paste onto a slide—no need to create a new table and key the data again. If you have created an outline on a subject in Word, you can use that outline to create a presentation—no need to rekey the information from the outline on the slides.

You have a number of options for exporting data from PowerPoint, too. You can send PowerPoint slides to Word to use as handouts or to create a Word outline. You can paste a PowerPoint slide in any of the other Office 2000 applications. If you know your PowerPoint presentation is going to be exported to a medium such as 35mm slides or overheads, you can adjust the slide layout to make the slide information fit those formats better.

This lesson introduces you to a number of ways to integrate your PowerPoint slide information with other applications.

Creating Slides from an Outline

One of the easiest ways to import information into PowerPoint is to create slides from an outline. There are several ways to do this:

- In PowerPoint, click Open, change *Files of type* to All Outlines (or All Files) in the Open dialog box, locate the outline, and click Open. PowerPoint creates slides from the outline headings and displays them in the default design template.

- With a presentation already open in PowerPoint, open the Insert menu, click Slides from Outline, locate the outline as above, and click Insert. PowerPoint creates slides from the outline headings and inserts them following the current slide.

- In Word, with an outline open, open the File menu, click Send To, and click Microsoft PowerPoint. PowerPoint opens, if necessary, and creates the slides from the outline headings.

These outline features are not installed for PowerPoint in a standard installation of Office 2000. You can quickly install the capability to use outlines using your Office 2000 CD-ROM.

For the import process to work correctly, the document outline should be prepared using the word processor's outline feature. PowerPoint follows the outline's headings structure to create titles and bulleted lists at various levels. PowerPoint creates only Bulleted List layout slides, so you might have to change the slide layout to create a Title slide for the beginning of your presentation.

S TEP-BY-STEP ▷ 5.1

SCANS

ExperTech, Inc., encourages its employees to take part in community service projects. Each year, all employees attend informal roundtable discussions to determine what community service projects the company might undertake. You have been given an outline of this year's selections and asked to prepare a presentation showing the alternatives. Rather than rekey the information on slides, use the outline feature to create a new slide show.

1. In Microsoft Word, open **AP Step5-1** from the student data files.

2. Open the **File** menu, click **Send To**, and click **Microsoft PowerPoint**. PowerPoint opens, if it is not already open, and the slides are created.

3. Switch to Slide view. Change the slide layout of the first slide to Title Slide.

4. To apply the design template you customized in Lesson 4, follow these steps:
   a. Click the **Common Tasks** button on the toolbar and then click **Apply Design Template**.
   b. Change the *Files of type* entry to **All PowerPoint Presentations**. In the *Look in* box, locate your solution files for Lesson 4.
   c. Click **ET Manual 2** and then click **Apply**.

5. Scroll through the slides to become familiar with the community service proposals for the year.

6. Save the presentation as **ET Service** followed by your initials. Close the **AP Step5-1** document in Word.

Importing Slides from Another Presentation

Suppose you are creating a presentation and realize that you could really use slides you have prepared for another presentation. Do you have to re-create the slides? No way!

PowerPoint offers several easy ways to import slides from one presentation into another presentation.

- Using Copy and Paste: In Slide Sorter view, select the slides you want and then click Copy. Switch to the presentation where you need the slides. In Slide Sorter view, click Paste. The copied slides appear following the currently selected slide.

■ Using the Slides from Files command: Open the Insert menu and click Slides from Files. The Slide Finder dialog box opens. If you know the path to the presentation containing the slides you want to import, key it in the *File* box. Or use the Browse button to locate the file. Click Display to show thumbnails of the slides in the presentation, as shown in Figure 5-1. Click Insert All to insert all the slides in your current presentation. Or click each slide you want to include and then click Insert.

If the presentation containing the slides you want to import is large and you want to pick and choose among the slides, the Slides from Files command is probably the best choice. You can scroll through the entire presentation, selecting only the slides you want, and then insert them all in one step. Slides from Files has the additional advantage that you do not have to open the presentation file to import slides from it.

When you use either method to import slides from one presentation to another, the imported slides immediately take on the design template of your current presentation.

FIGURE 5-1
Display the slides to import in the Slide Finder dialog box

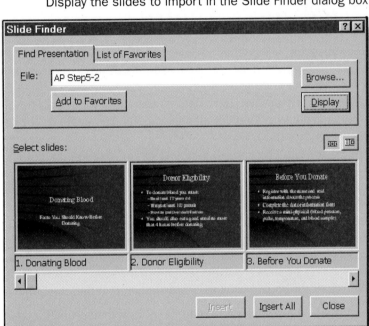

STEP-BY-STEP ▷ 5.2

SCANS

1. You remember that you have some additional slide information about donating blood that employees might want to take into account. You can import those slides into your current presentation. Move to slide 3.

2. Open the **Insert** menu and click **Slides from Files**. In the Slide Finder dialog box, click **Browse**.

3. Locate the data files for this lesson, click **AP Step5-2**, and click **Open**. Click **Display** to show thumbnails of the slides in the selected presentation.

4. You don't need the title slide, but the other four slides look useful. Click each one (scroll to the

(continued on next page)

right to see the final slides) and then click **Insert** to insert the four slides. Click **Close** to close the Slide Finder dialog box.

5. Check your slides in Slide Sorter view to make sure they are in the right order. Then run the presentation.

6. Save your changes and print the presentation as handouts with 6 slides per page. Close the presentation.

Integration: Sharing Data Among Office 2000 Applications

In Lesson 2 you briefly explored options for integrating Office 2000 applications: you inserted an Excel worksheet on a PowerPoint slide. There are many additional ways to share information among the Office 2000 applications.

The three most common ways to share information between any two applications are copying, embedding, and linking. Copying always works for all applications. You might not be able to link or embed data from one application to all others, however.

You will remember that when you *embed* on object on a slide, you double-click it to edit it in its original—or *source*—application. For example, when you double-clicked the Excel worksheet in Lesson 2, you actually used Excel's menus and tools to edit the worksheet. An embedded object is stored in the **destination application**—the application in which you embedded it.

When you *link* an object to a slide, you can edit it only in its source application. To edit a linked worksheet, for example, you must return to Excel. Changes you make in Excel are then automatically made to the linked object on the slide as well. A linked object is not stored in the destination application but in the source application. The linked object on the slide is only a "picture" of the actual object in the source application.

You might wonder when you should use these three integration options. Generally speaking:

■ Use Copy and Paste if you want to be able to edit the data in the destination application or if the application you are copying from does not support linking or embedding.

■ Use embedding if you want to be able to edit the source data from the destination application. Remember that an embedded object is stored in the destination document, so your destination document might become quite large.

■ Use linking if you want to maintain a relationship between data in the source and destination applications or if space for the destination document is limited.

Linking is not forever—you can easily break a link if you no longer want the linked object to update in the destination document. Once a link is broken, the linked object becomes just an object. You can still resize and move it like any other object, but you cannot edit it or update it.

In the following sections and in the projects at the end of the lesson, you will have a chance to perform a number of integration activities. These are not by any means all the ways you can integrate applications. You are encouraged to practice on your own or consult Help files for further information.

Copying Data from an Access Table

You cannot link or embed data from an Access table or form. You can, however, copy the data and paste it into anyother Office 2000 application. Though you might have to do some cleanup on the pasted data, it is usually quicker to do so than to key the data from the Access table into your destination document.

When copying data from an Access table to a Power-Point slide, you have several options:

Concept Builder

When you copy and paste any text, Office 2000 uses HTML format to maintain original formats during the process.

- If you paste the copied data on a slide with no placeholder open, the copied data appears as an object surrounded by selection handles, as shown in Figure 5-2. You can drag the object anywhere on the slide and resize it by dragging handles. But the text in the object remains small even when you have resized the object, and reading the text can be difficult.

- If you paste the copied data into an open bulleted list placeholder, the pasted text takes on the text formats for that placeholder. The data is copied in one long stream that you can easily separate into lines and align with tabs (see Figure 5-3). Some data formats also might change during the pasting process. The numbers in Figure 5-3, for example, should not have decimal places. You will probably want to remove the bullet from the first line of the pasted data. The field names will copy along with field data. You can remove these from your slide if desired.

FIGURE 5-2
Access data copied onto a slide as an object

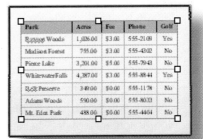

Unless you simply want to show a representation of the Access table data, you are better off pasting into a placeholder. You can then use text formatting features to spruce up the data on the slide.

FIGURE 5-3
Access data copied into a bulleted list placeholder

♦ **ParkAcresFeePhoneGolf**Rawson Woods1,026.00$3.00555-2109YesMadison Forest755.00$3.00555-4302NoPierce Lake3,201.00$5.00555-7943NoWhitewater Falls4,387.00$3.00555-8844YesBelk Preserve349.00$0.00555-1178NoAdams Woods590.00$0.00555-8033NoMt. Eden Park488.00$0.00555-4404No|

STEP-BY-STEP ▷ 5.3

You are beginning a presentation on the Madison County Park System for general distribution to the system's visitor centers. Some of the data you need for the presentation is stored in other applications. In this and subsequent Step-by-Steps you will use that data to help you complete your presentation.

1. Open **AP Step5-3** from the student data files. Save the file as **Park System** followed by your initials.

2. At present you have only two slides. You would like to add a third to give some selected

(continued on next page)

information about the main parks in the system. This information is stored in an Access database. First, add a Bulleted List slide to the end of the presentation. Give it the title **Selected Park Information**.

3. Start Access. From the data files for this lesson, open the **Madison County Parks** database. Then open the **Park Data** table.

4. You want to copy only the first five fields in the table (excluding the ID field). Drag the pointer across the field names to select the entire contents of the fields, as shown in Figure 5-4. Click **Copy**.

FIGURE 5-4
Selected Access table data

■ Park Data : Table					
ID	**Park**	**Acres**	**Fee**	**Phone**	**Golf**
▶ 1	Rawson Woods	1,026	$3	555-2109	☑
2	Madison Forest	755	$3	555-4302	☐
3	Pierce Lake	3,201	$5	555-7943	☐
4	Whitewater Falls	4,387	$3	555-8844	☑
5	Belk Preserve	349	$0	555-1178	☐
6	Adams Woods	590	$0	555-8033	☐
7	Mt. Eden Park	488	$0	555-4404	☐
* (er)		0	$0		☐

5. Switch to PowerPoint and open the bulleted list placeholder. Click **Paste**. The data appears in one long stream in the placeholder.

6. To turn off automatic bullets for the text in this placeholder, open the **Format** menu, click **Bullets and Numbering**, and select **None** for the bullet style. Click **OK**.

7. Press **Enter** after the boldfaced word **Golf** and then press **Enter** before each park

name to separate the text into individual rows of data. You should have eight rows, including the boldfaced column heads.

8. Do a little judicious editing at this point: remove the decimal places following the numbers and currency figures. Now align the text using tabs. Use a right-aligned tab for the *Acres* data so that the acreage figures will align right. Remember that you only have to set tabs in the first row of the text. Your completed slide should resemble the one shown in Figure 5-5.

FIGURE 5-5
Completed slide

Madison County Park System

Selected Park Information

Park	Acres	Fee	Phone	Golf
Rawson Woods	1,026	$3	555-2109	Yes
Madison Forest	755	$3	555-4302	No
Pierce Lake	3,201	$5	555-7943	No
Whitewater Falls	4,387	$3	555-8844	Yes
Belk Preserve	349	$0	555-1178	No
Adams Woods	590	$0	555-8033	No
Mt. Eden Park	488	$0	555-4404	No

9. Now that you can see the data clearly, notice that PowerPoint correctly converted Access's Yes/No field check marks into the words *Yes* and *No*. Print only the current slide as a handout with 2 slides per page.

10. Save your changes and leave the presentation open for the next Step-by-Step. Close the Access table and database.

Linking an Excel Chart to a Slide

In Lesson 2 you inserted an Excel worksheet object on a slide and entered text and values into the worksheet. In this section, you'll learn how to link an Excel chart to a slide.

To link an object, first copy it in the source document and then paste it into the destination document. You must use the Paste Special (or Paste Link) command on the Edit menu to set up a link. If you use the Paste tool, you embed the object instead of linking it.

FIGURE 5-6

Embed or link using the Paste Special dialog box

Clicking Paste Special opens the Paste Special dialog box, similar to Figure 5-6. By default, PowerPoint assumes you want to simply paste the object, so the *Paste* option is selected. If you accept this default setting, you will embed the copied object. Click the *Paste link* option to set up the link between the source and destination documents. The entries in the *As* list box depend on the object you have copied and what formats the destination application can accept. Notice that you have the option of displaying the embedded or linked object as an icon rather than at full size.

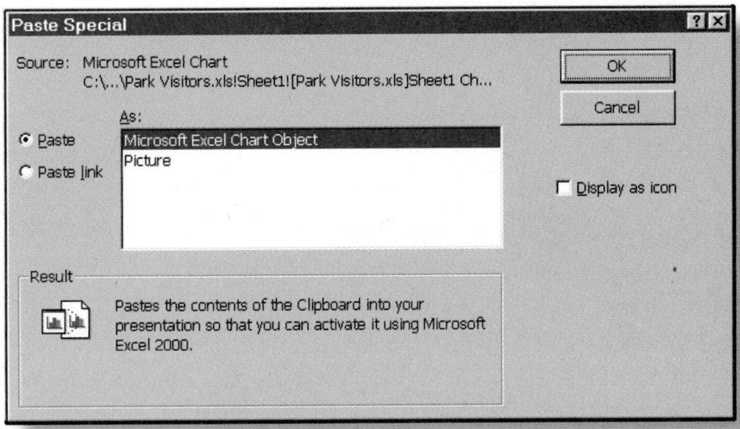

After you click OK in the Paste Special dialog box, your linked object displays on the current slide surrounded by selection handles. You can resize it or move it the same way you would any other object. You can also use the Object command on the Format menu to modify the object.

The object on the slide maintains a link to its original document. Any changes you make in that document that affect the linked object will appear not only in the source document but also in the object on the slide.

STEP-BY-STEP ▷ 5.4

You want to show a summary of annual attendance at the parks that charge entrance fees. That information is stored in an Excel worksheet that also shows a chart of the attendance figures to date. You can link the chart to your slide so that when the 4th Quarter figures are available, your slide will automatically show the final data.

1. First insert a new slide at the end of the show with the Title Only layout. Insert the title **Annual Visitor Summary**. Close the title placeholder.

2. In Excel, open **AP Step5-4** from the student data files. Save the file as **Park Visitors** followed by your initials. On the worksheet, click the chart's outside border to select the entire chart. Click **Copy**.

3. Switch to PowerPoint. Open the **Edit** menu and click **Paste Special**. In the Paste Special dialog box, click the **Paste link** option. Click **OK**.

(continued on next page)

4. Resize the linked object so that you can clearly read the chart labels.

5. The 4th Quarter figures have just arrived. Switch back to Excel and insert these values for the 4th Quarter. Then save and close the worksheet.

   1080
   1010
   1335
   1290

6. Switch back to PowerPoint. Notice that the 4th Quarter data now appears in the linked chart. Print only the current slide as a handout with 2 slides per page.

7. Save your changes and leave the presentation open for the next Step-by-Step.

Adding a Table from Word

Although PowerPoint offers a number of different ways to insert a table on a slide, you might sometimes want to take advantage of the ease of integration to insert a table from Microsoft Word. Word's table formatting features are more sophisticated than those of PowerPoint. After embedding a Word table on a slide, you can double-click it to format it using the commands on Word's Table menu. Adding a Word table to a slide in this way is also a way to save time if the table has already been prepared in Word.

To add a table from Word, select the entire table and copy it. In PowerPoint, open the Edit menu and click Paste Special. If you want to be able to edit the table in Word, you must select the Microsoft Word Document Object choice in the Paste Special dialog box.

STEP-BY-STEP ⇒ 5.5

1. You have a Word table with additional park information you want to add to the presentation. In Word, open **AP Step5-5** from the student data files and save the file as **Visitor Table** followed by your initials.

2. Select the entire table (open the **Table** menu, click **Select**, and then click **Table**). Click the **Copy** button on the Standard toolbar.

3. Switch to the presentation and add a new slide with the Title Only layout. Key the title **Come for a Visit** and close the title placeholder.

4. Open the **Edit** menu and click **Paste Special**. In the Paste Special dialog box, choose to paste the object as a **Microsoft Word Document Object** and click **OK**.

5. Double-click the table object to display the Word menus. Select the entire table again and change the font size to **26** pt. Use the up arrow key to move to the top of the table and merge the three cells in the first row to create one cell. Center the *Visitor Center* heading in the first row and boldface the text.

6. Boldface and center the headings in the second row. Adjust the column widths so that there are no runover lines. (You will have to expand the table by dragging the dark gray hatched border.) Center the phone numbers in the third column.

7. Sort the parks (not the headings) in ascending order. Remove the gridlines from the table. If necessary, drag the bottom dark gray hatched border upward, so it is close to the table.

8. Click outside the table to see it on the slide. If necessary, click the table object once to select it and move it to center it on the slide.

9. Save your changes. Print only the current slide as a handout with 2 slides per page. Leave the presentation open for the next Step-by-Step. Close the Word document and Word.

Copying Slides to Other Applications

Slides are not only full of information, they are also usually quite decorative. You can add both information and pizzazz to documents created in other Office 2000 applications by copying PowerPoint slides and pasting them into documents, worksheets, and database forms and reports.

Copy a PowerPoint slide in Slide Sorter view by selecting the slide you want and clicking the Copy button. Then switch to your destination document and click the Paste button. If desired, you can embed or link the slide using the Paste Special dialog box.

A slide pasted into Word or Excel has the same properties as any other object. You can move it, resize it, and control how text wraps around it. A slide pasted into an Access report or form needs a little more work. You must paste the slide into a band in Design view and then change its properties so you can resize it and move it easily.

In the next Step-by-Step, you'll learn the basics of pasting a slide into an Access form.

STEP-BY-STEP ▷ 5.6

1. In PowerPoint, switch to Slide Sorter view. Select slide 1 and then click **Copy**.

2. In Access, open **Madison County Parks**. Click **Forms** on the Object bar to see the forms in this database. Click the **Park Data** form and then click the **Design** button to open the form in Design view.

3. Click **Paste**. The slide displays, covering most of the form design. To begin the process of resizing the slide, right-click it and then click **Properties** on the shortcut menu.

4. On the **Format** tab in the Unbound Object Frame dialog box, click the **Size Mode** entry (it currently reads *Clip*). From the drop-down list, click **Stretch**. This setting allows you to resize the object freely. On the same tab, set a Width of **2.5** and a Height of **1.75**. Then click the dialog box's close box.

5. The slide object is now much smaller but still in the wrong place. Drag it to the right until its upper left corner is at the 2.5-inch mark on the horizontal ruler. Align the top of the object with the top of the first field. If any fields are covered by the slide object, click each one to select it and then drag the middle right sizing handle to the left to reduce the size of the field.

6. If necessary, drag the right border of the design grid to the left so that it extends about 1 inch past the slide. Drag the bottom border of the design grid upward to just below the last field. Scroll up to view the bottom border.

7. Change to Form view and scroll through the forms to see how the slide object appears on each form.

(continued on next page)

8. Select and print the first form. Save your changes and close the form and the database.

9. Save your changes to the presentation and close it.

Extra Challenge

Try pasting a slide into an Access report in Design view.

Sending Slide Information to Word

Word and PowerPoint have a special relationship insofar as sharing information goes. You have already seen how easily you can turn a Word outline into PowerPoint slides. You can just as easily export slide information to Word using the Send To Microsoft Word command on the File menu.

Click Send To and then Microsoft Word on the submenu. The Write-Up dialog box opens, as shown in Figure 5-7. This dialog box gives you a number of options for exporting the slide data. You can paste or link slides in four different layouts or you can export the outline only.

Slides pasted or linked to a Word document display in a table, as shown in Figure 5-8. You can easily resize the slides and adjust column widths as desired. Note, though, that Word files created this way can be quite large. If having the slides appear in color in the Word document is not critical, you can reduce the size of the file by choosing PowerPoint's Black and White command on the View menu. This command transforms your slides to grayscale versions that take much less room to store.

FIGURE 5-7
Use this dialog box to export PowerPoint data to Word

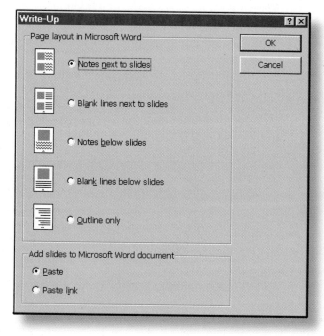

FIGURE 5-8
Pasted slides display in a table

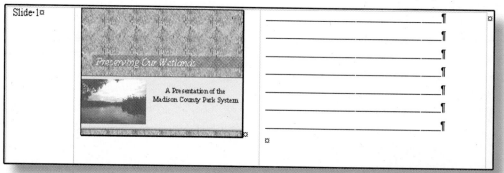

When you choose to export your PowerPoint data as an outline, Word opens and your slide information is displayed with outline heading styles. Depending on your system setup, you might see the Convert File dialog box during this process. You can click OK to accept the default conversion option (Rich Text Format).

Exported outlines contain no graphics, tables, or charts. You get only the slide text. Once you have the text in Word, you can modify styles to reduce the font size and remove unnecessary font styles.

STEP-BY-STEP ▷ 5.7

1. Open the **Wetlands 2** presentation you worked with in Lesson 3. You would like to send an outline of the text of this presentation to Word.

2. Open the **File** menu and click **Send To**. Then click **Microsoft Word** on the submenu.

3. In the Write-Up dialog box, click the **Outline only** option and click **OK**. If the convert File dialog box displays, click **OK** in the Convert File dialog box to accept the default conversion option.

4. The outline displays in Word. Modify the styles as desired to create a more traditional-looking outline of the text. (*Hint:* To remove the shadow font effect, open the Font dialog box and click to remove the check mark in the **Shadow** check box.)

5. Save the Word file as **Wetlands Outline** followed by your initials. Print the outline. Close the Word document and Word.

Sending PowerPoint Presentations to Others

Office 2000 has built in easy ways to send presentations via e-mail using the same Send To submenu you used in the last Step-by-Step. This submenu also gives you the option of sending a presentation to an Exchange folder where others can access it.

You have two options for sending a presentation via e-mail:

- If you click Mail Recipient on the submenu, you can then choose to send the current slide by itself as the body of the e-mail message or to attach the entire presentation to the e-mail message.

- If you know you want to attach the entire presentation, choose Mail Recipient (As Attachment) from the submenu. PowerPoint opens a new message with the presentation already attached, as shown in Figure 5-9.

FIGURE 5-9
A new e-mail message with an
attached presentation

If your system is a client of the Microsoft Exchange Server, you can use the Exchange Folder option to post a presentation to a public folder where others can access it. This is an excellent way for a workgroup to participate in a project. Each member of the workgroup can *subscribe* to the folder. Members then are notified of any changes to presentations stored in the folder.

S TEP-BY-STEP ▷ 5.8

1. If you have e-mail access from your computer, send slide 1 of the current presentation to a friend or colleague whose e-mail address you know. Open the **File** menu and click **Send To**. Then click **Mail Recipient** on the submenu and specify that you want to send the current slide as the body of the message.

2. Leave the presentation open for the next Step-by-Step.

Changing Output Options

By default, presentations are created for on-screen viewing. This means that the slides you see on your screen have been sized to fit the proportions of a monitor screen. However, PowerPoint gives you a number of other standard slide sizes to choose from.

To change the layout of your current presentation, open the File menu and click Page Setup. Then click the down arrow in the *Slides sized for* list box to see the list of preset slide layouts, as shown in Figure 5-10. If you want to have your presentation prepared as 35mm slides, click the 35mm Slides option and then OK. The proportions of your slides change to fit the requirement of 35mm slides. To prepare overheads, choose the Overhead option. The actual measurement of your slides is shown in the Width and Height boxes.

FIGURE 5-10
Choose from a list of preset layouts or create your own

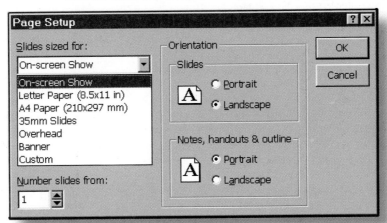

You can create a custom layout by clicking the Custom option and setting a desired width and height. You can also change the orientation of both slides and handouts in this dialog box. And should you want to start numbering your slides from a number other than 1, you can make that change in the *Number slides from* box.

Most graphics service bureaus can prepare slides and overheads directly from a PowerPoint file. If you do not have a service bureau in your area (or if you just like doing everything from your computer), you can use the Geni-

Concept Builder

If you are preparing a section of slides to fit into a larger presentation, you need to change the starting number for your slides to follow the last number of the previous section.

graphics option on the Send To submenu to send slides from your computer to an online service bureau whose business is presentations. PowerPoint includes a Genigraphics wizard to take you through the steps of selecting the services you want, placing your order, and sending your files.

You have another choice when preparing slides for others to use. You can save slides as graphic objects using a graphics format such as GIF, JPEG, Windows Metafile, or TIFF. To do so, open the File menu and click Save As. Click the down arrow in the *Save as type* list box and choose a graphic format. After you click Save, a message box opens to ask if you want to export all slides in the presentation or only the current slide. Graphics you create in this fashion are available for use as pictures in other applications or on Web pages.

1. To see how your slides would look as 35mm slides, follow these steps:
   a. Switch to Slide Sorter view.
   b. Open the **File** menu and click **Page Setup**. Click the down arrow in the *Slides sized for* list box and then click **35mm Slides**. Notice in the height and width boxes that the slide dimensions change (you could have used the extra width when creating that table!).

2. Change the setup to that for **Banner** and view the changes.

3. Change back to **On-screen Show**. Close the presentation without saving changes.

Summary

In this lesson, you learned:

■ You can easily create presentations from outlines you have already prepared in a word processing program such as Word. Once you have a presentation open, you can add slides to it either from a text outline or from another presentation.

■ There are many ways to share data between the major Office 2000 applications. Sharing information can take the form of copying, linking, or embedding data.

■ PowerPoint has specific options for sending data to Word and to e-mail clients.

■ By default, slides are sized for an on-screen presentation. You can change the width and height of slides in the Page Setup dialog box.

LESSON 5 REVIEW QUESTIONS

TRUE/FALSE

Circle T if the statement is true or F if the statement is false.

T **F** 1. As you create slides from an outline, you must specify a design template before PowerPoint will create the slides.

T **F** 2. You can select only one slide at a time in Slide Sorter view.

T **F** 3. You can easily embed data from an Access table in a PowerPoint slide.

T F 4. Slides pasted into Word from the Write-Up dialog box appear in a table.

T F 5. Slides prepared with a Banner layout will probably differ in size from those with a 35mm Slide layout.

WRITTEN QUESTIONS

Write a brief answer to the following questions.

1. What are two ways you can import slides from another presentation?

   1. insert slides from files
   2. Copy/Paste

2. In a linking operation, what is the source document? What is the destination document? How do you edit a linked object?

   Source contains data in the program it was created in
   Destination doc. will have a link to the data in the source file
   Edit menu → links object
   Select linked object
   Open Source

3. When might you want to display an embedded or linked object as an icon?

   to save space on the destination doc.

4. Give an example of when you might want to insert a single slide into a Word document.

   To use previously gathered information in the word doc.

5. You would like to send a presentation to a colleague. What are your options using e-mail for this task?

   Send for review
   Send as attachment
   Send to Routing recipient
   Send to Exchange Folder

A P - 9 5

SCANS

⚹ **PROJECT 5-1**   *do this at home.*

You and your partner at the Deer Creek Inn have an idea for boosting occupancy in the winter months: corporate conferences and retreats. You have outlined some ideas about a presentation you could use to persuade interested corporate clients.

1. In PowerPoint, click **Open** and locate the data files for this lesson. Change *Files of type* to **All Files** to see all the files. Click the Word file named **AP Project5-1**. Save the new PowerPoint presentation as **Deer Creek Conference** followed by your initials.

2. Apply the design template you customized in Lesson 4. Change the slide layout of the first slide to *Title*.

3. You realize you could use the slide from your previous Deer Creek presentation that describes the amenities available for each room type. Locate that slide and insert it after slide 2.

4. Save your changes. Run the slide show.

5. Print the slides as handouts with 6 slides per page. Close the presentation.

⚹ **PROJECT 5-2**   *Completed but didn't print*

You have some additional data you want to use in your weather presentation. The statistics are stored in other applications, so you will have to use integration techniques to import it into your presentation.

1. Open **Weather 3** from your solution files. Save the file as **Weather 4** followed by your initials. You'd like to create a chart showing weather disasters by year. You have the data you need for the chart in an Excel worksheet—all except the 1997 data, which you still have to tabulate.

2. Open **AP Project5-2** in Excel. Save the file as **Weather Disasters by Year** followed by your initials. Copy the cell range **A5:H9**.

3. Switch to PowerPoint and add a Chart layout slide following slide 3. Give it the title **Weather Disasters by Year**. Double-click the chart placeholder. Click the first cell in the datasheet (it is a blank cell). Open the **Edit** menu and click **Paste Link**. Click **OK** to replace current data. Close the datasheet.

4. You have some data on hurricane disasters that you think could contribute to the hurricane section of the presentation. Move to slide 7 and add a bulleted list slide following it. Give it the title **Costliest Hurricanes**.

5. In Access, open the database **Hurricanes** from the data files for this lesson. Open the table **10 Costliest Hurricanes**. You won't have room for all 10 in your placeholder, so select only the first seven. Copy the data and paste it into the bulleted text placeholder. Align the data using tabs. Close the database table, the database, and Access.

6. Return to slide 4 to make some further changes to the chart. Move the legend below the chart and add a label for the Z axis: **In Billions of $**. (*Hint:* Click **Chart Options** on the **Chart** menu to add the label. To choose an alignment for the label, double-click the label on the chart and choose

Alignment in the Format Axis Title dialog box.) And you've finally had time to tabulate the 1997 weather disasters. Leave the chart active while you return to Excel and insert these values:

```
Floods            2.0
Other Storms      1.5
```

7. Save the worksheet and close it. In the presentation, notice that the chart updated. Save your changes. (*Hint:* If the chart did not update, you did not leave it active while making changes to the Excel worksheet. Double-click the chart to update it.)

8. Print only slides 4 and 8 as handouts with 2 slides per page. Close the presentation.

PROJECT 5-3

You'd like to have copies of the slides you prepared for the Lead presentation. Export the slides to Word to make quick handouts.

1. Open **Lead 2**. You need only black and white copies of the slides in Word, so open the **View** menu and click **Black and White**.

2. Open the **File** menu and click **Send To**. On the submenu click **Microsoft Word**. In the Write-Up dialog box, click **OK** to accept the default settings.

3. Use the Object command on the Format menu to change the size of each slide to 2 inches wide. Reduce the space below each slide by dragging the table gridline upward to just below each slide. You should be able to fit five slides on the first page.

4. Change the font of the note text to Times New Roman 10 point.

5. Save the Word document as **Lead Slides** Followed by your initials. Print the document. Close the document.

6. Open the **View** menu and click **Black and White** to return to the color view. Close the presentation.

CRITICAL THINKING

ACTIVITY 5-1

Your workgroup has created an informative document to accompany a presentation. You would like to illustrate the document with slides from the presentation. Considering what you have learned in this lesson, what is the best way to accomplish this task? Write a description of the steps you would take.

ACTIVITY 5-2

You have linked an object to a slide but no longer want the link to be active. How do you break a link? Use PowerPoint's Help system to find out how and write a brief description of the steps you need to take.

USING ADVANCED PRESENTATION FEATURES

OBJECTIVES

Upon completion of this lesson, you should be able to:

- Hide slides.
- Set slide timings and rehearse timings.
- Add action buttons to slides and specify action settings.
- Record narration for a presentation.
- Use on-screen navigation tools during the presentation.
- Annotate slides during the presentation.
- Use Meeting Minder during a presentation to take notes and assign tasks.
- Set up online broadcasts and collaborate online with others in a group.
- Pack a presentation to be viewed on another computer.

⏱ Estimated Time: 2 hours

You are now ready to explore the advanced features available for presenting your slides. You have already done the hard work of preparing the content and the format of the slides. Now you can explore how to control those slides during the presentation.

PowerPoint 2000 also offers several online options for presenting slides. You can, for example, broadcast your presentation over your local area network or on the Web. You can also arrange an online meeting for the purpose of viewing or working on a presentation. And if you want to take your presentation somewhere else to present it, you can use the Pack and Go Wizard to gather all your presentation information into one file. You can even add the PowerPoint Viewer to use if the computer you're going to use for the presentation does not have PowerPoint available.

This lesson organizes all these topics into three areas: final preparations you make before the presentation, features you can use during the presentation, and other presentation options.

Before the Presentation

Before you actually give your presentation, you can make quite a number of adjustments to your slides to help you control them during the presentation. In this section, you'll explore many of those options, including hiding slides you don't want to show, setting slide timings, adding narration to the presentation, deciding what slide to start on, specifying action settings, and rehearsing your timing.

Hiding Slides

Slides you have prepared on a particular subject might not be suitable or necessary for every occasion on which you give the presentation. You can prevent slides from displaying during the presentation by hiding them. Hiding a slide does not delete it. You can unhide the slide the next time you want to use it in your presentation or even during the presentation, as you will learn later in this lesson.

You can hide a slide in any view, but you can see evidence that you have hidden it only in Slide Sorter view. A hidden slide has a diagonal bar across its number in Slide Sorter view, as shown in Figure 6-1. To hide a slide, select it or make it active. Open the Slide Show menu and click Hide Slide. Or click the Hide Slide button on the toolbar. To unhide a slide, use the same steps you took to hide it.

Setting Slide Timings and Effects

In Lesson 4, you customized presentations by creating animation effects for them. As part of the effect, you specified when the effect should occur.

You can create the same kinds of effects and timings for each slide in a presentation. The effects take place as each slide is displayed. As for the animation effects, you can specify whether you will advance the slides manually by clicking the mouse button or have PowerPoint advance them automatically according to the timings you set.

You can set slide timings and effects in any view by opening the Slide Show menu and clicking Slide Transition. When you do, the Slide Transition dialog box opens, as shown in Figure 6-2.

FIGURE 6-1
A hidden slide in
Slide Sorter view

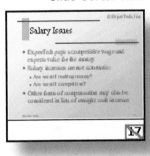

FIGURE 6-2
Set timings and effects in this dialog box

By default, no transition is in effect for a slide and the advance option is set for a mouse click. To see available transition effects, click the down arrow in the *Effect* list box and choose an effect. The preview picture immediately shows the effect. You can then choose a speed for the effect.

To have PowerPoint advance your slide automatically, remove the check mark from the *On mouse click* checkbox and click *Automatically after*. You must then set a time for the advance.

As for animation effects, you can also choose a sound effect to accompany your slide transition. Click in the Sound list box to see the available sounds.

To apply your effects and timing to the current slide only, click Apply. To apply the effects and timing to all slides in the presentation, click Apply to All.

The Slide Transition dialog box lets you set all transition options in one place. You can also use drop-down lists in Slide Sorter view to set transition and animation effects (see Figure 6-3). Your effects and timings are listed below each slide in Slide Sorter view.

> **Concept Builder**
>
> Using a large number of different transition effects can be distracting to the viewer.

FIGURE 6-3

Setting transition and animation effects in Slide Sorter view

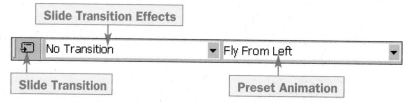

STEP-BY-STEP ▷ 6.1

You are ready to fine-tune your ExperTech employee manual for final release.

1. Open **AP Step6-1** from the student data files. Save the file as **ET Final Manual**.

2. With slide 1 on the screen, open the **Slide Show** menu and click **Slide Transition**.

3. Click the **Effect** drop-down list and locate the *Wipe Down* effect. Set its speed at *Slow*. Keep the manual advance option of *On mouse click*.

4. Click **Apply to All** to apply these settings to all slides. Or if desired, set other transition effects for individual slides. When you've finished

adding effects and sounds, switch to Slide Sorter view.

5. Notice the symbols below each slide to indicate that a transition effect has been applied. Symbols also indicate where you have already specified animation effects.

6. Management is rethinking some issues relating to salaries and raises. For now, you'd better hide slide 17: click slide 17 to select it and then click the **Hide Slide** button on the Slide Sorter toolbar.

7. Save your changes and leave the presentation open for the next Step-by-Step.

Adding Action Buttons and Action Settings

Action buttons are predrawn buttons that perform specific actions, such as taking you to the next slide or taking you to a Web site's home page. Action buttons are especially useful for presentations designed to be self-running or for presentations on the Web. Action buttons and settings are active only while you are running the slide show.

You insert action buttons in Slide view by opening the Slide Show menu, clicking Action Buttons, and selecting the button you want from the submenu of choices. After you select a button, the pointer changes to a cross. Click on your slide to insert the button. The Action Settings dialog box immediately appears, as shown in Figure 6-4. In this dialog box, you can customize action settings for hyperlinks, programs, and sounds.

FIGURE 6-4
Customize action settings in this dialog box

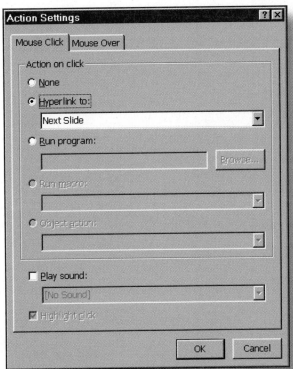

The *Hyperlink to* setting is automatically set for you if you have chosen one of the preset action buttons. If you chose to create a custom button, you can use the *Hyperlink to* list box to specify where you will end up if you click the button. Or, you can click the *Run program* option to have the button run a program or a macro or perform some other action. You can specify a sound to play each time the action button is clicked.

You can use action settings for hyperlink text on your slides. In Lesson 1, you inserted a hyperlink by clicking the Insert Hyperlink button on the toolbar. You can also set a hyperlink by selecting text or an object and clicking Action Settings on the Slide Show menu. In the Action Settings dialog box, use the *Hyperlink to* list box to specify where the hyperlink should jump to.

Notice the two tabs in the Action Settings dialog box. The Mouse Click tab lets you control action buttons or settings by clicking on them with the mouse. The Mouse Over tab gives you the same options as the Mouse Click tab, but you control the action buttons simply by passing the mouse pointer over the button. Having these two tabs makes it possible for you to assign two separate actions to a single button, one that you control with a click and one that you control by moving the mouse over the button.

After you have inserted the action button on your slide and specified your action settings, you can format the button as you like. Action buttons take their colors from the current color scheme. You can change the look of the button by dragging the small yellow diamond in or out. You can change the button's size by dragging one of the selection handles. You can move the button anywhere on the slide.

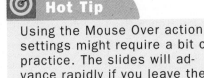

Hot Tip

Using the Mouse Over action settings might require a bit of practice. The slides will advance rapidly if you leave the mouse on top of the action button too long.

If you want the same button on the next slide (or a number of other slides), copy the button. When you paste it on another slide, it appears in the same location on the new slide as on the original slide. If you want a button to appear on every slide, place it on the slide or title master.

You want to insert hyperlinks on the Contents slide so that a user can jump immediately to the start of each section of the presentation. Also, you want users to be able to move easily forward and backward among the slides.

1. Switch to Slide view, if necessary, and move to slide 2. To insert the first hyperlink, click anywhere in the *Introduction* bulleted item. Open the **Slide Show** menu and click **Action Settings**.

2. Click the **Hyperlink to** option. Click the down arrow next to the hyperlink list box and choose **Custom Show**. Click the **Introduction** show. To allow viewers to return to the Contents slide after finishing this custom show, click in the **Show and return** check box. Then click **OK**. Click **OK** again to close the Action Settings dialog box.

Hot Tip

If you select *Show and return*, you must click the mouse at the end of the custom show to return to the agenda slide.

3. Set up hyperlinks for the other two bulleted items. To create the hyperlink for *Company Policies*, select both words before opening the Action Settings dialog box.

4. Now insert action buttons for the slides. On slide 1, you need an action button letting users move to the next slide. Slides 2 through 17 should have both a "next slide" and a "previous slide" button. And slide 18 should have only a "previous slide" button. Follow these steps to insert the buttons:

a. With slide 1 on the screen, open the **Slide Show** menu and click **Action Buttons**. On the submenu, click the right-pointing **Forward or Next** button. Click at the bottom middle of the slide. Don't worry if the button falls off the edge of the slide—you can move it later.

b. In the Action Settings dialog box, the default setting for the hyperlink is *Next Slide*, which is what you want. Click **OK**.

c. Resize the action button so it is small. Make sure it is entirely on the slide. To place it on the next slide as well, click **Copy** on the toolbar.

d. Move to slide 2. Click **Paste**. On the same slide, use the procedure above to insert the action button for Back or Previous. Make sure to select **Previous Slide** if necessary in the hyperlink list box. Size the second button to look like the first and arrange it near the Next button.

e. Group the two buttons using the **Group** command on the **Draw** pop-up menu. Position the grouped buttons at the bottom middle of the slide (so you don't hide the date or slide number) and then copy the group. Paste the group on all remaining slides.

f. On slide 18, ungroup the buttons. Click the **Next** button to select it and then press **Delete**.

5. Save your changes. To see how your presentation is looking so far, run the slide show. Try out the hyperlinks and the action buttons.

6. Leave the presentation open for the next Step-by-Step.

Recording Narration

If your computer has a voice recording option, you can record narration for your presentation. This is a useful option for a slide show that will run automatically at an information kiosk or on the Web.

Concept Builder

You must have a microphone and a sound card to record narration on your slides.

Open the Slide Show menu and click Record Narration. The Record Narration dialog box opens, as shown in Figure 6-5. Before you begin your narration, you can check to make sure your microphone is working properly by clicking the Set Microphone Level button. You can set quality for the recording as Telephone Quality, Radio Quality, or CD Quality. You can choose to link the narration to the slides.

FIGURE 6-5

Start in this dialog box to record narration for your presentation

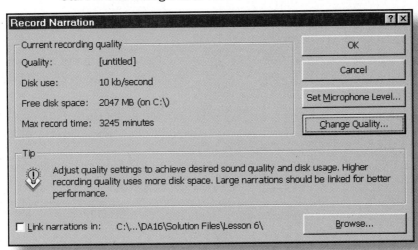

After you have selected your settings in the Record Narration dialog box, PowerPoint plays the slide show so that you can add your narration. After you have finished, PowerPoint tells you that the narration has been saved for each slide and asks if you want to save your slide timings as well. If you have set up automatic slide timings, you might want to choose Yes here to adjust your slide timings to match your narration.

Each slide that contains narration displays a sound object in the lower right corner. Voice narration takes precedence over any other kind of sound on your slides, so if you have recorded narration, you will not hear other sounds you have inserted.

S TEP-BY-STEP ▷ 6.3

Try this Step-by-Step if your computer has a microphone and a sound card.

1. Open the **Slide Show** menu and click **Record Narration**. In the Record Narration dialog box,

make sure the sound quality is set for telephone quality: Click the **Change Quality** button and then select **Telephone Quality** in the *Name* drop-down menu. Click **OK** twice to close both dialog boxes.

(continued on next page)

2. When slide 1 appears, say **Welcome to Exper-Tech!** When slide 2 appears, say **Click the hyperlink to move to a section of the manual**. Speak clearly, not too close to the microphone.

3. Right-click on slide 2 and choose **End Show** from the shortcut menu. When asked if you want to save slide timings, click **No**.

4. Run the show again and listen for your narration. After you have heard the narration on slide 2, end the show.

5. Select the sound objects in the lower right corner of slides 1 and 2 and delete them to remove the narration from the presentation.

6. Leave the presentation open for the next Step-by-Step.

Rehearsing Slide Timings

If you have set automatic slide timings, you can use the Rehearse Timings command to find out if you have allowed enough time for each slide. This feature is also useful if you want to know how long it might take a person to go through the show slide by slide.

When you choose Rehearse Timings on the Slide Show menu, the presentation immediately starts running. A "stopwatch" appears on the screen to show you how much time you have spent viewing each slide and the presentation as a whole (Figure 6-6).

You can stop timing by pressing the Pause button. If you have already set automatic slide transition timings, you can click the Next button to move to the next slide. After you have finished the presentation, PowerPoint tells you how long it took you to progress through the slides and asks if you want to use your rehearsal timings the next time you view the slides.

FIGURE 6-6

The Rehearsal dialog box lets you time each slide and the whole presentation

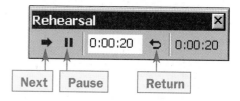

Setting Up the Show

Before you actually present your slides, you should use the Set Up Show command to make sure of your current settings and to specify additional settings. Open the Slide Show menu and click Set Up Show. The Set Up Show dialog box opens, similar to Figure 6-7.

In this dialog box, you can specify the show type and instruct PowerPoint how to show it—looping continuously, without narration, or without animation. If you have recorded narration for the slides, for example, you can tell PowerPoint in this dialog box

FIGURE 6-7

Specify settings for the show in this dialog box

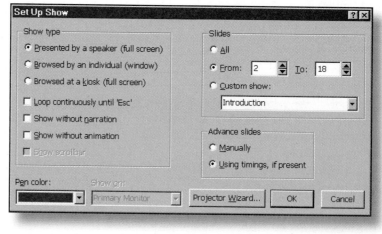

to run the show without that narration. You can also select a range of slides to display. To start the show from a slide other than 1, change the number in the *From* box. If you want to show only one of your custom shows, click the *Custom show* option and then select the show. Make sure this dialog box also shows your choice for advancing slides, either manually or automatically.

If you plan to write notes on your slides as you present them, you can choose what color your pen will write. To get help connecting your computer to a data projector, click the Projector Wizard button.

STEP-BY-STEP ▷ 6.4

1. You don't have automatic timings set for this slide show (except for some animation effects), but you can see how the rehearsal feature works anyway: open the **Slide Show** menu and click **Rehearse Timings**. Progress through each slide, reading all text. How long did it take you to complete the show? Click **No** when asked if you want to record the new slide timings.

2. Make sure your show is set up for your final presentation to the Manual Committee: open the **Slide Show** menu again and click **Set Up Show**. Your Set Up Show dialog box should indicate that you want to show all slides and that the presentation will use timings if they are available. Click **OK**.

3. Leave the presentation open for the next Step-by-Step.

During the Presentation

You have already used at least one of the tools available to help you during the presentation: the shortcut menu that displays when you right-click. This menu contains a number of commands you can use while presenting your slides. Some, such as End Show, are obvious. You'll learn about some of the less obvious ones in this section.

Navigating During a Presentation

Hyperlinks and action buttons help you to control the way a viewer will progress through the slides on his or her own. If you are presenting the slides yourself, though, you might want more control over your next slide. If an audience member asks a question that you know can be answered by showing a particular slide, you want to be able to go immediately to that slide.

The Go command on the shortcut menu gives you three options for finding a specific slide or group of slides during a presentation: Slide Navigator, By Title, and Custom Show. The Previously Viewed option can also take you back to the slide you viewed right before the current slide.

Slide Navigator (Figure 6-8) lists the slides in the presentation by title. Click on the slide you want to jump to and click Go To. A quicker way to jump to a slide whose title you know is to click By Title. A submenu opens with all slide titles listed. Click one to jump immediately to that slide. To jump to the beginning of a custom show, click Custom Show and select the show you want to start.

FIGURE 6-8
Slide Navigator

You can show a slide you have hidden using the Slide Navigator. In the Slide Navigator list, numbers of hidden slides are enclosed in parentheses. Select the hidden slide and click Go To to go to that slide.

Annotating Slides During a Presentation

You might occasionally want to draw or write on your slides as you present them. You can do so using the pen pointer, which you turn on from the shortcut menu. It's not all that easy to write with the pointer, but you can certainly use it to underline or circle important items.

On the shortcut menu, click Pointer Options and choose Pen. You can also choose a pen color from this submenu. The pointer changes to a pen shape. You can erase any scribbles you've made on a slide by clicking Screen on the shortcut menu and then clicking Erase Pen. If you don't erase, however, the marks disappear when you advance to the next slide. You need to change the pointer back to Automatic before you can click to advance to the next slide.

Another way to annotate your slides during a presentation is to click Speaker Notes on the shortcut menu. A dialog box opens to allow you to key notes for the slide you are viewing. Those notes are attached to the slide just like notes you create in the notes pane in Normal view.

Teamwork

One good way to practice presenting slides is to work with one or two friends. Take turns presenting the material on the slides and offer a critique to each person.

Hot Tip

To draw a straight line with the pen, hold the Shift key as you draw.

Using Meeting Minder

PowerPoint's Meeting Minder is a useful feature to have running when you are presenting slides as part of a meeting. Not only can you take notes on topics discussed during the meeting, you can prepare a list of items that need further action.

Start the Meeting Minder by clicking Meeting Minder on the shortcut menu during a slide show. (You can also access the Meeting Minder from the Tools menu in any other PowerPoint view.) The Meeting Minder dialog box opens. Notice the two tabs in the dialog box.

Use the Meeting Minutes tab to record notes for a meeting, as shown in Figure 6-9. To schedule a meeting or see schedule information, click the Schedule button. An Untitled Appointment dialog box opens, similar to one you would see when setting up an appointment in Microsoft Outlook. You can export your minutes to Word for further formatting by clicking Export in this dialog box and then Export Now in the Meeting Minder Export dialog box.

FIGURE 6-9
The Meeting Minder

The Action Items tab, shown in Figure 6-10, lets you assign tasks that come up in the course of the meeting. Tasks you insert in this dialog box are combined on a slide at the end of the current presentation. To schedule a task in greater detail, click the Schedule button. To export the tasks, click the Export button. You can export tasks to Word or post them to your Outlook task list for further action.

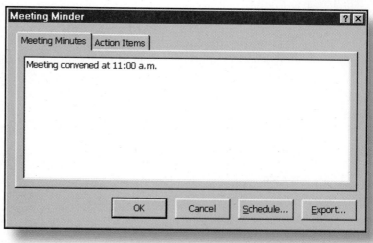

FIGURE 6-10
The Action Items tab

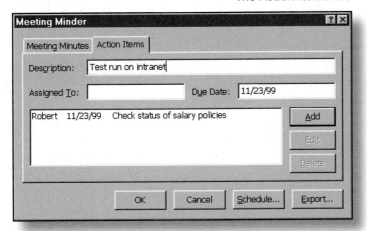

Adding an action item is easy. Key a brief description of the task, insert the name of the person you want to assign the task to, and specify the date by which the task should be completed. Then click Add. You can always go back and edit a task or delete it by selecting it and then clicking Delete.

STEP-BY-STEP ▷ 6.5

1. Run the slide show. On slide 1, right-click to open the shortcut menu. Click **Meeting Minder**. In the *Meeting Minutes* text box, key the following entries:

   ```
   Manual Committee meeting
   convened at 2:00 p.m.
   Present: Robert, Anne, and
   [your name]
   ```

2. Drag the Meeting Minder dialog box to the bottom right corner of the screen to be out of the way.

3. In previous meetings, the committee had some issues about wording on the Holidays slide. Go to that slide to make sure the wording is now acceptable: Right-click to open the shortcut menu. Click **Go** and then click **Slide Navigator**. Scroll in the list of slides, select slide 13, and then click **Go To**.

4. You want to discuss further the dress code policies on slide 11. Use the Slide Navigator to jump to that slide. Underline the topics you want to discuss using the pen:

   a. Right-click to open the shortcut menu and click **Pointer Options**. Then click **Pen**. Click **Pen Color** to choose a bright color for the pen lines.

   b. Use the pen to underline *professional business clothing*. (You think this concept might need to be spelled out for new employees used to more casual clothing options.)

   c. Underline *neatly and cleanly dressed*. (Neat, clean clothes might still be inappropriate—further explanation might be needed here.)

(continued on next page)

d. Circle *Casual* in the last bullet item. (Does the committee need to spell out what *casual* clothing is?)

e. Open the shortcut menu and select the **Automatic** pointer option.

f. Make a note in the meeting minutes:

```
Clothing issues were discussed.
Further guidelines should be
prepared and linked to locations
noted on slide 11.
```

5. Assign Anne the task of preparing guidelines and linking the resulting document to the slide text:

a. Click the **Action Items** tab.

b. Key the following description: **Prepare clothing guidelines and links**

c. Assign the task to **Anne** and choose a due date one week from the current date. Click **Add**.

6. Salary policies are still up in the air. To see the original salary policies slide, right-click again to open the shortcut menu. Click **Go** and then **By Title**. Click the title of the hidden slide (its number is in parentheses) to move to that slide.

7. Assign **Robert** the task of finding out what's up with the salary negotiations: On the **Action**

Items tab in the Meeting Minder dialog box, key the task description: **Check status of salary policies**. Robert should complete the task no later than three days from the current date.

8. The meeting adjourns at 3:00 p.m. Make a note of this for the minutes.

9. So all participants can have a list of the minutes and tasks, export the Meeting Minder information to Word: click **Export**, remove the check from the *Post items to Microsoft Outlook* box, and make sure there is a check in the option for exporting to Word. Click **Export Now**. If a Convert Text dialog box opens, accept the default conversion format of RTF.

10. Save the new Word document as **Manual Committee Minutes** followed by your initials. Print the document. Close Word.

11. Close the Meeting Minder dialog box by clicking **OK**. Scroll through the slides to the last slide. The last slide has been prepared from the action items you inserted in the Meeting Minder. Print this slide as a handout with 2 slides per page.

12. Save your changes and close the presentation.

Other Ways to Present Slides

As you have been working through this unit, you have probably been thinking of a few ways that slides can be presented to an audience. The most traditional way is for a speaker to stand up in front of the audience and control the slides so that the whole audience sees each slide at the same time. Another way is for a presentation to be set up on a computer that will run the slides automatically so that anyone who happens to be in the area can look at the slides as they flash on the monitor or viewing screen. Another way is for a presentation to be set up on a computer or network so that anyone with access to that computer or network can open and run the presentation at his or her own speed.

Improvements in multimedia devices for computers and the surge in popularity of networks and particularly the Internet have made it possible to expand presentation options beyond these traditional methods. With the right hardware and software, you can now broadcast a presentation over a local area network or on the Internet. You can now schedule an online meeting at which all participants can view and annotate slides. You can now pack up your presentation and take it to a different computer in a different location altogether and run it even if that computer does not have PowerPoint installed.

Broadcasting a Presentation

Broadcasting is a way to present slides to an audience that cannot convene in one location for the presentation. If, for example, you work in a very large company or for a company that has branch offices located over a wide geographic area, broadcasting is a sensible way to reach all your potential viewers. A broadcast presentation is saved in HTML format, which means your viewers do not need Power-Point to view the slides. Instead, they view the slides using their standard Web browser.

Hot Tip

You can use Outlook to schedule the broadcast for all viewers just as you would schedule an online meeting.

For audiences of more than 15 viewers, or for presentations containing video, you must use Windows NT Server NetShow Services. NetShow Services distribute streaming audio and video content that viewers display using the Windows Media Player. NetShow Services can be set up locally on a LAN, allowing you to broadcast to an unlimited number of users on the LAN. To reach users on the Internet, you can use a third-party NetShow service provider. When setting up a NetShow broadcast, click the Server Options button on the Broadcast Settings tab in the Schedule a New Broadcast dialog box. In the Server Options dialog box, choose a shared location for your presentation that has write access for the NetShow server. Then, specify the name of the local NetShow server on your LAN, or specify a third-part NetShow service provider. If you specify a NetShow service provider, follow directions from the provider on how to set up and schedule a broadcast. You can get more information on NetShow services by clicking the About NetShow Services button in the Server Options dialog box.

You can schedule a broadcast on your local area network for up to 15 people with no additional hardware or software requirements. To set up a broadcast, follow these steps:

- Open the Slide Show menu and click Online Broadcast. Then click Set Up and Schedule from the submenu. In the Broadcast Schedule dialog box, click the *Set up and schedule a new broadcast* option and then click OK.

- The Schedule a New Broadcast dialog box opens, as shown in Figure 6-11. On the Description tab, key the title and a description of the presentation. Indicate the speaker's name and the name of the contact person. Click Preview Lobby Page to see the introductory page that will appear in each viewer's browser before the presentation begins. The lobby page also gives a countdown until the presentation is scheduled to start.

FIGURE 6-11
Schedule your broadcast in this dialog box

Schedule a New Broadcast

Description | Broadcast Settings

This information will appear on the lobby page for the new broadcast:

Title: Wetlands Final

Description: This presentation explores wetland characteristics and rates of loss

Speaker: [Your Name]

Contact: [Presenter Name]   Address Book...

Preview Lobby Page   Schedule Broadcast   Cancel

- Click the Broadcast Settings tab to check settings for the broadcast. If you intend to broadcast over a local network, click the Server Options button to specify a shared folder on the network where all participants can access the presentation.

- Click the Schedule Broadcast button to set up a time for the broadcast and to invite viewers to the presentation. You can also set up reminders for each person you have invited.

- To start the broadcast, open the Slide Show menu, click Online Broadcast, and then click Begin Broadcast.

Depending on your hardware and software, you can enable chat so that viewers can discuss the presentation with others. You can archive presentations on your Web server to create "presentations on demand," so that people who could not view a particular broadcast can view it at their leisure.

Collaborating on a Presentation Using NetMeeting

If you need to discuss a presentation with other people not in your immediate area, you can set up and run an online meeting. This is a useful tool if members of a workgroup or committee are not all at the same corporate site. To set up an online meeting, you use the NetMeeting application that comes with Office 2000. You must also have access to a directory server that allows you to participate in real-time meetings with others.

During the meeting, you can control how the meeting participants work on the presentation. If you turn the collaboration option on, participants can take turns controlling the presentation to insert, modify, or suggest changes. Turning collaboration off lets you control the presentation yourself, but participants can watch your changes, send messages to one another, and work on a whiteboard. Only the host of the meeting must have the PowerPoint presentation stored on his or her computer.

You have two options for hosting an online meeting. You can start a meeting at any time by opening the Tools menu, clicking Online Collaboration, and then clicking Meet Now. You will see a list of all persons currently logged onto your directory server. Key or select names from the list to become participants in the meeting. PowerPoint displays the Online Meeting toolbar, similar to the one shown in Figure 6-12. This toolbar gives you control over the chat window and the whiteboard, lets you call or remove a participant, and lets you turn collaboration on or off.

FIGURE 6-12
The Online Meeting toolbar

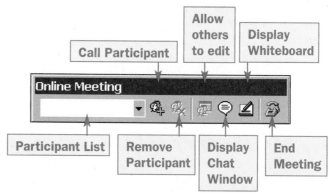

You can also schedule a meeting using the Schedule Meeting option on the Online Collaboration submenu. When you first choose this option, you will be asked to fill out a form with your name, e-mail address, and the directory server you use for online meetings. Then a dialog box similar to the one shown in Figure 6-13 opens. Here you can schedule the meeting and invite attendees. Attendees will be reminded about the meeting if you specify a reminder.

Running a Presentation on Another Computer

PowerPoint includes a handy feature called Pack and Go that can help you to organize all the materials you need to transport your presentation to another computer. If you know the computer from which you intend to run the presentation does not have PowerPoint installed, you can pack the PowerPoint Viewer as well. The PowerPoint Viewer lets you show your presentation on any computer. Some features, such as bullets created from pictures and automatic paragraph numbering, are not supported in the Viewer. If you know you will be using the Viewer, check your slides for these features and modify the slides accordingly.

FIGURE 6-13

Schedule a meeting in this dialog box

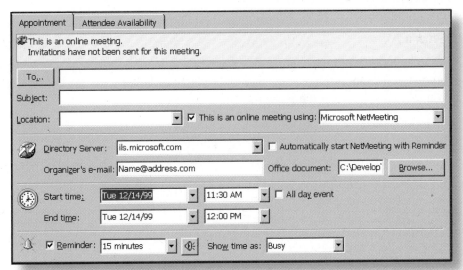

If you are not sure the computer you will be using has the fonts specified in your presentation, you can *embed* your presentation fonts. To do so, open the File menu and click Save As. In the Save As dialog box, click the Tools menu and select Embed TrueType Fonts (Figure 6-14). The fonts used in your presentation will then be available no matter where you run the presentation.

The Pack and Go feature supplies a wizard to help you pack your presentation and any files that must accompany it, such as clip art files or sound object files. To start the wizard, open the File menu and click Pack and Go. The first wizard dialog box displays as shown in Figure 6-15. The wizard's remaining dialog boxes require you to supply the following information:

FIGURE 6-14

The Tools menu in the Save As dialog box

FIGURE 6-15

The Pack and Go Wizard

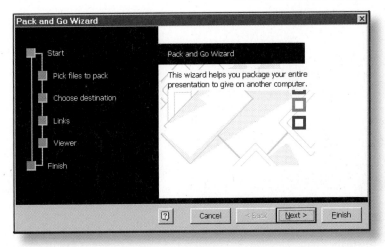

- Which presentation do you want to pack? Choose the active presentation or browse to locate a different one.

- What is the final destination of your packed files? By default, the wizard suggests a floppy or removable disk drive.

- Do you want to include linked files and embed fonts? These options ensure that linked data will be displayed correctly and that original fonts will be used even if those fonts are not resident on the computer you're going to use for the presentation.

- Do you need to include the PowerPoint Viewer?

After you click Finish, the Pack and Go Wizard will compress your files to take up less room and copy them to the destination you specified. If your file is too large for one disk, PowerPoint will prompt you to insert additional disks. This process might take a minute or two, but eventually you should see an information box that tells you the presentation has been successfully packed.

Once you reach the computer you want to use to run your packed presentation, you must unpack it. To do so, access the disk you packed the presentation on and double-click the Pngsetup file. A dialog box opens similar to the one shown in Figure 6-16. This setup file decompresses the files you packed to a location on the computer you specify. You can then start the presentation immediately or close the dialog box and run the presentation later.

FIGURE 6-16
Set up your packed presentation

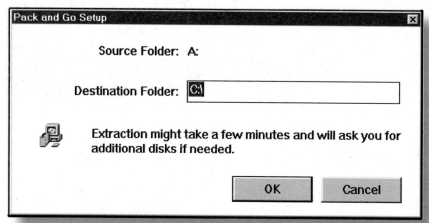

STEP-BY-STEP ▷ 6.6

Your **Wetlands** presentation is ready for a trial run at one of the park system's visitor centers. Pack the presentation to take it to that center. Have ready a high-density disk to pack the presentation.

1. Open **Wetlands 2** from your solution files and save it as **Wetlands Final** followed by your initials.

2. Open the **File** menu and click **Pack and Go**. The Pack and Go Wizard displays.

3. Proceed through the wizard's dialog boxes. Choose to pack the files of the current presentation on a floppy disk. Choose to include linked files and embed TrueType fonts. You know the

visitor center has PowerPoint available, so you do not need to pack the Viewer.

4. Insert your disk into the proper drive. When the process is finished, click **OK**.

5. If desired, take the disk to another computer that has PowerPoint available. Unpack the files and run the presentation.

Extra Challenge

Try packing the PowerPoint Viewer and running the presentation on a computer that does not have PowerPoint installed.

6. If you are going on to the Lesson 6 Projects, leave the presentation open. Otherwise, close the presentation.

Summary

In this lesson, you learned:

■ You can use a number of features to fine-tune your presentation before presenting it. You can hide slides, set automatic slide timings, add action buttons to help you control the slides during presentation, record narration, rehearse your timings, and specify options for the running the show.

■ During the presentation, you can use shortcut menu commands to jump to specific slides, annotate slides, and record meeting minutes and action items. Minutes and action items can be exported to Word. You can also send action items to Outlook to be included on your task list.

■ PowerPoint 2000 contains several features to allow you to broadcast a presentation or host a meeting for persons in different geographical locations. Using networks and Office 2000 applications, you can participate in constructing or editing a presentation with others in a workgroup.

■ You can easily pack a presentation to take it to another computer. The computer need not have PowerPoint installed for you to run the presentation. Use Pack and Go to gather the files necessary for the presentation, and include the PowerPoint Viewer if you must run the presentation on a computer that does not have PowerPoint.

LESSON 6 REVIEW QUESTIONS

TRUE/FALSE

Circle T if the statement is true or F if the statement is false.

T **F** 1. Once you hide a slide in a presentation, there is no way to see it when you run the presentation. *(go to use right click on any slide*

T F 2. You can apply a slide transition effect to a single slide or to all slides in the presentation.

T F 3. Voice narration takes precedence over any other sound object on a slide.

T F 4. Presentations are broadcast in HTML format so that viewers only need a browser to view the presentation.

T **F** 5. The PowerPoint Viewer works only on computers with PowerPoint installed.

FILL IN THE BLANKS

Complete the following sentences by writing the correct word or words in the blanks provided.

1. _action buttons_ are predrawn buttons that perform specific actions.

2. The two tabs in the Action Settings dialog box are _mouse click_ and _mouse over_.

3. Before you actually present your slides, you should use the _Set up show_ command to make sure of your current settings and specify any other necessary settings.

4. One way to jump to a particular slide is to open the shortcut menu, click _Go to Slide_, and choose the slide name on the submenu.

5. The _meeting mind_ feature lets you keep track of notes and action items during a presentation.

LESSON 6 PROJECTS

✳ PROJECT 6-1

1. If **Wetlands Final** is not on your screen, open it.

2. Add automatic slide timings so that this presentation will run on its own. Add transition effects as desired.

3. Rehearse the timings of the presentation, making sure you have time to read all text and understand the charts. Change the slide timings if necessary.

4. Set up the show to loop continuously until Esc is pressed. (*Hint:* Click **Set Up Show** on the **Slide Show** menu and click the **Loop continuously until 'Esc'** check box.)

5. Run the show. Let it loop at least twice before you stop it.

6. Save your changes and close the presentation.

✳ PROJECT 6-2

1. Open **Weather 4** from your solution file. Open the **File** menu and click **Save as** dialog box, click **Tools** on the menu bar. Click **Embed TrueType Fonts.** Key the new file name **Weather Final** and click **Save.**

2. You're not sure that slide 3, which discusses weather-related fatalities, will be appropriate for your audience. Hide the slide.

3. On slide 1, insert a text box in the lower right part of the slide and key the text **Hurricanes**. Format the text as desired. To the left of the text box, insert a custom action button. Set this button up to take you immediately to the first slide of the hurricane section.

4. Create a similar button and text box for the *Lightning* section of the presentation.

5. Set transition effects for the slides but leave the advance setting on manual.

6. Run the slide show and check your transitions and action settings.

7. Print only slide 1 as a handout with 2 slides per page. Save your changes and close the presentation.

PROJECT 6-3

1. Open **Lead 2** and save it as **Lead Final** followed by your initials.

2. You are ready to run this presentation for your neighbors. Begin the presentation.

3. You expect to have to record comments and further actions the neighborhood group will want to take, so start Meeting Minder.

4. Record the first item in the Meeting Minder: **Date: [current date]**

5. As you present slide 3, a neighbor asks a question. Record it in the minutes: **Question: What kind of developmental delays are typical of lead poisoning?** Create an action item to find out, and assign it to Roger, the person who asked the question. Roger should find the answer to his question within a week of the current date.

6. As you present slide 7, Gail reminds you that the neighborhood playground was built on the site of an old house. Would there still be lead in the soil of the playground? Record the question in the minutes and create an action item for Rani, who is acting as liaison with the health department. Rani should set up a time with the health department to test the playground soil in the next month.

7. On slide 9, use the pen pointer to underline the lead level that everyone should have to be healthy. Corazon wants to know where to have blood lead tests done. Assign her the task of finding out within the next week.

8. Export the meeting minutes and action items to Word. Save the document as **Lead Meeting Minutes** followed by your initals and print the document.

9. Save your changes to the presentation. Print the last slide in the presentation as a handout with 2 slides per page. Close the presentation.

SCANS

ACTIVITY 6-1

As part of a presentation, you want to be able to open another application with the click of a button. Can you do this? If so, how? Write a brief report in Word.

ACTIVITY 6-2

You do a lot of your office work on your laptop, because you can take it with you anywhere. You have prepared a presentation on your laptop's version of PowerPoint. You're wondering if you need to transfer the file to another computer to run the presentation on a data viewer.

Use the online Help system to find out if you can run a presentation from your laptop. If so, what steps must you take? Use Word to write a brief report on the results of your research.

Advanced Microsoft PowerPoint

·COMMAND SUMMARY

FEATURE	MENU COMMAND	TOOLBAR BUTTON	LESSON
Action buttons	Slide Show, Action Buttons		6
Action settings	Slide Show, Action Settings		6
Animation, custom	Slide Show, Custom Animation		4
Animation, preset	Slide Show, Preset Animation		4
Background, modify	Format, Background		4
Broadcast presentation	Slide Show, Online Broadcast		6
Chart, change options	Chart, Chart Options		2
Chart, change type	Chart, Chart Type		2
Chart, insert	Insert, Chart		2
Chart, view datasheet	View, Datasheet		2
Clip art, crop			3
Clip art, format	Format, Picture		3
Clip art, insert	Insert, Picture, Clip Art		3
Clip art, recolor			3
Color scheme, modify	Format, Slide Color Scheme		4
Custom show	Slide Show, Custom Shows		4
E-mailing slide data	File, Send To, Mail Recipient		5
Exporting data to Word	File, Send To, Microsoft Word		5
Find	Edit, Find		1
Hiding slides	Slide Show, Hide Slide		6
Hyperlinks	Insert, Hyperlink		1
	Slide Show, Action Settings		6
Linking data	Edit, Paste Special *or* Paste Link		5
Masters, modify	View, Masters		4

FEATURE	MENU COMMAND	TOOLBAR BUTTON	LESSON
Meeting Minder	Tools, Meeting Minder *or* Meeting Minder (shortcut menu)		6
Movie, insert	Insert, Movies and Sounds, Movie from Gallery *or* Movie from File		3
Narration	Slide Show, Record Narration		6
Navigating during show	Go (shortcut menu)		6
Number paragraphs	Format, Bullets and Numbering	▤	1
Object, insert	Insert, Object		2
Online meeting	Tools, Online Collaboration		6
Outline, slides from	Open		5
	Insert, Slides from Outline		5
	(In Word) File, Send To, Microsoft PowerPoint		5
Pen pointer	Pointer Options, Pen (shortcut menu)		6
Picture, insert	Insert, Picture, From File		3
Picture, scan	Insert, Picture, From Scanner or Camera		3
Presentation on another computer	File, Pack and Go		6
Replace	Edit, Replace		1
Slide setup	File, Page Setup		5
Slide show, set up	Slide Show, Set Up Show		6
Slide timings, rehearse	Slide Show, Rehearse Timings		6
Slides, import	Insert, Slides from Files		5
Sound, insert	Insert, Movies and Sounds, Sound from Gallery *or* Sound from File		3
Summary (agenda) slide		▣	4
Symbols	Insert, Symbol		1
Table, draw		▤	2
Table, insert	Insert, Table	▦	2
Text box	Insert, Text Box	▣	1
Transitions	Slide Show, Slide Transition		6

MATCHING

Match the correct term in Column 2 to its description in Column 1.

Column 1

Column 2

_____ 1. A palette of eight colors that work well together.

A. Order

_____ 2. An integration option that requires you to edit an object in its source application.

B. Color scheme

C. Datasheet

_____ 3. Drawing command that lets you control what layer a drawing object appears on.

D. Action button

_____ 4. Worksheet-like grid in which you enter text or numbers to create a chart.

E. Linking

F. AutoShape

_____ 5. Predrawn shapes that let you jump to a specific location in a presentation.

MULTIPLE CHOICE

Select the best response for the following statements.

1. To insert a foreign-language character in a text placeholder, open the Insert menu and click
   A. Language
   B. Character Set
   C. Symbol
   D. New Symbol

2. The best type of chart to use to show how parts of an item relate to each other is a
   A. Pie chart
   B. Line chart
   C. Column chart
   D. Bubble chart

3. To modify the colors of a clip art graphic, use
   A. Slide Color Scheme
   B. Format Colors
   C. Recolor Picture
   D. You cannot modify colors of a clip art graphic.

4. To change the color of a bullet for every bulleted list slide in a presentation, modify the bullet color on the
   A. Title master
   B. Slide master
   C. Bullets and Numbering dialog box
   D. Format Bullet dialog box

5. To create an Excel chart on a slide, you can use the _____ command.
   A. Paste Special
   B. Cut
   C. Object
   D. Make Chart

APPLICATIONS

SCANS

APPLICATION 1

In reviewing the **Solar System** presentation you prepared in Lesson 3, you have decided the material is a little skimpy. You'd really like to know more facts about these planets, and you think the Brown Bag Forum audience will too.

1. Using your Web browser or an online encyclopedia, research some basic facts about the planets listed in the presentation. You can choose which facts to stress, but include the following for all planets:

   ■ Rotation time—that is, how long it takes the planet to complete one revolution on its axis.

   ■ Orbit time—that is, how long it takes the planet to circle the sun.

   ■ Temperature of surface or atmosphere. If the planet has extremes of temperature, either figure an average or list the extremes.

2. You decide how to present the data and insert new slides to do so. Then run the presentation to see how your new data looks.

3. Copy the *forum* macro you created in Lesson 1 to this presentation by following these steps:
   A. Open **Coasting** from your Lesson 1 solution files. If you receive a message about macros in the presentation, click the **Enable Macros** button.
   B. Open the **Tools** menu and click **Macro**. On the submenu, click **Visual Basic Editor**.
   C. If the Project Explorer pane is not open, click **Project Explorer** on the **View** menu.
   D. In the Project Explorer pane, click the **Coasting** project if necessary to expand it so you can see all macro modules.
   E. Click **Module1** under the **Coasting** project and drag it on top of the **Solar System** project. **Solar System** should now have a **Modules** folder with **Module1** inside it.
   F. Close the Visual Basic Editor.

4. Run the macro. Save the revised presentation as **Solar System 2** followed by your initials. Print the presentation as handouts with 6 or 9 slides per page.

APPLICATION 2

You work on a part-time basis for the Richmond Heights Recreation Center. After finding out that you know how to create dynamite presentations, the recreation center coordinator has asked you to help her get the word out about classes and programs planned for the fall.

1. First, create a design template you will use only for RHRC presentations. Use an existing design template as a starting point or start from scratch. Choose a new background and refine the color scheme.

2. Create a logo for the RHRC using those letters in an AutoShape and insert the logo on the slide and title masters. Add slide numbers to each slide.

3. Save the design template as **RH Template** followed by your initials.

4. Open data file **AP App2**. Save the file as **RH Music** followed by your initials. This presentation gives details of a music appreciation course being offered by the recreation center.

5. Apply your template to the slides. On slide 4, align the compositions using tabs as has been done on other slides.

6. Insert proper foreign-language symbols in the names of the following composers and their works: on slide 3, Saint-Saëns; on slide 7, Gymnopédie, Fauré, and Thaïs.

7. Locate Windows' music files (the Media folder in the Windows folder) and insert an appropriate musical sound on slide 1.

8. Add clip art to illustrate at least two of the slides in the presentation. Resize and recolor the graphics as desired.

9. You think *Respighi* is spelled wrong in the presentation. Use the Find command to locate the phrase *Resp* and then correct the spelling of *Respighi*.

10. The class instructor has sent you an urgent bulletin that he will not be able to do the *The Seasons* section of the course this time, but he will in future. Hide the *The Seasons* slide for now.

11. Set up automatic slide timings and effects for the presentation. For the sound object, set a custom animation option to continue the slide show while the music is playing. Rehearse your timings and change them if necessary.

12. The director would like to have an outline of the class on file at the center. Export an outline of the presentation to Word. Format the outline if desired and save it as **Music Appreciation Outline** followed by your initials. Print the outline.

13. Print your slides as handouts with 9 slides per page. Save your changes and close the presentation.

✳ APPLICATION 3

ExperTech, Inc., is preparing a presentation of its annual corporate review. This presentation will eventually be available on the company's intranet with access for all senior management employees. You need to prepare some of the financial data to be inserted in the presentation as well as set the presentation up for online viewing.

1. Open PowerPoint data file **AP App3**. Save the file as **ET Corporate Review** followed by your initials. Apply your ExperTech design template or format the presentation with another design template.

2. Some slides you created for the ExperTech Employee Manual would work well in this presentation. From **ET Final Manual** insert slide 4 (The ExperTech Mission) following slide 2 of the current presentation. Insert slide 7 (Our Current Staff) following slide 5 of the current presentation. Remove the action buttons from the new slides.

3. Move to slide 9. You need to insert financial data here and give viewers the option to see the income statements for the current and previous years. Follow these steps:
   A. Open Excel data file **AP App3(a)**. Save the file as **Current Income Statement** followed by your initials. Copy cell **E36**. Switch to PowerPoint and paste the copied cell data at the end of the first bullet item. Reformat the copied text with the same font as the bullet items and remove the extra spaces between the dollar sign and the number. The currency amount will wrap to the next line. Close the Excel file.
   B. Open Excel data file **AP App3(b)**. Save the file as **Last Year's Income Statement** followed by your initials. Copy cell **E36** and paste it into the third bullet item on slide 9. Format the copied data as instructed above. Close the Excel file.
   C. Select the phrase *click here* in the second bullet item on this slide. Set up a hyperlink from this text to **Current Income Statement**.
   D. Select the phrase *click here* in the last bullet item on the slide. Set up a hyperlink from this text to **Last Year's Income Statement**.

4. Move to the next slide. On this slide, you'd like to insert a column chart showing the earnings over the current year by each department. The 4th quarter earnings are not yet posted, but you can build the chart anyway and link the chart data to the worksheet where the earnings will be posted. Follow these steps:
   A. Open Excel data file **AP App3(c)**. Save the file as **Quarterly Earnings** followed by your initials. Copy the range **A6:E9**.
   B. Switch to PowerPoint. Click the **Insert Chart** button on the toolbar. In the datasheet, click in the first cell, open the **Edit** menu, and click **Paste Link**. Click **OK** to replace existing data with the copied data.
   C. Format the chart as desired.

5. Move to slide 11. On this slide, you'd like to insert two pie charts showing the percent of total sales by department for the current year and the previous year. You can find this data in **Last Year's Income Statement** and **Quarterly Earnings**. Follow these steps:
   A. Click the **Insert Chart** button on the toolbar. With the datasheet displayed, open the **Chart** menu and click **Chart Type**. Choose the second pie option in the first row (the plain 3-D pie chart). Click **OK**.

B. On the More Buttons tool palette, click **By Column** to change the direction PowerPoint will chart the data.

C. Open the Excel file **Last Year's Income Statement**. Copy cell range **B7:B9**. Switch to PowerPoint and click in the datasheet cell that currently reads *East*. Click the **Paste** button. Switch back to the Excel file and copy the cell range **D7:D9**. Close the Excel file. In the PowerPoint datasheet, click in the cell that currently reads *20.4*, to the right of *Training*. Paste the copied data. Remove the remaining sample data in the datasheet. Close the datasheet.

D. Remove the legend and the border around the plot area. Insert data labels to show the label and percent. Reduce the size of the entire chart by about one-quarter and move it all the way to the left of the slide.

E. Click **Insert Chart** to insert the second pie chart. Change the chart type and options as in steps 5a and 5b, above. Create the pie chart using **Quarterly Earnings** cell ranges **A7:A9** and **F7:F9**. Because all the earnings are not yet posted in this file, use the **Paste Link** option to paste the second cell range into the PowerPoint datasheet.

F. Format the second pie chart the same way you formatted the first. Make any adjustments necessary to both charts to make them more readable and attractive.

G. Add two text boxes that label the pies as **Last Year** and **Current Year**.

6. Create custom shows for sections of the presentation, as you wish. Then create an agenda slide titled **Contents** and link each contents item to the appropriate slide.

7. Customize animation options for text and charts in the presentation.

8. You have the final 4th Quarter earnings ready—finally! Open the Excel **Quarterly Earnings** worksheet and add the following earnings:

```
125000
75800
34700
```

9. Save and close the Excel file. Exit Excel. Scroll to the charts in the presentation. Double-click each chart containing linked data to update the charts.

10. Run the presentation and take the following notes in the Meeting Minder:

```
Preliminary review - [current date]
Add Beginning and End action buttons on all slides.
```

11. Add the action buttons specified on each slide (except no Beginning button on slide 1 and no End button on slide 14).

12. Test your action buttons by running the presentation again.

13. Save your changes and print the presentation as handouts with 6 slides per page. Close the presentation.

APPLICATION 4

You have been volunteering at your town's Civic Garden Center. Come spring, the Civic Garden Center will be sponsoring a sale of trees. The Garden Center wants to create a presentation for your town's annual spring Home and Garden Show to advertise the benefits of planting trees and the tree sale.

1. Start a new presentation and give it the name **Trees** followed by your initials. Apply a suitable design template.

2. Key the title **Made in the Shade** and the subtitle **A Presentation of the Civic Garden Center**.

3. You remember you have an outline of general information about trees: benefits, types, shapes, and so on. Perhaps that outline could generate some slides for your show. Open the **Insert** menu and click **Slides from Outline**. In the Insert Outline dialog box, locate the data files for the Unit Review and open **AP App4**.

4. Scroll through the slides to see the new content. Change the slide layout for slide 7 to the 2 Column Text layout. Drag or cut and paste the summer-flowering trees into the right column.

5. Replace the Arial font throughout the presentation with a serif font such as Times New Roman.

6. Now for the tree sale items. First, insert a Title Only slide announcing **Civic Garden Center Tree Sale** as slide 8. Next, insert a slide 9 with the Table layout and title it **Deciduous Trees**. Insert the following table of trees for sale:

Name	Foliage	Height	Price
Red maple	Maroon	50 ft	$25.95
Sugar maple	Spectacular fall color	50 ft	$24.45
Red oak	Rusty red in fall	75 ft	$30.95
Willow	Lacy, graceful	50 ft	$18.45

7. Insert another slide, slide 10, for **Evergreen Trees** and insert the following table:

Name	Foliage	Height	Price
White pine	Long-needle	20 ft	$9.95
Blue spruce	Gray-blue	50 ft	$9.95
Douglas fir	Short-needle	75 ft	$9.45

8. Insert one last slide, slide 11, for **Flowering Trees**. Insert the following table:

Name	Flower	Height	Price
Crabapple 'Robinson'	Red	30 ft	$18.45
Dogwood 'Cloud White'	White	20 ft	$25.45
Weeping cherry	White	15 ft	$30.45

9. Format the tables as desired.

10. If you have Web access, search the Clip Gallery Live online site for pictures of trees. Adorn at least one slide with a tree picture.

11. Add automatic slide transitions. Run the presentation.

12. Print the slides as handouts with 6 slides per page. Use Pack and Go to pack the presentation for use at another location (no need to pack the PowerPoint Viewer). Close the presentation.

APPLICATION 5

Choose one of the presentations you have worked with in this unit and publish it for Web use. Explore formatting options and try making simple modifications to the HTML code.

ON-THE-JOB SIMULATION

You work in a very small production services company that has just been awarded a large writing and production contract—larger than you and your co-workers can easily handle. You got the job, however, by promising that you could complete the project in six weeks or less.

In this simulation, you will create two presentations that will help you to plan the project and review the project after it is completed.

✳ JOB 1

SCANS

Your colleagues like to hash out strategies as a group, so you have prepared a presentation that describes the scope of work for the Orion Project, problems that you foresee, solutions, and strategies for completing the project. The current date is April 3, 2000.

1. Open data file **AP Job1(a)**. Save the file as **Orion Strategy** followed by your initials.

2. Apply a new design template to the presentation. Customize the color scheme, background, and masters as desired.

3. Insert several appropriate clip art graphics on the slides. Recolor and modify the clip art as desired.

4. Insert the current date in a text box on slide 1.

5. You think the project summary on slide 2 might give your colleagues a more step-by-step feel if the bulleted text were numbered. Change the bulleted items to numbered items.

6. On the same slide, insert the following text at the end of the first numbered item: (**±350 final pages**). (*Hint:* The symbol is the sixth row down, sixth across in the Symbol dialog box.)

7. On slide 3, the writing challenge should come first. Move it to the top of the list. You might need to reapply left alignment to the bullet item after you move it.

8. You need to insert a tentative schedule of how the work is going to get done in six weeks. Add a slide after slide 4 and insert the following table. (*Hint:* The two First pages items can go in the same table cell. Key the first item and then press **Enter** and key the second item. Do the same for the First pages dates.)

```
Item                    Internal    To Client    From Client
Manuscript              4/14        4/17         4/19
First pages (1)         4/24
First pages (2)         4/28
Proofed pages (all)     5/3
Corrections             5/4         5/5          5/9
Files and copy out                  5/12
```

9. Format the table as desired. Title the slide **Schedule**.

10. You want to show your colleagues the proposed project team. Insert an organization chart as slide 6, containing the following project team:

Top level:	Paula Project Manager

Second level:	Tom Writing Team Leader	Fuji Proofer	Irina Production Team Leader

Subordinate to Tom:	Sharon Writer	J. Craig Writer

Subordinate to Irina:	Kristi Pager	Jeff Pager	Ron QA Spec

11. Format the organization chart as desired. Don't forget to add the slide title **Proposed Team**.

12. You have prepared a rough budget of hours available for the job. Add a slide following the organization chart with a Title Only layout. Insert the title **Hours Budgeted**. Open the Excel data file **AP Job1(b)**. Save the file as **Orion Budget** followed by your initials. Copy the budgeted and actual data and link it on the PowerPoint slide. Make any changes to the linked object necessary to display it properly on the slide.

13. Insert slide numbers. Insert the current date for handouts.

14. Add animations and sound effects to distract your colleagues from the hard work ahead.

15. Run the presentation to check your effects. Save your changes.

16. Print the slides as handouts with 9 slides per page. Close the presentation.

✳ JOB 2

You and your colleagues have successfully survived the Orion Project. It is time to hold a "post-mortem" session to discuss what went right, what went wrong, and how to prevent problems from occurring in the next big project. You also have some financial figures to share with your co-workers. The current date is May 19, 2000.

1. Open **AP Job2**. Save the file as **Orion Review** followed by your initials.

2. Choose an appropriate design template and customize the color scheme, background, and masters as desired. Or, apply the design from Job 1 to the current presentation.

3. You'd like to show the actual hours used on the project to compare to the budgeted hours. Following slide 4, insert the slide from **Orion Strategy** that contains the budget worksheet.

4. In the **Orion Budget** worksheet, insert the following actual hours for the tasks:

   ```
   Technical writing    110
   Technical review     60
   Paging               203
   Proofing             38
   QA review            38
   Support              8
   ```

5. On slide 6, create a column chart of the budget data to show the budgeted versus actual hours. Click **By Column** to change the way the data is plotted. Modify the chart as desired.

6. Set up animation for the chart so that you can display each data series with a mouse click.

7. Run the presentation. During the presentation, assign the task of creating and maintaining a free-lancer database to Sharon. Give her a month to set up the database. Assign the equipment update schedule to Irina. Give her a month to set up the schedule.

8. Save your changes. Print the slides as handouts with 9 slides per page. Close the presentation. Close the Excel worksheet.

email etiquette.
www.dtcc.edu/cs/rfc1855.html

UNIT

ADVANCED MICROSOFT® OUTLOOK

Estimated Time for Unit: 4 hours

CUSTOMIZING AND SHARING OUTLOOK INFORMATION

OBJECTIVES

Upon completion of this lesson, you should be able to:

- Use options to organize views of various folders.
- Create a custom form.
- Find items in any folder.
- Use a number of productivity tools in Outlook.
- Share information between folders and use attachments.
- Access the Web through Outlook.   ⏱ **Estimated Time: 2 hours**

Introduction

Microsoft Outlook is a very powerful tool designed to help you organize your business and personal life. Besides allowing you to schedule appointments and tasks, organize contacts, send and receive e-mail, and create notes, Outlook gives you many options to customize your views of these items. Outlook offers many more options for customizing and working with folders, in fact, than can be covered in this unit. The lessons in this unit cover a number of important features, but you are encouraged to explore Outlook on your own to develop a full appreciation of its capabilities.

Many customizing features work in approximately the same way for all of Outlook's folders. For example, as you will learn later in the lesson, you can assign any item—appointment, task, contact, journal entry, note, or e-mail message—to a category such as Business, Favorites, or Personal. All items can be archived or deleted in the same way.

Other customizing features and productivity tools are specific to a folder or can only be used with specific software configurations. Sharing items and working with offline folders, for example, require you to be connected to a network.

Before you begin learning about Outlook's advanced features, you need to insert some Outlook items to work with. The instructions in Step-by-Step 1.1 will help you to review basic Outlook concepts while supplying information to work with in this unit.

You work in the Human Resources department at ExperTech, Inc., a firm specializing in software training, technical support, and computer repair services. ExperTech is a dynamic work environment with a lot going on at all times. Outlook can help you to keep track of your various work tasks. The current date is July 11, 2000.

1. Open Outlook and click **Calendar** in the Outlook Bar. Move to the "current date" of July 11, 2000.

   a. Set up an appointment at 2:00 p.m. with Carol Herrerra to discuss the hiring of two new trainers. The meeting will take place in Conference Room A and will probably last an hour. Set a reminder for yourself 15 minutes before the meeting.

   b. Set up appointments with the training interviewees: Jon Applegate can arrive at 10:00 a.m. on July 13. Pen McCarthy has agreed to arrive at 2:30 on July 14. Interviews usually take at least an hour and a half. You don't need a reminder for either interview.

   c. While you're working in Calendar, you remember you agreed to play in a charity golf game on July 21. Add this new all-day event to the calendar. You don't need a reminder, and you should show this time as *Out of Office*.

2. Click **Tasks** on the Outlook Bar. Insert the following tasks:

   a. You need to review the new online training manual. You think you can start the task tomorrow, July 12 (remember you are in the year 2000), and finish it in a week. This task has normal priority. You don't need a reminder.

   b. You've been intending for weeks to gather some training materials for a friend who wants to teach a class on a particular software in an elementary school. (ExperTech allows this kind of sharing for elementary educators.) Remind yourself to get materials for Clare by the end of the work week, and give the task high priority. You don't need a reminder.

3. Click **Contacts** on the Outlook Bar. Insert the new ExperTech clients shown in Figure 1-1.

4. Create a note for yourself for an all-important event on Friday: **Don't forget to bring chili for the Chili Cookoff on Friday!**

5. Leave Outlook open for the next Step-by-Step.

FIGURE 1-1

Insert the contact data shown here

Auyang, Min	
Full Name:	Min Auyang
Job Title:	Operations Manager
Company:	Min Productions
Business:	753 Apple Creek Road Ross, OH 45061
Business:	(513) 555-0404
Business Fax:	(513) 555-4404
E-mail:	M_Auyang@iac.net
Web Page:	http://www.minprods.com

Gunther, Sam	
Full Name:	Sam Gunther
Job Title:	Training Coordinator
Company:	Joseph-Simon, Inc.
Business:	509 Roundtree Court Walnut Hills, OH 45219
Business:	(513) 555-3440
Business Fax:	(513) 555-3443
E-mail:	Sgunther@jsimon.com

Using Organizing Options

If you have only a few items in each of your Outlook folders (such as the ones you added in Step-by-Step 1.1), you will probably have no difficulty with organizing those items. You might even be able to see them all on the screen at one time. In a real-world situation, however, you might have a great many more items: dozens of contacts, a whole slew of e-mail messages (and more arriving every hour), any number of tasks you are working on, and so on. In this situation, you will appreciate being able to organize your items in different ways to help you get the best picture of your work commitments.

Each Outlook folder contains several organization options. Some folders contain more options than others, but most contain two basic options: Using Categories and Using Views. Some folders also contain the Using Folders option, and the Inbox folder lets you organize Using Color. You'll learn more about these options in the sections below.

To see the organizing options for any folder, click the Organize button on the standard toolbar. The Organize pane for that folder opens, as shown in Figure 1-2. Your choices for organizing are listed in the pane. Click a choice to see further options.

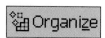

FIGURE 1-2
The Organize pane for a selected folder

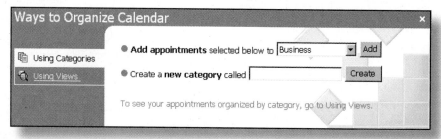

Adding Items to Categories

A *category* is a keyword or phrase you can assign to an item. Assigning categories makes it easy for you to sort and group items, as you will learn in the next section. Outlook supplies a list of standard category names, such as Business, Personal, Favorites, Miscellaneous, Hot Contacts, and so on. You can also create your own category name. For example, you can create a category for a particular project so that you can assign items relating to that project to that category.

In the Organize pane, click the down arrow next to the category name (Business, by default) to see a list of available categories (Figure 1-3). To add an item to a category, select it in the folder pane, choose the proper category, and click Add.

FIGURE 1-3
The list of available categories

To create your own category, simply type the category name in the new category text box and click Create. Outlook adds the category to its standard list so you can use it in any folder.

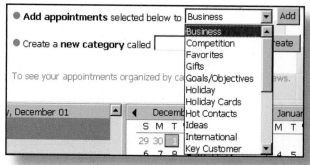

Changing and Customizing Views

Clicking the Using Views option in the Organize pane shows you a list of standard views for that folder. Each folder has a number of standard views available. Figure 1-4 shows the list of views available for the Tasks folder and the way the currently selected view (Active Tasks) displays the tasks you entered in Step-by-Step 1.1. To change the current display to one of these available views, simply click Using Views and then the view you want. The folder's items instantly display in the new view.

FIGURE 1-4

Selecting one of Outlook's standard views for Tasks

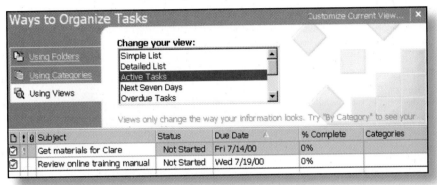

If none of the standard views is quite what you want, or if you want to organize the items in a particular way, click the Customize Current View button in the upper right corner of the Organize pane. A dialog box similar to the one shown in Figure 1-5 opens. The View Summary dialog box offers the following customizing options:

FIGURE 1-5

The View Summary dialog box

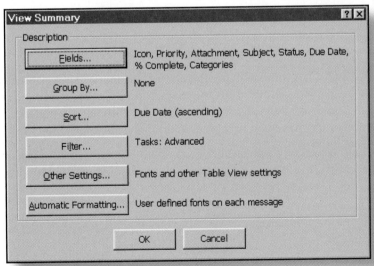

- **Fields**. Click this button to display the Show Fields dialog box. This dialog box contains a list of fields displayed in the current view as well as a list of fields you can add to the current view. If you don't need a particular field, select it and click the Remove button. Your folder will then no longer display that field or its contents.

Concept Builder

Changes you make to fields will stay in effect for the current view unless you change them again.

- **Group By**. Click this button to display the Group By dialog box. In this dialog box, you can choose how to group the folder items, such as by category, by contact, by date, and so on. You can group by more than one criterion, and you can choose a sort order for each grouping criterion.

- **Sort**. If you just want to sort the items in the folder, click the Sort button. In the Sort dialog box, choose the field you want to sort by and the sort order. You can sort by more than one field.

- **Filter**. Click this button if you want to display only the items that match certain criteria (similar to filters used in databases). The Filter dialog box that displays contains filter options specific to the current folder. Use the options on the three tabs to filter items according to words that appear in particular fields, according to fields in the folder or categories, according to categories, or according to more specific criteria. The Filter dialog box shown in Figure 1-6 will display only appointments in which the word *Carol* is used.

FIGURE 1-6
Filter dialog box for Calendar

- **Other Settings**. Click this button to change fonts, grid options, and other display options used in the current view.

- **Automatic Formatting**. Click this button to set up formatting that will automatically display for each item meeting a particular criterion. For example, you can specify in the Automatic Formatting dialog box that overdue tasks will always be displayed in Times New Roman colored red. You can also set additional conditions here and then indicate how items that meet those conditions will be displayed.

After you have finished setting your organizing options, click the Organize pane's close box (or click Organize again on the toolbar) to close the pane and see your new organizing options in the folder pane.

STEP-BY-STEP ▷ 1.2

1. To keep your Outlook items tidy, you'd like to add them to categories:
   a. Click **Calendar** in the Outlook Bar. Click **Organize** on the standard toolbar, click **Using**

Views, and then **Active Appointments**. All your appointments should display in table form. Select the first three appointments and then click **Using Categories** in the Organize pane. The *Business* category should be displayed. Click **Add** to add the appointments to the Business category. Add the Charity Golf Game event to the *Personal* category.

 Hot Tip

To select more than one item, click the first and then hold **Shift** and click other items.

b. Click **Tasks** in the Outlook Bar. Display the Organize pane. Add the first task to the *Personal* category and the second task to the *Business* category. If you cannot see the categories, change your view to Detailed List.

c. You are soon going to begin work on arranging the corporate business retreat. In the new category text box, key **Retreat** and then **Create**. Create a new task with low priority and name it **Start thinking about retreat**. Give the task no due or start date, and add it to the Retreat category by clicking Categories in the Task dialog box and selecting *Retreat*.

 Concept Builder

You can easily add an item to a category in the form in which you create the item. Click the Categories button at the bottom of the form and click in the proper category check box.

2. You want to see your business-related appointments in a specific order:

   a. Click **Calendar** on the Outlook Bar. Click **Organize** to open the Organize pane. Click **Using Views**.

   b. Click **Customize Current View** at the top right of the Organize pane. In the View Summary dialog box, click **Sort**. In the Sort dialog box, scroll down the *Sort items by* list and select **Subject**. Click **OK**.

   c. Click **Filter**. In the Filter dialog box, click the **More Choices** tab. Click **Categories** and click in the **Business** check box. Click **OK** three times to close the open dialog boxes. You should now see only the appointments in the Business category, sorted by subject.

3. Remove the filter by clicking **Customize Current View** again. Click **Filter**. In the Filter dialog box, click **Clear All**. Click **OK** twice. You should now see all your appointments.

4. Print the appointments in table style. Leave Outlook open for the next Step-by-Step.

Creating a Form

All Outlook items are entered into their folders using *forms*. The standard forms generally give you all the options you need to insert items. But you might, on occasion, want a form customized for a particular kind of item. Or you might want to simplify one of Outlook's standard forms for your own use.

You can design your own forms for each Outlook folder, placing on them only the fields you want, where you want them. After you have created the form, you can save it as a template so that you can use it whenever you want.

To design your own form, first open the Tools menu and click Forms. On the submenu, click Design a Form. In the Design Form dialog box, you can select what kind of form to design. Outlook then displays the form in Design view, as shown in Figure 1-7. You work in this view the same way you do in Access's Form or Report Design view: click on any item to select it, and then move or delete

FIGURE 1-7
A new Contacts form in Design view

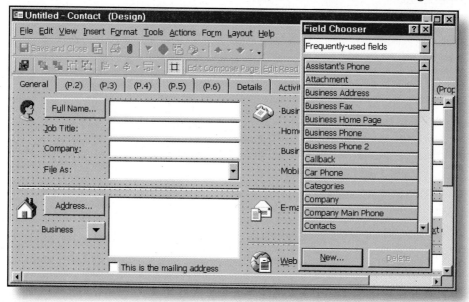

the item as desired. To add specific fields to the form, click the field you want to add in the Field Chooser and drag it to the form. The Field Chooser offers many collections of fields that you can see by clicking the drop-down list arrow. You can also add your own fields by clicking the New button on the Field Chooser. Notice that the form design has a number of blank tabs on which you can insert additional fields to customize your form.

When you are satisfied with your form, use Save As on the File menu to save the form. If you save it as an Outlook template, it will be stored with other templates. You can then open it the next time you want to use it by clicking the drop-down arrow next to the New button and then selecting Choose Form. In the Choose Form dialog box, choose User Templates in File System in the *Look in* box.

S TEP-BY-STEP ▷ 1.3

You'd like to create a Contacts form for personal information about your colleagues so you can speed up the process of sending cards during the holidays.

1. Click **Contacts** on the Outlook Bar. Open the **Tools** menu and click **Forms** and then click **Design a Form** on the submenu. In the Design Form dialog box, click **Contact** and then **Open**.

2. Create the form shown in Figure 1-8 by adding and deleting fields on the General tab of the form. Remember, add a field by dragging it into place from the Field Chooser. You will find most of the fields you need in the *Frequently-used fields* group. You will find the Spouse field in the *Personal fields* group.

FIGURE 1-8
Create this form in Design view

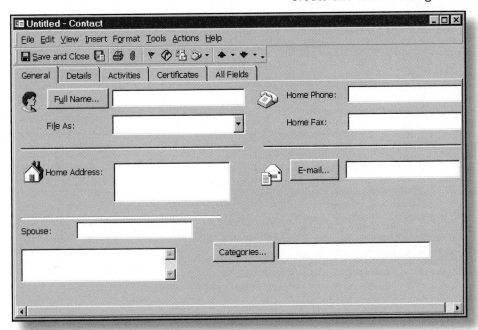

Concept Builder

To align and position your fields and boxes, use the commands on the Layout menu.

3. Open the **File** menu and click **Save As**. Give the form the name **Colleagues** followed by your initials, and choose the Outlook Template file type. Click **Save** to save the form along with other Outlook templates. Close the form design on your screen, clicking **Yes** to save changes. If you are asked whether you want to save the form with an empty File As field, click **Yes**.

4. Click the down arrow next to the **New** button on the toolbar. Then click **Choose Form**. In the Choose Form dialog box, locate **User Templates in File System** in the *Look in* box. Click the **Colleagues** form and click **Open**. Your new form opens, ready for use.

5. Using the form, insert the information shown in Figure 1-9. You will have to reopen the form each time using the step above. Add each contact to the Holiday Cards category.

6. Change the view to Detailed Address Cards and print the contacts in the card style. To avoid printing blank card forms along with your contacts, click **Page Setup** in the Print dialog box. In the *Blank forms at end* box, change the entry to *None*.

7. Leave Outlook open for the next Step-by-Step.

FIGURE 1-9
Insert the following contacts using your new form

Bradford, Hunter		Sinclair, Larry	
Full Name:	Hunter Bradford	Full Name:	Larry Sinclair
Home:	1212 Yarrowwood Lane Terrace Park, OH 45174	Home:	9002 Heath Cliff Drive Blue Ash, OH 45240
Home:	(513) 555-3471	Home:	(513) 555-6654
E-mail:	Hbradford@iac.net	E-mail:	Sinclarry@aol.com
		Spouse:	Yolanda

Logan, Beth		Talbot, Jeff	
Full Name:	Beth Logan	Full Name:	Jeff Talbot
Home:	3110 South Lebanon Rd Lebanon, OH 45036	Home:	67 Turner Lane #27 Loveland, OH 45140
Home:	(513) 555-7886	Home:	(513) 555-2001
Home Fax:	(513) 555-7886	Home Fax:	(513) 555-2001
Spouse:	Jack	E-mail:	JJ_Talbot@email.msn.com

Rojesh, Anne	
Full Name:	Anne Rojesh
Home:	8890 Crown Court Loveland, OH 45140
Home:	(513) 555-0888
Home Fax:	(513) 555-0889
Spouse:	Raj

Finding Items in a Folder

The Find button on the standard toolbar lets you search any folder for text or other items. When you have a lot of items in a folder, using Find can save you time when you are looking for a particular task, contact, or appointment.

Clicking the Find button opens a pane similar to the one shown in Figure 1-10. This pane will look slightly different for each of the Outlook folders, but the feature works the same way in all. Key the text you want to find in the text box and then click Find Now.

FIGURE 1-10
The Find pane for Contacts

To refine a search, click the Advanced Find button. In the Advanced Find dialog box (Figure 1-11), you can specify many more criteria for the search. After Outlook conducts the search, it displays additional information in the Find pane. You are instructed to go to Advanced Find if you didn't find what you were looking for. To see all items again, click Clear Search.

FIGURE 1-11
The Advanced Find dialog box

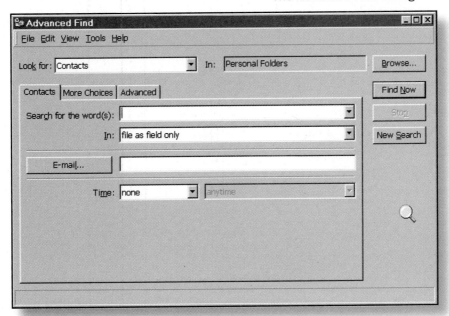

S TEP-BY-STEP ▷ 1.4

1. You want to know which two of your colleagues live in Loveland. You can use Find for
this. Click the **Find** button on the toolbar to
open the Find pane.

2. Key **Loveland** in the *Look for* box and then click
Find Now. Outlook displays the names of Anne
Rojesh and Jeff Talbot.

3. Click **Clear Search** in the Find pane to redisplay all contacts. Click the **Find** button on
the toolbar to close the Find pane.

4. Leave Outlook open for the next Step-by-Step.

Other Productivity Features

As you can probably tell by now, Outlook is chock full of features you can use to make organizing
tasks simple and fun. Outlook contains many other features that can enhance your productivity. Several
of these are discussed in the following sections.

Flagging Items for Follow-Up

You can add a flag to a message or contact item to remind you to take some further action with
regard to that item. To flag an item, click the Flag for Follow Up button on the toolbar. The Flag
for Follow Up dialog box opens, similar to Figure 1-12.

In this dialog box, you can choose what kind of action to take in the *Flag to* list box. You can set a date by which to perform the action you choose and you can check the *Completed* box when you have taken the action. You can clear the flag by clicking Clear Flag.

Concept Builder

Flags are only visible in views that have a table format.

FIGURE 1-12
The Flag for Follow Up dialog box

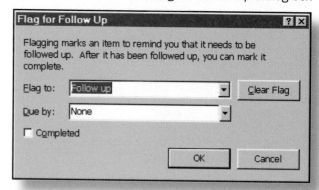

STEP-BY-STEP ▷ 1.5

1. Min Auyang has requested that the two of you get together to discuss training classes for her company. Click her contact card to select it.

2. Click the **Flag for Follow Up** button on the toolbar. In the Flag for Follow Up dialog box, click the **Flag to** drop-down list and choose **Arrange Meeting**.

Give yourself until July 18 (remember, you are in the year 2000) to arrange the meeting. Click **OK**.

3. Change the Contacts view to **By Follow-up Flag** to see the flag.

4. Leave Outlook open for the next Step-by-Step.

Creating New Folders

Though grouping, sorting, and filtering can help you display items in your folders so that you see only what you want, you might eventually find that you have simply too many items in a folder to work efficiently. In this case, you can cut down on some of the bulk by creating new folders within your Outlook folders. You can then move items into those folders to further organize Outlook.

Create a new folder by clicking New on the File menu (or the New button's down arrow) and then clicking Folder. In the Create New Folder dialog box, key a name for the new folder and select the folder in which to store your new folder (see Figure 1-13). You can also specify what kinds of items will be stored in the new folder.

After you click OK, Outlook asks if you want to store a shortcut to the new folder in the Outlook Bar. If you say yes, Outlook stores the shortcut in the My Shortcuts section of the Outlook Bar.

FIGURE 1-13
The Create New Folder dialog box

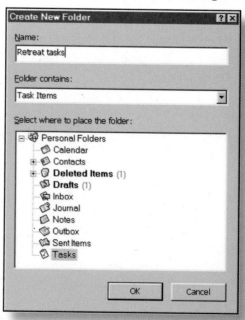

After you have created a folder, you can delete it at any time. Open the View menu and click Folder List to see a list of the Outlook folders. Right-click your folder and choose to delete it. The folder and its contents will be moved to the Deleted Items folder. Remove the shortcut by right-clicking it and choosing to remove it from the Outlook Bar.

Extra Challenge

Try adding a new folder for Retreat tasks in the Tasks folder. Let Outlook create the shortcut and then try clicking the shortcut to go to your new task folder. Then delete both the folder and the shortcut.

Archiving and Deleting Items

There are two other ways to reduce clutter in your Outlook folders. The first is by regular archiving, and the second is by permanently deleting items.

Archiving is the process of removing items from their original folders and storing them in a file that you can access later if you need them. Archiving can be either a manual or an automatic process, depending on your choice and Outlook's settings. To archive at any time, open the File menu and click Archive. The Archive dialog box opens, similar to Figure 1-14. Here you can choose particular folders to archive and you can specify a date that items must be older than in order to be archived.

Outlook's AutoArchive feature archives some items automatically. To see the current AutoArchive settings, open the Tools menu, click Options, click the Other tab, and click AutoArchive.

Archived items are stored in personal folder files with the .pst extension. As long as the archive file remains intact, you can retrieve an item stored in an archive file. Use either the Import and Export command or Open to locate the .pst file.

Deleting items is a simpler but more drastic way to rid your folders of clutter. Any time you delete an item from a folder, it moves to the Deleted Items folder. You can open that folder at any time to view a deleted item and move it to an-

FIGURE 1-14
Choose what to archive in this dialog box

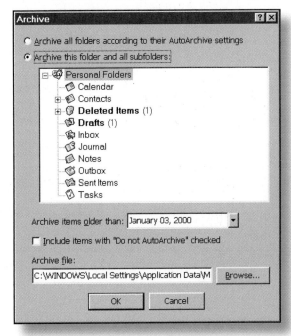

other folder, if necessary. Once you are sure you no longer want the item, select it and click Delete. Outlook will remind you that you are permanently removing the item, so you still have one last chance to change your mind.

Archiving and deleting can result in sweeping changes to your Outlook folders. Be careful when undertaking either of these tasks.

Integration: Sharing Information in Outlook

Like all the Office 2000 applications, Outlook makes it easy to share information among its folders. You can create new Outlook items from existing ones by dragging or the Using Folders option. You can use attachments to add information created in a different application to any item. If you are working on a network or have access to the Internet, you can share information in specified folders with your colleagues.

Using AutoCreate and the Move Option

Outlook's *AutoCreate* feature makes it possible for you to create a new Outlook item from an existing one of another type. For example, you can create a note from a contact or an appointment from a task. To use AutoCreate, simply select the item you want to use to create the new item and drag it onto the icon in the Outlook Bar where you want the new item to appear. Outlook then opens the appropriate form for that folder so that you can add or modify the item as necessary.

Another way to transfer information from one folder to another is the Using Folders option in the Organize pane. Not all folders offer this option, shown in Figure 1-15 for the Tasks folder. To move an item this way, select the item, click Using Folders, and select the folder to move the item to in the drop-down list. Then click Move. As with the AutoCreate feature, Outlook displays the appropriate form so that you can fine-tune the new item.

Hot Tip

You can create a new folder to move to by clicking the New Folder button in the top right corner of the pane.

FIGURE 1-15
Using Folders lets you move an item to another folder

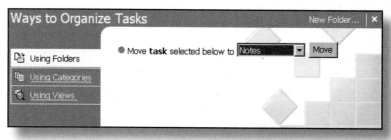

Attaching Items and Files to Outlook Items

You can attach an Outlook item or a file from another application to most Outlook items. Using attachments is a good way to provide additional information about a contact, an appointment, or a task.

You attach items or files in an item's form by opening the Insert menu and clicking Item or File. You can attach an item or file at the time you first create the item or you can open the item at a later date to add the attachment.

When you choose to insert an item, Outlook opens the Insert Item dialog box, similar to Figure 1-16. Here you can select the folder that contains the item you want to insert and then select the item itself. You have three choices for the insertion: You can insert the item as text only, as an attachment, or as a shortcut. If you choose Text only or Attachment, Outlook copies the data from your selected item. If you choose Shortcut, Outlook creates a pointer to the original item. Use this option only if the person who might be using that shortcut has access to the computer from which the item was inserted.

When you choose to insert a file, Outlook opens the Insert File dialog box, similar to an Open dialog box. Here you can browse for the file you want to insert and then click Insert to create the attachment. The attachment then appears as an icon on the form, as shown in Figure 1-17.

Hot Tip

Quickly attach a file by clicking the Insert File button on the toolbar.

To see the attachment, double-click it. Outlook asks if you want to save the file to disk or open it. If you trust the file's creator, you can go ahead and open it. If you are uncertain, save the attachment to disk and inspect it with antivirus software before you try to open it.

FIGURE 1-16
Use this dialog box to insert an item

FIGURE 1-16
Use this dialog box to insert an item

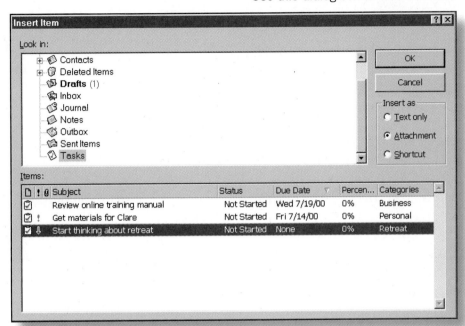

FIGURE 1-17
An attachment appears as an
icon on the form of the item

Concept Builder

You can use the Link command
on the Action menu to link
items or files to specific
Outlook items.

STEP-BY-STEP ▷ 1.6

1. You'd like to give yourself yet another reminder
about gathering those files for Clare. You can
create a note from your task:

   a. Click **Tasks** on the Outlook Bar. Select the
   task involving getting materials for Clare.

   b. Drag the task and drop it onto **Notes** in the
   Outlook Bar. A new note appears with the
   task information. Close the note.

2. You need to schedule that meeting with Min
Auyang. You can do so by moving her contact
information to Calendar:

   a. Click **Contacts** on the Outlook Bar and
   select Min Auyang's card.

   b. Open the Organize pane and click **Using
   Folders**. In the list box, choose **Calendar**
   and then click **Move**.

(continued on next page)

c. In the meeting form, key the subject **Meeting with M. Auyang**. Schedule the meeting for Tuesday, July 18, at 10:00 a.m. The meeting should last an hour. Notice that Ms. Auyang's e-mail address appears automatically. To avoid sending an invitation to this meeting, click **Cancel Invitation** on the toolbar. The meeting now appears in your list of active appointments. Add the item to the Business category. Save and close the form. Close the Organize pane.

3. Return to Contacts and select Min Auyang's card. Click the **Flag for Follow Up** button. In the *Flag for Follow Up* drop-down list, mark the flagged item as completed.

4. Larry Sinclair has been assigned to help you with the corporate retreat project. To get his creative juices flowing, attach your Retreat task to his contact card:

a. Double-click Larry Sinclair's card to open the form.

b. Open the **Insert** menu and click **Item**. In the Insert Item dialog box, click the **Tasks** folder. Then select the **Start thinking about retreat** item and click **OK**. The task appears on Larry's form. Double-click the item to see the task associated with it. Then close the task form.

5. You have some additional retreat information you want to share with Larry. Attach the file to his card:

a. If necessary, double-click Larry's card again to open the contact form. Open the **Insert** menu and click **File**.

b. In the Insert File dialog box, locate the data files for this lesson. Select **Retreat Sites** and then click **Insert**.

c. Double-click the file's icon and choose to open the file. Read the file and then close it. Save and close the contact form.

6. Leave Outlook open for the next Step-by-Step.

Sharing Information Using Net Folders

If you have access to the Internet, you can use Net Folders to share some of your Outlook folders with any colleague who is using Outlook. Net Folders can be used to share messages, calendars, tasks, notes or contacts. You cannot share information from your Inbox, your Outbox, or from offline folders. (You will learn more about offline folders in the next lesson.)

When you set up a Net Folder, you specify colleagues with whom you want to share the information in a specific folder. These colleagues are said to *subscribe* to the shared folder. A copy of your shared folder then appears in the folder list of those colleagues. Any item you create in the shared folder on your computer is automatically sent to the persons who subscribe to that folder. As you modify an item, the item is updated for all subscribers.

As you set up the shared folder, you assign permission levels to the subscribers. Permissions determine how a subscriber can work with the items in the folder. For example, the Reviewer permission allows a subscriber to read items but not create, modify, or delete items. The Editor permission allows a subscriber to read, create, modify, or delete any item.

You can add or remove subscribers at any time, and you can also change permission levels for any subscriber. To prevent an item from being published to a shared folder, click in the *Private* check box in the item's form.

Be careful when using shared folders. These folders are not secure! You risk losing control of any item you publish in a Net Folder.

Outlook and the Web

Like all other Office 2000 applications, Outlook makes it easy to work on the Web. For instant access to the Web, display the Web toolbar by opening the View menu, clicking Toolbars, and choosing Web from the submenu. (Or right-click any toolbar and click Web on the shortcut menu.) From this menu, you can search the Web, key an URL to go to a particular Web site, or go to your designated start page (for example, Figure 1-18).

FIGURE 1-18
A Web page open in Outlook

With a Web page open in Outlook, you can quickly send the page via e-mail by opening the Actions menu and clicking Send Web Page by E-Mail. If you find yourself going to a Web site frequently, you can add a shortcut to the Web page to your Outlook Bar by clicking the down arrow next to the New button and then clicking Outlook Bar Shortcut to Web Page. The shortcut is added in the My Shortcuts section of the Outlook Bar, handy for you to access any time you are working in Outlook.

1. If you have Internet access, try the following steps:
   a. Open the Web toolbar and key a Web address you are familiar with or key Microsoft's home page address (http://www.microsoft.com).
   b. Open the **Actions** menu and click **Send Web Page by E-Mail**. Address the message to someone whose e-mail address you know. Be alert for any application requirements, such as browser version requirements.
   c. Click the down arrow next to the **New** button on the toolbar and choose **Outlook Bar Shortcut to Web Page**. Click **OK**.
   d. Close the Web page by opening one of the other Outlook folders.

2. Locate your shortcut in the My Shortcuts section of the Outlook Bar. Click to see the Web page.

3. Remove the shortcut by right-clicking it and selecting **Remove from Outlook Bar**. Answer **Yes** to remove the item.

4. Leave Outlook open if you are going on to the Lesson 1 Projects. Otherwise, close Outlook.

Summary

I n this lesson, you learned:

■ Outlook offers many different ways to organize and view information. Use the Organize pane to choose a standard view or customize the current view to display items just as you want. You can also use the Organize pane to add items to categories. Categories help you to organize and group your items for ease of viewing.

■ Outlook's standard forms contain many options for capturing information, but you can create your own form to store only data items you want or need.

■ You can find text or other information in any Outlook item by clicking the Find button on the toolbar. If a simple search does not work, use the Advanced Find options to locate your item.

■ You can flag contacts or messages to remind you to follow up with some further action. To help organize items in your folders, you can create new folders within each folder to store specific items. Outlook's archiving feature lets you periodically store items in a personal folder file to remove them from your Outlook folders. You can retrieve items from archive folders. To remove items permanently, select them in the Deleted Items folder and press Delete.

■ Like other Office 2000 applications, Outlook gives you a number of ways to share information among folders. Using AutoCreate, you can create a new Outlook item from an existing one of another type. You can also move items from folder to folder to create new items. To add information to an Outlook item, you can attach either files or items. If you have Internet access, you can publish items in a Net Folder for others to share.

■ Like other Office 2000 applications, Outlook gives you easy access to the Internet. You can send displayed Web pages as e-mail messages. You can create shortcuts to Web pages you open frequently.

LESSON 1 REVIEW QUESTIONS

TRUE/FALSE

Circle T if the statement is true or F if the statement is false.

T F 1. Most Outlook folders contain the Using Categories and Using Views organizing options.

T F 2. To use a custom form again, you should save it as an Outlook Template.

T **F** 3. You can add a follow-up flag to any Outlook item.

T **F** 4. When you delete an item from an Outlook folder, it moves to the Outbox folder.

T **F** 5. You can attach files only to e-mail messages.

FILL IN THE BLANKS

Complete the following sentences by writing the correct word or words in the blanks provided.

1. A(n) _____category_____ is a keyword or phrase you can assign to an item.

2. To display only the items that match certain criteria, click _____filter_____ in the View Summary dialog box.

3. To refine a search, click the _____advanced find_____ button in the Find pane.

4. The _____autocreate_____ feature makes it possible to make a new Outlook item from an existing one of another type.

5. To attach a file to an item, you first open the _____insert_____ menu.

LESSON 1 PROJECTS

PROJECT 1-1

1. Create a new contact card for Martha Gately, the meeting planner at the Deer Creek Inn, one of your potential retreat sites. Add the following important information: The Deer Creek Inn's address is RR #3, White Springs, OH 41003. The telephone number is (614) 555-1543 and the fax number is (614) 555-1555. Add the card to the Retreat category.

2. Add two new appointments to your calendar:
   A. The first is with Martha Gately. Drag her card to the Calendar icon. Outlook informs you that no e-mail address exists, so the name will be used instead. Click **OK** to continue. Add

this additional information: You will be traveling to the Deer Creek Inn for this meeting on August 3, 2000. Allow 3 hours for travel time and the meeting. You need to start out at 11:30. Assign this appointment to the Retreat category.

B. The second appointment is with your boss John, to discuss your thoughts on the potential trainers you interviewed. John wants to meet next Wednesday at 8:30. The meeting will probably take about an hour.

3. Create a new category named **New Hires**. Add to this category your interviews and the two meetings you have scheduled to discuss new hires. (*Hint:* To delete the Business category from these items, view them as Active Appointments, click in the Category field, and delete Business.)

4. If you have not already done so, change the Calendar view to Active Appointments. Customize the view by grouping the appointments according to Category. Sort the appointments by Start in ascending order.

5. Print your appointments in table style.

PROJECT 1-2

1. Add contact information for the meeting planners at the other two proposed retreat sites. Assign these contacts to the Retreat category.

```
Hal Green                    Jane Grayfeather
Possum Lodge                 Miami Sweetwater Lodge
18 Lake Valley Rd            7901 Sugar Ridge Rd
Brandywine, OH  41087        Ross, OH  45061
Phone: (513) 555-3890        Phone: (513) 555-2121
Fax: (513) 555-3891          Fax: (513) 555-2122
```

2. You want to create a phone list of the retreat meeting planners only. Change the view to Phone List. Customize this view by clicking **Customize Current View** and then clicking **Fields** in the View Summary dialog box. In the Show Fields dialog box, click the **File As** field in the *Show these fields in this order* list and click the **Remove** button. Remove the Home Phone and Mobile fields as well. Apply a filter to show only contacts from the Retreat category.

3. Print the phone list. After you have printed the list, return the File As, Home Phone, and Mobile fields to the *Show these fields in this order list* in the Show Fields dialog box.

4. Add a flag to follow up with a call to Martha Gately, to confirm the appointment. Attach the appointment item to Larry Sinclair's card.

5. You seem to remember you know someone from Ross, Ohio, where the Miami Sweetwater Lodge is located. Maybe that person could give you some information about the lodge. Display all your contacts again in Phone List view and use Find to locate the person from Ross. Drag that person's name to Tasks and create a new task to call for further information. You should complete the task in the next week or so, and it has low priority. (*Hint:* You are not assigning this task to your contact, so click the **Cancel Assignment** button on the toolbar.)

SCANS

6. You guess you have started thinking about the retreat, so mark that vague task as completed. You have also located the training materials for Clare. Mark that task as completed. Then select both tasks and delete them.

PROJECT 1-3

Create a custom form for an item in Outlook. After you have created the form, insert several items using the form and print the items.

CRITICAL THINKING

ACTIVITY 1-1

You are troubled about assigning three hours to your meeting with Martha Gately. Is there a way you can indicate travel time for your appointments? Use Outlook's Help files to find out how to handle this kind of scheduling and write a brief summary of your findings.

ACTIVITY 1-2

You have generated a huge number of contacts in your Contacts folder. It is now becoming troublesome to scroll through them, and even using Find to locate specific information is a challenge. What options do you have to organize your contacts so that you can view them more efficiently?

ADVANCED OUTLOOK FEATURES

OBJECTIVES

Upon completion of this lesson, you should be able to:

■ Use advanced Calendar features.

■ Use advanced Tasks features.

■ Use advanced Contacts features.

■ Customize e-mail options.

⏱ Estimated Time: 2 hours

In the previous lesson, you learned about advanced features that apply to all or many of the Outlook folders. In this lesson, you will explore advanced features for Calendar, Tasks, and Contacts. You will also learn how to customize e-mail messages and read about some advanced mail-handling options.

Advanced Calendar Features

So far in your scheduling of items in Calendar, you have concentrated on creating appointments and simple events. Calendar allows you great flexibility in scheduling your time, however. You can schedule events that last more than one day, and you can plan meetings that range from simple to very complex. When scheduling events or meetings that involve persons in different time zones, you can display times from a second time zone in Calendar to help you keep track of time differences.

Scheduling Multiday Events

Scheduling a multiday event is just as easy as scheduling a single-day event. In Calendar, open the Actions menu and click New All Day Event. Then, in the event form, specify the starting day and the ending day for the event. A multiday event displays in Calendar as a banner across the top (or through the middle, depending on the view) of the scheduled days.

Using Two Time Zones

Displaying times from a second time zone in your Calendar's Day view is also easy. Right-click anywhere on the calendar's times to display a shortcut menu and then click Change Time Zone. In the Time Zone dialog box, click *Show an additional time zone* and then select the time zone from the *Time zone* list box, as shown in Figure 2-1. You can choose labels for each time zone to keep you from getting mixed up. If you work frequently with contacts in other time zones, you can swap time zones so that the other time zone is closest to your appointments.

To remove the additional time zone, right-click it, click Change Time Zone again, and remove the check from the additional time zone's check box.

FIGURE 2-1
Add a new time zone

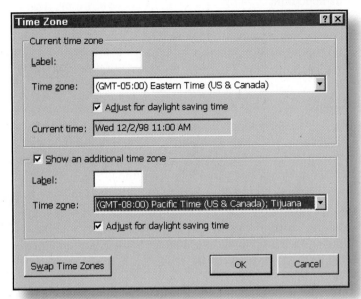

STEP-BY-STEP ▷ 2.1

The current date is now July 12, 2000.

1. Even though you don't yet know where the ExperTech corporate retreat will be, you want to schedule a tentative time for the three-day event. This will help you to focus on tasks you need to accomplish before the retreat. Schedule the multiday event:

   a. Move to January 17, 2001. Open the **Actions** menu and click **New All Day Event**. Set the starting day as January 17 and the ending day as January 19.

   b. View those days in Day, Week, or Month view to see the scheduled event.

2. Return to the current day. You and a couple of colleagues will soon be attending a conference in Europe and you will need to make reservations and other arrangements in Paris. To keep straight what time it is in Paris when you're drinking your first cup of café at your desk, add an additional time zone to your calendar:

   a. In Day view, right-click any time in the Appointments pane. On the shortcut menu, click **Change Time Zone**. In the Time Zone dialog box, click **Show an additional time zone**. In the *Time zone* list, locate **(GMT+01:00 Brussels, Copenhagen, Madrid, Paris, etc.)**.

   b. In the label box, key **Paris** to identify the second time zone. Click **OK**.

3. Schedule a call to the Hotel de Ville on Friday at 3:00 p.m. Paris time. Then remove the Paris time zone by right-clicking it, clicking **Change Time Zone**, and removing the check from the *Show an additional time zone* check box. Click **OK**.

4. Leave Outlook open for the next Step-by-Step.

Planning Meetings

Meetings differ from appointments in that you must invite several other people to join you. You must not only invite them, you must also let them know where and when the meeting is. Outlook lets you handle all of these chores online to save time in calling and faxing. Some online features are not available, however, if you are not using the Microsoft Exchange Server. The Exchange Server lets users view each other's calendars when scheduling meetings.

Concept Builder

Exchange Server is a Microsoft application designed for messaging and collaboration among users. It can only be used with a Microsoft NT network server.

To plan a meeting, open the Actions menu and click Plan a Meeting. The Plan a Meeting dialog box opens, similar to the one shown in Figure 2-2. Here you will see your name as the meeting organizer and a grid showing the day of your meeting. The vertical bars outline the amount of time you specify for the meeting. Invite the other participants by clicking Invite Others. This action opens the Select Attendees and Resources dialog box, shown in Figure 2-3. In this dialog box, you can choose the persons you are inviting from your contacts list. Or if necessary, you can add a new contact here. Click the contact and then the Required-> or Optional-> button to add the contact to the list of attendees.

After you have selected your attendees, click OK. If you have access to the calendars of the persons you have invited, the Plan a Meeting dialog box shows whether those persons are busy or out of the office at the time you have chosen for the meeting. You can then attempt to choose another time that will suit all attendees.

When you have refined your attendees list, date, and time, click Make Meeting. Outlook then displays a meeting form with the names of your attendees in the *To* box (Figure 2-4). You must add the subject of the meeting and the location and make sure the date and times are correct. To invite the attendees, click the Send button in the toolbar. Outlook sends the invitations via e-mail if your contacts have e-mail addresses. Note that you can specify whether the meeting is an online meeting and if so what the meeting software application is.

FIGURE 2-2

Start your planning in this dialog box

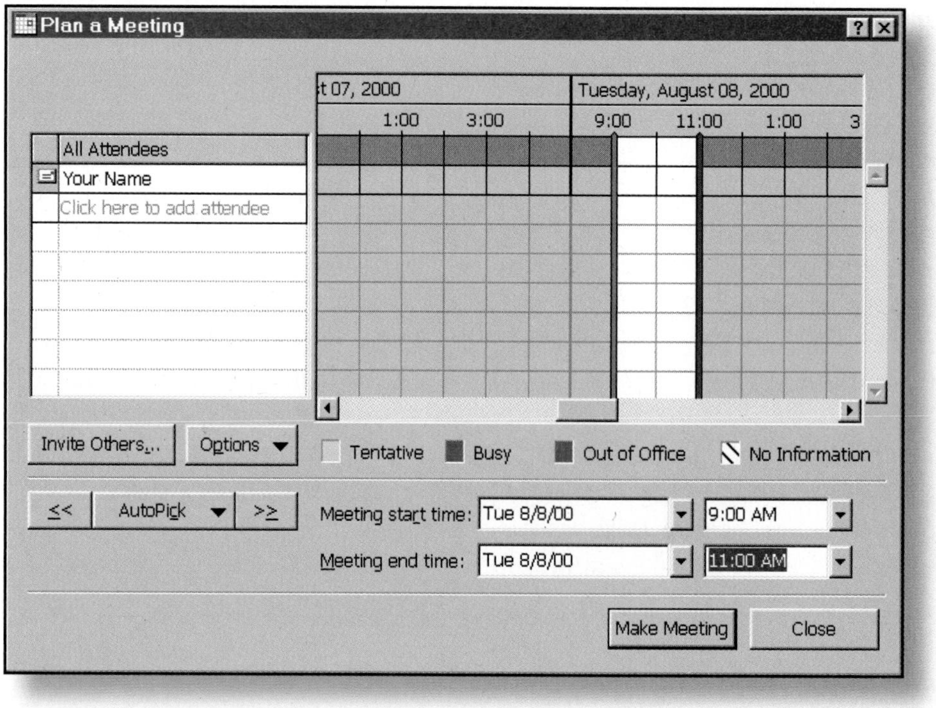

FIGURE 2-3

Choose attendees in this dialog box

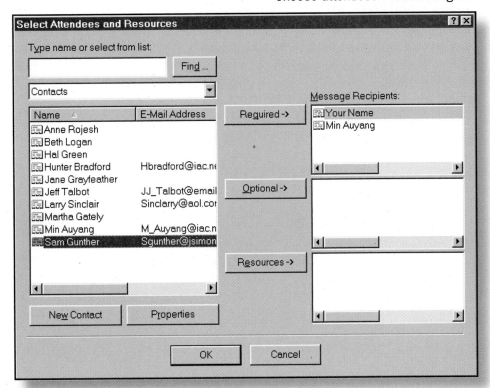

FIGURE 2-4

Send invitations to your attendees

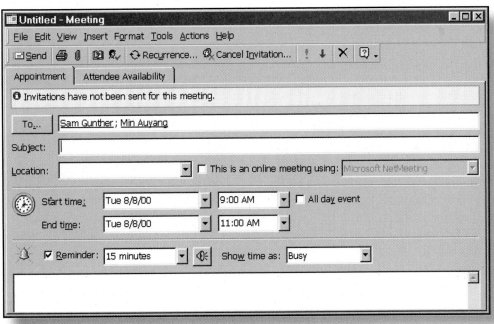

When your attendees receive a meeting request and open it in the Inbox, they will see toolbar buttons for Accept, Tentative, and Decline. Clicking one of these buttons lets the recipient check his or her calendar and send a response back to you. As your attendees reply to your meeting request, you receive a report in your Inbox showing their responses. You can track these responses on the Attendee Availability tab of the meeting form (Figure 2-5).

Hot Tip

You can easily turn an appointment into a meeting by opening the appointment's form and clicking the Invite Attendees button on the toolbar. Then click To and select names of attendees.

FIGURE 2-5
See responses to your meeting requests on this tab

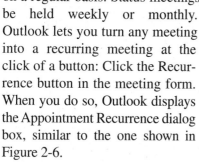

You can bypass the planning stage, if desired, and simply issue a meeting request to the persons you want to participate in the meeting. Do so by opening the Actions menu and clicking New Meeting Request. Outlook then displays a form similar to the one shown in Figure 2-4. Click the To button and add the names of your meeting participants.

In real-world situations, meetings on a particular subject are often held on a regular basis. Status meetings or sales conferences, for example, might be held weekly or monthly. Outlook lets you turn any meeting into a recurring meeting at the click of a button: Click the Recurrence button in the meeting form. When you do so, Outlook displays the Appointment Recurrence dialog box, similar to the one shown in Figure 2-6.

You can choose a number of options for your recurring meeting: the pattern of recurrence (how often and what day of the week), when to start the recurring meetings, and when to end them.

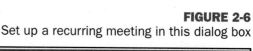

FIGURE 2-6
Set up a recurring meeting in this dialog box

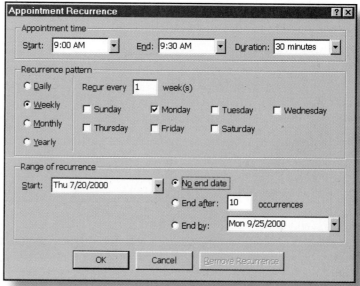

You would like to invite several of your local clients to a meeting to explore ways that ExperTech could be more responsive to client needs.

1. Open the **Actions** menu and click **Plan a Meeting**. In the Plan a Meeting dialog box, you should see your name (or the name on the current e-mail account). Click **Invite Others**.

2. In the Select Attendees and Resources dialog box, click Min Auyang's name and then click **Required->**. Click Sam Gunther's name and add him to the list of required attendees. Click **OK**.

3. Specify that the meeting take place on August 11 at 10:00 a.m. and last an hour and a half. Then click **Make Meeting**.

4. In the meeting form, key the subject of the meeting: **Meeting to outline ways ExperTech can serve clients better**.

5. You cannot send this invitation as you would in the real world, so simply save the meeting and close the form. Answer **No** when asked if you want to send the invitations. Locate the meeting in your calendar to see the results of your planning.

6. Leave Outlook open for the next Step-by-Step.

Extra Challenge

Create a new meeting request using the e-mail address of a classmate. Explore how to respond to a meeting request and tally responses.

Advanced Tasks Features

So far, you have created simple tasks with a subject, a starting date, and an ending date. If you find you are creating the same task on a regular basis, however, you should consider creating a recurring task. You control how often the task should recur. You can also choose to regenerate the task each time you complete it. This feature is perfect for scheduling tasks such as monthly reports. If you are in a supervisory position, you can also delegate tasks to others and then monitor their progress. If budgets are important for a particular task, you can record billing information for the task.

Setting Up Recurring Tasks

Setting up a recurring task is similar to setting up a recurring meeting. In the task form, click the Recurrence button on the toolbar to display a dialog box similar to the one shown in Figure 2-7. Notice that in addition to setting up the recurrence options, you can tell Outlook to regenerate the task at a specified interval. When you ask Outlook to regenerate a task, the task reappears in your task list each time you complete it. If you don't set a number of recurrences, it becomes the task that never ends!

Delegating and Tracking Tasks

Delegating a task is also as easy as clicking a button. In the task form, click the Assign Task button on the toolbar. When you do, Outlook opens a dialog box similar to the one shown in Figure 2-8. Click the To button and select the name of 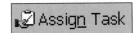 the person to whom you want to assign the task and then insert the other information about the task. Notice toward the bottom of the dialog box two options you can select to monitor the task. You can choose to keep an updated copy of the task on your own task list and/or request a status report when the task is complete. As the person you assigned the task updates information on the task, you will see changes to the task in your

FIGURE 2-7
Set up a recurring task in this dialog box

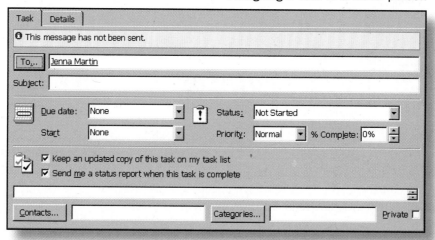

FIGURE 2-8
Assigning a task to another person

task list. After the task is complete, you will automatically receive a status report on the task.

Tracking Task Information

The Details tab in the task form (Figure 2-9) gives you options for recording billing information for a task. You can record estimated hours (Total work), actual hours (Actual work), a job code (Billing information), and mileage.

Concept Builder

Once you assign a task to someone else, you can no longer make changes to it. Only the person you assign the task can change it.

FIGURE 2-9
Record billing information on this tab

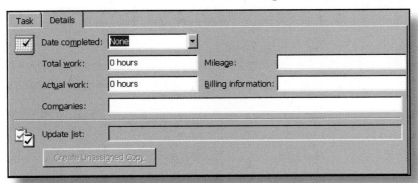

FIGURE 2-9
Record billing information on this tab

STEP-BY-STEP ▷ 2.3

SCANS

1. You spend plenty of time nagging other employees to file their expenses in a timely manner, but you are just as bad about filing your own. Set up a recurring task to prompt you to do better. *Note:* For the regenerating feature to work properly, you should use today's date (that is, the *real* date, not July 12, 2000) in this step.

   a. Click **Tasks** on the Outlook Bar. Click the **New** button to open a new task.

   b. Key the subject **File expenses**. Assign tomorrow as the due date. Click the **Recurrence** button on the toolbar.

   c. Click the **Monthly** option for the recurrence pattern and then the **Regenerate new task** option. Click **OK** and then **Save and Close**.

2. To see the regenerating feature at work, switch to Calendar and move ahead two days from the current date. In the Taskpad, click the File expenses task to mark it complete. Notice that the task regenerates to stay active in your Taskpad.

3. A new employee has just been hired to help you out. Enter the information shown in Figure 2-10 on a new contact card (not your Colleagues template). Your fellow employees have decided

FIGURE 2-10
Information for a new employee

Martin, Jenna	
Full Name:	Jenna Martin
Job Title:	Resources Specialist
Company:	ExperTech, Inc.
Business:	6790 Westlake Blvd Blue Ash, OH 45242
Business:	(513) 555-3400
Home:	(513) 555-8729
Business Fax:	(513) 555-3401
E-mail:	J_Martin@expertech.com

they want to donate blood as part of their community service. Make Jenna feel at home by instantly assigning to her the task of organizing the blood drive:

   a. Open a new task and key the subject **Call Foxworth Center to schedule donations**. This task should be completed by August 11, 2000.

   b. Click **Assign Task** on the toolbar. Click **To**. Locate Jenna's name in your Contacts list, click **To->**, and click **OK**.

(continued on next page)

c. You want to keep a copy of the task on your file list, but you don't necessarily care about the status report. Remove the check from the *Send me a status report* check box.

d. You cannot send this message as you would in the real world. Save the task and close it.

4. Leave Outlook open for the next Step-by-Step.

Advanced Contacts Features

You have already discovered a number of ways to store and use contact information in Outlook. There are many other Contacts options, however. In the following sections, you will explore some additional Contacts features.

Options for Adding and Filing Contacts

Creating new cards for contacts can be a tedious business if you have a lot to add at any one time. Fortunately, a shortcut is available to enter more than one contact from the same company. Also, you might want to customize the way a contact's name is filed in Contacts. You can specify exactly how a contact is to be filed, even if the filing name is different from the full name. If you have contact information stored on another computer, you can use the Import and Export command to avoid having to rekey all the cards.

Adding several contacts from the same company is an easy process. In the contacts form, key the information for the first contact. Then open the Actions menu and click New Contact from Same Company. Outlook creates a new contacts form with all the company information already inserted. All you need to do is enter the name and title (Figure 2-11).

By default, Outlook files contacts according to last name, using the name you key as the filing name. You can customize how Outlook files contact names by clicking the down arrow of the *File as* list box. This list lets you choose to file a contact by first name, by company name, by name and company, or by company and name. You can also key a name or other filing option in the list box.

You can import and export contacts to move them from computer to computer if you do not have sharing options in place. When you export Outlook items, you do so using a .psf file similar to the file created when you archive items. During the export process, you have the opportunity to indicate which folder you want to export items from and even apply a filter to select only the items you want. Outlook creates a Personal folder at the location you specify and stores the items in it. When importing, you specify the location of your .psf file. The easiest way to import is to place items in a folder with the same name as the folder you exported from.

Concept Builder

To change the default options for filing, click Options on the Tools menu and then click Contact Options in the Options dialog box.

Exporting and importing can be somewhat tricky, even using the Import and Export Wizard. The Outlook Office Assistant supplies timely help as you work through the process. You will use this feature in the Unit Review applications.

FIGURE 2-11

Adding a new contact from the same company

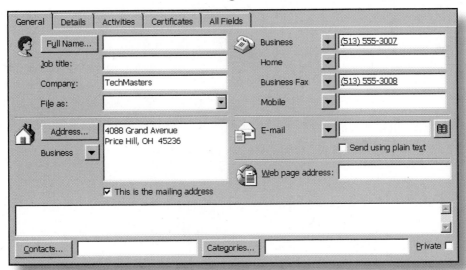

1. ExperTech is developing a relationship with a new company, TechMasters. Insert information for two contacts from that company:

a. Open a new contact form and insert the information shown in Figure 2-11. Insert the Full Name **Yanni Costas** and the title **Training Coordinator**. Insert the e-mail address **Ycostas@techmasters.com**.

b. Click the down arrow in the *File as* list box and choose the **Costas, Yanni (Tech-Masters)** option. Assign the contact to the Hot Contacts category.

c. Open the **Actions** menu and click **New Contact from Same Company**. Insert the name **Ben Jarvis** and the title **Trainer**. His e-mail address is **Bjarvis@techmasters.com**. Make the same change in the *File as* list box and add the contact to Hot Contacts.

2. Click **Save and Close** twice. Notice the way the two new contacts are filed in the File As column. Leave Outlook open for the next Step-by-Step.

Communicating with Contacts

Once you have created cards for your contacts, you can communicate with them in a number of ways. You already know how easy it is to set up a meeting by simply dragging a contact's information to the Calendar. You have also learned how to assign a task to a contact. There are a number of other ways to communicate with contacts, as you will learn in this section.

CALLING A CONTACT

If you have access to a phone line through your computer, you can call a selected contact by clicking the Dial button on the toolbar. A drop-down list gives you the option to call any of the numbers you have entered for that contact (business, home, fax, mobile, etc.). Clicking one of these options opens a dialog box similar to the one shown in Figure 2-12. This dialog box gives you many options for setting properties necessary for the phone connection. Notice that you can create a journal entry when you place the call, so that you can keep track of call time and duration.

FIGURE 2-12
Placing a call to a contact

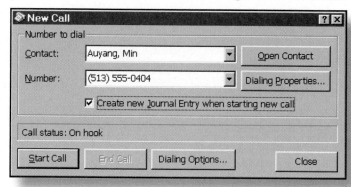

E-MAILING A CONTACT

Sending a message to a contact is also a matter of clicking a button. Click the New Message to Contact button on the toolbar to open a new e-mail message with the contact's name already displayed in the *To* box.

SENDING A LETTER TO A CONTACT

To send a letter to a selected contact, open the Actions menu and click New Letter to Contact. Microsoft Word opens and starts the Letter Wizard. You can decide on a style for the letter and insert information that will be used for date, salutation, return address, and complimentary close. After you have made your decisions, Word displays a letter similar to the one shown in Figure 2-13, ready for you to add text.

FIGURE 2-13
A letter to a contact prepared using the Letter Wizard

Yanni Costas
Training Coordinator
TechMasters
4088 Grand Avenue
Price Hill, OH 45236

Dear Yanni,
Type your text here.

Best regards,
[Your Name]
Human Resources

USING CONTACTS FOR MAIL MERGES

You can even use your contact list to prepare form letters or labels. On the Tools menu, click Mail Merge. The Mail Merge dialog box opens, similar to Figure 2-14. Here you can choose options for the merge, including how many contacts to use, what fields to use, whether to start a new merge document or use an existing one, and other merge options. Notice that you can merge all contacts or only selected contacts. To choose only specific contacts, apply a filter to the contact list.

After you make your selections and click OK, Microsoft Word starts and sets up a merge document for you, complete with Mail Merge toolbar, as shown in Figure 2-15. Insert the fields from your contacts, your text (if you are creating letters), and then click a merge option on the toolbar. Your contact names are already set up as the data for the merge, so your merged items appear immediately.

Concept Builder

To avoid having to scroll through many field names, you can customize the Contacts view to remove unused field names.

FIGURE 2-14

Set up a merge operation in this dialog box

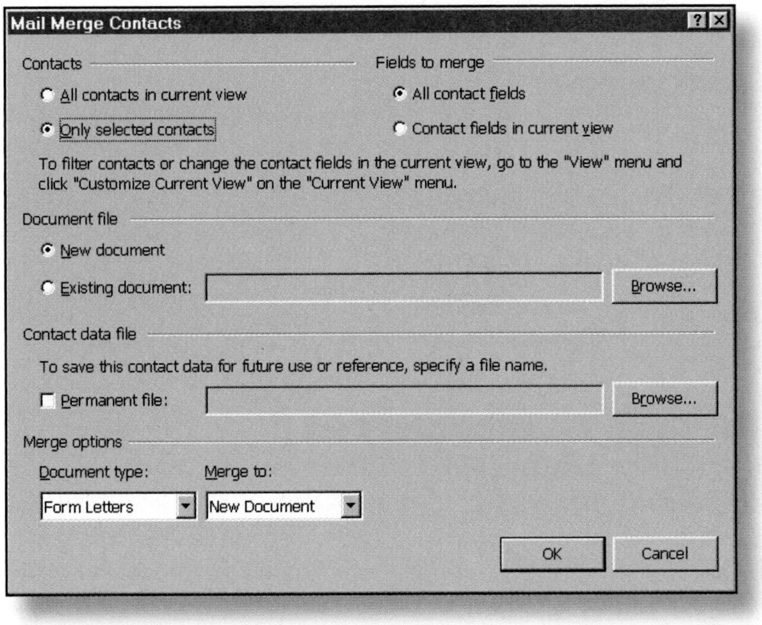

FIGURE 2-15

Merge fields inserted in the new document

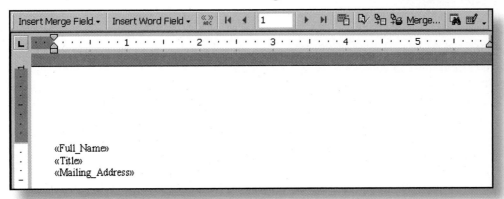

STEP-BY-STEP ▷ 2.5

1. Select both Yanni Costas's card and Ben Jarvis's card and click **New Message to Contact**. Insert the subject **Thanks for thinking of us!** Then key a brief message thanking the two new contacts from TechMasters for considering ExperTech as a way to improve their training programs. You

cannot send this message, but print it and then close it without saving.

2. Send a letter to Sam Gunther to thank him for agreeing to come to the meeting you planned earlier in this lesson:

(continued on next page)

a. Select Sam Gunther's card. Open the **Actions** menu and click **New Letter to Contact**.

b. Follow the steps in the Letter Wizard to provide information for the letter. Use your own judgment on what to supply. Then key a brief letter thanking Sam and looking forward to seeing him on the meeting day (August 11).

c. Print the letter and close it without saving. Exit Word.

3. Leave Outlook open for the next Step-by-Step.

Extra Challenge

If your computer has access to a phone line, create a contact whose phone number you know and then try dialing that contact using the Dial button on the toolbar.

Creating a Personal Distribution List

As you work with your contacts, you will no doubt find that you often have to deal with specific groups of contacts. For example, you might often need to send messages to all members of the Development Team. Or you might need to schedule a meeting with all support personnel. You can save yourself many minutes, if not hours, of time by grouping contacts into personal distribution lists. After you have created a personal distribution list, messages and other Outlook items you create can be automatically sent to all persons on the list.

Create a personal distribution list by clicking the down arrow next to the New button on the toolbar and choosing Distribution List. A dialog box similar to the one shown in Figure 2-16 opens. Key a name for the list. This name will appear in your Contacts list. Then click the Select Members button to open the Select Members dialog box. Choose names to add to the distribution list and then click OK.

The names and e-mail addresses you have chosen appear in the distribution list. You can always add new names to the list by opening the list in Contacts and clicking the Select Members button. You can also add contacts not currently in your contacts list by clicking the Add New button and inserting the necessary information. Note that you can add a distribution list to a category, just as you add any other Outlook item.

FIGURE 2-16
Creating a new distribution list

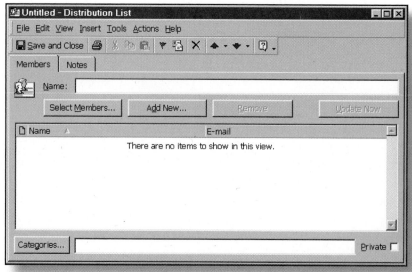

S TEP-BY-STEP ▷ 2.6

1. Create a distribution list of your training clients. You have only two in your contacts list right now, but this number is sure to grow! Follow these steps:
   a. Click the down arrow next to the **New** button on the toolbar. Click **Distribution List**.
   b. In the Distribution List dialog box, key the name **Training Clients**. Click the **Select Members** button below the *Name* text box.
   c. Click **Min Auyang** and then **Add->**. Add **Sam Gunther** in the same way and then click **OK**. Click **Save and Close**.

2. Scroll if necessary to find the Training Clients distribution list. To see how you can send a message to all members of the distribution list, select the distribution list and click **New Message to Contact** on the toolbar. The distribution list name appears in the *To* text box. Close the message without saving.

3. Leave Outlook open for the next Step-by-Step.

Customizing E-Mail Messages

Outlook's e-mail capabilities are extremely rich, and any discussion of even advanced features will not begin to explore all of them. And, as for other Outlook features, many e-mail features have been designed specifically for use with Microsoft's Exchange Server. The sections below discuss some fun and interesting e-mail features as well as some options available only in a shared environment supplied by Exchange Server.

Using Stationery

If you have chosen to send your e-mail messages in HTML format rather than as plain text, you can customize your messages using stationery. Stationery adds visual interest to your e-mail messages, as shown in Figure 2-17. Stationery supplies a background and a font, font size, and font color for the message text. Your recipient must be able to read HTML messages to get the full effect of your stationery.

FIGURE 2-17
An e-mail message formatted with stationery

Jenna,

Welcome to ExperTech! We work hard but we have fun, too! I know you'll enjoy working with your new friends in Human Resources.

Specify your mail format and stationery by clicking Options on the Tools menu. In the Options dialog box, click the Mail Format tab. Choose the format for your messages in the *Message Format* area, and then click the *Stationery* drop-down list to see available stationeries. Click the Stationery Picker button to see how the stationery will look in the message. The choice you make here will be the default stationery for all your e-mail messages.

Concept Builder

A number of these stationery choices are not currently installed and will install as you use them. Be prepared with your Office 2000 CD.

Adding a Signature

You can direct Outlook to add a "signature"—that is, a name, not a handwritten signature—to your e-mail messages. You insert the text for the signature and select it as the default signature. Then you can insert the signature in any message by clicking Signature on the Insert menu.

Create your signature on the Mail Format tab of the Options dialog box. Click Signature Picker and then New in the Signature Picker dialog box. In the Create New Signature dialog box, insert a name for your signature item and then click Next. In the Edit Signature dialog box (Figure 2-18), key the signature text. Then select it and format it using the Font or Paragraph button. Click Finish and then OK to return to the Mail Format tab. You can select a signature as the default and then click OK.

FIGURE 2-18
Insert and edit your signature text here

You can create more than one signature. You can also create entire paragraphs of "boilerplate" text—text that you might insert in any number of messages, such as the company address or a standard response to requests for information.

Creating E-Mail Templates

If you know that you will often be sending a particular kind of e-mail message—such as the welcome message shown in Figure 2-17—you can create the message without a recipient and save it as an Outlook template to be used again and again. To do so, click Save As on the File menu, change the file type to Outlook Template, and give the message a name you will remember.

By default, the template will be stored with other Outlook templates. You locate it for use in the same way you located your custom form in the previous lesson: Click the down arrow next to the New button, click Choose Form, and locate the template in User Templates in File System.

S TEP-BY-STEP ▷ 2.7

1. Specify a default stationery for your e-mail messages:
   a. Click **Inbox** on the Outlook Bar. Open the **Tools** menu and click **Options**. Click the **Mail Format** tab. If your message format is not set to HTML, click the message format down arrow and choose **HTML**.
   b. Click **Stationery Picker**. Scroll through the list to find a stationery you like (and that is suitable for business messages). Then click **OK**.

2. While you are in the Options dialog box, create a new signature:
   a. On the Mail Format tab, click **Signature Picker**. In the Signature Picker dialog box, click **New**.

   b. Type a name for the signature (your own name will work fine) and then click **Next**.
   c. In the Edit Signature dialog box, key your name in the *Signature text* area. (*Hint:* You will not see an insertion point—just start keying.) Select the text and format it as desired and then click **Finish**.
   d. Click **OK**. Make sure your signature appears as the default signature on the Mail Format tab and then click **OK**.

3. Create a new message to Jenna Martin. Insert the text shown in Figure 2-17 and add your signature: Open the **Insert** menu, click **Signature**, and choose your name on the submenu. Print the

message. (Your background will not print, but you will see the chosen fonts and your name.)

4. Leave Outlook open for the next Step-by-Step.

Using the Rules Wizard

Outlook has a number of rules in place to handle your e-mail messages, but you can, of course, customize these rules. To do so, you use the Rules Wizard. The Rules Wizard, with the help of the Office Assistant, will step you through the process of creating new rules for handling your messages. Figure 2-19 shows a number of rules you can add easily by clicking. Edit a portion of the rule by clicking on the underlined words in the lower pane. You can then set specific conditions for when to apply the rule, list any exceptions to the rule, and give the rule a name. The rule is turned on by default and ready to be used.

Tracking E-Mail

You can track your e-mail to find out when it was delivered and when it was read. To track all messages, in the Options dialog box click E-Mail Options and then Tracking Options. Click *Request a read receipt for all messages I send.* After you put this option in place, recipients of your messages will be notified that you have requested a receipt for the message. They can answer yes or no to this request. If they respond with Yes, you will receive a report in your Inbox telling you the date and time your recipient received the message. Figure 2-20 shows a portion of such a report.

To track individual messages, click the Options button on the message's toolbar. In the Message Options dialog box, click in the *Request a read receipt for this message* check box.

FIGURE 2-19
Creating a new rule in the Rules Wizard

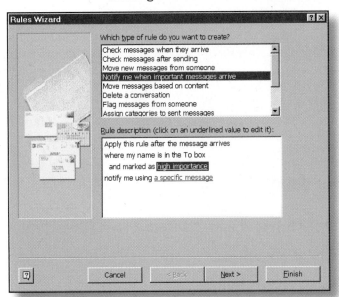

FIGURE 2-20
A read report tells you when a message was read

> Your message
>
> To: Cat Skintik
> Subject: Are you awake?
> Sent: 12/3/98 3:31 PM
>
> was read on 12/3/98 3:34 PM.

Options...

S TEP-BY-STEP ▷ 2.8

1. Open a new e-mail message. Address it to someone else in your class or someone whose e-mail address you know.

2. Click the **Options** button on the toolbar. In the Message Options dialog box, click the **Request a read receipt for this message** check box. Click **Close**.

3. Compose a brief message and add your signature. Send the message.

4. Check later for the report in your Inbox. Depending when the message was received and read, you might need to check later in the day or even the next day to see the report.

Other E-Mail Options

As indicated previously, many e-mail features can only be used if Outlook is being used in a networked environment with Exchange Server. Some of these features are discussed below.

Using E-Mail as a Voting Tool

If you are working in a networked environment and running Microsoft's Exchange Server, you can use e-mail messages as a voting tool. Explain to your recipients in the body of the message the subject of the vote. Click the Options button on the message's toolbar to open the Message Options dialog box. Click the *Use voting buttons* check box and select from the drop-down list the wording that should appear on the buttons. You can also delete the default choices and key your own voting options.

When a recipient opens the message in the Inbox, he or she will see toolbar buttons with the voting options on them. The recipient simply clicks the desired button. The responses are then stored with the sent message.

Recalling Messages

If you are using Exchange Server, you can recall or replace a message you have already sent, as long as your recipient has not already read the message or deleted it from the Inbox. To do this, reopen the message you sent. Open the Actions menu and click Recall this message. Then click the *Delete unread copies of this message* option. If you want to replace the message with another one, click the *Delete unread copies and replace with a new message* option. Then click OK and key your new message. You can ask Outlook to notify you whether you have successfully recalled messages you have sent.

Using Remote Mail and Offline Folders

If you are working in a networked environment, you do not necessarily have to be at your office computer to work with your e-mail messages. Outlook has several important options that give you great flexibility in working with Outlook items.

If you are connected to Microsoft Exchange Server, you can use *offline folders* to manage your Outlook items while not connected to the server. You store your Outlook items in the offline folder so that you can work with them anywhere. You can then synchronize your offline folder with the server folder by clicking Synchronize on the Tools menu. This feature is similar to the way you work with a Briefcase in Windows 98.

If you work on a network but do not use Microsoft Exchange Server, you can still manage your e-mail from a remote location using the Remote Mail feature. Remote Mail allows you to connect to your office computer by using a modem, telephone, dial-up networking software, and a mail delivery service.

Using Remote Mail, you can view the message headers (the name of the sender, the subject, and the date and time) of messages in your Inbox and decide which messages to download to your local computer. This feature saves downloading time (and possibly connection costs).

Summary

In this lesson, you learned:

- Calendar includes options for setting up multiday events and using more than one time zone in the Calendar view. Calendar also offers a complete meeting planning feature that lets you choose attendees, determine their availability, and send invitations. Invitees can respond automatically to your request, and you can tally their responses on the Details tab of the meeting request.

- You can set up a task that will recur at a specified interval. If desired, you can instruct Outlook to regenerate the task so that you have a constant reminder of the task. You can delegate tasks to others and be informed of progress on the task.

- Contacts has many advanced features to help you work with your contacts. You can easily add contacts from the same company, choose how to file contacts, call a contact, send a message or a letter to a contact, and even use a contact list in a mail merge. To further organize your contacts, you can create a personal distribution list of all contacts who belong to a particular group.

- E-mail messages can be customized in a number of ways. You can use stationery to liven up your messages and you can add a signature or other text to each message at the click of a command. You can create templates of e-mail messages you use frequently. To fine-tune the way Outlook handles your e-mail messages, you can specify rules using the Rules Wizard. To find out when your e-mail messages were read, you can specify tracking options.

- If you are using Outlook on a network with Microsoft Exchange Server, you can use e-mail messages to gather votes from recipients and recall messages you have already sent. You can also work with offline folders at another location (or when your network is down) and then synchronize your offline folders with your server folders to keep your work up to date. If you have set up Remote Mail, you can work with your mail messages from another computer.

LESSON 2 REVIEW QUESTIONS

TRUE/FALSE

Circle T if the statement is true or F if the statement is false.

T F 1. You can swap time zones to display the second time zone closest to your appointments.

T F 2. You cannot specify an ending date for a recurring task.

T F 3. When you send a letter to a contact, the Letter Wizard opens to help you create the letter.

T F 4. To use stationery, your e-mail messages must be set up for HTML format.

T F 5. When you track an e-mail message, you have the option of recalling the message before it is read.

FILL IN THE BLANKS

Complete the following sentences by writing the correct word or words in the blanks provided.

1. To simply invite attendees to a meeting, click _____ on the _____ menu.

2. To group contacts for ease of communication with them, use a(n) _____.

3. Create a signature by clicking the _____ tab in the Options dialog box.

4. To customize the way Outlook handles e-mail messages, use the _____ to establish new guidelines.

5. If you are connected to a network, you can use _____ to manage your Outlook items and then synchronize them later.

SCANS

PROJECT 2-1

The current date is July 19, 2000.

1. Add contact information to Contacts for your boss, John Freitag, and for Larry Sinclair (right now you have only his home information). To speed this process, open Jenna Martin's contact form and use the New Contact from Same Company command. John's title is Human Resources Director and Larry's is Resources Specialist. John's e-mail address is J_Freitag@expertech.com and Larry's is L_Sinclair@expertech.com. When you save Larry's contact form, you will receive a message asking if you want to update Larry's existing form or add this one as a new contact. Choose to add this one as a new contact.

2. You, John, and Larry are going to have a lot to discuss about the corporate retreat in January. Schedule recurring weekly meetings from sometime this week until the last week before the retreat. Invite John and Larry to attend each meeting. You choose the time for the meeting, the duration, and the day of the week. Do not send invitations, just save and close the meeting.

3. You and John have decided to hire both the prospects you interviewed last week. Both can begin work in two weeks, so their starting date will be July 31. Schedule a two-day training workshop for the new hires to take place at the end of their first week. Send a memo to John Freitag to let him know the days you have scheduled. Don't forget to use your signature in the message. Print the message, save it, and close it.

4. Print your apointments and meetings for July on a monthly calendar.

PROJECT 2-2

SCANS

1. Part of your job is to sweet-talk your colleagues into presenting Brown Bag Forums on Fridays. (The Brown Bag Forums allow employees to prepare presentations or lectures on subjects of interest to them.) To help you keep this task in mind, set up a recurring task on a weekly basis to find Brown Bag speakers. Use the current date for this task, so the task will regenerate properly. Delete the task sometime next week and confirm that the task regnerates.

2. While you're thinking of those Brown Bag Forums—create an e-mail template to invite all employees to each Forum. The body of the e-mail message should tell employees where the Forums are held (the Auditorium) and when (Fridays at 12:00 noon). Remind employees that they can bring their lunches and that coffee and soft drinks are on the house. Print the message and then store it as a template with your solution files for this course.

3. Since Jenna has already made a good start at scheduling the blood drive, give her another task. Employees have decided they want to work in groups at the local food bank. Set up a task to contact the food bank director to discuss times. Assign the task to Jenna and ask for a status report only. Schedule a due date of July 26, 2000.

4. You have finished reviewing the online manual. Mark the task as complete. Print your current tasks in table form.

PROJECT 2-3

1. You'd like to organize your Contacts folder a bit. Create a personal distribution list for all the persons in the Holiday Card category. Name the distribution list **Holiday Cards**.

2. Use a filter to display only the Holiday Cards contacts. Click **Mail Merge** on the **Tools** menu. In the Mail Merge Contacts dialog box, click the **Document type** down arrow in the *Merge options* area. Choose **Mailing Labels** from the drop-down list. Click **OK**.

3. When prompted, click **OK** again to set up your main document. Click the **Setup** button in the Mail Merge Helper dialog box. In the Label Options dialog box, scroll in the *Product number* list to locate and click **5162 - Address labels** for the contacts. Click **OK**.

4. Insert merge fields for first name, last name, and home address. Then click **OK**. In the Mail Merge Helper dialog box, click **Merge**. Then click **Merge** again to merge to a new document.

5. Print the labels on plain paper. Save the labels as **Holiday Label** followed by your initials. Close Word and any remaining Word documents.

6. Remove any filters or sorts you have used in this lesson. Follow the directions of your instructor to remove Outlook items.

CRITICAL THINKING

ACTIVITY 2-1

You know that a lot of holidays are going to intrude before your corporate retreat, and you want to account for them in your schedules. Is there a way to display holidays in your calendar? Use Outlook's Help files to find out if you can do this, and if so, how. Write a brief report of your findings.

ACTIVITY 2-2

Your company regularly receives e-mail messages containing résumés of persons who are interested in working for the company. Standard practice is to inform all persons submitting résumés that their résumés will be reviewed and kept on file, with a follow-up contact if a job is available for which a particular person is suited.

How could you streamline this process using Outlook's customizable e-mail options? Write a brief report on your ideas.

COMMAND SUMMARY

FEATURE	MENU COMMAND	TOOLBAR BUTTON	LESSON
Archive items	File, Archive		1
Attach file	Insert, File	📎	1
Attach item	Insert, Item		1
Contact, call	Actions, Call Contact	☎ ▼	2
Contact, in mail merge	Tools, Mail Merge		2
Contact, new from same company	Actions, New Contact from Same Company		2
Contact, send e-mail	Actions, New Message to Contact	📧	2
Contact, send letter	Actions, New Letter to Contact		2
Distribution list	File, New, Distribution List		2
E-mail, recall	Actions, Recall This Message		2
E-mail, track		Options...	2
Event, schedule	Actions, New All Day Event		2
Find, advanced	Tools, Advanced Find		1
Find item	Tools, Find	Find	1
Flag item for follow up	Actions, Flag for Follow Up	🚩	1
Folder, new	File, Folder, New Folder		1
Form, create new	Tools, Forms, Design a Form		1
Form, use new	File, New, Choose Form		1
Items, import/export	File, Import and Export		2
Meeting, plan	Actions, Plan a Meeting Actions, New Meeting Request		2
Rules Wizard	Tools, Rules Wizard		2
Signature, insert	Insert, Signature		2
Task, delegating	Actions, Assign Task	Assign Task	2

FEATURE	MENU COMMAND	TOOLBAR BUTTON	LESSON
Task, recurring	Actions, Recurrence	⟳ Recurrence...	2
Template, save	File, Save As		1
Time zone, display second	Change Time Zone (on shortcut menu)		2
View, change	Tools, Organize	⊞ Organize	1

REVIEW QUESTIONS

MATCHING

Match the correct term in Column 2 to its description in Column 1.

Column 1

_____ 1. Button to select to show only items that match certain criteria.

_____ 2. Keyword or phrase you can assign to an item.

_____ 3. A name or paragraph of text you can add to an e-mail message.

_____ 4. Option to change how a contact is filed.

_____ 5. Feature that makes it possible to make a new Outlook item from an existing one.

Column 2

A. File as

B. Signature

C. Group

D. Category

E. Filter

F. AutoCreate

MULTIPLE CHOICE

Select the best response for the following statements.

1. The process of removing items from their folders and storing them in a file is called
    A. Moving
    B. Archiving
    C. Deleting
    D. Recalling

2. All Outlook items are entered into their folders using
    A. Dialog boxes
    B. Attachments
    C. Forms
    D. Categories

3. To set up a meeting, you can use
    A. Plan a Meeting
    B. Create New Meeting
    C. New Meeting Request
    D. either a or c

4. When you create a mail merge using contacts, you also use
     A. Microsoft Access
     B. Microsoft Word
     C. Microsoft Excel
     D. Microsoft Publisher

5. To customize the way Outlook handles your e-mail messages, use the
     A. Rules Wizard
     B. Letter Wizard
     C. Import and Export Wizard
     D. Message Wizard

APPLICATIONS

APPLICATION 1

Your job at the Civic Garden Center requires you to keep track of a number of contacts, tasks, appointments, and meetings—Outlook can help you manage your time and resources efficiently. The current date is September 13, 2000.

1. First import a list of contacts you will use in the applications in this unit review. You should have no other contacts in your Contacts folder.
     A. With the Contacts folder open, open the **File** menu and click **Import and Export**. In the first Import and Export Wizard dialog box, choose *Import from another program or file* and click **Next**.
     B. Scroll down in the *Select file type to import from* list to locate and select *Personal Folder File (.pst)*. Click **Next**.
     C. In the *File to import* box, use the Browse button to locate the data files for this unit. Click **AO App1.pst** and then click **Next**.
     D. Make no changes in the final wizard dialog box and click **Finish**. The contacts should import into the Contacts folder.

2. This contacts list represents a partial list of the contacts you would have if you really worked at the Civic Garden Center. But there are still enough to require you to take some steps to organize them. First, sort the current view by the *File as* field so that the cintacts are in alphabetical order.

3. Your contacts fall into three rough groups: your colleagues at the Civic Garden Center, persons from landscaping companies you work with, and members of neighborhood committees with whom you work to improve the urban landscape. Change the view so you can see each person's "business" and assign them to categories. You can use existing categories or create new ones.

4. You need to set up a meeting with an arborist you have worked with before (one of the elms on the Garden Center property looks as if it might have Dutch elm disease). Find the arborist. (*Hint:* You will need to use Advanced Find to locate the title in a frequently used field.) Drag the contact to the Calendar. Schedule the meeting for the following Monday at 10:00a.m..

SCANS

5. You have interested the local morning newspaper in events at the garden center. To keep your contacts at the newspaper informed of other events, add them to your contacts list:

```
Toni Fellowes              Morgan Jones
Metro Editor               Garden Editor
Post Dispatch
Phone: (513) 555-6425
Fax: (513) 555-6466
76 N. Broadway
Cincinnati, OH 45204
E-mail: Toni_Fell@dispatch.com    Morg_Jones@dispatch.com
```

6. *Morgan Jones* is the name that Morgan Januszewski uses for her column, but she quite often addresses correspondence with her real name. In her contact form, change her last name to **Januszewski** but maintain the *Jones, Morgan* File as entry by keying **Jones, Morgan** in the *File as* box.

7. Create a personal distribution list for your neighborhood urban landscape committee contacts. Send a memo to these contacts to remind them of the Civic Garden Center tree sale, which will take place in the spring (you don't have a date yet, but you will inform them later). If desired, use stationery to jazz up your message. If you have already completed the PowerPoint unit review applications, attach the **Trees** PowerPoint presentation you completed in that unit review to the message. Print your message and close it without saving.

8. Print your contacts list as desired.

APPLICATION 2

SCANS

1. You are required to review revenues and expenses for the Garden Center's Gift Shop in your job. Currently, you review them whenever you have a spare moment (not very efficient). Set up a recurring task to review the Gift Shop accounts on a monthly basis, say, the first Friday of each month. Have the task regenerate. (Remember that you have to use the current date for tasks to regenerate properly.)

2. The last time you reviewed those accounts, you were befuddled by some items. Set up a meeting with your accountant and the Gift Shop manager to hash out proper accounting procedures. Plan the meeting for September 27 at 10:00 a.m. Better give yourselves a good hour and a half for the meeting. Do not set a reminder and specify the Garden Room as the location for the meeting.

3. Plan another meeting with the Gift Shop manager, your assistant Pat Tomita, and your boss Ben Goldman to brainstorm holiday decorations. Plan the meeting for September 25 at 11:00a.m. Do not set a reminder and specify the Garden Room as the location for the meeting.

4. You need to call Tokyo about an order of bonsai junipers you want to feature for the holiday season. Add a second time zone to your calendar and find out if there is a time you can call Tokyo from work. If so, create a reminder in the calendar to call in the next day or so. If not, create a reminder to send a fax.

5. You'd better think about scheduling that tree sale. Schedule the three-day event starting on April 11 of the next year (2001). The sale takes place at the Garden Center.

6. Assign your associate Pat the task of informing the newspaper editors of the sale. Pat will have to decide when to send out the details. Keep a copy of the task in your task list and request the status report at the conclusion of the task.

7. Print your current tasks as desired.

8. Print your current calendar in monthly form.

9. Remove any sorts or filters you have put in place in this review unit. Follow your instructor's directions for removing items from the Outlook folders.

SCANS

APPLICATION 3

In your job, you are always looking for new suppliers and interesting garden sites on the Web. Use a search engine to find three or four good sites related to gardening or landscape design. Write a brief report on how you could add these URLs to your Outlook shortcut bar so they will be easy to access. If desired, insert the URLs in your report file.

ON-THE-JOB SIMULATION

You work in the small production company called Min Productions, owned and managed by Min Auyang. In the PowerPoint unit review, Min Productions completed a job for Orion, Ltd. In this simulation, you will work with Outlook items that might have been generated during that job.

JOB 1

SCANS

The current date is March 21, 2000.

1. Using the instructions given in Application 1, import the contacts contained in data file **AO Job1.pst**. A total of 12 contacts should import into the Contacts folder.

2. Add the following Orion, Ltd., contacts to your contacts list. Create a category called Orion and add these contacts to the category:

```
John Cappel                     Elaine Guerrero
Project Manager                 Operations Manager
Orion, Ltd.
87 University Park Dr
University Heights, OH   45219
Phone: (513) 555-8763
Fax: (513) 555-9900
E-mail: Jcappel@orion.net       Eguerrero@orion.net
```

3. Send a letter to Elaine Guerrero thanking her for the opportunity to bid on the job. Save the letter as **Bid Letter** followed by your initials. Print and close the letter. John Cappel spent a lot of time with you making sure you understood the job you were to bid on. Flag his contact card to remind yourself to call him and thank him for his kind attention. You ought to make this call in the next day or so.

4. Create a personal distribution list of the persons who will be in charge of various parts of the Orion project: Paula, Tom, Irina, and Fuji. Schedule a meeting with the persons on this list to discuss the bid you need to prepare for Orion. Suggest March 22 as the date for the meeting and choose a time in the morning.

5. Create a task list of the jobs required for the project: Technical writing, Technical review, Paging, Proofreading, Corrections, QA review, and Final corrections. You will fill in starting and completion times and projected hours if you actually win the bid.

JOB 2

The current date is March 29, 2000.

1. Congratulations! You have been awarded the contract. Now you have a lot of work to do and not much time to do it. Schedule a meeting with the entire staff to discuss the project. The meeting should take place on April 3 at 9:00 in the morning. You need not send invitations for this meeting.

2. In conjunction with the team leaders and designated project manager, you hashed out a tentative schedule and projected hours for completion of each task. Insert the following information for the tasks you set up in the previous job. You do not need reminders for these tasks. (*Hint:* Insert the Total Work numbers on the Details tab of each task.) Assign the tasks to the Orion category. Create a custom view that adds the Start Date, Total Work, and Actual Work fields. Then sort the task list in ascending order by Start date.

Task	Start	Complete	Total Work
Technical writing	4/3	4/14	120
Technical review	4/17	4/25	75
Paging	4/19	4/28	124
Proofreading	4/24	5/3	40
Corrections	4/28	5/4	36
QA review	5/5	5/10	35
Final corrections	5/10	5/12	16

3. You will need to make weekly status reports to John Cappel at Orion during the project. Set up a recurring task to create the status report every Wednesday from the current date (March 29) to May 10. Have the task regenerate each week so you don't forget to do it next week. Assign the task to the Status category.

4. Schedule weekly meetings on Mondays at 9:00 a.m. with the project manager and the team leaders. Assign these meetings to the Status category.

SCANS

5. Paula reminds you that the Writing Team needs at least one freelancer to help out. There is one good freelancer among your contacts. Find the contact card and send an e-mail message asking if the freelancer can come in Friday of this week at 2:00 to discuss the Orion project. Print the e-mail message. You do not need to save the e-mail message. Tentatively schedule this appointment.

The current date is April 28, 2000.

6. The technical writing, technical review, and paging portions of the project are done. The proof-reading is half done. Record the status of these jobs in the task list.

7. Schedule a meeting with the entire staff to review the project when it is complete. Tentatively schedule the meeting for May 19 at 2:00 p.m. You do not need a reminder for this task.

JOB 3

The current date is May 17, 2000.

1. Well, you and the staff have survived the Orion project. Mark all the Orion tasks as complete and enter the following actual hours for each. Print only the tasks in the Orion category.

Task	Actual work
Technical writing	110
Technical review	60
Paging	160
Proofreading	38
Corrections	35
QA review	38
Final corrections	8

2. Send a follow-up letter to Elaine Guerrero thanking her for the opportunity to work with Orion. Save the letter as **Thanks Letter** followed by your initials. Print and close the letter.

3. Assign Jeff Branson the task of following up with Orion to see if more work might be available. Jeff should complete this task within the month. (You might have to clear the filter to see this task.)

4. Remove any filters or other changes you made to views in this unit review. Follow instructions from your instructor to remove items from Outlook.

The Alexander Pharmaceutical Company

Estimated Time: 10 hrs.

SCANS

For the past several months, Bonnie Petersilge, the vice president of marketing for The Alexander Pharmaceutical Company, has spearheaded a project to recommend technology purchases for the marketing staff. Bonnie's team includes you, Rob, Shawn, Paula, and Halli. After much analysis and research, the team is prepared to present its recommendations to the company's board of directors. As a member of Bonnie's team, you will compile all the information and prepare final documents for the acquisition proposal.

JOB 1

Rob drafted a proposal and then routed the document to Bonnie and Halli, who each added comments and edited the document. All revisions were tracked. Your first task is to review these revisions and comments and then accept or reject the changes.

1. Open **CS Job1a** from the student data files and save the document as **Proposal** followed by your initials.

2. Accept all the revisions except the change of *should* to *will* under the *Results and Benefits* heading. Turn off revision tracking.

3. At the end of the third sentence, which begins, *We are long overdue . . .*, delete the comment and then add the following autonumbered footnote: **A chief goal in the new fiscal year is to maximize the potential of the marketing staff.**

4. Move the insertion point to the end of the paragraph following the heading *Results and Benefits*. Delete the comment. Insert a blank line, and then insert the file **CS Job1b** from the student data files.

5. Format the table as desired using an AutoFormat or any other formatting options you want. To make the items easier to read, change the font size of the table to 11 point and change row height to 0.25 inch.

6. Sort the table in ascending order by the *Benefit* column. Delete any blank paragraphs below the table.

7. Check spelling and grammar and make any necessary corrections.

8. Save your changes and leave the document open.

JOB 2

To keep track of your work on the proposal, you will be scheduling and tracking various items. Use Outlook to complete the following tasks.

1. Open Outlook and insert the following names and e-mail addresses in the Contacts folder:

Bonnie Petersilge	B_Petersilge@alexander.com
Rob Yasbek	R_Yasbek@alexander.com
Shawn Hilliard	S_Hilliard@alexander.com
Paula Manzanilla	P_Manzanilla@alexander.com
Halli Shurgar	H_Shurgar@alexander.com

2. Create a distribution list for the members of the team. Name the list **Proposal Team**.

3. Plan a meeting on Monday of next week at 10 a.m. to discuss the status of the proposal. The meeting will probably take about an hour and should be scheduled for Conference Room A. Use the Proposal Team distribution list to send invitations to the meeting. You do not need a reminder for this meeting.

4. Bonnie has asked you to provide regular status reports. Create a regenerating task starting next Monday to provide weekly status reports to Bonnie.

5. Close Outlook.

JOB 3

You decide the document will be easier to read and understand if you create and apply some styles.

1. Apply the **Heading 1** style to the proposal's title. Modify the style to center the title and change the font to Times New Roman 18 pt bold. Specify 18 pt space above and 6 pt space below.

2. Apply the **Heading 2** style to the remaining headings in the proposal. (Use the Style list box on the Formatting toolbar to apply this style.) Modify the style to change the font to Times New Roman 14 pt bold. Specify 12 pt space before and 6 pt space after.

3. Create a style for the text paragraphs named *Text*. The style should have left alignment, a first-line indent of 0.25 inch, and a 6-pt space after the paragraph. Apply the style to all text paragraphs (but not to bulleted paragraphs).

4. Create a style for the bulleted paragraphs named *Bullets* that sets the bullet at the left margin with a 0.25 inch hanging indent and adds a 6-pt space after each bulleted paragraph. Apply the bullet style to all bulleted paragraphs.

5. Two bullet items under the *Proposed Solution* heading have subentries. To keep the subentries with the main bullet items, apply the *Keep with next* text flow option to the bullet item and *all but the last* subentry in each group. Align the subentries with the first word of the bullet items above them by selecting each group of subentries and clicking the **Decrease Indent** button on the Formatting toolbar one time. Format the last subentry in each group to have a 6-pt space after the paragraph.

6. Hyphenate the entire document.

7. Save your changes and leave the document open.

JOB 4

Bonnie started a worksheet to itemize the projected expenses for the technology acquisition, but she didn't finish the worksheet. She attached the worksheet to an e-mail message to you and asked you to include the worksheet in the proposal document. Before you can do so, you need to complete and format the worksheet.

1. From the student data files, open the **CS Job4** data file in Excel. Save the workbook as **Technology Proposal Worksheet** followed by your initials.

2. The items listed in this worksheet are grouped into three general categories: Hardware (cells A6:D10), Application Software (cells A12:D16), and Other Costs (cells A18:D21). You need to create subtotals for these items in the blank rows below each group of items. In cell A11, key **Hardware**. In cell B11, use AutoSum to total the hardware expenses in the column above. Copy the formula to cells C11 and D11. In cell E11, use AutoSum to total the subtotals in cells B11, C11, and D11.

3. Shade A11:E11 with Light Turquoise and boldface the entries to make them stand out from the rest of the worksheet. Format the subtotals for currency with a dollar sign and no decimal places.

4. Add subtotals for *Application Software* in row 17 and subtotals for *Other Costs* in row 22. Apply the same formats as you did to the Hardware row.

5. In cell E6, use AutoSum to total the costs in cells B6, C6, and D6. Total the costs of the other hardware items over the three-year period. Total the expenditures for application software (cells E12:E16) and other costs (cells E18:E21) in the same way.

6. Sum the *Total Capital Expenditures* for each year in row 23 by adding the subtotal amounts for each year. Then in cell E23, sum the total capital expenditures for the three years.

7. Use Auto Outline to outline the worksheet so that you can easily collapse portions you are not currently working with. Collapse the outline to show only the subtotals for each group of expenses. Save your changes to the worksheet. Then select and copy the cell range A4:E23.

8. Switch to the **Proposal** document. Position the insertion point at the end of the paragraph below the heading *Proposed Capital Expenditures*. Press **Enter** once to insert a blank paragraph with the **Text** style. With the insertion point in the blank paragraph, embed the copied worksheet cells using the **Paste Special** command on the **Edit** menu. Choose the *Paste* option and choose to embed the object as *Microsoft Excel Worksheet Object*.

9. With the worksheet object selected, open the **Format** menu and click **Object**. On the **Layout** tab, choose the *Center* horizontal alignment option. Click the **Advanced** button and specify *Top and bottom* text wrapping if necessary. In the *Distance from text* area, change the *Bottom* measurement to 0.3 inch.

10. Save the **Proposal** document and leave it open for the next Job.

JOB 5

The document is almost final, but as you read through it, you decide that the text needs to be rearranged.

1. Select the heading and all the text under the heading *Impact of Deferral* and move the selected material so that it follows the table below the heading *Results and Benefits*.

2. Add an autonumbered footnote at the end of the word *benefits* above the table. The footnote should read **Based on current fiscal year data.**

3. Search for the words *slump*, *disappointed*, and *discontented* and use the Thesaurus to find synonyms to replace them.

4. Just when you think you are almost finished, Bonnie sends you an e-mail message telling you she is exploring lease options and might want to revise her worksheet figures. She suggests you add the following paragraph in Text style below the embedded worksheet object:

   ```
   Pursuing advantageous leasing options might reduce expenditures in
   the first year. Proposed leasing options could result in the following
   bottom-line expenditures:
   ```

5. Press **Enter** after keying the paragraph above. You might need to adjust the embedded object to make the paragraph fall below the object.

6. Paste another copy of the worksheet below the new paragraph. This time, use the *Paste link* option in the Paste Special dialog box. Link the object as *Microsoft Excel Worksheet Object.* Format the object in the same way you did the embedded object.

7. Save your changes and leave the document open.

JOB 6

Bonnie asks that you prepare a draft of a slide presentation because she will need to present the proposal at the upcoming meeting of the board of directors. She has already created an outline of the proposed presentation.

1. Open a new blank presentation. Apply the Whirlpool design template. If desired, customize the color scheme and the background. Name the presentation **Technology Proposal Presentation** followed by your initials.

2. On the slide and title masters, insert a text box centered at the top of the slide and key **The Alexander Pharmaceutical Company** so the company name will appear on each slide.

3. Locate clip art in the ClipArt Gallery or on Clip Gallery Live that relates to the pharmaceutical or medical field. Insert the clip art somewhere on the title master. Resize and recolor the clip art as necessary.

4. Specify that slide numbers print on the slides.

5. Use the **Slides from Outline** command on the **Insert** menu to create slides from the **CS Job6** data file from the student files.

6. Adjust the slides as follows:
   A. Delete the current blank title slide and make the first slide from the outline a title slide. Change the size of the title to 48 pt. Add the subtitle **Presentation by Bonnie Petersilge**.
   B. If desired, change the Tahoma font throughout.
   C. Change the layout of slide 9 to Title Only.

7. **Technology Proposal Worksheet** should still be open in Excel with the outline collapsed. Copy the worksheet data in cells A4:E23. Switch to PowerPoint and display slide 9 if necessary.

8. Click **Paste Special** on the **Edit** menu and choose the *Paste link* option. Click **OK**. Adjust the size of the worksheet object to be large enough to read easily on the slide.

9. Bonnie is sure the Board will want to know what items are included in the *Other Costs* item. Create a table to show this information:

   A. Add a new slide following slide 9 with the Table layout. Key the title **Other Cost Components**.

   B. Create a table with four columns and five rows. Insert the following data in the table:

Cost	Year 1	Year 2	Year 3
Training programs	$21,000	$10,500	$12,300
Maintenance	3,000	6,500	8,500
Insurance	12,500	13,500	14,500
Supplies	5,000	6,000	7,000

   C. Adjust column widths and text size to display all data without wrapping text. Right-align the numbers. Make any other alterations to the table desired to display the data attractively.

10. Save your changes and close the presentation.

JOB 7

Bonnie left you a list of figures for a possible hardware lease deal. In order to give the Board information on both lease and purchase expenses, she would like you to create a couple of scenarios in your Excel worksheet to show costs both ways.

1. Switch to the Excel worksheet and expand the outline for the hardware section of the worksheet.

2. First create a scenario for the current figures. Click **Scenarios** on the **Tools** menu and then click **Add**. Name the new scenario **Purchase**. Specify the changing cells as $B$6:$B$10. Click **OK** twice.

3. Now add a new scenario for the lease option and name it **Lease**. Specify the same changing cells and change their values as follows:

   194500
   48900
   19500
   7800
   3400

4. You might want to see the Purchase and Lease values side by side at some future date, so create a scenario summary. In the Scenario Manager, click **Summary**. Then click **OK** to create a Scenario summary. Return to Sheet1, collapse the outline for the hardware section, and show the Lease scenario.

5. Switch to the **Proposal** document and notice that the linked object has now changed to show the figures for the **Lease** scenario.

6. Save your changes to the Word document and the Excel worksheet. Leave both items open.

JOB 8

You decide a chart would help the viewers of your presentation see how costs will be spread over the three-year period.

1. In the Excel worksheet, copy cell range A5:D22.

2. Open your PowerPoint presentation **Technology Proposal Presentation**. Click **OK** to update links and move to slide 9 to see how the linked object has been updated.

3. Add a slide following slide 10 with the Chart layout. Key the title **Costs over Project Period**.

4. Double-click in the chart placeholder. In the datasheet, click in the first cell and then select **Paste Link** on the **Edit** menu. Click **OK** to replace all data with your copied worksheet data.

5. Place the legend at the bottom of the chart.

6. Add slide transitions and custom animations as desired. Run the slide show to see your presentation in action.

7. Save your changes. Print the presentation as handouts with 6 slides per page. Close the presentation and PowerPoint.

8. Expand the outlines in the Excel worksheet and print the worksheet. Collapse the outlines again and save your changes. Close the worksheet and Excel.

JOB 9

Halli has done some research on the types of hardware equipment that the team is proposing to the Board and has stored the findings in a database table. You need to determine some approximate costs for equipping each sales representative with the hardware listed in the Excel worksheet.

1. From the student data files, open the **Alexander Pharmaceutical** database and then the **Equipment** table.

2. Apply a filter to sort the table by Item first in ascending order and then by Price in descending order.

3. This doesn't give you the best view of the data. And you notice that some of the items offer quantity discounts, which would be a big savings to the company. Create a query that shows only the items for which quantity discounts are available. The query should show Item #, Item, Name, Price, and Quantity discount. Sort the query results by Item in ascending order.

4. Modify the query to see the prices of the items after the discount has been subtracted. Create a calculated field named **Total** to show the discounted price. Show Item#, Item, Name, Price, Discount, and Total in the query results. Save the query as **Discount**.

5. Create a simple report using the Discount query. Name the report **Sample Costs**.

6. In Design view, adjust the Price, Discount, and Total detail items to display two decimal places. Display the report again and click the down arrow next to the **OfficeLinks** button on the toolbar. Click **Publish It with MS Word**. If you are asked for a file format, accept the default Rich Text Format option.

7. A new Word document opens named **Sample Costs**. Cut the tabular material from this document (do not cut the heading *Sample Costs*) and paste it in the **Proposal** document below the linked worksheet object on the last page. Delete the tabs at the beginning of each row.

8. Convert the text to a table and format it to match the table you created on page 2 of the proposal. (*Hint:* To remove space above the column headings, change space above for this text in the Paragraph dialog box to 0.) Sum the items in the *Total* column. Add any other formatting you think is appropriate.

9. Insert the following text above the new table:

   The following table shows some proposed costs to equip each sales representative, using discounted prices from reputable suppliers:

10. Save your changes to the Access report and close it. Close the **Sample Costs** Word document without saving changes. Save your changes to the **Proposal** document and leave it open.

JOB 10

You suspect that Bonnie will want to check your database information, and she might offer the database to others involved in the project at a higher level. To make it easy for Bonnie and any other interested persons to find your database material, create a switchboard to guide them.

1. In the **Alexander Pharmaceutical** database, create macros to open the Equipment table, the Members table, and the Discount query.

2. Create a new form for the switchboard. Insert the company name on the form and, if desired, the same clip art graphic you used on the presentation.

3. Insert command buttons on the form to run the macros you created. Save the form as **Switch**.

4. Click **Startup** on the **Tools** menu and specify that the **Switch** form be used at start-up. Test your switchboard by closing the database and then reopening it. Use the switchboard to open each item.

5. Leave the switchboard form open.

JOB 11

You need to prepare a form cover letter to accompany the proposal when it is mailed to Board members. You will use the **Members** table in the **Alexander Pharmaceutical** database as the data source for the merge.

1. Open the **CS Job11** data file from the student data files and save it as **Proposal Letter** followed by your initials.

2. Insert the current date and press **Enter** twice.

3. Start the mail merge process and specify **Proposal Letter** as the main document. Choose to open the data source. In the Open Data Source dialog box, change the *Files of type* to **MS Access Databases**. Select the **Alexander Pharmaceutical** database and then choose the **Members** table.

4. When prompted, set up the main document. Insert appropriate merge fields for the inside address. For the salutation, key **Dear** and then insert the Title and Last Name fields.

5. Click the **Mail Merge Helper** button and click **Query Options**. Set up a filter to merge only records for members of the Financial Policy Committee. Sort the records by last name.

6. Merge the letters to a new document. You should have three form letters. Save the document as **Alexander Form Letters** followed by your initials. Print the letters. Close the document.

7. Save your changes to **Proposal Letter** and close the document.

8. Close the **Alexander Pharmaceutical** database and Access.

JOB 12

You are ready to finalize the **Proposal** document. To do so, you want to create a table of contents and a title page with a watermark.

1. Insert a Next page section break at the beginning of the document. On the new, blank first page, create the table of contents by clicking **Index and Tables** on the **Insert** menu and then clicking the **Table of Contents** tab. Use a format of your choice.

2. Insert a blank line above the contents fields and key **Table of Contents**. Apply the Heading 1 style.

3. To create the title page, insert another Next page break at the beginning of the contents page. On the new, blank first page, key **Technology Acquisition Proposal** in Heading 1 style. Press **Enter** twice and key the following information:

```
Prepared by

The Technology Proposal Team

Bonnie Petersilge
Rob Yasbek
Shawn Hilliard
Paula Manzanilla
Halli Shurgar
[Your Name]
```

4. Center the text and format it as desired. Center all text on the page vertically.

5. Use the clip art you located for the PowerPoint presentation to create a watermark on the title page only.

6. On the contents page, insert a lowercase roman numeral page number for page ii at the bottom center of the page. If necessary, delete the watermark on this page.

7. In the body of the proposal, add a header to print on all pages. The header should include the title of the document (*Technology Acquisition Proposal*) and the word *Page* and the page number. Begin the body of the proposal on page 1.

8. Update the fields in the table of contents to show the correct page numbers by clicking just to the left of the first table of contents entry to select the entire table and then pressing **F9**. Choose to update page numbers only. (If you update the entire table, Word will add the headings from the title page and the table of contents heading. If your entire table updates, click **Undo** and try again.)

9. Preview the document to make sure everything looks the way you want it to. Save your changes and print the document. Close the document.

APPROVED COURSEWARE
EXPERT

APPENDIX A

THE MICROSOFT OFFICE
USER SPECIALIST PROGRAM

What Is Certification?

The logos on the cover of this book indicate that the book is officially certified by Microsoft Corporation at the **Expert** user skill level for Office 2000 in Word, Excel, Access, and PowerPoint. This certification is part of the **Microsoft Office User Specialist (MOUS)** program that validates your skills as knowledgeable of Microsoft Office.

The following grids outline the various Expert skills and where they are covered in this book.

MICROSOFT WORD 2000 EXPERT
TOTAL OBJECTIVES: 42

Standardized Coding Number	Activity	ICV Performance based?	Lesson #	Pages	Exercise #
W2000E.1	**Working with paragraphs**				
W2000E.1.1	Apply paragraph and section shading	No	5	87	SBS5.8
W2000E.1.2	Use text flow options (Windows/Orphans options and keeping lines together)	**Yes**	**6**	**103**	**SBS6.5**
W2000E.1.3	Sort lists, paragraphs, tables	**Yes**	**1**	**2–8**	**SBS1.1, 1.2, 1.3, 1.4, P1-1, 1-2, 1-3**
W2000E.2	**Working with documents**				
W2000E.2.1	Create and modify page borders	No	5	85	SBS5.6
W2000E.2.2	Format first page differently than subsequent pages	**Yes**	**10**	**210**	**SBS10.8, P10-2**
W2000E.2.3	Use bookmarks	**Yes**	**10**	**201**	**SBS10.2**
W2000E.2.4	Create and edit styles	**Yes**	**6**	**106, 109**	**SBS6.6, 6.7, P6-2, 6-3**
W2000E.2.5	Create watermarks	No	5	84	SBS5.5, P5-1
W2000E.2.6	Use find and replace with formats, special characters and non-printing elements	No	4	72	SBS4.9, P4-3
W2000E.2.7	Balance column length (using column breaks appropriately)	**Yes**	**4**	**67, 68, 71**	**SBS4.2, 4.3, 4.7, P4-1**
W2000E.2.8	Create or revise footnotes and endnotes	**Yes**	**6**	**114, 116**	**SBS6.4, 6.13, P6-3**

Standardized Coding Number	Activity	ICV Performance based?	Lesson #	Pages	Exercise #
W2000E.2.9	Work with master documents and subdocuments	No	7	142-143	SBS7.12, 7.13
W2000E.2.10	Create and modify a table of contents	**Yes**	**10**	**205, 210**	**SBS10.6, 10.7, 10.9, P10-2**
W2000E.2.11	Create cross-reference	**Yes**	**10**	**203**	**SBS10.3**
W2000E.2.12	Create and modify an index	**Yes**	**10**	**198, 204**	**SBS10.1, 10.5, P10-1**
W2000E.3	**Using tables**				
W2000E.3.1	Embed worksheets in a table	**Yes**	**2**	**28**	**SBS2.10**
W2000E.3.2	Perform calculations in a table	No	1	9	SBS1.5, 1.6, 1.7, P1-3
W2000E.3.3	Link Excel data as a table	**Yes**	**2**	**29**	**SBS2.11**
W2000E.3.4	Modify worksheets in a table	No	2	28	SBS2.10
W2000E.4	**Working with pictures and charts**				
W2000E.4.1	Add bitmapped graphics	**Yes**	**5**	**80**	**SBS5.1, P5-1**
W2000E.4.2	Delete and position graphics	No	5	82, 83	SBS5.3, 5.4
W2000E.4.3	Create and modify charts	**Yes**	**2**	**30**	**SBS2.12, P2-3**
W2000E.4.4	Import data into charts	No	2	33	SBS2.13, P2-3
W2000E.5	**Using mail merge**				
W2000E.5.1	Create main document	**Yes**	**3**	**40**	**SBS3.1, P3-1**
W2000E.5.2	Create data source	**Yes**	**3**	**42**	**SBS3.2, 3.3**
W2000E.5.3	Sort records to be merged	**Yes**	**3**	**50**	**SBS3.6, P3-1, 3-3**
W2000E.5.4	Merge main document and data source	**Yes**	**3**	**49**	**SBS3.5, P3-1**
W2000E.5.5	Generate labels	**Yes**	**3**	**53**	**SBS3.7, P3-3**
W2000E.5.6	Merge a document using alternate data sources	**Yes**	**3**	**56**	**SBS3.8, P3-3**
W2000E.6	**Using advanced features**				
W2000E.6.1	Insert a field	**Yes**	**10**	**200, 207**	**SBS10.7**
W2000E.6.2	Create, apply and edit macros	**Yes**	**9**	**179, 182, 185**	**SBS9.4, 9.5, 9.7, P9-1, 9-2**
W2000E.6.3	Copy, rename, and delete macros	**Yes**	**9**	**187**	**SBS9.8**
W2000E.6.4	Create and modify form	**Yes**	**8**	**153–157**	**SBS8.1, 8.2, 8.3, P8-1, 8-2, 8-3**
W2000E.6.5	Create and modify a form control (e.g., add an item to a drop-down list)	No	8	158, 162	SBS8.5, 8.7, P8-2, 8-3
W2000E.6.6	Use advanced text alignment features with graphics	**Yes**	**5**	**82**	**SBS5.3**
W2000E.6.7	Customize toolbars	No	9	177	SBS9.3

Standardized Coding Number	Activity	ICV Performance based?	Lesson #	Pages	Exercise #
W2000E.7	**Collaborating with workgroups**				
W2000E.7.1	Insert comments	**Yes**	**7**	**137**	**SBS7.9, P7-2**
W2000E.7.2	Protect documents	**Yes**	**7**	**140**	**SBS7.11**
W2000E.7.3	Create multiple versions of a document	**Yes**	**7**	**129**	**SBS7.4, P7-2**
W2000E.7.4	Track changes to a document	**Yes**	**7**	**131**	**SBS7.5, P7-1, 7-2**
W2000E.7.5	Set default file location for workgroup templates	No	7	124	SBS7.1
W2000E.7.6	Round Trip documents from HTML	No	5	94	SBS5.14

MICROSOFT EXCEL 2000 EXPERT
TOTAL OBJECTIVES: 50

Standardized Coding Number	Activity	ICV Performance based?	Lesson #	Pages	Exercise #
XL2000E.1	**Importing and exporting data**				
XL2000E.1.1	Import data from text files (insert, drag and drop)	**Yes**	**7**	**86-90**	**SBS7.1, 7.2, 7.3, 7.5**
XL2000E.1.2	Import from other applications	**Yes**	**7**	**86-90**	**SBS7.1-7.5**
XL2000E.1.3	Import a table from an HTML file (insert, drag and drop - including HTML round tripping)	**Yes**	**7**	**89-91**	**SBS7.4, 7.5, 7.7**
XL2000E.1.4	Export to other applications	No	7	90-91	SBS7.6
XL2000E.2	**Using templates**				
XL2000E.2.1	Apply templates	**Yes**	**8**	**96-97**	**SBS8.2**
XL2000E.2.2	Edit templates	**Yes**	**8**	**97**	**SBS8.3**
XL2000E.2.3	Create templates	**Yes**	**8**	**95-96**	**SBS8.1**
XL2000E.3	**Using multiple workbooks**				
XL2000E.3.1	Using a workspace	No	9	112-113	SBS9.7
XL2000E.3.2	Link workbooks	**Yes**	**9**	**113-115**	**SBS9.8**
XL2000E.4	**Formatting numbers**				
XL2000E.4.1	Apply number formats (accounting, currency, number)	Yes	1	2-4	SBS1.1, 1.2
XL2000E.4.2	Create custom number formats	**Yes**	**1**	**5-6**	**SBS1.3**
XL2000E.4.3	Use conditional formatting	**Yes**	**1**	**6-7**	**SBS1.4**
XL2000E.5	**Printing workbooks**				
XL2000E.5.1	Print and preview multiple worksheets	**Yes**	**9**	**111-112**	**SBS9.5**
XL2000E.5.2	Use the Report Manager	No	5	55	
XL2000E.6	**Working with named ranges**				
XL2000E.6.1	Add and delete a named range	**Yes**	**11**	**136-137**	**SBS11.5**

Standardized Coding Number	Activity	ICV Performance based?	Lesson #	Pages	Exercise #
XL2000E.6.2	Use a named range in a formula	Yes	11	136-137	SBS11.5
XL2000E.6.3	Use Lookup Functions (Hlookup or Vlookup)	Yes	11	137-138	SBS11.6
XL2000E.7	**Working with toolbars**				
XL2000E.7.1	Hide and display toolbars	Yes	12	144	SBS12.1
XL2000E.7.2	Customize a toolbar	Yes	6	77-78	SBS6.3, 6.4
XL2000E.7.3	Assign a macro to a command button	Yes	6	78-79	SBS6.5
XL2000E.8	**Using macro**				
XL2000E.8.1	Record macros	Yes	6	74-75	SBS6.1
XL2000E.8.2	Run macros	Yes	6	74-75	SBS6.1
XL2000E.8.3	Edit macros	No	6	76-77	SBS6.2
XL2000E.9	**Auditing a worksheet**				
XL2000E.9.1	Work with the Auditing Toolbar	Yes	5	56-58	SBS5.2
XL2000E.9.2	Trace errors (find and fix errors)	No	5	56-58	SBS5.2
XL2000E.9.3	Trace precedents (find cells referred to in a specific formula)	Yes	5	56-58	SBS5.2
XL2000E.9.4	Trace dependents (find formulas that refer to a specific cell)	Yes	5	56-58	SBS5.2
XL2000E.10	**Displaying and Formatting Data**				
XL2000E.10.1	Apply conditional formats	No	1	6-7	SBS1.4
XL2000E.10.2	Perform single and multi-level sorts	Yes	3	34-35	SBS3.6
XL2000E.10.3	Use grouping and outlines	Yes	11	131-133	SBS11.1
XL2000E.10.4	Use data forms	No	3	31	SBS3.2
XL2000E.10.5	Use subtotaling	No	11	134-136	SBS11.3
XL2000E.10.6	Apply data filters	Yes	4	41-42, 47-50	SBS4.1, 4.2, 4.7, 4.8
XL2000E.10.7	Extract data	No	4	41-50	
XL2000E.10.8	Query databases	No	4	49	
XL2000E.10.9	Use data validation	Yes	1	8-9	SBS1.5
XL2000E.11	**Using analysis tools**				
XL2000E.11.1	Use PivotTable autoformat	No	5	62-Concept Builder	
XL2000E.11.2	Use Goal Seek	No	5	67-68	SBS5.6
XL2000E.11.3	Create pivot chart reports	Yes	5	63-66	SBS5.5
XL2000E.11.4	Work with Scenarios	No	5	54-56	SBS5.1
XL2000E.11.5	Use Solver	Yes	5	68-69	SBS5.7, ACT5-1
XL2000E.11.6	Use data analysis and PivotTables	Yes	5	59-62	SBS5.3
XL2000E.11.7	Create interactive PivotTables for the Web	Yes	5	62-63	SBS5.4
XL2000E.11.8	Add fields to a PivotTable using the Web browser	No	5	62-63	SBS5.4

Standardized Coding Number	Activity	ICV Performance based?	Lesson #	Pages	Exercise #
XL2000E.12	**Collaborating with workgroups**				
XL2000E.12.1	Create, edit and remove a comment	**Yes**	**10**	**122-123**	**SBS10.2**
XL2000E.12.2	Apply and remove worksheet and workbook protection	**Yes**	**10**	**123-125**	**SBS10.3**
XL2000E.12.3	Change workbook properties	**Yes**	**10**	**122-123**	**SBS10.2**
XL2000E.12.4	Apply and remove file passwords	**Yes**	**10**	**124-125**	**SBS10.4**
XL2000E.12.5	Track changes (highlight, accept, and reject)	**Yes**	**10**	**119-121**	**SBS10.1**
XL2000E.12.6	Create a shared workbook	No	10	119-122	SBS10.1
XL2000E.12.7	Merge workbooks	No	10	119-122	

MICROSOFT ACCESS 2000 EXPERT
TOTAL OBJECTIVES: 44

Standardized Coding Number	Activity	ICV Performance based?	Lesson #	Pages	Exercise #
AC2000E.1.	**Building and modifying tables**				
AC2000E.1.1	Set validation text	**Yes**	**1**	**8**	**SBS1.3**
AC2000E.1.2	Define data validation criteria	**Yes**	**1**	**8**	**SBS1.3**
AC2000E.1.3	Modify an input mask	No	1	2	SBS1.1
AC2000E.1.4	Create and modify Lookup Fields	**Yes**	**1**	**10**	**SBS1.5**
AC2000E.1.5	Optimize data type usage (double, long, int, byte, etc.)	No	1	15	ACT1-2
AC2000E.2	**Building and modifying forms**				
AC2000E.2.1	Create a form in Design View	**Yes**	**3**	**37**	**SBS3.4**
AC2000E.2.2	Insert a graphic on a form	No	3	37	SBS3.4
AC2000E.2.3	Modify control properties	**Yes**	**3**	**37**	**SBS3.4**
AC2000E.2.4	Customize form sections (headers, footers, detail)	**Yes**	**3**	**37**	**SBS3.4**
AC2000E.2.5	Modify form properties	No	3	36	SBS3.3
AC2000E.2.6	Use the Subform Control and synchronize forms	**Yes**	**3**	**30**	**SBS3.1**
AC2000E.2.7	Create a Switchboard	**Yes**	**8**	**101**	**SBS8.4**
AC2000E.3	**Refining queries**				
AC2000E.3.1	Apply filters (filter by form and filter by selection) in a query's recordset	**Yes**	**4**	**51**	**SBS4.7**
AC2000E.3.2	Create a totals query	**Yes**	**4**	**46**	**SBS4.3**
AC2000E.3.3	Create a parameter query	**Yes**	**5**	**57**	**SBS5.2**
AC2000E.3.4	Specify criteria in multiple fields (AND vs. OR)	**Yes**	**4**	**49, 50**	**SBS4.5, 4.6**
AC2000E.3.5	Modify query properties (field formats, caption, input masks, etc.)	**Yes**	**4**	**46**	**SBS4.2**

Standardized Coding Number	Activity	ICV Performance based?	Lesson #	Pages	Exercise #
AC2000E.3.6 5.5	Create an action query (update, delete, insert)	Yes	5	59-64	SBS5.3, 5.4,
AC2000E.3.7	Optimize queries using indexes	No	5	59- Concept Builder	
AC2000E.3.8	Specify join properties for relationships	Yes	2	23	SBS2.7
AC2000E.4	**Producing reports**				
AC2000E.4.1	Insert a graphic on a report	No	6	72	SBS6.3
AC2000E.4.2	Modify report properties	Yes	6	73	SBS6.4
AC2000E.4.3	Create and modify a report in Design View	Yes	6	79	SBS6.6
AC2000E.4.4	Modify control properties	Yes	6	69-72	SBS6.1, 6.2, 6.3
AC2000E.4.5	Set section properties	No	6	72	SBS6.3
AC2000E.4.6	Use the Subreport Control and synchronize reports	Yes	6	79	SBS6.6
AC2000E.5	**Defining relationships**				
AC2000E.5.1	Establish one-to-one relationships	Yes	2	25	SBS2.8
AC2000E.5.2	Establish many-to-many relationships	Yes	2	25	SBS2.9
AC2000E.5.3	Set Cascade Update and Cascade Delete options	No	2	19	
AC2000E.6	**Utilizing web capabilities**				
AC2000E.6.1	Create hyperlinks	Yes	9	115	SBS9.1
AC2000E.6.2	Use the group and sort features of data access pages	Yes	9	120	SBS9.3
AC2000E.6.3	Create a data access page	Yes	9	118, 120	SBS9.2, 9.3
AC2000E.7	**Using Access tools**				
AC2000E.7.1	Set and modify a database password	Yes	10	131	SBS10.2
AC2000E.7.2	Set startup options	Yes	10	133	SBS10.3
AC2000E.7.3	Use Add-ins (Database Splitter, Analyzer, Link Table Manager)	Yes	10	134	SBS10.4
AC2000E.7.4	Encrypt and Decrypt a database	No	10	131	
AC2000E.7.5	Use simple replication (copy for a mobile user)	No	10	133- Did You Know?	
AC2000E.7.6	Run macros using controls	No	8	100	SBS8.3
AC2000E.7.7	Create a macro using the Macro Builder	Yes	8	109	SBS8.8
AC2000E.7.8	Convert database to a previous version	No	10	130- Concept Builder	
AC2000E.8	**Data Integration (New Skill Set)**				
AC2000E.8.1	Export database records to Excel	Yes	7	91	SBS7.2

Standardized Coding Number	Activity	ICV Performance based?	Lesson #	Pages	Exercise #
AC2000E.8.2	Drag and drop tables and queries to Excel	Yes	7	92	SBS7.3
AC2000E.8.3	Present information as a chart (MS Graph)	Yes	6	74	SBS6.5
AC2000E.8.4	Link to existing data	No	7	92	

MICROSOFT POWERPOINT 2000 EXPERT
TOTAL OBJECTIVES: 44

Standardized Coding Number	Activity	ICV Performance based?	Lesson #	Pages	Exercise #
PP2000E.1	**Creating a presentation**				
PP2000E.1.1	Automatically create a summary slide	Yes	1	14	**SBS1.10, P1-1**
PP2000E.1.2	Automatically create an agenda slide	No	4	67-68	SBS4.4
PP2000E.1.3	Design a template	Yes	4	72-73	**SBS4.7**
PP2000E.1.4	Format presentations for the web	Yes	4	74-75	**SBS4.8**
PP2000E.2	**Modifying a presentation**				
PP2000E.2.1	Change tab formatting	No	1	4, 5	SBS1.2, P1-1, 1-2
PP2000E.2.2	Use the Wrap text in AutoShape feature	No	3	50	
PP2000E.2.3	Apply a template from another presentation	Yes	4	73	**SBS5.1, P5-1**
PP2000E.2.4	Customize a color scheme	Yes	4	59-61	**SBS4.1, P4-1, 4-2, 4-3**
PP2000E.2.5	Apply animation effects	Yes	4	70-71	**SBS4.6, P4-1, 4-2, 4-3**
PP2000E.2.6	Create a custom background	Yes	4	62-64	**SBS4.2, P4-3**
PP2000E.2.7	Add animated GIFs	Yes	3	48-49	**SBS3.2**
PP2000E.2.8	Add links to slides within the Presentation	Yes	1, 6	12, 101	**SBS1.9, 6.2, P1-1, 1-3, 6-2**
PP2000E.2.9	Customize clip art and other objects (resize, scale, etc.)	Yes	3	46-47	**SBS3.1, P3-1, 3-2**
PP2000E.2.10	Add a presentation within a presentation	Yes	4	67	**SBS4.4, P4-1**
PP2000E.2.11	Add an action button	Yes	6	101	**SBS6.2, P6-2**
PP2000E.2.12	Hide Slides	Yes	6	99	**SBS6.1, P6-2**
PP2000E.2.13	Set automatic slide timings	Yes	6	99-100	**P6-1**
PP2000E.3	**Working with visual elements**				
PP2000E.3.1	Add textured backgrounds	Yes	4	63	**SBS4.2, P4-3**
PP2000E.3.2	Apply diagonal borders	No	2	26	

Standardized Coding Number	Activity	ICV Performance based?	Lesson #	Pages	Exercise #
PP2000E.4	**Using data from other sources**				
PP2000E.4.1	Export an outline to Word	**Yes**	**5**	**91**	**SBS5.7**
PP2000E.4.2	Add a table (from Word)	**Yes**	**5**	**88**	**SBS5.5**
PP2000E.4.3	Insert an Excel Chart	**Yes**	**5**	**87**	**SBS5.4**
PP2000E.4.4	Add sound	**Yes**	**3**	**54**	**SBS3.5, P3-1, 3-2**
PP2000E.4.5	Add video	No	3	55	SBS3.6
PP2000E.5	**Creating output**				
PP2000E.5.1	Save slide as a graphic	No	5	93	
PP2000E.5.2	Generate meeting notes	**Yes**	**6**	**106**	**SBS6.5, P6-3**
PP2000E.5.3	Change output format (Page setup)	No	5	93	SBS5.9
PP2000E.5.4	Export to 35mm slides	No	5	93	SBS5.9
PP2000E.6	**Delivering a presentation**				
PP2000E.6.1	Save presentation for use on another computer (Pack 'N Go)	**Yes**	**6**	**110-112**	**SBS6.6**
PP2000E.6.2	Electronically incorporate meeting feedback	**Yes**	**6**	**106**	**SBS6.5, P6-3**
PP2000E.6.3	View a presentation on the Web	No	4	76, 110	SBS4.8
PP2000E.7	**Managing files**				
PP2000E.7.1	Save embedded fonts in presentation	**Yes**	**6**	**111**	**SBS6.6, P6-2**
PP2000E.7.2	Save HTML to a specific target browser	No	4	75	
PP2000E.8	**Working with PowerPoint**				
PP2000E.8.1	Customize the toolbar	**Yes**	**4**	**68-69**	**SBS4.5**
PP2000E.8.2	Create a toolbar	**Yes**	**4**	**68-69**	**SBS4.5**
PP2000E.9	**Collaborating with workgroups**				
PP2000E.9.1	Subscribe to a presentation	No	5	92	
PP2000E.9.2	View a presentation on the Web	No	6	110	
PP2000E.9.3	Use Net Meeting to schedule a broadcast	No	6	110	
PP2000E.9.4	Use NetShow to deliver a broadcast	No	6	109	
PP2000E.10	**Working with charts & tables**				
P2000E.10.1	Build a chart or graph	Yes	2	30-31, 34-35	SBS2.6, 2.8, P2-1
P2000E.10.2	Modify charts or graphs	**Yes**	**2**	**32-34**	**SBS2.7, 2.8, P2-1**
P2000E.10.3	Build an organization chart	**Yes**	**2**	**37-38**	**SBS2.9, P2-3**
P2000E.10.4	Modify an organization chart	**Yes**	**2**	**39-40**	**SBS2.10**
P2000E.10.5	Modify PowerPoint tables	No	2	24	SBS2.3, P2-1, 2-3

Key: SBS: Step-by-Step   P: Project   ACT: Critical Thinking Activityx

GLOSSARY

A

Absolute reference An absolute reference is designated by a dollar sign before the column letter and the row number. This tells Excel to keep the cell's name the same regardless of where a formula or function containing this cell is copied.

Active cell Cell with the heavy border. Also called the selected cell.

Active window Window that you are currently using or that is currently selected.

Action buttons Predrawn buttons you can use to move from slide to slide or to other documents.

Agenda slide A slide that lists the titles of custom shows within a presentation.

Alphanumeric Sorted first by numbers, and then by letters.

Append query Query that adds records from one table to another table.

Archiving The process of storing folder items in a file that you can retrieve later.

Argument (Excel) Values that you give a function to compute. Arguments can be cell addresses or numeric data.

Argument A variable that supplies additional information, such as a file name. Arguments are enclosed in parentheses after the procedure name. You do not always need to use arguments but the parentheses will be added whether you add arguments or not.

Ascending order From the beginning of the alphabet, the lowest number, or the earliest date.

Auditing To check the results of information in a worksheet to be certain that it's correct.

AutoCreate An Outlook feature that lets you create a new Outlook item from an existing one of another type.

AutoFilter Allows you to easily display only a select group of records in a list.

AutoFit Widens the column to accommodate the long entries.

AutoForm A format that displays an entire record on the screen.

AutoFormat Predesigned format you can apply to a worksheet.

AutoFit An option that allows Word to automatically adjust table column widths to the size of the largest entry in the column.

AutoReport A format that displays records specifically for printing.

AutoSum Inserts the SUM function and selects the cells it plans to total.

Axis Lines in a chart used as a basis of measurement. The X-axis is typically the horizontal axis and the Y-axis is typically the vertical axis.

B

Boilerplate text Standard text used in various documents such as contracts and correspondence and in main documents for mail merge.

Bold Format makes the typeface appear thicker.

Bookmark Assigns a location in a document.

Bound control A control that gets its information from a table or query.

D

Calculated control A control that displays the results of the mathematical calculation that has been entered into it.

Case-sensitive (Excel) Refers to capitalization. Upper-case and lower-case letters must match.

Case sensitive In sorting, places uppercase before lowercase letters.

Category A keyword or phrase you can assign to items to group them.

Cell Basic unit of a worksheet. Cells are located at the intersection of columns and rows. You enter numbers, text, functions, and formulas into cells.

Cell comment Contains information or memos you've entered and is indicated by a red triangle in the upper-right corner of a cell. The comment is displayed when the mouse pointer moves over the triangle.

Cell name Name given to a cell and indicated by the column letter followed by the row number.

Chart Graphical representation of worksheet data.

Chart Wizard Guides you through creating a chart.

Clipboard Temporary storage area for text that is to be moved (cut) or copied and then pasted to another location.

Color scheme A set of eight colors that work well together. All the text, line, and fills in a design template are controlled by the color scheme. Most design templates have several color schemes to choose among.

Column Headings Headings at the top of each column. The columns are labeled alphabetically from A to IV.

Columns Cells that run vertically through the worksheet.

Command button Within a dialog box, a rectangle that executes an action, such as OK or Cancel.

Concatenation Combining text from two or more fields into one.

Conditional macro Macro that will run only if a condition is true.

Control This is an object that can be inserted into a form or report. There are three type of controls: bound, unbound, and calculated controls.

Criteria Information Excel searches for in a list.

Criteria range Area you create in a worksheet where you indicate what information Excel is to locate for you within the list.

Crop To remove a portion of a clip art graphic that you don't need.

Cross-reference Reference that directs the reader to another place in the text; cross-references in index entries and for text and page numbers can be created with fields.

Custom show A group of related slides within a presentation.

D

Data Information entered into cells.

Data access page Object in the database that lets you set up other objects, such as tables, forms, and reports, so that they can be published to the Web.

Data List Also referred to as a list. A data list is a collection of similar information entered into a worksheet. If this information is entered in a specific format using the rules of a data list, features such as filtering, sorting, and searching can be performed.

Data Map Uses geographic information in a worksheet and displays this information in a graphical (visual) format.

Data record Each row or paragraph in a data source containing information to be merged into a single copy of the form document.

Data source Document containing the records with variable information to be merged into a main document.

Data type The kind of information to be entered into a field, such as dates, currency, or text.

Database A list of related information arranged in a useful manner.

Database Wizard A step-by-step process of creating a database file.

Datasheet The worksheet-like grid where you enter data you want to chart.

Decrypting Removing the encryption. The decryption process unscrambles the encryption code so that a database file displays meaningful information.

Defragmenting Compacting a database by removing unused space within the database file.

Delete query Query that deletes records within a table.

Descending order Records sorted alphabetically "Z to A or numerically from highest to lowest, such as 3, 2, 1.

Destination application or document The application or document into which you want to insert data from another application or document.

Destination file The document in which a linked or embedded object is inserted.

Distribution list A list of contacts that belong to a particular group or team; you can use the distribution list to create items for all members of the list at the same time.

Document templates Determines the basic structure for a document and contains document settings.

Drop cap Enlarged capital letter used to emphasize the first letter in a paragraph; also called a display capital letter.

E

Edit To change existing information.

Embed To place information from one file or graphic into another file.

Embedded Describes an object from a source file that is inserted in a destination file, and becomes part of the destination file. The source file and destination file are not linked.

Embedded chart Chart created on the same worksheet as the chart data.

Embedded object An object that can be edited from the destination document by double-clicking the object. Embedded objects are stored in the destination document.

Exploded slice A slice of a pie chart that has been dragged out of the pie to emphasize it.

Encrypting Scrambling the code that makes a database file readable. When you encrypt a database, Access compacts the database file and then makes it indecipherable.

Event properties Similar to macro actions. It is the event or activity that takes place to trigger the conditional macro to execute.

Export To send information from Excel to another program.

Exporting Placing data from one program into another program.

Expression Typically a calculation in an unbound control or query.

Expression Builder The Access feature that helps you create calculations when you are not sure how to enter the expression.

External Reference Cell in another workbook that is referenced in a formula.

Extract To pull certain information out of a data list, such as all customers residing in California, and display this data in another part of a worksheet.

F

Field (Word) Set of codes to tell Word to insert items into a document; one piece of information in a data source record; or a column to be sorted.

Field Unit of information that contains one type of data. In a table, fields are displayed in columns. In a form, fields are represented by rectangles containing the information.

Field name (Word) Indicates variable text to be inserted in a main document; also called a merge field.

Field names (Excel) Names that represents a specific category of information in a record within a list.

Field names The name that represents a specific category of information in a record within a database.

Filter A method of screening out all records except those that match your selection criteria.

Font Appearance or design of text.

Footers Information that appears at the bottom of the printed page of your worksheet. This information can include the page number, name of the preparer, etc.

Formatting Changing the appearance of text or data. This may include such formatting as bold, italic, font size, currency format, etc.

Formula Instruction for how to perform calculations using table rows and columns.

Formula (Excel) Used to calculate data. For example, =B5 + C5 would add the information in cell B5 and C5 together and give an answer in the cell with the formula.

Formula bar Used for entering or editing text, data, and formulas in a cell.

Form Wizard A step-by-step process of creating forms.

Fragmentation Process in which parts of the database file become scattered over an area of the disk where the application is stored. This can cause the database to run slower and less efficiently.

Function A software routine that performs a task.

Functions (Excel) Used to simplify calculations using a function name. For example, =SUM(A5:A10) would add the information in cells A5, A6, A7, A8, A9, and A10 together and display the result in the cell with the formula.

G

Goal Seek Excel feature that finds one unknown value given a set of circumstances.

Global templates Templates that are available for all documents, not just the active document and not just documents based on the active template.

Graphic objects Various shapes and images you can produce on a worksheet.

Gridlines Lines within a chart that guide your eyes from the data series to an axis; also the background grid you see on a worksheet displayed on screen.

H

Header (Excel) Information printed at the top of each page of a workbook.

Header row The first row in a data source for a mail merge document.

Hidden text Formatted text that is not visible; it can be viewed or printed only if the Hidden Text option is turned on in the Options dialog box's View or Print tab.

Hyperlink An address embedded in a file that links the file with an object stored elsewhere in the computer or on the Internet.

Hypertext Markup Language (HTML) The standard document format used on the World Wide Web.

I

Import Bring a graphic or text into the application from another source.

Import (Excel) To bring information from another compatible program into Excel.

Importing Bringing information from one program into another.

Index List of words and phrases that provide a guide for references within the document.

Input mask Predetermined format for data entry.

Internet Explorer Browser program included in the Office suite, that gives you the capability to access, view, and download data from the Web.

L

Legends Information contained on charts that help identify the chart data.

Linked When an object is inserted in a destination file, a connection is created between the source file and the destination file. The object does not become part of the destination file. When the source file is updated, the destination file is automatically updated.

Linked object An object that must be edited in its source application. A linked object is stored in the source document and only a picture of it appears in the destination document.

Linking Refers to using information from various worksheets and workbooks in a formula.

List also referred to as a data list. A list of related data organized in a useful manner. A list is made up of records that are further divided into fields.

Lookup field field that pulls data from a field in another table or query in the database.

M

Macro Commands and instructions grouped together as a single command to complete a task automatically

Macro (Excel) Sequence of frequently performed tasks that you record. Excel plays the macro back and performs the recorded commands.

Main document Form document that contains boilerplate text and variable text.

Make-table query Query that creates a new table using the records found from one or more other tables.

Master document A document that groups several Word documents.

Merge fields Indicate variable text to be inserted in a main document.

Merging cells Combining two or more table cells into a single cell either horizontally or vertically.

N

Navigation buttons Buttons that allow you to move to different records in your table or form.

New Record button A button located with the navigation buttons that allows you to enter a new record.

Nonbreaking hyphen Used to indicate that a hyphenated word (such as the proper name Navarro-Cruz) should not be broken at the end of a line.

Nonbreaking space Used to indicate two words that should be kept together on one line (for example, "3 inches")

Normal template Word's default global template.

O

Offline folders Folders stored on your computer that you can use to work offline or when the network is down. You synchronize your offline folders with your server folders to keep your work up to date.

One-to-many relationship A relationship in which a table whose common field is a primary key field is linked to a table that does not have the common field as a primary key field.

One-to-one relationship A relationship in which each record in Table A can have only one matching record in Table B and each record in Table B can have only one matching record in Table A.

Operator Symbol that indicates the type of mathematical operation a formula is to perform.

Organization chart A chart that shows how the members of a group relate in the organization.

Orientation Determines the way a sheet prints. *Portrait* refers to printing on paper taller than it is wide. *Landscape* refers to printing on paper wider than it is tall.

P

Page (Excel) also referred to as a Web Page. This is a page of information that's been saved in an HTML (HyperText Markup Language) format. This format allows persons to view this page on the Internet or an Intranet.

Page (see also *Data access page*)An Access object that lets you create and display information for the Web.

Pane A separate part of a window when the window is split.

Panes (Excel) Used to display different parts of the worksheet on the screen at one time.

Parameter query Query in which you are prompted to enter the criteria each time you run the query.

PivotChart Displays data from a PivotTable report in a graphical (visual) format.

PivotTable Report Used to rearrange data in a worksheet.

Primary key A field designated by the user that uniquely identifies a record. Prevents duplicate information from being entered into a field.

Primary table A table with a primary key field that contains the same data as that stored in the common field of another table.

Protect To use passwords and other settings to control who can open and modify a document.

Q

Query An object used to find and display records that meet the criteria you specify.

Quick links Buttons on the Links toolbar in Internet Explorer that let you quickly connect to specific Web sites.

R

Range Rectangular group of cells.

Read-only recommended Used to prompt users to open a document as read-only. If the user edits the document, the file must be saved under a new name.

Record A collection of information (displayed in a row), such as name, address, telephone number for one person, within a data list. A database is divided into records. A record is further divided into fields.

Relative referencing When the cell name changes when a formula or function containing the cell name is copied.

Record selector The symbol that Access uses to identify the record your mouse pointer is currently in. This symbol is a triangle.

Records Collections of information about particular people or items. A database is divided into records.

Referential integrity Having Access check new data as it is entered into related fields.

Related table A table joined to another through a related field containing the same data type.

Relational database A database that can read information from other tables with a common field.

Relationships Links among two or more tables based on a common field.

Report A database object that is designed specifically for printing.

Report Wizard A step-by-step process of creating reports.

Revision marks Formats, such as strikethrough and underline, added to text to indicate editing changes that were made.

Row Cells that run horizontally through the worksheet.

S

Scenario Lets you view various results, such as a change to net income, if data within a worksheet is changed.

Selection handles Small boxes that appear on each corner and in the middle of each side of a selected object.

Shading Patterns used to shade the background of paragraphs and cells.

Search operators Mathematical symbols used in queries. Examples of operators are <, >, <=, >=, <>, and =.

Slide background The color, pattern, texture, and/or graphics that comprise the bottommost layer of a slide.

Solver Let's you find two or more unknown values in a formula.

Sort Rearrange the order of records in a list.

Source application or document The application or document in which you copy data you want to paste into another application or document.

Source file The original document containing the information that you link or embed in another document.

Spike Special AutoText entry for deleting text from various locations and inserting all of the text as a group in another location.

Splitting cells Dividing a single table cell into two or more rows and/or columns

Style (Excel) A collection of formats that's been saved with a name to provide instant formatting within a workbook.

Style A set of formatting instructions that tells Word how to format text in a document.

Subdocument A document that is contained within a master document.

Subform A form that is placed within another form. Usually these forms contain related information.

Switch A backslash in an index or table of contents entry that gives additional instruction such as bold format.

T

Table of contents A list that provides a guide to the contents of a document and their location.

Template Special document used as a pattern to create other similar documents; stores frequently used text, graphics, and formats.

Template (Excel) Special version of a worksheet document used to generate other, similar worksheets.

Text box A box you can draw on a slide to insert text.

Tick Refers to each label or mark on an axis.

Trace Dependent A dependent refers to a cell that is used in a formula. In Excel, for example, you can select a cell with data, click the Trace Dependents tool on the Auditing toolbar, and you will see an arrowhead appear in every cell that has a formula that uses this cells data.

Trace Precedents A precedent refers to a formula and which cells are used in this one formula. In Excel, for example, you can select a cell with a formula, click the Trace Precedents tool on the Auditing toolbar, and you will see an arrowhead appear in every cell that and a box appear. The box is drawn around the cells used in the formula.

U

Unbound control An unbound control does not get its information from a field in a table or query. An unbound control gets its information from other sources, such as Microsoft ClipArt.

Uniform Resource Locator (URL) A unique address for each Internet page that defines the route to that page.

Update query Query that changes the values of a specified field in a specified group of records.

V

Validation rules Properties applied to a database field that either require certain values to be entered or prevent them from being entered in the field.

W

Watermark A ghost image that appears behind the printed text.

Web Refers to the World Wide Web, the Internet, where you can access a wide variety of information using a computer and an Internet Service Provider.

Wildcard A symbol that stands for any character or a series of characters.

Workbook Excel file that contains worksheets. You keep related information together in a workbook.

Worksheet Grid-like structure in which you enter spreadsheet data. It consists of a series of columns and rows.

X

X-axis Typically the horizontal axis on a chart. This axis usually displays categories of data.

Y

Y-Axis Typically the vertical axis on a chart. This axis usually displays numeric data.

Z

Zoom To increase or decrease the view of data on a computer screen.